THE WARREN COURT
AND
AMERICAN POLITICS

THE WARREN COURT
AND
AMERICAN POLITICS

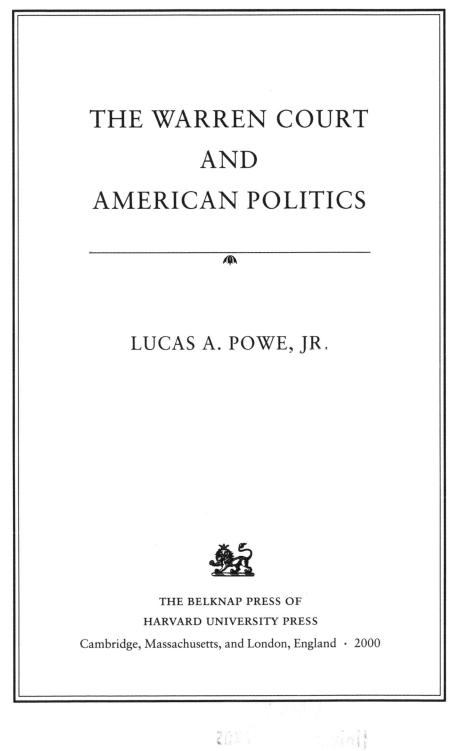

LUCAS A. POWE, JR.

THE BELKNAP PRESS OF
HARVARD UNIVERSITY PRESS

Cambridge, Massachusetts, and London, England · 2000

Library of Congress Cataloging-in-Publication Data

Powe, L. A. Scot.
The Warren court and American politics / Lucas A. Powe, Jr.
p. cm.
Includes bibliographical references and index.
ISBN 0-674-00095-1 (alk. paper)
1. United States. Supreme Court—History. 2. Law and politics. 3. Warren, Earl
1891–1974. I. Title.
KF8742.P68 2000
347.73′26′09045—dc21   99-047075

For Carolyn

Contents

─────────────── PART IV ───────────────

THE ERA ENDS

Illustrations

Preface

It is common to describe the judiciary as a "co-equal" branch of the government, but for much of American history this was a mere formal equality. Alexander Hamilton aptly described the judiciary in *The Federalist 78* as "the least dangerous branch" because it lacked both the sword to enforce its decisions and the purse to buy compliance. By the time Earl Warren retired in 1969 after sixteen years as chief justice, the name "Warren Court" had become a household word and there was no doubt in anyone's mind that the Supreme Court was a co-equal branch of government.

On the opening page of his short 1998 book, *The Warren Court and the Pursuit of Justice,* Harvard Professor Morton J. Horwitz writes that it is "increasingly recognized as a unique and revolutionary chapter in American Constitutional history" where the Court "regularly handed down opinions that have transformed American constitutional doctrine and, in turn, profoundly affected American society." David O'Brien's widely read *Storm Center* has a heading in its opening chapter that aptly conveys the modern reality: "No Longer 'the Least Dangerous Branch.'"

The Warren Court and American Politics has two goals. The first is to help revive a valuable tradition of discussing the Supreme Court in the context of American politics. The second seeks to replace stereotypes with information by synthesizing the numerous books and articles on the Supreme Court, its decisions, and its justices during Warren's tenure. While both of these goals are basically self-explanatory, perhaps a word or two about each is justified at the beginning.

There was once a flourishing genre of Supreme Court scholarship intertwining the Court and politics, led by major figures such as the holders of Princeton's McCormick Professorship of Jurisprudence—successively Edward S. Corwin, Alpheus Thomas Mason, and Walter F. Murphy—as

well as by Harvard's Robert G. McCloskey. There was a time when
political scientists had as much interest in the Court as did academic
lawyers and when the major journals of political science regularly published articles in this genre. But the genre vanished over a quarter century
ago; with its passing we have lost important perspectives on the Court.

Lawyers and law professors are Court-centered by both nature and
training. They tend to see law as more or less autonomous in relation to
the larger society. Political scientists have been more skeptical about that
and have typically seen the Court as subject to the trends and pressures
within the larger society. But in the 1950s and 1960s changes swept
through the discipline. First came quantification and its lure of precision.
Then, for those less enamored with statistics, came theory. At times political science departments seemed wonderfully divided. Some faculty
crunched numbers; others did theory; no one did politics. While this is
just a caricature, there was at least one area where, after the mid-1970s,
it was too close to true—public law with its focus on the Supreme Court
as a constitutional tribunal exercising the power of judicial review.

The shifts in political science further marginalized an already somewhat marginal public law and resulted in the declining numbers of public
law scholars choosing to analyze courts in terms of quantitative data or,
more likely, theory. The displacement of politics from Supreme Court
analysis and the decline in public law may be best seen by the facts that
although Harvard did replace McCloskey when he died in 1969 with
Martin Shapiro, his leading student, it made no further effort to keep the
tradition alive when Shapiro returned to California in 1974. Similarly,
Princeton has left the McCormick Professorship unfilled following Murphy's retirement. Today a nonquantitative article on the Supreme Court
and politics in a political science journal would stick out like an article on
physics in a law journal.

In 1969 political scientists Joel Grossman and Joseph Tanenhuas entitled the lead article in their edited volume *Frontiers of Judicial Research*
"Toward a Renaissance of Public Law." Their optimism was woefully
ill-timed for, in fact, public law was heading for the abyss. Corwin and
McCloskey were dead; Mason was retired; and Murphy's many scholarly talents were about to take him elsewhere.

Public law's "highly problematic status" was described more recently
by Shapiro in the American Political Science Association's update, *Political Science: The State of the Discipline II* (Ada Finifster, ed., 1993), a
collection of essays by senior professors reviewing their various fields.
Shapiro summarized and analyzed public law's unfortunate status

where, just before Murphy's retirement added Princeton to the list, a "striking proportion of top departments, including Harvard, Yale, Chicago, Michigan, and Stanford had no senior person devoted principally to teaching in the field." Yet in a real sense the gutting of public law did not matter because American politics scholars had stopped talking to their colleagues in public law anyway. "Public law thus dwindled into a marginalized constitutional law–Supreme Court ghetto of little interest to other political scientists." To complete the thought Shapiro might have added "and no interest to law professors" (who had long since stopped reading what their counterparts in political science wrote).

Large as the shifts within political science were, the Warren Court itself was an equally significant reason for part of the plight—"several generations of Ph.D.'s depleted"—that Shapiro described. The Warren Court galvanized a younger generation of lawyers and drew more students to law. At a time when a generational slogan was "never trust anyone over thirty," septuagenarians Earl Warren and William O. Douglas were icons on college campuses. Students interested in public law, who might have entered political science departments, mostly went to law school instead. Quite simply, because of the Warren Court, that was where the action was, and within law schools constitutional law stood alone and unchallenged at the top of the pyramid (and the Court's implicit promises to the present and the future assisted in marginalizing constitutional history). The results severely restricted public law enrollment within political science and helped continue the academic decline of public law whereby over time the Supreme Court was largely abandoned to the hands of law professors. Given the training and socialization of law schools, that meant that political events were given a minimal role in explaining judicial outcomes and behavior.

This book attempts to revive the genre of Supreme Court scholarship that focuses on the relationship between the Supreme Court's decisions and national politics. In seeking to explain what the Court did and why it did it, I have approached the task like the academic (and periodically practicing) constitutional lawyer that I am, someone who benefited (immensely) from a clerkship with William O. Douglas (the year after events in this book end). As a lawyer, I examine the distinctive facts of the cases, the arguments available to and made by counsel, and the legal tools available for the justices to respond as affected by prior decisions and institutional and personal arrangements within the nine-man body. I have supplemented the lawyer's look with insights from political science and history. Institutional arrangements matter. Decisions do not occur in a vacuum. Law is not just politics, but judges are aware of the political context of their decisions and are, like everyone else, influenced by the economic, social, and intellectual currents of American society.

The political science of judicial decisionmaking is better when supplemented by the insights of law and lawyers. Constitutional lawyering is better when supplemented by the insights of political science. There was a time when we understood this synergy. Therefore, in an important sense there should be nothing novel or surprising in the approach I have taken. But it is no longer clear that we know this synergy. Therefore, in another sense there must be something different since the approach I have taken has rarely been seen in over a quarter century.

There are some younger scholars in both law schools and political science departments who are similarly striving to combine law and political science, and I happily join their efforts. Just as there was a day when constitutional lawyers and their academic counterparts in political science read, comprehended, and profited from each other's work, so I would hope it would recur.

There is, in fact, lots of information about the Warren Court, and Supreme Court scholars are aware of it even if the general public is not. But no one has tried to synthesize the information into a general history, and by doing so I hope that even specialists may take a fresh look at the Court and here and there see new information.

There may be numerous reasons why there has yet to be a synthetic history of the Warren Court, but one certainly is that everyone seems to turn into a partisan once the Warren Court is mentioned. As a result, the Warren Court is so typically stereotyped, by both supporters and detractors alike, that what it really was and what it did have become casualties of quick generalization. The dominant feature of Warren Court literature is cheerleading. Writers typically come to praise the Court, although some come to bury it in contempt. In either case, the Warren Court is the window to the present, a touchstone for determining right and wrong today. This is the instrumental approach of lawyers and political scientists. One must realize that the Warren Court, like the Taft or Fuller Courts, has also become history. Anyone still in teaching who was teaching when Warren became chief justice has long since been eligible for retirement, and all teachers younger than fifty entered their graduate school after Warren had retired. With such a passage of time this Court, like its predecessors, also merits a more distanced historical perspective rather than instrumental subjugation to contemporary political goals.

I freely admit that I was once a partisan, celebrating liberal victories and despairing retrenchment. Years in academia, however, have given me a different perspective. My job is neither to cheer nor boo; it is to understand and explain. It no longer matters to me whether the *Reapportionment Cases* (1964) or *Miranda v. Arizona* (1966) was rightly decided; *Brown v. Board of Education* (1954) is different because it does matter to me that it was rightly decided. But all the cases should be understood for what the Court did and was trying to do. Whether we approve of the opinions has nothing to do with their import or with the forces working on the Court that produced them.

There are huge interpretive disputes about the legitimacy and efficacy of what the Warren Court did, but there are also important points of agreement. Scholars seem agreed that the Warren Court consisted of a group of powerful, talented men who were more sympathetic to claims of individual liberty while being simultaneously more egalitarian than their predecessors, more willing to intervene in contentious controversies, more prone to ignore the past, and more convinced that national solutions were superior to local solutions. My concern is not whether these changes were good or bad, but how they came to be, how far they reached, and how they eventually encountered limits. In the course of discussing these issues, I hope to eschew the law professor's traditional Court-centered focus and instead place the Court where it belongs as one of the three co-equal branches of government, influencing and influenced by American politics and its cultural and intellectual currents.

This book would not have been written without the friendship and encouragement of another of McCloskey's fine students, Sandy Levinson, who for two decades has proven to be the truly perfect colleague. This book still might not have been written had not the Government Department at the University of Texas extended a joint appointment to me. Jim Fishkin, the department chair, first induced me to teach a course on the Supreme Court and thereafter periodically needled me to put my ideas into book form.

In writing such a large book and discussing such a wide range of cases (mostly constitutional even though the nonconstitutional decisions of the Court far outnumber the more important constitutional ones), I have had to impose on numerous friends for time and advice, both of which were freely given. Sandy Levinson, Dick Markovits, and H. W. Perry have read every page of this book, sometimes more than once. Tom Krattenmaker has read most of the chapters. Walter Murphy, whom I met when this book was half written, has offered me comments on parts and, more important, access to his storehouse of knowledge. Walter Dean Burnham, George Dix, Cindy Estlund, Mark Gergen, Jack Getman, Mark Graber, Sam Issacaroff, Doug Laycock, David Rabban, Jordan Steiker, and Charles Alan Wright have commented on the parts of the work within their areas of specialization. I would love to state that any remaining errors are theirs, but I am afraid they are mine.

As always the excellent staff Roy Mersky has assembled at Tarlton Law Library has performed incredible feats for me. I am especially grateful to Barbara Bridges, the government documents librarian, Marlyn Robinson in reference, and Mike Widener, the archivist in charge of the Tom Clark papers. I am equally indebted to David Gunn, who has subsequently left Tarlton for the private sector. There is no adequate way I can convey my thanks to the Tarlton Law Library staff. They simply set the standards of excellence.

My longtime secretary, Consuelo Akin, took a manuscript that made sense to me and prepared it the way that the publisher wished to see it. She also found and corrected numerous errors that had escaped my many efforts at detection.

In addition to my friends, I must mention two younger scholars, Michael Klarman, a constitutional historian at the University of Virginia Law School, and Gerald Rosenberg, a political scientist at the University of Chicago, who have authored important work on the Court and social change. Their writings have periodically overlapped with mine and consistently helped me crystallize and clarify my thinking even when I disagreed with one or the other (or both). Their influence is present throughout the book even if unacknowledged in the notes to follow. Even more important was the inspiration given me by McCloskey's and Murphy's work. I still recall feeling "this is what scholarship is about" when I read their books three decades ago.

Finally, a word about endnotes. By choice, the notes in the book are sparse. They have been used for direct quotations but rarely anything else. The bibliography at the end acknowledges the sources that offered the most guidance. When the quotation is from a Supreme Court opinion, there is no note. The index of cases offers the relevant citations.

THE WARREN COURT
AND
AMERICAN POLITICS

Chapter 1

The Supreme Court, 1935–1953

The Warren Court created the image of the Supreme Court as a revolutionary body, a powerful force for social change. To note that the Supreme Court had not previously been seen that way is to make a gross understatement. Only a generation earlier, the Court that Franklin D. Roosevelt inherited during his first term had solidified the image of the Court in American history—old men wedded to the status quo ante; at their institutional best, conservative; at their institutional worst, reactionary.

The Court and the New Deal

As Roosevelt's first term went past its halfway mark, it was becoming apparent that the most serious opposition to his mélange of programs to tame the Depression was certainly not Congress, which during the 100 Days behaved as a rubber stamp, nor even the Republican Party, saddled with the blame for the Depression, but rather the Supreme Court. In the winter and spring of 1935, a series of decisions made clear that the Court opposed not only the particulars of New Deal legislation but the premises as well. By the time of the 1936 presidential election, the Court had signaled its intent to emasculate the New Deal. Roosevelt, in turn, decided to reciprocate by creating new positions on the Court and filling them with yes-men.

In 1935 and 1936, using a variety of constitutional doctrines, the Court informed the Roosevelt administration that fighting industrial and agricultural collapse from Washington, D.C., was unconstitutional because the Constitution did not grant the federal government the powers to deal with national economic problems. First, the Constitution had no Emergency Clause authorizing otherwise prohibited actions in dire times. Second, the power to regulate interstate commerce, which was

1

granted, did not extend to activities before the commerce commenced, like mining and manufacturing, or to activities after the commerce ended, like the final retail sale. Third, regulatory transfer payments, such as minimum wages or pensions, were compelled transfers from one private party to another, violating, according to the Court, the requirements of due process of law. Fourth, Congress had to specify the objectives of its laws; it could not simply delegate authority to the Executive with the instruction to do the right thing. Finally, in an overarching theory, even a regulation within national power—such as taxing and spending for the general welfare—was unconstitutional if it invaded areas that were properly within state control. Congress could not tax and spend to regulate the agricultural collapse because it constituted a "widespread similarity of local conditions" and thus was within state authority protected by the Tenth Amendment, which reserved to the states those powers not delegated to the federal government.

On the one hand, substantive due process, the name for the prohibition on regulatory transfers, severely limited the options available to the states. On the other hand, political and economic conditions made federal action the optimal solution. Thus, many states were paralyzed by the race to the bottom. If they regulated industry more severely than their neighbors during this time of economic collapse, they might wind up with no industry at all.

In 1935 and 1936 the Court struck down major New Deal measures, including the National Industrial Recovery Act, the Guffey Coal Act, the first Agricultural Adjustment Act, and the Railroad Retirement Act. In June 1936 it struck down a New York statute providing a minimum wage for working women. The votes in the cases ranged from 9–0 to a more typical 6–3 or 5–4, but the five justices were always solid. That meant that soon the National Labor Relations Act, the Social Security Act, the Tennessee Valley Authority, and maybe even the Public Utility Holding Company Act were all likely to be held unconstitutional. Whatever the New Dealers thought necessary or useful, the Court was going to find beyond the authority of the federal government or of state legislatures. Not since the Civil War had the nation faced such a constitutional crisis. Alabama Senator Hugo L. Black summed up the situation tersely: "120 million Americans are ruled by five men."[1]

The Court-Packing Battle

Working in complete secrecy after his landslide victory over Alf Landon, Roosevelt prepared his attack on the Court. On February 5, 1937, he proposed legislation adding a new justice for every one on the Court over the age of 70. At the time, the Court was the oldest in American history, hence the label "Nine Old Men," and Roosevelt was the first full-term president not to have made a single appointment. His plan would have given him six appointments all at once, enough to overwhelm the Court's conservatives and to guarantee, to the extent possible, the necessary votes to sustain the New Deal program.

The Constitution is silent on the number of Supreme Court justices. Washington had but six; Lincoln had the high of ten. Roosevelt's fifteen may have been inelegant or inefficient, but it was not barred by the Constitution. All he needed were the solidly Democratic majorities in the House and the Senate to continue to follow their leader.

Roosevelt initially and duplicitously stated the plan was intended to promote efficiency and help the Court stay abreast of its docket, but in a Fireside Chat on March 9 he told the truth: "Our difficulty with the Court today rises not from the Court as an institution but from the human beings within it. But we cannot yield our constitutional destiny to the personal judgment of a few men who, fearful of the future, would deny us the necessary means of dealing with the present. . . . We have, therefore, reached the point as a Nation where we must take action to save the Constitution from the Court and the Court from itself."[2] Maybe he had no difficulty with the Court "as an institution," but could the institution survive after the degradation to which he intended to subject it?

Roosevelt's Court-packing plan split the Democratic Party. Some, like Hugo Black and the youthful Texan, Lyndon Johnson, who rode the plan to victory in a special election, were enthusiastic supporters. Others, even progressives like Montana Senator Burton K. Wheeler, were opposed. It seemed not to matter. *Time* magazine reported that even "the staunchest foes of the President's plan were privately conceding that the necessary votes were already in his pocket."[3] In a like vein, Senator Carter Glass of Virginia, an opponent of the plan, explained why it would pass. "If the President asked Congress to commit suicide tomorrow, they'd do it."[4]

Charles Evans Hughes, the Jehovah look-alike chief justice, then demonstrated why, in his pre-Court career, he had been a brilliant and successful politician. Refusing an offer to testify in person before the Senate Judiciary Committee, he instead sent a letter (signed by the Court's two most senior justices, liberal Louis D. Brandeis and conservative Willis Van Devanter), noting that the Court was fully abreast of its work and that nine was an optimum number, while fifteen would make the work unwieldy. This was not bad for a letter stating that its authors took no position on the merits of the plan.

Even better were the Court's decisions that spring, as Owen Roberts pulled his famous "switch in time that saves nine." On March 29, in *West Coast Hotel v. Parrish,* the justices sustained, by a 5–4 vote, a Washington state minimum wage statute for women that was identical to the New York statute the Court had struck down the previous June. Two weeks later, by the same 5–4 margin, the Court sustained the National Labor Relations Act as a proper regulation of interstate commerce. Although no case was overruled, the decision was flatly inconsistent with the prior year's invalidation of the Guffey Coal Act. Then in late May the Court, again by a 5–4 vote, sustained the Social Security Act. A little over a week later, Van Devanter, who had dissented in each of these cases, announced his retirement.

Roosevelt now had the outcomes he wanted as well as a chance to replace one of the conservatives. Congress breathed a collective sigh of relief, assuming that Roosevelt would now pull down his divisive and unpopular plan, while Senate Majority Leader Joe Robinson of Arkansas received congratulations since it was well known that Roosevelt had promised him the Court's first opening.

In March Roosevelt could have achieved an easy compromise for two or three new justices, but he wanted all six. In June he was reluctantly willing to compromise, if necessary, but the Senate no longer was. Roberts had switched, Van Devanter had retired, and public opinion had "swung decisively against the President."[5] Moreover, the summer of 1937 was hot, Washington was without air-conditioning, and on July 14 Robinson was found dead in his apartment. So was Roosevelt's Court-packing hope; it might have survived with Robinson but could not without him. The president had only Van Devanter's seat to fill.

Roosevelt's Justices

On the night of August 11, Roosevelt called Hugo Black to the White House and told him that he was the choice for the Court and swore him to secrecy. The next morning Steven Early, Roosevelt's press aide, not knowing what had occurred, told the press that many people were under consideration and that a selection might not be made for weeks. Then Roosevelt sent a courier to the Senate with the notice of Black's appointment written in his own hand. When the president told Early, the latter responded with just two words: "Jesus Christ."[6] Roosevelt grinned because Early got it right. The Senate was outraged.

Roosevelt, bitter over losing, didn't care. Black "had" to be confirmed because of senatorial courtesy, and Black was Roosevelt's bitter pill for everyone else. The highly partisan Alabaman was not popular with his colleagues, had been publicly contemptuous of the Court, loved the Court-packing plan, had voted against Chief Justice Hughes's confirmation, and was anathema to business, always viewing it, whether in private practice or the Senate, as the enemy. He was just right for Roosevelt's idea of a diminished Court. If that were not enough, there were rumors—which, it turned out, were altogether accurate—that Black had belonged to the Ku Klux Klan early in his political career. No other organization was so rightly equated with lawless violence and bigotry.

Black refused to comment on his Klan membership but allowed Idaho Senator William Borah, who did not know the truth, to deny the rumors. The Senate, without serious investigation, followed tradition and confirmed Black by a vote of 63–16 only five days after his nomination. The Scripps Howard newspapers broke the Klan story a month later, but Black, already confirmed, weathered the furor and then spent most of his judicial career minimizing his prior association while atoning for it with his votes.

Roosevelt had wanted six appointments by the end of 1937. He got eight—nine if one counts moving Harlan Fiske Stone from associate to chief justice—by the beginning of 1943. The men he appointed served without the stigma of being the "yes-men" of the Court-packing plan. The eight new faces shared a common trait, however; they were New Dealers. The first seven—Black, Stanley Reed, Felix Frankfurter, William O. Douglas, Frank Murphy, James Byrnes, and Robert Jackson—were all loyalists. Black and Byrnes were senators, Reed, Murphy, and Jackson were from the Justice Department, and Frankfurter and Douglas were academic advisers of the president. Byrnes quickly went back into the Roosevelt administration and was replaced by Wiley Rutledge, a former law school dean and lower court judge. Murphy, Byrnes, and Rutledge served under a decade and are of no further importance. Roosevelt's five longer-serving justices all lasted until the Warren Court, and Black, Frankfurter, Douglas, and Jackson are genuinely important justices, in part because of their sheer force of intellect and commitment to one or another constitutional vision. Reed, the Kentuckian who argued a number of New Deal cases to the Court, was unimpressive, although a perfectly reliable vote for the federal government across the board and for state and local governments in domestic-security situations.

Frankfurter was the last immigrant to sit on the Court, yet he probably was the most qualified appointee of the century. He was a confidant of both Justices Oliver Wendell Holmes and Louis D. Brandeis, picked the law clerks for each, and taught the key public law courses at his beloved Harvard for two decades. He was incredibly active, helping found *The New Republic,* investigating the Bisbee Deportations, publicly castigating the fairness of the trials that condemned Sacco and Vanzetti, and funneling protégés into the New Deal administration (the "Happy Hot Dogs"), in addition to advising Roosevelt both as governor and president.

A complex and committed man who believed there was no higher calling than public service, Frankfurter was a classic progressive in believing fully in the role of disinterested experts. Whether consistently or not, he was also a firm believer in majoritarian democracy. He was a charismatic intellectual dynamo and a persistent, congenial proselytizer who befriended many an inquiring mind.

Douglas, who would eventually be the longest-serving justice ever, was unique among any group of Supreme Court justices. First, he was, in the estimation of all his colleagues, a true legal genius, capable of cutting to the heart of any problem instantly and impatient with those who could not (which included everyone). Second, he not only overcame polio as a child; he also knew poverty firsthand (and to an extent unequaled by other justices). These experiences gave him a strong empathy for society's downtrodden, which he never abandoned even as his own career skyrocketed.

After graduation from college in Walla Walla, Washington, then Columbia Law School where he was number two in his class because of a C in Constitutional Law, Douglas practiced on Wall Street and became a brilliant corporate scholar and, in his early thirties, Yale's highest paid professor and a leader among the emerging school of legal realists committed to creating a more accurate picture of the legal system. Too ambitious to settle solely for scholarship and teaching, Douglas moved to and up the New Deal, first as a protégé of Joseph Kennedy, then as a poker-playing adviser to Roosevelt. Ultimately, Douglas chaired the New Deal's showcase agency, the Securities and Exchange Commission, where he set standards for both toughness and competence that were (and remain) unequaled. When Roosevelt promoted the forty-year-old star, he was the youngest Supreme Court justice since 1810.

Jackson, a New York adviser to Governor Roosevelt, was another New Deal lawyer who moved rapidly up the Justice Department chain, eventually becoming attorney general before joining the Court in 1941. He was such a superb advocate as the government's lawyer before the Court that Brandeis believed he should have been appointed solicitor general for life. Once on the Court, he was probably the finest writer in its history. Unlike others, Jackson the justice was required to come to grips with positions that Jackson the government's advocate had previously taken. His opinions in these cases are models of wit, humility, and integrity.

Economic Regulation

The Roosevelt justices were a talented and fractious group, but they were united on one thing: Government had the authority to regulate the economy. Various doctrines, like restrictive interpretations on what was or what affects interstate commerce, substantive due process, or Tenth Amendment protections of localism, were unceremoniously discarded as rapidly as the justices could dump them. When the Court had sustained the National Labor Relations Act during the battle over the Court-packing plan, it did so in the context of a massive, vertically integrated steel manufacturing company that owned and operated ore, coal, and limestone properties, lake and river transportation facilities, and terminal railroads. No reasonable person could deny that a strike at one part of the business would have substantial effects elsewhere. Subsequent cases underscored the point that federal power reached beyond gigantic integrated businesses.

In 1942, in a breathtaking example of the new order, the Court authorized the federal regulation of wheat grown on a farm for consumption by that farm's animals. The justices unanimously reasoned that any homegrown wheat was a substitute for interstate wheat that would otherwise have to be purchased on the market. Accordingly, by not buying on the market, this farmer and others like him were affecting the interstate market. No wonder that just a year earlier the Court, again unanimously, stated that the Tenth Amendment was "but a truism that all is retained which has not been surrendered." Hence it was irrelevant.

The growth of federal authority did not render the states irrelevant regulators. The demise of substantive due process meant that they too could regulate as they wished just as long as they didn't get in the federal government's way. Businesses that had enjoyed a healthy constitutional protection just a decade before now in effect had none. That was the price of the revolution of 1937. It was a price that Roosevelt's appointees gladly paid, for in fact for them it was no price at all. Coming out of the New Deal, they wholeheartedly believed government was responsible for the economy and had to be free to take whatever measures were deemed necessary to promote economic stability and growth.

Civil Rights

Simultaneously with withdrawing constitutional protection from economic rights, the Court, in Footnote Four of *United States v. Carolene Products* (1938)—the most famous footnote in constitutional law—suggested that it might be more solicitous of civil liberties and civil rights.[7] The underappreciated *Buchanan v. Warley* (1917) had suggested some limits on "separate but equal," but the first overt movement away from *Plessy v. Ferguson*'s "separate but equal" doctrine of racial segregation came in 1938. It arose because Missouri made no pretense of equality in its law school. It had a state law school for whites but none at all for African-Americans. When an aspiring African-American law student, Lloyd Gaines, applied, the state offered to pay his tuition anywhere out of state or to consider opening an African-American law school for him and others. The Court, through Hughes, with two pre-Roosevelt holdovers dissenting, held this an unconstitutional denial of equal protection of the laws, although it did imply that creating an African-American law school, as opposed to thinking about doing so, would present a different case.

That different case was *Sweatt v. Painter* (1950), involving a newly created law school for African-Americans in Texas without permanent faculty, books, or, obviously, alumni. This too was held unconstitutional. A companion case involving an Oklahoma graduate student in English, physically separated from all his white classmates, reached the identical result. The change in personnel from 1938 made these unanimous decisions.

Ever since the Fifteenth Amendment was ratified to preclude racial discrimination in voting, the South had attempted to render it a nullity. A favorite early-twentieth-century tactic to prevent African-Americans from influencing an election was the all-white primary. Whites would select the Democratic Party candidate of their choice, and then African-Americans could vote in the general election where that winning primary candidate would run unopposed. The Court held the all-white primary unconstitutional in 1927 and seemingly granted African-Americans the right to participate in party primaries.

Southern states responded by deregulating primary elections. This let the Democratic Party operate as a private organization, controlling its own membership and, therefore, its own process of selecting candidates to represent the party. African-Americans, naturally, were barred from this exclusive organization consisting of all white citizens within the state. Amazingly, in a unanimous 1935 opinion by Roberts, this subterfuge was upheld. In 1944 the reconstituted Court, through Reed, held it unconstitutional.

Roberts was incredulous that his nine-year-old precedent was being discarded. He stated that, by overruling, the Court turned "adjudications of this tribunal into the same class as a restricted railroad ticket, good for this day and this train only," and he protested the intolerance of his Brethren toward those jurists who served before. Given the circumstances under which the Roosevelt justices were appointed, it is hardly surprising that they were intolerant of their predecessors, and Roberts, once the war ended, left the Court. President Truman replaced him with a Republican, Ohio Senator Harold Burton, a friend of the president's from their days on the War Investigating Committee.

In 1948, in *Shelley v. Kraemer,* a unanimous Court held unconstitutional racially restrictive covenants preventing the sale of housing to African-Americans. Like all the other decisions discussed, its effect was almost entirely symbolic. It meant a neighbor could not go to court to bar a home sale to an African-American, but it did not affect the seller's prejudices or those of a real estate agent or, indeed, give money to anyone to buy property in a white neighborhood. Similarly, the graduate-school cases affected only those eligible for graduate school. The white primary cases had greater effects, but African-American voting still could be hindered if not prevented by poll taxes, literacy tests (often enforced by semiliterate whites), and private pressure, like loss of credit, loss of employment, or even violence.

Yet symbolism matters, and within a judicial system (unless Roberts's complaint was valid) precedents build toward other precedents. The symbolism was running in favor of civil rights claims. So, too, were the politics of race. The New Deal had moved African-Americans out of the Republican Party and into a battleground between Republicans and Democrats. Politically aware justices knew this. Furthermore, everyone knew the wartime ideology of America's fight for freedom and against racial superiority, and everyone had seen Jackie Robinson integrate major league baseball, the national pastime. These intellectual, social, and political currents led the 1948 Democratic convention to adopt a civil rights plank and caused a Dixiecrat revolt, sealing the southern position as narrowly sectional. As such, it was more difficult for justices coming from the North and West to empathize with the southern position that the Constitution, with insignificant exceptions, left race to the states.

Criminal Procedure

Significant criminal procedure cases from the era were largely from the states. An exception, *McNabb v. United States* (1943), nicely highlights the differences between review of a federal criminal conviction and review of state convictions. The defendants were arrested at night on charges of murder. Instead of being brought before a judicial officer for arraignment, they were kept in jail for over fourteen hours during which time they were questioned individually and together. Eventually, they confessed. With only Reed dissenting, the Court, through Frankfurter, held that federal laws ordering that a person arrested be taken before a judicial officer had been violated. Accordingly, the Court, in its role as supervisor of the federal judiciary, held that the confessions obtained in violation of the statute were inadmissible. It was unnecessary to reach any constitutional issues.

State cases were different because in reviewing them the Court had no general supervisory power and had to rely exclusively upon the Constitution. These cases raised two classes of issues, the admissibility of confessions and whether the Bill of Rights bound the states in addition to the federal government. The Court concluded that due process required a voluntary confession, and the only way to determine voluntariness was to comb the facts of the case to see if the free will of the defendant was overridden.

Cases raising Bill of Rights issues attempted to substitute per se rules for multifactored rules (like "totality of the circumstances"). All these efforts failed. In *Betts v. Brady* (1942), *Adamson v. California* (1947), and *Wolf v. Colorado* (1949), the Court rejected claims that the provisions of the Bill of Rights applied directly to the states: in *Betts,* the Sixth Amendment requirement that indigents be provided with a lawyer; in *Adamson,* the Fifth Amendment's Self-Incrimination Clause; and in *Wolf,* the Fourth Amendment's rule excluding from trial evidence illegally seized by police.

The cases generated a remarkable jurisprudential debate between Frankfurter and Black. Frankfurter, who won the battle, argued that principles of federalism mandated that the states be free to develop their own systems of criminal justice rather than be forced into a potentially outmoded eighteenth-century straitjacket instantiated in the Bill of Rights. While Black agreed with Frankfurter that the Bill of Rights originally applied only to the federal government, he claimed that the framers of the Fourteenth Amendment intended to apply the Bill of Rights to the states. Black's position, wrongly derided at the time as historically fallacious, eventually peaked at four votes, his own plus those of Douglas, Murphy, and Rutledge. As a result of Frankfurter's victory, states could convict an indigent defendant at a trial where he had no legal assistance, allow prosecutors to argue to the jury about a defendant's failure to take the witness stand, and admit evidence that police illegally seized. Denial of counsel was a southern policy; the other two were national.

World War II

The first civil liberties clash of World War II came before the war and as a result of the patriotism of World War I. It involved a required flag salute, an idea dating from the time of the Spanish-American War but one that had gained momentum only when pushed by the American Legion, the Veterans of Foreign Wars, the Daughters of the American Revolution, and the Ku Klux Klan in the aftermath of the First World War. By the mid-1930s eighteen states required the opening of school to commence with a flag salute. In 1940, at a time when the British were evacuating Dunkirk, Frankfurter wrote a powerful opinion in *Minersville School District v. Gobitis* sustaining the compulsory flag salute— "'We live by symbols.' The flag is the symbol of our national unity"— over the objections of Jehovah's Witnesses. Only Stone, whose concern for conscientious objectors dated from the First World War, dissented.

The Jehovah's Witnesses believed that saluting the flag violated the biblical injunction against worshipping graven images, and accordingly they were placed in the unhappy situation of either disobeying the law— and facing jail time and potentially losing custody of their children—or their children facing eternal damnation. The former being the lighter penalty, the Witnesses opted for it.

Gobitis was widely condemned by the press and resulted, as many feared, in a virtual declaration of open season against the Witnesses. Over 2,000 were expelled from schools, but that was mild compared to the outbreak of vigilante attacks on them, over 350 in some 44 states. FBI Director J. Edgar Hoover publicly called for an end to the vigilante attacks as "having no place in America today."[8] The justices switched as rapidly as they could. In *West Virginia v. Barnette* (1943), Jackson held that no one could be forced to salute the flag. His opinion, over the dissents of Frankfurter, Roberts, and Reed, analogized the flag salute to the Nazi salute and implied those requiring it were narrow-minded individuals who could not understand that loyalty had to be won, not coerced. "If there is any fixed star in our constitutional constellation, it is that no official, high or petty, can prescribe what shall be orthodox in politics, nationalism or other matter of opinion or force citizens to confess by word or act their faith therein." Jackson's opinion in *Barnette* is aptly considered by many to be the most moving and powerful Supreme Court opinion ever written. It was announced on June 14—Flag Day.

No one would ever celebrate the opinions of Stone and Black sustaining the government's policies against the Japanese-Americans on the West Coast. Both deferred completely to the assertion that it was militarily necessary to round up all people of Japanese ancestry, whether citizens or not—citizens were labeled "nonaliens"—and remove them from their homes into detention camps for the duration of the war. It was a policy pushed by West Coast politicians like Earl Warren, the ambitious California attorney general, and John DeWitt, the commanding general on the West Coast (and an old Alabama friend of Hugo Black), along with DeWitt's civilian superiors like John C. McCloy in the War Department. Its justifications were fear, racism, and the desire by many to make a quick buck through the disastrous sales of homes and businesses forced on the hapless Japanese. Although Black's opinion sustaining the relocation stated that all racial classifications had to be subjected to strict scrutiny, what comes through is the idea that war is hell—so why are these people complaining? The justices joining the opinion were simply incapable of confronting their president over such a major policy during wartime; maybe no majority of a politically appointed Court would behave differently. Jackson, Murphy, and Roberts, however, did, refusing to go along with a decision that gave a constitutional imprimatur to a patently unjust policy.

That there were so few civil liberties cases during the war is a tribute not so much to the strength of the Court's jurisprudence as to Attorney General Francis Biddle, who resolved not to repeat the demands for conformity of World War I and had considerable success in following this resolve. Only the Japanese relocation, which Biddle turned over (because he recognized a juggernaut when he saw one) to Tom Clark in his Justice Department and McCloy in the War Department, was a major blemish on the record.[9] Indeed, this is the single greatest civil liberties blemish in the United States in the twentieth century.

The Justices and Politics

The war demonstrated that the Roosevelt appointees, to an unparalleled extent, did not think of the Court as a capstone of their careers nor even as an exclusive job. Possibly because of the political vacuum Roosevelt created in the Democratic Party, at least three justices—Black, Douglas, and Jackson—harbored presidential ambitions. Black and Jackson never had a prayer, but Douglas did. He was one of Roosevelt's two choices to replace Henry Wallace as vice president on the ticket in 1944 and was actually offered the vice presidency by Truman four years later. He turned it down because he refused to be a number two man to a man he perceived as a number two man. Black quietly seethed, believing Douglas was gaining opportunities that should have been his.

Byrnes left the Court for important posts running the domestic economy during the war and gained the label "Assistant President." Douglas had hoped to run the war economy, but Frankfurter had used his connections to thwart the appointment (although it appears Roosevelt made the decision independently). Frankfurter's diary is full of complaints about Douglas and politics, even as Frankfurter, through his numerous connections, had his fingers everywhere in the administration. He saw no problem with someone like himself, solely interested in the public good, doing what he condemned in others.

Two other justices were called to service while a third forlornly hoped to be called. At the beginning of the war, Roberts, a Hoover appointee, chaired, at Roosevelt's request, an investigation of preparedness at Pearl Harbor. At the end of the war, President Truman successfully prevailed on Jackson to be the first chief prosecutor at the Nuremberg War Trials. During the war, Murphy longed for a military appointment or another way to be of service.

With Stone's death, Truman had his second appointment, and he selected his friend, Fred Vinson of Kentucky, previously Secretary of the Treasury and veteran Democratic politician, to be chief justice. This caused Jackson, who was at Nuremberg, to publicly blast Black, who Jackson believed had lobbied against making him chief justice. Then, in the summer of 1949, Murphy and Rutledge, both energetic liberals, suddenly died, and Truman replaced them with two more of his friends, Sherman Minton, a former Indiana senator and federal judge, and Tom Clark from Texas. During the war, Clark was briefly the Justice Department's coordinator for the Japanese relocation and handled war fraud cases referred from Truman's Government Investigating Committee. Clark moved up through the ranks, heading the Antitrust Division and the Criminal Division; when Truman remade the Cabinet, Clark became the first Justice Department careerist to be named attorney general. As attorney general, he vigorously enforced the antitrust laws and enthusiastically put in place the government's domestic loyalty-security program; he was the founding attorney general of the ubiquitous "Attorney General's List" of subversive organizations.

Truman, like Roosevelt, knew his appointees well; indeed, of the men appointed by these two presidents, only Rutledge and Stone (elevated from associate to chief justice) did not know the president who appointed them. Furthermore, all except Burton were tied, in one way or another, to the national ruling coalition of the Democratic Party. Only Rutledge and Minton had prior judicial experience, and Minton's came after a partisan Senate career (where he had supported the Court-packing plan). Finally, Truman was unsuccessful in coming up with talented men for the Court; with the possible exception of Clark, Truman's appointees were a wholly undistinguished group. Joined by Reed, they were enthusiastic Cold Warriors, believing that the fight against domestic communism was essential to the nation's survival.

The Cold War

It is no small irony that with the glaring exception of the Japanese-Americans, civil liberties were far better preserved during World War II than after. The coup in Czechoslovakia and the Berlin Airlift in 1948, the "fall" of China and the Soviet A-bomb in 1949, and then the North Korean invasion of the South in 1950 reinforced an overwhelming belief among Americans that domestic communists were would-be traitors and a genuine threat to national security.

The federal government's domestic-security program used the Smith Act in seeking criminal sanctions against those holding the top leadership positions in the Communist Party and used loyalty review checks to rid public employment of all who were "disloyal"—a euphemism for past or present members of the Communist Party. It is essential to remember that joining the Communist Party had always been legal, if misguided, and that, in the course of the two decades prior to 1950, significant numbers of Americans did join the Party, both prior to the Molotov-Ribbentrop nonaggression pact and after the Nazi invasion of the Soviet Union placed the United States and Soviet Union in an alliance against Germany.

Testimony before the House Un-American Activities Committee (HUAC) and the Senate Internal Security Subcommittee (SISS) had painted a picture of every member of the Communist Party as under orders from above (all the way to Moscow) and awaiting the call to spy for the Soviet Union. However far-fetched this had once seemed, the indictment and then conviction of the handsome, urbane New Deal official Alger Hiss for perjury (over whether he had committed espionage while in the State Department) had rocked the country. A number of liberals went into a permanent state of denial: first, that HUAC and Richard Nixon could be correct; second, that an admitted ex-communist perjurer like Hiss's accuser, Whittaker Chambers, should be believed; and, third, that a man as educated and cultured and so representative of the New Deal could have been a spy. Most Americans rejected Hiss's implausible profession of innocence once a jury found to the contrary. They learned important lessons: there *were* communists; some of them had reached important positions in government; and they would commit espionage.

Immediately after the Hiss verdict, a British scientist, Klaus Fuchs, who had worked on the atomic bomb project at Los Alamos, confessed to English authorities that he had been a Soviet spy. But foreigners were not the only ones willing to ship atomic secrets to the Soviets. Shortly after Fuchs confessed, Ethel and Julius Rosenberg were indicted as atomic spies. After a jury convicted them, Judge Irving Kaufman sentenced them to death, blaming them for the American deaths in the Korean War, and the sentence was carried out early in the Eisenhower administration.

The Rosenberg case reinforced the ex-communists' HUAC testimony and the Republican claim that the higher loyalty of communists meant there was no crime too great for them to commit. Americans, very much including Supreme Court justices, viewed these trials against the backdrop of communist expansion in Europe and Asia, and an aggressive anticommunism became a staple of American politics and society.

Although tactics varied, ridding public life of communists was a non-partisan goal that had overwhelming public support, and states in varying degrees created loyalty programs paralleling the federal program. For the public the issue was not whether to have an effective program but rather whether the program was, in fact, working effectively and therefore whether improvements were necessary.

Sustaining the Domestic-Security Program

In three decisions in 1951 the Court sustained three of the four key elements of the federal policy and all but eliminated the First Amendment's guarantee of freedom of speech as a barrier to government action. The convictions of the top leaders of the Party were affirmed and the Smith Act sustained in *Dennis v. United States;* the authority to list organizations as subversive was sustained in *Joint Anti-Fascist Refugee Committee v. McGrath;* and this in turn provided authority to dismiss federal employees for membership in a listed organization, which was upheld in *Bailey v. Richardson.*

The Smith Act crime charged in *Dennis* was a conspiracy to *advocate* the overthrow of the United States government at some unknown future time. The Government did not charge a conspiracy to *attempt* to overthrow the government because there was no evidence of any steps taken toward such an attempt. Had the Government found such evidence, the case would have been easy, but because no such evidence existed, the case raised a huge First Amendment issue. All that the leaders had done was talk and hope. To be sure they wanted to overthrow the government, but they had not gone beyond advocating it and seeking to determine, according to Marxist-Leninist precepts, when the time for overthrow would be appropriate. Apparently, their failure to proceed reflected their failure to conclude (or, more likely, to be told from Moscow) that the time for action was ripe. As a result, *Dennis* arrived at the Court as the major First Amendment case of the century. How, absent a "clear and present danger" created by the Party's existence and its speech, could the leaders be sent to jail? By both the facts of the case and the jury charge, the lack of a *present* danger, except that posed by the Soviet Union, was clear.

The two lower federal courts that decided the case had done so by either ignoring or gutting Justice Oliver Wendell Holmes's famous test by which speech could not be penalized unless it created a clear and present danger to an interest the government had the right to protect. The Supreme Court followed suit. The danger from a communist overthrow was clear. It did not have to be present. It was sufficient that the defendants wanted to do it "as speedily as circumstances permit," whenever that might occur. Black wrote a short, blistering dissent; Douglas's dissent was a lengthy demonstration of why no clear and present danger was shown. After *Dennis* prosecutions of the second-tier leaders of the Party were initiated.

Joint Anti-Fascist Refugee Committee, involving the so-called "Attorney General's List" of subversive organizations, produced six opinions from eight justices. (Clark, who had been the attorney general, did not participate in any of the three cases, but would have voted with Vinson, Reed, Burton, and Minton if he had.) When the votes were totaled up, it was legitimate for the government to have and publicize such a list, but any listed organization had the right to contest being labeled subversive and thus could demand a hearing at which its actual nature would be determined. No one wanted that kind of a hearing, so the outcome was that the Attorney General's List would continue to be a blackballing mechanism. Known membership in a listed group meant the end of government employment. Indeed, that is exactly the result in *Bailey v. Richardson.*

Bailey was a 4–4 split and, therefore, by the Court's internal procedures, produced no opinions. Still, the opinion below, which was necessarily affirmed, upheld Bailey's dismissal because of her membership in a listed group. Had Clark been able to participate, his would have been the fifth vote to officially sustain the program and, more important, sustain the absence of trial-like procedures—especially to know what the charges were and to confront and cross-examine adverse witnesses—by which the finding of disloyalty was made.

The dominant facet of the post-1937 Court, then, was that it was composed of men who had served in the federal government and who believed in the beneficence of the federal government. When the federal government acted, even as egregiously as by ordering the Japanese relocation, the Court sustained it (albeit with three dissents). From the justices' points of view, the Court's prime role was to facilitate the policies ordained by the elected branches.

The states did not fare so well. In economic matters they gained real leeway after 1937—although that was always subject to Congress's paramount economic authority. But because of the diversity of the states—and because many southern racial practices were blatantly unconstitutional—states ran afoul of constitutional guarantees with some frequency (in contrast to the three trivial federal statutes struck down during the period).

Arguably the biggest case of the era came at its end when President Truman seized the steel mills to keep them running (and thereby avoiding a strike) during the Korean War. Truman claimed that the president had some form of inherent constitutional power to take necessary actions during national emergencies and that presidents from Lincoln through Roosevelt had similarly exercised such a power.

In those days, when the Court was filled with former presidential advisers, Vinson, cruising the Potomac on the presidential yacht *Sequoia,* agreed with Truman's position and told him that the Court would support him if he seized the mills. Armed with this knowledge, Truman went forward only to be stunned when Vinson's vote count was wrong. Only Reed and Minton joined Vinson in supporting Truman's position. Upon losing, Truman yielded, but his memoirs, written years later, showed he still was bitter about the vote.

Vinson's early guess probably went as high as six justices willing, without much further consideration, to sustain presidential power. In addition to the three Vinson got right, there was Clark, who as attorney general had told Truman that the president had inherent authority to temporarily seize essential industries; Jackson, who as attorney general had justified Roosevelt's doing so; and Burton, who was simply a friend. Furthermore, the Court always upheld presidential action in a crisis.

A recent book by Chief Justice William Rehnquist, who clerked for Jackson during *Youngstown Sheet & Tube v. Sawyer,* known as the *Steel Seizure Case,* discusses the case at length and suggests that Truman would have prevailed if he and the Korean War had not been so unpopular.[10] Rehnquist is probably correct although he misses an important point. In the fifteen years from 1937 to 1952, when the Court was sustaining everything a president did, the president and Congress were working in harmony. The Court was never asked to choose between the two. The justices were part of the national Democratic Party, sustaining actions of the national Democratic Party. That is what made the *Steel Seizure Case* different and difficult. It split the party, with influential members of Congress opposed to Truman's action. In splitting the party, the case split the Court as well.

Possibly, then, the *Steel Seizure Case* might presage the future, which by 1952 was already clear at the Court. The controversial cases that the Court would be forced to decide (or duck) were the next round of domestic-security cases, where greater numbers of federal employees were caught in the various programs' webs, and *Brown v. Board of Education* with its challenge to segregation in the public schools. Like presidential authority to seize the steel mills, both of these issues split the Democratic Party. Furthermore, if the constitutional claimants in these cases prevailed, the relief necessary for the result would not look to another branch's policy choice. Sustaining a constitutional claim in the domestic-security cases would mean blocking rather than implementing a congressional policy. Relief in the school segregation cases would entail a judicial rather than a legislative policy. Like the *Steel Seizure Case,* splitting the judiciary from the policy of the other branches of the federal government made these cases different and difficult.

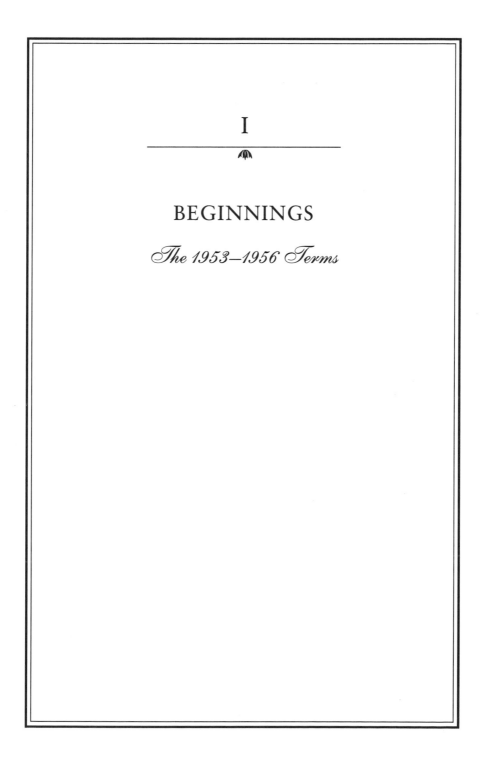

I

BEGINNINGS

The 1953–1956 Terms

Brown before Warren

Plessy v. Ferguson was the South's Magna Carta. The earliest cases arising under the post–Civil War amendments to the Constitution held that the amendments' overriding purpose was to protect the newly freed African-Americans. State-mandated discrimination against them was unconstitutional. *Plessy*'s charter to the South was its conclusion that officially but evenhandedly separating the races was not discrimination. The Court held this in a context where the evenhandedness of the separation seemed apparent—railroad cars. Whites had their own. African-Americans had an identical one. Homer Plessy was selected to challenge the law because he looked white and yet under Louisiana law he was deemed African-American even though seven of his great-grandparents had been white. With Plessy as the plaintiff the arbitrary nature of the racial classification should have been apparent on its face. Instead, the Court paid no heed for, as a best-selling novel of the period noted, "one drop of Negro blood makes a Negro."[1]

Plessy did three things. It found separate but equal public facilities to be consonant with the Fourteenth Amendment's requirement of equal protection of the law. It simultaneously denied that law could change attitudes. And it left racial issues to the states, right down to the determination of who was white. It did so within a requirement that legislation must be reasonable. In testing reasonableness, both legislatures and courts could "act with reference to established usages, customs and traditions of the people, and with a view to promote their comfort, and the preservation of the public peace and good order." Social equality being unattainable, the legislature could act to prevent a "commingling of the two races on terms unsatisfactory to either." Because whites would not believe a law requiring separation, enacted by an African-American legislature (as could be remembered from Reconstruction), would make whites inferior, so African-Americans should not perceive separate but equal to place a badge of inferiority on them. If they did, it was "not by reason of anything found" in the law but by their own doing.

However specious this reasoning appears today, it is worth remembering that *Plessy* was an 8–1 decision that was able to cite as authority an 1850 Massachusetts decision on segregated schools. The justices were fully aware of the contrary arguments because Justice John Marshall Harlan made them in a dissent comparing *Plessy* to the infamous *Dred Scott* case, and they rejected them by an overwhelming vote. There was no public outcry that indicated the Court got it wrong in the slightest. *Plessy* fully "embodied the conventional wisdom," and its author, Henry Brown, subsequently noted that in reaching the decision that Court experienced "little difficulty."[2]

The only dents in *Plessy* came when a state abandoned, as in fact they all did, even a pretense of equality. The African-American public schools of the South were not equal to their white counterparts, but they were not as bad as the graduate schools that the Court had dealt with, and the public schools were getting better. Furthermore, graduate-school integration threatened little since the students had already spent a lifetime becoming acculturated to the southern way of life; grade-school integration, affecting the young, threatened the cornerstone of white supremacy.

The consequences of holding school segregation unconstitutional were enormous. Yet that is what Thurgood Marshall and the National Association for the Advancement of Colored People were asking the Court to do in *Brown v. Board of Education* and four companion cases. Marshall had determined that in the post–World War II legal, political, and economic climate, the time had come to take *Plessy* head on. Even though Negro schools were nowhere equal to white schools, the NAACP intentionally eschewed any claims of inequality due to expenditures. If the time was ripe, then Marshall could short-circuit the tiring and possibly endless task of proving the inequality of resources in each school district in the South. Thus, the NAACP claimed that segregated schools, even if perfectly equal in resources, violated the Equal Protection Clause of the Fourteenth Amendment. And, of course, the NAACP won. (In fact the litigating arm of the NAACP was a separate organization, the NAACP Legal Defense and Education Fund, Inc., known to cognoscenti as either "the Inc. Fund" or the "LDF." The LDF was set up in the late 1930s to preserve the NAACP's tax-exempt status, but it was separate in name only until a southern-instigated Internal Revenue Service investigation in 1956 forced the two organizations to become truly separate.)

Decades after *Brown,* all constitutional commentators, whether on the left or the right, agree *Brown* was correctly decided, and any theory to the contrary is impossible to sustain. Most commentators also believe *Brown,* a unanimous opinion, was an easy case. That is ahistorical; it wasn't. That's why the Warren Court burst on the scene so dramatically and captivated two generations of law professors so completely.

The oral argument in *Brown* debunks the notion that it was easy. Felix Frankfurter informed one of the NAACP lawyers that "we do not argue for ten hours a question that is self-evident."[3] Then, after hearing those ten hours of argument in the fall of 1952, the Court ordered a new round of briefing and argument, complete this time with a request to the United States for full participation in the oral argument. Easy cases hardly need a second go-round.

The reason for reargument was that the Court, after the initial argument, was badly split. Hugo Black, William O. Douglas, Harold Burton, and Sherman Minton believed racial segregation was per se unconstitutional. Fred Vinson and Stanley Reed, both from Kentucky, did not believe separate but equal, with its long lineage, was unconstitutional. Tom Clark from Texas was similarly inclined, although less firmly so. Robert Jackson was in the middle, generally ambivalent about racial issues. He believed segregation was wrong but not that it was necessarily unconstitutional. Jackson was wrestling with the huge question of whether a decision striking separate but equal was consistent with law or an impermissible invasion of the political realm.

Frankfurter had similar concerns, but he was especially concerned with the Court's prestige. From his perspective, it was essential that any opinion be unanimous, and in 1953 unanimity looked all but impossible. At the optimistic best, a 7–2 vote to hold segregation unconstitutional was possible. The justices assumed that the more closely divided the result the more likely the South would engage in open defiance. A split that left all southerners (except Black) in the dissent with the northerners commanding the result might have looked like *Dred Scott* (where the seven in the majority consisted of five southerners and two northern doughfaces) on the one hand or the 1860 election (where Lincoln received no southern votes) on the other. In either case, it would be pure sectional politics, and in either case, southern whites would perceive the opinion as illegitimate northern aggression.

In order to buy more time, Frankfurter suggested new briefing and reargument devoted to ascertaining the circumstances surrounding adoption of the Fourteenth Amendment and the relationship between legislative and judicial power under the amendment (since counsel for Virginia had denied that even Congress could touch segregation). Maybe delay would help.

It did. On September 8, 1953, Vinson died from a heart attack. This was, Frankfurter commented privately to his law clerks, "the first indication that I have ever had that there is a God."[4]

Although he scarcely knew him, General Dwight Eisenhower had, just prior to being elected president, promised California Governor Earl Warren the first opening on the Supreme Court. Warren had campaigned for Eisenhower, and California's votes on a procedural issue at the convention had practically doomed the conservative Ohio Senator Robert Taft's chances. Warren had been Thomas Dewey's vice presidential candidate four years earlier and thus had gone down to the unexpected upset by Harry Truman. In 1952 Warren's chances for the nomination and probable November victory depended on at least a first ballot deadlock between Eisenhower and Taft. It didn't happen. Worse, California's youthful senator, Richard Nixon, outmaneuvered Warren to swing the California delegation to Eisenhower and came away with the vice presidency himself. Warren, a nonpartisan Republican, had never liked the partisan Nixon yet watched him being rewarded for helping deny Warren the prize he wanted most.

Then, of course, Vinson died suddenly. Attorney General Herbert Brownell flew west for a secret meeting with Warren, designed to convince him that the "first seat" did not mean the chief justiceship. Brownell then flew east with the response that the chief justiceship was the first available seat and, it being available, Warren was ready to accept the president's nomination. It was a wonderful consolation prize even though there appears never to have been an explicit quid pro quo or agreement between Eisenhower and Warren.

Warren was one of the century's most successful politicians. In California he won election as district attorney, attorney general, and then three times as governor. He was so popular that once he won both the Republican and Democratic gubernatorial primaries simultaneously. California was growing at a breakneck pace throughout his gubernatorial years, and he successfully dealt with the needs for new roads, schools, housing, and medical care, thereby assuring himself of electoral victory after victory. Although a committed good government progressive, he was hardly without fault. As a prosecutor, he could slight the rights of the accused. As attorney general, he was a leading advocate of Japanese relocation during World War II. As governor, he opposed any changes in California's rotten-borough senate.

No one praised Warren for his strong intellect, but almost everyone recognized a warm and gregarious man with a rugged sincerity. He was hardworking, principled, and honest. People liked him. All this held true on the Court where years of executive service had given him a strong philosophy of governing, of doing right as he understood the circumstances, and he continued to do so. Furthermore, just as when his California responsibilities broadened, so did his horizons, when he was placed in a national job, his horizons became national. That meant dealing with southern segregation, not when he thought the time was ripe but, rather, immediately.

Chapter 2

Brown

In the beginning there was *Brown v. Board of Education*. Writing for the Court, Chief Justice Warren concluded that "in the field of public education the doctrine of 'separate but equal' has no place." In placing his name on the opinion, Warren had done what chief justices since the legendary John Marshall had always done. In great and controversial cases, where the Court's prestige is on the line, the Court speaks through the chief justice. Those needs were apparent in *Brown*. The justices were not only overruling more than a half century of constitutional law stemming from *Plessy v. Ferguson*, they were going where no court had ever gone before: to dismantle an entrenched social order. Normally, such a transformation occurs only in the aftermath of wartime defeat. Accordingly, they knew that defiance and violence were likely by-products of their action. As Judge J. Harvie Wilkinson wrote, "*Brown* may be the most important political, social, and legal event in America's twentieth century history. Its greatness lay in the enormity of injustice it condemned, in the entrenched sentiment it challenged, in the immensity of law it both created and overthrew."[1]

The Process

Brown and its companion cases were reargued in December 1953, two months after Vinson's successor Warren took the center seat. During those two months, Warren had asked Black, the senior associate, to lead the Conference. But when *Brown* was discussed, Black was absent, and Warren for the first time exercised his prerogative to speak first in the conference room where the justices, with no others present, discuss cases.

Warren requested that the Brethren take no vote and avoid hardened positions, stating they would discuss the segregation cases in Conference each week. But then, when he offered his views, the other justices knew the cases' final outcome because Warren made it clear that he believed segregation could be sustained only on the fallacious theory of Negro inferiority. He did not "see how segregation can be justified in this day and age . . . we must act, but we should do it in a tolerant way."[2] There were at least five votes to hold separate but equal unconstitutional; only the final tally and the opinions stating why remained.

The year's delay that Frankfurter engineered through reargument had helped beyond replacing Vinson with Warren. Clark, who always liked to vote with the chief justice, now was willing to find separate but equal unconstitutional. Jackson had resolved his doubts too. Only Reed, who denied separate but equal was premised on Negro inferiority, held to *Plessy's* soon-to-be-discarded doctrine.

During the following months, Warren spoke privately with each of the justices about the cases, and the subsequent Conferences focused on what remedy the justices would order to dismantle the South's dual school system. As April was nearing its end, Reed remained the lone holdout. At a meeting with Reed, Warren went for the clinching argument: "Stan, you're all by yourself in this now. You've got to decide whether it's really the best thing for the country."[3] Reed switched.

The other potential holdout from joining a unanimous opinion was Jackson. He was writing a concurring opinion in which he wrestled with his concerns about changing so much settled law. Whether the opinion was intended as a way of cleansing his soul or to be delivered is unclear because on March 30 a heart attack hospitalized Jackson, and he never returned to the opinion. He did not leave the hospital until May 17, the day *Brown* came down. Indeed, he left the hospital to be present in the Courtroom to underscore the unanimity of *Brown*. Another heart attack would kill him before *Brown* was reargued yet again on the issue of remedy.

Jackson was not alone in wanting to be in the Courtroom that Monday. For several weeks it had been packed by people hoping to be at the Court on the day the historic opinion would be announced, and with the term approaching its end, every Monday had the chance to be *the* Monday. Warren recalled that as the justices came in on the 17th, "there was a tenseness that I have not seen equally before or since." Using his prerogative, he read the brief opinion in its entirety. "When the word 'unanimously' was spoken a wave of emotion swept the room; no words of intentional movement, yet a distinct emotional manifestation that defies description."[4]

The Opinion

Brown was short, a mere eleven pages in contrast to Warren's fifty-plus page opinions in *Miranda v. Arizona* (1966) and the *Reapportionment Cases* (1964), because he wanted it that way. A short opinion could be reprinted in full by any newspaper in the country. Warren, the politician, knew the importance of getting his message to as many people as possible. *Brown* was also short because it was nonaccusatory. Southerners weren't going to like the result no matter what the Court said, but Warren wanted nothing to unnecessarily inflame them; thus, the opinion was also nonrhetorical.

The initial three pages were devoted to an abstract and bland recital of the common legal challenge: that segregated public schools violate the Fourteenth Amendment's Equal Protection Clause because they are not equal and, more important, cannot be made equal. The next page was devoted to the reargument on the history of the Fourteenth Amendment. The opinion acknowledged that the history did not shed enough light to resolve the problem. At best it was "inconclusive."

Next the opinion bolstered its conclusion that history was not dispositive by noting the nature of public schooling in the North at the end of the Civil War as well as its primitive nature in the South. Therefore, little history of the Fourteenth Amendment touched education. The Court would return to this point but only after it disposed of its own precedents, a process that took but two paragraphs. It noted that at first the Court prohibited state-imposed discrimination against the Negro. Then, in 1896, *Plessy v. Ferguson* introduced separate but equal in transportation, not education, cases. The latter cases commenced thereafter. The first two education cases did not challenge *Plessy,* while the three most recent, all involving graduate school, found that specific benefits offered whites were denied African-Americans and hence separate but equal itself was violated. But, unlike the graduate-school cases, the records before the Court showed that tangible factors were being equalized and therefore the decision could not turn on them. In other words (which the Court did not write), although everyone knew that Negro schools had less of everything except leaky roofs than white schools, these cases were intentionally litigated on the assumption that everything except student assignments was equal. Therefore, the only question was "the effect of segregation itself on public education."

With that statement the Court returned to history to again reject it. The opinion stated it could not turn the clock back to 1868 and the adoption of the Fourteenth Amendment nor even to 1896 and *Plessy*. "We must consider public education in light of its full development and its present place in American life throughout the Nation." At this point, having rejected the turn to history on which reargument was based, Warren's opinion had but three pages and two lines remaining even though it had yet to offer a single word about segregation. And the next paragraph didn't either. Instead, that paragraph spoke to the importance of education; its topic sentence announced "education is perhaps the most important function of state and local governments." With the paragraph tying education to citizenship as well as success in life, the Court then stated the issue in the case once again. Here, however, the Court stopped with the hints and stated the result: Separate but equal education was unconstitutional. It is also at this point in the reading of the opinion in Court that Warren recalled the wave of emotion about unanimity. What Warren did not say is that he inserted "unanimously" orally; it does not appear in the Court's opinion.

The next two and one-third pages gave the entire reasoning. The opinion returned to precedent to show that the two most recent graduate-school cases had found that separated learning environments provided fewer of the "intangible" qualities that facilitate learning. "Such considerations apply with added force to children in grade and high schools." If children are separated solely "because of race," they will have "a feeling of inferiority as to their status in the community" that may never be corrected. The opinion then quoted the trial judge in the Kansas case:

> Segregation of white and colored children in public schools has a detrimental effect upon the colored children. The impact is greater when it has the sanction of the law; for the policy of separating the races is usually interpreted as denoting the inferiority of the negro group. A sense of inferiority affects the motivation of the child to learn. Segregation with the sanction of law, therefore, has a tendency to [retard] the educational and mental development of negro children and to deprive them of some of the benefits which they would receive in a racial[ly] integrated school system.

This finding was the key to *Brown*. Reargued on history, the articulated result turned on psychology.

The Court's conclusion expressly contradicted (without quoting) the well-known musings of the Court in *Plessy* that if "enforced separation of the two races stamps the colored race with a badge of inferiority," it does so "solely because the colored race choose to put that construction upon it." Hence, the Court now rid itself of those musings: "Whatever may have been the extent of psychological knowledge at the time of *Plessy v. Ferguson,* this finding is amply supported by modern authority." At the end of the sentence came Footnote Eleven, one of the two most famous footnotes in Supreme Court history. Footnote Eleven contained no text. It cited six professional studies, the most prominent of which was by NAACP consultant, Professor Kenneth B. Clark. After the six, the footnote gave a "see generally" to Gunnar Myrdal's mid-1940s classic, *An American Dilemma.*

The Court thus found separate educational facilities were "inherently unequal" because of their effects on Negro children. The plaintiffs prevailed on exactly the constitutional claim they raised. The case was not over, however; the last paragraph ordered yet another round of argument, this time on how to fashion "appropriate relief" now that the constitutional question was settled.

The opinion made two things clear: School segregation was unconstitutional, and the original understanding of the meaning of the Fourteenth Amendment had nothing to do with the holding. But that was it; the result was as clear as could be—the legal reasoning was not. The heart of the opinion, its sole reason, was the single paragraph holding that segregation generates feelings of inferiority, a holding backed by a lower court finding of fact (and not mentioning the contrary findings of fact in the other cases), a conclusion the Court asserted was "amply supported by modern psychology."

From his comments at the first Conference on *Brown,* we know that Warren believed segregation had to be premised on the inferiority of African-Americans. Had he gone further, he would have noted that an entire social structure had developed based on as complete a subordination of African-Americans as possible. The first Justice John Marshall Harlan had stated in his *Plessy* dissent that the Constitution "neither knows nor tolerates classes among citizens." Warren's *Brown,* without any rhetorical flair, was intended to make this real. Warren came closer to saying what he meant in a fifth case, *Bolling v. Sharpe* (1954), posing the same legal issue but in the context of the federal government and the District of Columbia schools.

Bolling v. Sharpe

The changed context meant changed constitutional text. The states are expressly forbidden to deny to any person within their jurisdiction the equal protection of the laws. The federal government is not; indeed, there is no comparable textual language. Lack of appropriate text was hardly a deterrent, however, because, as Warren wrote in *Bolling*, "it would be unthinkable that the same Constitution would impose a lesser duty on the Federal Government." Apparently it was also unthinkable to hold that segregation in the South violated the Constitution and then leave to Congress the option of retaining the only legally segregated schools in America. That being unthinkable, the Court, without considering it, foreclosed the option of making Congress act (and then potentially becoming something of a partner in ending segregation).

Because different constitutional duties could not exist, some textual hook had to be found, and the Due Process Clause of the Fifth Amendment (paralleled by identical language in the Fourteenth just in front of the Equal Protection Clause) was called into service. The Due Process Clause, Warren stated, stems from "our American ideal of fairness." So does the Equal Protection Clause. Therefore, while the clauses are not "always interchangeable phrases," neither are they "mutually exclusive." In this context both achieve fairness by forbidding segregation. Accordingly, because segregation in public education is "not reasonably related to any proper governmental objective," it is an arbitrary deprivation of liberty.

Equating the Due Process Clause and the Equal Protection Clause, even as limited, was nothing short of stunning. Due process traces its lineage back to Magna Carta, while the first use of equal protection of laws was in President Andrew Jackson's message to Congress announcing his veto of the rechartering of the Bank of the United States four decades after the Bill of Rights was adopted. Had Warren not been so disdainful of history, he could have shown that, prior to the Civil War, due process had a strong equal protection component, but this had been lost in history, and Warren did not rediscover it. He just asserted the point. Never before had a Supreme Court opinion found the two clauses banned similar governmental behavior. Nevertheless, the conclusion that segregation (in schools) was not related to any proper governmental objective spoke much more forcefully to the constitutional issue than had anything in *Brown*. (And in this it echoed the NAACP's brief: "When the distinctions imposed are based upon race and color alone, the state's action is patently the epitome of that arbitrariness and capriciousness constitutionally impermissive under our system of government.")[5] Furthermore, *Bolling* rested on no social science data and nestled, albeit uneasily, within existing doctrine that condemned wholly arbitrary actions as violations of due process. The uneasy fit came from the fact that this type of reasoning had fallen into disfavor, possibly rejection, and under the terms of the existing doctrine, there was an articulated reason for school segregation as facilitating learning, and therefore segregation could not be said to be wholly arbitrary.

The articulated rationale in *Brown* invalidated segregation because it generated feelings of inferiority. *Bolling* condemned segregation because it could not be justified by *any* reason. Anyone familiar with the rationales for segregation that white southerners offered for public consumption—it promotes racial harmony; it's better for everyone; in schools it promotes learning—would know that Warren had cut from the soothing facade of southern rhetoric to harsh reality. Segregation "elevated" whites by holding down African-Americans. That was its intent; after all, if it were so good for African-Americans, why weren't they consulted and allowed to vote on it (or anything else)? That was its effect. Maintaining second-class citizenship could not be a legitimate objective in America; yet promoting racial harmony is clearly a legitimate governmental objective. Therefore, implicitly, *Bolling* announced that the Court no longer would pretend to believe the official southern lie. But, as Warren knew, it would be *Brown,* applicable to the South and border states, not *Bolling,* limited to the District of Columbia, that would be reprinted and read, and *Brown* explicitly said none of this.

All the justices knew the Court was producing a state paper of enormous significance, one that would be read and was intended to be read. The opinion did not need to persuade the NAACP and many northerners who already believed official racism was banned by the Fourteenth Amendment, as the immediate moral cheering of the northern press would show. No opinion could possibly persuade unregenerate racists. In the middle were those amenable to persuasion. No other objective for the Court's opinion besides persuading the persuadable made sense. Thus, in a memorandum accompanying his draft opinion, Warren stated he had operated on "the theory that the opinions should be short, readable by the lay public, non-rhetorical, unemotional and, above all, nonaccusatory."[6] *Brown* was thus the Court's chance to bring as many southern whites as possible to the Court's view.

What would the readers of *Brown,* who would not see *Bolling,* conclude it would foreshadow about segregation, about education, about constitutional law? The answer to the middle question would be forthcoming within a year once the Court heard the new round of argument on remedy and then issued its ruling. Answers to the others would take longer. Because they affected the South directly and the opinion was written for Southern consumption, southerners would be those most interested in divining the underlying meanings.

National Reactions

Reaction to *Brown* was "electric and widely divergent"[7] and predictable. In the North and West, among African-Americans, and in the State Department the decision was welcomed. In the South, reaction was surprisingly mixed. The southern press did not go ballistic although the leading politicians did.

Americans believe the Constitution embraces and requires morally correct outcomes on key issues. America is good; the Constitution is good; therefore, the outcome of major constitutional cases should be good. When they are not, as with *Dred Scott* or the New Deal impasse with the Court in 1935–1936, there is a disconnection between the American people and the Constitution and the Court. A disconnection portends trouble.

World War II was less than a decade in the past, and the European theater had been devoted to wiping out a regime committed to racial superiority. C. Vann Woodward noted that the comparisons to the American South were "inevitably made in the American mind especially since American war propaganda stressed above all else the abhorrence of the West for Hitler's brand of racism and its utter incompatibility with the democratic faith for which we fought."[8] During Vinson's tenure Black had condemned segregation to his Brethren as "Hitler's creed—he preached what the South believed."[9] With *Brown*, the leading nation in the Free World was free at home. Once the decision was announced, the contrary result was unthinkable.

White southerners, not less than their northern brethren, believe the Constitution mandates morally right outcomes. Segregation was morally good and the Constitution, as correctly interpreted by *Plessy,* created a local option on race. Each community, understanding what was best for itself, should be free to handle racial issues as it chose. The Constitution, therefore, enshrined states' rights. With *Brown,* for the second time in less than a century the North and the federal government were acting the aggressor, demanding a national solution to a local problem, a problem southerners, even liberal southerners, knew the North could not comprehend. Thus, William Faulkner penned "A Letter to the North" urging slowing everything down so that the South could move on its own to remedy the problems. The Civil War should have informed the North that the South "will go to any length, even that fatal and already doomed one, before it will accept alteration of its racial condition by mere force of law or economic threat."[10]

The amicus—"friend of the court"—brief of the United States encouraged the Court to see segregation in the context of the Cold War struggle against communism. "The United States is trying to prove to the people of the world, of every nationality, race and color, that a free democracy is the most civilized and most secure form of government yet devised by man."[11] The Soviet Union, in its arguments to Third World countries, consistently emphasized racial discrimination in the United States, and other countries "cannot understand how such a practice can exist in a country which professes to be a staunch supporter of freedom, justice, and democracy."[12] Foreign diplomats and visitors to the nation's capital saw segregation firsthand because Washington "is the window through which the world looks into our house . . . and the treatment of colored persons here is taken as the measure of our attitude toward minorities generally."[13] Thus, segregation was a "constant embarrassment" that "jeopardizes the effective maintenance of our moral leadership of the free and democratic nations of the world."[14] Such arguments might not be decisive, but they could not fail to impress Cold Warrior patriots sitting on the Court.

While the new amicus brief filed by the United States for the second round of argument was not as forthright as the brief filed by Truman's Justice Department (because the new brief limited itself to answering the questions the Court had propounded), nothing suggested that the United States now favored the South.[15] At oral argument, Douglas asked Lee Rankin, who argued for the United States, whether the Government believed *Plessy* should be overruled. Rankin answered affirmatively, showing that the Eisenhower administration was perceiving the issue similarly to the Truman administration.

The United States Government made good its implicit promise of celebration. Within an hour of Warren's announcement, the Voice of America broadcast the decision to Eastern Europe in thirty-four different languages.[16] *Brown* was the "top priority" for several days, and accompanying analysis emphasized "the issue was settled by law under democratic processes rather than by mob rule or dictatorial fiat."[17] The *New York Times* concurred; it told its readers that *Brown* was a "blow to communism."[18]

Eisenhower's personal unease about *Brown* is well known and was demonstrated immediately when asked by a reporter if he had any advice for the South and he tersely replied, "Not in the slightest."[19] Warren's memoirs paint the president as a racist who favored the South. Indeed, while *Brown* was under consideration, Warren was seated at a White House dinner near John Davis, the 1924 Democratic candidate for president and lead counsel for the South, and Eisenhower told Warren at length what a great man Davis was and that southerners were not bad people, just concerned lest their "sweet little girls be seated alongside some big black bucks."[20] But Eisenhower had also personally signed off on Rankin's affirmative answer to the question about overruling *Plessy* and knew of Attorney General Herbert Brownell's strong feelings that the United States had to participate and had to oppose *Plessy*.[21] Eisenhower might have preferred the Justice Department to sit on the sidelines, but knowing what it would do, he gave his personal okay.

On May 18, 1954, the president ordered the District of Columbia Board of Commissioners to set an example of peaceful desegregation. Over the next five years Eisenhower had four appointments to the Court and made no effort to select someone who might question *Brown* even though in private he denounced the decision, believing, with the *Plessy* majority, that prejudices could never be overcome by law. Whatever Eisenhower's conflicting private views, his State Department knew it had a foreign policy victory and used it immediately; his Justice Department was equally happy.

The NAACP had prepared in advance two press releases to accommodate either result. Having had its careful litigation strategy vindicated, it was able to issue the one expressing its "delight" at the ruling and calling for leaders of both races to implement the decision in good faith.[22] The *New York Times* ran a story entitled "Capital's Negroes Slow in Reacting."[23] Maybe the realization that compliance remained all too dependent on the good faith of the South explains why the general reaction of the African-American community was, in Richard Kluger's conclusion, "muted."[24] To be sure, there were commendatory editorials, but there was also a wariness; African-Americans had a long history of dealing with white southerners.

The northern press, by contrast, greeted *Brown* as a momentous case deserving the nation's approbation. *Time* magazine ranked it at the top of the landmark cases in history.[25] The *Des Moines Register* stated it constituted "the erasure of one of democracy's blackest marks." The *Minneapolis Morning Tribune* found the decision "will be welcomed and embraced by all" who believe in equal rights for everyone. The *San Francisco Chronicle* editorialized that *Brown* represented the "majesty of the democratic idea that men are created equal and entitled to equal protection of the laws." For the *St. Louis Post-Dispatch*, it was a "great and just act of judicial statesmanship." The *Cincinnati Enquirer* editorialized that the Court had acted "as the conscience of the nation." The *New York Times*, which assigned fifty reporters and devoted seven full pages to the case, summed it up: "The highest court in the land, the guardian of our national conscience, has reaffirmed its faith and the underlying American faith in the equality of all men and all children before the law."[26]

Still, victory comes in many forms, with its declaration being one; full achievement of victory was in the future, when action, not praise, would be necessary. As Woodward subsequently observed, the North was "by no means aroused to the point of stern insistence on compliance."[27] A 1956 poll suggested that three-quarters of northerners favored desegregation;[28] how intensely was not measured. That it might not be too intense could be seen in one general reaction in the North as well as the South—a sigh of relief that the Court had ordered reargument on remedy. All concerned would have time to prepare for the new era. What seems surprising in retrospect is the unquestioning acceptance of the fact that constitutional rights could be placed on hold for at least another year.

The Southern Reaction

"In general the Southern response was surprisingly mild, in part, no doubt, because the court had decided not to order immediate desegregation of the schools."[29] In 1954 the South did not speak with one racist voice, as it so often had in its past, and the southern urban press was surprisingly conciliatory although no paper even began to approach the northern enthusiasm, much less rhetoric, about conscience, equal rights, and judicial statesmanship. The two leading newspapers, the *Louisville Courier-Journal* and the *Atlanta Constitution*, both suggested that ending segregation was not the end of the world and, more important, not a call for violence. The *New Orleans Times-Picayune* was sure of "ensuing strife" while the *Birmingham Post-Herald* foresaw using the legal system "to avoid the difficulties ending segregation presents to both races."[30]

Astute Southern academics, Woodward and Howard Odum, both saw reasons for optimism. The South of 1954 was not the South of 1934. The well-known race-baiting demagogues of the prewar era had basically passed from the scene. Previous judicial decisions over interstate commerce, the all-white primary, and higher education had not ignited an uprising. And the general postwar economic prosperity affected the South too, making it seem less different than its former backward existence. Woodward's autumn 1954 lectures at the University of Virginia, "The Strange Career of Jim Crow," were upbeat. He made the case that segregation had not been inevitable, with the implication that it was not basic to southern existence. Even more optimistic was Odum's prediction that the "South is likely to surprise itself and the nation and do an excellent job of readjustment."[31]

Southern politicians reacted differently. Not a single one defended *Brown*. Yet moderate border-state governors in Missouri and Maryland as well as the governor of Virginia all stated their citizens would work to comply with the Court's ruling. Liberal Tennessee Senator Estes Kefauver as well as Louisiana's Russell Long both offered more tepid statements indicating their unease with *Brown* but hoping there would be no strife.

More telling were statements from state leaders sweeping southward from Virginia down the former Confederate seacoast, all contradicting the Virginia governor and condemning *Brown* and the Court. Virginia's dominant senator, Harry Flood Byrd, called *Brown* "the most serious blow" struck against the states.[32] The governor of North Carolina was "terribly disappointed."[33] Governor James Byrnes of South Carolina, briefly a Roosevelt appointee on the Supreme Court, who was spearheading the equalization of resources in his own state's schools, was "shocked."[34] Senator James Eastland of Mississippi announced, with accuracy, that the South "will not abide or obey this legislative decision by a political court indoctrinated and brainwashed by Left-wing pressure groups."[35] Within weeks Virginia's governor switched and joined the dominant chorus of opposition.

Georgia was in the midst of a Democratic primary, and its politicians "maneuvered frantically to occupy the extreme segregationist position."[36] Thus, Georgia was the first state to say it would not comply with *Brown*. Governor Herman Talmadge referred to Georgia's successful defiance of John Marshall's Supreme Court in the *Cherokee Cases* (1831 and 1832) and noted it would take "several divisions of troops to police every school building in Georgia and then they wouldn't be able to enforce it."[37] *Brown* was, he proclaimed, "a step toward national suicide."[38] The lieutenant governor, who was running for governor, stated that the decision was no surprise to him and then proceeded to condemn the "meddlers, demagogues, race baiters, and communists who are determined to destroy every vestige of State's Rights."[39] Talmadge was the one who found the words that would come to dominate the South's attack: *Brown* was a judicial usurpation whereby the Court arrogated to itself powers to amend the Constitution and reduce that charter to "a mere scrap of paper."[40] Politics and ideology were such that Richard Russell of Georgia, "the most powerful and respected man in the United States Senate,"[41] also heaped scorn on the Court by branding the justices as "amateur psychologists."[42] The politicians knew their constituents; at least 80 percent of white southerners were opposed to ending school segregation. The Louisiana legislature, the only one in session when *Brown* came down, censured the Court.

Brown's Problem

Brown had two goals, declaring official government-mandated segregation unconstitutional and persuading the persuadable southerner. By results, the first goal was a success although the opinion left open whether *Brown* was a segregation case or an education case. Both *Brown* and *Bolling* were careful to condemn only segregation in the context of public education. Separate schools generate feelings of inferiority that may last a lifetime, as might the consequences of a segregated learning environment itself. Did officially segregated swimming pools or "back of the bus" rules have a similar effect? Would the Court compare their importance to that of public education? Would the Court wait for modern psychology to generate the relevant data? *Brown* didn't say, although if the Court was willing to take out schools, the cornerstone of white supremacy, there would be little basis for expecting it to defer on the other, necessarily less contentious, issues.

By challenging government-mandated segregation, the Court was challenging the foundations of the southern way of life. If the South was to be transformed, it would certainly be helpful if the South knew why segregation was wrong. Some southerners, who believed that African-Americans were an inferior, undeserving class, could not be expected to be persuaded. But others who accepted segregation in the same way that people accept air—it's there, why think about it?—might have a slightly milder view of African-Americans. To be sure, they had heard and probably accepted the ideas that without segregation the plight of African-Americans would be worse and that virtually everything African-Americans had achieved was a result of either luck or white beneficence. But they had never heard a contrary view. They might be persuaded to the contrary either by the Court or by those who agreed with the Court.

On exactly that basis the opinion was a failure. It seems inconceivable that not one of the very able jurists or politicians on the Court noted that the opinion as written would persuade only the already convinced. Nor did any of the justices subsequently, in any form or forum, ever comment on the opinion's having wholly failed to speak to southerners. Warren, for instance, never comprehended the criticisms of *Brown* and was mystified at the reaction to the opinion. There was some subsequent carping by justices about *Brown II* (the remedy opinion) but none about the *Brown* opinion itself. It was as if the need for unanimity and the fear of hostile reaction so blocked their vision that they could not focus on the real function of the opinion. In Wilkinson's apt conclusion, the opinion "simply existed."[43] In some circumstances that might have been enough, but not here.

Two of the most noticeable problems with the opinion were opposite sides of the same coin. When Warren found history unhelpful and precedent conflicting, he turned to psychology. Georgia's Russell was thus not off the mark when he claimed that the Court had "abandon[ed] law and precedents in favor of psychology."[44] The justices were appointed for life to the United States Supreme Court, not to the editorial board of the *Journal of the American Psychological Association.* Judges may claim, fairly or not, an expertise in law. They cannot claim an expertise in psychology. If the Constitution turns on psychology, then psychologists should be the appointed interpreters. Furthermore, one need not be a lawyer to understand this. Any layman can understand judges "do" law—not psychology. If judges are not doing law, why should their rulings be obeyed?

Thurgood Marshall stated that, in addition to winning, the "most gratifying" aspects of *Brown* were unanimity and the "language used."[45] He was right on the former, dead wrong on the latter. A lawyer reading *Brown* was sure to ask, "where's the law?" Where, using appropriate legal sources, is the justification for holding the Equal Protection Clause is violated by separate but equal? It couldn't be the text of the Fourteenth Amendment without more—because while the text might easily be construed to say no discrimination, it would take some interpretation to move from no discrimination to treating separate but equal as discrimination; otherwise *Plessy* could not have existed for over a half century. The next most likely source of reasoning would be to ask what those who created and adopted the Fourteenth Amendment thought they were doing. Indeed, it was exactly this question that Frankfurter had propounded for reargument. Warren wrote that history was inconclusive. Here his reasoning seems quite commendable. Warren did not torture the history to say it showed the Fourteenth Amendment was intended to bar segregation. The history didn't show that, and attempts to force it to do so would not persuade.

Nevertheless, there was one way history could have been used both successfully and honestly to reach the result in *Brown.* If we go back to 1866, we would find that the framers of the Fourteenth Amendment intended to protect the equality of all Americans from governmental action but especially that of African-Americans. The Fourteenth Amendment was in part a reaction to the South's adoption of the infamous Black Codes that attempted to reduce the newly freed African-Americans to serfdom. After the Fourteenth Amendment there was no doubt the Black Codes were unconstitutional, and the amendment by its very language required that all persons receive the equal protection of the laws. But we would also see, somewhat less clearly, that to the extent the framers thought about it, many also approved of segregation as well as equality. Based on their limited experience and the fact that they had not given the issues much thought, they believed that segregation was not inconsistent with equality.

What was apparent by *Brown,* but what the drafters of the Fourteenth Amendment did not know, was that de jure segregation and equality in American society were incompatible. Where there was legally enforced segregation, there was no equality. Under the circumstances of 1950, a choice between de jure segregation and equality had to be made. One could not have both simultaneously.

If, as Warren chose, the history of the Fourteenth Amendment was to be ignored, then the next best approach would be to rely on precedent. Since *Plessy* was obviously the dominant precedent, the Court would have to demonstrate either that *Plessy* was wrong when decided or that subsequent judicial developments had undermined its authority. In fact, the Court's decisions could support both these methods of attack, yet Warren eschewed both.

Footnote Eleven

Modern psychology and Footnote Eleven provided the unfortunate complement to the lack of traditional legal sources. Weak though the opinion was, it would have been far better without Footnote Eleven because the footnote, created by a law clerk to Warren and not thought particularly important, appeared to many to provide the articulated reason for the result in *Brown*. Thus, the towering James Reston of the *New York Times* entitled his May 18 column "A Sociological Decision." Reston wrote that the Court rejected history, philosophy, and custom and rested instead on "the primacy of the general welfare." "Relying more on the social scientists than on legal precedents—a procedure often in controversy in the past—the Court's opinion read more like an expert paper on sociology than a Supreme Court decision."[46] Reston was batting .500; the opinion didn't read like an "expert paper," as the South was quick to note.

Before reaching the substance of Footnote Eleven, there was the problem of who was cited in it. The first citation and the only one—contrary to then legal form at the request of Tom Clark—indicating more than an author's last name was to Kenneth B. Clark, the African-American psychologist consulting with the NAACP (and the prime witness on the harms of segregation in the South Carolina litigation). The final cite was to Swedish economist Gunnar Myrdal. His *An American Dilemma*, reflecting on the contrast between a commitment to democracy and the reality of a caste system in the South, however celebrated in the North, was largely ignored in the South.[47] Now it would be notorious. In a nonaccusatory opinion, Footnote Eleven was an accidental bomb. First, the South perceived it as an "in your face" attack by the Court because of who was cited. In addition to Clark and Myrdal, two of the other scholars had what passed for communist leanings during that era. Second, the footnote told the South, as Reston told the country, that the Court had abandoned law for psychology. Footnote Eleven was not only unnecessary; it was stupid.

When the Court moved from law to psychology, it opened itself to charges that it went beyond its own competence and may have therefore misinterpreted the materials. Worse, it implicitly suggested that if the teachings of modern psychology were different, so would be the legal outcome. One response to *Brown* was to develop a "modern Southern psychology" that would "prove" segregation was beneficial for African-Americans because they could not handle the faster learning environment of a white school.[48] That was not what the Court wanted.

Although Myrdal, the "foreign sociologist," became the lightning rod, Clark was the key figure and his scholarship proved the easiest to comprehend. If *Brown* rested on his primitive studies, segregation had a real good chance for a comeback.

Clark gave African-Americans, ages six through nine, in both the North and South, a white doll and an African-American doll and asked them questions such as which one was nice and which looked like you. The children knew which doll the latter was. Then when the children answered that the white doll was the nice one, Clark concluded that he had shown that segregation generated feelings of inferiority. He did not consider other potential causes such as low socioeconomic status or disparaging treatment by the dominant white society. He repeated his study in Clarendon County, South Carolina, using pictures of dolls and testified about the results in the trial court.

There are numerous problems with the study. First, the samples were too small and there was no control group. Second, the way the experiment was interpreted gave Clark a "heads I win, tails you lose" outcome. If the children picked the African-American doll as looking nice, he could conclude segregation reinforced feelings of race and isolation. But when they instead picked the white doll, he concluded that segregation generated feelings of inferiority (for otherwise they would have picked the doll that looked like them). Finally, the supposed outcome was greater in the North, that is, the children were more likely to pick the white doll as nice where the schools were not segregated than in the South where they were! Because of all the flaws, Clark only proved something about the primitive state of social science, but to the extent his research was relevant to the case, on Clark's chosen analysis, he showed African-Americans were better off in the South.

It is no wonder that some NAACP lawyers were uneasy about the social science evidence. William Coleman, the first African-American law clerk at the Supreme Court (with Frankfurter), thought the "tests" were a joke. At oral argument, John W. Davis, counsel for South Carolina, had taken the studies apart and there were no questions from the bench, an indication that the justices probably weren't interested in the discussion.

The Court and Warren's clerk should have known better than to cite them. Another ex-Frankfurter clerk, Alexander Bickel of Yale, stated of the terse opinion that it "was wise to present as small a target as possible to marksmen on the other side."[49] But the target, whether from lack of law or Footnote Eleven, was much larger than he perceived. By the end of the decade, even sympathetic northern academics found the opinion wanting. If friends felt that way, it is no wonder that its enemies felt it was unjustified. Footnote Eleven reduced both the legal and moral force of the opinion.

Unanimity

No scholar who has studied *Brown* has missed the pressure for unanimity among the justices nor the subsequent credit to Warren or Frankfurter (or both) for achieving it. The four, Black, Douglas, Burton, and Minton, who believed segregation was per se unconstitutional get slighted, first in the description of the process, second by Warren's opinion.

Frankfurter believed Marshall and the NAACP had moved too soon and, in refusing to make a claim about equalization of notoriously unequal facilities, was placing the Court in the unhappy dilemma of either reaffirming *Plessy* or ordering southern whites into inferior African-American schools (where they might not go). The South, and South Carolina in particular, was engaged in a massive effort to upgrade the African-American schools (an effort that if honestly pursued by the poorest section of the nation would necessarily take years to complete). Frankfurter thought the time to take on *Plessy* was later, after the upgrading was well along, not at the beginning. By bringing the cases too soon, the NAACP might lose, either by *Plessy*'s being reaffirmed or by the South's refusing to comply. Thus, Frankfurter was the prime exponent of delay to save the NAACP from itself.

Frankfurter's ire at Marshall would be a consistent cry from the white establishment over the coming years: "Why do they push it now? Why can't they wait until the time is right? Then we, as leaders of good will, can act and deliver." As Martin Luther King, Jr., would subsequently note about the Kennedys, it was never the right time for the white establishment. Marshall would have provided a practical argument as well. The NAACP did not have the time or resources to litigate the equality of schools in each district.

Nor is it clear why the early 1950s was not the right time. Jackie Robinson integrated baseball in 1947 (and the game was still being played). Truman ordered the armed forces integrated the same year (although it had not yet been accomplished at the outbreak of the Korean War). In 1948 the Democratic Party, the party of the Solid South, adopted a strong civil rights plank in its platform (and still won the election).

The continuing migration of African-Americans out of the South to the economic opportunities in the North away from state-mandated seg-regation made African-Americans a newly potent electoral force in a number of key states. The migrants cared about civil rights for them-selves as well as those left behind. The animus against the racial suprem-acy of the Nazis could hardly have been left in Germany, even if southern whites might have wished it could. So if Marshall had known of Frank-furter's query, he would have responded that the time was right, and it was not dependent on the pace at which the poorest, most backward section of the nation spent money to upgrade its inferior schools.

It is ironic that the justices had gone the extra mile to achieve unanim-ity only to join an opinion that failed in all its functions except result. Naturally, joining a collective statement involves some individual com-promise, but Warren's opinion compromised everything and then, with Footnote Eleven, blundered as well. Was unanimity that important?

Over the previous century most of the major and controversial opin-ions of the Court were not unanimous (although that is not to say that the majority would not have liked added votes). *Dred Scott* was 7–2; *Pollack v. Farmer's Loan and Trust,* holding the income tax unconstitu-tional in 1895, was 5–4; the New Deal invalidations were typically 6–3 or 5–4. Of course, it is conceivable that these decisions would have been less controversial had they been unanimous. A dissent, after all, immedi-ately demonstrates that an alternative result was plausible. Unanimity carries with it the suggestion that the issue has but one plausible correct answer.

Two decades after *Brown,* one of Richard Nixon's lawyers stated during Watergate that the president would obey "a definitive decision" of the Supreme Court on the issue of turning over his tapes. Implicit in the statement was the suggestion that Nixon might not obey a less-than-definitive decision. While definitive was not defined, one imme-diate thought was that a ruling by a badly split Court might not be deemed definitive by Nixon. (And when the time came, the Court ruled against him without dissent.) Maybe similar concerns were justified with *Brown.*

What if Reed or Jackson had dissented? The obvious answer is that there is no way to know if it would have made any difference. The South would have loved a dissent, and, indeed, many southerners wrote to the Court after *Brown* asking for a copy of the dissenting opinion they sup-posed had been issued. If there had been one, the South would have touted it for all it was worth (and in Jackson's case that might have been a lot, given his bluntness). But from the vantage point of time, as future

chapters will show, it is hard to imagine how the South could have fought
Brown any harder than it did, and it is difficult (although not as difficult)
to believe that the North, after the changes in the postwar nation, would
have come to the southern position just because one or two justices
took it.

A Changing Constitution

Southerners might wonder not only why the southern way of life was
unconstitutional but also how and when it became unconstitutional. In
his unpublished opinion, Jackson presciently wrote that "laymen as well
as lawyers must query how it is that the Constitution this morning forbids what for three-quarters of a century it has tolerated or approved."[50]
Bull's-eye. The South had erected its entire white supremacist social
structure under the regime of *Plessy*. If African-American schools needed
equalization, then the rule of *Plessy* was to bring them up to the standards of white schools, as Byrnes and others were trying to do. But
Marshall and the NAACP had completely eschewed the equalization
argument, and they won. What was constitutional from the presidency
of Grover Cleveland into that of Eisenhower was, overnight, unconstitutional. How could that be?

   In stating that the Court could not turn the clock back to 1896 (much
less 1868), the Court gave a direct answer. The Constitution must be
interpreted in light of current conditions to accommodate current needs.
And, of course, the Court itself, rather than other institutions consisting
of elected representatives, would evaluate the meaning of changed conditions and the needs of modern society.

   To some extent keeping the law up-to-date had always been the
case. Common law courts change legal doctrine to fit the needs of society
and so had the Supreme Court. *Plessy* was not the first case to be
discarded; overrulings by the Court happened about once every other
year. But there had never been anything like this: a case so big, the modern today versus the past so up front, and an opinion otherwise so without legal reasoning. The closest comparison would be the switch in
1937, when the Court also rather quickly brought the Constitution up-
to-date.

   Jackson's silent query received an immediate loud answer by Senator
Russell. In his "amateur psychologists" speech, Russell touched on a
deeper tradition, that we are a nation of laws and not men. *Brown*,
southerners claimed, had reversed that. The Court had "abandoned one
of the fundamental bulwarks of our form of government and went over

to the side of rule by men."[51] Instead of applying law, it had imposed its will. This became a dominant southern theme: a lawless Court, abandoning the Constitution ("a mere scrap of paper") for the personal and political values of unelected judges. In the words of the *Richmond News Leader,* the paper that would ultimately lead the southern attack on the Court, the justices "chose to throw away established law, . . . repudiated the Constitution, spit upon the Tenth Amendment, and rewrote the fundamental law of this land to suit their own gauzy concepts of sociology."[52]

Overruling prior cases always carries the downside risk of making observers wonder what has really changed. The Constitution? The society? The justices' views? The composition of the Court? The downside cannot be avoided; at best it can be explained. *Brown* didn't succeed in this regard either because the Court didn't try to succeed in this respect.

There is an upside to overruling as well. Presumably the new outcome is better, more attuned to current needs. That an injustice has occurred in the past is not a good reason for continuing it in the present and into the future. Overruling comes with the robes. It is necessarily going to happen some of the time. The questions are (1) how often and (2) with what justification? Reston's instant analysis of *Brown* captured the point even if the justices did not say it. The decision was based on the justices concept of the general welfare. They understood, although they did not say so, that segregation subjugated African-Americans because as practiced in the South its only meaning was white supremacy, an idea that, at a minimum, World War II had put to rest as incompatible with what the United States stands for.

Jackson made one final point relevant to overruling during oral argument. "I suppose that realistically the reason this case is here is that action couldn't be obtained from Congress."[53] Bull's-eye again. Congress at mid-century was dominated by a seniority system that gave the one-party South (with its virtually all-white electorate) inordinate power. Southern committee chairmen could block anything, and if that were not sufficient for the South, the Senate could be brought to a halt by a filibuster that, under then existing rules, could be broken only by a two-thirds vote. Congress was not going to pass a law dealing with segregated schools because Congress had not even been able to pass a law dealing with lynching!

So either the Court had to act alone or nothing would happen (or so it seemed to all concerned). Ultimately, this was *Brown*'s allure. Segregation was a massive blight on the United States, and yet our elected representatives were either unwilling or unable to do anything about it. Surely, some institution of government had to be able to do something. The judiciary was constrained too, but not in ways that precluded action. The Court was torn over whether its action would work, not whether it was correct.

Brown asked a lot. It asked the white southerners to give up their very privileged legal position as well as the southern tradition of race. It implicitly asked the Congress and the president to join with the Court. But in asking much, *Brown* promised more. It promised to end what Myrdal aptly called the American dilemma. All members of society could be brought under law and treated equally and fairly just as our jointly held values and ideals postulated. *Brown* promised a way of sidestepping legislative deadlock. When the representative branches would not act, the Court could where the Constitution and American ideals so held. The southern charge, that *Brown* rendered the Constitution a "mere scrap of paper," was wrong. *Brown* only lacked reasoning because Warren made a tactical choice about the opinion. The powerful need to eradicate second-class citizenship to accord with the equal protection of the laws was a more than sufficient, if unarticulated, reason. If the *Plessy* majority could not realize that segregation by law and equality under law were incompatible under American conditions, *Brown* could.

Jackson's concern that to do justice in *Brown* required the Court to abandon law for politics was misplaced. The task was great, but the Court had the necessary legal tools. It just left them unused and therefore left the Court vulnerable to the southern accusation of abandoning law. But because the southern accusation was inextricably linked to its understandable claim of white supremacy, the accusation could not stick unless it could be tied to decisions apart from race.

A more interesting basis for the claim that the Court did not feel bound by law would come in a year, and although he would never utter the words, the charge was implicit in Marshall's argument in *Brown II.* For in the aftermath of the nation's sigh of relief, the question of what must be done to remedy segregated schools would inevitably come. Jackson's death delayed it somewhat.

Harlan's Appointment

In a deserving and symbolic elevation, Eisenhower nominated the grandson (and namesake) of the lone dissenter in *Plessy,* John Marshall Harlan, to replace Jackson. The Congress was in recess for the 1954 elections, and after Congress reconvened in 1955, Eisenhower resubmitted the nomination.

Harlan was a fourth-generation lawyer, who, after Princeton, a Rhodes scholarship, and graduation from New York Law School, became the chief litigator in a prestigious New York firm, representing, among other clients, the duPont Corporation. He was a Republican but not a particularly active one. After brief service as chief counsel to the New York Crime Commission, he was appointed by Eisenhower to the federal court of appeals. The key to Harlan's promotion was simple. After Warren's appointment, Eisenhower turned the selection process over to his attorney general, Herbert Brownell, with the instruction that he wanted men with prior judicial experience who were under the age of 62.

Brownell was both a longtime personal friend of Harlan and, having begun his career in the same firm, was fully aware of how extraordinary a lawyer Harlan was. Indeed, Brownell had engineered Harlan's promotion to the court of appeals, both by presenting him to Eisenhower and more importantly by persuading Harlan to leave private practice. Brownell's memoirs stated that all the while he had hoped for Harlan's advancement to the Supreme Court.[54]

Senate confirmation was tied up for two months by southerners unhappy with *Brown* and conservatives worried about internationalism (and therefore communism) and the United Nations. Eventually, Harlan was confirmed by a 71–11 vote with southerners dominating the nays. The delay in his confirmation delayed the arguments in *Brown II*, for there was no way that the Court was going to hear the case without a full complement of justices.

In the meantime, *Brown* actually seemed to fade from view. The southern press was running virtually no stories on desegregation. A study of North Carolina newspapers in February and April 1955 found they devoted less than 1 percent of their newshole to racial stories.[55] It was as if the South had been wishing *Brown* away.

Chapter 3

Implementation

Constitutional rights and their remedies are intertwined, correlative, and immediate. Thus, when *Brown* held school segregation unconstitutional, the appropriate remedy was to end segregation immediately. Yet once the remedy is posed in this way, one must ask what seemingly is an obvious question. What is school segregation? Although the quickest answer is separation of the races mandated by law, *Brown*'s social science rationale implied an alternative. School segregation might be schooling without members of the other (white) race. If segregation meant forced separation by law, then it could be remedied by the removal of the law. But if segregation meant one-race schools (or classrooms), then it could be remedied only by racial mixing. *Brown* never addressed the issue. Possibly it was too obvious; possibly it was too explosive. Neither *Brown II* nor any other case for over a decade addressed what segregation meant either. Instead, the cases dealt with timing.

The Debate on Remedy

The law of constitutional remedies was clear at mid-century. When a constitutional claim was successful, the right was available immediately. There was a harmony between rights and remedies and an understanding that delaying a remedy was denying a right. Thus, in 1938 the Court ordered Lloyd Gaines admitted to the University of Missouri Law School and did not require him to wait until the state built and staffed a separate but equal one. Similarly, when Heaman Sweatt won his separate but equal suit against the University of Texas School of Law, the Court unanimously ruled that he had a "personal and present" right to be admitted. That was the rule of all the cases.

Brown was different. Its last paragraph commanded no specific relief at all, and argument was ordered on what would constitute a proper remedy. In 1955, as *Brown* was argued again, the talk was of delay. Marshall put the argument in perspective. "I don't believe any argument has been made to this Court to postpone the enforcement of a constitutional right. The argument is never made, until Negroes are involved."[1] Marshall was at his best, so obvious, down to earth, speaking with moral authority. But it was not his winning best, for everyone assumed delay— even Marshall himself for at least another year—and delay would be the meaning of *Brown II*. "All deliberate speed," a quotation from an opinion by Oliver Wendell Holmes, much beloved by Frankfurter, was the operative phrase; its operational meaning was delay. The only question was how much.

Despite the reargument over remedy, the justices had vetted remedy at length in their earlier deliberations. Once Warren had stated his position that separate but equal was unconstitutional (and could be sustained only by a belief in African-American inferiority), he tried to guide discussion away from the merits toward the remedy. The tactic, wonderfully successful, was to make the outcome on the merits seem inevitable (and unanimous) by focusing on a different issue that everyone agreed would be difficult. No court had ever ordered a society remade, and there was much speculation about how to do it wisely and successfully. It was an issue on which the justices were, as they had been on the merits under Vinson, profoundly divided.

The discussions over remedy were not formally about what was right. The justices believed they had ample leeway to do what would work best, and ultimately that was deemed to be what was right. The goal was to frame a remedy that would end segregated schooling in a reasonable time without violence. The reigning assumption was that violence would lengthen any process and simultaneously erode the moral (and legal) authority of the Court. Every justice participated in the discussions—for each was fully capable of guessing about the unknown. But the debate was dominated by the Court's giants: Black and Douglas on the one side, Frankfurter and (while alive) Jackson on the other. Ultimately, Warren cut the differences for the Court, but the victory was Frankfurter's. His need to play an important role in the landmark case was amply fulfilled.

Frankfurter, Jackson, and Black neatly framed the possibilities. For Frankfurter (and others), it was essential that whatever the Court ordered be obeyed. Accordingly, southern reaction had to be properly gauged and the decree carefully framed lest it be just a scrap of paper. "I think nothing would be worse . . . than for this Court to make an abstract declaration that segregation is bad and have it evaded by tricks."[2] Jackson wanted a decree that would set standards both to avoid a further generation of litigation and to avoid bringing "the Court into contempt and the judicial process into discredit."[3] Black, however, stated that was going to happen anyway because whatever the Court ordered was going to be ignored (at least in the Deep South). He argued that it simply did not matter what the decree said. That conclusion, offered consistently, "scared the shit" out of all the justices, especially Frankfurter and Jackson.[4] For if Black were right, nothing the Court could do would matter, and the justices were necessarily uncomfortable with a conclusion where they would have no influence on subsequent events. The Court was going to look both silly and impotent. Therefore, everyone assumed, as well as hoped, that Black was exaggerating; moreover, the two border-state southerners, Reed and Clark, were both more optimistic than Black.

Brown had invalidated the laws of twenty-one states (seventeen had required school segregation; four had established a local option) and, *Bolling,* those of the District of Columbia. By the time of reargument, it was clear the western states—Kansas, Arizona, New Mexico, Wyoming (in which no school district had ever exercised the segregation option)— and the District of Columbia would readily abandon segregation. The border states, Missouri, Oklahoma, Kentucky, Maryland, West Virginia, and Delaware, none of which had joined the Confederacy, would too, albeit without enthusiasm. The South, however, was something else again, as the unhappy reaction of its major political figures had shown. A huge difference between the border states and the Deep South (South Carolina, Georgia, Alabama, Mississippi, and Louisiana) was the percentage of African-Americans in the population. The border states ranged from West Virginia at 6 percent to Maryland at 17 percent. Excluding Texas (13 percent), no southern state had less than 22 percent, and in the Deep South the percentages of African-Americans went to almost double that. Still, the delay of oral argument had provided time for everyone to realize the end was coming. The cavalry had not saved the South in 1865 and would not be coming to do so in 1955.

The question of remedy in *Brown* involved several interrelated questions (beyond the unasked question about the meaning of segregation): Who was entitled to the relief to be granted? What options would be left to the school administrators? When would the remedy begin, and if it were not immediately complete, how long would it take? A further question remained. What institution would order and supervise the remedy?

The oral argument from the southern attorneys demonstrated one possible, albeit unacceptable, answer to the questions—segregation was not going to end. The lawyers were not trying to convince the justices; they couldn't. Instead, they exercised the supposedly radical and liberating prerogative of speaking truth to power. In a spirited exchange with Warren, the South Carolina attorney said that the whites in his district (which was overwhelmingly African-American) would not abide by any decree requiring sending their children to schools with Negroes. Warren asked, "But you are not willing to say that there would be an honest attempt to conform?" To which the attorney responded, "Let us get the word 'honest' out of there." Warren acidly replied, "No, leave it in," and got a blunt answer: "No, because I have to tell you we would not conform; we would not send our white children to the Negro schools."[5] As with many holding power, Warren didn't like it, but the answer was nevertheless true.

Marshall bore the burden of presenting his clients' case while attempting to assuage the justices' fears. First, he made the Court's task look both easy and normal; thus, he deemed segregation to be separation mandated by law. Therefore, all that was necessary was to forbid the use of race in student assignments. "This Court is not dealing with complexities, this Court is dealing with whether or not race can be used."[6] Marshall envisioned geographic school zones and had told the Court in the first argument that "in most of the Southern area—it might be news to the Court—there are very few areas that are predominantly one race or the other."[7] Marshall also addressed the argument that Negro children might be academically behind their white peers. There was an easy and obvious nonracial solution for that. "Put the dumb colored children in with the dumb white children and put the smart colored children in with the smart white children."[8]

Second, Marshall was willing to limit relief initially to the named plaintiffs in the cases. Instead of encompassing all African-Americans within a school district, relief could be limited to those willing to go to the courthouse and formally join the litigation. Third, the process should begin as soon as possible and in any event no longer than another year. Marshall made it clear that administrative problems were essentially trivial and easily solved; there were none that could not be worked out in a year. The process of ending segregation should also be completed as soon as possible. Reed asked about desegregating a grade a year, and Marshall responded that was unsatisfactory because the named plaintiffs might receive no relief at all.[9]

Finally, Marshall had more faith in the integrity of white southerners than their lawyers did. "I got the feeling yesterday that when you put a white child in a school with a whole lot of colored children, the child would fall apart or something. Everybody knows that is not true."[10] On a less humorous note, Marshall told the Court that "history" shows "that it is the inherent faith in our democratic process that gets us through, the faith that the people in the South are no different from anybody else as to being law-abiding."[11]

That was the public argument and it was a good one. In private, Marshall knew that it was going to take some time. By requiring individual African-Americans to join the lawsuit, Marshall knew that relief would be limited and staggered. In areas where their faith in the white southerner was less, African-Americans would be reluctant to come forward. As Marshall's astute biographer Mark Tushnet notes, immediate desegregation and gradualism were not that far apart in many parts of the South.[12]

The United States position had been developed by yet another ex-Frankfurter clerk, Philip Elman: Declare segregation unconstitutional and then delay doing anything about it. Although Elman talked freely and frequently with Frankfurter, he did not mention his brainchild prior to filing the brief because he feared Frankfurter's reaction. Elman's idea was, in his own words, "totally unprincipled."[13] Constitutional rights are not future expectancies. It is, indeed, totally unprincipled for a court to say to a litigant: "Your constitutional rights are being violated; we'll see that someone else's similar constitutional rights are protected later, and in the meantime you wait as you were." Yet that is exactly what the United States proposed because, as Elman noted, it might work. This argument looked all the better in the spring of 1955 when it was apparent that no one would be coming to the Court's rescue either. Eisenhower and the Congress were going to sit this one out.

Gradualism was exactly what the Court was going to try to implement. Elman had been right to worry about Frankfurter's (or any justice's) reaction to a suggestion that a flagrant, declared constitutional violation of individual rights need not be corrected until sometime later, but as it turned out, Frankfurter loved the idea. Gradualism, in Frankfurter's mind, was judicial statesmanship of the highest order, the exact type Frankfurter thought he represented best. The case, as Frankfurter conceived it, was no longer exclusively about constitutional rights. It was now about the sensitive adjustment to a new social system. Under the circumstances, courts could not behave like automatons. They must show their understanding of the fullness of the situation and bring about the desired outcome as intelligently and effectively as possible.

Black and Douglas both took positions closely matching Marshall's:

token desegregation—now. The now was essential for the always impatient Douglas. Although neither Black nor Douglas used the term "token," it was the natural outcome of their belief that the decree could be
limited to only the named plaintiffs. Surprisingly, especially since Black
always mentioned southern opposition, the other justices would not go
along with their position because it seemed not to take that opposition
sufficiently into account. And since any decision on remedy had to be
unanimous for the same reasons that *Brown* had to be unanimous, Black
and Douglas would have to go along with what the others wanted when
the others would not go along with them. The position on which all
justices finally agreed was that no date certain would be required, and the
cases would be sent back to the relevant district courts and those judges
would control the timing.

The Opinion

Brown II was initially drafted to require desegregation for the plaintiffs
to commence "at the earliest practicable date." But Frankfurter, gradualism's most ardent supporter, prevailed on Warren to use the now-famous
"all deliberate speed" formulation instead. The outcome, when it turned
out the decree was to be limited to "the parties to this case," was that the
Court was willing to accept token desegregation—later.

  Brown II shifted the burden from the Court back to the federal district
courts where the cases arose (Delaware excepted). Unable to enlist support from the president or Congress, the Court requisitioned the few
troops available to it—southern federal judges. They would man the
frontlines, albeit initially in a supervisory role. The local school boards,
all under political control, were given the first shot at doing something.
The Court's chosen solution here—because no other solution presented
itself—was placing southerners in charge of how *Brown* was implemented. First, the local school board would devise a plan; then the local
federal judge would approve or reject that plan. The Court was placing a
lot of faith in the southern establishment—if for no other reason than
there appeared nowhere else to turn.

  The opinion itself, like that of *Brown I,* was short, a mere four pages.
Like *Brown I,* it too was designed to avoid provoking the South. If the
Court showed appropriate sympathy, then maybe the South would show
appropriate restraint. It was both inevitable and necessary for the remedy opinion to refer back to *Brown I,* and the Court did so four times,
always blandly by referring to its date, May 17, 1954. The first reference

said that the earlier opinion declared the fundamental principle that racial discrimination in public education was unconstitutional; two of the references referred to the "constitutional principles" of the decision; and the final one noted the district courts would require the defendants in these cases to make "a prompt and reasonable start toward" compliance with the earlier decision. In context, however, "all deliberate speed" shifted the emphasis away from "prompt and reasonable" and to "start toward."

The Court stated that "it should go without saying that the vitality of these constitutional principles [from *Brown*] cannot be allowed to yield simply from disagreement with them." Yet that is what *Brown II* was about: the principles of *Brown* being delayed for an undetermined time because the Court feared the extent of southern disagreement with them. The Court was not willing to say so honestly; therefore, the Court had to offer reasons why delay was acceptable. One reason was that equity was flexible in adjusting private and public needs. The "private" needs of the plaintiffs were obvious—their constitutional rights not to be segregated because of their race. But what were the "public needs"? Well, there were "problems related to administration, arising from the physical condition of the school plant, the school transportation system, personnel, revision of school districts and attendance areas." The administrative problems—transportation and changed attendance zones—were those that Marshall had stated would not take longer than a year to fix, and he was right, unless opposition was itself the reason to delay. The Court's other two reasons—physical condition and personnel—seemed to speak obliquely to the fact that, contrary to the premise of the NAACP's litigation strategy that all facilities were equal, African-American schools were indeed inferior to white schools.

The Court, while telling the white South "we understand," was simultaneously telling the African-Americans that the dilapidated school house with a leaky roof or the African-American teacher with weaker credentials was good enough for them, but certainly not okay, at least for the time being, for their white counterparts. That is why equity would authorize the delay until the "variety of obstacles" could be eliminated.

The combination of *Brown I* and *Brown II* created the worst of all worlds. In attempting to stay within law, the Court concluded that it had the power to delay the effectuation of constitutional rights until those disagreeing became more willing to agree. Neither *Brown I* nor *Brown II* was long on legal reasoning. But on that score *Brown I* was better than *Brown II*. A careful reading of the latter showed that (1) opposition to rights could deny rights, and (2) although separate and unequal was bad, its consequences were too much for white children to take. If this was judicial statesmanship, it was neither legally nor morally costless. Indeed, maybe it wasn't statesmanship at all—just an ugly political compromise trying to pass itself off as something attractive. Different scholars have reached different conclusions. Since "shock treatment"—desegregate the whole South now—was not even argued by the NAACP, it seems futile to debate whether it would have worked. All we know is that the Court did nothing for over a decade and then, following the demise of the Warren Court at the end of the 1960s, the Court ordered a generation of busing.

The Immediate Reaction

Brown I failed in its goal of soothing the South. *Brown II,* with a similar goal, was initially more successful. Three times the Court emphasized local problems and needs. Not only did the Court say local conditions were a primary concern, it said that local people would evaluate them. The school boards, chosen from the white majority in the area, had primary responsibility. Then the local federal judge, who necessarily had been part of the state's establishment before his appointment, would offer his opinion. This amounted to local whites evaluating local conditions. Combined with the avoidance of a timetable—instead, it was "all deliberate speed"—the opinion read like a southern victory. And that is how it was initially perceived in the South. There was, as the *New York Times* stated, "a general feeling of relief."[14]

Florida's legislature was in session when *Brown II* came down, and the opinion was read aloud to both chambers as it came over the teletype. It was greeted with cheers. The *New Orleans Times-Picayune* concluded that it gave the South "pretty much what the Southern attorneys general had asked for." The *Atlanta Constitution* observed that it was "milder than expected." The *Tampa Tribune* referred to the Court's "wisdom." Louisiana Senator Allen Ellender expressed a common theme of the segregationists when he noted he was "delighted that they have left it to the local judges."[15]

The public reaction to *Brown II* was strikingly similar nationwide. African-American leaders "concealed their disappointment" and instead called the decision "gratifying,"[16] the exact characterization of the Eisenhower administration.[17] A few northern Democrats suggested that the Court had not done enough, but the bulk of congressional opinion was favorable. The *Los Angeles Times* seemed to put *Brown II* in perspective by stating that the decision would "not suit the extremists, but we think most reasonable people will agree with it."[18]

Wherever else the extremists might be, some were in Virginia. The very day *Brown II* was decided, the Prince Edward County school board, from the Virginia district before the Court, voted to cease funding its public schools. Two days later, a state judge ruled that bond money for school construction could not be expended on any schools that would be desegregated.[19] And on June 1, the *Richmond News Leader,* through its editor James Jackson Kilpatrick, fired what would turn out to be its opening shot against the Court with a lengthy editorial charging that *Brown* was not law and urging the South to see that "'as soon as practical' means never at all."[20] Georgia Governor Marvin Griffin concurred.

James J. Kilpatrick and Interposition

A year earlier, Georgia, with its election season in progress, had led the attacks on *Brown* while Mississippi came up with private muscle with the creation of white Citizen's Councils to maintain racial orthodoxy by both whites and African-Americans. With *Brown II,* Virginia took over the lead with public attacks on *Brown* while the Citizen's Council movement spread through and then out of the Deep South.

The political and intellectual problem facing the South was how to explain to itself and the rest of the nation why defying the Supreme Court of the United States was okay. Kilpatrick, within the pages of the *Richmond News Leader,* took up the task in a series of editorials through the winter of 1955–1956. His aim was, first, to push the Virginia legislature into full-scale revolt and, second, to bring the rest of the South along.[21] Acting as though the Civil War had never occurred, Kilpatrick reached back into antebellum southern history to revive the theory of interposition: that the Constitution is but a contract ("compact") among sovereign states and has no mechanism, except state agreement, for deciding important constitutional questions. Under this theory, the decisions of the Court—or of any other branch of the federal government—are not valid unless the affected states agree. Interposition, the *Richmond News Leader* proclaimed, did not preclude the Court from deciding cases, much less offering new constitutional meanings; rather, it empowers the states to approve or disapprove those meanings. Were it not so, the people of every state would be "compelled to lie down like sheep and be sheared by any court."[22]

Interposition had first been articulated by James Madison and Thomas

Jefferson in the Virginia and Kentucky Resolutions of 1798 and 1800. They posited that sovereign states could reject supposed federal usurpation by interposing the states' sovereign authority between the citizens of the state and the federal government. In the crisis of 1798–1800, the two state legislatures condemned the federal government and, quite unsuccessfully, asked other states to join them. But otherwise they did nothing. They articulated the theory of interposition but made no attempt (beyond asking other states for their opinions) to implement it. Three decades later, when John Calhoun led South Carolina to attempt to nullify federal law, Madison stated that South Carolina and the nullifiers were not acting within the "spirit of '98." Not surprisingly, after the Civil War, interposition became a dead letter.

Then the *Richmond News Leader* and Kilpatrick rediscovered interposition and claimed it offered a solution to this new crisis. The editorials, moving hand-in-hand with action in the legislature, recognized four objections to interposition. First, interposition does not exist; second, even if it once existed, it died with the Confederacy; third, the issue was not interposition but race; and, lastly, interposition is an open invitation to lawlessness. Kilpatrick took the antebellum examples of attempted interposition plus the statements from Jefferson, Madison, Calhoun, and John Taylor of Caroline as authoritatively establishing its existence and therefore its legitimacy. The Civil War was irrelevant; it just added three constitutional amendments but said nothing about interposition. Nor, Kilpatrick claimed, was interposition about race; rather, it was about principle, "the highest possible example of fidelity to the compact." Inconsistently, however, Kilpatrick played the ultimate southern race-card, that the "next wind that blows from the court will take with it a State's power to prohibit interracial marriage."[23] Of course, interposition was about race, but to admit the truth would result in an easy intellectual loss for the South.

It was lawlessness that drew most of Kilpatrick's attention because, after all, that was what he was proposing. He handled the problem in the obvious way: He charged the Court with lawlessness and therefore claimed the states "*'are in duty bound'* to interpose against the evil."[24] Indeed, the editorials had begun with the disingenuous suggestion that, in the current crisis, the South "has been handicapped by a fault that in ordinary times is among our highest virtues: It is our reverence for law, and our obedience to constituted authority."[25] Fortunately, the newspaper claimed, because interposition was the law of the compact, the South had no problems except gaining the will to use "honorable, legal and constitutional means"[26] to fight the battle with the Court and (perhaps) the federal government.

Virginia had the will. On February 1, 1956, it pledged, via a joint resolution overwhelmingly adopted by its legislature, to use all "honorable, legal and constitutional" means to "resist this illegal encroachment on our sovereign powers."[27]

Pleased with his intellectual revival of interposition, Kilpatrick enlarged it into a substantial book, *The Sovereign States: Notes of a Citizen of Virginia,* complete with 122 pages of footnotes. Walter Murphy drew the daunting task of writing a short, scholarly review of a book full of gaping intellectual holes. In the *Yale Law Journal,* Murphy adopted the conceit of wondering how someone as able as Kilpatrick could have produced such a work. Murphy's answer was that Kilpatrick was living in a closed society and thus was "under great social pressure to conform to local tradition." Nevertheless, Kilpatrick was seeking a way of protest. His vehicle was a book that, while pretending to defend the South, in fact demonstrated how indefensible segregation and states' rights were.[28]

The Southern Manifesto

C. Vann Woodward observed that "[s]omething very much like a panic seized the South toward the beginning of 1956, a panic bred of insecurity and fear."[29] Maybe the cause was the Montgomery Bus Boycott, which began in December 1955; maybe it was the fact that some schools in the border states were being desegregated. Maybe it was, potential delays or no, the reality of *Brown.* Just before the *Richmond News Leader* started its interposition editorials, the Court summarily (without as much as a word of justification) held that segregated beaches and bathhouses in Baltimore and segregated golf courses in Atlanta were unconstitutional. If that is what the Court now meant, then *Brown* was not about education; it was about race, and the Court was going to rule that the entire southern edifice of Jim Crow was unconstitutional. Harry Ashmore, the liberal editor of the *Arkansas Gazette,* offered the thought that the "Southerner's trouble in the middle of this disturbed twentieth century may be that too many generations have passed since the South won a victory—that we have rationalized defeat to the point where the hallmark of Southern success is a magnificent failure."[30] Maybe the panic that Woodward sensed reflected an awareness that the South was about to court yet another magnificent failure.

Strom Thurmond, Harry Flood Byrd, and Richard Russell brought together the southern Democrats in Congress to issue a frontal attack on *Brown,* combined with encouragement for official opposition to the decision. They drafted a "Declaration of Constitutional Principles," and it quickly became known as the "Southern Manifesto."[31] It began with the requisite attack on *Brown* as "a clear abuse of judicial power," encroaching on the legislative function. The aroused opposition of the South could not be unexpected since *Brown* was "now bearing the fruit always produced when men substitute naked power for law." Because the Court had abandoned the Constitution, it was the duty of other officials to reclaim it. The Manifesto, by supposed contrast to the Court, "reaffirmed reliance on the Constitution" and "commended the motives of those States" that were opposing *Brown,* and "pledged to use all lawful means to bring about a reversal of this decision which is contrary to the Constitution." As had the editorials of the *Richmond News Leader,* the Southern Manifesto took the position that the South was complying with law and the Court had abandoned law. In keeping with this, the Manifesto urged southerners to "scrupulously refrain from disorder and lawless acts." Not surprisingly, it did not say how there could be "lawful" means to oppose a Supreme Court decision.

The supposed "lawful means" of the Southern Manifesto was interposition, which was now being argued at the national level by political leaders who should have known better. Byrd explained that it was "a part of the plan of massive resistance we have been working on and I hope and believe it will be an effective action."[32] The Manifesto could not be written off as aberrational, representing only a handful of die-hard segregationists, because it was signed by 101 of the 128 men representing the South in Congress. The signers consisted of every single representative and senator from the Deep South (including future House Majority Leader Hale Boggs of Louisiana) plus Virginia (including both its Republicans) and Arkansas, and all but one (Representative Dante Fascell) from Florida. Senate Majority Leader Lyndon Johnson and House Speaker Sam Rayburn were not asked to sign. All other southerners were asked to sign and obviously most did. In the Senate, besides Johnson, only Tennessee's Albert Gore and Estes Kefauver did not sign; thus Arkansas's J. William Fulbright did. The House holdouts were all from the periphery: Texas (sixteen, including one Republican but without counting Rayburn), Tennessee (three, including Howard Baker and one other Republican), and North Carolina (three).

Anthony Lewis of the *New York Times* understood that the "true meaning of the Manifesto was to make defiance of the Court and the Constitution socially acceptable in the South—to give resistance to the law the approval of the Southern Establishment."[33] If the leaders of the South could label *Brown* contrary to law and therefore oppose it, then anyone could, and if anyone could, then maybe everyone should. The North Carolina primary came fast on the heels of the Manifesto. If the overwhelming support of the southern representatives was not enough to show that the Manifesto was calling for southern orthodoxy, the immediate defeat of two of the three nonsigners from North Carolina in the Democratic primary was a strong indication that it did represent a new orthodoxy, especially in an election year.

The 1956 Republican and Democratic Platforms

Neither the Republicans nor the northern Democrats condemned the Southern Manifesto. The initial draft of the 1956 Republican platform gave the Eisenhower administration credit for *Brown*. Eisenhower personally vetoed it on the official ground that the executive should not take credit for what the co-equal judicial branch did (and possibly because he believed the decision a huge mistake and therefore wanted no association with it). The final platform language stated that the Republicans "accepted" the *Brown* decision and "concurred" with *Brown II*.

The Democratic platform, reflecting the racial split within the party between its northern wing and its often solid southern base, tried to have it every possible way. It referred to *Brown* as a decision that had "brought consequences of vast importance to our Nation," as if that were a position. It reaffirmed its traditional northern commitment to nondiscrimination, but for the South it specifically opposed the use of force to implement any judicial decision on segregation. Finally, it "emphatically reaffirmed" the principle, which underlay the southern attack on *Brown* and the Court, that ours was a government of laws and not men. Yet it did so in the context of complaining that the Republicans were taking credit for unspecified judicial decisions, a position that made sense only if it was talking about *Brown*.

The platforms were thus perfect; no one could tell where either the Democrats or the Republicans stood. Both Eisenhower and his Democratic opponent Adlai Stevenson reflected their parties' empty and contradictory positions in simply stressing the southern commitment to oppose *Brown* only through "lawful means," as if that legitimized it.

The South and Graduate Schools

Autherine Lucy's case at the University of Alabama offered a useful example of what resistance to desegregation might mean. Lucy, an African-American, applied for admission to the graduate school at Alabama in 1952 when the law was already clear that use of race in graduate program admissions was unconstitutional. The university hired private detectives to search for information to discredit or blackmail Lucy. While it was unsuccessful, the process became routinized with future African-American applicants.

When Lucy's application was denied, she sued, and Judge H. Hobart Grooms, an Eisenhower appointee, ruled that she had been unconstitutionally rejected because of race. Grooms ordered her admitted. The university then successfully obtained a stay of his order from the federal court of appeals pending its decision on the university's appeal. Lucy then filed a motion at the Supreme Court to lift the court of appeals' stay, and on October 10, 1955, the Court unanimously ruled for her. But the university now refused to admit her because it was too late for enrollment for the fall semester; Grooms agreed. So Lucy entered Alabama at the beginning of the second semester.

When she arrived on campus, a mob greeted her, hoping to intimidate her into not enrolling; police protection caused the attempt to fail. But on February 6, 1956, with a mob nearly out of control, state police escorted Lucy off campus for her own protection. That evening the board of trustees suspended Lucy and expelled one of the mob's leaders. Suspending Lucy because a lawless group of whites opposed having an African-American in the university looked exactly like a violation of Grooms's order to cease using race to deny her admission. Unless lawless opposition were indeed a reason to deny rights, Lucy could expect an easy victory, and, moreover, her local lawyers also alleged that the university had been in a conspiracy with the mob; this charge, while true as to state officials, was one for which neither she nor the lawyers had any proof. Grooms invalidated Lucy's suspension as inconsistent with his orders. The university then expelled her for her unsubstantiated conspiracy charge. Grooms subsequently ruled that this was a valid action. Alabama's whites had won round one against the courts, and seven more years would pass before the next African-American student entered the University of Alabama.

While Lucy's case was in the news, the Court returned to the efforts of Virgil Hawkins, an African-American who had been trying since 1949 to enter the University of Florida Law School. In 1952 the Florida Supreme Court ruled that the African-American law school at Florida A&M was adequate and Hawkins should attend it. He then sought certiorari (the typical method by which a losing party in a lower court requests the Court to review the case), and the case was on the Court's docket during the arguments in *Brown*. A week after *Brown*, the Court vacated the judgment and sent it back for reconsideration. In Marshall's summation at oral argument in *Brown II*, he referred to Hawkins and the fact that five years after *Sweatt v. Painter*, he still could not get in to the University of Florida Law School because of the state's efforts in dragging out the inevitable. Marshall could not have guessed what was coming.

The Florida Supreme Court let the case sit until after the decision in *Brown II*. The court recognized that *Brown* had abolished separate but equal at all levels of schooling but read *Brown II* as holding that rights to end segregation were not immediate and depended on local conditions where the "public interest" could be weighed against Hawkins's personal interest. Reading *Brown II* as superseding *Sweatt v. Painter*, the court sent the case back to a trial court for a determination of how a systematic and effective transition to a nonsegregated law school could be accomplished consistent with the public interest.

Two weeks after the Southern Manifesto was issued, the Court, again unanimously, told the Florida court that graduate schools were to be desegregated immediately, just as the unquestioned Vinson Court decisions had required. Florida Governor LeRoy Collins, before *Brown* a moderate on race, responded that he was "as determined as anyone to maintain segregation" and appointed a panel to consider new rules for admission to the law school.[34] In March 1957, the Florida Supreme Court again took up the remand and demonstrated that its prior decision had been an example of bad faith, as it reaffirmed states' rights, the code name for segregation, "as vital to the preservation of human liberties." The court concluded that Hawkins could be admitted to the law school if he could show that his "admission can be accomplished without doing great public mischief." That was simply a repeat of its earlier rejected effort to string the case out. Hawkins returned once again to the Supreme Court, which now suggested he try to get relief from a federal district court. Hawkins tried, but the judge ruled against him. Hawkins then won in the court of appeals, but by then Florida had changed its admission standards for the law school and, with his wife pressuring him, he gave up.

In August 1958, nine years after Hawkins applied and eight years after *Sweatt*, an African-American finally was enrolled at the University of

Florida Law School. The Florida Supreme Court demonstrated in the Hawkins saga that with a little creative use of law and a little bad faith even the clearest constitutional rights could be delayed.

The South and Public Schools

If Florida, a peripheral state with a theretofore moderate governor, could go through hoops to keep Hawkins out of law school seven years after *Sweatt,* and Alabama could riot over Lucy even though African-Americans had previously entered southern universities, it is no wonder that *Brown,* dealing with younger children, was a virtual dead letter in the South. Statistics from the 1956–1957 school year tell an accurate story. The seventeen affected states had over 10,000 school districts and 2,700,000 African-American children enrolled in them. That school year only 723 districts, with about 300,000 African-American children, were engaging in *any* desegregation—and desegregation simply meant any African-American student in a formerly all-white school. Overwhelmingly, the desegregation that did occur was in the border states of Missouri, Kentucky, and Maryland. In the South, only three peripheral states had any desegregation: two rural districts in Tennessee, three rural districts in Arkansas, and over 100 districts in rural West Texas. All these districts had minuscule African-American populations. When the more urban schools in Fort Worth and Texarkana were ordered desegregated and there was some disruption, Governor Allan Shivers sent in the Texas Rangers to "preserve order" and to maintain segregation. In the Deep South plus Virginia, North Carolina, and Florida, three years after *Brown* schooling went on just as it had three years prior to *Brown.*

Nashville provides a useful glimpse of desegregation in a peripheral state. In response to an NAACP lawsuit, Nashville's school board adopted a desegregation plan in 1956 featuring neighborhood schools, grade-a-year implementation, and free transfers for any student. A federal judge approved. As implemented, only 115 of the 1,400 African-American first-graders lived within white attendance-zones. Only 55 of 2,000 white first-graders lived within African-American attendance-zones. All of the whites and about 100 of the African-Americans transferred to one-race schools to avoid desegregation. Nashville thus commenced desegregation with a dozen African-Americans in schools with whites; nevertheless, in 1959 a federal court of appeals upheld the plan, which supposedly complied with *Brown*—race not be used for pupil assignment—while clearly subverting it with the application of the transfer policy.

The border states were commencing compliance, but beyond them, the southern response split basically by region. Four states—Tennessee, Arkansas, Texas, and North Carolina—recognized *Brown* as law, albeit unwelcome law. They were not happy about complying and would evade it by whatever tricks might work—authorizing school closings in North Carolina or using the Texas Rangers in Fort Worth and Texarkana—but they did not go the way of Virginia, the Deep South, or Florida after *Hawkins.* In the latter states, interposition was the order of the day, the year, and hopefully the century. The Deep South, Florida, and Virginia shunned evasion; they engaged instead in total defiance because, in their constitutional eyes, *Brown* carried no legitimacy.

Southern Resistance—Laws

One of the standard evasive techniques of the states on the periphery was a pupil-placement law. Although the language varied, the substance of the laws did not. First, all pupils were to be assigned individually to the school appropriate for them. Second, until that assignment, all assignments would stay as they were (and for children entering the system, the school they would previously have been assigned to). Third, the burden of applying for an assignment to a different school was placed on the students. Finally, there was a lengthy appeals process designed to make sure it could not be completed within a single school year. Under the generally prevailing judicial doctrine of exhaustion of administrative remedies, a court could not intervene until the final administrative appeal was heard and decided. By then, it would be time to start again with the next school year. If pupil-placement laws worked as intended, and initially they did, then segregated schooling would continue as before, with every request for a transfer being rejected.

Most southern states were not content to rely solely on pupil-placement laws, and therefore they adopted a variety of backup measures just in case pupil placement did not work as intended. North Carolina offered tuition for private schools. Tennessee allowed free transfers from desegregated schools. There were threats, especially in North Carolina, of closings should a school board be silly enough to place an African-American in a white school.

The Deep South, Florida, and Virginia employed all the measures of the peripheral states and much more to preclude any end to segregation. Each state formally adopted interposition. Some offered private-school tuition, denied state funds to desegregated schools, or authorized closing schools that were desegregated, while Mississippi and Louisiana made it a crime to attend a desegregated school. Not since the Civil War had there been such a direct threat to national authority.

In February 1956, Marshall had told a Memphis NAACP audience, "We've got the other side licked. It's just a matter of time."[35] But as the year wore on, he became more pessimistic. Public opinion was clearly running against the NAACP. Southern whites agreed with their politicians; a 1956 poll showed over 80 percent opposed desegregated public schools. There was every reason for Marshall's initial optimism to wane.

The laws attacking *Brown* virtually ensured that the decision would go unenforced for years. Yet those laws were but one facet of what Harry Flood Byrd had aptly called "massive resistance." A second facet was attacking the NAACP. Politically, this was analogous to attacking the Communist Party anywhere else in the nation; the NAACP was so unpopular that no one lost by attacking it. The third facet was the formation—without government help, but with warm support—of Citizen's Councils to maintain segregation. By attacking the NAACP, the South was attacking the only organization (outside of the Court) attempting to enforce *Brown*. A Citizen's Council, by contrast, demanded a hegemony of thought and public action by citizens of both races. Its main function was to deprive the NAACP of plaintiffs and any other kind of support.

The NAACP and its Legal Defense Fund were vulnerable for three reasons. First, and obviously, it was highly unpopular and not deemed a part of the community—hence the ascription "outside agitators" to those who wished to end segregation. Second, many states, with the express approval of the Court, had been experimenting with ways to rid themselves of the Communist Party. All the South had to do was apply similar techniques to the NAACP, hopefully with similar results of driving the organization and its members underground or, better still, out of existence. Third, the LDF, unlike other organizations commencing legal action, openly solicited for clients. The LDF typically decided where to sue and then, and only then, found its nominal plaintiffs. There was a not insubstantial argument that this violated the applicable canons of legal ethics. To the extent that was in doubt, southern states were moving to clarify that the LDF's solicitations were illegal.

Alabama, Arkansas, and Florida attempted to obtain the NAACP's membership lists, while Virginia went directly after its lawyers. Different techniques had different success rates, but the net result was to put the NAACP and the LDF on the defensive for the rest of the decade—and out of business in Alabama until the mid-1960s. An organization fighting for its very life is hardly one that will be initiating lawsuits on other matters, like, say, ending segregation.

Southern Resistance—Citizen's Councils

The Citizen's Council movement began in Mississippi the summer after *Brown*. State judge Tom Brady wrote a ninety-page booklet, *Black Monday*, that argued it would be better to abolish the public schools than to desegregate them with all the attendant risks to "blue-eyed, golden-haired little girls."[36] Brady saw *Brown* as a virtual communist plot to mandate the amalgamation of the races. To counter any desegregation, Brady proposed the creation of a more establishment-oriented, nonviolent alternative to the Ku Klux Klan, and both houses of the Mississippi legislature officially commended him for his ideas and efforts in 1956. The Citizen's Councils had similar goals to the Klan, but they operated openly and peacefully. Instead of the Klan's killings, the Citizen's Councils would see that transgressors lost their jobs or couldn't get credit or, during that era of short-term mortgages, their mortgages renewed.

The techniques worked like a charm, as two early examples showed. When twenty-nine African-Americans in Selma, Alabama, signed a petition protesting Jim Crow, sixteen were quickly fired. In Yazoo City, Mississippi, fifty-three African-Americans endorsed an antisegregation statement; fifty-one withdrew their names after local Citizen's Council members suggested what the consequences of not doing so could be; the other two went North.

The Citizen's Council movement explains why southern states wanted the NAACP membership lists; the names could be made public and then private action by the local councils could extract the price of nonconformity. As Neil McMillen thoroughly documents, the councils demanded absolute conformity from whites and abject submission from African-Americans. Thus, neither race could publicly question the status quo. At the end of 1957, Hodding Carter III reluctantly concluded that the Citizen's Council "stands virtually unquestioned in its dominance of the white community in Mississippi."[37] "Between October and December 1955 membership in the Alabama Citizen's Councils grew from a few hundred to twenty thousand. After the mob forced Autherine Lucy off the campus, the number of 'Councilors' doubled then redoubled."[38] The Citizen's Councils were equally effective as the Klan—but unlike the Klan, everything they did may have been legal.

The same cannot be said for the companion legislation to the Mississippi legislature's commendation of Judge Brady. Mississippi created a Sovereignty Commission to operate as a public relations bureau for the southern way of life. But in the early 1960s, the Sovereignty Commission was transformed into a mini-KGB that conducted surveillance on civil rights workers and engaged in a variety of illegal activities—although their exact dimension is not known because many, if not most, of its key records were destroyed.

Under George Wallace, Alabama created both a Peace Commission and a Sovereignty Commission that, in conjunction with the state police, operated similarly to Mississippi's commission. A profile of Martin Luther King, Jr., by Peace Commission staffers told state law enforcement agencies that King was "totally under the direction of the Communist Party."[39]

White Supremacy and the Southern Woman

White supremacy, at bottom, was about a supposed purity: the purity of the southern woman, the purity of white blood, the purity of the South itself. "The purity of the white woman was the ultimate safeguard for the preservation of the white race and, in turn, white dominance. Take away that purity, that 'absolute taboo on any sexual approach to her by the Negro,' and 'the great heritage of white men' could not be guaranteed."[40] Brady's *Black Monday* stated that "the loveliest and the purest of God's creatures, the nearest thing to an angelic being that treads this terrestrial ball is a well-bred, cultured Southern white woman."[41] From the white southern perspective, nothing so threatened *everything* as interracial marriage, and all southern states, as well as several border states, prohibited it. The fear of "mongrelization" permeated white southern thought; it was assumed that if white and African-American children went to school together, they would grow to like each other, date each other, and ultimately some would marry each other. *Look* magazine editor William Attwood wrote that the southerner "will tell you that, sooner or later, some Negro boy will be walking his daughter home from school, staying for supper, taking her to the movies . . . and then your Southern friend asks you the inevitable, clinching, question: 'Would *you* want your daughter to marry a Nigra?'"[42] Attwood's hypothetical southern friend was hardly hypothetical; in the first national poll on interracial marriage, a bare 4 percent of white respondents said they approved.

Attwood explained that "sexual neurosis makes many whites impervious to logic,"[43] and perhaps this helps explain the irrationality and panic

Woodward saw at the beginning of 1956. If the existence of separate public schools was threatened, the South was certain that interracial marriages would follow as well, and this would be the end of southern civilization. This southern psychosis had partially underlined the NAACP litigation strategy of targeting graduate schools first. Marshall, with his characteristic humor, explained that "[t]hose racial supremacy boys somehow think that little kids of six or seven are going to get funny ideas about sex and marriage just from going to school together, but for some equally funny reasons youngsters in law school aren't supposed to feel that way. We didn't get it, but we decided that if that was what the South believed, then the best thing for the moment was to go along."[44] He was certainly correct; graduate students were not as threatening to southerners. They knew of the prohibition against miscegenation.

There was every reason to believe the South was deadly serious about its taboo on interracial sex. Virtually alone among the nation's states, southern states authorized the death penalty for rape—but of course not every convicted rapist was put to death. Southern juries, always all-white, reflected their communities well and imposed the death penalty at an extraordinarily high comparative rate for cases involving black-on-white rape to send the official message about how much worse a crime this was, the equivalent of killing someone. Indeed, the infamous Scottsboro cases ultimately illustrated the harshest feature of a charge against an African-American raping a white woman. There were but two outcomes. If the African-American was innocent, he would receive life in prison. Under all other circumstances, he would receive the death penalty.

Yet, even beyond rape, "white people were murderously sensitive to the character of attentions that an African-American man might pay to a white woman."[45] In the summer after *Brown II,* Emmett Till, a fourteen-year-old African-American from Chicago, was visiting relatives in the Mississippi Delta. One day Till "talked fresh" to a young, attractive, married white woman, concluding with "Bye Baby."[46] That night he was taken from his uncle's home, and subsequently his horribly beaten body was found floating in the Tallahatchie River. His murderers, the woman's husband and an in-law, were known to his uncle, and they were actually tried for killing Till. This itself was shocking; known murderers of African-Americans typically were not tried. The all-white jury needed just seventy minutes of deliberation, lengthened by a pause for sodas, to acquit.

Miscegenation at the Court

Like it or not, and the Court did not, miscegenation laws came to the Court in the wake of *Brown*. The first case involved Linnie Jackson, an African-American Alabama woman, sentenced to jail for marrying a white man. The case came to the Court by way of certiorari—that is, by a procedure (indeed, the typical procedure) whereby Congress had given the Court total discretion whether to hear a case. In November 1954, the Court refused review and let the conviction stand. A year later another case, *Naim v. Naim,* came for review, and this time by way of appeal— that is, by a procedure whereby Congress had mandated that the Court decide a dispute on the merits. The Court was going to have to rule, one way or another, on the constitutionality of laws barring interracial marriage.

The Naims were Virginians, a white woman and a Chinese man, who had gone to North Carolina to be married (under a less restrictive miscegenation law) and then returned to live in Virginia. Thereafter they separated, and Ham Say Naim moved to the District of Columbia. Ruby Elaine Naim then sought an annulment of the marriage based on Virginia's ban on interracial marriages. Mr. Naim, who faced deportation if his marriage to an American citizen was not valid, argued that the Virginia statute was unconstitutional. The Virginia Supreme Court of Appeals had no difficulty upholding the statute on grounds the whole South would recognize and approve. Laws prohibiting interracial marriage were designed "to preserve the racial integrity of [Virginia's] citizens," thereby avoiding "a mongrel breed of citizens." The Fourteenth Amendment did not require "the obliteration of racial pride" nor require "the corruption of the blood." "Both sacred and secular history teach that nations and races have better advanced in human progress when they cultivated their own distinctive characteristics and culture and developed their own peculiar genius." The law was therefore appropriate and more than reasonable.

Naim split the Court between justices ready to strike down the Virginia law and those who thought the symbolism of doing so would be a huge setback to *Brown*. Frankfurter argued as vehemently as possible not to hear the case, believing that to rule for Ham Say Naim would place *Brown* in jeopardy. (From the sidelines Thurgood Marshall had the identical thought.) The Court, with some reluctance, unanimously came to agree with Frankfurter and in a per curiam paragraph complained of the inadequacy of the record in showing the parties' relationship to Virginia both before and after their marriage. The Court vacated the judgment and remanded it "in order that the case may be returned" to the trial court. *Naim* was gone.

On remand, the Virginia Supreme Court of Appeals expressed its puzzlement. What couldn't the Court figure out? The Naims had been Virginia domiciliaries. They went to North Carolina to evade Virginia's law and were married there. They then immediately returned to Virginia as husband and wife. That was illegal, and when Mrs. Naim petitioned for annulment, it was the proper remedy. There was no need to send the case back to the trial court because the facts were clear and on these facts there was one appropriate remedy. Accordingly, once again, the annulment was granted. The Court's bluff had been called.

Naim was back at the Court when Ham Say Naim appealed again. With Frankfurter still leading the way, the Court again refused to hear the case, this time on the absurd fictitious ground that the case was "devoid of a properly presented federal question." When one of Clark's law clerks asked him how the Court could be doing what it was, the justice responded, "One bombshell at a time is enough."[47] Philip Elman, the ex-Frankfurter clerk in the Justice Department, had advised Naim's lawyer against taking the appeal (a choice that would have been unethical given the possibility of Naim's deportation) on the ground that the timing was all wrong. Elman recognized the Court's orders were "specious" but noted, "if the Supreme Court wants to duck, nothing can prevent it from ducking."[48] True enough, but if the Court does not feel it necessary to follow the rules when they pinch, why should others feel any more bound when different legal rules adversely affect them? Presumably the duty to follow the rules laid down is not a sometime thing.

Another ex-Frankfurter clerk, Alex Bickel, justified the Court's refusal to hear a case squarely within the category that Congress had stated it must hear. Bickel aptly noted that a judgment upholding the miscegenation statute would have been unthinkable but to strike down the statute, at that time, would have been unwise because that would have jeopardized *Brown*. The South would have understood that *Brown* did in fact mean the end of "racial purity," just what the South sensed and feared most. So an innocent African-American woman was in an Alabama jail (when the Court refused review), Ham Say Naim was subject to deportation, and the Court was forced into ignoring a jurisdictional mandate of Congress all so the Court could protect *Brown* from southern hysteria. *Brown* undoubtedly was worth that. But that doesn't mean it was necessary for the Court to do all it did to protect *Brown*. The Court's actions were not forced upon them. The justices had made a knowing choice—to commit an injustice and to disregard a law in order to do a larger justice and protect a more important law—or so they thought.

The Montgomery Bus Boycott

There was one victory over segregation in 1956. In December 1955, sparked by Rosa Parks's refusal to give up her seat at the back of the bus to a newly boarding white passenger, Montgomery's African-Americans began a boycott of the city's transit system. Initially, the boycott's aim was to protect the African-Americans' right to their seats in the back of the bus, but when it was apparent that no compromise was possible, the demand escalated to ending segregated seating altogether. The boycott walked hand in hand with litigation. Right after the 1956 election, in *Gayle v. Browder,* the Court in its now typical unsigned per curiam order ruled that Montgomery's segregation was unconstitutional.

Earlier, when the Court had considered segregated golf courses and beaches in November 1955, there had been some discussion of whether to write an opinion.[49] Apparently the South's reaction to the vacuity of *Brown* so startled the justices that they concluded any reasons in a desegregation opinion would set the South off again. Therefore, in *Gayle* there was no debate: A result without reasons was to be the method of announcing further unconstitutionality of separate but equal. Yet to the extent *Brown* itself had articulated reasons, they were the psychological effects of separated education on young children. Were there similar psychological effects on Atlanta's adult golfers, Baltimore's swimmers, or Montgomery's bus riders? Was not the North, if not the South, entitled to some reasoned elaboration in a Supreme Court decision? The shift to results without opinion began to make the legal academy nervous. The praise for *Brown* began to fade as Harvard-trained academics publicly wondered why the Court would not explain what it—always unanimously—understood and held. The complaint was a good one. Did not the exercise of the judicial—as opposed to legislative—function necessarily require a court to explain the decision, first to the loser, then to society?

Gayle literally came down while a collateral hearing was going on in a Montgomery trial court. When the decision was announced, a spectator explained, "God Almighty has spoken from Washington, D.C."[50] The transit system, already losing money and hoping for the return of its African-American patrons, yielded, and with the buses no longer segregated, the boycott was no longer needed. What was important, however, as Marshall's biographer Mark Tushnet aptly notes, was the boycott and the emergence of Martin Luther King, Jr., not the litigation. Direct action, with its empowering effect on the African-American community and monetary consequences on a business, spoke more cogently than a court decision and was easier to yield to. Yet, since no one could know whether direct action or litigation was the appropriate choice in any given situation, both would be used in the future. Furthermore, the justices had a natural propensity to think litigation was the appropriate and more effective solution than concerted action. So did Marshall, whose relationship with King was never good, and who "viewed the bus boycott and King's speeches as street theater that did not come close to equalling the main event"—the NAACP's litigation.[51] Thus, Marshall brushed aside the boycott: "All that walking for nothing. They might as well have waited for the Court decision."[52]

Montgomery was a victory. But in *Naim* the justices gave nothing. In *Lucy* their decision brought nothing, and similarly in *Hawkins*. *Brown* issued a great principle but in results yielded little except minimal desegregation in the border states, a bit in the rural areas of the periphery, and nothing except defiance in Virginia, Florida, and the Deep South.

Eisenhower, when he spoke at all, expressed concern over the "great emotional strains" placed on the white southerners; he never endorsed the Court—not his job—nor did he rebuke the southern leaders for attacking the Court. Indeed, in calling for patience, he decried "extremists on either side," thereby equating those, like the NAACP who wanted to see something happen quickly, with die-hard segregationists, as if there could be some equivalence.[53] Warren was unhappy and fumed at Eisenhower for not coming to the Court's defense. As a former executive, he was used to his orders being carried out. Eisenhower fumed right back, concluding that his nomination of Warren as chief justice was "the biggest damn-fool mistake"[54] he had made.

Chapter 4

Domestic Security

The Court understood the monumental nature of *Brown* and figuratively cleared its docket for three years to focus on school segregation. By comparison to what was decided in the years prior to *Brown I* and the years following *Brown II*, the three years when *Brown* was on the docket were largely devoid of other important cases. Once *Brown* arrived, the Court's focus on segregation was total. Once *Brown* left, the Court could refocus. Prior to *Brown I*, cases involving domestic security, the nice euphemism for hunting domestic communists, dominated the Court's docket. After *Brown II*, they dominated again.

The Domestic-Security Program in 1953

The domestic-security program in the United States was, in fact, several programs functioning primarily at the federal level (but supplemented by state programs) and using both criminal and civil sanctions. The latter were by far the more important because the criminal sanctions could reach only those who had been members of the Communist Party after 1948, and following the indictments of the leaders of the Party that year, membership declined precipitously. At best, only a few thousand people needed to fear prosecution, and, indeed, the number prosecuted was under 200. Therefore, the key elements of the various programs were those that operated to deprive communists and unrepentant former communists of their means of livelihood, especially public employment.

The civil domestic-security program had three features. First, there were loyalty investigations by the federal government with the express purpose of weeding out security risks. The investigations could easily turn up past membership in the Party or in front groups controlled by the Party as the Attorney General's List functioned to ban association with listed organizations. Past membership in the Party was deemed a security issue and therefore was always a ground for terminating government employment. Furthermore, membership in or association with front groups, no matter whether prior to or immediately after World War II, increasingly became grounds for termination of government employment. Second, there were legislative investigations, mostly, but not exclusively, by congressional committees, whose purpose came to be the public branding of individuals, one at a time, as communists or former communists. Typically, as a result of being so identified, the individuals lost their employment and often their friends. Third, there were loyalty oaths required of public employees, especially teachers. One could be terminated for refusing to take an oath, and to swear falsely exposed one to the criminal offense of perjury. Loyalty oaths were the least effective and least important part of the program overall.

The civil programs could ensnare the few remaining communists and the vastly more numerous former Party members. The programs might also ensnare socialists and the more left-leaning members of the Democratic Party. Furthermore, fear was an important factor. Former communists, fellow travelers, and even liberal Democrats might worry that something they said or did might trigger an investigation with the result being loss of employment, which inevitably meant no comparable employment in the future.

The underlying premise of the program was that communists were far more prone than any other Americans to have loyalties to Moscow, sufficient to commit espionage and maybe treason, and that it was neither possible nor worth the effort to sort the benign communists, if any, from the malignant ones. Hence, at a minimum, all should be denied sensitive government employment. As the trials of Alger Hiss and the Rosenbergs showed a stunned nation, given the opportunity, a communist would sell out the United States. Republicans were more than happy to note that Hiss was a prominent New Dealer who had been a Roosevelt adviser at Yalta.

Ever since 1932, the Democrats had been able to run against Herbert Hoover and successfully label the Republicans as uncaring and heartless. Being tough on communism at home and abroad was, finally, the Republicans' salvation. Without communism as an issue, the Republicans would be forced to run against the New Deal and seemingly be consigned to permanent minority status. With domestic and foreign communism to run against, coupled with the ever-present suggestion that the New Deal had been too close to communism, Republicans might become the majority party. Therefore, any challenge to the constitutionality of the domestic-security program was a challenge to the future of the Republican Party.

Republicans, along with some Democrats, believing Truman's program was insufficient, were intent on doing something big, and in 1950 Congress overrode a presidential veto to pass the McCarran Internal Security Act. The McCarran Act looked to force every communist organization and then every communist to register with the Subversive Activities Control Board whereupon the individual would be banned from government, defense, or labor union employment. The act also authorized the reactivation of the World War II detention camps, this time for holding supposed spies and saboteurs, during any national emergency declared by the president. The McCarran Act, for the first time, made it illegal to be a Communist Party member. If constitutional, the statute was so draconian that it could not help but be more effective than the Attorney General's List and the rest of the Truman program.

As described in the first chapter, in 1951 the Court sustained the greater part of the federal domestic-security program—hunting current communists was constitutional. What was left were the issues of the McCarran Act, legislative investigations, and former members and fellow travelers. These latter individuals, who had never joined the Party but nevertheless had similar views on key issues (especially foreign policy), lived in a legal netherworld. Supposedly, since they had not joined the Party, they were not targets. In fact, since their positions on key issues paralleled the Party's, they looked like communists. Most domestic-security conservatives could not distinguish them from members and did not seem to think it mattered. They "equated Communists with Soviet spies, fellow travelers with Communists, and liberal anti-Communists with fellow travelers."[1] Liberals wished to distinguish communists from fellow travelers but were far more intent on making sure that the line drawn on acceptable political behavior placed liberals safely and securely on the correct side.

Both HUAC (the House Un-American Activities Committee) and SISS (the Senate Internal Security Subcommittee) held hearings whose purpose appeared to be exposing witnesses as former communists. A witness would typically be subpoenaed when the committee had sufficient evidence of past membership. Then the witness would be asked the bingo question—"Are you now or have you ever been a member of the Communist Party?" A denial would lead to a perjury charge. "Taking the Fifth" was classified by everyone as a backdoor admission of guilt; hence the then-current term "Fifth Amendment Communist." Admitting past membership also had consequences because the hearings seemed designed to brand people as communists so that private employers and state and local governments could discharge them for their past associations. It was never clear that HUAC's operation was consistent with separation of powers—for the function of the legislature is to legislate. Even before the Eisenhower administration, HUAC had evolved into a mini-court, enumerating communists one at a time, where the punishment for the guilty, meted out by others, was loss of employment and social ostracism. Whatever HUAC's beginnings, by the mid-1950s producing legislation was no longer a consideration.

HUAC was a committee that everyone knew to be composed of "some of the most reactionary and bigoted men in public life."[2] Thus, one chairman, Mississippi Democrat John Rankin, claimed that "every member of the Politburo around Stalin is either Yiddish or married to one, and that includes Stalin himself."[3] Yet because of Richard Nixon's success and the fact that HUAC seemed to be where the action was, 185 Republican victors in the 1952 election asked to be on the committee. With domestic security as the Republican issue, HUAC had a natural attraction and would therefore continue to function at full speed. Its investigations left unexplored constitutional issues concerning whether exposure of ex-communists one at a time could be a legitimate legislative function and the extent to which the Bill of Rights might bar the questioning.

Although the trio of 1951 cases had not stated so explicitly, they were premised on the validity of congressional testimony of a number of ex-communists before HUAC and SISS to the effect that the Communist Party was not just another party like the Democrats, Republicans, or even Socialists. Its members, unlike the others, gave their loyalty to Moscow, not Washington. That justified the domestic-security program because in some sense every Party member was "guilty" of disloyalty—if not worse. Conservatives placed great stock in the testimony of former communists; liberals thought they were disreputable liars.

The Early Decisions under Warren

The first domestic-security case Earl Warren heard, *Barsky v. Regents* (1954), involved New York's punishing a recalcitrant HUAC witness. Dr. Edward Barsky had been a physician since the end of World War I. During the Spanish Civil War, he had gone to Spain to head a hospital for the Loyalist wounded. Following his return to New York, he headed the Joint Anti-Fascist Refugee Committee, which ostensibly was helping refugees from Franco but was also a communist front group—that is, an organization without formal ties to the Party that nevertheless was run by Party members who sought non-Party members.

Right after World War II, Barsky and others were ordered by HUAC to produce records of receipt and disbursement of funds of the Anti-Fascist Refugee Committee. They refused and unsuccessfully challenged the constitutionality of HUAC. Barsky paid twice: first, six months in jail (following the Court's refusal to hear the case) for failure to honor the subpoena and subsequently six months' suspension from his medical practice after the New York licensing authority used his federal conviction to lift his state license. That was an optional, but authorized, penalty under New York law—although the licensing authority seemed more interested in the subsequent decision to place the Refugee Committee on the Attorney General's List. What did the New York action have to do with Barsky's ability to practice medicine? Nothing. Did that matter? No. The Court affirmed his suspension over dissents by Douglas, Black, and Frankfurter. Warren, in his first domestic-security case, voted with the conservative members of the Court.

Douglas had a field day with the irrationality of the New York action, which he attributed to a national "neurosis." Could anyone seriously believe Barsky was unfit to practice medicine in New York because he supported Franco's opponents in Spain? Just what could be the relevance of Barsky's left-wing political beliefs to his ability to "set broken bones or remove ruptured appendixes, safely and efficiently?" Black joined Douglas in emphasizing that Barsky was being denied his right to earn a living because he was associated with a politically unpopular group, a clear violation of the First Amendment. Frankfurter also dissented because under New York law the decision to "list" the Refugee Committee was of no relevance and, accordingly, reliance on that law deprived Barsky of his right to earn a living in violation of due process of law.

Without mentioning the evils of supporting communists or opposing Franco, Harold Burton's majority found all the dissenters' concerns irrelevant. The practice of medicine was a privilege (and therefore not a right) granted by New York on conditions that the state deems appropriate. The state's legitimate interest in "maintaining high standards of professional conduct" was sufficient to justify the suspension.

Comparatively, Barsky got off lightly. Norhert Galven had been brought to the United States from Mexico at the age of six. He had been a resident alien for over three decades, with an American wife and four children. Yet he was so obscure that his first name appears in none of the judicial reports, and the Court simply referred to him as "Petitioner." Galven was ordered deported because he had joined the Communist Party in 1944 (when it was legal to do so). He had also left the Party in 1946, four years before Congress passed the McCarran Act, which, among its other provisions, made any prior Party membership by a resident alien ground for deportation.

Galven v. Press (1954) made two arguments. First, the McCarran Act should be construed to require that the member knew of and supported the unlawful aims of the Party. Second, the act was unconstitutional. Frankfurter's majority opinion disposed of both issues quickly. Congress did not intend a requirement of "knowing" (the legal term for knowledgeable) membership, and congressional power over aliens had been held to be plenary by prior Courts. Plenary means plenary, and "[w]e are not prepared to deem ourselves wiser or more sensitive to human rights than our predecessors, especially those who have been most zealous in protecting civil liberties." Therefore, any injustice about forcing the family to split up or else exit to a foreign land was not the majority's fault. Again, the majority included Warren.

Black and Douglas dissented, as they had two years earlier when a similar issue had been presented (albeit in the context of knowing membership), but their opinions have a tone of resignation and distance rather than their usual passion. For Black, Galven is the "Petitioner." For Douglas, he is "the alien Galven." Senator Joseph McCarthy was self-destructing on national television, and the Court was deciding cases by exactly the same voting patterns and analysis as it did prior to Warren's taking his seat. Maybe Black and Douglas, already known as "Black and Douglas dissenting," had reason to be discouraged.

In 1955, with McCarthy officially "condemned" by his Senate colleagues, the Court decided *Peters v. Hobby,* a challenge by Dr. John R. Peters, a professor of medicine at Yale and a consultant (without access to classified or sensitive material) to the Public Health Service, to the finding that there were reasonable grounds for believing him disloyal. Four aspects of *Peters* stand out. First, he was not a communist. Second, he had never been a communist. Third, he did not know the charges against him. Fourth, he did not know the source of the charges.

Peters offered the perfect case for dealing with the procedures of the domestic-security program. In 1949 Dr. Peters was informed that there was some derogatory information about him and was given a hearing, which cleared him. Then in 1951 the loyalty standard was amended to make it more stringent, and Peters's case was reopened to be redetermined under the new standard. At the hearing, no evidence was presented against him. It simply existed in his file. Peters answered all questions put to him. His testimony was supported by eighteen other witnesses and forty affidavits from prominent individuals so sure of Peters's innocence that they were willing publicly to stand up for him. The Agency Board determined there was no reasonable doubt about his loyalty.

Thereafter, the Loyalty Review Board, an interagency coordinating board, announced it would conduct a "post-audit" review of Peters's case, and it too held a hearing like the one just conducted. The difference was the outcome. The Loyalty Review Board overturned the prior decision, as it had in nineteen other cases, and concluded that "on all the evidence, there is a reasonable doubt as to Dr. Peters's loyalty to the Government of the United States." (By the time the case reached the Court, the Eisenhower administration had abolished the Loyalty Review Board, thereby leaving decisionmaking in the affected agencies.)

The Court knew from the beginning that there was something unusual about the case because the solicitor general, in an unprecedented action, refused to sign the Government brief and therefore refused to represent the Government in defending a procedure whereby the accused—and in some cases the Loyalty Review Board itself—had no idea of the identity (and therefore the veracity and motivations) of the accuser. The brief was signed and the case argued by the assistant attorney general in charge of the Civil Division, Warren E. Burger (who in turn was rewarded with a seat on the federal court of appeals for the District of Columbia). He was overmatched against the trio of Thurman Arnold, Paul Porter, and Abe Fortas. Still, the Court, through Warren, ducked all the constitutional questions, including the Kafkaesque hearing. The Court concluded that under the relevant Executive Order, the Loyalty Review Board could not conduct a "post-audit" review on its own. Therefore, it lacked jurisdiction, and its decision was ordered expunged. Peters won, but he did so on an issue that his lawyers had intentionally not raised because they wished to win not only for Peters but for everyone.

Douglas and Black concurred but reached the constitutional issues, which they did not find particularly difficult. Douglas offered his patented slam at the Government, stating that the procedure not only violated basic constitutional guarantees but "ape[d] the tactics of those whom we despise." Reed and Burton dissented without reaching the constitutional issues.

Douglas had written Black that "a decision on the regulations would, I fear, be tantamount to a victory for the Government. For their system of the Faceless Informer would continue."[4] He was right; therefore, the case caused no congressional comment. Had the Court been willing to reach the constitutional issues and decide them in favor of Peters, then it would have ended the domestic-security program, for the program could not exist in the light of day. Without hidden charges and secret informers, the domestic-security program would have ground to a halt.

After two terms, the Warren Court had left the loyalty-security program pretty much as it found it. That would change in the 1955 Term and dramatically so a year later when Sherman Minton retired. Just before the election, Eisenhower selected a Catholic Democrat, William J. Brennan, to fill his seat. The change would catch Congress's attention.

The 1955 Term

The change was not immediate or complete in the 1955 Term. The Court rejected a Fifth Amendment claim of privilege in sustaining the Immunity Act of 1954 in *Ullmann v. United States*. In *Pennsylvania v. Nelson* and *Slochower v. Board of Education,* it overturned a sedition conviction of an admitted Party member and protected a "Fifth Amendment Communist" from discharge. Furthermore, in *Communist Party v. Subversive Activities Control Board (SACB)* and *Cole v. Young,* the Court issued opinions that went against the Government although the opinions focused on technical issues and avoided constitutional questions. Nevertheless, the cases were setbacks to the federal loyalty-security program, just as *Nelson* and *Slochower* were setbacks to state programs.

William Ludwig Ullmann was a senior economic analyst under Harry Dexter White at the Treasury Department. Elizabeth Bentley, the "Red Spy Queen," had named White and Ullmann as part of a Soviet espionage ring.[5] The Government wanted Ullmann's story, and he took the Fifth; then, using a new 1954 law, the Government granted Ullmann immunity from prosecution, and a judge ordered him to answer questions before a grand jury. He still refused, claiming that immunity from prosecution was not a sufficient exchange for taking away his Fifth Amendment privilege.

In an opinion that was long on expressions of fidelity to all aspects of the Constitution and to civil liberties, Frankfurter, writing for all but Black and Douglas, nevertheless rejected Ullmann's argument. Although the Fifth Amendment "must not be interpreted in a hostile or niggardly spirit," a late nineteenth-century precedent, *Brown v. Walker,* held that immunity from prosecution was a fair forced-trade for the privilege, and Frankfurter interpreted the Fifth Amendment just as *Brown v. Walker* had. This easily sustained the granting of immunity and forcing Ullmann to testify on pain of contempt.

Possibly Frankfurter went out of his way to write like a civil libertarian because Douglas's dissent just shredded his opinion. Douglas focused on the realities of forced disclosure for an individual even in the absence of a threat of prosecution. An admitted communist will be denied federal government employment and employment as a teacher, doctor, or lawyer; if an actor, he will be blacklisted. His fate is "to find no employment in our society except at the lowest level, if at all." Disclosure of being a communist "practically excommunicates him from society." These are the necessary consequences of forcing him to testify, and as Douglas demonstrated, the Government's grant of immunity demanded far more than it paid for. "The crucial point is that the Constitution places the right of silence *beyond the reach of government.*" This dissent is the twentieth century's most eloquent apologia for the right to remain silent.

The *SACB* case involved a challenge to the SACB's order that the Communist Party register as a "communist action organization," the first step in triggering the disclosure and disability provisions of the McCarran Act. Three of the ex-communist witnesses who testified before the SACB had subsequently been found to have perjured themselves in other proceedings against Party members and the question arose over what to do about this. The court of appeals had concluded that, excluding the testimony of the three, the evidence about the Party remained sufficient for the registration order. Frankfurter's opinion nevertheless remanded the case back to the SACB to make certain the decision rested on untainted evidence. Clark, Reed, and Minton dissented sharply, stating that the remand was a waste of time since, even excluding the testimony, the "result could not have been different." So why not just get on with it? "The only purpose of this procedural maneuver is to gain additional time before the order to register can become effective." They were right, but the majority was beginning to have second thoughts about the benefits of the domestic-security crusade.

Those second thoughts were also apparent in *Cole v. Young,* where the Court held that federal statutes limited summary dismissal of civil service employees on loyalty grounds to those employees who had access to sensitive information. Clark, Reed, and Minton again dissented, accurately noting that John M. Harlan's construction of the federal statute "flies directly in the face of the Act and of the legislative history." As a result of the decision, over a hundred people, half of them Post Office employees, regained their former jobs.

The significance of the 1955 Term was epitomized in two major communist cases, *Nelson* and *Slochower,* handed down less than a month after the Southern Manifesto. These two were the most controversial since *Brown* and gave southerners an opening to legitimize their criticisms—an opening they gladly took.

For such a controversial case, Warren's *Nelson* opinion is quite bland. It rested on the technical doctrine of preemption, which concerns the interrelation of state law with a federal statute. Because of the Supremacy Clause, federal statutes are by definition "the supreme Law of the Land any Thing in the Constitution or the Laws of any State to the Contrary notwithstanding." Not only may state laws not conflict with a federal law; state laws may not even make the enforcement of the federal law more difficult. When a heretofore valid state law renders implementation of a federal law more difficult, that state law is preempted and henceforth unenforceable. *Nelson* held that the Smith Act and other federal laws regulating communists preempted Pennsylvania's sedition law. But beyond that bland façade was the reversal of a conviction of Steve Nelson (the Party's name for Steve Mesarosh), a leader of the Communist Party in western Pennsylvania, on charges of sedition against the United States.

Warren's opinion had two main thrusts, one regarding congressional intent, the other regarding the likely effects of the state laws. On intent, it recounted the various federal statutes dealing with subversive activity and concluded that Congress had left no room for parallel state laws (at least where they were designed to protect the United States). In effect, Warren's opinion stated that enforcement of the state laws "presents a serious danger of conflict with the administration of the federal program." This conclusion flatly ignored the contrary statement of the solicitor general's brief that state laws have neither "interfered with, embarrassed, nor impeded the enforcement of the Smith Act." The result was that laws of forty-two states (plus Alaska and Hawaii) were invalidated in one fell swoop. Reed, Burton, and Minton made the contrary case easily; obviously, Congress had not wanted to eliminate the power of the states in the field. The states were partners with the federal government in keeping the nation safe. Nevertheless, *Nelson,* as a preemption case, rested on congressional intent. If Congress wished to show the opposite intent, it was perfectly free to do so.

Harry Slochower was a tenured associate professor at Brooklyn College who was called to testify before SISS. He answered all questions about his post-1941 life but took the Fifth over questions about Party membership during 1940 and 1941. Under a New York anticorruption law, a municipal employee who refused to answer questions relating to his duties was deemed to have quit and therefore was automatically terminated. In a surprising 5–4 decision, Clark held that the New York action unconstitutionally penalized Slochower for his assertion of a constitutional privilege. The opinion "condemned the practice of imputing a sinister meaning to the exercise of a person's constitutional right under the Fifth Amendment" and rejected New York's presumption that took as confessed everything not answered. A "witness may have a reasonable fear of prosecution and yet be innocent of any wrongdoing. The privilege serves to protect the innocent who otherwise might be ensnared by ambiguous circumstances." There being no inference of guilt available from taking the Fifth, the Court found Slochower's discharge arbitrary. Reed, Burton, Minton, and Harlan dissented. The former three saw the case as one of choosing between a job and the privilege against self-incrimination where Slochower had chosen the latter over the former. Harlan, presaging the future, deemed the case as one of noncooperation, justifying termination.

The New Attack on the Court

Nelson and *Slochower* were a godsend to southerners. The decisions gave them allies against the Court—national security conservatives. The decisions also offered a potential legitimacy to anti-Court criticism. With a little care, the claim could be made on the newer and higher ground of anticommunism without mentioning race (although most southerners could not shake their ingrained habits).

The new attack on the Court had three strands. First, the justices went the extra mile to protect communists. Second, the justices undermined the states. Third, the justices weren't good lawyers and that explained their difficulties in properly interpreting the Constitution. The latter two fit squarely into the parallel attacks on the Court over *Brown* and together carried the message that the justices were over their heads and potentially endangering both American security and American liberty. The strands were nicely pulled together by Congressman George Andrews of Alabama when he asked the House, "How much longer will this Congress continue to permit the Supreme Court to usurp the power of Congress, write the laws of the land, destroy States' rights and protect the Communist Party?"[6]

At a pair of SISS hearings, Chairman James Eastland offered hanging curve balls to the tarnished but not vanished Joseph McCarthy, and, obligingly, McCarthy hammered them. Isn't there just one "pro-Communist" decision after another? "You are so right." Is there any explanation for the decisions "except that a majority of the court is being influenced by some secret, but very powerful Communist or pro-Communist influence?" "Either incompetence beyond words, Mr. Chairman, I would say, or the type of influence which you mentioned." Does Warren follow the Communist line? "Unfortunately, yes, Mr. Chairman although I do not accuse Earl Warren of being a Communist."[7]

Far more important than the accusation that the Court was following the communist line was the claim that it was stripping the country of its rights and its powers to protect itself. Shortly after *Nelson* and *Slochower,* Noah Mason of Illinois took to the House floor to denounce the "usurpation of States' rights" by the Court, concluding that "it is only a question of time before the States will be deprived of all power and sovereignty."[8] What followed was a southern lovefest as southern representative after representative took the floor to commend Mason's astuteness and add his own. Thus, James Davis of Georgia labeled *Nelson* "a brazen and irresponsible attack on the sovereignty of all the states" and an example of the Court's efforts to achieve "a complete judicial dictatorship."[9]

How could this be explained? South Carolina Governor, and former Supreme Court Justice, James Byrnes, took Lord Acton's route in *U.S. News & World Report:* "Power intoxicates men. It is never voluntarily surrendered."[10] Another alternative, increasingly offered, was that the justices were not competent. Thus, McCarthy's answer to Eastland's question about secret communist influences began with the possibility that the justices were "incompetent beyond words."[11] This was a perfect line for southerners, for if it were accurate, then it could explain not only the reliance on psychological evidence in *Brown* but the result itself. What better way to delegitimize *Brown* than attribute it to men who lacked legal training and understanding? In early April a former president of the American Bar Association informed a House committee that

"98 percent of the good lawyers of America had no respect for the legal ability of the present members of the Supreme Court."[12] Congressman Andrews could accurately note, "This is a sad situation in this country, when the leaders of the bar feel that way toward the present members of the Court."[13]

Warren, people quickly noted, lacked prior judicial experience, as was true of Frankfurter, Douglas, and Clark, the common members of the *Nelson* and *Slochower* majorities along with Black, whose prior judicial experience consisted of once being a lowly police court judge in Birmingham. Maybe that was why the justices did not know how to produce a legal opinion or achieve a sensible result. Without that maturation on the bench, the justices had, in South Carolina Congressman L. Mendel Rivers's mind, become a greater threat to the country than "Soviet Russia. They are not any more lawyers than the man on the moon."[14] This criticism of the Court was, as *Time* magazine aptly reported, "more emotional than cerebral"—although that did not make it less real.[15] Nor did it foreclose the possibility that it might turn out to be correct.

It had been almost two decades since the Court had been in the national spotlight with significant congressional opposition. Then, Roosevelt's (unsuccessful) Court-packing plan had more than captured the justices' attention. Although he did not know it, McCarthy's statements did spark Warren, who labeled the dying alcoholic a "querulous, disreputable liar."[16] McCarthy and Mason, as midwestern anticommunists, stood out in the group criticizing *Nelson* and *Slochower;* most of the talk came from those who had signed the Southern Manifesto. They were already in opposition, and anticommunism played especially well in the South. Still, they had acquired some dubious allies, who also now saw the Court's actions as threatening the America they wished to preserve.

In a second session of Congress, especially with summer rapidly approaching, there is little besides talk that can be accomplished with legislation starting from scratch. Karl Mundt of South Dakota tossed a "*Cole Repealer Bill*" into the Senate hopper,[17] but the only preexisting bill that could slap the Court was H.R. 3, introduced in January 1955 by Howard Smith of Virginia, the man who gave the Smith Act its name.

H.R. 3 was an antipreemption bill, declaring that unless there was a "positive conflict" or an "express" declaration by Congress of intent to preempt, state law should not be held superseded. Smith had two goals in introducing H.R. 3. First, the Pennsylvania Supreme Court had already found the state's sedition act preempted (its decision in *Commonwealth v. Nelson* coming two years before Warren's); Smith wanted to reverse that conclusion. Second, the bill would undo an increasing trend of preemption in labor cases, where state law more favorable to business interests had been deemed preempted by federal labor law that in operation was more favorable to labor. H.R. 3, by playing to both the antilabor and anticommunist constituencies, had a real chance of passage.

Shortly after *Nelson,* hearings were held in the House on H.R. 3. State attorneys general and business groups supported the bill. Labor groups were opposed and, interestingly, so was the Association of American Railroads, which worried about complying with dual systems of regulation. During the summer, the ABA's House of Delegates approved H.R. 3 in principle and the National Association of Attorney Generals specifically endorsed it. But the Interstate Commerce Commission and the Department of Justice strongly opposed it.

Chairman Emanuel Celler of New York would have liked to have kept the bill bottled in the Judiciary Committee but could not prevent a vote. He was successful in amending H.R. 3 to limit it to overruling *Nelson.* Smith and other supporters of the bill wanted the whole loaf and, after procedural wrangling, decided to wait until the 85th Congress convened in January 1957.[18]

With the 84th Congress adjourned, the Court, in its summer vacation, had escaped virtually unscathed. The southerners had their Manifesto and some well-directed cheap shots but, as yet, little else except the support of die-hard McCarthyites, a waning asset.

Warren's Shift

One further case in the 1955 Term, *Black v. Cutter Laboratories,* merits mention even though the Court concluded the case presented no constitutional question. The California Supreme Court had affirmed the right of a unionized employer to dismiss a union official under the "just cause" provision of a collective bargaining agreement simply for current membership in the Communist Party, which the employer had known about for two years prior to the firing. Clark's opinion ducked everything by concluding that the decision of the California Supreme Court was simply one construing that particular labor agreement and therefore not presenting a substantial federal question, a disputable conclusion but nevertheless one that rid the Court of the case. Douglas and Black dissented, demanding, as usual, that even communists be accorded the same rights as other members of the community. The majority's disposition stated that the case was of no particular importance. What was important, however, was that Warren switched his voting pattern to move from the center over to join Black and Douglas.

No one could know that Warren's change was permanent. When William J. Brennan joined the Court at the beginning of the next term, he joined with this threesome to add a fourth vote, thereby significantly changing the Court's balance in the domestic-security cases. Prior to *Cutter Laboratories* there were only two sure votes to hold the domestic-security program unconstitutional (occasionally joined by others). These votes were more than balanced by the three and often four contrary votes provided by Reed, Minton, Burton, and Clark. Thus, when Brennan replaced Minton, there were four sure votes to invalidate the programs balanced against at best three (depending on where *Slochower* was deemed to leave Clark) to sustain it; the tilt was more pronounced after Reed retired in February 1957. Either Frankfurter, Harlan, or Clark could provide the necessary fifth vote to cabin the various loyalty-security programs.

Brennan's Appointment

In September 1956 Minton announced his intention to retire on October 15. Eisenhower's immediate reaction, obviously with the pending election in mind, was to call Attorney General Herbert Brownell, who would conduct the search, and tell him to find "a very good Catholic" with judicial experience who was a "conservative Democrat."[19] This would accomplish several things. First, Eisenhower had come close to promising Francis Cardinal Spellman, the archbishop of New York, that the next appointee would be a Catholic (none having been on the Court since Frank Murphy's death in 1949). Eisenhower wanted, as always after Warren, someone with prior experience, and Eisenhower wished to show he was serious about the Court's being nonpartisan.

Brennan's name did not come up immediately, but it did not take long. Probably Deputy Attorney General William P. Rogers offered the name since Rogers had heard a major presentation by Brennan on court reform just the previous May. The decision to appoint Brennan was final by late September, before Eisenhower had even met him. Brownell claims to have sat and read all Brennan's New Jersey Supreme Court opinions. If he did so, then he knew Brennan was not a conservative Democrat but instead a liberal. Brownell professed, almost forty years later, to have known this and not been bothered by it, even though it conflicted with his instructions. After checking with Brennan's parish priest to make sure the judge regularly attended Mass, Brownell decided that Brennan was the man, right down to being fifty years old, well under Eisenhower's cutoff age of sixty-two. Thus, a Republican president placed a known liberal on the Court because he wanted a Catholic Democrat as part of his unnecessary nonpartisan push for reelection a few weeks hence. The Senate too was in a nonpartisan mood, and Brennan was confirmed with but a single dissent—that of fellow Catholic Joseph McCarthy.

While Brennan's liberalism, never concealed, may or may not have been known to the administration, everyone knew of his gregarious personality, which often masked his formidable intelligence. Without intending to do so, Eisenhower had elevated the man who would become the most important jurist of the second half of the century and Warren's best friend and ablest lieutenant.

The 1956 Term—Perjury

In fact, that fifth vote would always be there during the 1956 Term. There were twelve cases involving "communists" during the term, and all twelve were decided against the Government with the closest vote being 5–3. By the summer of 1957, the loyalty-security programs at both the federal and state levels were in shambles. On the one hand, this made sense. McCarthy had died, and Nikita Khrushchev had denounced Stalin. On the other hand, twelve for twelve is more than big-league hitting: It is an almost unheard of record at the Court. Furthermore, while McCarthy and Stalin were dead, anticommunism was not.

A day before Eisenhower's reelection, Steve Nelson won another complete victory, this time a reversal of his Smith Act conviction under his real name in *Mesarosh v. United States*. Just before argument, the solicitor general had filed a motion noting that a paid informer who testified against Mesarosh had committed perjury in other cases and requesting a remand for the trial judge to determine whether a new trial should be granted. Instead, Warren, over the dissents of Harlan, Frankfurter, and Burton, vacated the conviction, analogizing the situation to pollution and acidly informing a stunned Government that its "dignity . . . will not permit the conviction of any person on tainted testimony."

The perjuring informer problem returned in *Jencks v. United States*. Clinton Jencks, a president of a local of the "Communist-dominated"[20] International Union of Mine, Mill & Smelter Workers, had filed the requisite Taft-Hartley noncommunist affidavit so that the union could avail itself of the federal labor laws. Two government witnesses testified that Jencks was a communist during the period. On cross-examination they were asked what they had contemporaneously told the FBI about Jencks. When neither could recall, Jencks's counsel moved that the FBI files in question be turned over to the judge for inspection, with the judge then to turn any relevant information over to defense counsel. The judge denied the motion, and Jencks was convicted of perjury on the Taft-Hartley affidavit.

By the time *Jencks* was argued, the Court knew that one of the paid informers against Jencks had admitted to perjury, but the Government was, unlike *Mesarosh*, taking the position that the recanting was the perjury (and thus was thinking about prosecuting the informer for perjury for signing affidavits saying he had committed perjury at trial!). In context, Jencks's lawyer's request looked mild. How could defense counsel successfully cross-examine a potential perjuring witness without having the relevant information about the witness's prior statements to the law enforcement agency? If those statements were inconsistent with the witness's trial testimony, then maybe the witness was not credible. In fact, only the defense counsel, and therefore not the trial judge, would know if material in government files could successfully be used for impeachment purposes. Thus, the real issue before the Court in the context of the recanting witness was not whether Jencks should prevail but whether he should be given more than his lawyer asked for. In other words, the debate was between the judge reviewing the files to determine which should be given to the defense or giving the defense all the relevant files. Brennan opted for the latter, concluding that "justice requires no less." If the Government did not want to give up the information, that was fine; it could simply dismiss the prosecution. Whether this rule was a requirement of the Constitution or simply based on the Court's inherent supervisory power over the federal courts was not addressed. Burton and Harlan concurred, finding that Jencks's counsel's request contained the appropriate balancing of interests.

Dissenting alone, Clark wrote the most quotable and impassioned opinion of his career. Clark was a friend of FBI Director J. Edgar Hoover and admired him greatly. The Court had opened "a veritable Pandora's box of troubles" by granting communists (or their lawyers) the right to FBI files, and Clark called on Congress to reverse the decision quickly. If it did not, "intelligence agencies of our Government engaged in law enforcement may as well close up shop, for the Court has opened their files to the criminal and thus afforded him a Roman holiday for rummaging through confidential information as well as vital national secrets." Senator Charles Potter of Michigan outdid Clark by complaining that the decision made life a lot better for traitors by transforming "Government records into a free peepshow for alien powers."[21] (No one knew it, but no new prosecutions were to be initiated; hence, the "free peepshow for alien powers" was not a possibility.)

The 1956 Term—Bar Admission Cases

However hyperbolic the former ABA president's claim that good lawyers did not respect the Court, a pair of bar admission cases in May 1957, *Schware v. State Bar* and *Konigsberg v. State Bar,* left the organized bar seething. The Court not only questioned the bar's complete control over qualifications; it held that a former communist could posses the requisite good moral character to become a lawyer. The bar couldn't believe it, nor could the retired Minton, who wrote to Frankfurter asking, "Does the Supreme Court know better what good moral character is than the State Courts?"[22]

The overarching issue in the cases was whether membership in the Communist Party prior to World War II was per se evidence of the lack of good moral character in the present. For many people, including the leaders of the organized bar, the single transgression of joining the Party at any time was an indelible sin. It trumped everything else in a person's life and could not be explained away as error, "premature antifascism," support for progressive positions within the political system, or by the fact that, prior to 1950 (at least), it was legal to do so. The New Mexico bar had so found in Rudolph Schware's case where, in addition to Party membership, he had been arrested (but not prosecuted) and used aliases. He had served honorably in the paratroopers during World War II and offered witnesses, including his rabbi, attesting to his good moral character. Raphael Konigsberg's case in California was more complex because, unlike Schware, he had refused to answer two types of questions, one about membership, the other about his political affiliations and beliefs.

Black, for the Court, treated the two situations as if they were identical, where the bar had deemed membership as a per se disqualification. Such a conclusion, the Court held, was irrational. "There is nothing in the record that gives any indication that his association with that Party was anything more than a political faith in a political Party. . . . Assuming that some members of the Communist Party . . . had illegal aims and engaged in illegal activities, it cannot automatically be inferred that all members shared their evil purposes." With those statements, the Court took the props out from the basic premises of the loyalty-security program since the program assumed all who had been communists were necessarily evil (unless they had received HUAC or SISS absolution).

When Black treated *Konigsberg* as if it were *Schware,* he ignored the argument of the California bar that the denial of admission was based on Konigsberg's failure to cooperate with a relevant inquiry. That claim could be dealt with only by holding that Konigsberg was privileged, either by the First Amendment (which he claimed) or the Fifth Amendment, not to answer the bar's question or that past membership in the Party could never be a relevant inquiry. Black's opinion walked up to that first point and then straddled it with the statement that "the State could not draw inferences as to his truthfulness, candor or his moral character in general if his refusal to answer was based on a belief that the United States Constitution prohibited the type of inquiries which the Committee was making."

Frankfurter dissented on the ground that he could not tell if the California Supreme Court had passed on the constitutional question. Harlan and Clark took direct issue with the majority, finding, as bar associations nationwide also found, that the "decision represents an unacceptable intrusion into a matter of state concern."

The 1956 Term—"Red Monday"

With the capital digesting *Jencks,* two weeks later the Court had a once-in-a-generation day. On June 17, 1957, the Court handed down a quartet of extraordinary decisions, severely restricting the Smith Act, suggesting that communist-hunting legislative investigations were unconstitutional, and invalidating the loyalty dismissal of John Stewart Service, one of the "Old China Hands" of the State Department (who had mistakenly contrasted Chiang Kai-shek's corruption and weakness with the respect followers held for Mao Zedong). June 17 was immediately dubbed "Red Monday" in a takeoff on "Black Monday," the day a generation earlier when the Court had gutted the New Deal's legislative program on May 27, 1935. Furthermore, the votes of "Red Monday" were overwhelming. One was unanimous; two produced solo dissents by Clark; the other had a dissent by Clark and Burton. Warren wrote the two legislative investigation decisions; Harlan, the other two opinions.

When Service returned from China in 1945, a grand jury refused to indict him for espionage. From then until his discharge by Secretary of State Dean Acheson in 1951, he had undergone one continuous loyalty review after another. The Republicans, always more interested in Asia than in Europe, were blaming the State Department, and especially its China experts like Service (one of the few supposed State Department "communists" McCarthy actually named), for "losing" China to the communists. Although the goal was to affix blame on the Democrats generally, Service was a necessary first step up the chain of command.

Ultimately, Acheson discharged Service pursuant to the so-called "McCarran Rider" attached to every appropriation bill since 1947, authorizing the secretary of state to terminate any employee whenever the secretary might deem it "necessary or advisable in the interests of the United States." In a technical opinion, Harlan concluded that the secretary was bound by the internal procedures that he had promulgated to govern discharges (including those under the McCarran Rider); when Acheson summarily terminated Service without reviewing the record, he had violated his own procedures. The message, similar to the one of the perjured informers, was that the federal government was also bound by rules.

Harlan's other opinion was *Yates v. United States*, the Smith Act conviction of the West Coast second-tier leaders of the Communist Party. Following the sustaining of the Smith Act against the leaders of the Party in *Dennis v. United States* in 1951, the Court had denied review in second-tier-leader convictions coming from various parts of the country. Because *Dennis* had refused to review the evidence, *Yates* was the first time the Court would evaluate the necessary proof in a Smith Act case.

Dennis had held that the Smith Act satisfied the First Amendment's "clear and present danger" test and that advocacy of the objective to overthrow the government "as speedily as circumstances would permit" was soon enough. Harlan's opinion in *Yates* framed the issue as "whether the Smith Act prohibits advocacy and teaching of forcible overthrow as an abstract principle, divorced from any effort to instigate action to that end, so long as the advocacy or teaching is engaged in with evil intent." Is the dividing line between constitutionally protected speech and punishable speech the line between advocacy and incitement or the line between advocacy and discussion? Harlan construed the Smith Act to reach only "incitement"—speech that incites to illegal action. This left protected abstract advocacy—the belief in the doctrine of overthrow of the government. "The essential distinction is that those to whom the advocacy is addressed must be urged to *do* something now or in the future, rather than merely to *believe* in something." Harlan admitted that the distinctions were "subtle and difficult to grasp," but implicit in his line-drawing was the conclusion that it was mandated by the First Amendment.

Thus, Harlan required the prosecution to prove that a defendant incited others to engage in illegal action in the future. How this could be done was left unsaid because inciting people now to do something sometime later is almost impossible. Consider a rousing speech by a football coach at the opening of training camp whose purpose is to incite the team to beat its arch rival two years hence. Even Vince Lombardi would have had trouble doing that—which was the point of *Yates*.

The communists had been convicted because they believed in an evil idea and sincerely wished it would become reality. The United States was jailing men because it abhorred what they thought rather than because they had done anything wrong. Although Harlan never mentioned the First Amendment and smothered his conclusion in lawyer-like reasoning, he was construing the Smith Act in a way that would have reversed the *Dennis* convictions and was moving closer to Black and Douglas in result if not in tone.

The defendants, as had their *Dennis* predecessors, were also convicted under the "organize" provision, which prohibited organizing a group to advocate overthrow. The *Yates* defendants however, claimed that the organizing occurred in 1945 when the Party was reformed, and hence the three-year statute of limitations had run on the crime in 1948. The Government, more realistically, argued that to organize such a group was an ongoing process so that the statute of limitations had not run. After nine pages discussing the meaning of "organize," Harlan concluded that the Court could not ascertain Congress's intent in the Smith Act. Therefore, the Court followed the traditional rule of statutory construction, which was to interpret criminal statutes narrowly. The prosecution, commenced in 1951, was time-barred as the organizing occurred once, in 1945.

The Court also reviewed the evidence against the fourteen defendants. It consisted, as had the *Dennis* evidence, of lots of talk about revolution and not much else. "At best this voluminous record shows but a half dozen or so scattered incidents which, even under the loosest standards, could be deemed to show" advocacy reaching the quality of incitement. The Court ordered five defendants acquitted; the other nine had their convictions reversed. Subsequently, the Government dropped the case, believing that the Court's evidentiary standard could not be met. Harlan thought the Smith Act was "dumb,"[23] and he had rendered it useless.

The legislative investigation cases, *Watkins v. United States* and *Sweezy v. New Hampshire,* both involved quite cooperative witnesses who nevertheless refused to answer some questions on First Amendment grounds. John Watkins, a labor organizer, answered numerous questions, including inquiries about his own extensive relationship to the Party. But he refused to answer questions about individuals who were no longer members of the Party. Watkins was convicted of contempt for refusing to answer "pertinent" questions. Paul Sweezy was a classical Marxist economist; he refused to answered questions from the New Hampshire attorney general, acting as a one-man legislative investigating committee, about a lecture he had delivered at the University of New Hampshire and about activities of the Progressive Party during the 1948 presidential campaign. He too was found in contempt. Besides one being a HUAC case and the other a state case, the essential difference was that the questions propounded to Watkins dealt with communists and those to Sweezy concerned the Progressive Party. Thus, the latter touched the First Amendment fault line between the communists and everyone else.

Warren's opinion in *Watkins* spends a lot of time flirting with holding that the HUAC procedure of enumerating communists one at a time violates the First Amendment, but then as it nears its conclusion, it shifts gears to decide the case on the entirely fictitious ground that Watkins's not knowing what the investigation was about precluded him from understanding if a question was "pertinent" or not. Before reaching the pertinency holding, Warren wrote that the committee function was part of the legislative process and therefore subject to the Bill of Rights and specifically the First Amendment. Warren noted, with a tone of displeasure, the changes in legislative investigations since World War II and the current propensity to invade the private lives of citizens. He then refused to assume that every investigation was justified by a public need that overcomes a citizen's claims to privacy. In a rebuke clearly directed at HUAC, he stated "there is no congressional power to expose for the sake of exposure."

This would have been exactly the point where the opinion should have evaluated the need of Congress for the information tested by whatever standards the First Amendment mandated. Yet, instead, the opinion shifts to conclude that in the first instance Congress had to set the balance. That is, Congress had the duty to police its committees to make sure they were collecting information that related to a valid legislative purpose. This was not being done with HUAC. Its charter essentially told it to investigate "un-American propaganda" and groups that threaten

"the principal form of government guaranteed by our Constitution."
Just what are those, the Court asked? The "outer reaches" of HUAC's
"domain are known only by the content of 'un-American activities.'"
That is, they were essentially unknowable. The charter was too broad
and thus placed reviewing courts "in an untenable position if they are to
strike a balance between the public need for a particular interrogation
and the right of citizens to carry on their affairs free from unnecessary
governmental interference." Yet after reaching this point, the opinion
narrowed itself down to Watkins's supposed lack of knowledge about
the topic of the investigation (which, like all HUAC investigations, was
communism in America). Clark's dissent characterized the majority as a
"mischievous curbing of the informing function of the Congress."

Sweezy also avoided a First Amendment decision but with even less
justification. Warren concluded that New Hampshire should have limited the discretion of its attorney general to ask privacy-invading questions. The problem with this tactic is that there must be something in the
federal Constitution that demands this limit upon New Hampshire and if
that limit is not the First Amendment, it is difficult to see what else it
might be. As with Congress and HUAC, Warren noted that because New
Hampshire never specifically addressed the limits on the attorney general, the reviewing Court cannot discern how important the state deems
the inquiry. "[I]f the Attorney General's interrogation of petitioner were
in fact wholly unrelated to the object of the legislature authorizing the
inquiry, the Due Process Clause would preclude the endangering of constitutional liberties. We believe that an equivalent situation is presented
in this case."

Frankfurter, with Harlan, concurred and wrote the most powerful
First Amendment defense of academic freedom in the *United States Reports* that exists to this day. Furthermore, the opinion introduced for the
first time the concept that Brennan would subsequently perfect, that to
sustain a law entrenching on a constitutional right, a state must be acting
because of a compelling state interest.

Frankfurter stated that the "pages need not be burdened with proof,
based on the testimony of a cloud of impressive witnesses, of the dependence of a free society on free universities." Any governmental intervention "inevitably tends to check the ardor and fearlessness of scholars,
qualities at once so fragile and so indispensable for fruitful academic
labor." For New Hampshire to prevail in its request for this information,
"the subordinating interest of the state must be compelling." The state's
worry about the violent overthrow of the government in Concord was

just not enough. "When weighed against the grave harm resulting from governmental intrusion into the intellectual life of a university, such justification for compelling a witness to discuss the contents of his lecture appears grossly inadequate."

It is surprising that the stronger defense of the First Amendment came from Frankfurter than from Warren, Black, or Douglas. To some extent the animus that Warren and Douglas held for Frankfurter may have resulted in a reluctance to join his superior opinion. Another, and better, explanation is that Frankfurter's opinion seemed to rest on the fact that the Progressive Party was a legitimate political party (unlike the Communist Party). Warren, Black, and Douglas had already reached the point where they rejected the premise that the Communist Party was different, and since that premise underlay Frankfurter's confident opinion, they would not join it. As a result, the best opinion ever on academic freedom garnered two votes, and the holding of the Court was limited to an investigating procedure unique to New Hampshire.

Summing Up the 1956 Term

What the Court had done in two months was nothing short of astounding. It had opened FBI files to communists in *Jencks*. *Yates* made prosecution of Party leaders all but impossible. *Watkins* suggested that HUAC's operative policy of requiring witnesses to name other communists was unconstitutional. *Sweezy* protected fellow travelers. *Schware* and *Konigsberg* seemed to hold that the bar could no longer exclude communists. Over the entire term, the communist position had been sustained every time. It had been a long time since the Court had so challenged democratic bodies.

Nevertheless, a close reading of the decisions revealed more lecture than law. Neither *Jencks* nor *Yates* nor *Watkins* was a constitutional holding. Each was infused with constitutional values but, in theory at least, Congress could, with new legislation, rechart its original course. The state cases, *Sweezy, Schware,* and *Konigsberg,* were constitutional holdings but rather limited ones; their core was the conclusion that membership in the Communist Party a decade or more earlier could not, without more, justify the imposition of disabilities.

The day after "Red Monday," under an editorial entitled "A Day for Freedom," the *New York Times* stated that "the Supreme Court has shown itself by far the most courageous of our three branches of Government in standing up for basic principles."[24] I. F. Stone, speaking to and for liberals, was more direct. The decisions "promise a new birth of freedom. They make the First Amendment a reality again. They reflect the steadily growing public misgiving and distaste for that weird collection of opportunists, clowns, ex-Communist crackpots, and poor sick souls who have made America look foolish and even sinister during the last ten years."[25]

Renewing the Attacks on the Court

On June 19, at a press conference, Eisenhower was asked his opinion about the Court's decisions. He proceeded to give one of his patented circumlocutions that no one could decipher. A week later a reporter tried again, asking whether it was part of the president's duty to defend the Court. After noting the importance of an independent judiciary and that the justices lacked the means to defend themselves, Eisenhower added, "Possibly in their latest series of decisions there are some that each of us has very great trouble understanding."[26] In the summer of 1957 that almost amounted to a defense of the Court. All hell seemed to be breaking loose. Just as "Black Monday" helped precipitate Roosevelt's Court-packing plan, so "Red Monday" seemed to be leading to a new constitutional crisis between the elected branches and the judiciary.

During its summer meeting, the National Association of Attorneys General debated the Court. Louis Wyman, the losing advocate as well as the losing party in *Sweezy*, offered a resolution calling on Congress "to re-affirm and reactivate Federal and state internal security controls rendered ineffective or weakened by recent decisions of the Supreme Court." After a brief floor fight where the concluding eleven words were accurately characterized as a "gratuitous insult" to the Court, the words beginning with "rendered" were deleted and the resolution passed.[27] The association also created a special committee to study the Court's decisions and recommend corrective legislation by Congress. Wyman was one of the five members.

The attorneys general were kind compared to the American Bar Association. In 1957 the ABA held two summer meetings; the first was a business meeting in New York. The second was a tax-deductible holiday in London to celebrate the common legal heritage of the two countries. Warren was prevailed upon to attend the London session as a fitting show of American respect for the common law system. Frankfurter, always the Anglophile, urged him to go, believing it "highly desirable that you should represent the Supreme Court on the one great occasion, namely, the meeting at Westminster Hall in which you would respond, as it were, to the Address of the Lord Chancellor."[28]

At the New York business meeting, the ABA voted down a resolution to express the bar's support for, and to condemn the recent criticisms of, the Court. That set the stage for London where, on the first morning, the ABA Committee on Communist Strategy issued a screed at the Court, concluding its decisions "have rendered the United States incapable of carrying out the first law of mankind—the right of self preservation."[29] Warren subsequently stated that the report "became the theme of the convention as far as the public was concerned and the press gave full coverage."[30] Indeed, the Paris edition of the *Herald Tribune* ran the headline "BAR ASSOCIATION TOLD HIGH COURT WEAKENS SECURITY AGAINST REDS" and then subheads stating "NEW LAWS TO PROTECT U.S. ASKED" and "DELEGATES ACCEPT COMMITTEE VIEW." The story elaborated that "the policy making body of the American Bar Association accepted without protest here today a report stating that recent Supreme Court decisions threaten the right of the United States 'to protect itself against communist subversion' and that 'serious consideration' must be given to corrective legislation."[31] That was true but incomplete. All reports are accepted. Yet no one from the ABA leadership offered any elaborations or corrections. Furthermore, there was no apparent reason the report could not have been delivered in New York. Thus, Warren believed he had been sandbagged into coming to London to garner publicity for a simultaneous attack on the Court. Already bitter over the ABA's silence on *Brown,* he quietly resigned his membership later in the summer.

The ABA was thus part of the bad publicity that the Court was suffering. To be sure, just as during the New Deal, the Court had supporters. The liberal press hailed its decisions as "especially needed and long overdue"[32] and a rejection of "know-nothingism."[33] In the Senate, Democrats Hubert Humphrey of Minnesota, Paul Douglas of Illinois, Joseph Clark of Pennsylvania, Richard Neuberger of Oregon, and Thomas Hennings of Missouri plus Republicans Wayne Morse of Oregon and Jacob Javits of New York were supportive. Morse called *Watkins* "one of the great landmarks in the protection of the rights of the individual citizen."[34] Hennings, as staunch a supporter as the Court had, stated that, rather than being denounced, "the Court should be praised for fulfilling its function as the ultimate guardian of human rights and freedom in our society."[35] Nevertheless, as Walter Murphy, who chronicled these events fully, observed, there was a "quiet but unmistakable undertone on Capitol Hill, a fear not only among conservatives but among moderates as well as some liberals that the Justices had gone too far in protecting individual rights and in so doing had moved into the legislative domain."[36] Now the segregationists had reluctant allies, but with that reluctance came credibility. If the Court had gone too far, maybe a rollback was in order.

Murphy was on the mark; respected members of Congress now felt the need to do something about the Court. Within days of *Jencks,* the Justice Department was receiving queries from regional district attorneys about how to treat the case. The Department moved with extraordinary dispatch to draft legislation. Yet, as it turned out, the Department's concern was less with Brennan's opinion and more with the potential expansive misinterpretation of it by trial judges. The senator who introduced the Justice Department's bill was neither a southerner nor a Republican. He was Joseph O'Mahoney from Wyoming.

There was important symbolism in O'Mahoney. He was a longtime liberal who was sponsoring a bill that would have the moderates and some liberals joining with the conservatives to carry the legislation. It took just two months, during a time when the major piece of legislation in the Senate was the first Civil Rights Act since Reconstruction, for the "Jencks Act" to go through all hearings, draft after draft, to passage in each house, conference committee, and final passage. In the debate virtually all the attacks on *Jencks* came from northern or western Republicans rather than, as with *Nelson* and *Slochower* a year earlier, southerners. Still, the opposition to the Jencks Act in the Senate was entirely by liberals who were uneasy with tampering with a liberal precedent and who ceaselessly complained that the legislation was moving too fast and was not well thought out. Liberals would have preferred no action at all, but with Hoover asserting the need for legislation to protect the FBI, doing nothing was not a political option.

The Jencks Act that passed was surprisingly close to a codification of Brennan's opinion, and liberals could take some comfort. Yet in context there was no doubt that, however mildly, the Congress had rebuked the Court, the type of action that says "think a little more carefully before you decide."

Congressmen who exploded over *Nelson* and *Slochower* were free riders on the Jencks Act; they let the moderates and liberals battle it out. But unlike many in the center, they did not trust the Court to think more carefully because they believed the headstrong justices were beyond that. They had a different idea—to prevent the justices from thinking at all.

Georgia's James Davis referred to the "wild orgy of usurpation of power" and stated that no random group of men "could possibly achieve such a record of error by fortuitous chance."[37] A host of bills were introduced to curb the Court, including eleven to change the way justices were selected. Strom Thurmond in the Senate and Representatives Andrews, Mason, and Claire Hoffman of Michigan called for impeachments.

During the debate on the Civil Rights Act, Indiana Republican Senator William Jenner gained the floor and, in a lengthy speech, introduced a bill to withdraw from the Court's appellate jurisdiction—that is, preclude the Court from hearing cases—five general domestic-security categories that corresponded with the decisions that Jenner condemned: *Watkins, Konigsberg, Cole, Nelson,* and *Slochower.* "By a process of attrition and accession, the extreme liberal wing of the Court has become a majority; and we witness today the spectacle of a Court constantly changing the law, and even changing the meaning of the Constitution, in an apparent determination to make the law of the land what the Court thinks it should be."[38] No one who signed the Southern Manifesto would have needed to change a word. Thus, the necessity for the legislation was apparent: "The Court has become, for all practical purposes, a legislative arm of the Government; and many of its feats are subject to no review."[39] Similar jurisdiction-stripping proposals were already bottled up in appropriate committees, but Chairman Eastland swung SISS into immediate action and held a hearing in less than two weeks where Jenner and SISS's director of research were the only witnesses. A week later Eastland brought the Jenner Bill before the full Judiciary Committee, but Hennings halted the process with a single question: How many witnesses had appeared at the subcommittee hearing? On receiving the answer he already knew, Hennings then proposed that full hearings, with the bar and other interested groups invited to participate, were the appropriate way to proceed on such an important matter. Jenner disagreed and moved to table Hennings's suggestion, but his motion failed by a single vote. With the passage of the historic, if toothless, Civil Rights Act, the first session of the 85th Congress ended.

Whittaker's Appointment

In light of the controversy surrounding the Court, it is perhaps surprising that a nomination to replace Stanley Reed sailed through the Senate virtually without notice in March 1957. With the election behind him, Eisenhower wished to place a midwestern Republican on the still Democratic-majority Supreme Court. Brownell selected Charles Whittaker of Missouri, who, after a successful career as a corporate lawyer, had already been appointed by Eisenhower to both a federal district court and a court of appeals. Unlike his Brennan nomination, Eisenhower had in fact met Whittaker once before the nomination, a pro forma meeting when Eisenhower appointed him to the court of appeals. The Senate Judiciary Committee held a quick hearing, and three days later Whittaker was confirmed without a roll call. Timing may explain the Senate's lack of interest. Whittaker was nominated and confirmed in March, and the controversial domestic-security cases started to come down in May.

Chapter 5

Glimpses of the Future

Brown and the domestic-security cases were so important, so central to American politics, that they dwarfed everything else. But that is not to say the dwarfs were unimportant. Consider the duPont Corporation, long a 23-percent owner of General Motors (America's largest corporation) and even longer an important GM supplier, learning that this combination was an antitrust violation. During Warren's first four years, the Court handed down important cases in criminal procedure, obscenity law, and economic regulation, and, in addition, invalidated federal statutes regulating military courts-martial of civilians. These decisions, when based on the Constitution, were cautious and generally reflected mainstream values. When, however, the Court rested its decision on a federal statute, the decision tended to be more far-reaching and decidedly more liberal.

Criminal Procedure

Patrick Irvine was a bookie in Long Beach, California. The local police knew it, but their problem was that they lacked any evidence beyond Irvine's having actually paid the federal gambling tax. The police met with the district attorney to go over tactics and decided to break into Irvine's home and see if that turned up incriminating evidence. First, they used a locksmith to make a key to the home. Then they drilled a hole through the roof so that they could run a wire to a mike they were illegally installing in the home. They broke into Irvine's home three more times, first to move the mike into the bedroom, then to move it again within the bedroom, and, finally, after a month of listening to conversations, often with his wife, to arrest him. They then ransacked his home.

Not once did the Long Beach police attempt to obtain a warrant for actions that if done by private citizens would lead to substantial jail time. Instead, Irvine got the jail time. "Long Beach is unusually free of gambling of all kinds," the police chief observed, "and we intend to keep it that way."[1]

Irvine was plenty guilty of bookmaking, and his only hope was to have all the evidence the police obtained through eavesdropping and the ransacking excluded from consideration. This need reopened two arguments at the Court. In the 1940s Black had claimed that all the provisions of the Bill of Rights, rather than just the substantive ones on freedom of expression and religion and the prohibition against uncompensated takings of property, were applicable to the states because of the Fourteenth Amendment. Under Black's "incorporation" theory, Irvine would have an easy victory because of the admitted police violations of the Fourth Amendment's search and seizure clause. But Frankfurter had been successful in limiting Black to a maximum of four votes for his theory. Instead of a Bill of Rights applicable to both nation and states alike as Black advocated, principles of federalism were deemed to give the states leeway that the Bill of Rights denied the federal government, with the result that the states had a largely free hand to admit evidence as they wished. The Court nevertheless found one limitation on the states in the Due Process Clause; evidence obtained by coercion, conjuring images of the rack and the screw, was barred. The Court also recognized that psychological coercion could operate like its physical counterpart; therefore, when a confession was obtained by psychological coercion, it too was inadmissible into evidence.

In 1952 Frankfurter elaborated on this in *Rochin v. California,* where the defendant quickly swallowed heroin to prevent the police from acquiring it. The police then took Rochin to a hospital and had his stomach pumped. This action, the Court ruled, shocked the conscience and therefore made the heroin inadmissible. Irvine could claim that *Rochin*'s recent "shock the conscience" test barred using the evidence, even if the Court would not undo its decision holding the Fourth Amendment's exclusionary rule did not apply to the states.

Only rarely had the Court reviewed such egregious police behavior as that in *Irvine v. California* (1954): "[T]hat officers of the law would break and enter a home, secrete such a device, even in a bedroom and listen to the conversation of the married occupants for over a month would be almost incredible if it were not admitted." It was, the Court concluded, a "flagrant, deliberate, and persistent" violation of the fundamental principles of the Fourth Amendment bar on unreasonable searches and seizures. With a conclusion like that, it would be easy to predict that the evidence would be held inadmissible. But instead just as the Court had sustained Galven's deportation and affirmed denying Barsky the right to practice medicine, so, too, it let Irvine's conviction stand. The Fourteenth Amendment, in its Due Process Clause, the Court concluded, only forbade the introduction of evidence obtained by "coercion, violence or brutality to the person." If Irvine had swallowed his markers and the police had pumped his stomach, then, as in *Rochin,* the Constitution would have been violated. But as it was, the only illegality went against his property, not his person. This was a violation of state law but not a violation of the Constitution.

The justices were not happy about the result. All nine found the police conduct outrageous, three saying it smacked of totalitarianism. Yet they could produce no opinion of the Court, even though six held the Fourth Amendment ought not apply to the situation and five held the conviction should be affirmed. Jackson and Warren, who voted to affirm, were so angry that they publicly implored the Justice Department to consider prosecuting the police. Reed and Minton, who also voted to affirm, refused to join the request, while Black and Douglas in dissent said prosecutorial choice was none of the Court's business under the doctrine of separation of powers. The result made the Court look both angry and impotent.

The necessary fifth vote to sustain Irvine's conviction was Warren's. As with *Galven* and *Barsky,* he subsequently attributed the vote to his feeling his way into the new job, and in one sense he was correct. His natural affinities in this and other areas were with the positions staked out by Black and Douglas that the Bill of Rights applied to the states. In another sense, however, *Irvine* indicated something basic about Warren's attitudes. He had a blind spot against those, like Irvine, who were involved in vice. He had extraordinary difficulty believing that the Constitution's protections applied to men who would voluntarily commit heinous crimes, such as exploiting sex or engaging in professional gambling, whereby they would necessarily harm innocent people. These were the people the vigorous District Attorney Earl Warren had prosecuted during Prohibition.

The two other criminal procedure cases the Court decided by the end of June 1957 were classic glimpses of the future. *Griffin v. Illinois* forced a state to place more resources into the criminal justice system to aid its poorest defendants. *Mallory v. United States* threw out a confession, the key evidence supporting a conviction and death penalty for a brutal rape.

Griffin involved a procedure unique to Illinois. To appeal a conviction, a defendant had to furnish a bill of exceptions, which invariably required producing the trial transcript. If the defendants were indigent, like Griffin, their inability to procure a transcript meant they could not appeal their conviction, which in Griffin's case meant five to ten years in jail. This was, as Frankfurter noted, suspiciously like Anatole France's ironic comment: "The law, in its majestic equality, forbids the rich as well as the poor to sleep under bridges, to beg in the streets, and to steal bread."

The prevailing opinion by Black joined by Warren, Douglas, and Clark held the procedure unconstitutional as violating both due process and equal protection. First, Black analogized the Illinois law to one that would forbid a "not guilty" plea to defendants who could not pay court costs. "Such a law would make the constitutional promise of a fair trial a worthless thing." Second, Black noted that indigents, no less than those with money, secure appellate reversals in other states where they are able to appeal their convictions. Thus, for Illinois to deny indigents appellate review creates a "misfit in a country dedicated to affording equal justice to all and special privileges to none." Black followed with one of the most famous sentences in the *United States Reports*. "There can be no equal justice where the kind of trial a man gets depends on the amount of money he has." Despite the lofty ideal, *Griffin* could not be demanding that a gold-plated defense team be assigned to every indigent—no matter how fair that might be. There was neither the money nor the will nor the lawyers and investigators to do that. Black made *Griffin* an egalitarian delight to read but an enigma to apply in new circumstances. Furthermore, any new circumstances were likely to affect more than just a single state.

Frankfurter, who pronounced the parallel to Anatole France, would not join Black's plurality opinion. Frankfurter feared emptying the Illinois state penitentiary of inmates previously denied an appeal by their indigence, so he voted to limit the result in the case to Griffin and the future but without retroactive application to those in jail. Frankfurter also believed that due process of law did not even require providing for an appeal in a criminal case, but since Illinois (and every other state) allowed appeals, the state could not produce "such a squalid discrimination" by allowing appeals only to those who come to the criminal process with enough money at the beginning.

Burton, Minton, Reed, and Harlan dissented. They didn't like the Illinois rule but thought that a state should have the freedom to structure its procedures as it wished. The Constitution required equal protection, but that did not require states "to provide equal financial means for all also." Furthermore, they saw Illinois as ameliorating the harshness of the rule by "granting special considerations" to those facing execution.

Mallory presented a classic example of a confession case. The District of Columbia police, reasonably certain Mallory was the rapist, took him and two nephews into custody for interrogation at the police station. The police began Mallory's interrogation by telling him that his brother had already named him as the rapist. After four officers questioned him for under an hour, he agreed to take a lie-detector test.

After an hour and a half of added questioning in a small room, alone with the polygraph operator, Mallory confessed. Thereafter, he repeated his confession to others and ultimately dictated the confession to a typist and signed it. The next morning he was arraigned. At trial, the confession was admitted over objections.

The case was classic because no one besides Mallory or the police knew what happened in the station, and there was no lawyer involved before the police wrapped the case up. Unlike the typical state case, the District of Columbia was governed by the Federal Rules of Criminal Procedure, which required a suspect to be brought before a magistrate for arraignment "without unnecessary delay." The Court held that the District of Columbia police had not complied with the rule; instead of the lengthy questioning of Mallory, he should have been arraigned. Therefore, the Court ruled that Mallory's confession was inadmissible.

The Court concluded that the purposes of prompt arraignment are threefold. First, to force the police to decide whom they wish to arrest. Second, to have a magistrate inform the accused of his rights. Third, to deny "an opportunity for the extraction of a confession." Extraction is a loaded word, implying overcoming someone's will. The opinion hinted that just that had occurred because Mallory was only nineteen and had "limited intelligence."

Mallory generated a sharp reaction because it had facts anyone could understand. A brutal admitted rapist went free. Southern Democrats and security-conscious Republicans, already attacking the Court, simply added *Mallory* to their ever-growing bill of particulars. Senator William Jenner asked, "How many more girls will be raped in 1957 because the United States Supreme Court was so zealous a protector of Andrew Mallory's rights as an individual?"[2] Senator Strom Thurmond, eschewing mention of *Brown,* stated that the Court was "handing down decisions to give greater protection to Communists and criminals" and "has now issued an edict which will give greater protection to such heinous criminals as rapists and murderers."[3] Both senators made clear their belief that the Court was acting without checks and that checks on "judicial tyranny" were needed.

The contrast with a similar ruling in *McNabb v. United States* is instructive. First, in 1943 the war was the focus of public attention, while in 1957 the Court was at the center of controversy. Second, the *McNabb* defendants were murderers, while Mallory was an African-American rapist.

Police did not like *Mallory* at all. It was a federal case containing a federal rule. Therefore, it did not affect the states. But if the Court decided the federal rule was constitutionally mandated, then the procedures of every single state would undergo a revolutionary change. The District of Columbia police chief stated that the rule in *Mallory* would create "a complete breakdown in law enforcement where most serious crimes would go unsolved and unpunished."[4] While this probably was political grandstanding, if it was true, then the Court's application of the Federal Rules had created a huge problem. The question was thus posed but not answered judicially: Was custodial interrogation necessary for solving the most serious crimes? The sharp response to *Mallory,* coming even from liberals like California Governor Edmund (Pat) Brown, indicated that many Americans thought so. Warren's reply to Brown—"Have you read it? Read it again."—did not provide an answer.[5]

Congress and Courts-Martial

Mallory was not alone in being freed even though he was guilty. In a series of cases over a two-year period, involving the courts-martial of civilians, the Court held the statutes authorizing the procedure unconstitutional and thereby freed murderers. The court-martial cases straddle the criminal procedure cases, like *Mallory,* and the national security cases discussed in the previous chapter. They are criminal procedure cases because, obviously, a court-martial is part of military policy (albeit approved by Congress) and operates by its own military procedures. There was no jury and the judge was a military officer (who civilians might feel lacked independence). There was a supposition that the outcomes were foreordained. In short, they bore little relation to the justice expected in either federal or state court.

Overseas courts-martial implicated national security because, but for the Cold War, they might not have occurred. This was the first time the United States military was being stationed overseas in time of "peace." Inevitably, either men in the military or civilian dependents allowed to accompany them were going to commit crimes, maybe against each other, maybe against the local population. Under whose laws would they be tried and by what agreements? The host countries were willing to allow the United States to try its own citizens in these circumstances. Congress made that possible by the Uniform Code of Military Justice (UCMJ) of 1950, which provided that for crimes committed overseas by either servicemen or civilian dependents, there would be trial by court-martial.

While on guard duty in South Korea in 1952, Robert Toth and another guard apprehended a South Korean near their air base. They took him before a lieutenant, the officer in charge, who told them to "take him out and shoot him."[6] They followed orders. Thereafter, Toth was honorably discharged and returned to the United States. The other guard and the lieutenant, still in the Air Force, were tried by courts-martial and convicted of the killing. The Air Force arrested Toth in Pittsburgh and flew him to Korea to stand trial before a court-martial as authorized by the UCMJ.

Toth v. Quarles case turned on whether Congress's constitutional power to make rules governing the armed forces was limited to those actually in the armed forces at the time of the trial. The case was argued first in the winter and then held over and reargued in the fall of 1955. Black's majority opinion deemed discharge as the transformative moment, severing the individual completely from military jurisdiction. The Court noted that over three million Americans were former servicemen and concluded they should not live with the threat of military arrest and transportation to a distant land where they would be denied what "the Constitution has deemed essential to fair trials of civilians." The "dangers lurking in military trials" necessitated the constitutional rule that American civilians, residing in America, could be tried only by civilian courts. If Toth went free, it was only because Congress had not authorized his trial by a federal court, something Congress could remedy if it wished. Reed, Burton, and Minton in dissent thought Congress had already provided an acceptable remedy and if it proved too "harsh or hurtful," then Congress could correct it.

What, then, of American citizens residing abroad? Clarice Covert and Dorothy Krueger were wives of American servicemen living, respectively, in England and Japan. Each killed her husband and was convicted for doing so by a court-martial. Thereafter, each was returned to the United States for imprisonment. Each sought her freedom with the claim that, as a civilian, only a civilian court could constitutionally try her.

The Court, with Clark and Harlan joining the *Toth* dissenters, rejected the claims for two reasons. First, since the turn of the century, the Court had held that Congress had the power to set up so-called "legislative courts" overseas to try Americans accused of crimes there. Second, what Congress had done here might well be considered "preferable to leaving American servicemen and their dependents throughout the world subject to widely varying standards of justice unfamiliar to our people."

Reid v. Covert and *Kinsella v. Krueger* had been argued in the first week of May and came down in mid-June. The dissenters—Warren, Black, and Douglas—stated that they needed more time to write their opinions and would do so during the Court's next term. Frankfurter took a similar position, although he did not formally announce that he would dissent. Surprisingly, the indecision and lack of finished opinions did not result, as it would in future years, in the cases being put over to the next term for reargument. Instead of writing their dissents for the next term, Warren and Frankfurter convinced Harlan to vote (with the four dissenters) to rehear the cases—that is, to ignore the prior vote and begin again with oral argument. On rehearing, the Court reversed and thereby overruled the first of its own precedents during Warren's tenure. The initial opinions in *Covert* and *Krueger* lasted less than a year, and their rapid demise would have been unnecessary had the Court simply ordered reargument when the dissenters were unable to complete their opinions.

The changing composition of the Court also contributed to a changed final vote. Harlan was the only justice to switch from affirming to reversal, albeit limiting himself to capital crimes. Brennan had replaced Minton and quickly found his place with Warren, Black, and Douglas (whom Frankfurter joined). Reed retired but Whittaker was not confirmed soon enough to participate. Thus, the overruling vote was 6–2, with Clark and Burton the only dissenters.

The Bricker Amendment

Black's plurality opinion continued his strong emphasis on civilian courts for civilian crimes. The Constitution provided each American guarantees of fair trials as specified by the provisions of the Bill of Rights, and these guarantees could not be evaded by resort to court-martial. Nor did the fact that the court-martial had been agreed to by our government and the host country change anything. With this conclusion, Black had reopened and answered an earlier controversy over the treaty power.

The creation of the United Nations and the various new global organizations in the wake of World War II, coupled with Franklin Roosevelt's use of executive agreements with other nations, caused conservatives and isolationists to express fears of the possibility of domestic rule by these new organizations as well as the possibility that a treaty (or executive agreement) might give added power to the federal government since by Article VI of the Constitution "all Treaties shall be the supreme Law of the Land." As expressed (and sometimes implied), the real fears were that communists would be choosing American governing rules and that international organizations, with so many third-world votes, would eradicate local customs and institutions (like segregation). There were two ways these untoward results might occur via treaties. One was through a self-executing clause in a treaty that would then supersede local laws; the other was by implementing a treaty through legislation that would otherwise be unauthorized by the Constitution (and therefore a violation of the Tenth Amendment).

These fears led to the Bricker Amendment, named for senator and 1944 Republican vice presidential nominee, John Bricker of Ohio. The amendment specified that no treaty or executive agreement with a foreign nation could supersede the Constitution itself. That is, no agreement with a foreign nation could deny Americans their constitutional rights nor enlarge the powers of either the executive branch or the federal government generally. Bricker got to the essence of his amendment when he reintroduced it in the Senate and stated that "I do not want any international groups, and especially the group headed by Mrs. Eleanor Roosevelt, which has drafted the Covenant of Human Rights, to betray the fundamental, inalienable, and God-given rights of American citizens enjoyed under the Constitution."[7]

The American Bar Association was an enthusiastic backer of the Bricker Amendment, and issues of its journal warned of the legal dangers of the new international order. Former ABA president Frank Holman was the organization's prime mover. He told a Senate subcommittee that he opposed treaties declaring a universal human right to "food, clothing, housing, and medical care, and necessary social services, and the right to security in the event of unemployment, sickness, disability, widowhood, or old age" because such treaties would transform the United States "into a completely socialistic state."[8]

In 1954 the Bricker Amendment came within one vote of the necessary two-thirds in the Senate, but with the Republicans' loss of Congress in the fall elections and Eisenhower's opposition to the amendment, its perceived urgency diminished. Nevertheless, in the anticommunist and Court-bashing climate of 1957 and afterward, it might have resurfaced. Black's opinion in *Covert,* however, showed that there was no need to resurrect it because no treaty could control the Constitution. "It would be manifestly contrary to the objectives of those who created the Constitution, as well as those who were responsible for the Bill of Rights—let alone alien to our entire constitutional history and tradition—to construe Article VI as permitting the United States to exercise power under an international agreement without observing constitutional prohibitions." To allow a treaty to change the constitutional rules would be to "permit amendment of that document in a manner not sanctioned by Article V."

The clash in the court-martial cases was basic: the fundamental fear of military justice controlling civilians versus the needs of a global power with far-flung military commitments. Black's opinions contain a consistent emphasis on the fear coupled with statements about what Congress could do to better solve the problem. Frankfurter voted similarly but without the rhetoric. The dissenters, whose numbers were shrinking, believed that given the complexities of the world, Congress had already done a pretty good job in balancing the interests. The decisions in *Covert* and *Krueger* ended the court-martial cases, which ironically had the most liberal members of the Court taking a position consonant with a major aspect of the Bricker Amendment. The domestic-security members of the Court took no position because they found, on balance, the Bill of Rights inapplicable to the situations before the Court.

Obscenity

Volume 354, covering the cases handed down on the last three Mondays of June 1957, is one of those rare volumes of the *United States Reports* that contains a set of blockbuster cases. It begins with the switched results in *Covert* and *Krueger,* moves on to the domestic-security cases of "Red Monday," and ends with *Roth v. United States* and *Alberts v. California.* There the Court held obscenity was not constitutionally protected even as the Court stripped existing law of much of its Victorian veneer.

Throughout the first half of the century, the Court had stated again and again that obscenity was not within the constitutional protections of the First Amendment. But that was all dicta; it had never decided an obscenity case. The closest the Court came was in 1949 when it reviewed a New York Court of Appeals decision that *Memoirs of Hecate County*, by one of the nation's leading literary critics, Edmund Wilson, was obscene. Frankfurter was a friend of Wilson's and so recused himself. The other eight split 4–4 and therefore affirmed the New York court without issuing an opinion.

Wilson was not the only major figure who discovered that his literature was another's obscenity. After World War II, Massachusetts, for example, held both Erskine Caldwell's *God's Little Acre* and Lillian Smith's *Strange Fruit* obscene. The censor for the Detroit Police Department ruled John O'Hara's *Ten North Frederick* obscene—two years after it won the National Book Award as the best novel of 1955. And earlier in the century, both James Joyce's *Ulysses* and D. H. Lawrence's *Lady Chatterley's Lover* had been deemed obscene.

A major question of obscenity law was how much of the British law, specifically the 1868 case of *Regina v. Hicklin,* was also American law. *Hicklin* stated that "the test of obscenity is whether the tendency of the matter charged as obscenity is to deprave and corrupt those whose minds are open to such immoral influences." Thus, if an isolated passage of a work was felt to exert an immoral influence on a susceptible person, then the work was obscene. As early as 1913, federal judge Learned Hand stated that "however consonant [*Hicklin*] may be with mid-Victorian morals, it does not seem to me to answer to the understanding and morality of the present time."[9] But he thought *Hicklin* was the law and applied it. Two decades later federal judge Munro Woolsey, in a case involving *Ulysses,* rejected *Hicklin* and concluded that a work must be judged in its entirety and that it was not enough to find that a book would deprave morals. Woolsey's test was whether the materials would tend "to stir sex impulses or to lead to sexually impure and lustful thoughts."[10] This liberalized test reigned in the federal courts in New York, but in the state courts across the nation, *Hicklin* remained dominant, and there often was no exception for the works of major contemporary authors, as Smith, Caldwell, and Wilson learned. *Roth*'s goal was to transform the law, ridding it of the vestiges of *Hicklin* and ensuring that literary works were no longer the subject of obscenity prosecutions.

Immediately prior to *Roth,* one facet of *Hicklin* was found constitutionally objectionable—testing the materials by their effects on the young. In *Butler v. Michigan* the Court invalidated a state law that prohibited the distribution to a general reading public of material "containing obscene, immoral, lewd or lascivious language or pictures, tending to incite minors to violent or immoral acts, manifestly tending to the corruption of the morals of youth." This protection was in addition to Michigan's obscenity law. It was, in Frankfurter's words for a unanimous Court, "quarantining the general reading public against books not too rugged for grown men and women in order to shield juvenile innocence." The effect, "to reduce the adult population of Michigan to reading only what is fit for children," was unconstitutional. *Butler* did not say what materials were obscene, but it did hold they must be tested by their effects on adults.

Four months later, the Court turned to *Roth* and *Alberts*. Both cases involved criminal convictions where the defendant raised two questions. The first related to whether any government had the power to criminalize obscene materials. Assuming the answer was affirmative, the second question was whether the materials the defendants distributed were the type that the Constitution allowed government to proscribe—that is, were they obscene? Amazingly, the Court granted certiorari on the first question while denying review of the second. Thus, the Court was to decide whether government could punish obscenity (and send Roth and Alberts to jail) without considering whether the materials in the case were obscene. By not checking the materials, the Court was going to rule on obscenity in a factual vacuum.

The outcome of the first question was a foregone conclusion. Did the Constitution protect obscene materials? Of course not. Imagine the headlines if the answer were yes. This Court was being hit from too many sides to now bring every minister in the nation into battle against it. Only Black and Douglas, with their absolutist position on speech, believed the Constitution wholly barred government in this area.

The Court had long assumed that obscenity was not protected by the First Amendment, but it is one thing to assume that, another to explain it. Simply saying that "we haven't given this much thought in the past, so we need not think about it now either" is not a satisfying analysis; the Court would have to do more than cite its prior dicta and, for the Court, Brennan was up to the task. His prime rationale was historical; the Framers intended to exclude obscenity. Like any other use of history to decide a constitutional question, this raised two questions. First, was the history accurate? Second, should it be decisive? Why should what some people thought a century and a half earlier, the proverbial dead hand of the past, bind us today? This was hardly an irrelevant question because Brennan's historical evidence showed with far more clarity that the Framers intended to exclude blasphemy from the First Amendment than did the evidence support their intent to exclude obscenity. No justice would have been willing to hold that a state could return to the world of the eighteenth century and prohibit blasphemy. How could the Court explain the difference? Apparently it couldn't; so the Court ignored it.

The evidence about the Framers and obscenity was, to put it charitably, skimpy. Brennan found a 1712 Massachusetts statute forbidding mocking a sermon by the use of obscenity or profanity. He found other prohibitions of profanity. These, he concluded, showed obscenity and profanity were "related crimes" and if a state could punish the one, it could punish the other. Additionally, Brennan cited some Jacksonian-era statutes, beginning with Connecticut in 1821, to demonstrate that there was "sufficiently contemporaneous" evidence to back up the conclusion about the Framers' intent. He did not mention that virtually all of the Founders, save Madison, Adams, Jay, and Jefferson, were dead by 1821. Nor did he realize that, in fact, he had asked a question—what is beyond the scope of the First Amendment's protection of freedom of speech?—that history could not answer. The reason was simple. The First Amendment was designed to preclude the federal government from regulating speech; only states could regulate speech under the Constitution in 1791. Under those circumstances, knowing what the states could do is hardly useful in knowing what the federal government could not do.

"Implicit in the history of the First Amendment is the rejection of obscenity as utterly without redeeming social importance." This unproven conclusion provided a bridge to the 1942 case of *Chaplinsky v. New Hampshire* where the Court had stated that utterances such as libel, the lewd, the profane, and the obscene "are no essential part of any exposition of ideas, and are of such slight social value as a step to truth that any benefit that may be derived from them is clearly outweighed by the social interest in order and morality." With that return to the Court's prior dicta, the issue of constitutional power was decided, saving the Court from confronting Holmes's "clear and present danger" test and explaining, as it could not, how obscenity constituted a "present" danger of anything. All in all, it was a sloppy, unpersuasive effort.

The Court refused to quit there, however, because it was about to embark on the key facet of *Roth,* rescuing obscenity from the Victorian age. It did so immediately. "Sex and obscenity are not synonymous." A simple, obvious statement and yet one that cut the heart out of obscenity law, for the law's prime underlying assumption was that sex and obscenity were synonymous. That is why censors balked at even the word "rape" or a discussion of abortion. The Court now demanded that obscenity be limited solely to discussions or depictions treating sex "in a manner appealing to the prurient interest."

Since the Court was intentionally breaking from the past, it did so as completely as possible. *Hicklin* was explicitly rejected. Works had to be considered in their entirety—that is, "taken as a whole." Nor could materials be declared obscene because of particularly susceptible prudish individuals. Instead, a work had to be tested by "contemporary community standards." If a jury found, as did Roth's and Albert's, that to the "average person, applying contemporary community standards, the dominant theme of the material taken as a whole appeals to the prurient interest," then that material is properly classified as obscene. Therefore, the material was "utterly without redeeming social importance" and unprotected by the First Amendment.

Roth is an early example of the soon-to-be-classic Brennan approach to deciding cases. He always acknowledged the legitimacy of the government's interest; therefore, unlike Black and Douglas, he never took the government head on. But having recognized the legitimacy of what government wanted to do, Brennan then would shift to conclude government had not done it appropriately in the case at bar. That always left open the possibility that, with added thought and effort, government could get it right. The technique of approving ends, but finding fault with the means, suited Brennan well, for it allowed everyone—save the absolutists—to take some consolation from the opinion, and in Brennan's hands this technique achieved his increasingly liberal and egalitarian objectives.

Roth was not the best example of Brennan's methodology because he was hopelessly confused about obscenity. He refused to discuss what was "wrong" with obscenity—that is, why is it appropriate for the government to regulate the material? Because of his conclusion that obscenity was not included within the First Amendment, it followed that obscenity could be regulated for any reason or no reason at all. The First Amendment requires a good, maybe a very good, reason to regulate speech, but by taking obscenity out, the need for the reason vanished. If the legislature thought regulation would set a better tone for society, that was enough. Since any or no reason would suffice, Brennan did not waste a word pursuing reasons. Yet presumably if one doesn't know why obscenity is evil, it is difficult to know what limits to place on its regulation. The definition of the prohibited materials is inextricably linked to the rationale for regulation, but Brennan severed the link, never finding the reasons relevant. As a consequence he was never able to define successfully what he was certain the government could proscribe. As a result, subsequent to *Roth* the justices would have to evaluate each book or movie for themselves to make their own determinations of obscenity.

Warren, Harlan, and Douglas, who was joined by Black, wrote separately. Warren "would limit our decision to the facts before us," even though the Court's grant of review specifically excluded the facts. Warren could state this because for him the content of the materials was not important. Warren knew the case did not involve "great art or literature, scientific treatises or works exciting social controversy." Once serious art and literature were protected—as Brennan's opinion guaranteed—Warren believed the Constitution was satisfied. Roth was a man who knowingly mailed materials "calculated to corrupt and debauch the minds and morals" of the recipients. Both he and Alberts were purveying materials "openly advertised to appeal to the erotic interests of the customers." They were bad people, and "[i]t is not the book that is on trial; it is a person." Pithy perhaps, and true enough, but if the book consists of material protected by the Constitution, then how does selling it become a crime? Warren could not answer because in this and subsequent cases, in his certainty that the defendant willingly chose an immoral life, inflicting harms on innocents, Warren could not get beyond the defendant to the materials (which he refused to view, trusting Brennan's judgment).

Harlan both concurred and dissented, with federalism as his central theme. The federal government was limited to the suppression of "hard core" pornography. Its interest in protecting morals was too attenuated, and any national legislation denied the states the opportunity to be "experimental social laboratories." A uniform rule of suppression in a democracy was dangerous because it would destroy the "prerogative of the states to differ in their ideas of morality."

Harlan's rationale for limiting the federal government explained why he did not limit the states. If one state banned D. H. Lawrence, it might be a mistake, but at least citizens in other states could read him. States had ample leeway to make their own moral judgments subject only to whether a decision "so subverts the fundamental liberties implicit in the Due Process Clause that it cannot be sustained as a rational exercise of power." Under this standard a state could readily conclude that "over a long period of time the indiscriminate dissemination of materials, the essential characteristic of which is to degrade sex, will have an eroding effect on moral standards." Harlan's due process approach allowed him to avoid, as had Brennan, the issue of clear and present danger. Under due process, state obscenity laws raised few if any questions.

Douglas and Black thought the whole enterprise violated the First Amendment. Douglas chided the majority for a test that made books illegal for "only the arousing of sexual thoughts." He noted that arousing such thoughts "happens every day in normal life in dozens of ways." Accordingly, the Court had granted "the censor free reign over a vast domain." Still chiding the majority for its concern about provoking sexual thoughts, Douglas also noted that even in the Smith Act decision of *Dennis* the Court had recognized there must be "some relation of the speech to action." Douglas, too, avoided clear and present danger but did so on an entirely different basis. No longer believing it offered speech sufficient protection, he offered a strengthened alternative: "speech brigaded with action." If a work does not provoke "illegal action as an inseparable part" of reading it, then it should be protected.

Douglas ended with his normal testament of faith in the American people without discussing how this seemed contradicted by the work of their elected representatives. No adult is ever forced to read a dirty book or a literary gem. "I have the same confidence in the ability of our people to reject noxious literature as I have in their capacity to sort out the true from the false in theology, economics, politics, or any other field." Thus, neither courts nor communities could censor obscenity any more than they could censor other unpopular speech; the First Amendment guaranteed that only the individual could censor for himself. Douglas's and Black's absolutism was no more effective here than in the domestic-security cases, but they raised questions that the other justices had difficulty answering.

The Court's obscenity cases would become enormously controversial. But *Roth* and *Butler* were not. *Roth* was a situation where the Court was dead certain where it was going but without much of a clue on how to get there. Its final destination was an easy compromise: eradicating the outmoded Victorian overlay of the American law to treat adults as adults, while nevertheless leaving society with the necessary leeway to protect its members from the debasement of excessive sex. Lawrence, Joyce, Wilson, Caldwell, but maybe not Henry Miller, were safe.

Of course, not everyone would get the message. The Chicago film censors demanded the deletion of the word "rape" from *Anatomy of a Murder*. Since rape necessarily implicates sex and sex is obscene, the film was obscene so long as the word "rape" remained.

Economic Regulation

Under *Roth,* since obscenity was not within the contours of the First Amendment, no reason was necessary for its regulation. That placed obscenity on a constitutional par with economic regulation generally. By the time of the Warren Court, it was close to perfectly clear that the Constitution placed no substantive limits on how governments chose to regulate businesses. That was the business of the legislature, not of any court. *Williamson v. Lee Optical* (1955) perfectly illustrated the Court's approach.

Williamson involved an Oklahoma law that prohibited opticians from, among other things, placing old lenses into new frames without a written prescription from an ophthalmologist or an optometrist. Douglas, for a unanimous Court, recognized that the "law may extract a needless, wasteful requirement in many cases." But that was irrelevant; if consumers or opticians had a complaint, they should take it to the Oklahoma legislature, not a court of law. The "day is gone when this Court uses the Due Process Clause to strike down state laws, regulatory of business and industrial conditions, because they may be unwise, improvident, or out of harmony with a particular school of thought." The Constitution, quite simply, did not apply here.

When the issue was a federal regulatory statute rather than the Constitution, the Court believed it faced no such limitations, and that it had ample leeway to interpret the statute to do justice in the economic sphere. The Federal Employers Liability Act (FELA), the Jones Act, and the antitrust laws provided striking examples.

FELA, covering railroad workers, and the Jones Act, covering maritime workers, provided statutory mechanisms for recovery for personal injuries on the job when the employer was negligent. The statute provided for a jury trial, and juries often found employer negligence on very thin to nonexistent evidence. In such cases, either the trial judge or the appellate court might rule as a matter of law that the evidence would not support a verdict, and the injured worker's judgment vanished.

These cases involved no important point of law. They were the routine work of lower courts. Nevertheless, the workers whose judgment had been taken away often petitioned for certiorari, and Black and Douglas always voted to grant the employee's request. They had considerable success in convincing at least two others to join them and set the case for review.

Frankfurter, to the applause of the Harvard faculty, argued this was a complete waste of the Court's precious docket. He felt so strongly about this that he refused to participate on the merits, despite the Court's "rule of four," which allows a minority to bind the majority to decide a case on the merits. In Frankfurter's view, by granting certiorari in FELA or Jones Act cases, the Court was flouting the Judges Act of 1925 whereby Congress delegated to the Court the ability to choose the vast number of cases it would hear in exchange for the Court's guarantee that it would hear cases of national legal importance. Frankfurter could not believe the FELA and Jones Act cases were such—and he was right. Nevertheless, the Court kept granting certiorari: twice in the 1954 Term, three times in the 1955 Term, and four times in the 1956 Term.

The invariable—although not exclusive—result on the merits was that the jury's verdict was reinstated. The Court either loved juries or believed that the party with the deepest pockets should pay for injuries regardless of negligence (and therefore regardless of the statutory language). There was little evidence it was anything but the latter.

Sympathy for the little guy was matched by a fear of bigness. In the duPont-General Motors case, the Court overturned a judgment for du-Pont and sent the case back for appropriate relief, which invariably would be at least some stock divestiture.

GM had encouraged duPont to purchase a substantial block of its stock, and between 1917 and 1920 duPont had done so. As GM's largest shareholder, with 23 percent of the outstanding shares, it controlled the larger company. In 1949 the Antitrust Division of the Justice Department charged duPont with a Sherman Act violation. Following a lengthy trial, as an afterthought, the Government spent 11 of its 777 pages in its post-trial brief also alleging that the ownership violated §7 of the Clayton Act, the antimerger provision. This was an afterthought because, prior to a 1950 amendment, everyone from the Federal Trade Commission to the Congress had assumed §7 applied only to horizontal mergers between competitors and not to vertical arrangements such as the du-Pont-GM relationship. The Court nevertheless held that §7 did apply to vertical mergers. In a more stunning conclusion, going flatly against the district court's findings of fact, the Court also held duPont's ownership of GM stock violated §7 by presenting the illegal threat of use of monopoly power whereby duPont could be a prime GM supplier by reason of stock ownership rather than product superiority. Brennan wrote the opinion—which Harlan in a note to Frankfurter labeled "the most disillusioning blot on the Court's process"[11]—and was joined by Warren, Black, and Douglas. Burton and Frankfurter dissented. Three justices were forced into nonparticipation: Clark because he had been attorney general when the suit was filed, Harlan because he had been a duPont attorney, and Whittaker because he had not been confirmed by the time of argument.

The business community was stunned by the holding and the seemingly cavalier opinion. The Court had ignored both the trial and any actual effects on competition. Instead, it assumed from the size of GM and the magnitude of its purchases that the duPont ownership must affect competition even though Ford, Chrysler, and others used alternate suppliers. Wall Street wondered how many other existing corporations might now find their prior mergers drawn into question by the government. As the *Wall Street Journal* noted, the decision was "so sweeping that it throws suspicion on any corporation that does business with any other company any of whose stock it may own."[12]

The same day as *United States v. duPont* came down, the Court handed organized labor a victory in *Textile Workers Union v. Lincoln Mills,* where a union sued the employer for specific performance of an arbitration provision in a collective bargaining agreement. Federal jurisdiction was predicated on §301 of the Taft-Hartley Act, which provided that suits between unions and employers could be brought in federal court. Yet the law governing labor agreements was state law, and giving the federal courts jurisdiction to decide cases of state law (absent diversity of citizenship of the parties) raised serious constitutional questions. The range of jurisdiction of federal courts is limited by Article III. Going beyond those limits would be similar to going beyond any other substantive provision of the Constitution. Frankfurter, who was normally reluctant to invalidate any reasonable statute, argued §301 was unconstitutional. Douglas, however, cut through everything and made the constitutional questions vanish. He concluded that Congress wished the federal courts to create a substantive law of labor contracts to displace state law, which had heretofore governed, and quite obviously the fact of federal courts creating and applying federal substantive law raises no constitutional questions. To the argument that there was no federal common law of labor agreements, Douglas tersely answered that "judicial inventiveness" would create it. (Indeed, it was easy. Three years later in the so-called *Steelworkers Trilogy,* the Court, through Douglas, simply held that, as a matter of federal labor policy, arbitration awards were to be upheld.)

Although the cases discussed in this chapter are largely unrelated, they offer a pair of themes that break down on lines between constitutional and statutory interpretation. The first is that when interpreting the Constitution the Court did not appear to be ahead of the country. *Griffin, Toth-Covert-Krueger,* and *Roth* and *Butler* all offer constitutional interpretations that, while new, nevertheless brought constitutional law into harmony with mid-twentieth-century American values. Denying someone even an opportunity for justice because of poverty was wrong, and Americans knew it. Seven years after *Griffin,* in *Gideon v. Wainwright* the Court held that indigents had to be furnished counsel at trial. The decision, alone among criminal procedure results, was popular. Had *Griffin* been better known, it would have been popular as well. As to *Covert,* everyone could tell the difference between a trial by jury and a trial by a military officer. There was no reason civilians should have been subject to the former when the latter could be made available. Finally, however, debasing as obscenity was, American conceptions in the 1950s were no longer those of Great Britain during the rule of Queen Victoria.

Looking back to the earlier chapters, *Brown* and its progeny, as we saw, also were in full harmony with national values. The same could not be said for the communist cases; the results had no constituency except the few civil libertarians. *Williamson v. Lee Optical* was an outlier, but the Court had no interest in revisiting the already firmly decided withdrawal of constitutional protection for business activities.

In contrast with the Court's constitutional decisions, those interpreting federal statutes are more assertive and more reflective of the justices' values. *Mallory* interpreted the federal rule quite literally because the Court was uneasy about station-house police practices leading to confessions (even if federalism operated as a check in Fourteenth Amendment cases). The FELA-Jones Act cases protected workers, as best the Court could, who needed protection. The decade of the 1950s, it ought to be remembered, was well before the explosion in jury awards in personal injury cases. The *New York Times* had labeled the prevailing justices in *duPont* as the "anti-big business bloc,"[13] and by any normal standards that was an accurate description. The Justice Department's Antitrust Division had no firmer friends than those sitting on the Supreme Court. The Antitrust Division was 8–1 during Warren's first four terms, the Federal Trade Commission was 2–0, and it is important to remember that the winning government was Republican. A general preference for little over large was not politically controversial, and the Eisenhower Antitrust Division and Federal Trade Commission were extraordinarily active in filing antitrust claims. The antitrust results were comparable to those for the FELA-Jones Act workers and African-Americans in discrimination cases. They were anything but random.

The statutory cases had more limited effects than the constitutional cases. The District of Columbia police were angry over *Mallory* and others were uneasy, but it was still just a federal problem. Wall Street didn't like *duPont,* but it is not clear that anyone else thought much about it. *Lincoln Mills* was a labor victory largely because it took the issues out of potentially hostile state courts. No one except those affected—and the Harvard Law School faculty who were lip-synching to Frankfurter's song—cared about the FELA cases. Largely freed from external constraints in statutory cases, the Court's majority did justice according to its own lights. Similar behavior in constitutional cases, especially those involving domestic security, would meet external pressure, and it would have profound effects.

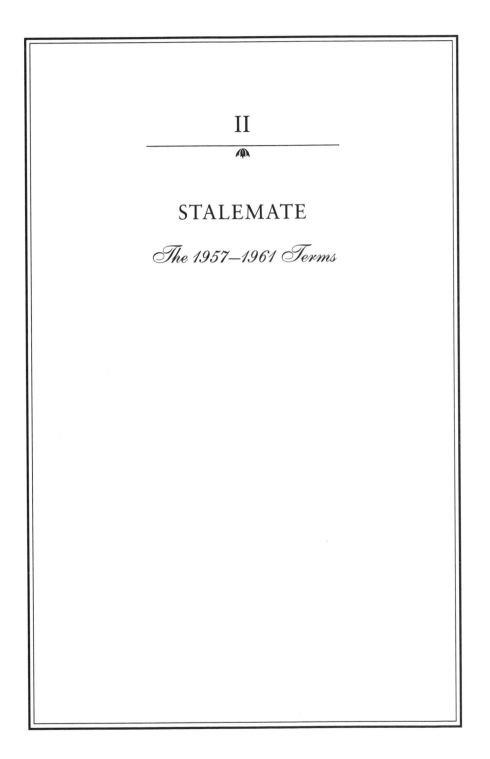

II

STALEMATE

The 1957–1961 Terms

"Dangerously, Shockingly Close"

During the 1961 Term, the Court voted 5–4 to allow a Florida legislative committee, created in 1956, to use communist-hunting tactics on the NAACP. This came after a term in which the Court undid everything it decided in the 1956 Term about domestic-security issues. It also came four years after the Court abandoned the field in school desegregation. These dramatic changes, especially the former, were keyed by events that occurred in the summer of the second session of the 85th Congress.

The Court tried not to send any tactical nukes toward Congress in 1958. Nevertheless, given the political sensitivities across the street, that was an almost impossible task. Basically, the domestic-security cases broke down three ways. First, there were true peace offerings, including a virtual road map around *Slochower v. Board of Education* to show how to fire "Fifth Amendment Communists." Second, in the middle, were cases that looked to the future but in the present didn't seem to matter much. Finally, there was *Kent v. Dulles*, echoing cases of the previous term, long on rhetoric but then holding that the State Department's policy of denying passports to suspected communists lacked statutory authorization. The peace offering wasn't enough.

Forty years later, the events to be discussed have so receded from memory that they are all but unknown. Yet they involve one of those great issues that dominated the jurisprudence of the time, the ability of Congress to control the jurisdiction of the Court.

The summer of 1958 witnessed a battle over judicial power not quite comparable to Roosevelt's Court-packing plan twenty-one years earlier but close enough for Court supporters. As with the battle over the Court-packing plan, the House of Representatives was less relevant than the Senate. The old coalition of convenience of southern Democrats and conservative Republicans that had formed to block the New Deal after

1938 had reassembled itself on the new issue of limiting the Court. The Court in 1937 was saved in the more deliberative Senate and especially in the Senate Judiciary Committee. In 1958 it would be saved again in the Senate, but not by the Judiciary Committee, which was headed by James Eastland, an implacable foe of the Court; instead, the Court was saved by Lyndon Johnson, whose unflagging support of Roosevelt's Court-packing had led to Johnson's first congressional victory.

There was also a huge difference at the presidential level. Roosevelt had just won a landslide victory, and he pulled out all the stops in attempting to get his way from a reluctant Congress. Eisenhower was a constitutional lame duck, and he did not put his prestige on the line. He seemed to oppose the efforts to attack the Court and that suggested a veto possibility, but during key votes the administration did not attempt to bring Republicans to his supposed position. Presidential politics were not absent, however; Johnson played his key role because he wanted to be president.

Eisenhower rarely spoke about the Court. His one statement about Senate bill 2646 came at a later time, when it would have stripped the Court of jurisdiction only in the bar admission cases and reversed the results in *Watkins v. United States* on pertinency in contempt of Congress cases and *Yates v. United States* on the meaning of the Smith Act. Once again, the President showed his verbal acuity when he did not wish to answer a question: "I do believe most emphatically in the separation of powers. But, let's not be too didactic, you might say, in exactly what the meaning of that expression is. . . . But on the other hand when we get down to this, just law interfering with the constitutional rights and powers and authority of the judiciary, I think that that will have to take a lot of studying, and by very fine lawyers, before I could see the justification of any law."[1] No wonder he once told his press secretary, "don't worry, if that question comes up, I'll just confuse them."[2]

Just as in the previous Congress, the House battle over anti-Court bills, especially H.R. 3, initially pitted the powerful Rules Committee chairman, Howard Smith, against his liberal Judiciary Committee counterpart, Emanuel Celler. Celler was outraged that H.R. 3 would apply its new antipreemption rules not only to future statutes but to ones already on the books. Wouldn't this, he asked Smith, "unsettle many, many cases that have been settled?" Smith didn't flinch: "I hope to goodness it will unsettle some of them. That is what I am trying to do."[3]

Celler's goal, as it had been in 1956, was to see H.R. 3 die in committee. But as Walter Murphy explained, Smith put "triple pressure" on

Celler. As Rules Committee chairman, he delayed a rule on legislation that Celler deemed important, which meant that the bill could not come to the floor. Furthermore, Smith let members of the Judiciary Committee understand that it was not only Celler's legislation that might not get a rule if there were no quick action on his pet. Finally and perhaps most significantly, he "made a veiled but unmistakable threat to exercise the Rules Committee's authority to take a bill out of the hands" of the Judiciary Committee.[4] Mirabile dictu, H.R. 3 sailed out of committee. Celler was left to join a minority report complaining it was "a horse-and-buggy formula applied to an atomic age."[5]

H.R. 3 was not the only anti-Court legislation finding its way to the floor. The Post Office Committee took a handy Senate bill and wrote in a repeal of *Cole v. Young* so that summary discharge applied to "nonsensitive" as well as sensitive government positions. The Judiciary Committee also rewrote the Smith Act to undo the part of *Yates v. United States* that limited "organize" to a one-time event. Finally, two measures changing criminal procedure decisions, specifically *Mallory v. United States,* also made it to the floor. All these provisions then passed the House. The broader definition of "organize" passed by voice vote, the "*Cole* Repealer" by 298–46. The only provision lacking a veto-proof two-thirds majority was H.R. 3, which passed 241–155.

The breakdown of the voting showed a huge chasm in the Democratic Party. Southern and border-state Democrats were with the majority; the northern liberals were on the losing side. Republicans, even with hints of an Eisenhower veto, supported H.R. 3 by 140–46 and the other measures even more so. Kansas Representative Wint Smith seemed to speak for them. "The Warren Court has now thrown its protective cloak around fellow travelers and Communists. The Court is simply blind to the reality of our time."[6]

The House action was an imposition of vision on the blind. Given these votes, the House would back anything the Senate could pass.

In February 1958, two astounding, contradictory events had occurred. At the Harvard Law School, Judge Learned Hand, whom the *New York Times* called "the most revered of living American judges,"[7] gave the Holmes Lectures to standing-room-only audiences. These lectures, collectively entitled "The Bill of Rights," were a stinging rebuke of the Warren Court, which was characterized as a "third legislative chamber," substituting its values for those of elected representatives.[8] In what was the most shocking statement, in the second lecture Hand characterized *Brown v. Board of Education* as impermissible second-guessing of legislatures.[9] In his third lecture, entitled "Guardians," Hand concluded with his rejection of the Court. "For myself it would be most irksome to be ruled by a bevy of Platonic Guardians, even if I knew how to choose them, which I assuredly do not."[10]

Alistair Cooke, writing for the *Manchester Guardian,* predicted that the lectures would "flutter the gowns" of the justices and make Hand "the latest idol of the South." David Lawrence of *U.S. News & World Report* publicized Hand's conclusions, and southern editorial writers did just as Cooke had predicted.[11] The South had acquired an ally of unquestioned and unquestionable stature.

Shortly after Hand delivered his lectures, the Senate Internal Security Subcommittee held the hearings that Thomas Hennings had demanded the year earlier on the Jenner Bill. At this time, S. 2646 still attempted to strip the Court of appellate jurisdiction in five domestic-security areas. The hearings produced an incredible split in the witness list. There were no Learned Hands, or for that matter anything close, in support of the Jenner Bill. With the exception of the Veterans of Foreign Wars, the organizational proponents of the bill—and they were numerous—were unrecognizable organizations, such as the Independent Farmers of Indiana. When it came to unaffiliated individuals, with a single exception, about the best the proponents could do was the McCarthy apologist L. Brent Bozell[12] of the recently founded, anticommunist *National Review.* But the exception was Edward Corwin, the well-known emeritus McCormick Professor of Jurisprudence at Princeton and, even though retired since 1946, still a leading analyst of the Constitution. The eighty-year-old Corwin did not specifically back the Jenner Bill because he felt it went too far but was in sympathy with its "general purpose." Shortly thereafter, in a letter to the *New York Times,* he elaborated that the Court needed its "nose well tweaked" because the "country needs protection against the aggressive tendency of the Court."[13]

Arrayed against the unknowns was their opposite, organizations anyone could recognize: the American Civil Liberties Union, the National Association for the Advancement of Colored People, Americans for Democratic Action, the American Jewish Congress, the AFL-CIO, and the Committee on Federal Legislation of the Association of the Bar of the City of New York. It was the same with individuals: Roscoe Pound, the dean emeritus at Harvard Law School, Jefferson Fordham, the dean of the University of Pennsylvania Law School, and Hoover's Solicitor General Whitney North Seymour, as well as written replies from the deans of virtually every large law school. Attorney General William Rogers described the bill as a "retaliatory measure" that "threatens the independence of the judiciary."[14] Finally, even the American Bar Association's House of Delegates at its February meeting opposed the Jenner Bill: "*Resolved,* That, reserving our right to criticize decisions of any court in any case, and without approving or disapproving of any decisions of the Supreme Court of the United States, the American Bar Association opposes the enactment of Senate bill 2646, which would limit the appellate jurisdiction of the Supreme Court of the United States."[15] Even if this was a rather mealymouthed show of support, it was enough to do the job. The ABA could and would criticize individual decisions, but one solution that was off-limits was jurisdiction-stripping.

Jenner understood that the opposing lineup made passage of S. 2646 unlikely. He denied Rogers's assertion. "I introduced this bill not out of any spirit of retaliation, but out of a deep concern for the preservation of the Constitution of the United States as it was meant to be, and our American way of life as we used to know it."[16] If a compromise that could restore constitutional balance was available, he would gladly support it.

Senator John Marshall Butler of Maryland, who wanted to pass the Jenner Bill, came up with the substitute that created a committee majority. The new Jenner-Butler Bill dropped all the jurisdiction-stripping provisions except that relating to the organized bar's pet—admissions to the profession. In addition, other provisions changed *Watkins* by holding the committee presiding officer was the judge of pertinency, *Pennsylvania v. Nelson* on preempting state sedition laws, and two aspects of *Yates*. The first broadened the definition of "organize"; the second made it criminal to advocate overthrow of the government "without regard to the immediate probable effect of such action."

As amended, S. 2646 was voted out of committee 10–5, the five including Hennings's fellow Democrats Estes Kefauver of Tennessee and John Carroll of Colorado and liberal Republicans Alexander Wiley of Wisconsin and William Langer of North Dakota. The minority emphasized that with the exception of the single jurisdictional withdrawal, no hearings had been held on any part of the bill. They sought and received numerous letters and telegrams opposing the bill, including one from the president of the ABA. The best move, however, came when Hennings decided that he needed to blunt the majority's use of Hand's Holmes Lectures as a rationale for supporting S. 2646. Hennings solicited a letter from Hand, and the latter stated that, while his official position precluded offering constitutional analysis, as a matter of policy any statute removing the Court's appellate jurisdiction "would be detrimental to the best interests of the United States."[17] Without Hand, it really was the yahoos against the establishment.

Despite the committee vote, the minority held a singular advantage. Johnson opposed S. 2646 for numerous reasons: the merits, the fact it was a Republican measure that split the Democrats, the fact that he believed it would reflect badly on the Senate, and his own presidential ambitions, which necessitated distancing him from the South. He kept the bill off the floor for three months and hoped to keep the Senate from taking action on any of the House bills either. Ten liberals, led by Hubert Humphrey, made clear that they were adamantly opposed to any action that could be seen as taking aim at the Court and that they would fight as hard as necessary to protect the Court.

Conservatives saw it differently, and with a week to go in the session, Johnson's erstwhile friend and mentor, Richard Russell, forced Johnson's hand. If Johnson wished to get a key mutual-security appropriation passed, at least some anti-Court votes had to be taken first so that southerners could send home a message about their disgust for the Warren Court. Furthermore, Strom Thurmond informed Johnson that he intended to offer H.R. 3 as an amendment to every bill remaining. Johnson knew this was no bluff, and to prevent end-of-session chaos, he agreed to a vote; indeed, subsequently he had to make the same deal on Jenner-Butler.

Jenner-Butler came up first and after a brief debate, Hennings moved to table it. The motion carried 49–41, but it demonstrated an extraordinary amount of anti-Court feeling. Then came the debate and vote on H.R. 3, which John McClellan of Arkansas had attached to another bill. The liberals, believing with Johnson that they had the votes, cut short their speeches and got on with the motion to table. They lost 45–39. At that moment, Walter Murphy wrote that the Senate "was in a state of near pandemonium" with conservatives "on their feet excitedly shouting 'Vote, vote.' Johnson was pale and visibly shaken."[18]

When Johnson composed himself after a series of parliamentary maneuvers designed to give him a few minutes, he asked Carroll, who had the floor, "to yield to me for the purpose of making a motion to adjourn until 12 o'clock tomorrow."[19] Everyone knew what this meant—a night and a morning of "The Treatment"[20] to move seven votes. Yet it carried 70–18. When the arm-twisting was over, Johnson, with the assistance of the AFL-CIO, acquired the necessary votes, but it was a suspenseful count, which initially ended in a 40–40 deadlock. Then Republican Walter Bennett of Utah came out of the cloakroom to cast the tie-breaking vote so that Vice President Richard Nixon would not have to put his future on the line. Bennett, a supporter of Jenner-Butler, mistakenly concluded that to get Nixon off the hook he had to vote aye—which he did. Nixon would have been equally off the hook if Bennett had voted nay—which he wanted to. Thus, motion to recommit carried 41–40.

Joseph Rauh, a keen observer and at the time the vice chairman of the influential liberal Americans for Democratic Action, analogized the leaders of the attack on the Court to "the owners of a baseball team that hit the opposing pitchers all over the lot but ended up scoreless after repeatedly leaving the bases loaded. For the attackers had things all their own way except in the last half of the ninth inning; even the small band of Court defenders ended up somewhat astonished at their spectacular success in preventing the enactment of a single anti-Court bill."[21] They *should* have been astonished. If Bennett had not been so worried about Nixon's options that he confused himself into voting the wrong way, H.R. 3 would have passed.

In context, beyond Bennett's selfless confusion, the key was the overwhelming vote to adjourn, a move actually suggested to Johnson by a southern supporter of H.R. 3. Why, if southerners wanted H.R. 3 passed, did they back adjournment? Murphy offers several reasons, one of which was institutionally oriented senators backing their leader. Another reason was that for some senators the anti-Court goal was neither to upset the balance of federal-state relations nor to engage in massive retaliation on the Court. Rather it was to send a message home and, as Whit Smith implied, provide vision across the street to the Court's Marble Palace. Finally, and importantly, H.R. 3 did nothing about race, and that was what the southerners really cared about.

Corwin's hope that the Court would have its "nose well tweaked" was more than fulfilled. Thus, while the Court had prevailed in a technical sense, there was no masking the extent of congressional hostility. The anti-Court measures, though not as all-encompassing as the Court-packing plan, had come far closer to passage than Roosevelt's initiative. Black, Frankfurter, and Douglas had been there in 1937 and had joined the Court shortly thereafter. They knew, or should have known, what Congress was saying. Warren wrote in his memoirs that the "legislation, evoking as it did the atmosphere of the Cold War hysteria, came dangerously close to passing."[22] That was exactly Robert McCloskey's conclusion: "The 1958 counter-attack on the Court, even though it failed, can still be regarded as a firebell in the night: it did come shockingly close to succeeding."[23]

Yet, while cloaked in "Cold War hysteria," the summer of 1958 was four years after domestic anticommunism peaked in Congress and McCarthy's public disgrace. More than domestic security was at work. Southerners had found the rhetoric of anticommunism brought allies, but the southern concern was blacks, not reds. What had been drawing together in the 84th and 85th Congresses was a coalition that wanted the Court brought to heel for decidedly different reasons.

Chapter 6

Domestic Security after Red Monday

Less than three years after being condemned by his Senate colleagues, Joe McCarthy drank himself into an early grave. A year later in 1958, liberal Democrats prevailed in the midterm elections, setting the stage for John Kennedy's victory over Richard Nixon. Yet all the while the Court was running away from the domestic-security decisions of its 1956 Term as fast as it could. It was as if domestic communism were the key national issue, and the Court wanted no part of thwarting the anticommunist program in any form. As a result, the decisions of the 1956 Term were replaced by a new set that bore an uncomfortable resemblance to those of the Hiss-Rosenbergs-*Dennis v. United States* era.

The 1957 Term

It would be hard for any term to have as many important domestic-security cases as the Court decided during the 1956 Term, and the 1957 Term not only had few domestic-security cases but the ones decided were of less importance than those of the prior term. As noted in the Prologue, the cases fell into three groups. There were major victories for government; there were cases of no immediate significance; and there was *Kent v. Dulles,* which invalidated the Passport Office's creation of its own limits on travel by suspected subversives.

One of the middle group was a set of cases, under the name *Speiser v. Randall,* invalidating a California procedure whereby a tax exemption was conditioned in part on a loyalty oath. Under California law, veterans were entitled to a property tax exemption; they had to file a loyalty oath with the assessor, who then made his own determination on eligibility. As would be his style, Brennan conceded *arguendo* the power of the state to limit the exemption to those who do not advocate overthrow of the

135

government. In doing so, he was following Frankfurter, whose opinion in *Sweezy v. New Hampshire* the previous term drew a bright line between communists and fellow travelers. In finding the procedure unconstitutional, Brennan wrote a lawyer-like opinion on the problems of mistaken fact-finding (which in context meant placing a fellow traveler on the wrong side of the constitutional divide). Furthermore, given the importance of the fact-finding, the state must bear the burden on proof. "The vice of the present procedure is that, where particular speech falls close to the line separating the lawful and the unlawful, the possibility of mistaken fact-finding—inherent in all litigation—will create the danger that the legitimate utterance will be penalized. The man who knows that he must bring forth proof and persuade another of the lawfulness of his conduct necessarily must steer far wider of the unlawful zone than if the State must bear these burdens." In operation, the procedure "can only result in a deterrence of speech which the Constitution makes free."

Clark's dissent accurately notes that Brennan's approach was "a wholly novel doctrine, unsupported by any precedent." In the future, however, *Speiser* itself would be the precedent for what would become known as the chilling effect. Because Brennan drew a line between protected and unprotected speech, rather than a line between speech and action, Black and Douglas refused to go along; instead, they concurred separately, denying that California had any power to penalize beliefs, no matter how abhorrent they might be.

The other set of middle cases, *Perez v. Brownell* and *Trop v. Dulles,* were about involuntary expatriation rather than domestic security, but because the theories offered by Warren and Frankfurter spoke so directly to domestic security, they merit discussion. By statute, Congress stripped of citizenship those, like Perez, who voted in a foreign election and those, like Trop, who were convicted by court-martial of desertion during wartime. The cases proved especially difficult and were set over from one term to the next for reargument. Essentially, two voting blocs and two diametrically opposed theories emerged. Warren, for Black, Douglas, and, to a lesser extent, Whittaker, found that the definition of citizenship in the first sentence of the Fourteenth Amendment created an absolute, unqualified, "fundamental" right, leaving Congress wholly without power to sever the relationship between citizen and nation. It could punish, even capitally, transgressions such as desertion, but it could not end the political bonds of community. Involuntary expatriation "is a form of punishment more primitive than torture, for it destroys for the individual the political existence that was centuries in the development." It is therefore banned by the Eighth Amendment prohibition on cruel and unusual punishments.

Frankfurter's approach, for Burton, Harlan, and Clark, was to ask first where congressional power lay and then whether its exercise was unreasonable under the circumstances. Once he found that Congress had authority under its foreign affairs and war powers, the rest was easy. These were not irrational judgments by Congress.

Most importantly in the context of 1958, Warren and Frankfurter also lectured each other on the judicial function. To sustain the law was to "respect the actions" of the elected branches, Frankfurter asserted, in a reaffirmation of his traditional views. The "awesome power" to invalidate congressional laws "is bounded only by our prudence" and "must be exercised with the utmost restraint." Frankfurter ended by quoting the canonized Holmes, as if by tying himself to the great jurist he could end debate. With Holmes, Frankfurter claimed that "the United States would not come to an end if we lost our power to declare an Act of Congress void. I do think the Union would be imperiled if we could not make that declaration as to the laws of the several states."

Warren's retort was that the judicial duty runs not to prudence but rather fidelity to the Constitution, to which the justices took an oath. "The judiciary has the duty of implementing the constitutional safeguards that protect individual rights."

The actual results split the cases. Voting in a foreign election cost citizenship; desertion during wartime did not, a ruling that led to the third federal statute during Warren's tenure being held unconstitutional. Brennan, more or less following Frankfurter's approach, nonetheless found no rational relationship of expatriation to the war power and thus cast the fifth vote for each result. In a private performance that presaged the future, Whittaker switched his votes in the cases three different times.

The Court's major peace offering came in a pair of cases, *Beilan v. Board of Education* and *Lerner v. Casey*, that gutted *Slochower v. Board of Education*. Both Beilan, a public school teacher, and Lerner, a subway conductor, had taken the Fifth on questions about Party membership and been fired. The 5–4 majority opinions, one by Burton, the other by Harlan, found the dismissals perfectly proper. Neither Beilan nor Lerner was fired, as Slochower had been, for "taking the Fifth." Instead, the Court concluded, Beilan was fired because he was incompetent; Lerner, because he lacked candor, which raised questions about his "trust and reliability." Only lawyers could believe this distinction without a difference. *Slochower* was not overruled; it was rendered useless. Had New York terminated Slochower not because he refused to answer, but because his refusal to answer showed he was uncooperative, then he too could have been fired successfully (and, indeed, on remand in the actual case, that is what happened).[1] The four liberals dissented, Douglas and Black stating that a "teacher who is organizing a Communist cell in a schoolhouse or a subway conductor who is preparing the transportation system for sabotage would plainly be unfit for his job. But we have no such evidence in the records before us." The only evidence was the bare refusal to testify.

The other peace offering, *International Association of Machinists v. Gonzales,* was a straightforward labor preemption case. Could state law provide a remedy for wrongful expulsion from a union or did the Wagner and Taft-Harley Acts preempt the field? With H.R. 3 in the near background, Frankfurter, over a dissent by Douglas and Warren, quickly and easily held that state law was not preempted.

Balanced against the peace offerings was *Kent v. Dulles.* In 1856 Congress had passed legislation centralizing the issuance of passports in the State Department, where passports were issued as a routine matter. Then in 1952 Congress made it a crime to leave the United States without a passport, and more or less contemporaneously the State Department imposed security criteria on the issuance of passports. Rockwell Kent, the well-known artist, was denied a passport for two reasons: He was a communist and he had "a consistent and prolonged adherence to the Communist Party line." The first obviously reached communists, although, after *Dennis v. United States,* Khrushchev's denunciation of Stalin, and the suppression of Hungary, there were precious few left. The second reached fellow travelers, also a dwindling breed. Douglas's opinion for a 5–4 Court sings the praises of a right to travel abroad as indispensable to liberty because it "may be as close to the heart of the individual as the choice of what he eats, or wears, or reads. Freedom of movement is basic in our scheme of values." But, in an uncharacteristic move for Douglas, he then shifted to a more limited ground. The Court was "hesitant to impute to Congress" the intent to leave the secretary of state with "unbridled discretion to grant or withhold a passport from a citizen for any substantive reason he may choose." Clark, for Burton, Harlan, and Whittaker, had no such qualms; of course Congress knew and wanted the State Department to use security criteria. Freedom to travel is always limited during times of war and in "a wholly realistic sense there is no peace today, and there was no peace in 1952. . . . It is not a case, then, of judging what may be done in peace by what has been done in war."

As the account of the congressional session in the Prologue showed, the Court's peace offerings were too little, too late. There is no indication they influenced anyone in Congress. Nor, as it turned out, did they influence other critics. Both the ABA and the Conference of State Chief Justices came down on the Court, the latter at the end of the summer, the former at its winter 1959 meeting.

The Legal Profession on the Court

At their tenth annual meeting in Los Angeles, the State Chief Justices issued a *Report of the Committee on Federal-State Relationships as Affected by Judicial Decisions,* accompanied by several scholarly background-papers by very able law professors. The *Report* concluded that the Court was responsible for a rapid extension of federal powers at the expense of the states. It never mentioned segregation and relied instead on labor and criminal procedure decisions. On its own legal terms, the *Report* is inexplicable. Its rhetoric was inflammatory and yet neither the listed transgressions nor the scholars' background papers came anywhere close to justifying the language used. The chief justices adopted the *Report* by an overwhelming 36–8 vote. Its condemnation of the Court was strong.

> We believe that in the fields with which we are concerned, as to which we feel entitled to speak, the Supreme Court too often has tended to adopt the role of policy-maker without proper judicial restraint.
>
> It has long been an American boast that we have a Government of laws and not of men. We believe that any study of the recent decisions of the Supreme Court will raise at least considerable doubt as to the validity of that boast. . . .
>
> These frequent differences and occasional overrulings of prior decisions in constitutional cases cause us grave concern as to whether individual views of the members of the court on what is wise or desirable do not unconsciously override a more dispassionate consideration of what is or is not constitutionally warranted. . . .
>
> It is our earnest hope that that great Court exercise to the full its power of judicial self-restraint by adhering firmly to its tremendous, strictly judicial powers and by eschewing, so far as possible, the exercise of essentially legislative powers.[2]

Time magazine, quoting most, but not all of the above, called this "the most meaningful criticism yet of the highest federal court."[3]

There are echoes in the *Report* of the justices' lack of competence, claims that connect to the earlier debates in the 84th Congress. Those debates had received an interesting supplement in December 1957 when William Rehnquist, a young Phoenix lawyer and former Jackson law clerk, tried to lay part of the blame for the Court's handiwork on the justices' law clerks. Writing in *U.S. News & World Report,* Rehnquist claimed that the clerks were politically to the left of both the Court and the country and showed "extreme solicitude for claims of Communists and other criminal defendants, expansion of federal power at the expense of state power."[4] While the clerks could hardly control the justices, Rehnquist felt that the clerks subtly influenced the Court's work. Rehnquist's article hit the Court three ways. First, it suggested there were left-wingers in the Marble Palace. Second, it reminded people that the justices could not do all their work alone. Third, it hinted that the justices were not quite up to the task of policing the handiwork of their bright, left-leaning employees. Senator John Stennis took up the theme briefly in the spring of 1958, when, in a move calculated to embarrass the Court, he called for an investigation of the clerks.[5]

Finally, the ABA once again weighed in against the Court. While the organization had opposed and continued to oppose jurisdiction-stripping bills, it supported efforts to undo the Court's domestic-security decisions in other ways. Its Committee on Communist Strategy, Tactics and Objectives kept pouring out criticism of the Court, whose decisions it deemed to "encourage an increase in Communist activities in the United States."[6] The Committee then offered a set of legislative solutions (including jurisdiction-stripping), similar to those that had died in the Senate at the end of the 85th Congress. The House of Delegates approved the Committee recommendations. As the former chairman of the President's Commission on Government Security said in support of the resolutions, "[i]sn't it time we told the Court to read the law and stop writing ideological opinions?"[7]

But the resolutions of the ABA and the Chief Justices were going nowhere. In the 1958 elections, seven Republican senators who had supported one or more of the anti-Court bills either retired or went down to defeat. Court-curbing, however, had not been an issue in the defeat. The key issues in the election were the state of the economy and, in a decided Republican mistake, curbing labor. The new Congress, where Democrats had gained in the North, was decidedly more liberal than the outgoing one and therefore less likely to take action against the Court.[8] When Eastland offered his proposals to start up the process again, California

Republican Thomas Kuchel, who had supported H.R. 3, responded that the anti-Court bills had gone down to a "well-deserved death."[9] They had lacked the support of the people, and therefore there was no need to revive them.

The Court's New Critics

Kuchel's reply placed the opposition to the Court in a new perspective. The resolutions of the State Chief Justices and the ABA were the last gasps of a fading establishment anticommunism directed against the Court, one that was simultaneously replaced by a more virulent strain from right-wing fringe groups, like those that had testified for the Jenner Bill. They were supplemented by a group of commentators, like David Lawrence, George Sokolsky, and Fulton Lewis, Jr., and the *National Review.*

The most notable among the right-wing groups was the newly formed John Birch Society. What made the Society different from other similar groups was the money of its founder, Massachusetts candy-maker Robert H. Welch, who saw a communist conspiracy everywhere. Thus, President Eisenhower spent his adult life "knowing, accepting and abiding by Communist orders, and consciously serving the Communist conspiracy."[10] Small wonder that Welch also thought Warren a dupe.

With the John Birch Society's money came a campaign for impeachment. Over the next few years, billboards sprouted across America, imploring "Impeach Earl Warren." These became so ubiquitous that in 1965 a *New Yorker* cartoon showed Whistler's Mother embroidering "IMPEACH EARL WARREN." Warren hung the cartoon in his library.[11]

Frankfurter's Switch

The anti-Court bills caused Frankfurter to get religion again. His exchange with Warren in *Trop* was a reversion to where he had been in *Dennis* in 1951. He had always believed in a very strong presumption of constitutional validity for government action, but he held himself out as ready to limit arbitrary excesses of legislative power. Frankfurter interpreted the 85th Congress as having questioned whether an independent judiciary might be too high a price to pay when the cost was the eradication of the loyalty-security program. Thus, one of the two would have to give way either voluntarily or involuntarily. Frankfurter was ready to save the Court; prudence dictated the Court yield in this area. His dalliance with the four liberals, as shown by *Watkins, Sweezy, Yates, Slochower,* and even *Kent v. Dulles,* was over.

On a sharply divided Court the centrist justices are the law, and no one from then on voted with the Court's majority in key cases as often as Frankfurter. Beginning in 1959 until he retired three years later, he cast but a single dissenting vote in the loyalty-security area (in a nonconsequential, nonconstitutional case, *Vitarelli v. Seaton*). When he switched his voting behavior between 1957 and 1959, he switched the results as well. The new trend was immediately observable. Thus, the *New York Times* unhappily editorialized in March 1960 that "what Senator Jenner was unable to achieve the Supreme Court has virtually accomplished on its own."[12] Little did the *Times* realize that the retreat had only just begun.

Frankfurter had an outcome—the Government wins. What he needed was a theory to produce that outcome. He had that too; as he had said in the face of the First Amendment challenge in *Dennis,* government action is constitutional if it is reasonable. Reasonableness involves a consideration of all relevant factors; it is a balancing of interests. Only a fool—like Black or Douglas—could believe in absolutes, and once absolutes are rejected, a fair and complete balancing of interests naturally leads to the correct constitutional outcome.

Frankfurter's switch was apparent in *Vitarelli* where he was one of four dissenters against a Harlan opinion that applied the *Service v. Dulles* rule that an agency must follow its own procedures. Frankfurter and the dissenters agreed but thought the action dismissing the employee was independently justified. A week later Frankfurter became a permanent member of the new majority when the Court revisited legislative investigations, specifically HUAC and New Hampshire, once again, and this time by a 5–4 vote sustained the contempt convictions.

Stewart's Appointment

Joining Frankfurter in the *Vitarelli* dissent was Eisenhower's final nominee to the Court, Potter Stewart. When Harold Burton announced his retirement, Eisenhower met with Attorney General William Rogers and stressed that because of the mistake with Brennan, Rogers should be "most careful" in this selection. The only name that came up at the meeting was another Ohioan, Potter Stewart, who, like Whittaker, Eisenhower had appointed in 1954 to the court of appeals. Eisenhower commented on Stewart's age, just forty-three, and cautioned Rogers again that he wanted a "conservative attitude" in the appointee.[13]

Stewart had been born into affluence, the legal profession, and a Republican family. His father was mayor of Cincinnati and subsequently a member of the Ohio Supreme Court. Stewart graduated from Yale and Yale Law School just before the war. Following Pearl Harbor, he joined the Navy and served in the Atlantic theater. After the war, he returned to Cincinnati where he was a litigator and, on the side, a local politician. He fit the president's requirements well, and like Warren and Brennan he was given a recess appointment (the last ever for a Supreme Court justice). Six months later on April 9, 1959, his confirmation hearings commenced only to be quickly recessed so that everyone could attend the opening game of the American League season. When the hearings were reconvened five days later, southern senators, especially North Carolina's Sam Ervin, engaged in noticeably sharp questioning, having found yet another forum to denounce *Brown v. Board of Education*. The southerners were the overwhelming part of the nays in the 70–17 vote to confirm.

On the divided Court he joined, Stewart fit right in with the middle, and on domestic-security matters he voted just like his predecessor, Burton. Accordingly, in this area his appointment had no effect.

Legislative Investigations—the 1958 Term

As the senior justice in the majority in all the remaining cases, Frankfurter was able to choose who authored each. The key cases went to Harlan, who was already closely associated with him. More than anything else, Harlan's opinions in *Barenblatt v. United States* and its bar admission counterparts in 1961 sealed the initial conclusion that he was, in more modern parlance, "Frankfurter-lite."

Barenblatt represented the new breed of witnesses, like Watkins and Sweezy before him, who eschewed the Fifth Amendment and based their refusal to answer HUAC questions specifically on the First Amendment. After distinguishing *Watkins* by concluding the questions put to Barenblatt were pertinent, Harlan developed his balancing test. There were several aspects of the test that merit note. First, there was a difference between the First Amendment and the Fifth Amendment. The latter "affords a witness the right to resist inquiry in all circumstances." The former simply cannot. This was at least 50 percent wrong. Harlan had been in the majority in *Ullmann v. United States*, where the Court held there was no right to resist in the face of a limited grant of immunity. Second, Harlan asserted that the government interest was the "right of self-preservation" and, thus, in *Dennis*'s conclusion, "the ultimate value of any society." How this was involved in asking a former psychology instructor at Vassar about meetings when he was a graduate student at the University of Michigan was never explained; it was assumed. The assumption would continue in all subsequent cases. Third, ending the possibility suggested by *Watkins,* Harlan held that the judiciary "lacks authority" to inquire into motives and thereby could not rule that the "true objective" of the HUAC hearing was "exposure for exposure's sake." Fourth and finally, "the record is barren of other factors which in themselves might sometimes lead to the conclusion that the individual interests at stake were not subordinate to those of the state." Harlan had not mentioned a single interest on Barenblatt's side, so it was no wonder Barenblatt lost.

Barenblatt and balancing so outraged Black that over the next two years he wrote his greatest opinions tearing Harlan and balancing apart and offering his alternative: First Amendment absolutism. He was decidedly more successful in the former endeavor than in the latter.

Black read the First Amendment as if the "no law" part were all there was to it; in other words, he never considered the scope of "the freedom of speech." So far as balancing goes, the Framers did it all when they wrote "no," and the First Amendment "means what it says." Really? Is perjury absolutely protected because the witness is engaging in speech? No one else, including Douglas, could take absolutism seriously. Frankfurter's cheering section at Harvard Law School demolished it with Dean Erwin Griswold's observation that it reminded him of a sign on a church in New Orleans: "God said it. We believe it. That's all there is to it."[14] Academic liberals had come to love Black's and Douglas's courage but could not support their supposed absolutism, which their ablest defender downsized from a universal outcome to an attitude toward the First Amendment.[15]

Black's problems justifying absolutism vanished when he shifted to his attack on balancing. Black stripped Harlan's opinion of its pretenses when he restated Harlan's interests; the Court "balances the right of the Government to preserve itself against Barenblatt's right to refrain from revealing Communist affiliations." The balancing therefore was not a serious undertaking. If it were, Barenblatt's interests would actually be mentioned. Furthermore, Black believed, the government interest was wildly overstated because the possibilities of valid legislation touching speech and association in the field of education were low. And Baren-blatt's interest was not just to remain silent. On his side was "the interest of the people as a whole in being able to join organizations, advocate causes and make political 'mistakes' without later being subjected to governmental penalties for having dared to think for themselves. It is this right, the right to err politically, which keeps us strong as a Nation." Warren, who did not pretend to be an absolutist, joined Black and Douglas, while Brennan dissented on the ground that there was no purpose for the investigation except "exposure purely for the sake of exposure."

A companion case, *Uphaus v. Wyman*, featured the return of Attorney General Louis Wyman as New Hampshire's one-man legislative investi-gating committee charged to find out whether there were any "subver-sives" in the state. He had subpoenaed the executive director of World Fellowship, Inc., an organization that maintained a summer camp in the state where it presented discussion programs, open to the public, on political, economic, and social themes. Uphaus, like Sweezy before him, was partially cooperative. He was willing to discuss his own activities but would not provide a list of the names of all the people who attended the camp during 1954 and 1955. Clark quickly distinguished *Sweezy*'s aca-demic-freedom basis "since World Fellowship was neither a university nor a political Party." Thereafter Clark's ham-handed opinion flowed simply. New Hampshire wanted to know if anyone attending the camp "posed a serious threat to the security of the State," and New Hampshire had reason to be concerned because at least nineteen speakers at the camp were affiliated with groups on the United States Attorney General's List. The "governmental interest in self-preservation is sufficiently com-pelling to subordinate the interest in associational privacy."

Brennan wrote a long dissent for the four liberals suggesting that both the individual and the government interests were important and should be accommodated "with minimum sacrifice of either." The accommoda-tion could best be done by testing the connection between the investiga-tion and a "discernible" legislative purpose. Brennan could find none; indeed, the record "not only fails to reveal any interest of the State sufficient to subordinate appellant's constitutionally protected rights, but affirmatively shows that the investigatory objective was the impermissi-ble one of exposure for exposure's sake."

Black and Douglas, apparently looking for an alternative theory, added that Brennan's opinion demonstrated that the New Hampshire practice was an unconstitutional bill of attainder—a legislative determination of guilt. They were a bit right and a bit wrong. Bills of attainder were a seventeenth- and eighteenth-century practice whereby the legislature determined, without trial, that a person was guilty and meted out the appropriate (and severe) punishment. New Hampshire, at best, had done the former. Still, Black and Douglas were on to something. Exposure for exposure's sake, for the purpose of facilitating punishment by private individuals, is not a legitimate government function, and the analogy to bills of attainder best explains why.

Aliens

Barenblatt and *Uphaus,* with only a single addition, *Fleming v. Nestor,* during the 1959 Term, set the stage for the 1960 Term, which was a replay of the 1956 Term. This time, however, the cases would be decided on constitutional rather than technical grounds; more significantly, by 5–4 votes, they came out the other way. Instead of the 1956 Term's twelve-for-twelve for the communists, albeit mostly on nonconstitutional grounds, it was six-for-seven for the Government on constitutional issues.

Fleming v. Nestor is a unique case. Ephram Nestor had come from Bulgaria to America in 1913. He lived here continuously for forty-three years but had never become a United States citizen. During the 1930s he joined the Communist Party, leaving it, with so many others, in 1939. Because of the McCarran Act's retroactive application to membership, the sixty-five-year-old Nestor was deported in 1956. At this point, a 1954 amendment to the Social Security Act kicked in, which denied social security benefits to aliens who were deported because of their communist past—in Nestor's case the $55.60 a month he had begun receiving in 1955 for the nineteen years he and his employers had paid into the fund. His wife, who remained in the United States, received the notification of the cutoff.

Harlan's opinion justified the law by rejecting the argument that a vested social security benefit is a property right that would receive protection under the Fifth Amendment's Takings Clause. It is not a property right; it is a real expectation of continuing benefits, but that is not enough to bring the Takings Clause into play. Nor was the Court overly bothered by the retroactivity. The result, although admittedly harsh, was not punishment because the Court refused to find that Congress so intended it.

The liberals in dissent found the social security amendments in their retroactive application an ex post facto law, inflicting a punishment for behavior not criminal when committed. Black's separate dissent was angry and evokes memories of his *Dennis* dissent. He found that the law in question, along with so many other statutes, was based on the "fear that this country is in grave danger if it lets a handful of Communist fanatics make their arguments and discuss their ideas." He chastised the majority for illustrating "the extent to which people are willing to go these days to overlook violations of the Constitution perpetrated against anyone who has ever even innocently belonged to the Communist Party."

Legislative Investigations—the 1960 Term

The 1960 Term began with a pair of HUAC cases, *Braden v. United States* and *Wilkinson v. United States.* After *Barenblatt,* it was easy to think there wasn't much of a defense against a HUAC demand to testify, and that, in fact, was what the Court thought too. Yet there were differences, for until Braden and Wilkinson appeared before the committee, HUAC had always had reasonable evidence tying the recalcitrant witness to the Communist Party. Forcing the witness to confirm it, add other names, or risk perjury was the point. Wilkinson and Braden were different because the inference was unmistakable that HUAC was using its contempt powers against them because they were vocal advocates of abolishing the committee. Wilkinson was a member of the Emergency Civil Liberties Committee, which was dedicated to HUAC's abolition.

Braden was a field secretary to a civil rights organization (and had been convicted of sedition for promoting racial integration in Kentucky). He believed HUAC was being used by segregationists to attack their opponents as communists. Braden had written letters to Congress in opposition to reversing *Nelson* (because sedition statutes could too readily be used against those opposing segregation) and also requesting the House of Representatives not to let HUAC hold hearings in the South. HUAC apparently believed that the purpose of the letters was not to further integration (or to petition for redress of grievances) but rather to further the interests of the Communist Party by fomenting racial strife and interfering with a HUAC investigation. HUAC thus subpoenaed Braden to appear at its Atlanta hearings, where he was asked whether he had been a member of the Party "the instant" he signed the letters to Congress.

Wilkinson had journeyed to Atlanta to protest holding the hearings there. He was not subpoenaed until he checked into an Atlanta hotel. He too refused to answer whether he was a Party member.

Stewart's opinion found the First Amendment claims of Braden and Wilkinson "indistinguishable" from those in *Barenblatt*. Thus, the Government's interest remained self-preservation and the individual's interest was, at best, the right not to answer whether he was a communist. The dissenters, through Black, reminded the Court that "the noble-sounding slogan of 'self-preservation' rests upon a premise that can itself destroy any democratic nation by a slow process of eating away at the liberties that are indispensable to its healthy growth." Black saw the Court's decision as a "dangerous trend" that needed correction lest it prove impossible to stop.

Bar Admissions

Braden and *Wilkinson* were decided in February; the trend continued in April when the Court revisited the issue of bar admission, for the 1957 *Konigsberg* case was back again. Previously Black had treated *Konigsberg* as if it were similar to its companion case of *Schware v. Board of Bar Examiners;* that is, he concluded that California had denied Konigsberg admission solely because it found that any past membership in the Party was disqualifying. On remand, Konigsberg presented evidence of his good moral character but persisted in his refusal to answer the membership question. The California Supreme Court reaffirmed Konigsberg's exclusion from the bar on the ground that his refusal to answer the communist question cut short a relevant inquiry. Had he said that he had been a member in the past, then he could have been questioned about when he quit the Party and what he had done while a member of the Party. Refusal to answer obstructed the inquiry, and thus the bar had no choice but to refuse his application.

In affirming California, Harlan again applied the balancing test, and the analysis was as short and sweet as it had been in *Barenblatt*. The state had a legitimate interest "in having lawyers who are devoted to the law in its broadest sense, including not only its substantive provisions, but also its procedures for orderly change." This interest was "clearly sufficient to outweigh the minimal effect upon free association occasioned by compulsory disclosure."

A companion case to *Konigsberg, In re Anastaplo,* offered a situation somewhat removed from Konigsberg's. The Illinois bar asked George Anastaplo about membership only after he had written a short required essay on the "principles underlying the Constitution." After mentioning separation of powers and protecting liberties, Anastaplo wrote, "And, of course, whenever the particular government in power becomes destructive of these ends, it is the right of the people to alter or abolish it and thereupon to establish a new government." Anastaplo's statement was taken substantially from the Declaration of Independence. When the Committee on Character and Fitness read the statement, it held a hearing and asked Anastaplo whether he was a member of the Party or any organization on the Attorney General's List. All agreed that there was no evidence whatsoever, except his invocation, without citation, of the Declaration of Independence, that indicated he might have subversive tendencies.

Harlan treated *Anastaplo* as if it were *Konigsberg* (just as Black had treated *Konigsberg* as if it were *Schware* four years earlier). The state had the right to demand of any prospective lawyer an answer to whether he had been a communist. His interest in not answering was always outweighed by the state's interest. Nor was there any particular injustice on the facts because all he need do is cease obstructing the Committee. "In short, petitioner holds the key to admission in his own hands."

Black's dissent in *Anastaplo* for all the liberals, aided by the can't-miss facts that the bar seemed to think Thomas Jefferson was a little too subversive for America, was the best of his career. "The effect of the Court's 'balancing' here is that any State may now reject an applicant for admission to the Bar if he believes in the Declaration of Independence as strongly as Anastaplo and if he is willing to sacrifice his career and his means of livelihood in defense of the freedoms of the First Amendment."

Brennan also separately dissented, drawing on his *Speiser* opinion to shift the burden of proof onto the state because of the difficulties in establishing innocence in such a sensitive area and the risk that even innocent, innocuous words might be mistaken for advocacy. Thus, he claimed that neither Konigsberg nor Anastaplo could be forced to answer a question about political beliefs and associations until the state had made out a prima facie case that the applicant lacked good moral character.

The Smith and Subversive Activities Control Acts

The 1960 Term continued with the two Smith Act convictions, *Scales v. United States* and *Noto v. United States*, and, eleven years after Congress passed what it deemed its key anticommunist legislation, the Subversive Activities Control Act (SACA), the Court finally rendered a decision affirming the order by the Subversive Activities Control Board (SACB) to the Party to register as a "Communist-action" group. A "Communist-action" group is distinguished from a "Communist-front" group in that the latter conceals its true character "to obtain support from persons who would not extend their support if they knew the nature of the organization" while the former does not. A Communist-action organization was required, after an order to register, to disclose the names of all its officers and members while a front group need disclose the names only of its officers. In addition, thereafter the SACA stigmatized the Communist-action organization by requiring it to disclose on all publications that it was a communist organization. The SACA also had an extended set of disabilities, ranging from denial of passports to denial of government employment to denial of employment in the private sphere in either defense or labor. The act also recognized that the compulsory registration requirement raised serious self-incrimination problems. It sought to get around them in §4(f) by providing that membership per se in the Party was not a violation of the SACA "or of any other criminal statute."

The registration order was sustained in a 115-page opinion by Frankfurter over 87 pages of dissents with each of the liberals writing separately. Frankfurter's opinion, in Harry Kalven's conclusion, "embodies both the best and the most debatable features of his judicial work."[16] It separately analyzes, with care, each individual feature of the act, decides the constitutional questions he deems present, and avoids the ones he deems avoidable. Frankfurter sustained the Government's approach against the Party's First Amendment challenges while not dealing with its Fifth Amendment contentions. The First Amendment issues were whether the disabilities the statute imposed were justified by the fact that there was substantial evidence indicating that unlike normal political parties, the Communist Party was subject to foreign domination, and further whether a statutory scheme like the SACA constituted a form of unconstitutional "outlawry." Making clear once again that registering communists was different from registering socialists or Republicans, Frankfurter found the Party's claim that Congress cannot require disclosure of a foreign-dominated group operating primarily to advance the objective of overthrow of the government "a travesty of that Amendment and the great ends for the well-being of our democracy that it serves."

Frankfurter refused to reach the self-incrimination claims because he found them conjectural. He concluded that the Party, a foreign-dominated criminal conspiracy, might decide to comply voluntarily with the law; furthermore, its members might decide never to travel abroad or to seek employment from the government, defense contractors, or labor unions. At best, the conclusions blink reality. They suggest that the communists, dedicated to overthrowing the government, will, upon learning that overthrow is illegal, cease and desist and indeed quit their jobs. The only way this conclusion could be brought anywhere near reality would be if there were no true communists left in the Party—the only remaining members being FBI agents. Nevertheless, it was necessary to avoid striking down the penalty provisions of the SACA—unless the Court would downsize substantially the scope of the Fifth Amendment too.

The four dissents show an interesting divide among the liberals. Warren wrote an opinion arguing there are technical errors that justify a remand to the SACB. Brennan limited himself to the Fifth Amendment. Douglas and Black voted differently on the First Amendment for the first time since 1947. Douglas found the registration requirement consistent with the First Amendment although unconstitutional under the Fifth Amendment for its failure to grant immunity. Black rested entirely on his First Amendment absolutism.

Douglas focused on the overwhelming evidence of foreign domination, which he concluded took the case out of the First Amendment because the activity was not speech but instead "speech-plus." First he noted that disclosure may cause a serious loss of First Amendment rights for unpopular groups. "In logic then it might seem that the Communist Party being at the low tide of popularity, might make out a better case of harassment than almost any other group on the contemporary scene." Then came the "however." The SACB's "findings establish that more than debate, discourse, argumentation, propaganda, and other aspects of free speech and association are involved. An additional element enters, viz., espionage, business activities, or the formation of cells for subversion, as well as the use of speech, press, and association by a foreign power to produce on this continent a Soviet satellite."

In his Dennis dissent, Douglas had stated that "the freedom of speech is not absolute." He had noted the overtones of sedition in the Government's Dennis argument and acknowledged that that would make a different case if it were true. "But the fact is that no such evidence was introduced at trial." The record in Communist Party v. SACB showed, however, that the Communist Party was not just "another" political party. Douglas, applying his "speech brigaded with action" test, found the registration requirement consistent with the First Amendment.

Black stuck to his absolutism. He was willing to protect even the Party leaders and wrote a powerful opinion that the SACA was unconstitutional, as he expressed concern about the precedent of a free country for the "first time banning an association because it advocates hated ideas."

Scales and *Noto* were handed down the same day as *Communist Party v. SACB*. They involved a different Smith Act provision from the one used in *Dennis* and *Yates*. Scales and Noto were convicted under a provision making it a crime to have "knowing membership" in any organization that advocates the overthrow of the government. A natural attack on the provision was that it was guilt by association. Harlan rejected the claim that the provision was therefore invalid, concluding *Dennis* had already held that the requisite advocacy, "albeit under the aegis of what purports to be a political Party, is not such association as is protected by the First Amendment. We can discern no reason why membership when it constitutes a purposeful form of complicity in a group engaged in this same forbidden advocacy, should receive any greater degree of protection from the guarantees of that Amendment."

Still, Harlan construed the provision to exempt innocent membership, which "lacks the requisite specific intent" to overthrow. "Such a person may be foolish, deluded, or perhaps merely optimistic, but he is not by this statute made a criminal." It is dubious that Congress would have agreed; nevertheless, as *Yates* had construed congressional intent to preclude conviction for mere advocacy, so *Scales* construed it to preclude conviction for mere membership. A Communist Party member had to know of and support the Party's illegal aims. Both Scales and Noto, as second-tier leaders like Yates, met that test.

To prevent an end run around *Yates*'s stringent requirement of incitement, Harlan construed the requirement that the Party illegally advocate overthrow to meet the *Yates* standard of advocacy of violence as a rule of action rather than, as the Government hoped, theoretical advocacy of Marxist-Leninism. Harlan then turned to the evidence of the Party's— and not Scales's or Noto's—supposed illegal advocacy. In a conclusion that (for different reasons) outraged Clark and angered Black, Harlan found that the evidence of illegal advocacy by the Party was sufficient in *Scales* but not in *Noto*. Clark couldn't believe it; this was the same Communist Party, after all. Once the Court finds what everyone knows—it is an illegal conspiracy—then its knowing members, like Noto, can be convicted. Black, for his part, complained that the distinction between *Scales* and *Noto* turned on having a staff of informers ready to provide up-to-date information. Neither Black nor Clark (nor Warren,

Douglas, and Brennan) saw that the evidence on which Noto was ordered acquitted, Scales was convicted, and nine *Yates* defendants were remanded for a new trial (which never occurred) was remarkably similar, given the differing dispositions of the cases.

The major dissent was Brennan's. Drawing on §4(f) of the SACA, which stated that neither "the holding of office nor membership in a Communist organization shall constitute a per se violation" of the SACA or "any other criminal statute," Brennan claimed that the SACA superseded the Smith Act's membership provisions. He may well have had the better of the debate with Harlan on this point. If the membership clause of the Smith Act remained in force, then the compulsory disclosure required under the SACA registration requirement would necessarily compel disclosure of a crime. Therefore, it would run afoul of the Fifth Amendment's privilege against self-incrimination unless the Court decided to create new doctrine, resembling the First Amendment, whereby a claim of privilege would be tested by the Government's need for the information.

Employment Discharges

Finally, on the last day of the 1960 Term, the Court for the first time wrote on the constitutional merits of a summary discharge case. Rachel Brawner was a short-order cook at the Naval Gun Factory and needed a security badge to enter the premises. One day the security officer of the installation withdrew her badge. Thereafter, she was refused admission and lost her job. The commanding officer refused to meet with her and her union on the ground that it would "serve no useful purpose." This was the first time the Court faced a summary dismissal where the relevant statute and regulations authorized what occurred. Stewart's majority stated that Brawner could not have been similarly treated because she was a "Democrat or a Methodist." But a security risk was different. There was no constitutional infirmity in summary action because there was no stigma attached (so the Court concluded), and she could find alternative employment elsewhere. In a short, somewhat lifeless, dissent for the liberals, Brennan stated that the Government's actions were arbitrary. Brawner had a sufficient "property" interest in her job to require the Government to give a reason (and not just a conclusion) for its termination. The lack of enthusiasm in the dissent may have stemmed from the fact that the majority's decision was of quite uncertain reach, given the fact that the installation in question was under military supervision and therefore the case might have no application elsewhere.

Four years earlier, after Red Monday, the domestic-security program seemingly was in shambles, thus matching the status of the American Communist Party itself. But the 1957 decisions had largely been on non-constitutional grounds. When the issues reappeared in 1961, the solid five-man majority was willing to reach the constitutional merits and hand down decisions that reached the opposite results from the earlier cases. Thus, with the limited exception of the Smith Act, the program was almost fully restored. A decade after the important 1951 decisions, the Court had once again validated the domestic-security program as consistent with the Constitution.

The Court did not fully turn the clock back to 1951. *Yates, Scales,* and *Noto* were not *Dennis,* and there were some recognized limits. Thus, in December 1961 in *Cramp v. Board of Public Instruction,* a unanimous Court held unconstitutionally vague a Florida loyalty oath that required teachers to swear they had never lent "aid, support, advice, counsel, or influence" to the Communist Party. Would claiming communists had constitutional rights be "support," Stewart asked? Stewart's opinion recognized, as no majority a decade earlier would have, "that there are some among us always ready to affix a Communist label upon those whose ideas they violently oppose."

In his *Anastaplo* dissent, Black charged the balancers with being absolutists; he was correct. When the issue was disclosure of a person's behavior, there was no point during the era that the balancers ever found the individual to have any chance. When they relied upon national self-preservation as the ultimate value, they announced that they were absolutists because they held, as they had to, that this interest always trumps. This conclusion eventually led the balancers to support application of the anticommunist tactics to the civil rights movement, indeed to the NAACP.

What seems inconceivable in retrospect is the extent that the Court's majority held to the religion to which Frankfurter was reborn again in 1958, acting as if domestic communism were too hot an issue to touch. These cases are about as good an example of the dead hand of the past ruling the Court as one gets. The Soviet Union remained a threat to the United States; but, with the huge exception of J. Edgar Hoover, few national leaders claimed domestic communism was (with its membership at 5 percent of its 1947 peak). The *New York Times* was correct when it editorialized that authorizing the SACB to go to work could "only serve again to divert public attention to the virtually nonexistent internal communist threat. The real communist challenge is from abroad; and the sooner Americans get over the idea that we can solve the problem by persecuting the tattered remnants of American communism at home, the better able we will all be to face the really hard decisions and hard problems posed by the genuine menace of communism" abroad.[17]

Yet concluding that Frankfurter and his four cohorts overreacted to a fear that a new outbreak of McCarthyism could sweep them away may be unfair. A far better politician, Lyndon Johnson, entertained similar fears of a renewed McCarthyism should the United States suffer defeat in Vietnam.[18] Those who had watched the rise of McCarthyism after the "fall" of China would naturally be apprehensive.

In as much as Black and Douglas had been willing to stand against the real McCarthyism, it is no wonder that they were ready to stand against its revival. Furthermore, this time around, they had partners in Warren and Brennan. They knew that 1958 was not 1949 and that race, no less than a potential new McCarthyism, was a motivating factor in the anti-Court politics. The South, quite naturally, tried to tie the two.

A major public relations tenet of the southern defense against civil rights, which southerners may have myopically believed, was that southern Negroes were happy in their condition and that those pushing change were "outside agitators" and communists. Such claims operated to disarm some northern criticism of the South and to maintain hegemony at home.

In December 1961 in *Gibson v. Florida Legislative Investigating Committee,* the effort of Florida to acquire information from the NAACP membership list was argued before the Court. At the Conference the same 5–4 voting pattern that came into existence in 1958 prevailed. The NAACP was going to have to provide Florida with the names of some of its members so that Florida could determine if the NAACP had been infiltrated by communists. It was every segregationist's dream, going back at least to Strom Thurmond's Dixiecrat run for the presidency in 1948 when he charged civil rights agitation had "its origin in Communist ideology and was designed to create the chaos and confusion which leads to communism."[19] The Court was offering the South the chance to take out the NAACP by painting the organization red. If the price of self-preservation against domestic communists in 1962 was turning the NAACP over to southern legislators or Citizen's Councils, then the price was high indeed. It was never paid, however, because five months later, Whittaker followed his doctor's advice into retirement, and *Gibson,* now evenly divided, was put over for reargument the following term.

Chapter 7

Little Rock and Civil Rights

The flip side of Eisenhower's ability to obfuscate was his ability to answer questions directly whenever he wished. Thus, Warren chaffed at Eisenhower's refusal to place either moral or political authority behind *Brown v. Board of Education.* On July 17, 1957, Eisenhower was asked a civil rights question that he answered without ambiguity. Federal force was not going to back up desegregation orders. "Now I want to say this: I can't imagine any set of circumstances that would ever induce me to send Federal troops into a Federal court and into any area to enforce the orders of a Federal court, because I believe that the common sense of America will never require it."[1] Maintaining law and order was a state, not a federal, function.

Little Rock

A little over two months later, in what was "the most repugnant of all his acts" as president, Eisenhower ordered 1,100 troops from the 101st Airborne into Little Rock to enforce a court-ordered desegregation plan.[2] That plan came from the school board and federal court feeling out the meaning of *Brown II.* The board responded to a NAACP desegregation suit with an offer of a minimalist plan where for the 1957–1958 school year nine African-Americans would be admitted to the 2,000-student, all-white Central High School. The NAACP challenged the plan as far too little but, like the Nashville plan, the courts approved it, down to its 1963 date for full desegregation of the system. The plan that was too little for the NAACP was far too much for others, and that is why Eisenhower had to commit troops.

Little Rock was a strange place for a showdown: Arkansas was not part of the Deep South; Little Rock was a moderate community; and

157

other Arkansas communities, including Fort Smith, had already commenced the desegregation process. Governor Orval Faubus was not a race-baiter, and his 1956 reelection had been seen as a liberal (or at least an anticorporate populist) victory. But Faubus took to television the day before the school year commenced to announce he had ordered the National Guard to come to Central to protect the African-American students who were about to enter and desegregate it. In fact, the Guard's job was to prevent them from entering the school.

Opening day, September 3, the African-Americans accepted the advice of the school board and stayed home. The next day, when they came to school, they were met by a crowd of taunting whites, and the Guard prevented them from entering the school. While the school board went to federal court to seek an injunction against the governor, Faubus talked with Eisenhower by phone and even flew to Newport to meet with him. The nine African-Americans stayed at home awaiting an outcome. On Friday, September 20, the federal judge ordered the Guard removed, and Faubus complied.

On Monday the nine African-Americans came to Central again. So did "a mob of belligerent, shrieking and hysterical" whites.[3] The African-Americans entered via a delivery entrance. "'Oh God,' said a woman, 'the niggers are in school.'"[4] The crowd got angry. There was shouting, murmurs about rushing the school, and attacks upon both local African-Americans who were on the street and "Yankee" reporters and photographers. At noon the students were ordered withdrawn from Central, and thereafter the mob dispersed. The mayor asked for federal troops.

Daisy Bates, the head of the Arkansas NAACP, stated that the African-Americans "will not be out there again until they have the assurance of the President of the United States that they will be protected from the mob."[5] The next day they stayed home, but the mob didn't. Eisenhower, on the advice and urging of Attorney General Herbert Brownell, ordered the 101st to Little Rock and federalized the National Guard. It was the first time since Reconstruction that federal troops had been sent South to protect African-Americans. Senator Richard Russell offered the exaggerated southern response by comparing the 101st to "Hitler's storm troopers."[6] Senator Herman Talmadge was more restrained. "We still mourn the destruction of the sovereignty of Hungary by Russian tanks and troops in the streets of Budapest. We are now threatened with the spectacle of the President of the United States using tanks and troops in the streets of Little Rock to destroy the sovereignty of the state of Arkansas."[7]

The courageous African-Americans, who could not have known what would happen, reentered Central on Wednesday. Eight of the nine lasted the entire year in a situation where white toughs enforced a strict code of no contact. The eight were protected by the federalized Guard, who continued to guard the school and patrol its halls after the 101st was withdrawn at the end of November. Minnie Jean Brown, an eleventh-grader, was the ninth. One student called her a "nigger bitch." She responded with "white trash" and was expelled.[8] White students then distributed cards reading "One Nigger Down, Eight to Go."[9]

Cooper v. Aaron

In February the school board asked the district judge to end the experiment of desegregation until the 1960–1961 school year. The school board argued that Faubus had inflamed the city and convinced many people to believe Arkansas had a way to overcome federal law. Thus, the board felt that violence was probable without troops and that education with troops was not worth it. The court agreed, citing "chaos, bedlam and turmoil" in and around Central High School. The court of appeals reversed. In a highly unusual step, the Court agreed to come back for a summer session in Washington to hear arguments and presumably decide the controversy before the school year commenced.

Marshall had an easy time at oral argument for the NAACP. The Court hounded his opposition but left him alone. In a voice of sorrow but moral authority he told the Court, "I am not worried about Negro children at this stage. I don't believe they're in this case as such. I worry about the white children in Little Rock who are told, as young people, that the way to get your rights is to violate the law and defy lawful authorities. I'm worried about their future. I don't worry about those Negro kids' future. They've been struggling with democracy long enough. They know about it."[10]

The school board was in the unhappy position of arguing that it acted in good faith, but that Faubus and others had created a mob situation where there was nothing to do but retreat until passions calmed. Not surprisingly, the justices understood the school board argument to mean that if state officials could incite opposition to federal law and if they were successful in creating a climate of violence, then the federal court order must yield to the mob. Even Eisenhower rejected that theory, and so did the Court. To do otherwise would be to offer southern segregationists a way to permanently avoid *Brown*—just be lawless enough.

"[C]onstitutional rights of children not to be discriminated against in school admission on grounds of race or color declared by this Court in the *Brown* case can neither be nullified openly and directly by state legislators or state executives or judicial officers, nor nullified indirectly by them through evasive schemes for segregation whether attempted 'ingeniously or ingenuously.'"

Cooper v. Aaron was a very important case. Yet the Court could reach only one conclusion unless it was prepared to run up a white flag in disgrace. The importance of the case had less to do with its expected result than with the lecture the Court's opinion gave Faubus and other southern officials. Over a century and a half earlier, in *Marbury v. Madison*, the Court had successfully claimed the right to interpret the Constitution and invalidate government action in a case properly presented for adjudication. *Cooper* was different, for it claimed not only the right to interpret the Constitution but also the right to be final, that is, to bind not only the parties but everyone else. The Constitution, the Court asserted, meant exactly what the Court said it meant. Therefore, because of the oath of office taken by every government official "to support the Constitution," all officeholders, from president to governor, to legislators, to judges, were controlled by the Supreme Court's interpretation and duty-bound to obey it. The *New York Times* approvingly noted the Court's "clear language, understandable even to the most fanatic segregationist."[11]

The Aftermath

Faubus knew how to send messages too. He immediately ordered the Little Rock schools closed, and they were. Then, in the November elections, he was overwhelmingly reelected, while Little Rock Congressman Brooks Hays, a signer of the Southern Manifesto who nevertheless worked for calm during the crisis, was defeated by a write-in campaign for a militant segregationist. In a December Gallup Poll, Americans placed Faubus among Winston Churchill, Albert Schweitzer, Jonas Salk, and Eisenhower as one of the ten most admired men in the world.[12]

A year later, when things were calmer, the desegregation process started slowly again. The idea of depriving whites of their education lest there be African-Americans in the schools had limited utility, especially since it was not easy to set up a successful and complete "private" school system. Furthermore, having no public schools was a perfect proxy for backwardness; it guaranteed that no new business would locate in that community (as both Arkansas and Virginia learned). Thus, while districts in Virginia closed their schools during massive resistance, only Prince Edward County, one of the original *Brown* cases, abandoned its public schools completely. Influential business interests successfully raised the question of whether white supremacy in the form of massive resistance really was worth abandoning public education, and the answer was no. If there were alternative legal ways of avoiding desegregation, that would be okay.

In the Little Rock of 1959, instead of nine African-Americans attending Central High School, three African-Americans were assigned to each of the two white high schools. Elizabeth Ann Eckford, one of the original nine, once more entered Central. The demonstrators were there too, but this time police maintained order. Elsewhere, this might have been seen as progress, for in fact desegregation had come to a halt across the South, having never been started in the Deep South.

This was not what the Court expected. Like all other race cases, *Cooper* was slated to be an unsigned per curiam, but upon the justices' realization of its importance, that changed. The justices wanted to send a signal to the South, and they decided the best way to proceed was to make an unprecedented move. Instead of issuing the opinion as they always did by its author, they decided to issue it in each of their names. This was deemed an effective way of showing that the three post-*Brown* additions, Harlan, Brennan, and Whittaker, no less than the others, agreed fully with the principles of *Brown*. The message intended was something to the effect of "even stronger than unanimity." Maybe that would finally show the South that the Court was serious.

Frankfurter, as always, believed the key to the South was the southern moderate. Although he had been instrumental in coming up with the idea of the jointly signed opinion, he decided to write separately as well, and the opinion began by stating that he "unreservedly participated" in the joint opinion. Thereafter, he said virtually the same thing as the Court's opinion although he did so slightly better. Frankfurter explained his reasoning in a contemporaneous letter to a longtime correspondent. Unlike the opinion of the Court, his was addressed to lawyers and law professors in the South, "an audience which I was in a particularly qualified position to address in view of my rather extensive association, by virtue of my twenty-five years at the Harvard Law School, with a good many Southern lawyers and law professors."[13] Apparently, Frankfurter thought that school ties meant that Harvard graduates were moderates and that they needed to hear from him to know of their responsibilities. His appeal to southern moderates was just as effective as *Brown*'s appeal had been.

In the four years since *Brown*, the southern moderates had become either extinct or invisible, moving, as Faubus had, to a much more hard-line position on race or being retired. Brooks Hays and other southerners knew why; it was *impossible* to lose votes by being too rabid a segregationist. Old-line southern race-baiters, like Eugene "Bull" Connor in Birmingham, whose time had passed in the late 1940s and early 1950s, enjoyed a comeback as did a newer breed of virulent racists. Alabama's youthful George Wallace was defeated in the 1958 gubernatorial race by a blatant racist and vowed that he was "not goin' to be out-niggahed again."[14]

Black, Warren, and Brennan (who had in fact drafted the *Cooper* opinion) were furious at Frankfurter, succeeding only in convincing him to delay his opinion until after the Court's opinion had come down. Warren thought Frankfurter's action detracted from the Court's opinion, and the breach, already wide, between the two justices became insurmountable after Frankfurter's opinion came down. They too missed the fact that there were no moderates publicly left to appeal to. Contrary to its intent, *Brown* had created a political tidal wave that had washed away those who might support the decision.

The refusal of business to accept school closures as official policy set a limit on how far the South could go in fighting *Brown*. In Virginia it caused the official policy of massive resistance to end. Schools would remain open. Two different methods were used to keep the schools segregated. One was the pupil-placement laws. The other was the frontal attack on the NAACP with the goal of putting it out of business.

Pupil Placement

While the Court was focusing on *Cooper*, a challenge to Alabama's pupil-placement law appeared on the docket. The Alabama statute was typical of such laws. Every child in every system was to be individually assigned to the school appropriate for the child. Until those assignments were made, students would continue at the school they would have attended before the law was passed, that is, a legally segregated school. Lest anyone still have missed the point, the Alabama pupil-placement law was tied in with other contemporaneous acts declaring *Brown* null and void.

Shuttlesworth v. Birmingham began in 1957 when the Reverend Fred Shuttlesworth, Birmingham's civil rights leader, tried to move his children from their segregated school to the school closest to their home, which just happened to be all-white. Although the children took the placement test, school officials would not process it within the statutorily required thirty days. After sixty days, Shuttlesworth filed suit. He then received a letter from the state superintendent of education, informing him that African-Americans were doing just fine in Alabama and that the lawsuit threatened public education in the state should the law be struck down. Shuttlesworth was not deterred; his argument was obvious. The law was a response to *Brown* and part of massive resistance to preclude any desegregation.

Shuttlesworth's problem is less obvious today but was decisive then. Essentially it was the problem of allowing a court to know what everyone else knew. In the 1950s and 1960s, as the legislative investigation cases demonstrated, the Court had not developed a doctrine of illegal motivation. That is, the Court would not hold that an action was unconstitutional simply because the government actor had an unconstitutional purpose in acting. In context, this meant that the Court had difficulty justifying a ruling in a South Carolina race case when it would be unwilling to make a similar ruling in a South Dakota race case.

The legislative investigations were "exposure for exposure's sake," but the Court's majority could not bring itself to say so because that would accuse the legislators of behaving unconstitutionally in violation of their oaths of office. That same problem reappeared in the pupil-placement situation; indeed, it would reappear in virtually all the remaining cases discussed in this chapter. To declare the law unconstitutional—before any Alabama official had done anything (except write a threatening letter as the superintendent had)—required a court to say that the law was passed for an unconstitutional purpose and would be administered in the same way.

The federal judges who passed on the Alabama law were not segregationists. But because of the problems just stated, they sustained the law. "We cannot say, in advance of its application, that the Alabama Law will not be properly and constitutionally administered." After all, executive officials and school board members had taken an oath to support the Constitution, and "no court, without evidence, can possibly presume that they would violate their oath." Thus, the state prevailed, and plaintiffs were told to come back later if they could show the law was being unconstitutionally applied.

Shuttlesworth appealed, but with *Cooper* and its declaration that *everyone* was bound by *Brown*, the justices were finished. Only Warren and Douglas wanted to hear (and reverse) the case. The others, however, didn't order briefs and argument in *Shuttlesworth*. Instead, the Court issued a one-sentence per curiam affirming the court below on exactly the grounds relied on by that court. The pupil-placement law was constitutional on its face. When *Shuttleworth* was filed, there was not a single African-American child attending school with a white in Alabama. In 1963, five years after the Court's summary affirmance, there was not a single African-American child attending school with a white in Alabama. But then again there were virtually no African-Americans attending school with whites anywhere in the South. In the 1961–1962 school year only .24 percent of African-Americans in the South were attending a school with whites. Once Tennessee and Texas are factored out, the number falls to an infinitesimal .07 percent.

The decision in *Shuttlesworth* was, like that of *Brown II,* a statement that constitutional rights of African-Americans could be delayed as necessary. Privately, the justices were unhappy about the result, but they felt they had no alternative except allowing Alabama officials to implement the law even though it was not going to achieve the effectuation of *Brown* either in the present or "with all deliberate speed." With *Shuttlesworth,* the Court was out of business in the school area.

The justices might have hoped the North Carolina experience would prevail. The opinion of the federal court in *Shuttlesworth* stated that the North Carolina pupil-placement law was being constitutionally applied and has a footnote reciting a colloquy between Judge Richard Rives, one of the southern judges who truly believed in *Brown*, and counsel about how well North Carolina was doing. North Carolina was deemed a "good" southern state, in sharp contrast to Virginia and the Deep South. North Carolina did not adopt, as those states had, a program of massive resistance. North Carolina's pupil-placement law, like Alabama's, did not mention race and had been sustained, while Virginia's and South Carolina's had mentioned race and had been struck down by lower courts. Prior to *Shuttlesworth,* the Court had denied review in all three situations.

In 1958 North Carolina offered a temporary mirage. In 1964 Virginia, which had implemented massive resistance right down to the closing of schools, had three times as many African-Americans attending schools with whites as North Carolina did. Neither had many. Virginia's percentage was but 1.63; North Carolina's was .537. The difference between pupil-placement laws and massive resistance was purely cosmetic.

The Attack on the NAACP

Since school boards never voluntarily commenced desegregation, it always took a court order. This meant there had to be a lawsuit, which necessarily entailed both a lawyer and a plaintiff. Marshall's NAACP Legal Defense Fund, as the legal arm of the civil rights movement, provided both. Even if there were plaintiffs galore willing to brave economic and physical threats, the NAACP had limited resources. It could not file lawsuits everywhere and therefore it concentrated on urban areas.

Knowing the importance of the NAACP, the South moved on it with a vigor that exceeded the domestic-security program against communists. The parallel was apt. The NAACP was a domestic threat to the South, and the South adopted a program similar to those used by Congress against communists to hamstring the NAACP. The key was a demand to make NAACP membership lists public. If that occurred, Citizen's Councils would take care of the rest; the NAACP would be out of business because its members would be out of employment, credit, and maybe even life. Although the South was ultimately legally unsuccessful, the tactics bought a decade of segregation.

In contrast to Mississippi, which relied upon terror, including assassination, no state used "law" to disable the NAACP better than Alabama. Beginning in 1956, Alabama put the NAACP completely out of business until the summer of 1964. The Alabama Supreme Court was in the forefront of the effort, and its interest was never law; it was to see that the NAACP lost. Like the rest of the Deep South, the Alabama Supreme Court was at war to protect white supremacy from all foes.

On June 1, 1956, the Alabama attorney general, John Patterson, went into state court claiming the NAACP was violating state law by doing business without registering. The judge had no interest in hearing from the NAACP on the issue, and so he enjoined it without waiting for a response, announcing "I intend to deal the NAACP a mortal blow from which they shall never recover."[15]

In fact, the NAACP was willing to register if that is what state law required, but the judge wouldn't allow it. Instead, he ordered the NAACP to produce its records, including its membership list. That the NAACP could not do without subjecting its members to the mercies of

Citizen's Councils. When it refused, the judge hit the organization with a $10,000 fine, increased to $100,000 after five days, and naturally he continued the injunction.

The NAACP then filed a motion with the Alabama Supreme Court to suspend the injunction so that it could register. The court responded that the NAACP must follow the "established rule" and file for a writ of certiorari. A week later the NAACP did. The court then said the allegations in the NAACP filing were insufficient. So the NAACP refiled with more detailed allegations. Then, taking a page from Kafka, the court announced that the way to challenge the injunction was by mandamus, not by certiorari, and it was too late to file for that. Thus, the NAACP was still enjoined from operating, even though it had never had a hearing to determine whether it had done anything illegal.

The NAACP now went to the United States Supreme Court. Its legal position was somewhat tenuous. The Court cannot review state cases when an "adequate and independent" state-law ground supports the decision. Patterson claimed that the NAACP did not comply with Alabama procedures and therefore the decision could not be reviewed. The NAACP also had problems on the merits. The whole point of the legislative investigation cases was that membership in organizations was relevant information. Furthermore, a 1928 decision held that a state could require the Ku Klux Klan to turn over its membership list.

The Court had no trouble recognizing the blatant lawlessness of the Alabama Supreme Court, and for the first time it also recognized that disclosure of membership was not as benign as the communist cases suggested. *NAACP v. Alabama* came down in June 1958 with Harlan stating, for the first time, that it was "beyond debate that the freedom to engage in association for the advancement of beliefs and ideas is an inseparable aspect of the 'liberty' assured by the Due Process Clause." While Alabama had taken no direct action to restrict rights of association, even "unintended" abridgments require close scrutiny. Thus, it is "a hardly novel perception that compelled disclosure may constitute an effective restraint on freedom of association." At times, "inviolability of private association" is "indispensable." Given the constitutional rights, the state could prevail only if it has "a subordinating interest which is compelling." Alabama did not have one, and that distinguished the 1928 KKK case (and presumably the communist cases) where the state was concerned with lawlessness.

The Alabama Supreme Court did not take the reversal well. It simply reaffirmed its decision. The Court again reversed. Next the Alabama court refused either to lift the injunction or to send the case back to the trial judge to give the NAACP a hearing. Another trip to the Court, this time through the federal courts, was necessary to prod the Alabama Supreme Court to let the case go to trial.

Naturally, at trial, the NAACP lost. It appealed again. For over a year the Alabama Supreme Court refused to hear the case, and, when it finally did, it created a new fictitious procedural rule that it declared the NAACP had not satisfied. Accordingly, the trial court's judgment was affirmed without reaching the NAACP's constitutional claims. For the fourth time, an exasperated NAACP went to a now angry Court, and for the fourth time it won. After writing the book on lawless judicial cynicism, the Alabama Supreme Court finally yielded in June 1964.

Arkansas too tried to force the NAACP to make public its membership list. One vehicle was the so-called "Bennett Ordinance," named after Arkansas Attorney General Bruce Bennett, who tried to prevent Faubus from grabbing all the political pay-dirt of attacking the NAACP. A "Bennett Ordinance" was a municipal requirement that all organizations operating in a city provide a list of members and contributors. The ostensible purpose of the ordinance was to facilitate the city's determination of whether the organization was entitled to an exemption from a business licensing tax. The NAACP immediately lost members, and Daisy Bates and Birdie Williams were convicted for refusing to turn over the lists to Little Rock and North Little Rock, respectively.

Bates v. Little Rock, decided in the spring of 1960, reversed the convictions. Stewart's opinion drew heavily on *NAACP v. Alabama.* Freedom of association "for the purpose of advancing ideas and airing grievances" is "protected not only against heavy-handed frontal attack, but also from being stifled by more subtle governmental interference." Stewart used the "compelling state interest" test first articulated by Frankfurter in his *Sweezy v. New Hampshire* concurrence and then brought into majority doctrine by Harlan in *NAACP v. Alabama.* The Bennett Ordinance lacked anything close to a compelling interest since disclosure of the members' identities has little, if anything, to do with whether the organization must pay a licensing tax. At most, the cities needed to know the purposes and activities of an organization to make the necessary tax determination; therefore, under the test, disclosure of membership lists could not be required.

In 1956 South Carolina passed a law banning NAACP members from government employment. As a challenge to the law headed for the Court, South Carolina repealed the law and replaced it with a law copied from

Mississippi requiring all teachers to declare the organizations to which they belonged. During the Little Rock crisis, Arkansas went whole hog and adopted both laws. Furthermore, since Arkansas teachers did not have tenure, any teacher who belonged to the NAACP was finished teaching under the laws. Failure to file the requisite disclosure operated to terminate employment, while filing and admitting NAACP membership would, because of the other statute, have the same effect. Filing an erroneous affidavit, of course, was perjury.

Evidence at the inevitable trial showed that one plaintiff, who had taught for twenty-five years, was not a member of the Communist Party but was a member of the NAACP. That would have resulted in his being barred from employment, but the federal judge struck that particular statute down while simultaneously upholding the disclosure provisions because they did not mention the NAACP. *Beilan v. Board of Education* implicitly and *Barenblatt v. United States* explicitly held that membership in some organizations was a legitimate cause for state concern. What better way for a state to know if there was a potential problem than just asking?

Shelton v. Tucker brought this highly intriguing situation to the Court and split the Warren Court for the first time in an NAACP-desegregation case. Stewart, who clearly saw a difference between the Communist Party and the NAACP, joined with the four liberals to strike down the Arkansas disclosure requirement. While acknowledging the state's legitimate interest, he concluded that Arkansas should have asked for less information because he believed those asked to disclose had very real interests at stake. Given the teachers' interests, Arkansas had been too unfocused. "Public exposure, bringing with it the possibilities of public pressures upon school boards to discharge teachers who belong to unpopular or minority organizations, would simply operate to widen and aggravate the impairment of constitutional liberty." Because of the teachers' interests, the state must proceed "more narrowly" and use "less drastic means." Interestingly, Stewart did not suggest what less drastic means were available to Arkansas, and this is exactly the focus of the dissents by Frankfurter and Harlan, who were joined by Clark and Whittaker.

Harlan stated that he believed "it impossible to determine *a priori* the place where the line should be drawn between what would be permissible inquiry and overbroad inquiry in a situation like this. Certainly the Court does not point that place out." Frankfurter went farther and demonstrated why the Arkansas solution was not unreasonable.

For the dissenters, the statute was valid unless and until the state misused it. The NAACP was living by law and therefore should expect no special favors from the law. Indeed, in the Virginia lawyer regulation case to be discussed momentarily, Frankfurter told the others he couldn't "imagine a worse disservice than to continue being guardians of Negroes."[16]

One is tempted to conclude that the majority knew Arkansas would misuse the law but, lacking a way to articulate the conclusion, came up with the neutral idea that by asking too much, Arkansas created a chilling effect on associational rights, which must be remedied by asking for less. A not unreasonable conclusion was that Stewart, as the decisive justice in this area, was drawing a constitutional line between the Communist Party and the NAACP, just as the Court had attempted to maintain between communists and fellow travelers.

The NAACP Loses

If Stewart was drawing such a line for the NAACP, *Gibson v. Florida Legislative Investigating Committee* erased it two years later, just as *Braden* and *Wilkinson* had erased the similar line for fellow travelers in the previous year. In 1956 the Florida legislature began an investigation of supposed communist infiltration of the NAACP. The legislative investigation committee subpoenaed the entire membership list of the Miami branch. The Florida Supreme Court found that to be excessive but held that the committee could compel the custodian of the lists to appear and to refer to them in answering questions propounded about specific individuals. The NAACP's petition for certiorari was denied in 1959.

Theodore R. Gibson, the custodian, appeared at the hearing but refused to bring the records with him. He stated that he would be willing to answer questions from personal knowledge—and indeed, when given names or photographs of fourteen individuals who were supposedly communists, he stated he could associate none with the NAACP—but that to bring the membership lists would be to interfere with the associational rights of NAACP members. He was found in contempt, sentenced to six months in jail, and fined $1,200, and the Florida Supreme Court affirmed the conviction. As stated at the end of the previous chapter, the Court reached the same conclusion. When the line between communists and the NAACP became so blurred, Stewart shifted to vote with Frankfurter, Clark, Harlan, and Whittaker to require the information to be provided. Then Whittaker's retirement caused the case to be restored to the docket for reargument the following term.

The Court responded similarly to Virginia's attempt to regulate the

NAACP lawyers. As part of massive resistance, Virginia, South Carolina, Georgia, and Mississippi had taken the direct tack of going after the NAACP lawyers. Virginia passed two laws expanding the definitions of its already existing rules of professional ethics against solicitation of clients and lawyer-financed litigation and made clear these rules applied to the NAACP Legal Defense Fund. If valid, they would have brought the NAACP's litigating arm to a halt, for the LDF did solicit plaintiffs for desegregation cases and it did fund and control the ensuing litigation. Furthermore, with a single exception, the new rules were facially neutral and appeared to be attempts to maintain the integrity of the legal profession.

The NAACP and the LDF challenged the Virginia laws in a three-judge federal court. That court held three statutes dealing with registration unconstitutional, while agreeing to let the Virginia courts construe the reach of the other two, which regulated the practice of law. In the aftermath of *Cooper* and *Shuttlesworth,* the Court held that the federal court should have "abstained" from deciding any questions at all and instead let the Virginia courts initially construe all the statutes and establish what they meant. Given the time it would take to secure an interpretation from the Virginia courts through litigation, this holding guaranteed that the statutes would be in operation for at least two more years, although Harlan's majority opinion stated that the Court "understood" that the state would not go against the NAACP until the litigation had ended.

Douglas, Warren, and Brennan dissented, arguing that the statutes should be held unconstitutional immediately and that if the federal court had erred at all, it was in allowing the Virginia courts to have a chance to construe the two remaining statutes. "Where state laws make such an assault as these do on our decisions and a State has spoken defiantly against the constitutional rights of citizens, reasons for showing deference to local institutions vanish."

Abstention is premised on the idea that an unclear statute might be valid if it were construed one way and might be unconstitutional if construed the other. Therefore, one possible interpretation by a state court might make the constitutional issue go away, and to some extent this happened in the subsequent Virginia proceedings because the state supreme court of appeals found only one provision valid and applicable to the NAACP. Nevertheless, that was the key provision, Chapter 33, whereby the NAACP's activities in seeking out plaintiffs constituted improper solicitation of legal business because the ensuing litigation was such that the plaintiffs bore no costs and had no control over the lawyers.

By the same 5–4 vote as *Gibson,* the Court in Conference affirmed the Virginia decision and thereby offered a way for the South to use law to put the NAACP Legal Defense Fund out of business. But, as with *Gibson,* Whittaker's retirement moved the vote back to 4–4, and the justices restored the case to the calendar for reargument in the fall of 1962.

Direct Action

By 1960 the NAACP, with its emphasis on change through litigation, was being rendered irrelevant. On the one hand, southern "law" was paralyzing the organization. On the other hand, the great victory in *Brown* had little follow-up. To be sure, there were numerous lower court decisions striking down segregation ordinances, but more sophisticated laws, such as the Alabama pupil-placement law, seemed to prevail, and segregation persisted without letup in the Deep South. As a result, the leadership of the southern movement for civil rights passed from the NAACP to newer organizations with their youthful emphasis on direct action and their disdain for litigation. Lawyers worried about how courts would react. Activists didn't; they acted. If courts went along, that was fine; if they didn't, that was tough but nowhere as tough as Mississippi sheriffs.

The prototypical example of direct action was the "sit-in" where students, drawing on Martin Luther King, Jr.'s Gandhian nonviolence, sat, requested service, and then submitted to arrest. Sit-ins were effective because in many situations merchants would rather yield and make money than have disruptions or boycotts that would cost them business.

Sit-ins began on February 1, 1960, when four freshmen from the all-African-American North Carolina A&T College in Greensboro entered a Woolworth's to protest. Woolworth's was a typical department store in the South. All departments were open to everyone—except that the lunch counter was for whites only. The four went to the lunch counter at 4 P.M., took seats, and refused to move. No one served them, and an hour later the store closed early. Back on campus, the four freshmen were local heroes, and the next day twenty-four students were sitting in at Woolworth's. By the fourth day, white women from the local University of North Carolina Women's College joined in.

Within two weeks there were fifty-four sit-ins underway in nine southern states. The four Greensboro African-Americans, Ezell Blair, Jr., David Richmond, Franklin McCain, and Joseph McNeil, "prompted a volcanic response."[17] While only lawyers could direct litigation, anyone willing to risk it could sit in. Those risks fell into two categories. First, there was always the risk of violence, whether by the police, the Ku Klux Klan, or white bystanders. Some states (Mississippi and Alabama jump out) were more prone to violence than others. Indeed, the patterns of violence functionally limited sit-ins to the Upper South. Second, the legal response to a sit-in was to arrest the demonstrator for trespass, followed by an undetermined amount of jail time, for conviction always followed arrest. In 1960 alone, some 3,000 sit-in demonstrators were arrested.

The legal issues coming out of the sit-ins divided in two ways. If the relevant law required the business to refuse to serve African-Americans, then the decision to arrest flowed from state law and the case was classic racial discrimination, and the Court would reverse. If there were no applicable state law requiring the segregation, then the decision to have the demonstrators arrested was a decision of the business manager that the unwanted individuals were committing a trespass. In the latter circumstance the rights of private property were on one side of the ledger with the rights to demonstrate and be free of racial discrimination on the other. Marshall's legal background led him quickly to recognize this was a very tough balance, one where the protesters would likely lose.

The Court tried to force cases into the first mold, to find some applicable law that required the police to arrest the demonstrators. After the sit-ins commenced, but well before any case came into the appellate chain, the Court decided two cases that offered a prelude by showing how solicitous of one side the Court could be when it wanted. *Boynton v. Virginia* involved an African-American law student on a Trailways Bus trip from Washington, D.C., to Alabama who went into the whites-only restaurant for service at a stopover at the Trailways terminal in Richmond. He was convicted for refusing to leave. Black's opinion found that the Interstate Commerce Act required all facilities of interstate transportation to be free of discrimination; just as the bus could not be segregated, neither could the terminal. Clark and Whittaker dissented.

Then, in *Burton v. Wilmington Parking Authority* in the spring of 1961, the Court held that a restaurant operating under a lease in a public parking-authority in Delaware was so intertwined with the financial success of the authority that action by the lessee-restaurant was in fact action by the authority itself. The Court even mentioned the wholly irrelevant fact that an American flag flew atop the garage, as if somehow that made the lessee's actions those of the lessor. But since the authority as a public entity could not discriminate, neither could the restaurant. Clark's opinion for the Court, over a dissent by Harlan and Whittaker, was a real stretch of the "state action" doctrine, one that was used to transmute private discrimination into government discrimination. It was also an indication that the Court would continue to strike at segregation wherever it felt able to do so.

Boynton led to the "Freedom Rides" of the late spring and summer of 1961, as African-American activists decided to test whether the South— or, more important, the new Kennedy administration—would enforce the decision. Racially integrated groups would buy bus tickets and head to the Deep South, intent on using all facilities, from water fountains to restrooms, at bus terminals on the way. James Farmer, head of the Congress of Racial Equality, who organized the Freedom Rides, stated that "[o]ur intention was to provoke southern authorities into arresting us and thereby prod the Justice Department into enforcing the law of the land."[18] Farmer also rightly expected national media attention if violence ensued. He was right to expect violence; the Freedom Rides initiated the bloodiest period of the civil rights movement. Over the next four years, twenty-six civil rights workers were killed in the South.

The first Freedom Riders were savagely beaten in Rock Hill, South Carolina, and Anniston and Birmingham, Alabama. The Justice Department had to provide a plane to fly them out of Alabama to safety. Another trip followed.

The Birmingham KKK had worked out a deal with Public Safety Commissioner "Bull" Connor (who was also Alabama's Democratic National Committeeman) whereby the Klan would have fifteen minutes to attack the riders before the police would intervene. Klansmen with baseball bats, pipes, and bicycle chains attacked the civil rights activists. One rider, who was sixty-one years old, was left permanently brain-damaged. Connor explained the lack of protection to reporters by noting it was Mother's Day and no police were available. The bus went on to further beatings in Montgomery. The remaining riders, who continued to Jackson, Mississippi, were arrested and jailed there for exercising rights under federal law, but Robert Kennedy had secured a pledge from Senator James Eastland that they would not be beaten, and they weren't.

The Freedom Rides brought forth no Court decisions, but they did force a reluctant Kennedy administration to pressure the Interstate Commerce Commission to adopt regulations to force compliance with *Boynton*. The message was not lost on the activists. When the ICC adopted the relevant regulations in September, the Freedom Rides ended. King explained to the attorney general, "I am different than my father, I need to be free now."[19] Still, he knew that the Kennedys could not comprehend that, and he was right. The attorney general told Harris Wofford: "This is too much. I wonder whether they have the best interests of their country at heart."[20]

The Freedom Rides provided the northern public with the initial shocking pictures of brutality from the South, pictures that would be repeated for the next four years. The southern racists could hardly have realized that they were laying the seeds in the North of a political movement that would produce the first major civil rights statutes in a century. Indeed, the initial evidence was that the southerners did not. According to a May 1961 Gallup Poll, 64 percent of respondents who had heard of the Freedom Rides disapproved and only 24 percent approved. Yet as historian Robert Weisbrot concluded—with understatement—as a result of the Freedom Rides, sit-ins, and nonviolent demonstrations "the veneer of racial harmony in Southern cities cracked, then fell away to reveal a core of racial antagonism."[21]

Marshall, ironically like the attorney general, was wholly out of sympathy with the generational and tactical shift to direct action. Looking at it as a lawyer, he found sit-ins and therefore "jail-ins" were both impractical and expensive. He was correct about the latter but wrong on the former. The sit-in movement energized youthful activists, typically but not exclusively African-American, and gained publicity. What happened in the South could, all of a sudden, be seen and seen consistently in the North. Eventually, it became impossible to sustain the idea, so dear to southern ideology, that African-Americans liked segregation and their second-class citizenship. But eventually was not immediately. Even in 1963 when the Gallup Poll asked if any group in America was being treated unfairly, a whopping 80 percent of respondents said "no." Five percent said "the Negroes," but 4 percent said "the whites."

Eventually, civil rights leaders learned how to play the media. With the failure of protests in Albany, Georgia, in 1962, King had come to understand that there was no hope of convincing southerners of the errors of their ways. Instead, as Birmingham in the spring of 1963 would show, he had learned perfectly "how to use television to make the protests of African-Americans irresistibly appealing to a large majority of the American people who were mostly indifferent to segregation when it remained distant but disliked it when forced to face the unpleasant measures needed to maintain it."[22]

In the fall of 1961, the first sit-in case, *Garner v. Louisiana*, reached the Court's docket. *Garner* was unusual in that it did not involve a trespass conviction. Instead, it was a breach of the peace case. But, as in all sit-ins, the African-Americans never breached the peace; they just sat there. Nor was this a situation where some white onlookers became so incensed at seeing African-Americans demand service that they broke the peace. The arresting officer testified that the students did nothing except sit, although one student asked for a glass of tea. The officer stated he believed they were disturbing the peace "by sitting there." *Garner* was an easy case because under Louisiana law, as articulated by its supreme court, peaceful conduct could never be breach of the peace. On its admitted facts, there was no evidence of breach of the peace, and while the Court ordinarily will not review evidence, it had already held that it would reverse a conviction in a case if there were no evidence at all that the defendant had committed the crime. *Garner* was such a case, as Warren's opinion showed. The students may have committed a trespass, but they had not disturbed the peace. Frankfurter, Douglas, and Harlan all wrote separately, reaching the same result but for different reasons, and by their opinions showed that the sit-in cases of the future could prove difficult.

The Right to Vote

By 1962 the various civil rights organizations in the South were attacking the different facets of white supremacy in different ways. All agreed, however, that bringing African-Americans to the polls was a must. It was also difficult, given the decades of stratagems the South had developed to defeat the Fifteenth Amendment. In 1940 only 5 percent of southern African-Americans were registered to vote; in 1960 the percentage had jumped to 28 percent. Nevertheless, the percentages were decidedly lower in the Deep South.

The favorite southern legal device for preventing African-Americans from voting was the literacy test, whereby a person attempting to register to vote had to demonstrate an ability to read and write and occasionally interpret state law. Such laws were racially neutral; that is, as written they applied equally to whites as well as African-Americans. Their success in precluding African-American voting came from how they were administered. Stories and jokes were legion about semiliterate white officials turning away better-educated African-Americans. Anthony Lewis of the *New York Times* described a white applicant in George County, Mississippi, who was asked to interpret, as most whites were, a simple provision of the state constitution stating "There shall be no imprisonment for debt." He wrote: "I thank that a Neorger should have 2 years in collage before voting because he don't under stand."[23] Voila, a new white voter. Still, being able to read was hardly unrelated to the ability to cast an intelligent ballot and that posed the legal problem: Reasonable laws did not violate equal protection if they were racially neutral.

That is exactly what a unanimous Court held in 1959 in *Lassiter v. Northampton Board of Elections*. Louise Lassiter attempted to register to vote but refused to read any section of the North Carolina constitution. When she was denied registration, she sued, claiming the literacy test violated the Fourteenth, Fifteenth, and Seventeenth Amendments (direct election of senators). Beyond what has just been stated, there were no facts developed and no showing that the North Carolina test was—or even had been—discriminatorily applied. Lassiter did show that North Carolina had a grandfather clause and that there might be illiterate white voters over the age of seventy in the state, but she did not produce any. Douglas's characteristically quick pen resulted in a short opinion that came down less than three weeks after the case was argued. It sustained the literacy test because it was reasonable: racially neutral, related to the desire to raise voter standards, and without evidence that it was discriminatorily applied.

Ascertaining whether individuals were discriminatorily denied the right to vote was one of the charges of the Civil Rights Commission, which had been created by the Civil Rights Act of 1957. The Commission had received numerous complaints from Louisiana African-Americans that they were being denied their right to vote, and on not receiving satisfactory responses from Louisiana officials, it decided to hold hearings in Shreveport during the summer of 1959. By statute, the Commission had subpoena power, and the Commission operated much like House and Senate investigating committees—that is, like a grand jury, except it was in public, but without the power to indict. Under Commission rules, subpoenaed witnesses would not know the specific charges against them nor the identity of their accusers. Therefore, they would not have rights of confrontation or cross-examination. The Louisiana attorney general, on behalf of state voting registrars, challenged the rules as violations of due process of law.

Hannah v. Larche presented an unusual clash of rights because the Commission was publicly putting the voting registrars on trial, yet to require unveiling the identities of the complainants would put those individuals at risk. Warren concluded that due process was "elusive" yet flexible, and that these proceedings, like many administrative investigatory proceedings, looked fair enough. Douglas, with Black, dissented and remained true to positions articulated in cases like *Peters v. Hobby*. Important though civil rights are, "it will not do to sacrifice other civil rights in order to protect them. We live and work under a Constitution. The temptation of many men of goodwill is to cut corners, take short cuts, and reach the desired end regardless of the means. Worthy as I think the ends are which the Civil Rights Commission advances in these cases, I think the particular means used are unconstituitonal." For Warren and Brennan, however, the ends were so good that means questionable elsewhere seemed fine here.

No commission was needed to know that Alabama's redrawing of the municipal lines of Tuskegee "from a square to an uncouth twenty-eight sided figure" resulted from discrimination. The redrawn boundary moved outside the city all but four or five of the city's 400 African-Americans, while not removing a single white from the city. The local newspaper quipped that Tuskegee's African-Americans had moved out of town. The African-Americans challenged the law as a violation of their preexisting rights to vote in Tuskegee municipal elections since they had been thrust into an unincorporated area still within Tuskegee's extraterritorial jurisdiction. Frankfurter's majority opinion in *Gomillion v. Lightfoot* is short and simple, and quotes from an older case: "The Fifteenth Amendment nullifies sophisticated as well as simple-minded modes of discrimination." That said it all although Whittaker, concurring, ignored the facts and thought the Fourteenth Amendment was the appropriate provision (even though its history plus the text of the Fifteenth Amendment illustrated that it was not intended to reach voting).

The Court's race cases from 1958–1962 were in a holding pattern. In the school area, the Court was missing in action. After *Cooper* and *Shuttlesworth,* it decided no more cases, and school desegregation in the South was at a standstill. As a not unrelated matter, so was the NAACP, which was fighting for its legal life in a number of southern states. The only voting cases indicated that the Court and courts generally lacked the tools to help African-Americans register and gain some political power.

The NAACP cases had recognized, as the domestic-security cases had not, that rights of political association were important, fragile, and threatened by legal mechanisms that demanded disclosure and publicity. For a while, the race and domestic-security cases moved in opposite directions on parallel tracks. With *Shelton v. Tucker,* however, and the first fissure on race cases, eight of the nine justices were committed one way or another. It was only Stewart who distinguished between subsequent race and domestic-security cases. With *Gibson* and the Virginia lawyer regulation case, Stewart joined Frankfurter, Clark, Harlan, and Whittaker to sustain the state's regulation of the NAACP. Legally, this would have been an ominous move. Given the changes in the civil rights movement, it might not have mattered. In any event, Whittaker's retirement caused the cases to be reargued.

As the Court ceased being an important player in the area and the NAACP tried to sustain itself, the role of law and lawyers diminished. King's nonviolence pointed in a different direction and, as the four Greensboro African-Americans had shown, it offered a way that enabled anyone who was willing to join in the struggle for equal rights. As the period under discussion closed in the summer of 1962, it was unclear where direct action would lead in the immediate future. A snapshot at the time would have shown the local chief of police in Albany, Georgia, preventing white mobs from forming while simultaneously arresting and incarcerating African-American demonstrators. But the snapshot would not be sent North for, without violence, there was no "story" for national television. As John Morton Blum summarized the situation, Albany's "public schools, interstate bus terminal, and municipal library remained segregated. In spite of that clear violation of federal law, the president and attorney general made no helpful gesture. The failure of African-American nonviolence in Albany contrasted with the success of white violence in Mississippi."[24]

Chapter 8

The Transition

Stalemate as a description of the Court's work for 1958–1962 applies best to civil rights. The Court would not retreat but could not go forward. The domestic-security cases are better described as retreat. The congressional debates and votes in the summer of 1958 convinced Frankfurter that the Court could not sustain itself against such intense opposition and led him to join the more conservative justices to create an impregnable five-vote bloc. In other areas, however, the Court did not face such an actively hostile and organized opposition, and in these areas the Court began to chart new courses. The leaders were the four liberals—Warren, Black, Douglas, and Brennan—and they typically found one or another of the remaining five justices to go along with them. Thus in 1961 and 1962, the Court decided cases in church-state relations, criminal procedure, and voting rights that were striking new initiatives, true harbingers of the future, that at a minimum canceled out the domestic-security retreat. For the first time since the 1956 Term, and only the second time since Warren joined the Court, governments lost over half their public-law cases before the Court. In each area, the eventual opposition was caught by surprise and needed some time to organize, and indeed was not able to do so prior to the changes in the Court's personnel in 1962.

In two other areas the Court continued what it had been doing. In antitrust, the Justice Department could not lose. And in the first gender discrimination case of the era, the justices saw no problems, just as they had not a decade before.

Gender Discrimination

Gwendolyn Hoyt was in an unhappy marriage with an unfaithful air force officer. After her final attempt at reconciliation was spurned, she took a broken baseball bat and bashed her husband's head in. He died the following day. The facts were never in dispute, and Florida tried her for second-degree murder. She defended with temporary insanity. An all-male jury rejected her defense and convicted with just twenty-five minutes of deliberation. She was given a thirty-year sentence.

Hoyt argued that her defense would have been better understood by women and that Florida's jury-selection procedure, basically excusing any woman from jury service unless she affirmatively volunteered, was a violation of equal protection because of how differently men were treated. Men were automatically placed on the jury list, and at the time of Hoyt's trial, there were 9,990 men along with ten women (out of 223 volunteers) in the relevant pool.

Florida was not alone in treating women differently from men with respect to jury service. Women were ineligible for jury service in Alabama, Mississippi, and South Carolina. Louisiana and New Hampshire had statutes identical to Florida's, requiring women who wished to serve to volunteer. Thirteen other states plus the District of Columbia offered a woman an absolute exemption if she so wished.

The case was handed down in November 1961, one month after it was argued. Harlan's opinion in *Hoyt v. Florida* found that the treatment of women was reasonable because "woman is still regarded as the center of home and family life"; furthermore, Florida had taken no "arbitrary" steps to exclude women from jury service. Warren, Black, and Douglas considered dissenting but instead wrote a one-sentence concurring opinion announcing that on the record before them they could not say Florida was not making a good-faith effort to include women. If African-Americans rather than women had been required to affirmatively volunteer, these three (and the other six) would have defined a good-faith effort rather differently.

It would be another decade, and therefore beyond Warren's tenure, before the next gender discrimination case appeared on the docket. *Hoyt* is thus a useful reminder that the Court does not create social movements; it responds to them. It took Betty Friedan and the sexism of the civil rights movement to create the modern women's movement.

Antitrust

The Court decided two antitrust cases that continued the Government's incredible victory streak. One was the necessary follow-up to the duPont-General Motors case discussed earlier where the Court had held that duPont's ownership of General Motors stock violated the antitrust laws. When the case returned four years later in 1961 on the issue of remedy, the Court ordered duPont to divest itself of all of the GM stock. Harlan and Clark could not participate, and the decision ran exactly on the liberal-conservative split. Brennan wrote for the four liberals; Frankfurter for Whittaker and Stewart.

In *Brown Shoe v. United States,* the Court blocked a merger between Brown Shoe and G. R. Kinney because it feared that the merged company would put small retail competitors at too much of a disadvantage. It is hard to imagine today, when a Boeing can merge with a McDonnell Douglas, that the merger between Brown and Kinney could have caused difficulties. Both companies manufactured shoes and owned retail stores. Brown was the fourth largest manufacturer of shoes, with 4 percent of the nation's production, Kinney was the twelfth largest, with 0.5 percent of national production. Between them they would also own about 2.3 percent of the 70,000 retail outlets in the country and become the second largest national retailer.

The tone of Warren's opinion foreordained the result. The merger would "force Brown shoes into Kinney stores." Other manufacturers' brands would possibly be excluded as the new company preferred its own. Rejecting Brown's litigation-created argument that there would not be any efficiencies flowing from the merger, the Court correctly found there would be efficiencies that would result in lower prices to the consumer. Consequently, independent shoe retailers might be at a competitive disadvantage and therefore eventually forced out of business. According to the Court, Congress wanted to protect small, locally owned retail outlets from competition from larger national firms, regardless of consumer benefit. If this merger were approved, competitors might be encouraged to engage in similarly efficient mergers, which presumably would have to be upheld. The Court behaved like a frontier sheriff heading off the potential villain at the pass. "In light of the trends in this industry, this is an appropriate place at which to call a halt." Whatever the accuracy of its view of congressional intent behind the 1950 amendments to the Clayton Act, the majority, like Louis Brandeis before them, believed bigness, even of the Brown Shoe variety, was an evil that needed to be combated, and it was more than happy to assist. When asked what businessmen thought of the Warren Court, the general counsel of a major corporation replied, "Well, it pays to be a Negro or a Communist if you want justice from the Warren Court. Business just doesn't get it."[1]

Church-State before Warren

The Court's modern entry into church-state separation came in 1947
when in *Everson v. Board of Education,* all nine justices agreed that the
First Amendment's ban on "establishment of religion" was best subsumed in Thomas Jefferson's metaphor of a "wall of separation" between church and state. In rhetoric that carried the metaphor further,
Black wrote that the "wall must remain high and impregnable." Still,
forecasting the ultimate chaos—and many would say outright incoher-
ence—of the metaphor as constitutional doctrine, a 5–4 majority upheld
the New Jersey subsidy for bus transportation to parochial schools that
was at issue.

The reaction to *Everson* showed that centuries after the Reformation,
religion remained a volatile issue. Catholics generally condemned the
rhetoric of the decision even though they prevailed in the case. Jews and
nonbelievers hugged the wall, while Protestants were split. Because decisions in the church-state area were a zero-sum game—government either
could or couldn't adopt the program—there would likely be an outcry no
matter what the Court did.

Black's rhetoric in *Everson* was simultaneously inflammatory and un-
sustainable. It was inflammatory because it seemed to embody Jefferson's hostility to religion, and the Court triggered opposition from those
who believed that government and religion had much to do together.
It was not sustainable because the United States, in drawing contrasts
between itself and the totalitarian Soviet Union, often emphasized
American religiosity, including a public embrace of God. Indeed, to distinguish Americans from the era's redundant "godless atheistic communists," the Pledge of Allegiance was modified in 1954, with Eisenhower's
support, to include "under God." Two years earlier Congress enacted legislation calling upon the president to proclaim each year a "National Day of Prayer." And should anyone study money before using it,
that person would learn that "In God We Trust." (This dates from
1865.)

The Court decided no church-state cases of any consequence during
Eisenhower's presidency. Then in the spring of 1961 it decided five cases,
and a year later it handed down a decision on school prayer that was
almost as controversial as *Brown v. Board of Education.* Four of the
1961 cases involved Sunday closing laws, the fifth a requirement that
Maryland officials—right down to notary publics—affirm a belief in
God.

Sunday Closing Laws

In 1960 every state except Alaska had some form of blue law that criminalized engaging in activities on Sunday that were legal if done on any other day of the week. These laws had their origins in facilitating Christian religious observances. Over time, however, they acquired new rationales. Essentially, they operated as a restraint of trade and a union benefit. Small merchants and department stores supported them against discounters, who challenged them. Labor unions also were supportive because they did not have to bargain for that day off. Indeed, the myriad exemptions to a typical state's blue laws were a remarkable tribute to various interests that had put together coalitions to exempt themselves from the generally applicable law.

The four cases the Court decided in 1961 had two different types of litigants. One set involved highway discount-stores that were allowed to open but only on a restricted basis; they could sell some items but not others. The other set involved Orthodox Jewish merchants, who already closed for religious reasons on Saturday and thought they should not be required to close on the Christian Sabbath as well.

The cases presented three different constitutional issues. Did the blue laws, with their Christian heritage, constitute an establishment of religion? Did the laws abridge the free exercise of religion of the Jewish merchants or their customers? And, finally, did the crazy-quilt network of exceptions show the laws had no basis except as the outgrowth of ugly pluralist coalition-building and therefore violate the equal protection of the laws? The Court, through Warren, rejected all the constitutional claims. Frankfurter, joined by Harlan, wrote a concurring opinion that said the same things as Warren's majority but did so far more verbosely. Douglas dissented in each case on Establishment Clause grounds; Brennan and Stewart dissented in the cases involving the Orthodox Jews on free exercise grounds.

Warren's opinion in the principal case, *McGowan v. Maryland,* agreed with an important aspect of the Establishment Clause challenge. If the purpose of the blue laws were to support or facilitate religion, then the laws would be unconstitutional. Warren admitted that the laws had once had such an illegal purpose but said that over time their purpose changed. The states had gone from believing that the family that prays together stays together to asserting the family that plays together stays together—a wholly acceptable secular purpose of creating a "family day of rest." Thus, for Warren and the Court—even if not for Moslems,

Jews, atheists, and devout Christians—Sunday as a day with minimal commercialism had lost its Christian meaning. Nor did a state need to tailor its laws to create exceptions for those who celebrated other Sabbaths since doing so might undermine the goal of uniformity. As for the equal protection challenge, which focused on the myriad exceptions to the blue laws, Warren was similarly upbeat. Of course, there was "some inequality" but that was okay and might be necessary to promote the day as one of relaxation. Underlying the dismissal of the equal protection argument was the reality that the Court had no interest whatsoever in reviving any constitutional protections for economic claims; in any event, equal protection was a race-based doctrine.

Douglas's dissent rejected the Court's newfound rationale for the existence of Sunday closing laws. "No matter how much is written, no matter how much is said, the parentage of the laws is the Fourth Commandment." To be sure, a state could mandate a day of rest but not Sunday because the blue laws "force minorities to obey the majority's religious feelings of what is due and proper for a Christian community; they provide a coercive spur to the 'weaker brethren,' to those who are indifferent to the claims of a Sabbath through apathy or scruple." Douglas asked if there would be any doubt that Christians would be "strongly opposed if they were prosecuted under a Moslem law that forbade them from engaging in secular activities on days that violated Moslem scruples?" Not surprisingly, no one rose to the bait.

Braunfeld v. Brown decided the free exercise claims in a case involving a kosher grocery store owner and some of his patrons. The store owner argued he was placed at a competitive disadvantage because he was closed Saturday for religious reasons and then on Sunday because of state law, while his competitors were operating six days a week. Similarly, his kosher customers could not shop for food from Friday evening until Monday morning, while Christians and nonbelievers did not suffer such disabilities.

Warren, for the Court, was unimpressed. "[W]e are a cosmopolitan nation made up of people of almost every conceivable religious preference. . . . Consequently it cannot be expected much less required" that the states accommodate everyone. Braunfeld's disadvantage came because he chose not to work on Saturday, not because the state required that he close on Sunday. In other words, Warren concluded that it was his religion, not the law, that was responsible for his predicament. This was, however, just a bit facile. Braunfeld did not mind closing on Saturday for his God; it was Pennsylvania's legal requirement that he close on Sunday that caused his problems.

Brennan, in a rare split from Warren, thought the Court was justifying the states by "mere convenience," and in his emerging jurisprudence, states needed a bigger and better reason for disadvantaging a person who exercised his constitutional rights. He found the supposed difficulties about accommodating everyone to be "fanciful." Free exercise was being unnecessarily slighted. Stewart thought so too, finding that a "cruel choice" was being imposed on Orthodox Jewish merchants but not on Christians and stating that this was "not something that can be swept under the rug and forgotten in the interest of forced Sunday togetherness." Maybe free exercise was being swept under the rug momentarily, but societal trends, including secularization and increasing suburbanization, were combining with the unwillingness of police to enforce the laws, with the result that, despite the Court's okay, they were passing into the history books.

Affirming a Belief in God

The Court was unanimous in *Torcaso v. Watkins,* holding that Maryland's constitutional provision requiring all public officers to affirm a belief in God was unconstitutional. The Maryland provision was so blatantly unconstitutional that it is hard to think of ways it could have been sustained. One possibility might have been that the Establishment Clause simply forbids a state from preferring one religion but does allow a preference for religion over no religion (although this is contrary to its history). Yet even here Maryland was in trouble because it preferred theistic religions to nontheistic religions.

After quoting *Everson* about the "wall of separation," Black wrote that "neither a State nor the Federal Government can constitutionally force a person 'to profess a belief or disbelief in any religion' . . . and neither can aid those religions based on a belief in the existence of God as against religions founded on a different belief." The opinion then footnoted that "Buddhism, Taoism, Ethical Culture and Secular Humanism" were religions in America "which do not teach what would generally be considered a belief in the existence of God." Black's listing of Secular Humanism as a religion would come back to haunt the Court via opponents to the Court's future religion-in-the-school decisions. Frankfurter and Harlan, having written at length just to agree in the Sunday closing cases, did not join Black's opinion; instead, they concurred in the result without saying why.

School Prayer

A year after the Sunday closing cases the Court returned to church-state relations in a case that at the time was the most controversial the Court had decided since *Brown v. Board of Education. Engle v. Vitale* involved a twenty-two-word prayer: "Almighty God, we acknowledge our dependence upon Thee, and we beg Thy blessings upon us, our parents, our teachers and our country." School days in a number of New York districts began with its recitation.

The "Regents Prayer" had been adopted by the New York Board of Regents in 1951 as part of the larger anticommunist efforts, including changing the Pledge of Allegiance and creating a Law Day observance juxtaposed against May Day to highlight American differences from the Soviet Union. The Regents, a thirteen-member body, had five attorney members, and in an accompanying press release they announced that they were aware of the Establishment Clause and that the prayer was "clearly constitutional." At the venue that counted, only Stewart agreed.

Black wrote a short opinion that is easily summarized. The prohibition of an establishment of religion "must at least mean that in this country it is no part of the business of government to compose official prayers for any group of the American people to recite as part of a religious program carried on by government." Religion should be left "to the people themselves and to those the people choose to look to for religious guidance." The opinion totally eschewed the Court's prior cases, focusing instead entirely on history, and the history relied on was the history of religious conflict prior to the adoption of the First Amendment. The implication was clear. If government and religion get involved, conflict is inevitable. Without citing *Everson* (except in a footnote), Black got to the same place.

Douglas wrote a concurring opinion that, like his *McGowan v. Maryland* dissent, was looking for bigger game. Since the teacher was on the public payroll and the prayer didn't take long to recite, he concluded the case implicated financing of religion in any circumstances. Douglas cited James Madison's *Memorial and Remonstrance* for the proposition that public money devoted to religion "brings the quest for more" and with it religious divisiveness, as each religion tries to cut itself in and cut the others out. This was a more explicit version of Black's position, and in hearings before Eastland's Judiciary Committee that summer, Douglas's opinion was treated as if it were the opinion of the Court.

Stewart wrote a noninflammatory dissent that, like Black's majority, rested on history. Presidents recognize God; Congress opens its sessions with a prayer; the Supreme Court begins sessions with "God save the United States and this Honorable Court"; the "Star Spangled Banner," the national anthem by an act of Congress, mentions God. These were all part of America's postconstitutional history of accommodation and recognition of religion. Why shouldn't schoolchildren who wish to do so be allowed a similar privilege at the beginning of the school day? None of these examples constitutes an "official religion"; rather, they recognize the "deeply entrenched and highly cherished spiritual traditions of our Nation." So does school prayer.

Reaction to *Engle*

The Court received more mail complaining about *Engle* than any other case,[2] and a later study found more widespread opposition to *Engle* than to any other case. Taken at face value, Black's opinion should not have been controversial. Virtually no religious people, raised in a pluralistic society, would believe it should be the function of a government body to sit around a table drafting religious exercises and attempting to come up with the necessary compromise language on prayers so that no one would be offended. That is what Black's opinion both stated and held. But another way of reading *Engle,* and one that would prove accurate within a year, was that prayer in the public schools was wrong (and not merely unconstitutional). And that is how many did read it. Warren noticed what he believed to be an absurd headline in a newspaper: "Court outlaws God."[3] The *New York Herald Tribune* commented about "so many otherwise responsible newspapers getting completely swept off their feet by the tide of emotionalism."[4] The newspapers reacted to *Engle* more intensely than normal, but basically along the lines they were already taking on the Warren Court.

Liberal papers liked *Engle;* conservative ones did not. Thus, the *New York Times* approved of the decision and announced that "prayer is personal."[5] The *Wall Street Journal,* by contrast, saw the decision as a "violent wrecking of the Constitution's language" and "symptomatic of a broader move in the nation toward the rigid exclusion of all traces of religion in the public schools."[6] The *Times* was offering as universal a view of prayer that was hardly universal, while the *Journal* was on the mark in comprehending what was occurring in the wider society.

The religious comment on *Engle* also predictably split, and, as with the press, there was a shrillness to those who thought the decision wrong. Spokesmen for the Catholic Church, now happily a part of the American mainstream, were especially vehement. The Jesuit weekly *America* characterized the decision as "asinine," "stupid," "doctrinaire," and "unrealistic."[7] *Catholic News,* the archdiocesan paper for New York, found the "implications appalling."[8] Those implications were illustrated by New York's Francis Cardinal Spellman when he asserted that *Engle* "strikes at the heart of the Godly tradition in which America's children have for so long been raised."[9] Richard Cardinal Cushing of Boston simply called the result "ridiculous."[10] On the other coast, Los Angeles's James Cardinal McIntyre stated that the decision was "positively shocking and scandalizing to one of American blood and principles."[11]

Southern Protestants agreed. The Reverend Billy Graham was "shocked and disappointed."[12] Like many others, he thought Douglas's concurring opinion best understood *Engle*'s implications; taken to its logical conclusion, *Engle* was going to eradicate a lot of heretofore accepted practices. "God pity our country when we can no longer appeal to God for help."[13] A Methodist bishop from Georgia analogized *Engle* to "taking a star and stripe off of the flag."[14]

Jewish and mainstream Protestant leaders, happily supporting a high wall of separation, applauded the decision. It was, an editorial in the *Christian Century* said, a decision that "protects the integrity of the religious conscience and the proper function of religious and government institutions."[15]

The *New York Times* reported that congressmen "questioned the justices' honesty and patriotism."[16] South Carolina's Mendel Rivers was the most flamboyant, announcing that nothing in his lifetime, presumably including Yalta, had given "more aid and comfort to Moscow than this bold, malicious, atheistic, and sacrilegious twist by an unpredictable group of uncontrollable despots."[17] George Andrews of Alabama, however, was the one who best explained southern hostility. "They put Negroes in the school and now they've driven God out."[18] Actually in Alabama at that time not a single Negro was in the schools with whites, and one could doubt whether the Supreme Court could drive God out of any place He wished to be. But for quick, serviceable rhetoric, it was hard to top Andrews. Angry over *Brown*, he was willing to attach anything else to it. But for that reason *Engle* did not create additional opposition to the

Court from southern Democrats; rather, it added another reason for believing the Court was out of control.

The southern opposition to *Engle* caused the NAACP, which rarely took a public position on issues not in some way affecting African-Americans, to join the fray. It unanimously passed a resolution supporting *Engle* at its national convention. Martin Luther King, Jr., as well praised the decision as "sound and good, reaffirming something that is basic in our Constitution."[19]

Some northern Democrats chimed in as well, and Long Island Republican Frank Becker, a devout Catholic, offered a constitutional amendment to undo the result the very day *Engle* came down. At the National Governors' Conference, a resolution passed unanimously (with Nelson Rockefeller abstaining) supporting such an amendment. While only a handful of congressmen, like Emanuel Celler and Jacob Javits, came to the Court's defense publicly, Republican Senate leader Everett M. Dirksen accurately predicted that "the proposition of separation of church and state is so ingrained into our people that I doubt that such an amendment would be adopted."[20] What did pass instead was a resolution in the House to place the motto "In God We Trust" behind the Speaker's desk. In an election year, no one could vote no, and no one did.

One politician's views—the president's—counted more than any other's. Unlike Eisenhower, Kennedy forthrightly defended the Court. To a planted question at a press conference, he acknowledged that there would be people who disagreed, but "I would hope that [the people] will support the Constitution and the responsibility of the Supreme Court in interpreting it, which is theirs, and given to them by the Constitution."[21] For Kennedy, *Engle*'s result was perfect. In 1960 many people thought the country was not ready for a Catholic president because they feared that his loyalties would run to Rome, not to the Constitution. These people believed "that Catholics do not accept, or accept grudgingly, the implications of the Establishment Clause. While many Americans can speak with deep feeling about the separation of church and state, the impression is that Catholics would prefer some form of union of church and state."[22] Kennedy had needed a way to separate himself from the way Protestants felt about the Catholic Church, and in September 1960 he went to the very Protestant South for the convention of the Greater Houston Ministerial Association where he made clear that if there were any conflicts between his religion and the Constitution, the Constitution would control. Knocking religion out of the campaign as a respectable issue was essential for his victory.

For the election in 1964, Kennedy wanted the issue of religion well behind him. The last thing he needed was a way it could be revived and he could once again be associated with the discomfort Protestants felt about his church. Given those political needs, it was hardly surprising that he supported a decision like *Engle* that seemed to be driving religion out of public political life. The Court was doing what he wanted done, pushing religion away so that elections would be fought over something else, like getting (or keeping) America moving again, his 1960 theme. Thus, he stated, in language that tracked the mainstream Protestant position, that every family had "a very easy remedy and that is to pray ourselves, and I would think it would be a welcome reminder to every American family that we can pray a good deal more at home and attend our churches with a good deal more fidelity, and we can make the true meaning of prayer much more important in the lives of our children."[23]

Just as political opposition to *Engle* was nothing to worry about, neither was the possibility that the religious opposition would translate into new political opposition. The southern Protestants were the people who had bequeathed the country the Monkey Trial. Who would want them as allies? The Catholic Church was not a problem either. As noted, mid-century Americans were suspicious of the church. Elites were often downright hostile. "A Who's Who of mid-century American intellectuals offered research, analysis, or opinion to support the theory that Catholicism was inimical to democracy and conducive to fascism or other forms of authoritarian government."[24] Several members of the Court, perhaps a majority, were aware of this multidisciplinary research, and both Black and Douglas, as classic mid-century liberals, found anti-Catholicism an acceptable and respectable prejudice.

Opponents of the Court went through the motions of proposing a constitutional amendment to overturn *Engle*. But they lacked the clout to move the amendment in committee. Their political time in the sun was either in the distant past or the distant future.

Morality Cases

The Court also decided two minor cases that, while not formally about church-state issues, were in fact about statutes strongly backed by the Catholic Church. *Kingsley Pictures v. Regents* struck down part of New York's film-censorship scheme while *Poe v. Ullman* created a fictitious ground for avoiding a ruling on Connecticut's ban on the use of contraceptives.

The Catholic Church's Legion of Decency had always been active in movie censorship. It suffered a major defeat in 1952 when *Burstyn v. Wilson* held that a state lacked the power to ban a movie just because the state deemed it sacrilegious. In 1959 in *Kingsley Pictures v. Regents*, *Burstyn*'s holding was extended to immorality. New York had banned the 1957 movie version of D. H. Lawrence's *Lady Chatterley's Lover*, not on the ground of obscenity, which had greeted the book thirty years earlier (and would have been unconstitutional under *Roth v. United States*), but rather on the ground that the movie was "immoral" because it presented "adultery as a desirable, acceptable and proper pattern of behavior." New York wished to ban the false doctrine lest it corrupt its citizenry.

Stewart was given the opportunity to write the slam-dunk opinion supporting freedom of expression. "The First Amendment's basic guarantee is the freedom to advocate ideas. The State, quite simply, has struck at the very heart of constitutionally protected liberty." The First Amendment's protections are "not confined to the expression of ideas that are conventional or shared by a majority." One can advocate a single tax, socialism, or adultery; the state cannot take areas of life off the table as unchangeable. Nor does a Lawrence lose constitutional protection because he was an effective writer. "In the realm of ideas, the First Amendment protects expression which is eloquent no less than that which is unconvincing."

Surprisingly, there were a number of concurring opinions. Black and Douglas joined Stewart but wanted to go further and be rid of film censorship. Frankfurter, Harlan, Clark, and Whittaker agreed that New York had gotten carried away but wanted to leave as much of the film censorship in place as possible. They were successful a year later when Stewart joined them to create a 5–4 majority in *Times Film v. Chicago*, which was a direct challenge to the requirement that films be submitted to a licensing board prior to their first exhibition. Clark acknowledged that the ordinance was a prior restraint and would be unconstitutional if applied to magazines or books, but concluded that films were not "necessarily subject to the precise rules governing any other particular method of expression."

Poe v. Ullman (1961) represents a classic example of not reaching out to decide a constitutional question. Two married couples and their doctors challenged Connecticut's ban on the use of contraceptives or the providing of advice about contraception. The statute, adopted in 1879, tested once and sustained in 1940, had not been enforced, although the state attorney general claimed he would prosecute violators. The state court had refused to hear the challenge to the statute, on the ground that it had not been enforced. The statute thus looked like a dead letter. Yet, if so, it was an effective one. There were no birth-control clinics operating within the state.

Behind the dead-letter question was, for this era, a truly difficult constitutional question. Ever since the Court's retreat in 1937, the use of the Due Process Clause to invalidate statutes had been abandoned, and if Connecticut's statute was invalid, the Due Process Clause seemed to be the likely explanation.

There was one other possibility, but it would be a huge reach. That was to find the law unconstitutional because the Catholic Church liked it so much and now prevented a legislative repeal. In one sense this was the reverse of the Sunday blue laws, for the Connecticut statute had been passed well before the Catholic Church had any political power. Initially, the statute, patterned after an 1873 federal law, was part of Anthony Comstock's Calvinist crusade against pornography as anything that dealt with sex. The statute had acquired its Catholic veneer decades after it had been placed on the books. No one, not even Black or Douglas, would touch a theory like this, condemning a statute simply because a given religion had found it genial.

The posture of the case and the difficulty of the questions caused five justices to duck. Frankfurter ignored the effectiveness of the statute in precluding birth-control clinics and concluded there was a tacit agreement it would never be enforced. Accordingly, there was no need to decide the case; it was really "nonjusticiable"—that is, an inappropriate vehicle for a judicial ruling.

The most liberal justice and one of the most conservative justices, Douglas and Harlan, wrote full-scale impassioned opinions on why the statute was unconstitutional and the Court should decide rather than duck the case. Harlan had a robust theory of due process tied to the traditions of the American people, and he thought the statute an outrageous invasion of marital privacy. The "full scope of the liberty guaranteed by the Due Process Clause cannot be found in or limited by the precise terms of the specific guarantees elsewhere provided in the Constitution. This 'liberty' is not a series of isolated points pricked out in terms of [the various guarantees in the Bill of Rights]. It is a rational continuum which, broadly speaking, includes a freedom from all substantial arbitrary impositions and purposeless restraints and which also recognizes, what a reasonable and sensitive judgment must, that certain interests require particularly careful scrutiny."

By the 1960s, Douglas, with his two decades of service, had thought through all the issues normally appearing on the docket. His restless mind had turned to wondering about protecting the individual from new government abuses unanticipated by an eighteenth-century culture. He perceived the twentieth century as posing twin threats to the individual, one from corporations, the other from government, and he believed that "freedom" was like pure air—one could never have enough. *Poe* offered him the first opportunity to explore the problem from the bench. He seemed to find the statute unconstitutional without regard to the Constitution's text. To enforce the Connecticut law would necessitate "an invasion of the privacy implicit in a free society" and "allowing a state that leeway is congenial only to a totalitarian regime."

Douglas and Harlan persuaded Black and Stewart that the case ought to be decided on the merits although not necessarily that the law was unconstitutional. But, as always on the merits, five beats four. If the parties wanted to know whether the statute was unconstitutional, they could violate it and, if prosecuted and convicted, bring the issue back to the Court.

Criminal Procedure

The closely divided nature of so many cases of this period where the four liberals hoped to attract just one more vote was also prevalent in the criminal procedure area. The Court ruled 5–4, first, against a double jeopardy claim where the defendant was tried first by the federal government and then by the state for the same offense and, second, on the lack of need for a search warrant when health or building inspectors wished to see a home. But on the issue of applying the federal rule excluding illegally seized evidence to state proceedings, the liberals struck pay dirt.

The Fifth Amendment protects a person against being tried twice for the same crime. The reasons for the Double Jeopardy Clause are numerous and historical but come down to the realities that trying a person twice undermines the presumption of innocence, wears down the accused, and gives the government an inordinate advantage in the second trial. Black offered an example right out of the newspapers. A man who was trying to break into a store killed an officer who was trying to prevent the crime. The criminal was convicted and given ten to twenty-five years. The public was outraged at the leniency of the sentence. Responding to the outrage, the government retried the defendant, and he was sentenced to death. It occurred in Moscow.

Bartkus v. Illinois was decided in 1959, just five months after the proceedings in Moscow. Bartkus was convicted of robbing a bank in Cicero; the conviction came shortly after he was acquitted of the identical offense in a federal trial. Frankfurter rejected the double jeopardy claim on a "dual sovereignty" ground—that is, that in fact Bartkus could have committed two crimes in the same incident, one against the federal government and one against Illinois. Therefore, trying him twice was not double jeopardy. Essentially, Frankfurter held that federalism required respect for the decisions of each sovereign. He noted that with a single exception every state supreme court that had passed on the same question had ruled against the double jeopardy claim. This was "irrefutable evidence" that courts had disagreed with Bartkus's position, and Frankfurter thought it would be wrong to disregard "a long, unbroken, unquestioned course of impressive adjudication."

Black, Warren, and Douglas agreed with Bartkus, and Black footnoted the Soviet story to back up his point that double jeopardy was not respected in lands "torn by revolution or crushed by dictatorship" but had been part of our "heritage of freedom." Brennan dissented as well but on the very limited ground that the federal government had been too involved in assisting the state prosecution.

Over a thirteen-month period from May 1959 to June 1960, the Court twice considered so-called administrative searches of private dwellings. *Frank v. Maryland* involved a $20 fine imposed on Frank for denying entrance to his home to a health inspector who had overwhelming evidence of a rodent infection there—a house in an "extreme state of decay" with a half-ton pile of rodent feces, straw, trash, and debris visible in the backyard. Frank's claim was that the inspector needed a search warrant to gain entrance (although under *Wolf v. Colorado* and *Irvine v. California* if he searched without a warrant, any evidence taken would be admissible in a state trial). The question presented to the Court was whether the routine nature of health inspections and the lack of criminal consequences could justify a lack of a warrant. As in *Bartkus*, Frankfurter put together a majority for relying on "the long history of this kind of inspection and of modern needs."

Douglas, for the dissenters, also relied on history, albeit the different one that respected the right against unwanted intrusion. The dissent condemned the "dilut[ion] of the right of privacy which every homeowner had the right to believe was part of our American heritage." Douglas was unimpressed with the relevance of the fact that the fine was piddling because it was "not the measure of the right"—here one of the "indispensable ultimate essentials of our concept of civilization."

Two weeks later, the Court considered an Ohio case, *Eaton v. Price,* on the same issue, but with the homeowner, after refusing admission, sitting in jail awaiting trial because he could not make bail. This was a real punishment, not the de minimus fine in *Frank.* Furthermore, if one were convicted for denying admission to the home, the law carried a thirty-day jail sentence plus a $200 fine. There was one further difference from *Frank.* Stewart's father was on the Ohio Supreme Court and so Stewart could not participate.

The *Frank* dissenters voted to hear the case, and the four remaining members of the *Frank* majority voted to affirm summarily without briefs or a hearing. Since the Court operates by a "rule of four" whereby all justices are bound to hear a case (but not necessarily decide it on the merits as *Poe* showed) if four justices wish to, *Eaton* was set for argument. Frankfurter's four took the unprecedented step of writing their views and issuing the opinion with the Court's order granting review. They let Eaton know that he would lose (by a 4–4 vote) because they stated that his case was fully controlled by *Frank.*

A year later, *Eaton* was argued and indeed came down 4–4, thereby affirming the lower court. This time the dissenters broke with precedent and wrote opinions in a 4–4 situation, arguing that *Eaton* demonstrated how dangerous *Frank* was because *Eaton* showed that the state could demand a homeowner let the inspector in or face criminal jail-time should he refuse.

Bartkus, Frank, and *Eaton* were dwarfed by *Mapp v. Ohio,* which a year later held that the states were bound by the federal exclusionary rule in cases of illegally seized evidence. *Mapp* overruled the 1949 decision of *Wolf v. Colorado* and its validation of the well-settled state procedure of allowing evidence from illegal police behavior into the trial against the accused. This set in motion the criminal procedure revolution of the 1960s. The astute Washington lawyer and future justice, Abe Fortas, characterized *Mapp* as "the most radical decision in recent times."[25]

Mapp was Dollree Mapp, a Cleveland woman who had a number of run-ins with the police. This time the police suspected her of harboring a fugitive wanted in a bombing. They arrived in force, but she refused them entrance, after phoning her lawyer who told her not to admit them. Meanwhile, the police called headquarters, gained substantial reinforcements, and broke down her back door. Mapp demanded to see a search warrant and someone showed her a piece of paper, which she took and quickly thrust into her bra. An officer successfully "went down after it" and then very forcefully handcuffed her. Her lawyer arrived while the police were ransacking her house, but they would not let him in. They did not find the fugitive, but they did find in a trunk what they deemed obscene materials—which Douglas described as "four little pamphlets, a couple of photographs and a little pencil doodle." There was no warrant, but under the 1954 decision in *Irvine v. California* the evidence was admissible.

Mapp was convicted of possession of obscene materials and sentenced to seven years in jail. Her defense was that the statute was unconstitutionally vague and that she did not have the materials in her possession because they belonged to a former roommate and she was just storing them (with his other possessions) until he picked them up. The Ohio Supreme Court (Stewart's father now retired) found the defense irrelevant since they were in her home and the former roommate was not; that was possession enough. Mapp then appealed the constitutionality of the statute to the Court.

Neither Mapp nor the state wrote as much as a comma about excluding the evidence because of the lack of a warrant. The American Civil Liberties Union filed an amicus brief, and in the last paragraph, as sort of an "oh, by the way," the ACLU mentioned the illegal search and said *Wolf* should be overruled. It offered no reasons for doing this. At oral argument, one justice asked Mapp's attorney about *Wolf*, and he expressly disavowed wanting the case overruled.

There was little doubt that the Ohio obscenity-possession statute, as applied to the facts, was unconstitutionally vague. Although Douglas, looking for the broadest result, was attracted to overruling *Wolf*, the rest of the justices were content with invalidating the statute. Warren assigned the case to Clark who, in the process of drafting the opinion, became intrigued with overruling *Wolf*. In one sense, this is not surprising. In *Irvine*, he had indicated his view that *Wolf* had been wrongly decided and that had he been on the Court he would have dissented. Clark greatly respected J. Edgar Hoover and the FBI, and Hoover did not complain about obtaining search warrants.

Clark could expect Douglas, Warren, and Brennan to agree, but needed a fifth vote. Black would seemingly be a natural but for his past. From his Senate investigating days on, he had seen the Fourth Amendment as Wall Street's amendment and therefore entitled to no respect. Thus, he had agreed with the result in *Wolf*. In *Mapp*, he nevertheless decided that he had been in error in 1949. He now concluded that the Fifth Amendment's privilege against self-incrimination was a sufficient supplement to the Fourth to "not only justify but actually require" that illegally seized evidence be excluded at trial. Only Black could have concocted and believed such a preposterous theory. It was, however, an essential step to his objective of having all of the Bill of Rights apply exactly to the states as it did to the federal government.

The remaining four justices were appalled that the majority should "simply reach out" and overrule *Wolf* so cavalierly. They were quite right in claiming that, before *Wolf* was dispatched, its fate should be subject to briefs and oral argument. That, after all, is the established and proper judicial practice. Nevertheless, the Court did it, and *Mapp* became the tenth case in which the Warren Court overruled a precedent. Stewart agreed with the dissenters that the majority was just reaching out but concurred in the result because he thought the Ohio obscenity statute unconstitutional.

Clark's opinion had to explain why a twelve-year-old case, validating a fairly uniform practice among the states, should now be discarded. The thrust of Clark's opinion was that *Wolf* had been in error in separating the exclusionary rule from the Fourth Amendment itself. Once the rule is understood as part and parcel of the Fourth Amendment, then *Wolf*'s recognition that states could not abrogate the citizen's privacy necessarily meant that the exclusionary rule was part of that privacy. Quite simply, this was, as Harlan's dissent stated, "a syllogism." The exclusionary rule is part of the Fourth Amendment. The Fourth Amendment applies to the states through the Fourteenth Amendment. Therefore, the exclusionary rule applies to the states through the Fourteenth Amendment. Not only was it a syllogism, it was exactly what Black and Douglas had been arguing in the 1940s—full incorporation of a provision of the Bill of Rights into the Fourteenth Amendment to make the federal rule bind the states as well. Harlan's dissent noted this too.

Clark buttressed his conclusion three different ways. First, when *Wolf* was decided, two-thirds of the states rejected the exclusionary rule; now, one-half the states accepted it, including California. Second, Clark concluded that without the exclusionary rule, there was no way to deter illegal police conduct. Third and last, there was the issue of judicial integrity. Government teaches by example. If it becomes a lawbreaker, it breeds contempt for law. Courts cannot be a party to lawbreaking without threatening "that judicial integrity so necessary in the true administration of justice."

The reasons were not equally persuasive. Clark was reasonably accurate in concluding that the exclusionary rule was a necessary deterrent to illegal police conduct. Without the exclusionary rule, the Fourth Amendment guarantee of privacy in the home was "an empty promise." Neither criminal nor civil sanctions were ever brought against police who did not get warrants, and there was ample reason to believe that the practice of illegal searches was widespread. Possibly, if the evidence could not be admitted in a subsequent trial, police would be more careful in respecting subjects' rights. At the very least, the exclusionary rule does not encourage police violations of the Fourth Amendment.

The half of the states adopting the exclusionary rule included Alaska and Hawaii, which formerly had been territories and therefore were required to follow the exclusionary rule. Furthermore, how a more or less fifty-fifty split meant that those adopting it were right and those holding to their older positions were wrong was unstated, although probably Clark was following the assumption of *Elkins v. Unites States* a year earlier that the movement toward the exclusionary rule was "inexorable." Since history inexorably pointed one way, the Court was going to help history out.

After chastising the majority for its lack of restraint in deciding a question not properly before it, Harlan's dissent defended *Wolf*. The defense was federalism. States should have a choice on how to structure their criminal trials rather than be forced into a federal straitjacket. The fact that half the states reject *Wolf* is fully balanced by half the states following its invitation to reject the exclusionary rule. Nor, Harlan concluded, was the prediction of history such a useful guide. The dissenters were not so sure that "time has set its face against" allowing illegally seized evidence in a criminal trial (although the majority's view became a self-fulfilling prophesy because of the outcome).

Mapp was the first of the important Warren Court criminal procedure cases; nothing before it even comes close. A prime reason is that virtually all criminal procedure cases of the previous quarter-century were thinly disguised race cases coming from the South. *Mapp* was not a race case, and it had national implications because, by its own admission, it was changing the law in half of the states, including New York, then the most populous one. Furthermore, the Court was requiring local police and local trial judges to comply with a federal rule that many people thought wrongheaded and often worked to free an accused who had clearly committed the crime. After all, evidence seized, unlike confessions coerced, is not untrustworthy.

Almost four decades earlier, the great Benjamin Cardozo had summarized the opposition to the exclusionary rule in a terse sentence: "The criminal is to go free because the constable has blundered." For many citizens, that seemed too high a price for deterring blundering. Implicit in

Clark's majority opinion was the view that the police were not really "blundering"; they were willfully ignoring the constitutional requirement of obtaining search warrants. And why shouldn't they? As the Deputy New York City Police Commissioner stated, "[e]vidence obtained without a warrant—illegally if you will—was admissible in state courts. So the feeling was, why bother?"[26] Prior to *Mapp*, New York City spent no time whatsoever training police about the law of search and seizures.

Police behavior could be changed to match the professionalism of the FBI, and setting the occasional criminal free was not too high a price to pay for compliance with the Constitution because once the states complied, the dichotomy would vanish. Thus, California's Chief Justice Roger Traynor, the most respected mid-century state court jurist, and the author of the 1955 *Cahan* ruling adopting the exclusionary rule for his state, stated the "objective is certainly not to compensate the defendant for the past wrong done to him any more than it is to penalize the officer for the past wrong he has done. The emphasis is forward."[27]

The federal government knew best and offered the states an example of how to do it right, an example half of the states were too lazy (or backward) to follow. Once the states changed their behavior to match the federal practice, they would, like the FBI, get their man and respect the Constitution as well. *Mapp* was thus doubly good in the majority's eyes.

Traynor recognized from his *Cahan* experience that after *Mapp* there would be "ill-informed and emotional debate."[28] He knew that inevitably there would be talk of guilty criminals going free on "mere technicalities" because police and prosecutors had already adopted this litany. Thus, William H. Parker, the chief of the Los Angeles Police Department, had, prior to 1954, found the causes of crime to be complex and stated there was no "easy formula for preventing crime."[29] After *Cahan*, he claimed that police tactics were too constricted, so no wonder there was so much crime. In Minneapolis, a burglary wave that hit the city in late 1962 was blamed by local police on the new restrictions imposed by *Mapp*.[30] Traynor was on the money, and these stories would increase, especially when supplemented by the powerful reinforcement of *Escobedo* and *Miranda*. But that was in the future.

The Political Thicket

The first of the Warren Court blockbuster cases was, of course, *Brown*. Eight years later, *Baker v. Carr* was the second. In Warren's own estimation, *Baker,* setting in motion the redistribution of legislative power nationwide, was "the most important case of my tenure on the Court."[31]

Baker began when Memphis voters, soon joined by others from Nashville, Knoxville, and Chattanooga, challenged the way Tennessee was allocating seats in its legislature. The Tennessee constitution stated that seats should be apportioned each decade more or less on the basis of the number of qualified voters within a county. But the state legislature had never changed its turn-of-the-century apportionment despite (or maybe because of) the fact that in the ensuing six decades the number of qualified voters had jumped from 487,380 to 2,092,891. The result was that cities, especially Memphis, were grossly underrepresented in the state legislature. Moore County, in the south-central part of the state with its 2,340 voters, had one seat in the state house, while Shelby (Memphis) with its 312,345 voters had only seven seats. Districts with 40 percent of the state's voters could elect sixty-three of the ninety-nine members of the house, and districts with 37 percent of the voters could elect twenty of the thirty-three members of the senate. In the words of the Nashville mayor, the state was ruled "by the hog lot and the cow pasture."[32] In this, Tennessee was hardly alone; rural control of mid-century state legislatures was a political fact of life.

Tennessee lacked initiative and referendum so there was nothing the voting majority of the state could do about the apportionment. That's why *Baker* was brought in federal court. The case didn't last long. The court threw it out, believing that precedent, especially the Court's 1946 decision in *Colegrove v. Green,* had established that the federal courts lacked the power to hear this type of case.

Colegrove was a 4–3 case without a majority opinion, but everyone had assumed that Frankfurter's opinion for Reed and Burton stated the holding of the case. That opinion, expressing Frankfurter's most deeply held views, was that issues of apportionment were nonjusticiable "political questions," that is, not appropriate for judicial resolution. Frankfurter thought they were "of a peculiarly political nature," the type that the judiciary must eschew in order to protect its own independence. Should courts get involved, the elected branches of government would strike back hard because the "controversy concerns matters that bring courts into immediate and active relations with political party contests." Thus, Frankfurter concluded, "Courts ought not enter this political thicket." As a final although not as important point, these cases were also nonjusticiable because a court could not remap a state since there could be no judicially enforceable standards developed for deciding what to do.

Subsequent to *Colegrove,* the Court had disposed of a number of cases summarily, reinforcing the belief that Frankfurter's position was the Court's position. Reapportionment was a political question and therefore its solution lay with the legislature or, if that failed, *Colegrove* stated "the ultimate remedy lies with the people."

Baker arrived at the Court in November 1960, a week after the decision in *Gomillion v. Lightfoot* on the Tuskegee racial gerrymander. The four liberals wished to hear the case. It was set for oral argument in the spring of 1961, with the solicitor general invited to participate to express the views of the United States. After oral argument, the liberals voted to reverse, and Frankfurter "unleashed a brilliant tour de force"[33] that analogized entering the political thicket with the recent fiasco at the Bay of Pigs. Stewart could not make up his mind, and with the others split 4–4, he asked that *Baker* be put over to the next term so that he could have more time to think about it.

Baker was reargued at the beginning of October 1961. By that time, Stewart had virtually made up his mind that the Tennessee apportionment was "utterly arbitrary without any possible justification in rationality" and therefore unconstitutional, although he was not ready for "one person, one vote." When Brennan learned he had Stewart's vote, he was jubilant.

There was one further switch. Frankfurter encouraged Clark to explain why the voters of Tennessee had everything within their control, as Frankfurter's theory postulated. But when Clark researched the point and found to the contrary, he too switched. Like Stewart, he thought the Tennessee apportionment was "a crazy quilt without rational basis." By the time the case came down, Whittaker had decided to retire, so instead of being 5–4 one way or another, *Baker* was a 6–2 mandate for courts to enter Frankfurter's heretofore forbidden political thicket. It marked the eleventh time the Warren Court had overruled prior decisions.

The "political questions" label is inherently amorphous, and that constitutes both its allure and its vice. Frankfurter saw it as a way of protecting the judiciary from public backlash. The public needs confidence in the moral authority of the Court, which "must be nourished by the Court's complete detachment, in fact and appearance, from political entanglements and by abstention from injecting itself into the clash of political forces in political settlements." Applied literally, that would mean that the Court could never decide a controversial case if by doing so one political group would be angry. Why invalidating state legislative apportionment was a dangerous political entanglement, but invalidating the

New Deal or intervening between president and Congress in the steel seizure crisis was not, presented a question that was not considered because it could not be answered.

Brennan's task for the majority was either to rid the Court of the "political question" doctrine or else to cabin it. Douglas was ready for the former, but no one else was, so Brennan did the latter. "Much confusion results from the capacity of the 'political questions' label to obscure the need for case-by-case analysis." Confusion applies as well to Brennan's opinion, whose cumbersome strategy was to recategorize all the political questions cases in such a way that no prior case, *Colegrove* included, appeared to cover the present situation. In essence, Brennan treated the political questions doctrine as creating a closed class of situations, none of which fit legislative apportionment. Hence, the opinion backs in to its conclusion that apportionment was not a political question. It was not entirely pretty, but it did cut the former doctrine down to a reasonably manageable size.

Apportionment would be nonjusticiable only if there were no judicially manageable standards. Creating standards was no problem, Brennan asserted, though he failed to state what they would be. "Judicial standards under the Equal Protection Clause are well developed and familiar, and it has been open to courts since the enactment of the Fourteenth Amendment to determine, if on the particular facts they must, that a discrimination reflects *no* policy, but simply arbitrary and capricious action." Coming just a year after *McGowan v. Maryland* and *Hoyt v. Florida* showed the helplessness of equal protection in the non-race context, this statement is breathtaking. There were so few non-race equal protection cases that no one could confidently assert what the equal protection standard was. Yet Brennan said just the opposite; the reason was Stewart. *Baker v. Carr* is a perfect illustration of Brennan's willingness to say virtually anything (or nothing) if a key member of his majority requested it, so long as the opinion reached the right outcome.

When the Court effectively held the Tennessee apportionment unconstitutional, it had to have some idea of what a constitutional plan would be. Brennan's Court papers contain a contemporaneous University of Virginia study showing that nationally "big city voters have less than one-half the representation of people in open-country areas."[34] Although the opinion gave no hint of what the equal protection rationale was, the solicitor general's brief, filed by Harvard Law Professor Archibald Cox, did. "One of the most basic rights in any democracy is the right to fair representation in one's own government."[35] Urban voters were having this right abridged with the twin results that state legislatures were refusing to address urban needs and therefore the urban areas "now tend to by-pass the states and enter directly into cooperative arrangements with the national government which reinforces the debilitation of state governments."[36] Thus, *Baker* would signal the end of rural domination of state legislatures and the beginning of states dealing with the problems of their urban majorities.

The Reaction to *Baker*

Unlike *Mapp* and *Engle*, *Baker* was highly popular. Brennan had it just right. Writing six months later (as the only political scientist invited to write the *Harvard Law Review* "Foreword"), Robert McCloskey contrasted the immediate and enthusiastic efforts to implement *Baker* with those where the public disapproves of the Court's decision. In the latter situation, "the tendency is at best to abide by the minimum compulsion grudgingly interpreted. The tendency suggested by the early reactions to *Baker* seems very different from this, and it may warrant the conjecture that the Court here happened to hit upon what students of public opinion might call a latent consensus."[37] While Frankfurter worried about the political thicket, the public understood representative democracy. The Court was not operating to thwart the legislatures; it was making them more democratic.

At bottom, Frankfurter had said America must live with rotten boroughs for "in a democratic society like ours, relief must come through an aroused popular conscience that sears the conscience of the people's representatives." While that summarized a lifetime of Frankfurter's thought, it also left urban majorities subject to rurally dominated legislatures even as the problems of urbanization grew more compelling. For the Court's majority, and indeed the majority of the nation, these problems could not be tabled until the consciences of rural representatives were so seared that they ceded their places at the table. Frankfurter's willingness to defer to majority will as expressed by legislation seems inconsistent with his lack of concern over whether the legislature itself represented a majority of the people. In contrast to Frankfurter's lack of interest, the Court had held that democracy entails majority rule, and in the America of 1962, majority rule beat rotten boroughs hands down. Thus, a survey of the sixty-three leading metropolitan newspapers showed that thirty-eight favored the decision and did so quite strongly, while only ten were opposed and only mildly so; the other fifteen were either neutral or confused.[38]

Richard Russell, always ready to attack the Court in the hopes of derailing *Brown*, pronounced *Baker* "another major assault on our constitutional system. If the people truly value their freedom, they will demand that the Congress curtail and limit the jurisdiction being exercised" by the Court.[39] Russell was speaking for southerners, not conservatives. Thus, Republican Barry Goldwater of Arizona, who in 1964 would frequently attack the Court, called *Baker* a "proper decision."[40] McCloskey concluded: "[I]t has been as if *Baker* catalyzed a new political synthesis that was already straining, so to speak, to come into being."[41] (McCloskey, however, also emphasized his hope that the Court would move very cautiously when actually faced with the task of giving content to *Baker*.)

The reaction that mattered most came not from segregationist senators or soon-to-be-redistricted state representatives but rather from the Kennedy administration. Since the solicitor general had vigorously pushed for the result in *Baker*, the fact that the reaction was favorable is hardly surprising. But saying it was favorable does not catch its flavor. The administration too understood the elemental appeal of *Baker* as well as its potential to provide solutions to the problems of the cities. In a conversation with Dean Acheson, the president, echoing his opinion while a senator that apportionment "has either been deliberately rigged or shamefully ignored" at the expense of the cities,[42] defended *Baker* on the grounds that the legislatures would never reform themselves and that only the Court was capable of handling the issue. At his next press conference, Kennedy publicly supported the decision. "The right to fair representation and to have each vote count equally is, it seems to me, basic to the successful operation of a democracy."[43] Attorney General Robert Kennedy was even more enthusiastic, calling *Baker* "a landmark in the development of representative government."[44] At a Law Day speech, Nicholas Katzenbach, who had just moved up to deputy attorney general, characterized *Baker* as "historic" and "a great example of the rule of law in our society."[45] Rarely, if ever, had the Executive Branch come out so enthusiastically for a decision to which it was not even a party; this is a remarkable tribute to the latent consensus the Court unearthed.

Negative decisions are resented more than popular decisions are liked. So, three months later, *Engle* swamped *Baker*. Some months later, Alan Westin wrote that "during the past six months, hardly a day has gone by without some influential figure in American public life denouncing the Court."[46] But it did not matter because unlike the controversies over domestic security or civil rights, the Court could more than balance any opposition to its actions by active support of the most prominent politician in the United States—John Kennedy. Furthermore, behind Kennedy's defense of *Engle* and *Baker* was more than politics and approval of the new approaches taken. Kennedy and Warren genuinely liked each other. Warren had at first thought Kennedy was "too young for the job" and rooted for Adlai Stevenson.[47] But Warren would have supported anyone against Richard Nixon, and during Kennedy's presidency, Warren's biographer Ed Cray concludes he came to "idealize" the president, especially for Kennedy's "capacity for growth."[48]

Their relationship began that frigid day of the Inaugural when Warren and his wife stayed on an empty reviewing stand with the president until he chose to leave. For his part, Kennedy restored Warren to a favored place on the White House guest list, and the two pols liked to talk politics. Just two months after the inauguration, the President dropped in unexpectedly, to the obvious delight of everyone, on a dinner party given by Warren's past and present law clerks to celebrate the chief's seventieth birthday. Two years later, on Warren's birthday, he expressed gratitude "for the dignity and wisdom of your judicial leadership in the past ten years. Although it is not possible for all of us to be your clerks, in a very real sense we are all your students."[49] These were honest views and the result was that Warren knew that, unlike under Eisenhower, there would be no flak, either public or private, from the White House over the decisions of the Court. Furthermore, when the vacancies on the Court occurred, Warren was consulted and thereby gained the opportunity to influence the choices of who his future colleagues might be.

One vacancy occurred immediately before *Baker,* when Whittaker, emotionally exhausted by the work of the Court, took his doctor's advice and retired. Warren had assigned Whittaker *Brown Shoe,* and the complex antitrust case, like so much of the Court's work, was more than he could handle.

A second vacancy came immediately thereafter. The lengthy, intense defeat in *Baker* was too much for the eighty-year-old Frankfurter. Like many older public figures, he was shocked that what seemed to him to be eternal truths were being rejected as outmoded leftovers from an earlier and forgotten era. Less than two weeks after *Baker,* he suffered a stroke while working in his chambers, followed by a second, more serious one in the hospital. When Cox went to see his former mentor, Frankfurter, who could no longer speak clearly, "conveyed in substance the message that it had been *Baker v. Carr* that had been responsible" for his strokes.[50]

III

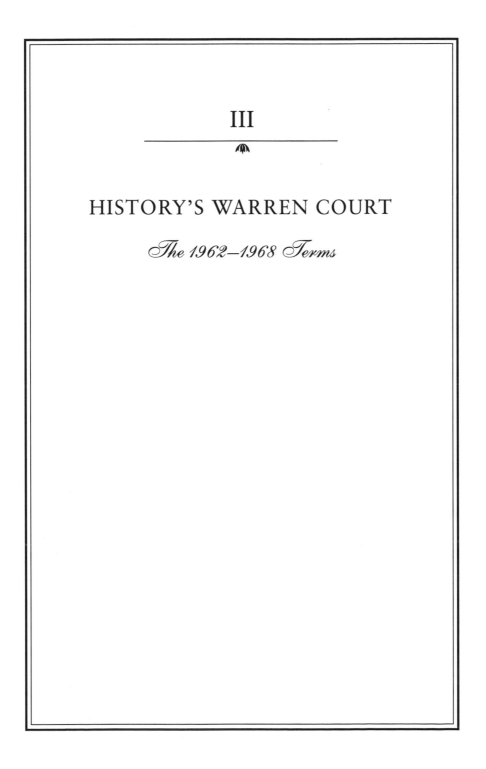

HISTORY'S WARREN COURT

The 1962–1968 Terms

The Fifth Vote

In the spring of 1962, two opinions in cases involving southern efforts to hamstring the NAACP were scheduled to come down 5–4 in favor of the states. In the spring of 1963, those two cases did come down 5–4 but instead in favor of the NAACP. In the interim, the Court's composition had changed, and, with the change, the Court the public currently identifies as "the Warren Court" came into being. Specifically, it came into being because Frankfurter spurned John Kennedy's entreaties about retirement and then suffered a debilitating stroke that forced his retirement and created the necessary one-vote swing.

In some senses, the Warren Court was an accident of history. It might have been Black, almost as old as Frankfurter, who suffered a stroke, for, indeed, Black's own heart problems commenced at this time. Or Douglas might have gotten his wish (never seriously considered by Kennedy) to become secretary of state. Or, for that matter, the horse that rolled over Douglas in 1950, breaking twenty-three of his ribs, might have killed him, thereby giving Truman another slot for one of his friends. With any of these possibilities, history's "Warren Court" would not have come into existence in the 1962 Term. On the other hand, heart attacks had killed two liberals, Wiley Rutledge and Frank Murphy, both in their fifties, in 1949. Had they lived, Warren himself would have been the "fifth vote" whenever he so chose. But, of course, none of this happened. Instead, Kennedy exercised two of what he assumed would be many appointments, and one of the two loyal New Frontiersmen he elevated provided the "fifth vote." Yet his own actions and statements show that the way he went about his decisions might well have failed to change the outcomes.

In late March 1962, after five painful years of being over his head, Whittaker announced his retirement. Within two weeks, Frankfurter had the strokes that caused him, in August, to leave the Court. Although he moved quickly, Kennedy did take the time to consult with Warren and Douglas about some of the handful of men under consideration. Both urged Kennedy to reject the initial front-runner, federal court of appeals judge William Hastie, an African-American, because he would be "just one more vote for Frankfurter."[1] Warren and Douglas were equally cool, for the same reason, on another potential nominee, Harvard Law Professor Paul Freund.

After a brief flirtation with Hastie and Freund, and worried about southern pressure from Richard Russell (who might have tried to extract true believers, as James Eastland had for the lower federal courts), Kennedy nominated Byron White, the man who had put together the able Kennedy Justice Department. Robert Kennedy was initially reluctant to lose White but switched when his ego was put on the line, that is, when the implication surfaced that he might not be able to run the Justice Department without White. "I'm not going to stand in Byron's way. I can run the Justice Department without Byron."[2]

Although "the best and the brightest" is now a pejorative label for the Kennedy-Johnson foreign policy advisers, it applies, without the pejorative, to Kennedy's domestic team as well—especially White, the ex-all-American halfback and Rhodes scholar, who not only led the National Football League in rushing but was at the top of his Yale Law School class, and the first ex-Supreme Court clerk to make it back to the Court with life tenure. White, who had met John Kennedy in both England and the navy, perfectly exemplified all that the New Frontier aspired to; indeed, Kennedy thought of him as "the ideal New Frontier judge."[3] He was confirmed, without a roll call, to universal acclaim.

White reflected the values of the postwar Yale Law School and the Kennedy Justice Department. He was pragmatic, always a realist, and believed in the beneficence of the federal government. Once on the Court, this translated into a preference for the national government, for equality when the states were parties, but, like the Kennedy Justice Department, showing little concern for claims of individual liberty. There was no coherent constitutional philosophy yielding those results because White had no interest in theory. He believed in "good" outcomes, and that was sufficient. His vote in constitutional cases never varied from his views on the merits of the underlying policy. What was good was constitutional; what was bad was not. White, as a justice, perfectly mirrored what White, as a senator, would have done had he been one (although he never wished to be one). Yet White's vote did not matter. He reinforced the already strong preference for equality, but the "tough on crime, tough on communism" line of the Kennedy administration was reflected in his inability to support the "liberal" criminal procedure or domestic-security claims being pressed on the Court.

The vote that did matter and the one that transformed the outcomes came from White's fellow New Frontiersman, Arthur J. Goldberg, Frankfurter's replacement. In the instant aftermath of the steel contract settlement and before Big Steel's double cross, Kennedy had seriously considered Goldberg for Whittaker's seat but did not want to lose such a valuable Cabinet member.

Before Frankfurter's strokes, when it nevertheless seemed that he was slipping, Kennedy asked Frankfurter's biographer Max Freedman to sound out the justice on retiring if he and Kennedy could agree on a suitable replacement. Because of the patriarch, Joseph Kennedy, Frankfurter wholly distrusted the administration. His response, in Kennedy's words, was that "I guess he decided he was indispensable to the Court."[4] Had Frankfurter taken the president's offer, Freund, whom Kennedy intended to appoint at some time anyway despite Warren's and Douglas's criticism, would have been the choice. Had that happened, the "fifth vote" would have waited at least until Clark retired (in 1967). But once Frankfurter suffered his strokes after the *Baker v. Carr* decision, the justice recognized, over the long summer, that he would have to leave the Court.

Because of the proximity of this appointment to that for Whittaker's seat, Kennedy knew his options. He also knew Frankfurter's was the Court's so-called "Jewish seat." He had been willing to have two Jews on the Court, but having none was not an attractive option for a Democratic president. Thus, when Frankfurter's seat opened up, Kennedy, knowing already that Goldberg wanted a seat on the Court, quickly rewarded him—although the president would have preferred Goldberg to turn down the opportunity and to remain in the Cabinet.

Goldberg told his wife prior to taking his seat that he intended to be an activist justice,[5] and he immediately settled in with Warren, Black, Douglas, and Brennan. His 89-percent liberal voting record during his brief tenure was the era's second highest (behind Douglas). Like the other four liberals, he had not been raised in middle-class comfort but through determination and ability rode the escalator of upward mobility in American society. As one of the intellectuals of the labor movement and supremely confident in his own abilities, Goldberg had always been enamored with, and strove for, the Swedish "middle way" as the sensible organization for an industrial democracy. He was able to translate his understandings, once a justice, into a robust view of rights, and during his brief tenure he maintained an untamed exuberance for constitutional claims of both liberty and equality. In so doing, he became the long-awaited fifth vote.

The five-vote bloc did not change in the slightest when, just three years later, Goldberg was replaced by Abe Fortas, another Jew who started at the bottom but moved upward through talent and determination. In each of his three years on the Court, Goldberg had voted with Warren between 85 to 89 percent of the time. During their four years together, Fortas and Warren agreed between 83 to 92 percent of the time. Likewise both had a percentage of agreement with the Court in the high 80s.

The replacement was triggered by Adlai Stevenson's sudden death in July 1965 and the resulting vacancy at the United Nations. Johnson wanted a "Kennedy liberal" at the United Nations to deflect any criticisms of the widening war in Vietnam. His initial call went to Harvard economist John Kenneth Galbraith, Kennedy's ambassador to India. Galbraith wanted no part of the job but, unwilling to turn the president down immediately, he instead suggested Goldberg, who was reputedly wishing for more action than the Court offered, for the post. The suggestion hit Johnson as sheer genius. He could offer Goldberg the United Nations and provide Fortas, his most trusted friend and adviser, with a reward matching his talents.

There were problems at both ends. Goldberg had to be moved out of a life-tenured job. Fortas had to be convinced to leave a practice he enjoyed into a job his wife, Washington tax attorney Carol Agger, was adamant against because it would necessitate a big pay cut and possibly a corresponding cut in their lavish lifestyle. Convincing Goldberg proved the easier of the two.

Anyone who knew Goldberg understood that, although he was highly intelligent, his ego dwarfed his brain. Johnson gave Goldberg the full treatment, promising him that he would be a principal adviser in all decisions leading to a Vietnam settlement. Johnson's biographer, Robert Dallek, reports that Johnson dangled the vice presidency in front of Goldberg. Goldberg's biographer, David Stebenne, says it was the chief justiceship, all part of a much larger plan that would bring peace to Vietnam and return him to the Court as chief justice when Warren retired. Whichever, Goldberg saw the trade as highly desirable; maybe it was delusional. Had Goldberg stayed, the liberal bloc would not have collapsed so quickly with Warren's retirement.

Fortas turned Johnson down and rejected entreaties from both Douglas and Goldberg to change his mind. Then on July 28, Johnson called Fortas to the White House, ostensibly to aid with drafting Johnson's statement announcing that 50,000 more troops were being sent to Vietnam and, for the first time, that the troops were actually to be engaged in ground combat. On the way to the press conference, Johnson told Fortas, "I'm sending all these boys to Vietnam, and they're giving their life for their country and you can do no less. If your president asks you to do something for your country, can you run out on him?" Years later Fortas recalled, "To the best of my knowledge, and belief, I never said yes."[6]

Fortas was a protégé of Douglas, first as a student, then as a young Yale faculty member, and then following Douglas to the New Deal. At the end of World War II, Fortas and two other New Dealers, Thurman Arnold and Paul Porter, moved into private practice in Washington to do good and well, and they did, building a great law firm with Fortas as managing partner. Fortas was known as a "lawyer's lawyer" because of his brilliance both as a strategist and an advocate. One of his earliest clients had been Johnson, in need of assistance because of a challenge to his victory in the 1948 Texas senatorial primary. Just like Goldberg, Fortas not only voted liberal but also did not have the slightest doubt about his own abilities or the efficacy of the Court acting as the engine of reform.

Fortas and White received unanimous Senate votes while Goldberg missed by one. How ironic it seems that Warren, Brennan, Goldberg, and Fortas, the appointments that were essential to the formation of the liberal bloc of the Warren Court, were so uncontroversial when nominated that but two dissenting votes, one by Joseph McCarthy against Brennan, the other by Strom Thurmond against Goldberg, were cast.

The four liberals had outlasted their critics and, furthermore, the liberals and their critics were on different political trajectories. By 1962 the critics were better understood as a disreputable and discredited lot. The segregationists could convince no one that they were correct, and Birmingham and then Selma would seal their fate. Time also had taken care of the domestic-security conservatives. Red-baiting had lost its political salience nationally, and those worrying about the Court's being soft on communism were a shriveling group often subsumed under one of two labels: "Bircher" or "right-wing nut." The South remained an exception; in unknowing homage to Occam's razor, southern politicians attacked civil rights leaders as communist-inspired.

These traditional opponents of the Court had gained some other allies, but they were not helpful in 1962. Conservative Protestants were unhappy over the decision banning school prayer, but they were as yet unorganized, small, and, in any event, clustered in the South. Police were unhappy but nowhere near as much as they would be in mid-decade. Finally, *Baker* had placed some political careers in jeopardy, but its victims were losers who would pass from the scene.

Even the American Bar Association was quiescent. The prior criticism of the Court that crossed political lines—the justices weren't really all that competent—faded. Its prime exponents had been those objecting to the results reached, especially *Brown*. As those who opposed the results generally were discredited, so was their critique. Claims of lack of competency passed from the political scene and were relegated to Frankfurter's acolytes in the legal academy.

Not only were the Court's critics vanquished and therefore the pressure from Congress removed, but the Court had finally found friends in high places. For different reasons, both Kennedy and Johnson were publicly supportive of the Court's controversial decisions and friendly with liberal justices, a reversion to the pre-steel seizure days. Thus, for the first time in years, the Court decided cases in a political climate in which there was no serious opposition to its decisions. Yet to leave this at a negative would miss the changed nature of the mid-1960s and the Warren Court's role therein. American policymaking in the 1960s was a heady experience, fueled with the confidence that had never tasted failure. The liberal-majority justices, like the Kennedy-Johnson foreign policy team, but with the justifications of age, experience, and knowledge the latter lacked, were supremely confident in their ability to fashion a better world. The best description of the period is that all three branches of government believed they were working harmoniously to tackle the nation's problems. It was simply a matter of determining which institution was best-suited to handle a specific problem, and each went forward in its own way knowing the others also were seeking complementary results.

When historian John Morton Blum described the decisions of the Warren Court in *Years of Discord,* he summarized the dominant legal view of the Court. According to this consensus, the Warren Court was implementing a theory of constitutional adjudication that Justice Harlan Fiske Stone had laid out in Footnote Four of a 1938 decision, *United States v. Carolene Products* (sustaining a regulation of filled milk).[7] According to Footnote Four, the Court should scrutinize carefully the electoral process to make it fair because, once a legislature is properly functioning, its legislation is entitled to a presumption of constitutionality and therefore is overwhelmingly likely to be constitutional. A Footnote Four Court would guarantee that impediments to majority rule are corrected and that citizens may fully discuss the public issues of the day so that they can accurately select and guide their representatives. Additionally, a Footnote Four Court must enforce the specific limitations on governmental power found in the Bill of Rights.

Unfortunately, even with a perfect electoral process, some groups may be shut out because of prejudice against their members. Footnote Four mentioned African-Americans and Jehovah's Witnesses in this regard and offered the phrase "discrete and insular minority" as a more general description of those who might find themselves as legislative targets. The theory of Footnote Four suggests that even if African-Americans in the South could vote, they could not win elections and might be subject to such prejudice that legislation hostile to them would be forthcoming. When that occurs, the Court must step in to protect the discrete and insular minority that otherwise lacks the normal means—joining electoral coalitions—that we expect to protect people.

Brown is a classic Footnote Four case. So is *Baker*. So, indeed, are a number of other Warren Court decisions (although quite clearly the domestic security cases are not), and it is no wonder that scholars have identified Footnote Four as the dominant feature of Warren Court jurisprudence.

A consensus is not always correct. There is an alternative and also plausible (if less complimentary) reading of the Warren Court decisions. Under this view, the Court was not worrying about constitutional theory but rather reaching results that conformed to the values that enjoyed significant national support in the mid-1960s, a period when Americans believed the nation was capable of anything. The Depression had been licked. World War II had been won. The two-decades-plus trans-Atlantic focus had significantly eroded. American resources and know-how seemed limitless. Like their counterparts in the New Frontier and the Great Society, the liberals on the Court had no doubts about their own abilities. They were the experts in understanding where American constitutional law needed to go to bring to Americans the rights that a free people deserved. The goal of government was to match America's ample resources with good and able men working together to solve society's problems and supply its needs.

One problem for a Footnote Four explanation is that the majority justices were not constitutional theorists. They were men of action, ready and willing to act. Furthermore, even though they coalesced as a majority, they had differing preferences and perceptions. Warren believed the Constitution mandated a just society, one where things were fair. Brennan, who would increasingly emerge as the key justice, eventually concluded that the Constitution was designed to promote human dignity. But this was years after Warren's retirement, and for the period of the Warren Court, he saw the Constitution pretty much like Goldberg. Fortas placed less emphasis on liberty and more on the ability of government to foster community.

Black and Douglas, who had served for a decade and a half before Warren arrived, had faced different issues and developed different responses. Unfortunately, Black had reached the end of his intellectual road and increasingly shoehorned new issues into older categories that he had developed in other circumstances. In the process, the robust individualism of his prior years waned. Douglas, both physically and intellectually restless, would shortly, with the Vietnam War, shift one more time to the left. Always the most individualistic of the justices, Douglas came to the ahistorical conclusion that the Constitution was designed to get government off the backs of the people.

Most of the issues coming to the Court allowed a merging of the views into a majority opinion, increasingly one by Brennan. But both because the justices were not interested in theory and because their preferences varied, it is difficult to speak of an overriding jurisprudence apart from the results reached.

Part III will allow the reader to choose between the conventional wisdom, often expressed by law professors and well described by Blum, and the less idealistic alternative that these were men with power happily exercising it to promote the values of what were, at least during the 1960s, the dominant national elites. Whether the driving force was Footnote Four or the imposition of national values on institutions needing upgrading, with the roadblocks finally cleared and the fifth vote finally secured, the Court was on its way.

Chapter 9

To the Civil Rights Act

Like Eisenhower during the summer before the Little Rock crisis, the Kennedys did not believe there could be a situation necessitating federal troops. As Robert Kennedy, who would be the administration's civil rights crisis-manager, stated: "I cannot conceive of this administration's letting such a situation deteriorate to that level."[1]

At the end of September 1962, after winning the inevitable court battle, James Meredith prepared to enroll as the first African-American at the University of Mississippi. Governor Ross Barnett had other ideas, and stated no school in Mississippi would be integrated while he was governor. "We will not drink from the cup of genocide."[2]

Violence looked likely as white extremists arrived at Ole Miss by the truckload. Among them was retired Army General Edwin A. Walker, the man who now regretted leading the 101st Airborne into Little Rock just five years earlier. Walker urged southerners to "Bring your flags, your tents, and your skillets! It is time! Now or never!"[3] The Kennedy administration moved federal marshals into Oxford and readied federal troops at Memphis.

Still holding to a policy of reasoning with Deep South politicians, the attorney general tried to negotiate a peaceful solution with Barnett and James Eastland. Kennedy believed that he had an agreement whereby Meredith would register and Barnett would be content to "just raise cain about it,"[4] with state troops keeping the crowds under control. Because of the assurances, Kennedy had limited the number of marshals. More, many more, were needed.

The night of September 30, a crowd that peaked at 3,000 began to throw bricks and Molotov cocktails at the marshals, injuring eight. The marshals defended themselves with tear gas. Then the state police withdrew, gun shots sounded, and the riot ensued in earnest leaving three dead, a couple of hundred injured, and the marshals all too soon running low on tear gas. With the marshals perhaps thinking of the Alamo, federal troops took endless hours, including an astonishing full hour to cover the last half-mile, to move the sixty-five miles from Memphis. But when they arrived, order was restored, and Meredith registered in the morning. Although he needed constant protection during the school year, he graduated in the spring.

The television pictures of rioting southerners provided a contrast to the measured approach of the Kennedy administration and gave it national approval. Martin Luther King, Jr., dissented; he thought President Kennedy, still unwilling to support a civil rights bill even as strong as the one Eisenhower backed in 1957, "lacked moral conviction."[5] King was on the money. The Kennedys "believed abstractly in the goal of better civil rights, but they felt no passionate attachment to the cause"[6] nor did they wish civil rights to interfere with the important objectives of the administration.

The new Alabama governor, George C. Wallace, felt the passion. In his inaugural speech in January 1963, he proclaimed "in the name of the greatest people that have ever trod this earth, I draw the line in the dust and toss the gauntlet before the feet of tyranny and I say . . . segregation now . . . segregation tomorrow . . . segregation forever."[7]

The NAACP Cases

A little over a week after the Battle of Ole Miss, the Court heard the reargument in the two cases involving southern attacks on the NAACP that had been restored to the calendar after Whittaker retired. The first of the two to come down was *NAACP v. Button,* dealing with Virginia's attempt to curtail the way the NAACP and the Legal Defense Fund handled litigation. Brennan wrote for the liberals and liberated the NAACP. Harlan dissented, joined by Clark and Stewart. White tried to split all the differences.

The Virginia Supreme Court of Appeals had struck down several laws but sustained the key provisions that regulated the soliciting of litigation by the NAACP, the financing by the NAACP of that litigation, and the control of the litigation, once begun, by the NAACP lawyers rather than the named plaintiff. The statutes reinforced standard rules of professional responsibility but, as applied to the NAACP, they would preclude the organization from controlling the timing and method of attack by litigation as the key part of its strategy of dismantling segregation.

All nine justices found a new First Amendment right to pursue redress by means of litigation. Brennan explained that "groups which find themselves unable to achieve their objectives through the ballot frequently turn to the courts [because] under the conditions of modern government litigation may well be the sole practicable avenue open to a minority to petition for redress of grievances." Harlan agreed that the First Amendment "must include the right to join together for the purposes of obtaining judicial redress."

Yet neither Brennan nor Harlan would hold that the NAACP's recruitment and control of civil rights litigation was the type of activity the state could not reach. Indeed, Harlan was certain the state could, while Brennan finessed the issue by claiming the Court could not tell exactly what Virginia would allow and what it would forbid. He asserted that Virginia had forbidden even the act of advising individuals of their rights and recommending an attorney—and implied it had done a lot more. Thus, the Court concluded that Virginia had done too much and that the NAACP, given southern feelings, would be well advised to steer clear of potential sanctions. But since "First Amendment freedoms need breathing space to survive, government may regulate in the area only with narrow specificity." Furthermore, government had to show a compelling state interest and it had none here. Fear of conflicts of interest seemed unfounded given the history of the NAACP and the fact that other lawyers did not wish to handle similar litigation.

Harlan's dissent came straight from his normal First Amendment stance: Interests must be balanced with a heavy hand placed on the state's side. Harlan believed that Brennan had been unfair to the Virginia Supreme Court of Appeals and that potential conflicts of interest were a sufficiently compelling reason for the state to regulate. Harlan's implicit premise was that the Court must be blind to the fact that the regulating state was Virginia, not Vermont. Under some circumstances neutrality might be correct, but it strains credulity to believe that in the Virginia of "Massive Resistance" the state was really concerned about protecting African-American litigants from the overbearing NAACP. Harlan's offer to the NAACP was one he rejected in the Connecticut contraceptive case, *Poe v. Ullman*—go about your business and come back here if and when you have a real complaint.

White stated that he would, like Harlan, uphold a narrowly drawn statute, and he would, like the majority, strike down this application against the NAACP. Where he differed from the majority was on the issue of any regulation of the NAACP's way of conducting its legal business. He would allow it but could not tell where the majority stood, probably because the majority, now finally in a position to protect the NAACP from southern actions, did not wish to take a stand on the issue that might encourage any southern hope that a further harassing of the NAACP might succeed.

The harder of the two NAACP cases was *Gibson v. Florida Legislative Investigating Committee*. After the litigation was pared down, Gibson had refused to bring the NAACP records to a legislative committee hearing to use when answering a question about whether or not a particular person, named as a communist, was also a member of the NAACP. Gibson would, however, answer the question to the best of his knowledge from memory. At one level it seems as if he was claiming, in Harlan's dissenting words, a right to provide "partial and inaccurate testimony." *Gibson* was unlike any of the prior communist-investigation cases where the dispute was over the invasion of privacy that disclosure of organizational affiliation would cause. The real issue in *Gibson* was an attack on the NAACP by indirection, via the claim that at least some NAACP members were communists. If the state could show that, then it could suggest there might be more communist members. Therefore, a full investigation of this communist-harboring organization would be necessary; such an investigation would bring the NAACP to a halt. First, it would tie up resources: time, energy, money. Second, it would result in a loss of members. Third, it would tarnish the image of the organization. The South could hardly ask for more.

The NAACP and Florida appeared to agree on the appropriate legal standard for deciding the case: whether there was a substantial relation between the information desired and an overriding and compelling state interest. With the legal standard agreed, Goldberg distinguished prior legislative-investigation cases; they concerned asking the witness about his own associations with the Communist Party. Given that the Party was so evil, the compelling interest was automatically established. But here, the state already claimed to know who the communists were. Florida was not investigating communists; rather, it was investigating a legitimate organization, and that made all the difference in the world—and in the result. Florida had no evidence of a relationship between the Communist Party and the NAACP and, lacking that, it had no compelling interest. There simply was no foundation for the questions to Gibson.

Douglas and Black joined Goldberg but also wrote separately to reemphasize their long-standing views. "Government is not only powerless to legislate with respect to membership in a lawful organization; it is also precluded from probing the intimacies of spiritual and intellectual relationships in the myriad of such societies and groups that exist in this country, regardless of the legislative purpose to be served. Government can intervene only when belief, thought or expression moves into the realm of action that is inimical to society."

Harlan's dissent for Clark, Stewart, and White began by stating that the "Court's reasoning is difficult to grasp." He was correct; Goldberg's opinion was looking for a way to protect the NAACP without having to overrule all the legislative-investigation cases. Harlan did not believe that the prior cases, many of which he had authored, were based on a distinction between "Communist infiltration *of* organizations and Communist activity *by* organizations." He claimed that *Gibson* did not "really present any serious question of interference with freedom of association." What Harlan did not see was that it represented a threat to the NAACP, and this was reason in itself for the result because there was no reason to believe that Florida, any more than Virginia in *Button*, was trying to be helpful.

White's separate dissent focused so thoroughly on the communist side that he lost sight of the NAACP. Thus, he professed bewilderment why the NAACP, instead of fighting Florida, was not embracing the state's efforts. The decision "insulated from effective legislative inquiry the time-proven skills" of the Communist Party in taking over an innocent organization. Thus, until the Party is successful, the majority denies the legislature the facts necessary and "records another victory for the Communist Party."

Gibson, like *Button*, had easily adopted the compelling state interest test rather than the straight "balancing" test favored by Frankfurter and Harlan. In so doing, they reflected Brennan's preferred approach of conceding the legitimacy of the state objective but finding that the reasons for invading a right were insufficient on the facts. Furthermore, *Gibson*, like *Button*, introduced a new phrase into First Amendment adjudication. *Button* marked the first time the Court had stated that the First Amendment needed "breathing space." For its part, *Gibson* introduced the phrase "'chilling' effect." The two are complementary concepts dealing with the fear that individuals may have of prosecution and therefore the likelihood that they will shy away from activity that might result in criminal sanction. This is the "chilling effect" (which after *Gibson* lost the single quotation marks around chilling). The "breathing space" is the necessity that the law be narrowly confined to avoid the chilling effect.

Mass Demonstrations

First Amendment doctrine had developed with the paradigm of the lone dissenter protesting government activity. When the dissenter combined with others, the degree of protected freedom seemed to shrink, and when the others were communists, to vanish. The civil rights demonstrations of the 1960s put the lone dissenter to a test, for the key to the demonstrations was numbers. The more demonstrators, the more publicity, and the more publicity, the more chance to prick the northern conscience. The lessons of 1961 and 1962 were that southerners were not troubled by segregation (or by some violence), but northerners, who would otherwise not be overly concerned about a distant local custom, did not like to see what was necessary to sustain segregation. Laurie Pritchett, the sheriff of Albany, Georgia, figured this out. Thus, he took care to order nonviolent arrests, which had little effect on the North, but as bail money and bodies became scarce, dispirited King and other leaders. The Court's prior cases reflected, albeit imperfectly, the idea that the bigger the crowd, the more likely disorder would break out. Yet, from the perspective of King and others, that was not necessarily bad so long as northerners watched.

Edwards v. South Carolina was the first mass-demonstration civil rights case decided by the Court. One hundred and eighty-seven high school and college students, after protesting at the state capitol, were convicted for disturbing the peace. They picketed the capitol building when the legislature was in session "to protest our dissatisfaction with the present condition of discriminatory actions against Negroes." The African-Americans carried placards announcing "I am proud to be a Negro" and "Down with segregation." There were about thirty law enforcement officers at the capitol, and a curious crowd of about 200–300 onlookers collected over the next half hour plus. The onlookers, like the demonstrators, were peaceful.

After forty-five minutes the police told the demonstrators that they would be arrested if they did not disperse within fifteen minutes. The demonstrators were, in the city manager's testimony, "boisterous," "loud," and "flamboyant." What he meant was that the demonstrators had the élan to sing "The Star Spangled Banner" and other patriotic and religious songs. At the end of the fifteen minutes, they were arrested.

Stewart's opinion had no difficulty reversing the convictions. What the African-Americans were doing was exercising First Amendment rights "in their most pristine and classic form." This was a stunning conclusion, given the lone dissenter paradigm. The Court asserted its right to review the facts *de novo*—that is, for itself, as new—to ensure that First Amendment rights were not accidentally (or intentionally) lost to mistaken fact-finding. The Court's review showed that the onlookers were not threatening and there were no traffic or pedestrian problems; therefore, there was no reason to have ordered a halt to the demonstration.

Only Clark dissented. "It is my belief that anyone conversant with the almost spontaneous combustion in some Southern communities in such a situation will agree that the City Manager's action may well have averted a major catastrophe." In other words, because whites could break into violence at any time, African-Americans should not exercise their First Amendment rights since that might upset the whites. Clark's position, which the Court seemed to have adopted in *Feiner v. New York* (1951), is an unattractive, open invitation for a hostile audience to prevent, by threats of violence, peaceful demonstrations of views with which they disagree. The majority was wisely rejecting a doctrine that would instantly have put a legal (but not an actual) end to civil rights demonstrations in the South.

Ironically, one of the dissenters in *Feiner* had been Black, and yet he was moving toward Clark. Black felt that mass demonstrations ran the risk of violence, and he unknowingly agreed with Thurgood Marshall's conclusion about direct action, that it deflected action from the courts, the "route by which the only lasting civil rights will come."[8] The mass demonstrations combined with the sit-ins had finally pushed him past his First Amendment breaking point, and in the future his vote would be opposed to the demonstrators unless some discriminatory facet of state law was present.

Birmingham

King was determined to force the civil rights issue in 1963 and, with thorough preparation, he picked Birmingham as his target. It was perfect. In all of downtown Birmingham there was no general restaurant where African-Americans could sit and eat and no public restrooms to use. If it was not the most systematically segregated city in the South, it was close enough. When ordered to integrate parks and swimming pools, it had closed them instead. Furthermore, Birmingham had the notorious "Bull" Connor as its public safety commissioner, and it was the dynamite capital of America. In 1961 Connor had allowed the Klan fifteen free minutes to bloody the "Freedom Riders," "until it looks like a bulldog got a hold of them,"[9] and King expected Connor to overreact big-time. If all worked to plan, Connor would place Birmingham on national television, and this would force the North to pressure the Kennedys to do something.

The stated goal of the Birmingham campaign—"Project C" for confrontation—was to desegregate downtown businesses and obtain promises to hire African-American clerks. Both the mayor and the Kennedy administration unsuccessfully urged King to call the whole thing off before it started. Two days before the scheduled kickoff Good Friday march, a state judge used a flagrantly unconstitutional city ordinance to grant an ex parte injunction against King and others, forbidding them from marching without Connor's permission. The symbolism of Good Friday was too good to pass up; rather than file a useless appeal to an Alabama appellate court or to postpone the march, King defied the injunction. As a result, he was immediately held in contempt of court and spent a week in jail, where he penned his classic nonviolent creed in "Letter from a Birmingham Jail" with its pointed reminder that "wait" meant "never." Yet, after he was out, mass demonstrations met with mass arrests and threatened to deplete King's dwindling supply of volunteers. Furthermore, King himself, still under the court order, could not join in the marches. As Taylor Branch notes, "Birmingham's white leadership grew more confident that its united noninflammatory toughness was subduing the Negro protest."[10]

Facing defeat as he had in Albany the previous year, King unleashed a new tactic, his children's crusade. King persuaded a thousand school children, right down to the age of six (the Baptist age for a church commitment), to skip school and march on May 2. "Singing, laughing, praying, the children climbed without resistance" into police vans and off to jail.[11] King rejected the argument that he was endangering them with the statement that the children had a "sense of their own stake in freedom" and a right to influence their own futures.[12]

On May 3, King had hundreds more ready to go, and Birmingham's jails were already bulging. Bull Connor was finally ready to play his assigned part in prime time.

The children were met with fire hoses on the assumption that a solid dousing would keep them at the Sixteenth Street Baptist Church, but when that did not stop them, the fire department shifted to special high-pressure hoses designed for long-range firefighting. These could knock bricks loose from mortar or strip bark off a tree at 100 feet or, as it happened, roll a child down the middle of the street. The hoses "made limbs jerk weightlessly and tumbled whole bodies like scraps of refuse in a high wind."[13] Other children met Birmingham's K-9 units, and an Associated Press photographer captured the first of the decade's legendary still images, one that the president said made him sick: "a white policeman in dark sunglasses grasping a Negro boy by the front of his shirt as his other hand gave just enough slack in the leash for the dog to spring upward and bury his teeth in the boy's abdomen."[14] Like horrifying summer reruns, the pictures went on day after day with police violence met occasionally with African-American violence as well. Finally, after white bombings in the African-American community, including the residence where King was supposedly staying, and a riot, quiet, if not peace, returned.

David Vann, a lawyer who negotiated the surrender for the white business community, stated that "in marching one block the demonstrators could get enough news film to fill all the newscasts of all the television stations in the United States."[15] Birmingham not only filled the still-fifteen-minute national news, it was also often carried live, and millions of Americans watched, stunned and outraged, wondering if the pictures could actually be coming from a part of the United States. The children's crusade focused the *New York Times* on race; during the first two weeks of May, the *Times* published more stories about race than it had during the previous year.

The Civil Rights Bill and the March on Washington

When Governor George Wallace tried to imitate Ross Barnett and bar African-Americans from the University of Alabama, the Kennedy administration vigorously intervened, and Wallace backed down. President Kennedy used the occasion to take to the airwaves and discuss civil rights with a ready nation. Birmingham had caused Kennedy to find his eloquence, and he stated that in America it ought to be possible "for American students of any color to attend any public institution without having to be backed up by troops. It ought to be possible for American consumers of any color to receive equal service in places of public accommodation, such as hotels and restaurants and theaters and retail stores, without being forced to resort to demonstrations on the street, and it ought to be possible for American citizens of any color to register and to vote in a free election without interference or fear of reprisal. . . . In short, every American ought to have the right to be treated, as one would wish his children to be treated. But this is not the case."[16] The Justice Department was already drafting a strong civil rights bill, and Kennedy promised he would send it to Congress.

That night, Medgar Evers, an NAACP organizer in Mississippi who had been working late, was shot in the back by a high-powered rifle as he stepped out of his car at his Jackson home. He died en route to the hospital. The assassination came at the midpoint of a ten-week period where civil rights demonstrations in 186 cities produced almost 15,000 arrests.

A week after his speech, Kennedy's civil rights bill arrived on Capitol Hill, with his urging that it be passed "not merely for reasons of economic efficiency, world diplomacy and domestic tranquillity—but above all because it is right."[17] It required desegregation of all places of public accommodation, authorized the Justice Department to initiate suits for school desegregation, and gave the executive power to withhold federal funds from facilities where discrimination occurred. This was a real bill. First, it would demand of everyone what the Birmingham demonstrators had risked so much to achieve in that city. Second, it would substitute the resources of the United States for those of the NAACP in school desegregation and would not require brave plaintiffs to come forward and place their names before the public. Finally, if money talks to segregationists, then some school districts would voluntarily initiate desegregation upon receiving a threat to eliminate federal funding. It was more than a real bill. Short of including voting—as Kennedy's speech had—it was a bill that might signal the end of the southern way of life.

There is no doubt that Birmingham was the catalyst for the Civil Rights Act of 1964. Had not the North seen the white South so vividly, a strong civil rights bill would have waited in the womb of time. According to a Gallup survey in April 1963, immediately before Birmingham, when asked what was the most important problem facing the country, about 5 percent of the respondents named civil rights. By July, over 50 percent of the respondents would name civil rights. Burke Marshall, head of the Civil Rights Division, stated that "the Negro and his problems were still pretty much invisible to the country until mass demonstrations of the Birmingham type."[18] *Brown v. Board of Education* had brought out the worst in the American South, and King had learned how to reflect that southern behavior to the American North to bring out the best in the country.

For many liberals, that best was on display in the March on Washington on August 28, 1963, when a quarter million Americans, between a third and a fifth of them white, listened to gospel singers and folk singers and to many speeches, the most memorable of which by far was King's. When he seemed about ready to sit down, Mahalia Jackson came out from behind him and called out, "Tell them about your dream, Martin! Tell them about your dream!"[19] In so doing and in bringing many of the crowd to tears, he demonstrated why he was the most powerful orator of his time.

Liberals fell in love with the March on Washington. "News outlets gushed over scenes of harmony—'White legs and Negro legs dangle together in the reflecting pool.'"[20] It helped move civil rights as the nation's principal issue even higher in the Gallup Poll. But it left some African-American activists unhappy about the administration's constant efforts to tone down the demonstration. And it did not change Kennedy's view that his tax bill was the administration's number-one domestic priority.

Sit-Ins Again

The sit-in cases of 1963 and 1964 presented the same clash of ultimate issues as their predecessors. The African-American defendants claimed a constitutional right to sit in; the owners of the targeted establishments claimed a right to exclude whomsoever they chose. The only variables were the state law used to convict and the background state laws, if any.

As with *Garner v. Louisiana* the previous term, the Court avoided addressing the underlying issues in the five principal cases decided in the spring of 1963 in the immediate aftermath of King's Birmingham victory. With only Harlan breaking ranks, Warren found something about state law or executive action in each of the cases that allowed the Court to conclude that the action of the property owners was really not theirs but rather mandated by law. These cases were apt predictors of the future as they showed that the Court intended to free the demonstrators if it possibly could.

One, *Lombard v. Louisiana,* provided a different window to the future in a concurring opinion by Douglas. Drawing on but not citing his dissent in *Poe v. Ullman,* he wrote that "[i]f this were an intrusion of a man's home or yard or farm or garden, the property owner could seek and obtain the aid of the state against the intruder. For the Bill of Rights . . . casts its weight on the side of privacy of homes. . . . But a restaurant, like the other departments of this retail store where Negroes were served, though private property within the protection of the Fifth Amendment, has no aura of constitutionally protected privacy about it." Under Douglas's view, a business simply could not ask for the help of law in backing up a racially discriminatory policy—period.

The 1963 Term had fourteen sit-in cases, nine of which were disposed of summarily. The two that looked the most significant, *Robinson v. Florida* and *Bell v. Maryland,* were argued in October 1963. They lacked the technicalities on which the Court had previously relied, and the justices therefore voted on the merits of the constitutional right to sit in.

Despite Brennan's plea at the Conference to reverse the convictions lest the Court accidentally derail the civil rights bill, Black, Clark, Harlan, Stewart, and White voted to affirm the convictions. In moving to join the more conservative justices, Black was quite clear that either the state or federal government could mandate that restaurants serve everyone, but if the law was neutral, then the property owner prevailed. The Fourteenth Amendment "does not destroy what has until very recently been universally recognized in this country as the unchallenged right of a man who owns a business to run the business in his own way so long as some valid regulatory statute does not tell him to do otherwise." He saw the situation in terms of his father's store in Ashland, Alabama, and related that he believed "Pappy" would have the right to decide whom he was going to serve in the store.

Douglas, who had been inseparable from Black in the earlier periods, was now his opposite, and he was hardly interested or impressed with Black's childhood or his father's store because they were irrelevant to the issues before the Court. Douglas had no tolerance for the idea that S. H. Kress or Woolworth's or McCrory's was a mom-and-pop store where ownership and management merged. "The corporation that owns this restaurant did not refuse service to these Negroes because 'it' did not like Negroes. The reason 'it' refused service was because 'it' thought 'it' could make more money by running a segregated restaurant." Distinguishing a business from a home as he had in *Lombard,* Douglas concluded that when the state allowed a person to operate a business via a charter, it had the duty to require nondiscrimination. Goldberg agreed, and Warren and Brennan were willing to go along. But Brennan really wanted a reversal of the convictions, and he could care less about the theory used to reverse. Why an affirmance of the convictions would have hurt rather than helped (or left unchanged) the chances for passage of the civil rights bill is unclear. Possibly Brennan feared the unknown as more dangerous than the known, and since the Court had yet to affirm any convictions of African-American demonstrators anywhere in the South, the consequences of an affirmance were necessarily unknown.

Phase one of Brennan's effort to head off his opposition came a month after argument, when the Court asked the solicitor general to submit a supplemental brief on the broader constitutional questions in the cases. Archibald Cox was given thirty days to file the brief, but he then requested and received thirty more. The new brief turned up a Florida statute requiring segregated toilets and that was enough for the Court to get rid of *Robinson* on the usual technicality. But *Bell* remained 5–4, and

Black finished his opinion in mid-March. He informed the Conference that the Court owed it to the country to decide the cases quickly. Given how the Court was going to decide the cases, Brennan could not have disagreed more, and he indicated he would do his utmost to delay the cases. As Black's wife wrote in her diary, the dissenters feared "Hugo's enormous prestige would work adversely to the bill's passage."[21]

Phase two was writing the dissents. Warren, Douglas, and Goldberg did so on the merits, while Brennan searched for a vote to flip the result. Much like Frankfurter in *Poe v. Ullman*, he concocted a reason to avoid the merits. He argued that the case should be sent back to the Maryland courts for them to consider the effect of a Baltimore ordinance and a state law each prohibiting discrimination in Baltimore restaurants. Both laws had been adopted after the Maryland court of appeals had affirmed Bell's conviction. Brennan successfully blocked Black's opinion from coming down, as Black wished and expected by early May, by demanding more time to answer new editing in Black's opinion.

Normally an intervening state law, at best, would cause the Court to vacate rather than reverse convictions, but Brennan wanted a reversal, and he convinced Clark, in Black's words, "to desert."[22] Eventually, Stewart followed suit. After a month of internal wrangling, some of which was tense, the convictions were reversed on intervening-laws grounds even though six justices continued to argue (and so wrote) that the cases should be decided on the merits.

Bell v. Maryland, with 120 pages of the *United States Reports* occupied by the opinions, was announced three days after the Senate passed the Civil Rights Act of 1964. Brennan had won because he had refused to lose; *Bell* did not derail Congress; and sit-ins as a legal issue was behind the Court because henceforth there was a federal statutory prohibition against discrimination in places of public accommodation.

Marshall's initial observation about the sit-ins, that they presented an extraordinarily difficult legal issue, one which could well go against the African-Americans, proved true. As *Bell*'s internal deliberations showed, had the Court ever reached the merits, the demonstrators would have lost instead of won. That they did not is largely the result of Brennan's abilities and his doggedness.

School Desegregation

Beginning in 1963 the Court returned to school desegregation after an almost five-year voluntary absence, and it began to exhibit impatience publicly with the lack of results. *Watson v. Memphis*, even though a case involving the city's parks and not its schools, was the entering wedge. Memphis had taken the position that opening its parks to all races had to be accomplished slowly and carefully, just as *Brown II* seemingly suggested. Amazingly, both lower federal courts agreed with that position.

Goldberg's unanimous opinion made clear that only schools could take the benefit of *Brown II* and that every other facility was required to desegregate now. "The second *Brown* decision is but a narrowly drawn, and carefully limited, qualification upon usual precepts of constitutional adjudication and is not to be unnecessarily expanded in application." Furthermore, the Court questioned the continued applicability of *Brown II* as a justification for delay. "Given the extended time which has elapsed, it is far from clear that the mandate of the second *Brown* decision requiring that desegregation proceed with 'all deliberate speed' would today be fully satisfied by the types of plans or programs for desegregation which eight years ago might have been sufficient."

That sentence presaged *Goss v. Board of Education*, which a week later set aside a transfer plan that allowed students who were in the racial minority in a school to transfer to a school where they would be in the racial majority (but not vice versa). The transfer policy could have no other effect except to "perpetuate racial segregation." That was it; "all deliberate speed" was no longer a good excuse. Clark wrote that "now . . . nine years after the first *Brown* decision the context in which we must interpret and apply the second *Brown* decision has been significantly altered." Those were nice words, but *Goss* was a Tennessee case; in the Deep South, schools remained 100 percent segregated just as they always had.

Interestingly, a companion case to *Goss*, *McNeese v. Board of Education*, did speak to the South. *McNeese* was of interest because it was an Illinois case, where African-American students were claiming they were being illegally segregated within a school. The lower courts held that the case should be dismissed without a hearing because the plaintiffs had not yet exhausted state administrative remedies. *McNeese* thus offered a northern opportunity to deal with the exhaustion issue that predominated in southern pupil-placement laws. Douglas wrote an opinion holding that exhaustion of administrative remedies was not a federal requirement in suits brought under §1983 of the Ku Klux Klan Act of 1871. Since §1983 was the foundation of all desegregation suits, this meant that exhaustion was not necessary in the South even though Douglas never mentioned the fact. (In 1961 Douglas had written *Monroe v. Pape*, holding that §1983 created a damage action against state and local officials, but not their employers, for violations of constitutional rights. *Monroe,* so important for the past three decades, remained an obscure case until after the Warren era.)

In 1964 the Court decided again one of the original *Brown* cases, *Griffin v. Prince Edward County.* Ten years later, there were no African-Americans in public schools with whites because there were no public schools. Like the rest of the state, Prince Edward County, in rural south-central Virginia, had closed its public schools as part of massive resistance. Unlike every other county, however, Prince Edward did not reopen them when massive resistance collapsed. A private school system for whites had been established, complete with many of the teachers from the now-closed public schools. State and county tuition grants were available for any child, white or African-American, attending a private school. There was no private school for African-Americans because their leadership made the decision that they must battle for reinstitution of the public schools. Hence, the tuition grants benefited whites alone. James J. Kilpatrick was so enthusiastic about the Prince Edward solution that he donated eighty books to the library of the private school. With a school available for the white children of the area, the County Board of Supervisors stopped levying the taxes for public schools. An overly sympathetic federal judge found there was no need to do anything about the situation.

Black's impatient opinion completed *Goss*'s thought: "[T]he time for mere 'deliberate speed' has run out." The duty of the federal court was to see that African-Americans got a public education. The easy part of the order told the district court to enjoin the tuition grants. The more significant part came in authorizing the district court "if necessary to prevent further racial discrimination, to require the Supervisors to exercise the power that is theirs to levy taxes to raise funds adequate to reopen, operate, and maintain without racial discrimination a public school system." Ordering taxes was a whopper. Black cited no authority for the proposition that a federal court could order state officials to levy taxes. He could have found relevant authority in the late nineteenth century, but there was none in the twentieth. The tone of *Griffin* matched its result. The Court was serious.

All the justices agreed that what Prince Edward County had done was unconstitutional. But Clark and Harlan broke ranks for the first time in a school desegregation case. In a one-sentence statement they joined Black's opinion except on the ability to order public officials to levy a tax.

The Civil Rights Act

The momentum toward a civil rights bill began with the violence in Birmingham and yet needed more violence to advance. Hubert Humphrey sadly concluded that the March on Washington had not added a single vote for the bill. Then on September 15, 1963, Birmingham came back to the headlines. A huge bomb at the Sixteenth Street Baptist Church, headquarters of the civil rights movement there, killed four girls and injured twenty other children. The massive stone and brick construction of the church prevented a slaughter of worshipers. African-Americans rioted and the police responded with guns and tanks, killing two children. Still, the civil rights bill remained bottled up with the prospects of a killing filibuster in the Senate should the bottle open. According to liberal activist Joseph Rauh, the civil rights bill "was absolutely bogged down."[23]

Then, in the aftermath of Dallas, President Lyndon Johnson, speaking to a joint session of the mourning Congress, stated that "no memorial oration or eulogy could more eloquently honor President Kennedy's memory than the earliest possible passage of the Civil Rights Bill for which he fought so long. We have talked long enough in this country about equal rights. It is time now to write the next chapter—and to write it in the books of law."[24] Unlike his ironic and detached predecessor, Johnson had moral conviction. He knew what racial discrimination was, and he intended to do something about it now.

On February 10, 1964, the Civil Rights Act passed the House of Representatives by the overwhelming bipartisan margin of 290–130, 104 of the dissenters being southern Democrats, who fully understood that this bill was aimed directly at the white South. There had been only one substantive amendment to the bill. Rules Committee Chairman Howard Smith, an ardent foe, tried to make the bill unpalatable by extending its employment antidiscrimination principles to women as well as African-Americans. A Georgia representative "gallantly observed that no Southern gentleman could vote to leave women deprived of employment rights guaranteed to Negroes."[25] Judiciary Committee Chairman Emanuel Celler, who was managing the bill along with Ohio's William H. McCulloch, the ranking Republican on the committee, was ready to oppose Smith, but nine of the ten women members of the House rushed to support Smith. In the words of Republican Representative Katharine St. George of New York: "We are entitled to this little crumb of equality."[26] (Democrat Edith Green of Oregon was the dissenter. She felt gender discrimination imposed nowhere near the humiliation and disabilities of racial discrimination.)

No one expected the Senate to be easy. Southerners, led by Richard Russell, would filibuster the bill to death if they could because to fail against the strong bill meant its passage without their having any opportunity to water it down. Under the then-existing Senate rules, they held an enormous advantage since a cloture vote needed a two-thirds majority. Beginning in 1938, Russell had led eleven filibusters against civil rights bills, and he was batting one thousand.

To prevail, Johnson needed the support of a majority of the thirty-two Republicans in the Senate and specifically that of Minority Leader Everett M. Dirksen of Illinois. A normal way to gain support is to compromise, but Johnson felt he could not. There was a "fit between his personal needs and his political needs."[27] Kennedy's base had been with northern liberals; Johnson's base was in the South. To be successful, Johnson had to transcend that base. "I had to produce a civil rights bill that was even stronger than the one they'd gotten if Kennedy had lived. Without this I'd be dead before I could ever begin."[28] Accordingly, he spent many a night drinking and swapping stories with his old colleague Dirksen and offering him "favors which ranged from personal notes to federal projects, from photographs to judgeships."[29] So did Humphrey, the Democratic floor leader for the bill. "I courted Dirksen almost as persistently as I did my wife."[30]

The filibuster was the longest on record, eighty-two days, and takes up 63,000 pages of the *Congressional Record*. Russell deployed his troops into three platoons of six each, using a fresh platoon each day. "They talked on and on—about the 'amalgamation and mongrelization of the races,' the source of grits that people in Minnesota eat, the living habits of Hungarian immigrants, sometimes about the bill itself, calling it, to use the phrase of Senator Russell Long, 'a mixed breed of unconstitutionality and the NAACP.'"[31] They did not talk about the fact that there were more hotels and motels in the South that would accept animals than there were that would take African-Americans. But Humphrey did.

Eventually Dirksen gained some minor compromises and brought the Republicans to the cloture vote, which prevailed 71–29. Twelve days later the final tally was 73–27. Twenty-one of the dissenters were southern Democrats; they were joined by five Republicans, one of whom was Arizona's Barry Goldwater, soon to be the Republican presidential nominee.

What a difference a decade made. Instead of being isolated, the Court was being backed by virtually every nonsouthern politician in the United States. The principle of equality in *Brown* and subsequent cases was not only the law as declared by nine men, it was also the law as adopted by 70-percent votes in both houses of Congress and enthusiastically signed by the president of the United States. Furthermore, on the issues it covered, the Civil Rights Act was more potent than the Constitution, for enforcement would no longer be limited to private plaintiffs and federal judges in the South. The entire weight of the federal government was available to make equal opportunities a reality. The Supreme Court has often been told it blew it—*Dred Scott,* the invalidation of the income tax in 1895, the New Deal crisis—but never in American history has the Court been told it was so right. Indeed, Dirksen's quoting of Victor Hugo in explaining his behavior to the *New York Times* underscored the Court's steadfastness: "[N]o army can withstand the strength of an idea whose time has come."[32]

Southern senators knew they had been defeated, just as Johnson had told Russell would happen. After years of decrying *Brown,* they offered a different tune. Allen Ellender, J. William Fulbright, and Russell all acknowledged that the Civil Rights Act was the law of the land and, in Russell's words, "as long as it is there it must be obeyed."[33]

The Constitutional Question

Goldwater and the southern Democrats, in increasingly strident language, had argued that the Civil Rights Act was unconstitutional. They believed that it exceeded federal powers and thereby invaded the reserved rights of the states and that requiring private businesses to open their doors to unwelcome customers took away the right to control property. In 1875 Congress had passed a public-accommodations provision. In the *Civil Rights Cases,* decided in the aftermath of Reconstruction, the Court had held it unconstitutional, as exceeding congressional power to enforce the Fourteenth Amendment. That old case, the southerners claimed, was still good law.

Constitutional challenges to the Civil Rights Act of 1964 were commenced immediately in Atlanta and Birmingham. The former involved a large motel readily accessible to two interstate highways and catering to an interstate clientele. The Justice Department welcomed the challenge and prevailed before a special three-judge district court. The Birmingham case involved Ollie's Barbeque, a family-owned restaurant situated on a state highway eleven blocks from the interstate. To the best of Ollie

McClung's knowledge, interstate travelers did not come to his restaurant. The Justice Department had never heard of Ollie's and didn't like the facts at all, so it tried to get the case dismissed by the three-judge district court. The court wouldn't do it and proceeded to hold the Civil Rights Act unconstitutional.

Both *Heart of Atlanta Motel v. United States* and *Katzenbach v. McClung* were argued October 5, the Court's first day of the new term, just three months after the president had signed the law. Not since the *Steel Seizure Case* had a case gotten to the Court so fast. Nine weeks after argument, the Civil Rights Act of 1964 was unanimously upheld.

There never was any doubt about *Heart of Atlanta*. The Civil Rights Act of 1875 had rested on congressional power under the Thirteenth and Fourteenth Amendments, invoking in the former the eradication of slavery, in the latter equal protection of the laws, though to no avail. The constitutional issue in the *Civil Rights Cases* ultimately turned on whether Congress could reach "private," nonstate actors in its enforcement capacity. The 1964 Act, instead, rested squarely on Congress's power to reach private actors as part of the regulation of interstate commerce. Thus, the *Civil Rights Cases*, in theory at least, could be distinguished without difficulty.

The congressional record reflected ample testimony showing the difficulty, if not outright impossibility, of African-American travelers finding places to eat or spend the night, thereby creating a deleterious effect on interstate commerce. At this point, the constitutional debate was over. Clark's opinion noted that Congress had plenary power to remove obstructions on commerce. That it did so because it believed that racial discrimination was morally wrong was irrelevant.

McClung presented by far the more difficult case, and Solicitor General Archibald Cox tried to get the Court to duck by arguing that a statute may not be enjoined on constitutional grounds when that claim can be raised as a defense in enforcement proceedings should they occur. He immediately ran into hostile questioning that revealed a desire by the justices to reach the merits.

The relevant public-accommodations provision of the act covered Ollie's under two circumstances, (1) if it served interstate travelers or (2) if "a substantial portion of the food which it serves has moved in interstate commerce." Ollie's purchased about $150,000 of food annually, $69,683 of which was meat that came from out of state. That was substantial enough to be covered by the act, so the issue was whether congressional power could reach Ollie's. If it could, it was hard to see what wouldn't be reached. The justices wanted to settle this once and for all; in sustaining the act as to Ollie, the Court was necessarily sustaining it, practically speaking, for everyone else as well.

The de minimus nature of Ollie's business was hardly a hindrance. When the Court held in 1942 in *Wickard v. Filburn* that federal power to regulate interstate commerce could reach homegrown wheat used to feed homegrown cows, the Court had functionally announced that Congress could reach anything, and Ollie's was encompassed under anything. Still, some might ask, what was the relationship between refusing to serve African-Americans and food traveling in interstate commerce? Clark said that because restaurants discriminated, African-Americans ate out less, and that behavior depressed the amount of food shipped interstate. "The fewer customers a restaurant enjoys the less food it sells and consequently the less it buys." Clark's conclusion would be accurate only if African-Americans did not eat unless they ate out or restaurants were more prone than grocery stores to have out-of-state products. A far better assumption is that the African-Americans who were refused service at Ollie's would nevertheless eat a meal elsewhere that night, most likely at home, and may well have bought food that had traveled in interstate commerce from the grocery store.

Despite Clark's newfangled sociological assumptions, the result in *McClung* can be justified. At one point, Clark did note that the Senate discussed the unwillingness of businesses to relocate to areas that practiced discrimination. That would be the necessary relationship between discrimination and commerce. Clark also could have, but did not, note that allowing local businesses to discriminate while forbidding those serving interstate customers to do so might give local businesses a competitive advantage in the local white trade, and Congress has the power to mandate a level playing field. Either of these rationales would have brought the result well within prior doctrine.

Clark's opinion had all nine justices, but Douglas and Goldberg wrote separately to state they would have sustained the Civil Rights Act as well under Congress's power to enforce the Fourteenth Amendment. Black too wrote a concurring opinion that noted it was unnecessary to discuss the Fourteenth Amendment issue because Congress's commerce power was clear. "It requires no novel or strained interpretation of the Commerce Clause to sustain the Act as applied in either of these cases." That might have come as a surprise to those who did not know Farmer Filburn, but Black was right.

In closing this brief era with an exclamation mark, the Court also decided its last sit-in case, *Hamm v. Rock Hill,* on the same day as *Heart of Atlanta* and *McClung.* Like *Bell v. Maryland,* there was no local ordinance that required the store to refuse service at its lunch counter. But unlike *Bell,* there was no new state law that the Court could latch on to suggest the case be reversed on that ground. So the Court latched on to the Civil Rights Act itself. First, Clark concluded the act should be construed to wipe out convictions still pending in the courts. Second, Clark held that since Congress had the acknowledged power to wipe out federal convictions, it could do the same with state convictions. The Supremacy Clause and all that.

Hamm's conclusion was a double stretch. First, there wasn't the slightest hint that Congress had even thought of the problem. Black, Harlan, Stewart, and White dissented on this basis. Still, the majority had a point. If Congress had thought about the problem, it ought to have done as the majority did. By far the more troubling point was the second, an unseen constitutional issue. Assuming Congress did intend to wipe out state convictions, where did it get its power? Given *Heart of Atlanta* and *McClung,* the answer had to be the Commerce Clause. But just what is the present effect on interstate commerce of a conviction two years prior to enactment of the Civil Rights Act? The majority, so happy finally to be rid of the sit-ins, never offered a word. Nor would anyone complain. This was a free shot at justice unencumbered by technicalities—such as constitutional power. Nor would the problem come back. The Civil Rights Act ended it prospectively. *Hamm*'s interpretation of the act ended it retrospectively. No one who peacefully engaged in a sit-in had a valid conviction registered on that basis. It was a clean sweep. Jack Greenberg of the LDF estimated that about 3,000 individuals and a shade under half a million dollars in bond money would be freed as a result of *Hamm.*

It is hard to pick the biggest winner in 1964: Johnson, the Democratic Party, the civil rights movement. A strong case can also be made that it was the Supreme Court of the United States. Just fifteen months earlier, Brennan bemoaned publicly that "there is sectional opposition because of the desegregation cases; state opposition because of recent decisions involving state powers as they relate to aspects of criminal law; rural opposition because of the reapportionment cases; and church opposition because of the prayer case."[34] He concluded the opposition represented a strong coalition in contrast to the Court's supporters, who were relatively weak and scattered. Seemingly everything had changed after the election. Congress had validated the Court's biggest case in history by voting margins that would have been unthinkable at any previous time. The president, who enjoyed such an electoral mandate, was a friend of the Court and its justices.

The Republican candidate had placed the Court in a presidential campaign for the first time by a major party candidate in the century—FDR had remained silent in 1936. Goldwater asserted that of all three branches of government, "today's Supreme Court is least faithful to the constitutional tradition of limited government, and to the principle of legitimacy in the exercise of power."[35] He specifically claimed that "law enforcement agencies—like the police, the sheriffs, the FBI—are attacked for doing their job. Law breakers are defended. Our wives, all women, feel unsafe in the streets"[36] and what mattered was "the make-up of the Supreme Court."[37] But he was drowned under a tidal wave of votes in November. That same tidal wave brought a net gain of thirty-seven Democrats in the House and one in the Senate to give the Democrats over two-thirds majorities in each, and a whopping 541 "Goldwater Freshmen" Democrats in state legislatures. The new face of legislatures nationwide largely ended the sharp incumbent discontent over the post-*Baker v. Carr* reapportionment decisions, which had even resulted in a less than expected pay raise for the justices. Finally, nominees to the Court who would tilt the balance to a more liberal stance would not produce more than a single dissenting voice or vote in Senate confirmation proceedings.

The unanimity of *Heart of Atlanta* and *Katzenbach v. McClung* had not been that startling, but, in fact, the level of agreement of the justices was incredibly high for the 1963 Term that ended in June 1964. Brennan had agreed with the Court 96 percent of the time, Warren 93 percent, Goldberg, Douglas, and White over 85 percent, Black, Clark, and Stewart over 83 percent. Only Harlan at 66 percent lagged. The justices were in agreement with each other, and seemingly the country agreed with them.

Chapter 10

Revamping the Democratic Process

Baker v. Carr was intended and was perceived as requiring a more "fair" apportionment system. Thus, President Kennedy stated that his "Administration has made clear its endorsement of the principles implicit in the Court's decision."[1] Yet it would be a mistake to think that the Court was the only or even the first political actor striving for voting fairness. In the early 1960s before *Baker* came down, Congress had sent proposed constitutional amendments to the states that gave the District of Columbia votes for president for the first time and abolished the poll tax in federal elections. The Twenty-Third Amendment, on the District of Columbia vote, had already been ratified.

According to the 1950 census, the District of Columbia had a population that was one-third African-American. The poll tax was an entirely southern phenomenon, functioning to depress African-American voting. Only five states still retained it, as six had recently repealed it. Race meant that neither amendment had a chance of getting out of James Eastland's southern-dominated Senate Judiciary Committee. The amendments were initially the result of floor changes to a proposed constitutional amendment dealing with the effects of nuclear war that would have allowed governors to appoint new congressmen in the event of deaths. Florida Democrat Spessard Holland, who had long advocated an amendment to abolish the poll tax as a means of heading off federal legislation over state voting regulation, attached the antipoll tax proposal. Then New York Republican Kenneth Keating attached a proposal to give the District of Columbia seats in the House of Representatives and presidential electoral votes on the same population basis as states. It passed 70–18 with the negatives from the South.

Emanuel Celler concluded the House would not adopt the entire Senate package, and he wanted a successful amendment, not the satisfaction of having fought for principle and lost. Thus, he focused entirely on the District of Columbia where he downsized the amendment to provide the District of Columbia with the same electoral votes as the least populous states even though the District had a population that was larger than that of thirteen states, one that would have justified either four or five electoral votes. In June 1960 the House passed the Celler proposal without a roll call vote, and the Senate followed suit two days later. Keating accepted the compromise by observing that "three-fourths citizenship or three-fifths citizenship is better than no citizenship at all."[2]

In the winter of 1961, the Twenty-Third Amendment was ratified easily. Every state outside the former Confederacy supported the amendment; of the latter, only Arkansas brought it to a vote, rejecting it.

In the new session, Holland lined up two-thirds of the members as cosponsors of his poll tax amendment, but while that was enough to pass the amendment under Article V, it was not enough to get it out of the Judiciary Committee. To successfully avoid the committee, Holland again had to wait for a propitious moment, which this time turned out to be a bill making Alexander Hamilton's home a national monument. Holland offered the poll tax amendment as a substitute, and the Senate then debated three different proposals: the southern do-nothing position, Holland's amendment, and New York Republican Jacob Javits's alternative of eliminating the poll tax by statute. The latter was far more threatening in its implications, and southerners did not mount a serious filibuster against the amendment, which passed 77–16. Fifteen of the sixteen negatives came from the South; only Wyoming Democrat John Hickey joined them. The administration supported the amendment happily for a number of reasons: It had a reasonable amount of southern support, it allowed the Kennedys to be for an actual civil rights law, and, it "could make a difference" in 1964 in both Virginia and Texas.[3]

Just as the problem in the Senate was the Judiciary Committee, the problem in the House was Howard Smith's Rules Committee. Virginia was one of the five states retaining the poll tax, joined by Alabama, Arkansas, Mississippi, and Texas. Smith kept the amendment bottled up for months. Then Celler tried the rarely used maneuver of a suspension of the rules. This took a two-thirds majority, would provide for only forty minutes of debate if successful, and would forbid amendments. Smith complained of a "farce" that had never been used before, and that it was treating the amending of the Constitution "with the utmost disrespect."[4] He lost 294–86.

The Twenty-Fourth Amendment took two years to be ratified, again without the South. Only Mississippi, which rejected it, and Tennessee, which approved it, brought it to a vote. It became part of the Constitution two weeks after the House voted favorably on the Civil Rights Act of 1964 and, like the act, was part of the effort to bring the South in line with national values.

Once the Twenty-Fourth Amendment was ratified, the governor of Virginia called the state legislature into special session to amend the state's poll tax law as it applied to federal elections. The new law allowed voters to either continue to pay the poll tax or to file a witnessed or notarized certificate of residence. In *Harman v. Forssenius* Warren invalidated the Virginia evasion under the newly ratified amendment.

This easy case would merit no attention if it had been handed down with several other cases on Monday, April 26, 1965. Warren had been urged, especially by *New York Times* reporter Anthony Lewis, to end the century-old practice of handing down opinions only one day a week, invariably Monday. Lewis rightly noted that the Court was doing a lot and that spreading opinions out would help both reporters and the interested public. That, Warren believed, would better serve the country by allowing a fuller reporting of what the Court said as well as what it did and what it might mean. *Harman* was the occasion for opening a new policy. It came down on Tuesday, April 27, 1965. Ironically, Fred Graham, Lewis's successor, wrote the *Times* story.

The Georgia Preliminaries

The first two reapportionment cases decided after *Baker* involved Georgia. *Gray v. Sanders* in 1963 dealt with its all-but-unique county-unit system of electing statewide officials. *Wesberry v. Sanders,* decided in early 1964, involved its drawing of congressional districts.

Georgia, along with Maryland and Mississippi, used an Electoral College analogy, dating from its end-of-Reconstruction constitution, for statewide elections. To be elected, a candidate must capture a majority of the county-unit vote where each county's vote is awarded on a winner-take-all basis to the candidate with the popular vote plurality in the county. At the time of *Gray,* Fulton County (Atlanta) had six units based on a population of over half a million. Echols, in east-central Georgia on the Florida border, with its population of under 2,000, received two units. That is a disparity of about 99–1. If a candidate won Atlanta by a landslide, he would get six votes; if he lost Echols in a close vote, his opponent would get two votes. As the Court described the system, "if a candidate won 6,000 of 10,000 votes in a particular county, he would get the entire unit vote, the 4,000 other votes for a different candidate being worth nothing and being counted only for the purposes of being discarded." It was thus very possible for a candidate to win the popular vote in the state, but lose when the units were counted. That is true of the Electoral College as well, but by contrast, the largest disparity in the Electoral College (at the time) was between New York (population 17 million, forty-three votes) and Alaska (population 226,000, three votes), a 5–1 disparity. And the Electoral College was not the most cheerfully celebrated part of the Constitution because the losing candidate's votes in each state were counted only for the purpose of being discarded as well.

While *Gray* was pending in the district court, the state legislature amended the unit scheme to give the urban counties more weight, reducing the disparity to 14–1. The district court held the new plan invalid as well, finding that the constitutional line was 5–1, that is, "not in excess of the disparity that exists against any state in the most recent electoral college allocation." Should the least populous states enjoy a boom, under the district court's reasoning the constitutional line would become tighter and, in fact, could change with each decennial census.

Knowing *Gray* was an easy case (given *Baker*'s dicta), Robert Kennedy chose it as his maiden appearance in any court and argued as amicus for the United States against the unit system. He demonstrated, to a Courtroom with more Kennedys than justices, that he had memorized the facts of the case, as a number of commentators gushed. More significantly, he became the first person in the Courtroom to utter the magic words "one man, one vote," which Douglas immediately changed to "one person, one vote."

In a typically breezy opinion, Douglas struck down the county-unit system completely. After stating that nothing in the case dealt with the design of geographical districts—that is, the *Baker* problem—Douglas rejected the Electoral College analogy. Georgia gave its adults the right to vote; then it weighed the votes before counting them. That was an unconstitutional infringement on the right to vote. "The conception of political equality from the Declaration of Independence, to Lincoln's Gettysburg Address, to the Fifteenth, Seventeenth, and Nineteenth Amendments can only mean one thing—one person, one vote."

Although Douglas did not explicitly say so, that explained why original intent was irrelevant. Douglas offered an evolutionary, not a static, history much the way Harlan had described in his due process dissent in *Poe v. Ullman.* Rather than using history to freeze 1963's answer in 1787, Douglas used history to give the answer for 1963. Still, ignoring the actual text of the Constitution, in an opinion that looked for authority in the Declaration of Independence and the Gettysburg Address, was breathtaking and harkened back to his dissent in *Poe*. The new living Constitution embraced far more than the text held in the National Archives. Indeed, it might not even cite that text.

Stewart and Clark joined the opinion for the Court but wrote separately to reemphasize that the case had nothing to do with legislative districting. Georgia was the district, and "[w]ithin a given constituency, there can be room for but a single constitutional rule—one voter, one vote." Harlan, in what would be a solo crusade, dissented, stating that there was not enough information before the Court to determine whether Georgia's plan was irrational.

In *Wesberry*, Fulton was attached with two neighboring suburban counties to make a huge congressional district, at least twice as populous as any of Georgia's other nine districts and three times more so than Georgia's smallest. Indeed, Atlanta was the second most underrepresented city in the nation in Congress, saved from first place because seemingly all Texas Republicans conveniently lived in Dallas where the Texas legislature could, and did, ring them by allocating a single congressman. Black's opinion displays his penchant for pairing literalism with his version of history, the technique that had worked so well with the First Amendment issues in the domestic-security cases. Textually, the Constitution demands that United States representatives "be chosen 'by the People of the several states.'" This, he concluded, means "that as nearly as practicable one man's vote in a congressional election is to be worth as much as another's." Why? "The history of the Constitution, particularly that part of it relating to the adoption of Art. I, section 2, reveals that those who framed the Constitution meant that, no matter what the mechanics of an election, whether statewide or by districts, it was population which was to be the basis of the House of Representatives." Black followed that statement with history and nothing but history. This is what the Framers did; we are just following it. It's really quite simple.

Clark wasn't so sure. He would have sent the case back to the district court for it to "apply the standards of *Baker*."

Harlan was sure Black's opinion was simple, and *Wesberry* marked the beginning of Harlan finding his voice in the reapportionment cases. In a lengthy history he challenged Black all the way. Harlan did not believe that the Framers "surreptitiously slipped their belief [that representation should be based on population] into the Constitution in the phrase 'by the People,' to be discovered 175 years later like a Shakespear-ean anagram." Furthermore, Harlan noted, by Black's own standards a full 398 members of the House of Representatives were sent from dis-tricts that were unconstitutional under the opinion of the Court. This was "to declare constitutionally defective the very composition of a coor-dinate branch of the Federal Government." He was right. *Gray* might have been breathtaking in analysis; *Wesberry* was breathtaking in result. Did any coordinate branch of government have that kind of power? Was it legitimate to raise questions about a coordinate branch's legitimacy?

Harlan enjoyed an article written a year later by historian Alfred Kelly. Discussing the Court and its uses of history, Kelly concluded with regard to *Wesberry:* "To put the matter bluntly, Mr. Justice Black, in order to prove his point, mangled constitutional history. Yet perhaps a constitu-tional historian may be forgiven if he views the entire performance with some astonishment, not unmixed with admiration for the Court's crea-tive historical imagination."[5]

In *Wesberry* Black mangled history to make it conform to what he believed the Framers should have believed, which not surprisingly was what he believed, and he then claimed that only history should count. Douglas's opinion in *Gray* may have been stunning in its use of noncon-stitutional materials, but he had not adopted a technique that required him to distort the past in order to get where he wanted to be in the present. Interestingly, Warren, Brennan, Stewart, White, and Goldberg joined both opinions, and Black and Douglas joined each other as well.

State Apportionment at Mid-Century

In the aftermath of *Baker,* legislatures were inordinately active in trying to ward off judicial intervention, and prior to the Court's six decisions in June 1964 over half the states had adopted new plans for apportioning their legislatures. That did not preclude a run to the courthouse, and lawsuits were filed in thirty-nine states seeking to reapportion their legis-latures. That there was so much action could not have been surprising. Only a handful of states had anything like equal population districts, while two dozen chambers in various state legislatures had not been reapportioned for at least three decades. Nationwide, counties with fewer than 25,000 people held twice the representative strength of coun-ties with over 100,000 people. In thirteen of the states "districts encom-passing one-third or less of the population corresponded to solid majori-ties in both houses of the legislature."[6]

Florida had senate districts ranging from 935,000 down to 9,500 and house districts from 311,000 to 2,900. Vermont had left its scheme unchanged since 1793. It assigned a representative to each town, even one, in 1960, with just thirty-eight people. Burlington, the state's largest city, with a population of 35,531 got equal representation with the former. Connecticut's house had remained unchanged since the constitution of 1818, with each city having one or two representatives. Both Hartford and Union had two, even though in 1820 Hartford had 9,789 people and Union 711. By the 1930s Hartford had grown to 164,072 and Union had shrunk to 196. In the 1936 election, Hartford went 70 percent to the Democrats and Union went 64 percent for the Republicans so each party had two seats. That pattern helps explain why in that year of Democratic landslides the Connecticut house was 100 Democrats to 167 Republicans, while in its properly apportioned senate, Democrats controlled 26 to 9.

Many people were especially familiar with California. Its constitution forbade any county from having more than one senator or combining more than three counties into one senate district. Thus, Los Angeles County with its 6 million inhabitants had one senator as did Mono, Inyo, and Alpine with their combined 14,294. When California had considered changing its apportionment in 1948, Governor Earl Warren had opposed it. "Many California counties are far more important in the life of the State than their population in the State. It is for this reason that I have never been in favor of restricting the representation in the senate to a strictly population basis."[7]

The 1964 Decisions

The plaintiffs "almost without exception were either front-men for a political party, or were politically active and politically ambitious citizens loosely classifiable as liberal Democrats or liberal Republicans."[8] Except in the one-party South, whichever party controlled the legislature, the other party filed the lawsuit. It seemed to be what Frankfurter had predicted and feared: the use of the judiciary for partisan political ends.

The moves from *Baker* to *Gray* to *Wesberry* reflected docket control by the Court in picking cases that progressed from easy to slightly more difficult. After *Wesberry,* the Court exercised further docket control in granting review in legislative apportionment cases from New York, Delaware, Maryland, Virginia, and Alabama. The cases chosen offered the

Court a wide-ranging array of facts and issues and essentially left the justices free to draw the constitutional line wherever they wished.

To assist the Court, Solicitor General Cox was invited to participate as amicus, and by his participation, the Court knew that the administration remained firmly camped in opposition to the state practices. Cox, in turn, coordinated the challengers' issues and became their chief theoretician. Thus, unlike the states, which did not consult with each other, Cox eliminated inconsistent arguments on the plaintiffs' side. Plaintiffs claimed that one of the two chambers had to be apportioned on an equal population basis, but that in the second house there was "considerable room" for recognition of other considerations. This point mattered to the states, and fourteen nonparty attorneys general banded together to file an amicus brief that relied on extensive historical materials to support the claim that states were within their authority to follow the federal analogy with respect to an upper house.

These five cases had been argued in mid-November and were being discussed at Conference the day that President Kennedy was killed. Warren had assigned the opinions to himself immediately before the justices received the tragic news. After President Johnson prevailed on him to head the commission investigating the assassination, Warren, not wanting to be a shirker, kept the assignments. He took a sixth in March when *Lucas v. Colorado 44th General Assembly* was argued and added to the mix a situation where the people rather than the legislature approved the districting plan that had a senate reflecting the state's geography.

The six cases presented three large issues. First, how equal must the population be to satisfy the requirement of equal protection? Second, could a state follow the example of the United States Senate and have one house represented on a nonpopulation basis? Third, from *Lucas*, would the Court allow more leeway to a plan adopted by popular vote than one adopted by the affected politicians? Cox, pushed hard by the Kennedys to advocate as egalitarian a position as possible, answered the questions with seeming reasonableness: (1) very; (2) yes, if rationally pursued; and (3) a wishy-washy yes.

Reynolds v. Sims was chosen to be the lead opinion. It came out of Alabama, which like Tennessee had last redistricted itself at the turn of the century. During oral argument, Warren had acidly asked counsel for the state, "How long can we wait?"—a question tied to the sixty years since Alabama had last redistricted.[9] The question and its tone answered one implicit question; there would be no *Brown II* "all deliberate speed" fiasco with redistricting. Indeed, oral argument foreshadowed other aspects of the Court's decisions. Counsel for Delaware, following the tack of the fourteen attorneys general and Black's opinion in *Wesberry,* argued history should be the touchstone. He was twice asked whether his logic did not entail overruling the untouchable *Brown I.* He was also asked by both Warren and Douglas why the logic of *Baker* did not apply equally to both houses of the legislature.

Warren's opinions in *Reynolds* and the companion cases held to a no-compromise approach throughout. The opinion took its tone from the race cases. Equal protection was an absolute or something pretty near thereto. Thus, unlike Cox, the Court's answers to the questions were: (1) very equal, indeed, "as nearly of equal population as is practicable"; (2) upper houses are held to the same constitutional standard as lower houses because the federal analogy has no application to states; and (3) the right and necessary remedy did not go to the process of redistricting, it went to the outcome of districting, and thus there is no dispensation for a popular vote. The Court was mandating change on the order of *Brown,* but unlike the first blockbuster, one of the victorious plaintiffs remarked two years later, "[w]e would have been satisfied with less than we got."[10] Warren, for his part, viewed *Baker* and not *Brown* as the most important case of his tenure; but when he said *Baker* he meant *Reynolds* for he saw the latter as "merely the application" of the former.[11] It was not, however, merely an application as Warren's expansive view took *Reynolds* far beyond what anyone thought that *Baker* had foretold.

The right to vote is a fundamental personal right, and any deprivations will be meticulously scrutinized, Warren stated. *Reynolds* begins as if this were a right to vote case, yet no one was being denied the right to vote and neither *Reynolds* nor any other case held that the Constitution itself guaranteed a right to vote. Thus, while the Court waxed eloquent about the importance of the right to vote "in a free and unimpaired manner as preservative of other basic civil and political rights," that wasn't the issue. Still, the basic thrust of the opinion was to equate the right to vote with the right of representation in districts of equal population.

Reynolds recognized that *Gray* and *Wesberry*—with their one person, one vote basis—represented different fact situations, "but neither are they wholly inapposite." Indeed, it turned out they were perfectly predictive. The most-quoted language from *Reynolds* is a crisp two sentences rejecting factors other than population in setting district lines. "Legislators represent people, not trees or acres. Legislators are elected by voters, not farms or cities or economic interests." Majority rule is essential to democracy: "Logically, in a society ostensibly grounded on representative government, it would seem reasonable that a majority of the people of a State could elect a majority of the State's legislators."

The perception of the case that it was about the right to vote, where a majority of the voters should have a majority of the seats in the legislature, was transformed into the redistricting area by the conclusion that one person, one vote should ensure that "each citizen ha[s] an equally effective voice in the election of members of his legislature." Equally effective voices, in turn, should promote a process that yields a "fair and effective representation" of the electorate as a whole. Anything else would be an invidious discrimination like those condemned in *Brown* or *Griffin v. Illinois*. The "Equal Protection Clause demands no less than substantially equal state legislative representation for all citizens of all places as well as all races."

Alabama, like Tennessee and Georgia (and others), was horribly malapportioned. From that conclusion the Court assumed that if the states were properly apportioned, then there would be "fair and effective representation" although that conclusion does not follow. Since the point of a contested election is to create winners, what can be said about those who voted for the loser and their right to "an equally effective voice"? The Court took a verifiable concept, equal population, and merged it with a subjective one, effective representation, and did so where on its own terms it could not be accurate, given loser-take-nothing elections.

A prime argument for overrepresenting rural areas was that to do so protected their voting minority rights and prevented their interests from being submerged under a sea of urban and suburban votes. But if urban and suburban majorities rule, what of the rights of the rural minority? One answer was that this was not the Court's focus. It was worried about minority capture, not the tyranny of the majority. But it offered the observation that minorities can be protected "amply" by other unstated means, which presumably were judicial enforcement of constitutional rights. And constitutional rights included those of the majority to hold a majority in a legislative body. That disposed of the first issue. Unlike *Wesberry*, which was a bad history lesson, or *Gray*, which used history as tradition, Warren used no history at all, just reasoning from the premises of the right to vote and majority rule. Nevertheless, the demand for equal population districts directly answered the Harlan-Frankfurter claim that there were no judicially manageable standards. There were; any judge can count and determine if the population among districts is equal.

The Court also believed that equal population districts provided an important check on partisan gerrymandering, though gerrymandering was not an issue in any of the six cases. It viewed unequal districts as "an open invitation to partisan gerrymandering." It is surprising that some-one as politically sophisticated as Warren would suggest equal popula-tion would check gerrymandering, especially in an opinion that elimi-nated existing political lines as appropriate guides. As the era's most astute scholar on reapportionment noted, given winner-take-all elec-tions, "all districting is gerrymandering."[12] Almost any number of equal population districts may be drawn, but each will have a different effect on the overall political balance within a state. Thus, despite the Court's myopic conclusion, *Reynolds* could not and did not prevent gerryman-dering.

Logically, as Warren and Douglas noted in oral argument, one person, one vote and the requirements of majority rule apply just as completely to the upper house of a state legislature as the lower house. But American constitutional development has never been driven purely by logic, and the federal analogy to the United States Senate suggested that upper houses could be based on something other than rule by pure majorities. In the Court's only brush with history it pronounced the Senate as "con-ceived out of compromise and concession indispensable to the estab-lishment of our federal republic." It grew out of "unique historical cir-cumstances." Since they were unique, there was no need to pursue them further because they could not be applicable to state bodies. Bicameral-ism is fine, and it is not "rendered anachronistic and meaningless when the predominant basis of representation in the two legislative bodies is required to be the same—population." So much for the second issue and for history. Yet if rural domination was preventing the solution of urban problems, it makes no sense to give one house a veto over needed legis-lation.

Reynolds is an absolutist opinion but one with a pragmatic cast. War-ren believed that had reapportionment occurred "fifty years ago we would have saved ourselves acute racial troubles. Many of our problems would have been solved a long time ago if everyone had the right to vote and his vote counted the same as everybody else's. Most of these prob-lems could have been solved through the political process rather than through the courts."[13] If there was no way to cure urban problems so long as the voters of the rural minority could block legislation, the chief justice dealt with the problem by largely taking them out of the equation. The urban needs that drove *Baker* applied no less to both chambers than to just one.

Lucas presented the most interesting situation because Colorado was not an example of a turn-of-the-century plan or an entrenched minority holding on to power. Its house was districted on a pure population basis, but its senate was not. The Colorado voters approved this plan by referendum in 1962. Indeed, the majority of the voters in each and every county in the state had approved the plan, and simultaneously, by better than a 2–1 margin, they had rejected a plan that would have districted the senate on a pure population basis. The majority had spoken—overwhelmingly by some 60 percent of the vote—and they wished to cede some of their legislative representation in the senate to the minority west of the Rockies. That, the Court informed them, was unconstitutional. *Reynolds* had held that everyone had a right to effective representation, which the Colorado plan denied. "A citizen's constitutional rights can hardly be infringed simply because a majority of the people choose that it can be."

Lucas displayed an absolutism that would increasingly dominate reapportionment. First, despite suggestions of flexibility in *Reynolds, Lucas* allowed none, even in the highly appealing example of a perfectly modern plan overwhelmingly approved by every geographical area in the state. Second, *Lucas* implicitly held there was but a single solution to the problem of reapportionment. The Court created that solution in *Reynolds,* and once it was created every part of the United States must conform. No state could attempt its own solution to its own problems because the five members of the majority had already come to their own solution. To suggest that the five liberals and White had a supreme confidence in their own judgment is to understate the situation.

Harlan dissented in all six cases, concluding that history foreclosed what the majority had done. "The history of the adoption of the Fourteenth Amendment provides conclusive evidence that neither those who proposed nor those who ratified the Amendment believed that the Equal Protection Clause limited the power of the States to apportion their legislatures as they saw fit." His history was correct; the Fourteenth Amendment was not intended to touch voting, as reading it in its entirety along with the Fifteenth Amendment shows. Thus, "when in the name of constitutional interpretation, the Court *adds* something to the Constitution that was deliberately excluded from it, the Court in reality substitutes its view of what should be so for the amending process." The majority, however, didn't care.

After Harlan finished with his history, he offered a few words on what the majority had done. He thought its reasoning was based "on the constitutionally frail tautology that 'equal' means 'equal'" and little more. While Harlan was willing to concede—who wouldn't—that "people, not land or trees or pastures, vote," he went on to state it is "more meaningful to note that people are not ciphers and that legislatures can represent their electors only by speaking for their interests—economic, political, social—many of which do reflect the place where they live." He was willing to live with what the American experience had provided but he was unwilling to read that experience generously, as one consistently expanding the franchise and striving toward the goal of electoral equality. Therefore, he believed there was nothing that precluded minority rural dominance of legislative bodies across the land unless those with power voluntarily surrendered it. His view that there were problems without practical solutions was the antithesis of the conclusions of the majority.

As a dissenter Harlan could expose the weakness of the majority's constitutional analysis and complain of the "current mistaken view of the Constitution," which "in a nutshell, is that every social ill in this country can find its cure in some constitutional 'principle,' and that this Court should 'take the lead' in promoting reform when other branches of government fail to act." On one hand Harlan was exaggerating. Some social ills were best cured by Congress, and the majority was more than happy to let Congress handle those problems. Where Harlan was correct was in his conclusion that when governments failed to act on a serious problem, the majority was likely to find a constitutional principle that justified judicial intervention.

Clark and Stewart concurred in some of what the Court had done while rejecting its absolutism. Clark felt the majority had gone "much beyond the necessities" of the cases, especially in completely rejecting the federal analogy. Stewart complained of the majority "converting a particular political philosophy into a constitutional rule, binding upon each of the 50 states . . . without respect for the many individualized and differentiated characteristics of each State, characteristics stemming from each State's distinct history, distinct geography, distinct distribution of population, and distinct political heritage." In a thoughtful, pragmatic opinion he charged the majority as resting on "the uncritical, simplistic, and heavy-handed application of sixth-grade arithmetic." His position was that a state must have a genuinely rational plan and that it "be such as not to permit the systematic frustration of the will of the majority of the electorate of the State." He thus approved the Colorado plan, adopted by the overwhelming majority of the state's voters. He also would have sustained the New York plan, which was up-to-date and tried to place a "reasonable limitation upon massive overcentralization of power," that is, giving upstate interests a break. In the other four cases he believed the plans violated his standard.

Reaction

Writing in the Sunday *New York Times* following *Reynolds,* Anthony Lewis observed that "even some liberal-minded persons, admirers of the modern Supreme Court, find themselves stunned."[14] In Court, on the day *Reynolds* came down, Lewis, not writing for the newspaper of record, had been more exuberant, and he passed a note to Cox "asking him how it felt to be present at the second American Constitutional Convention."[15] Cox, having gone as far as he thought possible and still having been nowhere close to Warren's position, responded, "It feels awful."[16]

Lewis's hyperbole was not that far off. In *Wesberry,* the Court put in issue 90 percent of the districts in the House of Representatives. *Reynolds* put in issue virtually every single seat in the upper houses of state legislatures and most of the seats in lower houses. Furthermore, the way *Reynolds* rejected the federal analogy was a direct slap at the United States Senate. Before *Reynolds,* one scholar had written of the federal analogy that "the question has been raised as to how an institutional scheme may be rational if it is the product of a compromise between equal forces and arbitrary when it results from a grant made within the discretion of the granting body."[17] A nice observation. There is no other reading of *Reynolds* except one that concludes the United States Senate's overrepresentation of the smaller states violates the nation's principles of political fairness. Could the nation's governments really have been as bad as the Court suggested? Had the nation really strayed so far from its principles? Or had the Court adopted newer and better principles and then imposed them on the nation in the name of the Constitution?

No one had any doubt that it was the latter, and professional politicians were somewhat more enamored with the status quo and the United States Senate than the Court appeared to be. Thus, they reacted strongly against the Court. Moreover, unlike the situation with *Baker* where the public instantly embraced the decision, there was no latent popular consensus that equal population districts in both houses were a good idea.

The national chairmen of both parties initially praised *Reynolds,* but that changed quickly as the Republicans went into opposition with a platform calling for a constitutional amendment to overturn the application of one person, one vote to both chambers. The Democrats were split, and nothing that split the party was being mentioned in Lyndon Johnson's platform.

With passage of the Civil Rights Act behind them, many members of Congress wished the nation's attention would switch to the plight of rural America's prospective loss of political power, and by the time of the conventions both the House and the Senate were trying to restrict *Reynolds*. The House, pushed by William Tuck of Virginia, was considering the draconian jurisdiction-stripping route. If the federal courts had no jurisdiction over reapportionment, then they could not order the dismantling of state senates or, more important, congressional districts. In the Senate, Everett Dirksen was calling for a two-year moratorium on enforcement of *Reynolds*. During that time he hoped the Constitution could be amended to authorize one legislative chamber to be based on a nonpopulation basis should a state so choose.

Celler, as always, was an enthusiastic defender of the Court, and he called the jurisdiction-stripping proposal the product of "deliberations of angry men, irate men" as well as "a rather vicious attack upon the Supreme Court."[18] Tuck, for his part, defended the bill as necessary to "preserve the Constitution of the United States, already bleeding from assaults made upon it by the Supreme Court."[19] Howard Smith suggested that members should think "about what this Court can do to you. You can come to live under just as much a dictatorship as any European country which has gone through the regimes of Hitler and Khrushchev."[20] The most useful perspective was that Tuck's proposal was a jobs bill. Under *Wesberry* a number of heretofore safe congressional seats were likely to be contested with the result that some members of the House could expect to be unemployed in January. Few things focus the political mind so well as a prospective loss of power, and Tuck's jurisdiction-stripping bill passed the House 218–175 in mid-August.

That shifted action to the Senate where Dirksen's moratorium, attached as a rider to a foreign aid bill, was quite mild by comparison to the House bill. Furthermore, Dirksen's was not a jobs bill like Tuck's. *Reynolds* meant a substantial transfer of power in Illinois from downstate to Chicago, something, given Chicago's politics, that made no sense to Dirksen, himself from the state's central area. He believed the federal analogy would be good not only for his home but for the nation as well.

Liberals wanted neither Dirksen's moratorium nor Tuck's end of federal intervention, so they filibustered just as southerners had when facing civil rights legislation. Unlike their sectional counterparts, the liberals prevailed, as those supporting Dirksen's moratorium did not have the votes for cloture. Eventually, the Senate compromised on a "sense of Congress" resolution that federal courts should give legislators one legislative session plus thirty days to comply with future court orders. The resolution passed 44–38, but the House found the tepid Senate response so unsatisfactory that they chose nothing rather than accede to the Senate's pious vacuity.

The Senate action was a devastating blow for those wishing to undo *Reynolds* by constitutional amendment. It is never easy to amend the Constitution, and supporters of the federal analogy would do far better with the then-existing state legislatures. To the extent that states were reapportioned, support for an amendment would necessarily wane because this would require politicians who had just gained office to relinquish it, an altruistic and absurd proposition. Furthermore, only fourteen state negatives would kill any amendment. Thus, time was of the essence, and the failure of both Dirksen and Tuck meant that time would be inexorably slipping away.

The only true slap at the Court that became law was a pay raise for the justices that was $3,000 less than that for the remainder of the federal judiciary. Congressmen who supported slicing the raise made clear they were unhappy about recent decisions, especially reapportionment. The *New York Times* aptly characterized the action as a "petty expression of Congressional resentment."[21] The justices' loss of part of a pay raise was more than compensated for by the losses suffered by their opponents as "Goldwater Freshman" poured into both the House of Representatives and state legislative chambers across the nation.

Dirksen, as his colleague Birch Bayh of Indiana noted, "was deadly serious" about allowing states the opportunity to have one house apportioned on a nonpopulation basis, and with the new Congress he sought to undo *Reynolds* by constitutional amendment.[22] By January 1965, he had thirty-seven cosponsors. Those opposing the amendment did so for one of two reasons: first, that *Reynolds* got it right and, second, even if *Reynolds* went too far, that malapportioned rural-dominated legislatures ought not be allowed to draw up plans to perpetuate themselves. Rather than deal with the Judiciary Committee, Dirksen used the same tactic as had been used for the District of Columbia and poll tax amendments, attaching his proposal to a measure already on the floor, in this case a bill to proclaim National American Legion Baseball Week. Although Dirksen had softened his proposal to mandate that all ratifications had to come from legislatures already apportioned on a population basis, he still could not get the necessary two-thirds vote in the Senate. Southerners and rural senators provided the bulk of his fifty-seven votes, but thirty-nine were opposed and he was seven short.

Dirksen refused to give in, tying up Senate business until he was promised that the Judiciary Committee would allow another vote the following spring. That vote was a virtually identical 55–38, and time was now running out. In the last gasp of the old order, a number of states attempted to implement for the first time in American history that part of Article V that provides that two-thirds of the states could "call" for a constitutional convention. There were numerous legal difficulties with this, not the least of which was whether any convention could be limited to topics in the "call," but the number of states involved peaked at thirty-two in 1967 and not all were "calling" for the same amendment—indeed, several dated to 1963 and were proposals to overturn *Baker,* and one was to make the fifty state chief justices a final court of review to rule on Supreme Court cases dealing with state powers.

The problem for those hoping to reverse *Reynolds* was that the federal analogy had never caught on—"the issue of reapportionment was almost invisible to the national public in 1964 and 1966"[23]—and as states came rapidly into compliance with *Reynolds,* there was neither a public outcry to return to the past nor a desire of the newly elected to return to private life. *Reynolds* created a self-fulfilling prophesy. Once its mandate was complied with, the objections to the decision largely vanished because, on the one hand, those objecting most on the state level were redistricted out of office and, on the other hand, the principles of *Reynolds* "rapidly became embedded in the national sense of democratic values."[24] *Reynolds* went from debatable in 1964 to unquestionable in 1968. The *New York Times* quoted reapportionment expert Robert McKay as stating that "the mood, even among politicians, is that the decisions are acceptable; the accommodations have largely been made."[25]

Freedom Summer

Mississippi was "the living embodiment of the potential for inhumanity and injustice."[26] Northerners who were concerned with the problem of civil rights felt, when they visited Mississippi, "that they had strayed into another time, another country where even more striking than the unimpaired external structure of white supremacy was the emotional atmosphere of the state."[27] While well over 40 percent of its population was African-American, the highest in the nation, not even 7 percent of the African-Americans were registered voters, the lowest in the nation, and far below Alabama, which was second at 19 percent. In November 1963 as white Mississippians chose the state's government, nearly 80,000 disenfranchised African-Americans cast "freedom ballots" in a demonstration of their desire to vote.

The Student Non-Violent Coordinating Committee (SNCC) and the Congress of Racial Equality (CORE) in conjunction with other more activist organizations then designated the summer of 1964 as "Freedom Summer" where northern students and southern activists would come into the state and attempt to conduct a massive voter registration drive. By subjecting whites to the terrors that African-Americans faced daily, SNCC hoped to rivet the national media on Mississippi. It worked. "The whole of Mississippi became the stage, its public officials and law-enforcement personnel unwitting, but perfectly cast, villains, its 400,000 disfranchised adult Negroes the principal players, and the nation at large the audience to which 'live' television presentations were offered each evening with the news."[28]

Freedom Summer began with the disappearance—and murder—of CORE volunteers James Chaney, Andrew Goodman, and Michael Schwerner. Senator Eastland and other Mississippi politicians claimed for six weeks—that is, until the bodies were discovered—that the three "were alive and well and perpetrating a hoax on the state's innocent citizens."[29] Goodman and Schwerner were the first northern whites killed by the Ku Klux Klan in the 1960s, and that guaranteed consistent and favorable media attention for all the civil rights workers. Thereafter segregationists burned or bombed thirty-five homes, churches, and other buildings, shot at three dozen activists (hitting three), beat eighty, and killed three more. The federal government's hands-off policy partially eroded, although SNCC leader Robert Moses acidly noted immediately after the first air strikes against North Vietnam that a country that declined to protect civil rights workers in the South "could galvanize so readily to do violence in Asia."[30] Moses's query occurred at the same time that the bodies of Chaney, Goodman, and Schwerner were found in an earthen dam. The constant favorable press attention had the intended effect; the Gallup Poll reported that over 40 percent of Americans continued (since Birmingham) to believe that civil rights was the most important question facing the country.

The climax of the voter registration campaign was a challenge to the all-white Mississippi delegation at the Democratic National Convention in Atlantic City. The interracial delegation of the Mississippi Freedom Democratic Party was led by Fannie Lou Hamer, a very eloquent African-American sharecropper. Johnson and his liberal allies arranged for a so-called compromise where the Freedom Democrats were given two at-large seats at the convention. The Freedom Democrats rejected the compromise with Hamer explaining, "We didn't come all this way for no two seats."[31] When friends of Humphrey tried to explain that the refusal to accept the compromise might cost Humphrey the vice presidency, Hamer turned to him and asked in disbelief, "Do you mean to tell me that your position is more important to you than four hundred thousand black people's lives?"[32] Many African-American activists never again trusted white liberals, and white liberals knew that the civil rights agenda remained incomplete.

Selma

Johnson understood the next step after the Civil Rights Act had to be a comprehensive protection of the rights of African-Americans to register and to vote. In January 1965 he told Attorney General Nicholas Katzenbach to begin the process of drafting the necessary legislation. His target was the second session of the new Congress. "Johnson's sense of timing told him that after the struggle over the Civil Rights Act of 1964, 1965 was not a propitious year to present more civil rights proposals. He felt that the American people wanted an intermission, a period without renewed conflict, in order to assimilate the political and social impact of the earlier bill."[33] King, fresh off his Nobel Peace Prize, had other thoughts; African-Americans needed the vote now, not later. The Gallup Poll suggested King may have understood the situation better than Johnson.

Just as he chose Birmingham to push for a general civil rights act, King chose Selma, Alabama, to push for a voting rights act. Selma was an old industrial town of 29,000 in the middle of Alabama's Black Belt that had been the location for the first meeting of the Alabama Citizen's Council. Selma had 15,000 African-Americans, but only 383 were registered to vote compared to 9,800 white registered voters. Most important, however, Selma had Dallas County Sheriff Jim Clark, "an unreconstructed segregationist who proudly displayed on his lapel a button, NEVER, to tell blacks that nothing would change."[34] Clark, who "habitually lost his self-control at the sight of a marching Negro," was slated for Bull Connor's former starring role on national television.[35]

King told his followers that they "must be willing to go to jail by the thousands," and in the first two months of 1965 they did.[36] Indeed, at one time King penned a letter to the American people noting that "THERE ARE MORE NEGROES IN JAIL WITH ME THAN THERE ARE ON THE VOTING ROLLS."[37] But, like all demonstrators in the Deep South, they risked more than jail time. Once, when Clark shoved an African-American woman, she shoved back. Deputies threw her to the ground and pinned her while Clark smashed her with a club to the clicking sounds of cameras. On February 10, Clark arrested 165 protesters and sent them on a forced march out of town, aided by electric cattle prods, again to pictures heading North. State troopers beat demonstrators in nearby Marion, and when twenty-six-year-old Jimmy Lee Jackson tried to protect his father, he was shot in the stomach at close range. He died eight days later.

Johnson was pushing the Justice Department for quicker action in drafting a voting rights bill. He wanted it "ready for Congressional action before King's demonstration got out of hand and either created backlash or made it appear that the administration was not moving fast enough."[38] The drafting was completed on Friday, March 5.

King decided to draw attention to Selma by organizing a march to the capital, Montgomery, some fifty miles away. This march commenced on March 7 with 600 marchers (but not King, who heeded the concern of Katzenbach about a plot on his life) reaching the Edmund Pettis Bridge at the edge of town. Across the bridge were Clark and his men on horseback, along with helmeted state troopers wearing gas masks. A bullhorn told the marchers they had two minutes to turn back. But that was a lie as almost immediately thereafter horses and tear gas moved. Clark's men charged with a rebel yell, swinging "bullwhips and rubber tubing wrapped in barbed wire."[39]

Johnson's biographer Robert Dallek notes that "the national reaction to what the press called 'Bloody Sunday' was everything advocates of a voting rights law could have wished. Television provided graphic descriptions of the police actions, and newspapers all over the country featured the story on their front pages."[40] ABC interrupted its feature film *Judgment at Nuremberg* to show footage of the carnage. It was then joined on Monday by CBS and NBC in rerunning the scenes again and again to a shocked national audience. SNCC's John Lewis who had his skull fractured by police, just as he had four years earlier as a Freedom Rider, was finally able to speak his mind (unlike at the March on Washington, where administration officials had pressured him to tone it down). In Selma, as he was taken to a hospital, he tied the South into the escalating Vietnam War. "I don't see how President Johnson can send troops to Vietnam and can't send troops to Selma, Alabama."[41] Unlike Birmingham two years earlier, northern whites began arriving in Selma to participate in history.

Within the next two weeks Johnson met with Governor George Wallace, who left the meeting stating, "If I hadn't left when I did, he'd have had me coming out *for* civil rights."[42] The president sent troops to Alabama to public applause and addressed a joint session of Congress to propose a voting rights act. The march to Montgomery finally began on March 21. With helicopters overhead and federal marshals and the federalized national guard protecting both sides of the road, thousands of marchers took four days to reach Montgomery where comedian Dick Gregory and folk singers Peter, Paul, and Mary entertained them, and the crowd of 25,000 modified the lyrics of the movement's anthem from "we shall overcome someday" to "we have overcome today."[43] To remind everyone that this was the South, later that night Klansmen murdered Viola Liuzzo, a white Detroit housewife, who had been transporting marchers to and from Selma in her car. The Gallup Poll reported that over 50 percent of all Americans considered civil rights the most important issue facing the nation. This was an all-time high.

Johnson's address to the joint session March 15 was the first such speech in a generation that a president personally delivered dealing with a domestic issue. It was televised live to an estimated audience of 70 million. Doris Kearns Goodwin best describes this, the high point of Johnson's presidency, as Johnson "at his best—homely, compassionate, audacious and noble—a hard practical appeal and a strong moral statement."[44] Johnson began by observing that "at times history and fate meet at a single time in a single place to shape a turning point in man's unending search for freedom. . . . So it was a century ago at Appomattox. So it was last week in Selma, Alabama." He demanded there be no compromise and no delay in bringing to the Negroes "the full blessings of American life. Their cause must be our cause too. Because it is not just Negroes, but really it is all of us who must overcome the crippling legacy of bigotry and injustice." Raising his arms, Johnson took from the anthem of the movement and placed it in his own cadence: "And . . . we . . . shall . . . overcome."[45] The audience, some in tears, gave a wild standing ovation. Even Supreme Court justices—Warren, Clark, Brennan, and Goldberg were in attendance—were standing and clapping.

The media had already adopted the message. Robert MacNeil of NBC stated, "[t]he tone of the network programming has been emphatically liberal, identifying the advancement of the American

Negro—toward equality as unquestionably linked to the health of the nation."[46]

The Voting Rights Act of 1965 was on its way. As Johnson had ordered, the act was comprehensive, indeed the most comprehensive of all the civil rights bills, and it was directed squarely at the South. It ordered the Justice Department to suspend literacy tests and any other registration tests in any county where fewer than half the eligible voters were registered or had voted. If necessary, the Justice Department could send federal employees to the states to register voters. No affected state could adopt any new test for registration to vote without first "preclearing" it, that is, getting permission from the Justice Department. The only thing the act failed to do was abolish the poll tax in its few remaining holdout states. On this, the act simply directed the Justice Department to file suit challenging the state laws.

The Voting Rights Act was passed in the House by the overwhelming regional vote of 333–85. Russell and his cohorts in the Senate knew the times had changed too much to block the bill, but offered a "desultory" filibuster that was "permitted out of deference to tradition more than anything else."[47] It lasted twenty-five days before Dirksen brought in the Republicans for cloture. Then the Senate approved the act 77–19.

Robert Weisbrot, who best chronicled the civil rights movement, wrote that the Voting Rights Act of 1965 "enjoyed broader, more sustained public support than any previous civil rights measure" and that it "fit perfectly with the liberal call for expanded federal action to protect the rights of all citizens."[48] It was, after all, hard to explain why American citizens were being denied such a basic right, enshrined in the Constitution for almost a century. Johnson signed the Voting Rights Act on August 6, and two days later federal registrars were in Selma and other Black Belt counties where the percentage of African-Americans registered shot up to 52 percent in Alabama and 60 percent in Mississippi. Sheriff Clark lost in the next primary election.

South Carolina v. Katzenbach

South Carolina led the southern challenge to the Voting Rights Act by invoking the Court's original jurisdiction so that the case could be decided as quickly as possible and in time for the 1966 elections. The justices who had applauded Johnson's speech a year earlier were equally happy to validate the product of that speech. Warren's opinion for the Court began by stating that "[t]wo points emerge vividly from the voluminous history of the Act contained in committee hearings and floor debates. First: Congress felt itself confronted by an insidious and pervasive evil which had been perpetrated in certain parts of our country through unremitting and ingenious defiance of the Constitution." Second, that all prior attempts to remedy the evil had been unsuccessful, so a new direction was necessary.

South Carolina's principal arguments were that the statute was too regional and that the congressional power under the Fifteenth Amendment to prevent racial discrimination in voting went no further than doing so in general terms. The Court easily and emphatically rejected the arguments. The Voting Rights Act was aimed at the South because the South was the area where racial discrimination in voting was most prevalent, and Congress "chose to limit its attention to the geographic areas where immediate action seemed necessary." Drawing on John Marshall's famous statement of congressional power in *McCulloch v. Maryland*, Warren wrote that Congress could use "any rational means to effectuate the constitutional prohibition"; given the evidence that the prior "case-by-case litigation was inadequate to combat the widespread persistent discrimination in voting," the act was fully rational. Nor was the prior upholding of the constitutionality of the North Carolina literacy test in *Lassiter v. Northampton Board of Elections* to the contrary. *Lassiter* itself recognized literacy tests "could" be used to discriminate, and the congressional record developed showed that literacy tests "have been instituted with the purpose of disenfranchising Negroes, have been framed in such a way as to facilitate this aim, and have been administered in a discriminatory fashion for many years."

Black dissented on the preclearance issue only. He believed that requiring a state to ask the federal government for permission to adopt a new law was inconsistent with the constitutional scheme and the dignity of the states. He was correct that Congress had chosen an extraordinary remedy, but after twenty-nine years on the bench he was increasingly splitting from the liberal coalition on issues affecting his native South.

It is impossible to state with any precision when Black had outstayed his time. It occurred at some point during the mid-1960s, and by the end Warren urged him to retire. But Black was blinded to what others could see by his own vision of closing in on a new career goal, one that all the true longtimers seemed to acquire—the Court's record for longevity, then just under thirty-five years, held by Stephen J. Field. (Not surprisingly, Field also had stayed beyond his time in order to pass John Marshall's then-record tenure.) The first John Marshall Harlan had subsequently

stayed past his abilities to try to edge Field but had fallen short. Now
Black, a frail octogenarian with failing eyesight, intended to surpass
Field. He died trying in 1971. (His longtime younger colleague, Douglas,
passed Field during Richard Nixon's shortened second term. That is
laden with irony, for Douglas was planning to leave the Court in 1970
and changed his mind only when Nixon and Gerald Ford concocted the
idea of impeaching him for being too liberal. Never one to run from any
fight, Douglas shelved his retirement plans.)

Katzenbach v. Morgan

A far more interesting and difficult challenge to the Voting Rights Act
was argued in April a month after *South Carolina v. Katzenbach* came
down. In *Katzenbach v. Morgan* the Court upheld §4(e) of the Voting
Rights Act, which provided that no person who had completed the sixth
grade in a Puerto Rican school where the instruction was in Spanish shall
be denied the right to vote because of an inability to read or write English. The intent of the provision, introduced as a floor amendment (and
therefore without committee hearings or reports) by New York Senator
Robert Kennedy, was to enfranchise several hundred thousand people
who had migrated to New York City from Puerto Rico and who had run
afoul of New York's English literacy requirement.

To understand how difficult *Morgan* was, it is useful to return briefly
to *South Carolina v. Katzenbach*. As Harlan, dissenting in *Morgan*, accurately described it, the Court first reviewed "the 'voluminous legislative
history' as well as judicial precedents supporting the basic congressional
finding that the clear commands of the Fifteenth Amendment had been
infringed by various state subterfuges." Then, "given the existence of the
evil, we held the remedial steps taken by the legislation" under the Fifteenth Amendment to be appropriate. The problem in *Morgan* was very
different.

Lassiter v. Northampton Board of Elections had held that the ability
to read English was not an irrational requirement for voting. Therefore,
it was not a violation of the Equal Protection Clause to distinguish between those who could read English and those who could not. If an
English literacy test was valid, how, absent a showing that it was used for
racial discrimination, could Congress displace it? One answer would be
that *Lassiter* was wrongly decided, and congressional fact-finding might
show that it is irrational to distinguish for the purpose of voting between
adults who can read English and those who can read Spanish. But there

were no such findings by Congress to assist the Court in reconsidering *Lassiter.* A second option would be for the Court on its own to reconsider and reverse *Lassiter,* but this was not taken. A third option would be that §5 of the Fourteenth Amendment gives Congress the right to overrule Supreme Court decisions that it believes are erroneous interpretations of equal protection and due process. Yet *Cooper v. Aaron* in 1958 emphasized—some would say created—the Court's role as ultimate interpreter of the Constitution. Accordingly, it was inconceivable that Congress could overrule the Court. With these as the plausible options, sustaining §4(e) of the Voting Rights Act seemed unlikely at best. Yet the Court did so with only Stewart joining Harlan's dissent. Brennan's majority opinion was nothing short of a constitutional tour de force, although when one reaches its end it is difficult to restate with accuracy how he did it.

Brennan began with the indisputable but seemingly irrelevant proposition that "the States have no power to grant or withhold the franchise on conditions that are forbidden by the Fourteenth Amendment." But *Lassiter*'s holding was that a requirement to read English was not a condition forbidden by the Fourteenth Amendment. Brennan's next move was to eschew reconsideration of *Lassiter.* "Thus our task in this case is not to determine whether the New York English literacy requirement as applied violates equal protection." Instead, the "task" was limited to determining "whether §4(e) is appropriate legislation to enforce equal protection." As was typical of Brennan, he had used a lot of space but still had not explained why the "task" was the latter rather than the former or, indeed, why the two were dissimilar.

Brennan's next move was to shift the case from discrimination in voting to discrimination in the delivery of government services. Maybe §4(e) wasn't really about English versus Spanish, but instead about a means of protecting the Spanish-speaking New Yorkers from being discriminated against by their government. By granting them the ballot, Congress provided the means by which they could protect their other rights, for as the Court frequently noted, the right to vote "is preservative of all rights." Brennan was undeterred by the fact that there were no hearings that demonstrated discrimination in the delivery of government services. It was up to Congress to weigh and assess the facts and not for the Court to review the weight Congress attached. "Any contrary conclusion would require us to be blind to the realities familiar to the legislators."

Brennan had successfully turned the case around. New York was treating Spanish speakers unequally in violation of the Constitution. Congress thought the best way to put a stop to this was ending English literacy tests. That was indeed a rational way to enforce the guarantees of equal protection. But having sustained §4(e), Brennan was only beginning. He had a powerful message he wanted to deliver.

Brennan's next paragraph begins with the statement that the "result is no different if we confine our inquiry to the question whether §4(e) was merely legislation aimed at the elimination of an invidious discrimination in establishing voter qualifications." This directly implicated *Lassiter,* for *Lassiter* held literacy tests were not invidious. In the paragraph that follows, sentences state that "Congress might well have." In each case Brennan is viewing Congress as having an identical and independent ability to interpret the Constitution for itself. The second half of *Morgan* finds §4(e) constitutional because Congress found literacy tests unconstitutional.

Harlan was concerned. If Congress has an independent ability to interpret the Constitution, are not constitutional rights thereby placed in jeopardy? For a Congress that can interpret equal protection to abolish a literacy requirement could also interpret due process to abolish the exclusionary rule in criminal cases. Brennan answered this in one of those few famous footnotes in Supreme Court opinions. Footnote Ten of *Morgan* announced that Congress's power went only one way. It could expand on rights the Court had recognized, but it could not contract or dilute them. Why? Because Footnote Ten said so.

The problem with Footnote Ten's one-way ratchet is knowing which way Congress was ratcheting rights. From Brennan's perspective, Congress had expanded the rights of the Puerto Rican minority in New York. But from the perspective of voters who could read English, Congress had diluted their rights to control the outcomes of elections by adding in a number of unqualified voters who might tip the election scales. The line between ratcheting up and ratcheting down might not be as clear to others as it was to Brennan. His conclusion stands as a monument to the proposition that any expansion of the right to vote is necessarily a step of progress toward a better country.

Cox, who had returned to Harvard as a professor after his resignation as solicitor general, wrote the prestigious "Foreword" to the *Harvard Law Review* in the fall. He analogized 1966 to 1937. "A newer theme is the strong declaration of congressional power. If the Congress follows the lead that the Court has provided, the last Term's opinions interpreting §5 will prove as important in bespeaking national legislative authority to promote human rights as the Labor Board decisions of 1937 were in providing national authority to regulate the economy." Cox understood how momentous this was, and he concluded that *Morgan* meant that "Congress, in the field of state activities and except as confined by the Bill of Rights, has the power to enact any law which may be viewed as a measure for correction of any condition which Congress might believe involves a denial of equality or other fourteenth amendment rights."[49]

Cox was correct. The Court was extending an offer to Congress to become a full partner in the Court's great tasks, just as Congress had become with the Civil Rights Act of 1964 and the Voting Rights Act of 1965. In making the offer the Court saw that its views and those of Congress were harmonious. Each was working as hard as it could to improve American life. The simple caveat that should Congress slip and dilute a right, the Court would invalidate the statute ought to be sufficient for anyone except people like Harlan and Stewart, who were otherwise out of sympathy with the new constitutional order, in promoting human liberty by expanding the understanding of equality.

The Poll Tax

The Court's other voting rights case from the 1965 Term served to pull everything together. *Harper v. Virginia Board of Elections* was a challenge to Virginia's poll tax of $1.50. In striking it down the Court overruled both a 1937 case sustaining Georgia's $1 poll tax and a 1951 case sustaining Virginia's, and indicated that the Twenty-Fourth Amendment had not been necessary because poll taxes violated equal protection and were thus unconstitutional without the new amendment. Nevertheless, Congress hinted they violated equal protection too because the Voting Rights Act of 1965 directed the attorney general to initiate challenges to the few remaining ones. The *New York Times* was mostly correct that once Congress passed on the issue, action by the Court "probably became inevitable."[50] Only the "probably" was wrong.

Douglas wrote an opinion that dispatched the past and encouraged the future. The easiest way to deal with the constitutional issue was probably to acknowledge, despite the Court's earlier statements, that the Constitution does guarantee the right to vote. But Douglas did not do so. Instead, he called the right to vote a fundamental right to make clear that it was different from a constitutional right. Exactly how it was different was not clear.

In creating doctrine out of whole cloth, Douglas stated, "Wealth, like race, creed, or color, is not germane to one's ability" to cast an intelligent ballot. And "lines drawn on the basis of wealth or property, like those of race, are traditionally disfavored." Traditionally? That tradition, which probably dates from *Harper* itself, could at best be no older than *Griffin v. Illinois* in 1956 with its requirement that indigent defendants be furnished transcripts for their appeals. *Griffin* was supplemented by *Douglas v. California* in 1963 with its guarantee of a lawyer on the first appeal. But that was all there was of the tradition that Douglas was so blithely pronouncing. What *Harper* seems to be doing is using the voting rights context to lay the foundations for a constitutional right to government assistance even though the opinion does not mention the problem.

To the charge by the dissenters that the majority was wrongly enshrining their own beliefs about good public policy in the Constitution, Douglas unpersuasively denied the charge. He also dismissed original understandings in a single sentence. "Notions of what constitutes equal treatment for purposes of the Equal Protection Clause *do* change." His emphasis let everyone know this was an up-to-date Constitution, and his opinion evoking tradition, not original intent, was like his earlier effort in *Gray v. Sanders*.

Black, by himself, and Harlan for Stewart dissented, finding that history showed that the poll tax, even if not good public policy, was at least rational policy. Harlan demonstrated that existing equal protection doctrine could not support Douglas's construction. He acknowledged that times had changed, but did not believe that was sufficient to justify "rigidly imposing on America an ideology of unrestrained egalitarianism." Yet somehow Black and Harlan missed the point. This was a poll tax in a southern state where every conceivable effort had been made to keep African-Americans as second-class citizens. Douglas understood, as the dissenters did not, that the Fourteenth Amendment was supposed to bring the Civil War and its issues to a close. *Harper,* by looking to tradition and not originalism, reached the right result.

Harper clarified *Reynolds* and *Morgan*. Original intent was not a guide, but evolving standards were. Whatever earlier generations thought, the right to vote was too precious to be limited. And Harlan was right; just as the infamous 1905 decision in *Lochner v. New York* supposedly incorporated Herbert Spencer's *Social Statics*, these cases were about unrestrained egalitarianism. But unlike *Lochner*'s rearguard action to invalidate progressive legislation, these cases were on the cutting edge, with the Court walking hand-in-hand with Congress. There was no judicial thwarting of the popular will. The Voting Rights Act of 1965 overwhelmingly passed Congress and supported both the outcome in

Morgan and the one in *Harper.* *Harper* was an example of *Morgan*'s tendered partnership.

Logical Extensions

Reynolds, Wesberry, and *Harper* were quickly and easily extended to their logical limits. Each of the new cases produced a thoughtful dissent questioning both the absolutism of the majority and the practical consequences of the decision.

Reynolds was extended to subunits of state government in 1968. Midland County's four commissioners, joined by a fifth elected at large, formed a governing body that set tax rates and adopted a county budget. Yet they came from three districts of under 1,000 people and a fourth, the city of Midland, Texas, of 67,000. White's opinion in *Avery v. Midland County* explained that "the Constitution permits no substantial variation from equal population in drawing districts for units of local government having general governmental powers over the entire geographic area to be served by the body." That was that. Harlan and Stewart dissented and, surprisingly, so did Fortas, who thought that the functions of local governments were too complex to be straitjacketed in the *Reynolds* principle. Because some citizens were more interested in county government than others—its jurisdiction was mostly rural—Fortas concluded that they were entitled not to have their votes submerged in the urban deluge.

A year later the Court decided two congressional districting cases, both adopting new plans and neither involving claims of gerrymandering, as well as a ballot restriction case. Opinions by Brennan and Warren had an unyielding quality to them as if there really were no alternatives available except the Court's outcome.

Kirkpatrick v. Preisler was the more important of the two redistricting cases where the Court adopted mathematical precision as the constitutional rule. Missouri's congressional districts varied from 3.13 percent above to 2.84 percent below the mathematical ideal for the state, and Missouri thought that meant it had done a pretty good job. It learned instead that *Wesberry*'s "as nearly as practicable" should be taken very seriously. Thus, the Court rejected any concept of "de minimus" entirely and stated that "practicable" did not mean "politically practicable"; rather it was a mathematical test. Nor was Missouri's argument that it was striving for compact districts a justification for population deviation because it was "based solely upon the unaesthetic appearance of the map of congressional boundaries. A State's preference for pleasingly shaped districts can hardly justify population variances."

New York had been divided first into seven regions and then each region was split into equal population districts. New York justified the deviations from 6.5 percent above to 6.6 percent below as necessary to keep the regions, with their similar interests, intact. In *Wells v. Rockefeller,* as in *Kirkpatrick,* Brennan was not impressed. What mattered was districting that approached the mathematical ideal, not any supposed commonality of interests of the voters. Harlan and White dissented in both cases, Stewart in *Wells* only.

In *Wesberry* Harlan had argued the Constitution did not support the Court's actions, but that case was on the books and so long as the Court was not going to undo it, Harlan considered its holding as binding upon him. So now, acting as the Court's conscience, he attempted to show that the majority had dropped off the deep end by letting ideology trump reality. Harlan's peroration accurately summarized Brennan's conclusions although not in complimentary terms. The majority "transforms a political slogan into a constitutional absolute. Strait indeed is the path of the righteous legislator. Slide rule in hand, he must avoid all thought of county lines, local traditions, politics, history, and economics, so as to achieve the magic formula: one man, one vote."

How perfect is perfection? Implicit in Brennan's opinion was the conclusion that if a plaintiff had a better plan, then that plan should be implemented. The plaintiffs in *Wells* had a plan calling for a maximum deviation of 4.7 percent from the state average. That was only 1.9 percent better than the state's plan. It was also unconstitutional under *Kirkpatrick* although no one was so unkind as to say so, possibly because no one yet had produced an even better plan for New York. The plaintiffs' plan would allow 49.8 percent of the state's population to elect a majority of the congressional delegation—a whopping 0.5 percent improvement on the state's plan. But given that *Kirkpatrick* had rejected any concept of de minimis, the plaintiffs' plan was better. Whether it was that much better was irrelevant. But to what avail?

The Court's "exclusive concentration on arithmetic blinds it to the realities of the political process." Harlan, the patrician lawyer, understood this aspect of politics better than Warren or Black or Douglas or Brennan or Thurgood Marshall. Mathematical precision is "perfectly compatible with 'gerrymandering' of the worst sort." Even in those days of primitive computers, Harlan was able to note that a computer "may grind out district lines which can totally frustrate the popular will on an overwhelming number of critical issues."

The Supreme Court, 1953 Term. Bottom row, left to right: Felix Frankfurter, Hugo L. Black, Earl Warren, Stanley Reed, William O. Douglas. Top row, left to right: Tom Clark, Robert H. Jackson, Harold Burton, Sherman Minton. (Photographer: Harris and Ewing. Collection of the Supreme Court of the United States.)

Earl Warren. (Photographer: Fabian Bachrach. Collection of the Supreme Court of the United States.)

Hugo L. Black. (Photographer: Harris and Ewing. Collection of the Supreme Court of the United States.)

Felix Frankfurter. (Photographer: Pach Bros.,
New York. Collection of the Supreme
Court of the United States.)

John Marshall Harlan. (Collection of the
Supreme Court of the United States.)

William J. Brennan. (Photographer: George Van, Newark, N.J. Collection of the Supreme Court of the United States.)

John Birch Society sign. (Collection of the Supreme Court of the United States.)

The Supreme Court, 1962 Term. Bottom row, left to right: Tom Clark, Hugo L. Black, Earl Warren, William O. Douglas, John M. Harlan. Top row, left to right: Byron R. White, William J. Brennan, Potter Stewart, Arthur J. Goldberg. (Photographer: Harris and Ewing. Collection of the Supreme Court of the United States.)

Earl Warren and wife, Nina, with President Kennedy at a White House reception. (Courtesy of John F. Kennedy Library.)

Thurgood Marshall with President Johnson. (Photographer: Yoichi R. Okamoto. Courtesy of Lyndon B. Johnson Library.)

The Supreme Court, 1968 Term. Bottom row, left to right: John M. Harlan, Hugo L. Black, Earl Warren, William O. Douglas, William J. Brennan. Top row, left to right: Abe Fortas, Potter Stewart, Byron R. White, Thurgood Marshall. (Photographer: Harris and Ewing, Collection of the Supreme Court of the United States.)

President Johnson giving Abe Fortas "The Treatment" the day after he was nominated to the Court. (Photographer: Yoichi R. Okamoto. Courtesy of Lyndon B. Johnson Library.)

William O. Douglas with fourth wife, Cathy, in his favorite environment. (Collection of the Supreme Court of the United States.)

Harlan noted that this was not a hopelessly malapportioned legislature resisting change. But once *Reynolds* freed legislators from traditional lines, "the demands of blatant partisanship will [no longer] be tempered by constraints of tradition and history. If the Court believes it has struck a blow today for fully representative democracy, it is sorely mistaken." Instead, the Court has offered the party "temporarily dominant" in the state an opportunity to maximize its advantages. Harlan, whose eyes were failing badly, found himself in the unaccustomed role as the prophet of the Warren Court.

In 1969 in *Kramer v. Union Free School District*, the Court invalidated a New York law that limited the franchise in rural school elections to adults of the district who own or lease property or who have children in the schools. Kramer was an adult living with his parents. Warren's opinion virtually denies the states power to restrict the franchise except on the basis of age, citizenship, and residency. "Statutes granting the franchise to residents on a selective basis always pose the danger of denying some citizens any effective voice in the governmental affairs which substantially affect their lives." *Kramer* became the first case where the Court explained its underlying rationale. Legislation is entitled to a presumption of constitutionality because it is the product of a democratic process. When the process itself is challenged, it cannot be entitled to any presumptions. "And, the assumption is no less under attack because the legislature which decides who may participate at the various levels of political choice is fairly elected. Legislation which delegates decision making to bodies elected by only a portion of those eligible to vote for the legislature can cause unfair representation." Therefore, mere rationality is not enough to support the restriction; the restriction must be subjected to "close scrutiny." No governmental action that had been subjected to such scrutiny had been held constitutional since the *Japanese Relocation Cases* of World War II.

Stewart, for Black and Harlan, dissented. He took the concession of the majority that residence was a valid voter qualification and stated that if a legislature could presume those who were residents were most interested in an election, then the legislature could equally think that those who own or rent property or who have children in school are the most interested in a school election. Warren's opinion, resting on bedrock absolutism, offered no response.

At the end of Warren's last term, he handed down the opinion in *Powell v. McCormack* holding that Congress could not exclude an election victor on any grounds except that the winner failed to meet the requirements of the Qualifications Clause: twenty-one years old, seven years a citizen, a resident of the electing district. Powell was Adam Clayton Powell, the notorious congressman from Harlem whose constituents, focusing on his militant stand on behalf of civil rights, seemed unconcerned about his transgressions and therefore kept electing him to Congress. A House Select Committee concluded that Powell had "asserted an unwarranted privilege and immunity from the process of the courts of New York," had "wrongfully diverted funds for the use of others and himself," and had "made false reports on expenditures of foreign currency to the Committee on House Administration." Either House may expel a member by a two-thirds vote, but the House determined instead to exclude Powell, and by a vote of 307–116 it did so and declared his seat vacant.

Powell, with some constituents joining him as plaintiffs, then sued for his seat and back salary. The House defended by arguing that courts had no business deciding such cases and that in any event the Constitution explicitly states that "each House shall be the Judge of the . . . Qualification of its own Members."

After the court of appeals in an opinion by Warren E. Burger affirmed the dismissal of the case, Powell's constituents elected him to the next Congress. The case thus bore an unhappy resemblance to that of John Wilkes and the British Parliament some two hundred years earlier, where Parliament refused three times to seat him while his constituents sent him back each time. The new Congress, understanding what would happen should Powell be excluded again, seated him, but also fined him $25,000. Warren's opinion for the Court showed that was not only the wise course, it was the course consistent with the Constitution.

To some extent, *Powell* was a replay of *Baker v. Carr*. The issue that took the most time was justiciability, not the merits. The House argued that this was a political question and that the courts had no business at all supervising what the House does about membership. The political questions doctrine had gotten no clearer since *Baker,* and like *Baker,* the Court was not impressed with the argument that it should stay its hand. In words that indicated the political questions doctrine could properly be interred, Warren stated that "it is the responsibility of this Court to act as the ultimate interpreter of the Constitution." The responsibility to interpret the Constitution is inconsistent with ducking cases because of an amorphous concept like political questions. To be sure that no one missed the point that this was not just modern doctrine, the quoted sentence cited John Marshall's famous *Marbury v. Madison.*

Like *Baker,* the assumption was that if the Court intervened the case would be decided in favor of the plaintiff. Like *Baker,* it was. "'The cry of "Wilkes and Liberty" echoed loudly across the Atlantic Ocean as wide publicity was given to every step of Wilkes's public career . . . Colonials saw him as a popular hero and a martyr to the struggle for liberty.'"[51] Just as the British learned they should have seated Wilkes, so Congress learned that it should have seated Powell. When the Framers wrote the Qualifications Clause, they intended to prevent a repeat of Wilkes by making the qualifications short and certain. The text about each House being the judge of qualifications simply meant that each House could ascertain age, citizenship, and residence. If they were in order and the election was not contested on the merits, then the winner must be seated in the Congress. Once seated, should a house wish to expel the member, well, that was another case and one not before the Court. Douglas concurred to indicate that he would have found no justiciable controversy if there were a two-thirds vote to expel. Stewart dissented on the grounds that with Powell in the new Congress the case was moot—even though Powell was suing for his full salary from the previous Congress. Perhaps Stewart was anticipating that Powell could not collect anyway. Representative Sam Gibbons of Florida, who had filed the charge against Powell, reacted to the decision: "The Supreme Court has created a very dangerous confrontation between the two branches of government, and I would hardly think that the House will bow to the wishes of the Court on this most important question."[52]

Powell fit perfectly with the voting cases, and there was no outcry that the Court had transgressed an impermissible barrier even though this marked the first time the Court had asserted jurisdiction to settle constitutional questions involving internal congressional matters; indeed, Harlan had joined the opinion. Under the Court's egalitarianism all adults got to vote and their votes were to be weighted equally. Unstated, but obvious, was that the candidate of the majority of voters got to represent them. Congressional refusals to seat had to be based on questioning the outcome of the election, not the quality of the voters' choice.

Powell also seemed to close out an era. The Court had entered the political thicket and answered every single question tendered. For a period at least, there did not appear to be more to do except apply to any arising litigation the principles settled in the previous five years, although anyone taking Harlan's dissent in *Wells* seriously had cause to worry about whether the outcome would be either easy or just. But why would anyone worry about taking seriously someone so out of touch with his times?

Chapter 11

After the Civil Rights Act

In 1961 African-American students in Columbia, South Carolina, and Baton Rouge, Louisiana, marched downtown in orderly fashion, carried placards protesting discrimination, and sang the "Star Spangled Banner" while attracting a large crowd of white onlookers before the police ordered the demonstrators to disband. In 1963, in *Edwards v. South Carolina,* the Court stated that "the circumstances of this case reflect an exercise of these basic constitutional rights in their most pristine and classic form." In 1965, in *Cox v. Louisiana,* the Court stated that the case did not involve speech "in its pristine form but with conduct of a totally different character" and proceeded to detail some of the dangers of "mob" rule. One could easily be amazed at how such similar protests produced such a drastic change in tone, but that was the prelude to a changed message. *Cox* emphatically "reject[ed] the notion . . . that the First and Fourteenth Amendments afford the same kind of freedom to those who would communicate ideas by conduct such as patrolling, marching and picketing as these amendments afford to those who communicate ideas by pure speech."

Mass Demonstrations

The ease with which Stewart's opinion had reversed the *Edwards* breach of the peace convictions was gone in *Cox* (which consisted of two docketed cases with the identical name). One factor may have been numbers. *Edwards* had involved under 200 demonstrators; *Cox* involved 2,000, although only the leader of the demonstration, the Reverend Elton Cox, was charged with violations of the law and no arrests were made on the day of the demonstration. Another factor stemmed from the Louisiana law. In addition to breach of the peace, Cox was convicted of violating statutes prohibiting obstructing public passageways and picketing near a courthouse; his sentences were cumulative, a year and nine months in jail plus $5,700 in fines. All the justices agreed the breach of peace conviction had to be overturned on the basis of *Edwards*. Goldberg's opinion reversed the obstructing passageways conviction because the Court, on the record before it, found evidence that the statute had been administered as an informal licensing scheme without any standards for the exercise of discretion, something long unconstitutional. The courthouse picketing conviction was overturned because Goldberg concluded, after watching a tape of the demonstration as part of the Court's de novo review of the evidence, that the police chief had given his permission for the demonstrators to be where they were. It was thus a case of administrative estoppel where the state was forbidden to deny that the demonstrators had a right to be that "near" the courthouse.

Goldberg's opinion explicitly found the courthouse picketing statute was valid. Thus, if the police chief had not given his permission, the conviction would have been affirmed. Furthermore, in the obstructing passageways case Goldberg stated that "the rights of free speech and assembly, while fundamental in our democratic society, still do not mean that everyone with opinions or beliefs to express may address a group at any public place at any time. The constitutional guarantee of liberty implies the existence of an organized society maintaining public order, without which liberty itself would be lost in the excesses of anarchy." Anarchy is not a pristine exercise of liberty.

Harlan and White dissented in both cases. Black and Clark joined them in the courthouse picketing case, while concurring in the obstructing passageways case on the ground that the statute violated equal protection by exempting labor picketing. The dissenters thought that Goldberg's methods to reverse the convictions were just evasions, "very vague evidence" in the first case and the police chief being faced with a fait accompli in the second. If the opinions were taken at face value, all nine justices agreed the state could prohibit picketing near a courthouse and obstructing sidewalks.

The Court's new attitude showed the next year in *Brown v. Louisiana*, when a small peaceful protest in a public library could garner but five fragmented votes for overturning the conviction. Five African-Americans had entered a segregated library, and Brown asked for a book that it did not have. He was told it would be ordered for him and he would be called when it came in. Then Brown sat down and his four companions stood nearby. They were peaceful and quiet. Shortly thereafter the sheriff arrived and asked them to leave. When they did not, they were arrested and convicted for breach of the peace. Fortas, for Warren and Douglas, concluded that the African-Americans had a right to be in the library and were engaged in "appropriate" protest. There had been no disorder or any circumstances indicating a breach of the peace and hence their conviction was unconstitutional. Brennan took the overbreadth route to invalidate the Louisiana statute and therefore found it "wholly unnecessary" to discuss the underlying rights.

White and Stewart switched their votes from *Cox,* and White therefore provided the fifth vote to reverse. He stated that even though this was a protest, it was so much like the normal use of a library that "it is difficult to avoid the conclusion that the petitioners were asked to leave the library because they were Negroes." Difficult meant impossible, so the state action had violated equal protection.

Black, for the four dissenters, had no doubts about the case. It was "high time to challenge the assumption in which too many people have long acquiesced, that groups that think they have been mistreated or that actually have been mistreated have a constitutional right to use the public's streets, buildings, and property to protest whatever, wherever, whenever they want without regard to whom it may disturb." Libraries were about books and reading, not about protest.

Cox and *Brown,* while reversing convictions, indicated that the era of seeing demonstrations as pristine exercises of First Amendment rights had passed. It was now the era of mobs and anarchy. Whether one looked to Berkeley or to Watts or to the Student Non-Violent Coordinating Committee in the South, there seemed unfortunate confirmation. Assuming White rejoined his normal allies, there were five votes to sustain future convictions of demonstrators.

Ghettos, Campuses, and the South

Selma had sent civil rights to an all-time poll high as the nation's most pressing problem for well over 50 percent of all respondents. By the fall of 1966, a like number had concluded the Johnson administration was moving "too fast" on civil rights. Urban riots provide a sufficient explanation for the switch in results.

On July 18, 1964, a white patrolman in Harlem shot a fifteen-year-old African-American in the course of a routine arrest. This set off the first major urban race riot since World War II, as mobs looted and burned. In retrospect the riot was mild. The reason for retrospect was Watts, a year later, which began the transformation of the image of African-Americans from "that of the praying long-suffering nonviolent victim of southern sheriffs" to that of "a defiant young hoodlum shouting 'black power' and hurling 'Molotov cocktails' in an urban slum."[1]

Six days after the Voting Rights Act passed, a white police officer in Watts stopped a twenty-one-year-old African-American motorist who was both drunk and hostile. A crowd gathered; the officer called for backups; and within an hour the crowd was throwing rocks and bottles at the police while shouting "Burn, Baby, Burn!" For four days the nation watched televised clips of "men, women, and children walking through broken plate-glass windows in department, grocery, and liquor stores, carrying out all they could handle."[2] The African-American writer Louis Lomax confronted one man carrying a sofa from a burning furniture store and asked "do you realize what you're doing?" The answer was simple. "Don't bother me now. I've got to hurry back and get the matching chair."[3] By the third day, a dull orange haze from a thousand fires hung over the city. Then the National Guard arrived and slowly restored order.

Over 30,000 African-Americans had participated in the looting, burning, and sniping while twice that had been in the streets as supportive spectators. There were thirty-four dead, including a deputy sheriff and a firefighter shot by a sniper, 1,072 injured, 977 buildings destroyed or damaged, and 4,000 arrests. Martin Luther King, Jr., visiting Watts in the aftermath, was, according to Bayard Rustin, "absolutely undone."[4] Lyndon Johnson asked the question so many others asked too: "How is it possible after all we've accomplished?"[5]

Watts was a beginning, not an ending. In the summer of 1966, thirty-eight riots destroyed ghetto neighborhoods from Providence to Cleveland to San Francisco although none approached the scale of Watts. That would wait a year for the "long hot summer" of 1967 where by the end of September there had been 164 riots, a fifth of them large enough to bring in state troopers. Two, Newark and Detroit, matched Watts.

Detroit's was the worst riot in a century. "Smoke rose over the commercial strips in the stillness of the hot, smoggy Sunday afternoon; after nightfall radios in the police commissioner's office reported with the crackle of static first one, then another, then still another square mile or so of ghetto being abandoned by the police and the National Guard to those who were setting it aflame."[6] The violence, unlike Watts, was indiscriminate as both African-American and white stores were burned and looted. Governor George Romney became the first governor in decades to ask for federal troops, and, with legal advice from Abe Fortas, Johnson dispatched 4,700 paratroopers from Fort Bragg to quell the riots. When it was over, Mayor Jerome Cavanaugh stated, "It looks like Berlin in 1945."[7] By the end of the three years of riots, there were over 200 dead, several thousand wounded, and tens of billions of dollars in property damage. And the rioting in Boston, New York, Newark, Trenton, Baltimore, Pittsburgh, Cincinnati, Detroit, Nashville, Memphis, Kansas City, Oakland, and more than a hundred small cities, and most spectacularly in the nation's capital, after King's assassination was yet to occur.

The ghetto riots could be explained, and many white liberals worked overtime doing it. Campus disturbances were something else again because they involved the most privileged group of young Americans. The Free Speech Movement at Berkeley initiated the new campus radicalism, and thereafter Berkeley remained a hotbed of campus activism. But there were many competitors, and the end of the Warren era witnessed the shutting down of Columbia and militant protests at dozens of other campuses in 1968. Tom Hayden, in *Ramparts,* enthusiastically proclaimed, "we are moving toward power—the power to stop the machine if he cannot be made to serve human ends," and he called for, in the title of his piece, "Two, Three, Many Columbias."[8]

The problems at Berkeley were initiated in the fall of 1964 by an insensitive bureaucracy headed by President Clark Kerr. The confrontation began when students returned to campus to learn that political activity was henceforth prohibited along the brick pavement creating Sproul Plaza even though it had always occurred there. When a civil rights worker set up a table in protest, a police car arrived to arrest him, and then hundreds of students spontaneously sat down around the car, holding the arresting officers captive, and using its roof as a platform for an open forum for well over a day. The Free Speech Movement was born. Its leader was the charismatic Mario Savio, back at Berkeley from Freedom Summer in Mississippi.

Two months into the demonstrations, Savio made a fiery speech, seizing on Kerr's then-current characterization of the modern university, especially California, as a "multiversity."[9] Savio instead characterized the university as a machine and told the crowd that "you've got to put your bodies upon the gears, upon the wheels, upon all the apparatus and you've got to make it stop."[10] With that a thousand students marched into Sproul Hall, the administration building, to sit in, "less to achieve free speech than to protest the oppressiveness of the liberal university."[11]

A day later Democratic Governor Edmund "Pat" Brown ordered the police in and there were 773 arrests. Students determined to strike over the free speech issues, the faculty backed the students, and the administration ran up the white flag. Students, soon faced with Vietnam, saw the Free Speech Movement as a positive model. Adults, more worried about the lines between authority and anarchy, had an opposite reaction, especially as the Free Speech Movement turned into an obscenity-spewing "Filthy Speech Movement," in Kerr's telling phrase.[12]

With the passage of the Voting Rights Act, the civil rights movement had achieved most of its formal legal goals, but just changing the law did not make the underlying problems vanish immediately. Robert Weisbrot, in his history of the movement, notes that "a malaise crept over the movement."[13] People were tired and burned out. Bob Moses left SNCC, moved north, and abandoned his name for the nonbiblical Robert Paris. Weisbrot continued by noting, "the mass saintliness that had sustained the nonviolent revolution was at last giving way to more common if less admirable human responses—frustration, blind rage, and perhaps inevitably, racial hate."[14]

In May 1966 Stokely Carmichael defeated John Lewis before the "exhausted remnants of the SNCC convention" to become the new chairman.[15] A month later, on seeing how effective the cry "Black Power" was in creating a frenzy in an audience, Carmichael picked it up himself and witnessed its magic. When King subsequently asked him to find something less divisive, Carmichael refused. No other slogan had such an appeal to African-American audiences or to white newsmen who found him more interesting than the Nobel Peace Prize winner. The press proceeded to anoint Carmichael as the new leader of African-Americans. Yet he lasted but a year, voluntarily stepping aside in May 1967 to be replaced by H. "Rap" Brown. Carmichael accurately told the press, "You'll be happy to have me back after you hear from him—he's a bad man."[16]

It took no time at all for Brown to become the nation's symbol of African-American rage. With the fires of Newark still smoldering, he urged Jersey City African-Americans to "wage guerrilla war on the honkie white man."[17] After Detroit he declared that "we live in the belly of the monster. So it's up to us to destroy its brain."[18] In Columbia, Maryland, he urged African-American youths to "burn this town down" and not to "love a white to death," but to "shoot him to death."[19] Maryland Governor Spiro Agnew began his ascent to the vice presidency by ordering Brown's arrest and declaring that "I hope they pick him up soon, put him away and throw away the key."[20] Brown had become the most hated man in America, and a federal law forbidding the crossing of state lines for purposes of riot was known as the "Rap Brown Law."

By the time Brown preached race hate and guerrilla warfare on national television, the damage that King feared was more than done. While Great Society liberals puzzled over explanations, others believed they already knew. House Republican leader Gerald Ford could ask an audience: "How long are we going to abdicate law and order—the backbone of civilization—in the form of soft social theory that the man who throws a brick through your window or tosses a fire bomb into your car is simply the misunderstood and underprivileged product of a broken home?"[21] Ford perfectly projected the Republican message of blaming "both riots and radicalism on the 'soft' social programs of the Democrats."[22] In the November 1966 elections the Republicans gained forty-seven House and three Senate seats—more than the new Democrats who had flooded in with Johnson's tidal wave—basically at the expense of liberal allies of the Great Society. Ronald Reagan swamped the incumbent Pat Brown by over a million votes for governor of California, and 540 new Republicans were elected to state legislatures.

The Court's New Attitude

Immediately after the 1966 elections, the Court decided *Adderley v. Florida*. White did rejoin his natural allies, and Black wrote an opinion enshrining into law the views he had been espousing since 1964: Trespass trumps the First Amendment. By a 5–4 vote.

Thirty-two Florida A&M students were convicted of trespass with a malicious or mischievous intent for peaceably picketing on the grounds of the county jail where a number of other students were held, having been arrested the previous day for protesting segregation. Black saw the case as nothing but trespass, and following his dissent in *Brown v. Louisiana,* he saw no difference between public and private property. The jail was under the sheriff's control and when he said leave, that was it. Black was explicit that it did not matter that the jail was chosen as the site of the protest because other students were held there. "Such an argument has as its major unarticulated premise the assumption that people who want to propagandize protests or views have a constitutional right to do so whenever and however and wherever they please. . . . We reject" that concept. *Cox* had begun the transformation of peaceable protest into the fear of the mob; *Adderley* completed it.

Douglas, for all the dissenters, wrote his best opinion in fifteen years. For him the case was about the ability of the poor as well as the rich to try to influence public opinion and gain their government's attention. "Those who do not control television and radio, those who cannot advertise in newspapers or circulate elaborate pamphlets have only a more limited type of access to public officials." And turning their protest into a trespass action does "violence" to the First Amendment.

Douglas agreed with the majority that not all demonstrations were constitutionally protected. "A noisy meeting may be out of keeping with the serenity of the statehouse or the quiet of a courthouse." But this was a jail and the students were peaceful—no shoving, no pushing, no disorder, no threat of riot. Furthermore, the jail was exactly the place to protest the unconstitutional arrest of their friends. "The jailhouse, like an executive mansion, a legislative chamber, a courthouse, or the statehouse itself . . . is one of the seats of government, whether it be the Tower of London, the Bastille, or a small county jail. And when it houses political prisoners or those whom many think are unjustly held, it is an obvious center for protest." Appropriateness of the site is defined by context, not by law enforcement officials.

Black had been lecturing protesters that they were not constitutionally free to do anything they pleased. In *Walker v. Birmingham,* Stewart lectured them about the need to respect the law. *Walker* was the penultimate chapter of the 1963 Good Friday march where King and the others had decided to march rather than delay even though there was an ex parte injunction from a local judge prohibiting the march.

Stewart's opinion is easily summarized. There was an order from a court that had jurisdiction over the parties, and so long as the order was not "transparently invalid" it had to be obeyed because "no man can be judge in his own case, however exalted his station, however righteous his motives." To be sure King's cause was a good one. "But respect for the judicial process is a small price to pay for the civilizing hand of law, which alone can give abiding meaning to constitutional freedom."

Warren, Douglas, and Brennan dissented, with Fortas joining each. They all said the same thing. First, the Birmingham parade ordinance was patently unconstitutional and everyone knew it. Second, an ex parte injunction tracking the words of a patently unconstitutional ordinance does not suddenly transmute the unconstitutional ordinance into a valid respected law. Third, judges too must respect the law, and the Birmingham trial judge had to know his injunction was unconstitutional. Surprisingly, it was Brennan who unleashed the strongest rhetoric. He thought the majority had let "loose a devastatingly destructive weapon for the suppression of cherished freedoms." King agreed, stating that the "use of the injunction as a crippling device could very well break the back of the nonviolent movement."[23] More significantly, Brennan charged that the majority's fears of riots and civil disobedience had diverted attention from the fact that it was Alabama, not King, that had behaved lawlessly.

In retrospect it seems strange to read an opinion of the Court that is a lecture at and to King. But he had already stated that he would "stir up trouble" in northern cities during the summer,[24] and as another "long hot summer" approached, many Americans believed that King too needed to be reminded of the importance of law. Oregon's moderate Republican Mark Hatfield had told an audience that civil rights leaders "including King" had "sowed the seeds" of the urban riots by preaching civil disobedience.[25] Black had said virtually the same thing two years earlier during Watts, and had even, like the Kennedys, opposed the March on Washington. "The demonstrations would lead to riots and anarchy; Watts was part of the lawless spirit of the times."[26] Stewart's lecture on law was a pointed reminder from the establishment that law (or at least the commands of judges) counted (even as that reminder had to ignore the fact that at the time King disobeyed the injunction the Alabama Supreme Court was in open defiance of the Court itself in the NAACP litigation.) Times had changed.

Walker was the only one of King's convictions that was not set aside on appeal. It was ironic that when the majority's patience ran out and their fears were heightened, it was King, not a real lawbreaker, who was the party.

Two years later, in *Shuttlesworth v. Birmingham,* the Court returned to the Good Friday march for the final time—now six years after it occurred. A unanimous Court, through Stewart, found the Birmingham ordinance that underlay the *Walker* injunction to be as unconstitutional as the *Walker* dissenters had claimed. Shuttlesworth, speaking about the affirmed contempt convictions in *Walker,* deserves the final word. "When you consider all that the Birmingham movement accomplished in advancing civil rights, I'm glad to pay the very small price of five days in jail."[27]

Protecting Civil Rights Workers

Just as in the late 1950s and early 1960s when the Court had a number of cases dealing with attempts to hamstring the NAACP, in the mid-1960s it began to see a new generation of cases brought by more activist, youthful organizations claiming that southern laws were being used to thwart their efforts at changing southern society. In the earlier era it took time, but the NAACP had invariably prevailed. The newer cases, with more far-reaching claims and coming in the post–Civil Rights Act era, did not invariably result in civil rights victories.

The organizations' one major success, *Dombrowski v. Pfister*, was a significant victory and produced a tour de force by Brennan over a dissent by Harlan and Clark. (Neither Black nor Stewart participated in the case.) The Southern Conference Educational Fund (SCEF) charged that Louisiana officials were using the state's Communist Propaganda Control Law and its Subversive Activities and Communist Control Law to harass SCEF in its pursuit of civil rights for African-Americans, and it sued for an injunction against enforcement of those laws. The complaint in federal court charged that state officials were threatening prosecution, which had no hope of securing valid convictions, and that they were using the laws and the threat of prosecution to discourage members, frighten potential members away, and bring the organization to a halt. James Pfister, chairman of the State Un-American Activities Committee, had helped the plaintiffs by an outbreak of candor when he stated their arrests resulted from "racial agitation." The SCEF offices had been raided and a truckload of their files and records seized at gunpoint, but a state judge found there had not been probable cause and therefore the seizures were unlawful.

The facts were appealing, but SCEF nevertheless faced serious hurdles in having its case heard by a federal court. One was a federal statute that prohibited enjoining state prosecutions. A second was a judicial policy of noninterference with state prosecutions because state courts are entitled to a strong presumption that they will follow the law and, in any event, eventual review by the Court could correct any errors and vindicate constitutional rights. *Dombrowski* took all of Brennan's imagination. He began by construing a second federal statute, §1983 from the Ku Klux Klan Act of 1871, which had been construed in *McNeese v. Board of Education* to authorize an exception to the exhaustion of state administrative remedies, to create also an express exception to the anti-injunction statute; so the case turned on policy. The Louisiana statutes were overbroad; that is, they covered much activity that was fully protected by the First Amendment. They were also vague; that is, a person could not be sure what activity they covered and what activity they left free. A single prosecution might not narrow the statutes sufficiently and so there would remain a chilling effect not only on SCEF activities but on the willingness of others to join SCEF, since to do so might expose them to prosecution. "The chilling effect upon the exercise of First Amendment rights may derive from the fact of the prosecution, unaffected by the prospects of its success or failure." Accordingly, abstaining from deciding the questions until review of any criminal convictions "is inappropriate in cases such as the present one where . . . statutes are justifiably attacked on their face as abridging free expression, or as applied for the purpose of discouraging protected activities."

Harlan's dissent rested on two points. First was federalism. He found the majority insensitive to the legitimate demands of the state courts. After all, the Louisiana courts had already upheld SCEF's claim about the illegal seizure of its books. Second was the unknown. Harkening back to his views about the ultimate value of self-preservation, Harlan asked what if the organization was really "conspiring to stage a forcible coup d'etat?" Harlan's federalism point was apt, although the majority was not in the mood to exalt federalism over civil rights. Harlan's concern about a conspiracy to overthrow the Louisiana government either looks like a throwback to the early 1950s or a prescient guess about the future formation of the Black Panthers. Since Harlan was no seer, it was an example of an overheated imagination. If the only cost to *Dombrowski* was leaving Louisiana at risk of a coup d'etat, there was little to worry about.

Harlan accurately read *Dombrowski* as authorizing an injunction against prosecution whenever civil rights workers were criminally charged under a vague or overbroad statute and no narrower ruling seems likely given the statute's language. Brennan had created a remedy for the 1960s. Just as *Brown II* had enlisted the federal courts, so too would *Dombrowski* as the means for freeing civil rights organizations from local harassment. This helps explain why Brennan referred to the *Walker* injunction as "devastatingly destructive." He knew the importance of an injunction and the ability of one side to legally freeze the other through its use. The only problem proved to be timing. *Dombrowski* was decided in 1965 just as the traditional civil rights protest was passing from the scene. In that sense it is fully related to *Walker*. *Dombrowski* was from the era of peaceful protest, *Walker* from the subsequent era of riots and disorder even though the facts of each date from the earlier era.

Civil rights and antiwar movement lawyers agreed with Harlan's reading as a minimum position, but they went one step farther. As Charles Alan Wright, the leading authority on the federal courts, described the situation, movement lawyers "read *Dombrowski* as meaning that every person prosecuted under state law for conduct arguably protected by the First Amendment could, by murmuring the words 'chilling effect,' halt the state prosecution while a federal court passed on the validity of the statute and the bona fides of state law enforcement officers."[28] Since all civil rights and antiwar protests had some element arguably protected, there were hundreds of such cases brought in the lower courts, which in turn decided them "in every possible direction."[29]

Cameron v. Johnson in 1968 showed that the broadest reading of *Dombrowski* was untenable. This should have been obvious at the beginning, since *Cameron* had been vacated and remanded a few weeks after *Dombrowski* came down, so that the court of appeals could reconsider it in light of *Dombrowski*. Black, Harlan, Stewart, and, most significantly, White dissented, with White bluntly stating that although he had joined *Dombrowski,* he found it inapplicable on the facts of *Cameron*.

Cameron involved voter registration picketing in Hattiesburg, Mississippi, at the courthouse, where the registrar's office was located. The picketing had begun in January 1964 and continued for months. Then the Mississippi legislature passed the Anti-Picketing Law, which prohibited "picketing in such a manner as to obstruct or unreasonably interfere with free ingress or egress to and from any courthouse." Arrests followed immediately, and *Cameron* was an attempt to enjoin enforcement of the statute. Brennan held that the statute was not invalid on its face, a conclusion foreshadowed by *Cox,* nor was there any showing of bad faith enforcement. Hence *Dombrowski* was inapplicable. The Court refused to infer bad faith from the claims that the picketers were innocent. Fortas and Douglas dissented, believing there was no showing that the picketers had blocked the courthouse and therefore the arrests and prosecutions were made in bad faith.

The outcome of *Cameron* matched that of civil rights removal, decided in 1966. Congress has provided in a number of statutes for removal of a case from a state court to a federal court. When removal occurs—and the decision is that of the federal court—the state court loses jurisdiction and can no longer proceed. The civil rights removal statute, dating from an 1866 predecessor, authorizes removal to federal court by defendants who cannot secure in a state court civil rights guaranteed to them by federal statutes or the Constitution. That seemed to fit most southern civil rights cases perfectly.

City of Greenwood v. Peacock, like *Cameron,* dealt with voter registration efforts in Mississippi both before and during Freedom Summer. Unlike *Cameron*, the twenty-nine defendants were charged with breach of the peace and disorderly conduct. In petitioning for removal, they alleged their arrests were for the sole purpose of harassment and that they would be tried in segregated courtrooms, before all-white juries, and by judges who had gained office in elections where African-Americans were denied the right to vote. The Court held that even so, the cases were not removable. Construing the removal statute, Stewart stated that it "is *not* enough to support removal . . . to allege or show that the defendants' federal equal civil rights have been illegally and corruptly denied by state administrative officials in advance of trial, that the charges against the defendants are false, or that the defendant is unable to obtain a fair trial in a particular state court." Cutting to the heart of the matter, Stewart concluded that federal law "does not require and does not permit the judges of the federal courts to put their brethren of the state judiciary on trial." That was the key. Had *Peacock* gone the other way, as Douglas, Warren, Brennan, and Fortas in dissent urged, every state charge against civil rights workers would have had to be tried first in federal court. Nevertheless, any civil rights case out of Mississippi was a case where the defendants stood no chance at all.

A companion case, *Georgia v. Rachel,* was truly the last pre–Civil Rights Act sit-in case. The Court authorized removal in *Rachel* because *Hamm v. City of Rock Hill* had already held that the Civil Rights Act wholly immunized the conduct at issue. Because of *Hamm* "any proceedings" in a state court would constitute a denial of the right conferred since the right itself included being free of the burden of defending a prosecution.

Peacock and *Rachel* made sense. It was asking too much to bring the criminal law of the South to a halt in all cases involving civil rights protests. To do so would have been to issue a blanket vote of no confidence in the southern state judiciary, perhaps a justified vote, but an extraordinarily difficult one nevertheless. *Dombrowski* could be read to offer much, but *Cameron* indicated it meant far less than movement lawyers thought. *Dombrowski* could not have been decided as it was before Frankfurter retired, when such a holding might have had an impact in the South. But when it did come down, its time had virtually passed. With the Civil Rights Act of 1964 and the Voting Rights Act of 1965 on the books and SNCC turning to Black Power, the political and legal landscape of the South had been radically transformed. The Court needed no hints from the representative branches of government to reach these results. In the technical area of federal jurisdiction, especially when the only affected region was the South, the Court had a free hand. It offered or withheld relief as it deemed the circumstances required.

Racial Discrimination

Ever since *Brown,* the Court had been happiest unanimously striking down clear examples of racial discrimination. After the Civil Rights Act and the Voting Rights Act were on the books, the core issues of white supremacy passed with but a single exception. In their place came more complex issues, two involving popular votes in referenda. More fundamentally, these were issues in which the South was not the target. And when civil rights moved out of the South, unanimity vanished. A City College of New York professor and student civil rights adviser explained the waning northern interest in civil rights in 1966 this way: It was "much easier to take a stand on civil rights when the issue was remote or abstract."[30]

Naim v. Naim had left one of the cornerstones of white supremacy—the prohibition on interracial marriage—standing. In 1964 in *McLaughlin v. Florida,* involving habitual cohabitation, and in 1967 in *Loving v. Virginia,* involving Virginia's miscegenation statute, the Court unanimously interred these final remnants of the southern legal order.

In 1883 *Pace v. Alabama* had sustained a prohibition against interracial fornication as consistent with equal protection because the law affected African-Americans and whites alike; neither could have sex with the other. Alabama was hardly alone. Even as late as World War II over 60 percent of the states had laws prohibiting interracial marriage. Then in the North and West a repealing movement commenced, and by the 1960s the South and the border states remained the lone holdouts.

White's opinion striking down the cohabitation statute is an unsure effort. After noting that the crime is based on the race of the parties, he states that "the central purpose of the 14th Amendment was to eliminate racial discrimination emanating from official sources in the States." Yet, as the opinion continues, White suggests that some racial classifications might be okay. "A law which trenches upon the constitutionally protected freedom from invidious official discrimination based on race . . . bears a heavy burden of justification and will be upheld only if it is necessary, and not merely rationally related, to the accomplishment of a permissible state policy." The structure of the opinion is one of looking for and being unable to find a sufficient justification for the statute.

Stewart, joined by Douglas, offered a terse contrast to the majority in condemning the Florida law without regard to possible justifications. He acknowledged that a law requiring public records be kept by race for statistical purposes would be valid, but a criminal law was something else. "I think it is simply not possible for a state law to be valid under our Constitution which makes the criminality of an act depend on the race of the actor. Discrimination of that kind is invidious *per se.*"

In 1958 Richard Loving and Mildred Jeter had gone to the District of Columbia to be married. Then they had returned to rural Virginia where they soon were rousted out of bed and arrested for violating Virginia's law, which dated from 1691 (and, while forbidding whites from marrying anyone except whites, made an exception for descendants of Pocahontas and John Rolfe). After they pleaded guilty, the judge suspended a one-year sentence on condition that they leave the state for twenty-five years. They headed back to the District, but after becoming homesick they secretly moved back to rural Virginia to raise a family. Still hiding, they subsequently began proceedings to have the statute set aside so that they could live openly without fear of jail.

Even as the Court was ducking *Naim v. Naim,* Warren privately characterized the decision to his law clerks as "total bullshit."[31] He kept *Loving* for himself to undo the decade-old blight, and, possibly because of his lingering anger, his opinion was far sharper than White's in *McLaughlin*. It held that the racial statutes must be subjected to the "most rigid scrutiny" and be shown necessary to the accomplishment of a permissible objective. Rather than hunt for one, Warren announced the obvious, that none was conceivable. Additionally, in two quick paragraphs Warren also found the law denied the Lovings liberty without due process because marriage was one of the basic civil rights of man and the state offered "so unsupportable a basis" as race for depriving them of the right to marry whomsoever they chose. Stewart concurred, reiterating his *McLaughlin* conclusion.

In *McLaughlin* the Legal Defense Fund cited the first Harlan's *Plessy* dissent for the proposition that the Constitution was "color blind" and hence race was a constitutional "irrelevance."[32] The LDF could have made a similar argument in *Loving* but did not. Indeed, *Loving* marked the first time the LDF filed a brief in a racial classification case that "omitted any reference to the inherently invidious nature of racial classifications or to race as a constitutional 'irrelevance.'"[33] The LDF was rethinking its views on race and moving from color-blindness to color-consciousness.

McLaughlin and *Loving* were easy, but three other cases, one from Georgia but with some national implications, and the others from California and Ohio, caused difficulties. The Court was split and the majority could not easily explain the outcomes beyond simple protection of African-Americans.

Evans v. Newton in 1966 was about Baconsfield, a segregated park in Macon created by former Georgia Senator Augustus Bacon's will in 1911. The city of Macon was named trustee of the park and had maintained it, but after *Brown* it determined it could no longer operate the park on a segregated basis, so it successfully petitioned a state court to appoint private successor trustees who could. Douglas blocked that move, stating that on the record before the Court, it still looked as if the city was maintaining Baconsfield as before. While that was enough for reversal, Douglas then went farther by noting that "the service rendered even by a private park of this character is municipal in nature . . . like a fire department or a police department that traditionally serves the community." Douglas was clearly suggesting that private activity paralleling a like government activity might be deemed governmental and therefore forbidden to discriminate on the basis of race. The problem of private schools jumps to mind.

Harlan, joined by Stewart, dissented, especially condemning the public function analysis, which he understood "at least in logic, jeopardizes the existence of denominationally restricted schools while making every college entrance rejection letter a potential 14th Amendment question." Black dissented as well, claiming the case was only about the appointment of successor trustees and not whether Baconsfield could be operated on a segregated basis. Under this theory, contesting segregation in Baconsfield would take a second lawsuit. Presciently, he noted that if successor trustees could not be appointed, Baconsfield should revert to Senator Bacon's heirs under a long-standing racially neutral Georgia law similar to that in all other states. (In 1970 he wrote *Evans v. Abney* reaching just that result over the dissenting votes of Douglas and Brennan.)

At the same time the nation was granting Lyndon Johnson his desired mandate, California voters, by an astounding and even greater margin of 4,526,460 to 2,395,747, adopted a new provision for their state constitution. Proposition 14 guaranteed to property owners the right to absolute discretion in selling or leasing property to whomsoever they chose. Proposition 14 by its own force repealed two existing fair housing laws and made future fair housing laws impossible to pass without first amending the state constitution. Three years later in *Reitman v. Mulkey* the Court divided 5–4 in striking down Proposition 14. A state is not constitutionally required to have fair housing laws, but if it does, then repealing them constituted a violation of equal protection. That was the stark outcome. If that was the meaning of what the Court was doing, then it would take a lot of explaining. To the extent that it was very difficult to explain, White was fully capable of the necessary obfuscation.

White took the legal conclusion of the California Supreme Court that the necessary effect of Proposition 14 would be to repeal the state's fair housing laws and therefore to authorize private discrimination in housing—and he treated it like a fact. Thus, he had the California court stating that Proposition 14, a part of the state constitution, authorized racial discrimination in housing. Neither California nor a Carolina could do that; that was an unconstitutional violation of equal protection. The problem with the conclusion was its overbreadth. Any state lacking fair housing laws "authorizes" discrimination in housing in the same sense that California did; that is, the state law, by not prohibiting discrimination, "authorizes" it.

Harlan, for Black, Clark, and Stewart, dissented and made the obvious argument that the people of California had objected to what their elected representatives had done and exercised their rights to repeal it and prevent the representatives from doing it again. There was nothing, the dissent urged, unconstitutional about that.

Two years later, with a huge assist from Charles Black in the "Foreword" to the *Harvard Law Review*,[34] the Court figured out how *Reitman* should have been written. Akron's voters, annoyed that the city council had passed a fair housing law, amended the city charter to provide that regulations of real estate transactions on the basis of race had to be approved by the city voters before taking effect. *Hunter v. Erickson* invalidated the referendum requirement. White noted that the classification was specifically racial and that it made it harder for those seeking an end to racial discrimination in housing to prevail in the political process than for those wishing to regulate real estate transactions in any other way. While the charter amendment drew no distinctions among racial groups, "the reality is that the law's impact falls on the minority."

Only Black dissented. He stated that the Court was using the Equal Protection Clause the way earlier Courts had used due process to strike down laws they did not like. Black stated that the Court "uses this granted right of the people to vote on this important legislation as a key argument for holding that the repealer denies equal protection to Negroes. Just consider that for a moment. In this Government, which we boast is 'of the people, by the people, and for the people,' conditioning the enactment of a law on a majority vote of the people condemns that law as unconstitutional in the eyes of the Court!" Somehow with his failing vision and failing health, Black would not see that the Akron voters had targeted minorities. Two years earlier, during oral argument in *Giles v. Maryland,* a rape case involving African-American brothers and a white woman, Black asked the Giles's counsel the totally irrelevant question: "Is there any indication how many times the victim consented with Nigra men?"[35] The Court reversed the Giles's convictions while Black dissented (with Harlan, Clark, and Stewart).

The NAACP suffered a huge defeat in *Swain v. Alabama* in 1965. Despite decades of rulings that states were forbidden to exclude African-Americans from juries, *Swain* refused to hold that it was unconstitutional for a prosecutor to use his peremptory challenges to remove all African-Americans from the jury. Alabama used a "struck" jury; that is, a procedure where the defendant and the prosecution alternate striking potential jurors, the defense having two strikes for every one by the prosecution, until only twelve jurors remain. More than any other decision, *Swain* had northern implications, for even though a "struck" jury was not the norm, it was common throughout the country for prosecutors and defense counsel to base peremptory challenges on the race of the potential juror.

Swain was a nineteen-year-old African-American youth convicted for raping a seventeen-year-old white girl and then sentenced to death. The group of eligible jurors was 74 percent white and the venire was about 85 percent white; the jury that convicted was all-white, the prosecutor having struck the six eligible African-Americans.

White, for the Court, recognized the long-standing principle that systematic exclusion of African-Americans was a violation of equal protection, but found it inapplicable since there were African-Americans available on the venire—even though no one alive could remember them having served on a jury. Peremptory challenges, exercised without having to provide any reason for their use, had a very long pedigree and were used in all the states. They could be used against anyone, for any reason, and therefore for no reason at all. "With these considerations in mind, we cannot hold that the striking of Negroes in a particular case is a denial of equal protection of the laws. In the question for an impartial and qualified jury, Negro and white, Protestant and Catholic, are alike subject to being challenged without cause." To prohibit racial strikes would "entail a radical change" and "establish a rule wholly at odds with the peremptory challenge system as we know it." The majority being unwilling to order the radical change, Swain's death sentence was affirmed.

Goldberg, for Warren and Douglas, dissented. The actual workings of the system showed its unconstitutionality and if preventing the prosecutor from systematically basing his peremptory challenges on race were a radical change, well, so be it. The defendant showed a systematic exclusion of African-Americans from juries, and applying prior law to the facts of the case required a reversal of his conviction.

In many respects *Swain* is one of the most surprising decisions by the Warren Court. It was a death penalty case for rape, and the showing of discrimination was plain. Yet White, Black, Clark, Harlan, Stewart, and, most surprisingly, Brennan were unmoved. On a Court that was inordinately willing to order radical change and to ignore a contrary history— just ask every malapportioned state legislature—peremptory challenges were deemed too grounded in the past and so it would be too radical for the Court to change the system. (In *Batson v. Kentucky* (1986) the Court overruled *Swain*.)

Marshall's Appointment

Black's "leaving" on the race issue was more than matched by a new arrival at the beginning of the 1967 Term—Thurgood Marshall. He fit in perfectly, voting with the majority 95 percent of the time. This was remarkable for the simple fact that it was only achieved by two others. Brennan did it for eight years running, an unbelievable record. The other justice to do it was Warren and he did it but once.

Six years earlier Marshall had left the NAACP Legal Defense Fund, concluding that he had outlasted his usefulness as the lead NAACP litigator in a changed world featuring more direct action. John Kennedy, looking for a cheap civil rights move, wanted to make Marshall a federal district judge, but Marshall successfully held out for the court of appeals. Kennedy nominated him to the Second Circuit in New York to appease southern senators who would not have tolerated him sitting on a court deciding their cases. James Eastland assured Robert Kennedy that the Senate "would be allowed to vote on Marshall's confirmation once the Southern Democrats had milked the nomination for its political benefit to them."[36] They delayed about as long as possible, and then Eastland let the Senate confirm Marshall.

After Johnson's election in 1964, Solicitor General Archibald Cox submitted his resignation believing that was the way to ensure he had

Johnson's support when, as Cox expected, Johnson would refuse to accept the resignation. Johnson instead called Marshall, told him he was "a patriot of very high ability," and stated "he wanted the public to see a Negro arguing cases for the Government of the United States at the Supreme Court."[37] Johnson was very persuasive, as Goldberg would soon note, but he was asking Marshall to surrender a lifetime job for one that was at the pleasure of the president. Marshall's biographer, Mark Tushnet, says his decision to yield life tenure on the court of appeals "was not very calculating,"[38] while Attorney General Nicholas Katzenbach noted it was inconceivable that Marshall would have given up his seat unless he understood Johnson as promising the Court. Surely that is true, although as Goldberg learned to his dismay, the unarticulated promise might not have been granted.

Of course, Johnson loved firsts, and he did want to appoint the first African-American to the Court. But to do so, he needed a vacancy. Just as he created one for Fortas, he created one for Marshall. Like a clever baseball manager, he moved certain players into unexpected positions that generated the hoped-for result. First, he moved Katzenbach from attorney general to undersecretary of state. Then he made Deputy Attorney General Ramsey Clark the acting attorney general. Six months later he nominated Clark—Tom Clark's son—as attorney general. Because of the Government's role at the Court, Johnson could assume that the father would have to yield his seat—as he did. All other presidents waited for vacancies, but Johnson was not like others. He created two vacancies because there were two people who, for entirely different reasons, he wanted to reward with the highest judicial office.

Apparently Johnson hesitated momentarily when his wife suggested he should appoint the first woman because he had already done so much for African-Americans. Then he did what he wanted to do, announcing "I believe that it is the right thing to do, the right time to do it, the right man and the right place."[39] Privately, when aide Larry Temple suggested he nominate instead federal judge A. Leon Higginbotham, also an African-American, Johnson responded that "the only two people who ever heard of Judge Higginbotham are you and his momma. When I appoint a nigger to the bench, I want everyone to know he's a nigger."[40] The symbolism was indeed the point, and Johnson expected thousands of mothers to name their sons Thurgood. Doris Kearns Goodwin's check of New York and Boston revealed that not a one did.[41]

The Senate hearings were a southern-only affair where Marshall's supporters laid low and allowed the South to have its verbal moment because, in fact, the nomination produced "hardly a ripple of adverse comment."[42] Marshall came out of the Judiciary Committee with a 11–5 vote and was confirmed 69–11 with all the negatives from the usual southern suspects like Eastland, Sam Ervin, and Strom Thurmond (although Richard Russell was one of those not voting). The *Washington Post* pronounced the day "an occasion for self-congratulation."[43]

It was also an occasion for the resolidifying of the liberal bloc. James J. Kilpatrick had accurately, if unaesthetically, complained that Marshall would immediately join the "horseblindered liberal ideologist faction," and he did.[44] Warren, Douglas, Brennan, and Fortas no longer needed to worry about the aging Black's hardening of the categories nor his defection in cases involving race. They had a secure fifth vote who, like the others, believed he had been placed on the Court to exercise his judgment about how best to solve society's conflicts.

School Segregation

For the first half of Warren's tenure, the Court decided few school cases, did not break segregation except in the border states and Tennessee and Texas, and did not state what it expected of the South. During the second half of Warren's tenure, those same three aspects—first, lack of participation; second, lack of results; and third, lack of candor—persisted.

First, the Court, having declared war in *Brown*, still remained largely absent without leave. After *Cooper*, it waited five years before deciding its next case, *Goss v. Board of Education*. After the Civil Rights Act of 1964, it decided two easy cases in 1965 both as per curiams. One ordered an end to faculty discrimination; the other announced that the time for grade-a-year plans had passed. The Court then waited three more years before deciding three cases on freedom of choice. A year after that it issued an opinion on faculty desegregation. That was it for the Warren years.

Nevertheless, when *Rogers v. Paul* ended grade-a-year programs, a legal noose was surrounding the white South. The three primary means of delay, massive resistance, pupil placement, and then grade-a-year, had run their course. African-Americans and whites were going to attend schools in some numbers together. As thinkable southern options to comply with *Brown* dwindled to freedom of choice or neighborhood schools, the day of constitutional reckoning was coming. Because residential segregation in the South did not match the North, neighborhood schools would produce considerable racial mixing, and whites would necessarily be assigned to formerly all-African-American schools.

As a consequence, the South embraced freedom of choice, whereby every schoolchild could choose which school to attend. What had been unthinkable just a few years earlier achieved, in Judge J. Harvie Wilkinson's words, "the status of holy prerogative."[45] An HEW official captured the new religious embrace of choice when he quipped, "One would find that freedom to choose one's own school was being talked about in the South in the same breath as the freedom of speech and assembly under the first amendment."[46]

Freedom of choice meant that whites could choose to continue as closely as possible to things as they had always been, and no white would go to a formerly all-African-American school. But that was only half the equation, for, as Wilkinson notes, the "opportunity for pressure, covert and overt, was built into every pore of the 'free' choice system." African-Americans, understanding the potential consequences full well, were reluctant to opt for the formerly all-white schools just as many in the pre-1964 era had been reluctant to offer their names to the NAACP as plaintiffs.[47]

Second, and probably relatedly, little had been accomplished in the years since *Brown*. The percentages of whites and African-Americans in school together remained astonishingly low. Excluding Tennessee and Texas, under one-half of 1 percent of African-American children attended school with whites at the time of the Civil Rights Act. For the 1965–1966 school year, the number increased to 3.8 percent. In June 1965 the Justice Department had launched a substantial legal attack on school districts in the South that had refused all federal aid rather than comply with Office of Education desegregation guidelines. A year later, the *New York Times* reported a "fresh wave of resistance" in the South to the guidelines.[48] They had been revised to require school districts with 8 to 9 percent of their African-American children in predominantly white schools to double the figure within a year, and districts with virtually no African-Americans in school with whites to make a substantial effort to catch up. Kilpatrick, in the *Richmond News Leader*, maintaining his segregationist stance, "denounced the 1966 guidelines as an 'arrogant edict' with a 'harsh, peremptory, commanding' tone."[49]

Right on the heels of the revised guidelines came the third of a trilogy of opinions by Judge John Minor Wisdom, the most distinguished of the excellent group of Eisenhower appointees to the Fifth Circuit. *United States v. Jefferson County School Board of Education* mandated that all judicial decrees within the circuit comply with the federal guidelines. Thereafter the percentages rose significantly so that, including Tennessee and Texas (which always previously would double the percentages), in 1968–1969 a third of the African-Americans attended a school with whites. Nevertheless, that necessarily meant that two-thirds did not.

Third, the Court intentionally avoided clarity. To the question "what is required?" the Court responded instead with, in Wilkinson's analysis, opinions that "were couched in the negative. Minority-to-majority transfer provisions, public school closings, public funding of private, segregated schools, racially biased faculty assignments all were impermissible. What exactly was permissible the Court never said. It simply policed the bare minimum, and that, rather belatedly."[50]

As early as 1955 Judge John Parker of the Fourth Circuit in *Briggs v. Elliot,* one of the *Brown* cases on remand, stated that "the Constitution, in other words, does not require integration. It merely forbids segregation."[51] For a decade, this would be the most famous lower court formulation of the requirement of *Brown.* Yet for that decade the South fought Parker's latter conclusion; after the Office of Education guidelines, it embraced his former. The South offered too little, too late.

Wisdom's trilogy was designed to reject all of *Briggs v. Elliot.* In *Singleton v. Jackson Municipal School District* (known as *Singleton II*), he stated that school authorities "are under the constitutional compulsion of furnishing a single, integrated school system."[52] He explained *Brown II* and the delay authorized by "all deliberate speed" as a recognition that *Brown* had been about group rights, not individual rights. Thus, *Brown II* "subordinated the 'present' right in the individual plaintiffs to the right of Negroes as a class to a unitary, nonracial system—some time in the future."[53] Wisdom's trilogy required the Office of Education guidelines to be followed in order to "liquidate" the states' system of de jure segregation.[54] "The only adequate redress for a previously overt system-wide policy of segregation directed against Negroes as a collective entity is a system-wide policy of integration."[55] In Wisdom's lexicon, a unitary school system was an integrated system.

Wisdom was reading the Court exactly right. It had just lacked the candor to be so blunt. Ever since *Cooper* the Court had meant integration rather than just desegregation (the removing of offending laws), but for prudential reasons it never said so. In his first draft of *Goss,* Clark had written "integrated" instead of the usual "desegregated." Brennan then sent him a heretofore undiscovered memo asking him to change the wording. "I recall," Brennan wrote, "that when we had *Cooper v. Aaron,* we thought that it would be well to avoid the use of the word 'integrated' and to use instead 'desegregated.' I remember that there was a feeling that the latter is a shade less offensive than the former."[56] Just three days earlier, with reference to *Watson v. Memphis,* Harlan had sent Goldberg a similar request: "I do not think that we ought to use the word integration in our opinions."[57] These memos demonstrate that the Court intentionally chose to obfuscate. Of course, Clark and Goldberg each made the change after receiving the respective memos.

The justices were striving for integration but would not say so. Because *Briggs v. Elliot* was such a famous opinion, they knew that the South saw an important difference between "desegregation" and "integration." The Court dealt with the problem by adopting the South's language—desegregation—but slowly infusing it with a different meaning—integration. All of this, beginning with *Cooper* and continuing through *Goss,* was unknown to the outside. It took *Green v. New Kent County* to bring the Court's meaning to the public, and even there the Court's avoidance of the hot-button word "integration" was studious.

With the exception of *Brown,* Wisdom's trilogy was far more important than anything the Court had done on school desegregation until *Green* and two companion cases in 1968. *Green,* resting on the simplest of facts, was one of the Warren Court's major decisions; therefore, it was no surprise that its author was Brennan, who Warren hoped could hold Black and therefore maintain the Court's stance of unanimity. With just the most cursory cite to *Jefferson County* and without Wisdom's candor, the Court wholly adopted Wisdom's views with its own code words for integration—"unitary" and "results."

New Kent County is a small rural county east of Richmond. It had two schools, New Kent in the east, Watkins in the west. Prior to the Civil Rights Act, the two schools had remained segregated, New Kent for whites, Watkins for African-Americans, and the district's twenty-one buses traveled overlapping routes to the two schools. With the threat of a federal funds cutoff, the county decided to do something. It could have drawn two geographical districts and, given the lack of residential segregation, the schools would have been integrated. Or it could have made one of the schools a first through seventh and the other eighth through twelfth, and the schools would have been perfectly racially balanced. Instead, the county adopted a freedom-of-choice plan.

No whites elected to attend Watkins. In the first year of the plan, thirty-five African-Americans went to New Kent. Then the number climbed to 111 in 1966 and finally to 115 in 1967. That left approximately 85 percent of all the African-Americans at Watkins in an identifiably one-race school that looked as it always had. That was the fatal defect. *Green* wanted "results" and by results Brennan did not mean a perpetuation of the past.

All prior cases always returned to *Brown* as stating the key principle; *Green* marked the emergence of *Brown II* and its supplanting of *Brown* in the school desegregation area. The reason was that *Brown* seemingly rested on a pure nondiscrimination principle, that the taking of race into account was wrong much the way the first Harlan had concluded in his famous *Plessy v. Ferguson* dissent. *Green*, however, mandated taking race into account because, unlike prior cases that said what was prohibited, *Green* finally addressed what was affirmatively required. Desegregation was now to be measured by actual results. That looks suspiciously close to "integration," the word the Court still avoided.

The only mention of integration came in the school board's argument. The board claimed "its 'freedom-of-choice' plan may be faulted only by reading the Fourteenth Amendment as universally requiring 'compulsory integration,' a reading it insists the wording of the Amendment will not support." The Court tersely rejected the argument without expressly dealing with its underlying theory. The "argument ignores the thrust of *Brown II* [which] was a call for the dismantling of well-entrenched dual systems." School boards were "clearly charged with the affirmative duty to take whatever steps might be necessary to convert to a unitary system in which racial discrimination would be eliminated root and branch."

Here Brennan had slipped Wisdom's synonym for integration into the opinion. What was a "unitary" system? It was one where schools are not "racially identifiable," a system "without a 'white' school or a 'Negro' school, just schools." Such a system was not achieved by leaving Watkins all-African-American. The school board could have used geographical zoning or divided the two schools by grade. Either of those concepts would have worked, and that was the requirement of *Green*. "The burden on a school board today is to come forward with a plan that promises realistically to work, and promises realistically to work *now*."

Monroe v. Board of Commissioners was a helpful companion case because of its slightly different facts. Jackson, Tennessee, was a medium-sized city with 7,650 school children, some 40 percent African-American, in its system. The city had eight elementary schools (five formerly all-white), three junior high schools (two formerly all-white), and two high schools. Under a plan adopted by the school board, the city was divided into geographical zones but with a "free transfer" provision whereby any student could transfer to another school if space was available. In fact, the geographical zoning was gerrymandered to keep the schools as close to one-race as possible, and whites were the first accommodated in the free transfers.

Monroe was about the three junior high schools where every single white transferred out of the formerly all-African-American junior high. Only seven African-American students remained in one of the formerly all-white junior highs. The second of the two had 349 whites and 135 African-Americans. Brennan easily invalidated the free transfer. Quoting *Green*, Brennan wrote, "'Rather than further the dismantling of the dual system, the ["free transfer"] plan has operated simply to burden children and their parents with a responsibility which *Brown II* placed squarely on the School Board.'" Like freedom of choice, the Court did not forbid free transfer. Instead, it said of each that if it would "further rather than delay conversion to a unitary, nonracial, nondiscriminatory school system," then it could be used; otherwise, not. By extending *Green* from a rural system to a city of 40,000 without as much as a comment on the differences, *Monroe* signaled it would be applicable to larger cities as well.

When Warren joined Brennan's opinion, he wrote that "[w]hen this opinion is handed down, the traffic light will have changed from *Brown* to *Green*. Amen!"[58] He was right about *Green* supplanting *Brown* as the governing principle. *Green* ended all deliberate speed; the time was now—and in italics. *Green* placed the duty to achieve its unitary system not on the children but on the public officials running the system (as supervised by a federal judge). And while *Green* eschewed use of "integration," there seemed no way of achieving "results" and the end of "Negro" schools without the affirmative duty to integrate. Wisdom had said it with more clarity in *Jefferson County*, but the Court seemingly had come to the same place. As interpreted in *Green*, *Brown* and *Brown II* were not about removing laws on race; they had been about bringing African-American and white children together to learn with and from each other. Black's wife wrote in her diary: "The 'Freedom of Choice' school case came up. Bill Brennan rendered the opinion, and it looked like nobody had freedom of choice, especially the school boards."[59]

In the Warren Court's last school case, *United States v. Montgomery County Board of Education*, the Court took the huge step of embracing racial quotas for faculty assignments to schools without considering the merits of the determination. *Montgomery County* had three salient features. First, the district judge, Frank Johnson, was one of the most respected in the South and had an excellent record on race issues. Second, the school board, being from Alabama, had done nothing but maintain segregation for the first decade after *Brown*. Third, and surprisingly, the Court stated how happy the justices were that there was so little difference between the parties. The United States and the LDF supported Johnson's quota. His order had required the school board to assign teachers to schools so that the ratio of white to African-Americans in each school would eventually be substantially the same as for the system as a whole. As a first step, Johnson mandated that each school must have at least one faculty member of each race and for schools with more than twelve teachers, he ordered a 5–1 ratio. The school board supported the Fifth Circuit modification of Johnson's order to require only substantially or approximately the 5–1 ratio. It referred to Johnson's order as requiring quotas. The Government and the LDF never used quotas; their preferred term was "ratios." The Government asserted that the ordering of set racial ratios in each school was appropriate because it was just creating the faculty assignment pattern that would have existed but for segregation.

The Court viewed Johnson's order as "adopted in the spirit of this Court's opinion in *Green,* in that his plan 'promises realistically to work, and promises realistically to work *now.*'" But *Montgomery County* was not *Green.* In *Green,* the Court used racial statistics to invalidate the county's freedom-of-choice plan. But *Montgomery County* rested on the fact that previous plans had not achieved their desired end, so that racial quotas were justified as a means of ensuring that the schools would have the desired outcome. Lost in this was the issue of quotas. Where did the requirement or need for racial balance among faculty in all schools come from? The Court did not answer the question beyond noting Alabama's sorry history (and thereby perhaps implicitly agreeing with the Government that but for segregation random assignment of teachers would create ratios in each school matching the ratio for the system as a whole). A year before the "Philadelphia Plan" on racial set-asides, the Court "sanctioned minimum racial quotas in the public workplace without any independent discussion of the merits of such a course."[60]

Scholars have debated up to the present whether the Court knew what it was doing in the school area between *Brown II* and *Green.* The Brennan memo to Clark is a strong indication it did. It was biding its time with its eyes on an integrated ending. It can also be debated whether the Court understood what it was doing in *Montgomery County.* It is likely it did not. *Montgomery County* was written by Black, who, as has been detailed, was out of sympathy with the Court's race jurisprudence generally. Furthermore, he was the most reluctant vote in *Green,* having "initially voted to uphold the freedom-of-choice plan."[61] It is unlikely he comprehended the new era he had opened, and since *Montgomery County* produced no dissents, it seems unlikely that either Harlan or Stewart paid much attention.

Statutes Old and New

Two cases at the end of Warren's tenure seemed to be answering ghetto unrest by the extension of federal law. In decisions out of Missouri and Arkansas the Court twice reversed the Eighth Circuit Court of Appeals and in the process pushed two civil rights acts to their limits. In *Jones v. Alfred H. Mayer,* the statute dated from the 1866 Civil Rights Act. In *Daniel v. Paul,* it was the Civil Rights Act of 1964.

After the House of Representatives passed an "open housing" bill in 1967 but before the Senate had acted, the Court granted certiorari to review a decision that a company selling homes in a housing development was under no obligation to sell to African-Americans. Judge Harry Blackmun for the Eighth Circuit had reasoned that no federal law reached private discrimination in housing and that there had been no "state action" involved in the company's refusal to sell to African-Americans. The Court heard oral argument in *Jones* three weeks after the Senate passed a version of the Open Housing Act that was different from the House's version. Then King was assassinated in Memphis, and another round of urban riots commenced, with more than 20,000 federal troops and 34,000 National Guardsmen called for antiriot duty. The House decided to accede to the Senate bill rather than delay with a conference committee, and the president signed the law a day later. The most logical decision in *Jones* would have been to dismiss certiorari as improvidently granted due to the intervening federal law; instead, the Court construed the century-old statute as also barring racial discrimination in housing. The Court too wished to do its part to help quell the urban violence.

On its face, the century-old statute belied Blackmun's interpretation. It simply stated that "[a]ll citizens of the United States shall have the same right as is enjoyed by white citizens thereof to inherit, purchase, lease, sell, hold, and convey real and personal property." Stewart concluded that it meant exactly what it said. The reason Blackmun had construed it as he did was the concern that if a statute passed under the Reconstruction Amendments reached private action it was unconstitutional, as a 1906 case had previously concluded. In a major, but relatively easy, constitutional holding, Stewart noted that the statute had been passed under the *Thirteenth,* not the Fourteenth, Amendment and that the Thirteenth Amendment reached private action. Since discrimination in housing could be deemed a badge or incident of slavery, the statute was valid. The new Open Housing Law was not to go into effect until January 1969, and there is a "let's fill in the six-month gap" quality to *Jones.* Harlan and White were dubious all the way but took the sensible position that the Court should have dismissed the writ of certiorari rather than compete with Congress in creating new remedies for housing discrimination. *Jones* marked a record-breaking seventh time in a single term that the Court had overruled a previous case. The previous record, six, set in the 1941 Term, had been tied the term before.

In 1969 *Daniel v. Paul* returned to the problem posed by Ollie's Barbeque. How far removed from interstate commerce does a business have to be before it is beyond the reach of the public-accommodations provisions of the Civil Rights Act of 1964? The opinion in *Daniel v. Paul* seemed to answer the question with "totally." The case was an action by two Little Rock African-Americans against the Lake Nixon Club, a for-profit 232-acre outdoor park located twelve miles from Little Rock that refused to admit any African-Americans. The so-called club was accessible only via a six-to-eight-mile stretch of country road and served about 100,000 people annually. There was no evidence that any interstate travelers had visited the facility.

Brennan first concluded that since the club advertised in a magazine distributed at local hotels and motels, it was trying to attract interstate travelers. "It would be unrealistic to assume" that none of the patrons was an interstate traveler. Then Brennan went on to note that the club's snack bar served hot dogs and hamburgers "on buns" along with soft drinks and milk. "Thus, at the very least, three of the four food items sold at the snack bar contain ingredients originating from out of state." There could be "no serious doubt" that this was substantial.

There was one more provision of the Civil Rights Act not discussed in *Katzenbach v. McClung.* It covered places of entertainment affecting commerce. The Lake Nixon Club was easily deemed a place of entertainment. Did it affect commerce? Sure. Fifteen paddle boats were leased from an Oklahoma company. The jukebox had been manufactured out of state. So had the records played. This one-two-three punch knocked out Lake Nixon's claim to be exempt from congressional power.

Black filed a lone dissent. He would have gone along if Congress had used its Fourteenth Amendment powers to pass the Civil Rights Act, but Congress instead chose commerce, and the conclusion that this affected commerce was absurd. "The milk was even produced by an Arkansas cow!"[62]

As the 1968 Term, Warren's last, was commencing, an NAACP attorney wrote an explosive article in the *New York Times Magazine*. It was entitled "Nine Men in Black Who Think White."[63] The title is descriptive and explains why it caused so much controversy. If the Court, the leading body in government pushing for the end of racial discrimination, was itself racist, what hope was there?

The critique took for granted the recent Kerner Commission *Report on Civil Disorders* and its most-quoted sentence: "[O]ur nation is moving toward two societies, one black, one white—separate and unequal." What, the author asked, had the Court done to prevent that? It decided *Brown;* then it said the South "merely had to comply 'with all deliberate speed.'" It refused to tackle de facto segregation in northern schools and "as a result, the schools of the North have become segregated faster than the Southern schools have been desegregated." It clamped down on civil rights demonstrations in ways that can "be explained only in terms of a judicial concession to white anxieties." It refused to protect civil rights groups in *Cameron v. Johnson* by "accepting the protestations of good faith made by racist public officials." While it decided *Reitman,* it refused to consider a claim of racial use of urban renewal funds in Chicago. It seemed to have caved to public opinion, yet in other areas it was oblivious to public opinion. The only reason appears to be that down deep the Court was part of white society.

That was quite a critique and demonstrated at least two things. First, the Court wasn't as perfect on the issues of race as the NAACP wished; indeed, it wasn't. Second, it shows the wonderful 1960s faith, both at the NAACP and elsewhere, that litigation and court decisions are the way to change society. That the Court itself would have agreed with this view did not make it correct. Had the Court done everything wished in the article, the hard facts of riots and the war in Vietnam would have left the situation much as it was. As hard as it was for litigators to understand, the problems facing America at the end of the 1960s could not be solved by more law, however quick and satisfying it might be to think so.

Riots and Vietnam had put a grip on money. The escalating war was eating every available dollar while the escalating crime statistics and urban riots cut the constituency willing to spend for Great Society programs. Hamilton's *Federalist 78* explains the predicament. Even if the Court's goal was the judicial transformation of American race relations, both the sword and the purse were in other hands and those hands were dominating the American agenda.

This does not mean that the executive and judicial branches were immune to arguments that extending law was a key to making a better society, for they weren't. The Court's dominant theme for the post–Civil Rights Act race cases was that if instead of rioting African-Americans would follow the law, they would reap rewards. Leave the law and lose.

Stewart said it all in *Walker* when he affirmed King's and Shuttlesworth's contempt convictions because they had not followed the law. The message of playing by the rules was not just that of the Court. From *Evans v. Newton* to *Reitman* to *Hunter* to *Green* to *Montgomery County* to *Jones* to *Daniel v. Paul* the United States, through the solicitor general, urged the Court to support the claims of the African-Americans, no matter how far-reaching they were, in each of the cases. The problem of racial discrimination was a national problem, and both the executive and the Court were going as far as the law would allow to demonstrate that reliance on the good faith of the government was the appropriate means for achieving the necessary social change. If it wasn't perfect or wasn't as much as some wanted, it stands up well compared to any other period.

Chapter 12

Freedom of Expression

New York Times v. Sullivan in the spring of 1964 signaled Brennan's emergence as the author of the liberal majority's legal doctrine. Warren trusted Brennan and always turned to him in a jam as the peer and friend with whom he felt most comfortable. Furthermore, their level of agreement was astounding, between 92 and 97 percent from the 1962 Term until Warren's retirement. This was an agreement rate that the two other well-known Warren Court pairs, Black-Douglas and Frankfurter-Harlan, never achieved during a single term.

When the liberals came to dominate, Brennan's time arrived. As seen in earlier chapters, Brennan embraced a technique of conceding in principle the government's power to pursue its objective, while simultaneously making it extraordinarily difficult for the government to do so. The concession deflected criticism of absolutism, while the decision accomplished the task. Strict scrutiny, compelling interests, the chilling effect, and the need for breathing space constituted the vocabulary of unconstitutionality in Brennan's jurisprudence.

Brennan was the only member of the liberal majority capable of performing the role of principal doctrinalist; indeed, he may have been the only one to care, and none of the majority justices, Brennan included, seemed to care about theory during this era. Warren was a wonderful practical politician and was on a par with the legendary John Marshall in working his magic in small groups, but he was ham-handed with opinions and found theory foreign. Black was on the downslide in his career, and his reputation would match reality if he had left the Court with Frankfurter, the indispensable foil who brought out the best in him. Black's well-developed constitutional theories, based on his good versus evil law-office history, were too idiosyncratic to convince anyone else. Furthermore, given the centrality of race, his view of civil rights demonstrations necessarily separated him from the liberals in a key area.

Douglas had the ability and once might have articulated a jurisprudence based on evolving tradition, but he no longer had the interest. A
solo dissent was as satisfying as a majority opinion for him, perhaps even
more so because it symbolized the role of the lone individual he so cherished. While he was occasionally labeled lazy, that was a misnomer. His
second wife perfectly classified him as Max Weber's Calvinist. But when
the Court could not occupy his attention, he turned elsewhere, to chasing
young women and saving the environment; the Court represented, at
best, a poor third.

Goldberg had not been around long enough and therefore had not
found a theory to back his intensely liberal views. Fortas, even more than
his mentor Douglas, had contempt for the explanatory process; his was,
one of his clerks concluded, "the opportunistic outlook of a good lawyer"; that is, once he knew his desired outcome, he couldn't care less how
he got there.[1] Furthermore, he treated the Court as a part-time job. His
truly important job was that of presidential counselor.

The remaining four only occasionally joined the liberal majority and
so did not matter, although Stewart would have liked to. Harlan, who
had the talent, was wedded to a jurisprudence that could explain only
incremental change and so became the Court's official dissenter. White,
Kennedy's "ideal New Frontier judge,"[2] held a job for which his talents
were ill-suited.

Because *Sullivan* was a First Amendment case—indeed, Harry Kalven,
the leading First Amendment scholar of the era, immediately pronounced
it "the" First Amendment case[3]—the press took instant notice. *Sullivan*
protected the press from libel judgments and therefore created a powerful supportive constituency overnight. As a result, Brennan became identified with the First Amendment, previously a preserve occupied exclusively by Black and Douglas, and his importance to the press was
understood.

The Advertisement

Sullivan began when veteran civil rights leaders A. Philip Randolph and
Bayard Rustin joined with entertainer Harry Belafonte to spend $4,800
for a full-page advertisement in the *New York Times* of March 29, 1960,
to appeal for funds to assist Martin Luther King, Jr., with legal fees. The
ad tied together King, the initial sit-in demonstrators, and the effort to
register African-American voters. The point was that King was integral
to the "total struggle for freedom in the South."[4] In placing these to-

gether, the ad reminded everyone that African-Americans were asserting a right to "live in human dignity as guaranteed by the U.S. Constitution" and that their efforts had been "met by an unprecedented wave of terror by those who would deny and negate that document which the whole world looks upon as setting the pattern of modern freedom."

Alabama was introduced when the ad noted that after college students sang "My Country, 'Tis of Thee" at the state capitol, they were expelled, and police armed with shotguns and tear gas "ringed" the Alabama State College campus where state authorities tried to starve students into submission. King too had his peaceful protests met with violence. "Southern violators" bombed his home, assaulted him, and arrested him seven times. Their real purpose was to remove King physically from his leadership position, "to destroy the one man who more than any other, symbolizes the new spirit now sweeping the South."

The ad was a strong, effective attack on the intransigence of the South. It was "signed" by sixty-four civil rights figures. Additionally, there was a one-sentence statement of "warm endorsement" for the appeal signed by twenty others, mostly African-American ministers in the South, many of whom were wholly unaware of the use of their names. The ad achieved its purpose; it was highly effective in raising money.

At the time, Alabama was waging its unconstitutional war on the NAACP. The ad caused state officials to expand the enemy to include the *Times* and CBS. After an angry editorial in the *Montgomery Advertiser*— "lies, lies, lies and possibly willful ones"—brought the ad's existence to the attention of state officials,[5] the state attorney general announced that Governor John Patterson had instructed him to study suing the *Times*, and he did, recommending that "proper public officials" file "multimillion dollar" lawsuits against the *Times*. Immediately there were two questions. The *Times*? And who were the proper plaintiffs? Legally the *Times*'s responsibility was clear. Even if the statement was prepared by others, the *Times* published it, thereby making the *Times* equally responsible for any damages (indeed, under tort law entirely responsible if the plaintiffs so chose). Identifying proper plaintiffs was the more difficult problem since the ad had not mentioned a single state official.

Before the summer began, Montgomery Police Commissioner L. B. Sullivan, Commissioner Frank Parks, former Commissioner Clyde Sellers, the Montgomery mayor, the Birmingham mayor and two of its commissioners, and Governor Patterson all wrote to the *Times* demanding a "full and fair retraction of the false and defamatory matter" about them in the ad. Under Alabama law the request for a retraction was the neces-

sary predicate for initiating a libel suit—a tort action for harm to reputation caused by the defendants' statements. The *Montgomery Advertiser*
accurately concluded that "State and city authorities have found a formidable legal bludgeon to swing at out-of-state newspapers whose reporters cover incidents in Alabama."[6]

The legal bludgeoning was not over either. The distinguished *Times*
correspondent Harrison Salisbury was hit with a forty-two-count indictment for criminal libel based on stories he had written about racial conditions in Birmingham and Bessemer. CBS was also on the receiving end
of libel suits based on its Birmingham coverage.

As a consequence, the *Times* retreated out of Alabama and instructed
its reporters not to reenter the state. It was not that the *Times* maintained
a big presence there. Only the New York-based Salisbury and the At-
lanta-based Claude Sitton had even been in the state in 1960. Furthermore, only 394 out of about 650,000 copies of the *Times* came into
Alabama each day. Thirty-five of them went to Montgomery.

A century after Fort Sumter, Alabama officials were attempting to
secede intellectually from the Union by barring the northern press from
the state on penalty of huge fines. In our era of seven, eight, and even nine
figure verdicts, $500,000 sounds diminutive. But in 1964 it was "real
money," enough to buy three dozen Rolls Royce Silver Clouds at their
then-current price.[7] Furthermore, the *Times,* like the other New York
City newspapers, was in a precarious financial position. A former vice
president of the *Times* observed that once the $500,000 verdicts started
to roll in, "there was a reasonable question of whether the *Times,* then
wracked by strikes and small profits, could survive."[8] Libel promised a
bloodless route for the South to rid itself of the meddlesome national
press.

As the NAACP litigation showed, the Alabama courts would go to any
lengths to protect white supremacy. Yet in Sullivan's case they really
didn't have to twist the law, which in fact was similar to that in most
states. If Sullivan could convince a jury that the references to "Southern
violators" who were engaging in brutality and illegal actions were "really" the police, then the ad could be deemed to be referring to Sullivan,
who, as the Montgomery police commissioner, was the supervising
official. If that was so, he was home free because the ad had factual
errors. Some were trivial, like saying the song was "My Country, 'Tis of
Thee" instead of the National Anthem or stating that King had seven
arrests when the number was only four. More significantly, the claim that
the Alabama State College dining room had been padlocked to starve the

protesting students into submission was not only false, it was ludicrous. Alabama's defamation law, like that of other states, withdrew the defense of good faith when statements were not 100 percent true, and that spelled huge trouble for the *Times.*

Under these circumstances, the key issue at trial was whether the ad could be deemed "of and concerning" Sullivan. This was a jury question, and Sullivan introduced sufficient evidence that people understood the ad to refer to the police department and therefore to Sullivan. Those witnesses also stated that they didn't believe the truth of any statements about Sullivan nor did they think less of him because of the ad, but this was legally irrelevant. Once Sullivan proved the ad referred to him and was false, Alabama law—like that of the other states—presumed he had been damaged. It was therefore up to the jury to determine how much. Sullivan had asked for $500,000—ten times the largest libel judgment in Alabama history—and the jury came back with a $500,000 verdict. It was but the first of several similar verdicts in the libel suits against the *Times,* and the Alabama Supreme Court, as expected, affirmed it completely.

New York Times v. Sullivan

Sullivan's lawyer was confident. "The only way the Court could decide against me was to change one hundred years or more of libel law."[9] Yet a Court that was in the process of declaring 90 percent of the congressional seats were unconstitutionally apportioned and that the analogy to the United States Senate was wholly inapplicable to the state legislatures was quite capable of changing a mere century of law if that was deemed necessary. If Alabama could place the *Times* on the verge of bankruptcy with millions of dollars in verdicts, then it could successfully isolate itself from national scrutiny. Criticizing the South, at least for news organizations with people in the South or papers or broadcasts going to the South, could be made too expensive to bear. Given *Brown,* the NAACP saga, and the fact that the Court needed allies, changing a century of libel law to protect the northern press was a small task, much smaller than that of the segregation or reapportionment cases, and Brennan was more than up to it.

Ridding itself of Sullivan's prime argument—that for a century libelous utterances have been deemed unprotected speech—was easy. Brennan announced that "mere labels" of state law cannot protect speech from the application of First Amendment standards. Libel could "claim no talismanic immunity" from the Constitution, and the *Times*'s ad must be measured by the demands of free speech, which require an "unfettered interchange of ideas." In a statement that would become famous, Brennan summarized prior cases as creating "the background of a profound national commitment to the principle that debate on public issues should be uninhibited, robust, and wide-open, and that it may well include vehement, caustic, and sometimes unpleasantly sharp attacks on government and public officials."

The discussion of racial events in the South in the ad "would seem clearly to qualify" for First Amendment protection. Therefore, the questions were whether it lost that protection because of the falsity of some of its statements or because of its harm to Sullivan's reputation. The answers were no.

Truth could not be the sole guide to the protection of speech because error in free debate is inevitable. Anyone can make a mistake; if held strictly accountable, people will watch their words more closely, thereby denying the full benefits of free debate. Drawing from his opinions in *NAACP v. Button* and *Speiser v. Randall,* Brennan first noted that speech needs "breathing space" for survival and, second, that any requirement of truth would "dampen the vigor and limit the variety of public debate."

Nor did the reputational interests of the public official change the calculus. The Court had already held that, even in the interests of dignity and reputation, judges could not silence debate over their actions. That conclusion applied a fortiori to other officials.

At this point, Brennan made one of the most interesting moves found in the *United States Reports.* Following the lead of the *Times*'s appellate counsel, Columbia law professor Herbert Wechsler, Brennan reopened the controversy over the Sedition Act of 1798, a statute that had expired by its own terms on March 3, 1801, some 163 years earlier. Relying on Thomas Jefferson's and James Madison's opposition to the Sedition Act, the Court concluded, in Madison's words, that "we shall find that the censorial power is in the people over the Government, not in the Government over the people." With Jefferson and Madison deemed correct in theory, they were also deemed correct in practice, and the Sedition Act was posthumously held unconstitutional. This marked the first time in history that a federal statute, living or dead, had been held to violate the First Amendment.

Brennan then applied the Sedition Act conclusion to the problem of defamation of public officials where neither the criminal law burden of proof nor the limitations of double jeopardy apply. "Plainly the Alabama law of civil libel is a 'form of regulation that creates hazards to protected freedoms markedly greater than those that attend reliance upon the criminal law.'" He therefore concluded that the Constitution imposed a requirement on state libel laws that preclude public officials from recovering damages to reputation for statements about their official conduct unless those statements were false and were made with "actual malice." The Court then defined actual malice in the terms of gross negligence, that is, "with reckless disregard" of whether the statement is true or false.

Furthermore, Brennan seemed to indicate that the falsity in the ad, even if made with actual malice, must be significant. Thus, without deciding the issue, the Court indicated its doubts about whether the discrepancy between seven and four or about whether state troopers actually "ringed" the campus would have supported a verdict even if made of and concerning Sullivan and with the requisite malice.

As a final twist, justified by the Court's duty in First Amendment cases to examine the facts independently for itself, Brennan applied his new standard to the ad and concluded that the facts could not support a judgment. Given Alabama in 1964, this conclusion was necessary because otherwise the state judiciary would have done whatever was necessary to maintain a judgment against the *Times*. Application of the new legal standard to the facts was the only part of the opinion that offered a hint that *Sullivan* was about anything except the First Amendment.

Both Black and Goldberg wrote concurring opinions and Douglas joined each. Black restated his view that the First Amendment was absolute and therefore the whole law of defamation was unconstitutional. Unlike Brennan, Black mentioned what was truly at issue, "huge verdicts" of millions of dollars against the *Times* and CBS, and he believed that "malice" no matter how defined would remain an elusive concept, providing "at best an evanescent protection" for freedom of expression. Goldberg was more limited than Black, more expansive than Brennan, finding the First Amendment "affords to the citizen and to the press an absolute, unconditional privilege to criticize official conduct despite the harm which may flow from excesses and abuses."

The reaction to *Sullivan* was one-sided. The press, having found a champion, was in love. Because it was in love, the press was blinded. *Sullivan* was a race case first and foremost. This was obvious on its facts, and in its companion case, *Abernathy v. Sullivan,* the Reverend Ralph Abernathy, one of the twenty endorsers of the ad and therefore a defendant as well, explained the libel suits perfectly as "part of a concerted, calculated program to carry out a policy of punishing, intimidating and silencing all who criticize and seek to change Alabama's notorious political system of enforced segregation."[10] Secondly, *Sullivan* was a case about citizenship, the rights of the "citizen-critic of government." That was the point of the seditious libel discussion. Americans have the right to criticize their government without fear of retribution. Third and last, it was the press case the press thought it was.

Later, when *Sullivan* moved more generally into libel, questions of whether the Court had undervalued reputation or mistakenly overlooked damages or too enthusiastically wiped out state law surfaced. For the time being, however, what mattered was that the Court had recognized the importance of free debate and a free press within the American constitutional system and protected reporting that was simultaneously making race the most important issue facing the country and thereby providing the momentum for the Civil Rights Act of 1964.

Domestic Security

Up to Frankfurter's retirement, the domestic-security cases, with only de minimus exceptions, had been one government victory after another for four years. Then, when *Gibson v. Florida Legislative Investigating Committee* was reargued, race triumphed over security. *Gibson,* however, soon was treated as a domestic-security case and assisted in undermining the whole program. Thus in June 1964, the Court decided *Baggett v. Bullitt,* striking down two loyalty oaths at the behest of University of Washington professors. Three years later, in *United States v. Robel,* the Court held that it was unconstitutional to fire a Communist Party member employed at a defense facility. *Baggett* and *Robel* bracketed the complete evisceration of the domestic-security program. *Baggett,* with its loyalty oath for public employees, typified the remaining state domestic-security programs. Only the ubiquitous New Hampshire attorney general was doing anything else. The existing federal program was more varied but was dominated by the disabilities imposed on Communist Party members by the requirement that the Party register with the Subversive Activities Control Board.

The oaths in *Baggett* required university employees to file affidavits stating they would promote, by teaching and example, "respect for the flag and the institutions of the United States of America and the State of Washington" on the one hand and to disavow membership in any "subversive organization" on the other. White's opinion, like Stewart's 1961 opinion in *Cramp v. Board of Public Instruction,* found the oaths unconstitutionally vague even though the oaths were narrower than the Florida oath in *Cramp.* White asked the same question that Stewart had used— would voting for a communist in an election violate the oath?—and came to the same conclusion that the oath was too vague, leaving those affected unable to know what was covered and what was not. The opinion ended by stating that the Court did "not question the power of the State to take proper measures safeguarding public service from disloyal conduct." Clark and Harlan dissented, believing the narrow oaths made *Cramp* distinguishable and placed the situation within the ambit of a 1951 case, *Gerende v. Board of Supervisors,* where a somewhat similar oath had been sustained.

Two years later, *Elfbrandt v. Russell* abandoned the vagueness approach for a straight constitutional ruling on what a state could not do. *Elfbrandt* involved an Arizona oath requiring state employees to support the Constitution based on another statute that made it perjury to falsely swear as well as making it grounds for discharge for an employee to be a member of the Communist Party. Douglas's opinion was the exact opposite of the Harlan opinions from 1959–1961 that relied on the preservation of the state as the ultimate value of society and ignored the individual's interest. In striking down the Arizona oath as an example of guilt by association, Douglas never acknowledged that the state had an interest that would justify an oath and therefore, unlike *Baggett,* Douglas did not offer even a palliative about state power. Turning to the Smith Act cases, Douglas noted that they distinguished between knowing membership in the Party by one who subscribes to the illegal aims and membership in the Party by one who does not. "Those who join an organization but do not share its unlawful purposes and who do not participate in its unlawful activities surely pose no threat, either as citizens or public employees." Therefore, Arizona's law "threatens the cherished freedom of association protected by the First Amendment."

White wrote the dissent for Clark, Harlan, and Stewart. They believed, as prior cases had held, that a state was free to condition public employment on abstaining from joining the Communist Party. Thus, they rejected application of the Smith Act criminal cases to the employment context where the state's interest in loyal employees was broader than the state's interest in jailing those who joined the Party.

A year after *Elfbrandt,* the same 5–4 pattern struck down New York's Feinberg Law, with its prohibition on the employment of "subversive persons," which had been sustained in *Adler v. Board of Education* fifteen years earlier. *Keyishian v. Board of Regents* challenged the law in the context of a refusal to sign a "Feinberg Certificate," an affidavit stating that the employee was not a member of the Party and that if he ever had been a Party member, he had communicated that fact to the president of his university. The best explanation for what Brennan's opinion did came from Clark in dissent, who quipped that "no court has ever reached out so far to destroy so much with so little."

Brennan's opinion elides between a number of statutes so easily and quickly that before it stops at any one, it has proceeded to find trouble in the next. The Feinberg Law was designed to implement two laws. One criminalized "the utterance of any treasonable or seditious words" or acts. The other disqualified from public employment anyone who advocated overthrow of the government or was a member of an organization that did. The Board of Regents was to maintain a list of prohibited organizations, and membership in any of them was deemed to be prima facie grounds for discharge. Brennan's premise is that the nation is "committed to safeguarding academic freedom, which is of transcendent value to all of us and not merely to the teachers concerned." Accordingly, there is a special need for "precision" not found in the "regulatory maze" New York has created. Brennan then found that "seditious" utterance was too vague a concept and, using standard chilling effect analysis, concluded that it would cause teachers to shy too far from the exercise of "vital First Amendment rights." Using *Elfbrandt,* he also found that innocent membership in a listed organization would result in a prima facie case for disqualification even though the Constitution protected the membership. Thus, this law, as applied to teachers, was overbroad. Between these two holdings, which resembled the technique he used to authorize federal intervention in *Dombrowski v. Pfister,* he moved back to the Feinberg Law and found it unconstitutional.

Clark, for all the dissenters, concluded that the Court had "swept away one of our most precious rights, namely, the right of self-preservation." He could not believe that the state could not fire a communist after notice and hearing and proof that he had personally advocated overthrow of the government. Therefore, he believed it was the Court, not the Feinberg Law, that was engaging in overbreadth.

In the spring of 1966, Douglas invalidated New Hampshire's anticommunist investigating committee in *DeGregory v. New Hampshire.* The opinion was terse even by Douglas's standards. DeGregory had stated that since 1957 he had not been a member of the Communist Party but refused to answer questions about any earlier period. Using *Gibson v.*

Florida Legislative Investigating Committee, Douglas noted that "[t]here is no showing whatsoever of present danger of sedition against the State itself, the only area to which the authority of the State extends. . . . New Hampshire's interest on this record is too remote and conjectural to override the guarantee of the First Amendment that a person can speak or not, as he chooses, free of all government compulsion." Harlan, for White and Stewart, dissented. They believed that the state did not have to show any present evidence because the state was seeking evidence about the present by first demanding evidence about the past.

The dissents refused to say "as a constitutional matter that inquiry into the current operations of the local Communist Party could not be advanced by knowledge of its operations a decade ago." That statement wholly explains the divide between the majority and the dissenters. The majority believed there had been no serious domestic communist menace at the end of the 1950s; the dissenters were not sure the domestic communist menace did not exist in the mid-1960s. The divide parallels whether one believed J. Edgar Hoover's continuing reports on domestic communism, and the majority, correctly, did not.

The federal domestic-security program was obliterated in five cases in which the Court used four different constitutional provisions: Due Process, First Amendment, Self-Incrimination, and Bill of Attainder. The easiest of the five was *Albertson v. Subversive Activities Control Board,* which dealt with the issue left open from *Communist Party v. SACB—* whether requiring individuals to register with government as communists (as the SACB was ordering Albertson to do), once the Party itself did not register, violated their rights of self-incrimination by exposing them to prosecution where the registration would provide material evidence against them. Given the Smith Act, no one seriously doubted that the answer was yes—Clark as attorney general in 1948 had reached that conclusion as well—and *Albertson,* decided in 1965, was a unanimous Brennan opinion.

Albertson was handed down a year after the first invalidation of the federal program, *Aptheker v. Secretary of State,* which involved revocation of a passport by a person required to register with the SACB. Because Aptheker was a knowing communist and therefore likely to meet the *Scales* standard, Goldberg treated the case as a right to travel, rather than a freedom of association, case. As a result, *Aptheker* is a confused opinion.

Goldberg constantly intertwines the right to travel, held constitutionally protected in *Kent v. Dulles,* and the right to freedom of association,

protected by the First Amendment. He concluded that abandoning freedom of association is too high a price to place on the right to travel
especially since the statute renders irrelevant the "member's degree of
activity in the organization and his commitment to its purpose." These
factors, Goldberg concluded, are relevant to a ban on foreign travel
because they go to the likelihood that the travel would be for Party
purposes rather than personal purposes. Therefore, Congress could have
employed less drastic means, and the ban is overbroad.

Black concurred, restating his First Amendment views. Douglas joined
Goldberg but also wrote a concurring opinion. Douglas, like Goldberg,
intertwined travel and the First Amendment but did so far more persuasively, for Douglas saw the two as inseparable components of freedom.
Harkening back to his standard 1950s technique of complaining that the
domestic-security program aped that of communist societies, Douglas
wrote that totalitarian governments, afraid of their people, restricted
travel. Thus, "riding boxcars carries extreme penalties in Communist
lands." But in a free country there is free movement. "Like the right of
assembly and the right of association, it often makes all other rights
meaningful—knowing, studying, arguing, exploring, conversing, observing and even thinking. Once the right to travel is curtailed, all other
rights suffer."

Clark dissented for Harlan and White on the ground that as applied to
Aptheker, an officer of the Party, the ban was valid and Goldberg's musings were fanciful, just "irrational imaginings: a member of the Party
might wish 'to visit a relative in Ireland or to read rare manuscripts in the
Bodleian Library.'" Furthermore, international travel could not be an
absolute right, and therefore precluding communists from traveling in-
ternationally was reasonable.

The final domestic-security case to avoid First Amendment grounds
was *United States v. Brown*. Since the Taft-Hartley Act of 1947 union
officials had been forced to sign a noncommunist affidavit in order that
their union have the right to invoke the National Labor Relations Act.
The affidavit was sustained against a First Amendment challenge in
1950, and in 1959 Congress amended it to require an official to swear he
was not a member of the Party and had not been one for the previous five
years. Warren's opinion in *Brown* found this requirement to be an unconstitutional bill of attainder on the ground that Congress was actually
finding the Party and its members prematurely guilty of a crime. Stripping them of their union leadership positions was therefore punishment.
By crossing the line between legislature and judiciary, Congress violated
the Attainder Clause.

Warren's opinion was both novel and unsatisfying. The rationale for the affidavit was that union officials who were communists were therefore more likely to engage in political—rather than economic—strikes; indeed, the statute was partially premised on the idea that communist union officials had an inherent conflict of interest on the point. Congress had previously adopted just this rationale in prohibiting employees of underwriting firms from becoming directors of national banks. As with the Taft-Hartley ban it named no individuals and left everyone free of the penalties by giving up one of the two positions. Warren's majority tried to distinguish the conflict of interest analogy by the fact that the Communist Party is named in the legislation while no specific underwriting firm was named in the other legislation and was concerned that Congress was attributing illegal characteristics of some members of the group to all the members of the group. Yet, as White for the four dissenters noted, that is the very nature of conflict of interest legislation.

Neither *Aptheker* nor *Brown* was a model of clear analysis. Black and Douglas could have offered a solution with their First Amendment views, but few justices find absolutes in the Constitution. For the others something less was necessary, and in 1964 and 1965 Brennan's chilling effect provided the likely alternative but was, in situations like *Aptheker,* not factually plausible because the Party leaders were not chilled.

In 1965, in *Lamont v. Postmaster General,* the Court for the first time struck down a live federal statute on the grounds that it interfered with freedom of expression. The statute barred the Post Office from delivering "communist propaganda" via second-class mail to an addressee unless the addressee made known to the Post Office the desire to receive the information. The chilling effect of the statute was obvious. Few citizens are likely to go to their government and affirmatively express a desire to receive communist propaganda even if they wish the materials for scholarly or other purposes. Douglas wrote a terse opinion invalidating the law without even mentioning the second-class mailing subsidy. Brennan, for Goldberg and Harlan, wrote a better and equally terse concurring opinion that explained the chilling effect for those who read Douglas's opinion and needed some analysis. Douglas's opinion assumes there is a First Amendment right to receive ideas; Brennan makes this explicit. "It would be a barren marketplace of ideas that had only sellers and no buyers."

The coup de grace of the domestic-security program was delivered in *Robel* where the Court invalidated the prohibition on banning communists from working in defense facilities. This conclusion, which was obviously not unthinkable in 1967, certainly would have been just five years earlier. That times had changed generally could be seen from the facts. After Robel was indicted and arrested for violating the McCarran Act, he was released on his own recognizance and immediately returned to his job as a machinist at the Todd Shipyards and continued to work there while his case was in the courts.

As a domestic-security matter, if communists can be treated as potential security risks anywhere, a defense facility would seem to be a prime site, but the majority was long past believing that any relic of the McCarthy Era should be allowed to stand. Warren applied a technique similar to that used by Goldberg in *Aptheker* to bring down this provision of the McCarran Act. The act did not distinguish among types of membership in the Party and adherence to the Party's illegal goals. The district court had narrowed the statute by reading into it a requirement of specific intent, but Warren rejected the effort to save the statute, concluding it was for Congress, not the courts, to decide the intended scope of a statute's sweep. The majority had no desire to save the statute; it wanted to be rid of the whole area. The majority was also troubled that the act did not distinguish among jobs at a defense facility. The McCarran Act was prophylactic, treating all defense jobs as sensitive. Therefore, the act was an overbroad restraint on freedom of association and was on that account unconstitutional.

Surprisingly, Brennan, whose opinions from *Speiser* to *Button* to *Dombrowski* had created and perfected ideas of overbreadth, would not join the majority. He found the act unconstitutional but rested his views on the unregulated nature of Congress's delegation of authority to the secretary of defense to name covered defense facilities. Implicit in Brennan's concurring opinion is that finally there was something serious going on. Robel was an admitted Party member and the Todd Shipyards were a defense facility. Maybe the government had a true interest, worthy of respect, for a change. White for Harlan—Clark having retired—dissented and made the point explicit as they protested the Court's exercising "an independent judgment of the requirements of national security."

Robel brought the domestic-security apparatus to a halt. The Subversive Activities Control Board had been rendered a functionless sinecure where Richard Nixon's appointees had the principal tasks of choosing new carpeting and reading the *Washington Post*. After trying to find something more substantive for the SACB members to do, Nixon ended its life on June 30, 1973, by zero-budgeting the agency. Unlike the earlier periods, no one cared about what the Court had done. Thus, after *Al-*

bertson, James Eastland offered only a tepid criticism of the decision, noting it was not the first time that the Court had "overthrown a provision of the law enacted by the Congress as protection against subversion" and stating he would ask his committee to meet.[11] More interesting was the statement of Postmaster General John Gronouski after *Lamont* praising the decision and stating it would "free 40 postal employees for other work at an estimated saving of $250,000 a year."[12] The Court was operating with a free hand; domestic communism had long since ceased to be a live political issue.

Libel after *Sullivan*

If *New York Times v. Sullivan* was a true libel case, then it demanded major changes in state libel law. But maybe it was not really a libel case; after all, its actual context was race relations in one of the two most recalcitrant states in the nation. Furthermore, even if it was a libel case, the Court's use of the seditious libel analogy might prove a limiting factor. Only when a libel judgment created risks similar to those of seditious libel—that is, where the attack on the press is really because the press was criticizing the government—might *Sullivan* then apply.

For whatever reasons, state courts read *Sullivan* very narrowly. As a result, a number of cases were available to the Court to interpret the meaning of *Sullivan.* The cases demonstrated that *Sullivan* was a libel case; the seditious libel analogy had been fortuitous and therefore was not limiting.

Given the delays in the legal system, the cases the Court decided were all tried prior to the decision in *Sullivan* and then (with the exception of *Garrison v. Louisiana*) affirmed by an appellate court after the decision. These cases raised the simple legal issue of whether the Court's "actual malice" standard should be applied in their new factual contexts.

The Court was often quite fractured, in no small part because Black and Douglas, maintaining their position that all libel was an unconstitutional restriction on speech, refused to join opinions of any of the other justices. Nevertheless, a majority of the justices had come to believe that a vigorous press, largely freed from the specter of libel judgments, was an essential component of the proper functioning of the democratic process. Yet the Court did not fully explain how its results were fitting into and promoting that process.

The easiest of the cases was *Garrison v. Louisiana,* decided eight months after *Sullivan,* because it was the only case in which the seditious libel analogy worked. Garrison was the irresponsible, publicity-seeking

New Orleans district attorney whom Oliver Stone imagined as a mythical hero in the movie *JFK*. At a press conference in 1962, Garrison issued a statement charging that a large backlog in pending criminal cases was due to the inefficiency, laziness, and excessive vacations of the judges and that by refusing to authorize disbursements for investigations of vice, they hampered his enforcement efforts. "This raises interesting questions about the racketeer influences on our vacation-minded judges."

In context, Garrison's conviction for criminal libel, which supposedly served similar interests to civil libel, looked a lot like a conviction for seditious libel—punishment for excessive criticism of government. Under the logic of *Sullivan*, posthumously invalidating the Sedition Act, that was unconstitutional. Brennan's opinion held that Garrison's conviction could not stand unless the state proved his words were false and uttered with actual malice. *Sullivan* had suggested that falsehoods always had some value; *Garrison* wisely repudiated that. "Calculated falsehood" has no value at all. Brennan was implicitly stating that a new seditious libel statute would be valid if it contained the *Sullivan* limitations of falsity and actual malice. Black, Douglas, and Goldberg each dissented from that implicit conclusion, claiming that the First Amendment, properly understood, precluded punishment under all circumstances for libeling a government official for official conduct.

Sullivan was quickly extended to all public officials, even as minor as the supervisor of a ski resort in *Rosenblatt v. Baer*. Brennan explained that "criticism of government is at the very center of the constitutionally protected area of free discussion" and that "the 'public official' designation applies at the very least to those among the hierarchy of government employees who have, or appear to the public to have, substantial responsibility for or control over the conduct of government affairs." Although Brennan wrote for a majority, there were five short separate opinions.

The splits of *Rosenblatt* became full-blown in *Curtis Publishing v. Butts* and *Associated Press v. Walker* where the Court extended *Sullivan* to public figures, in particular to University of Georgia Athletic Director Wally Butts and retired general Edwin A. Walker. The facts of *Butts* and *Walker* were decidedly different. In *Walker's* situation, an Associated Press reporter filed a story about the riot at Ole Miss over James Meredith's admission, stating that Walker "had taken command of the violent crowd and had personally led a charge against the federal marshals." A Texas jury returned a verdict of $500,000 in compensatory and $300,000 in punitive damages, but the trial judge set the punitives aside. In *Butts*, the *Saturday Evening Post* had published an article claiming that Butts had provided Alabama football coach Paul "Bear" Bryant with Georgia's defensive plans as well as other secrets prior to the Georgia-Alabama game. The article was entitled "The Story of a College Football Fix." A jury returned a verdict of $60,000 compensatory and $3,000,000 in punitives, which the trial judge reduced to $460,000.

The cases thus offered a couple of distinctions. *Walker* was about breaking news; *Butts* was less timely, more investigative, where there was considerable doubt about the quality of the information relied upon, and the magazine never checked anything with a football expert who might have wondered what help the highly favored 'Bama team needed in winning 35–0. *Walker* was about public affairs; *Butts* was not (although it may have been about a secular religion in some locales). These distinctions suggested that Walker should lose and Butts might win, and that is how the Court voted, 9–0 in *Walker,* 5–4 in *Butts.*

Four justices, Harlan, Clark, Stewart, and Fortas, opposed extending *Sullivan* to the public-figure situation although they would demand that the plaintiff show "highly unreasonable conduct constituting an extreme departure from the standards of investigation and reporting ordinarily adhered to by responsible publishers." The *Saturday Evening Post* had crossed that line and therefore the verdict for Butts should be affirmed, but given the "hot news" at Ole Miss, the AP had not transgressed this standard. Black and Douglas thought the First Amendment forbade libel. In between were Warren, Brennan, and White.

Warren wrote that increasingly "the distinctions between governmental and private sectors are blurred. . . . It is plain that although they are not subject to the restraints of the political process, 'public figures,' like 'public officials,' often play an influential role in ordering society." They could command media attention to "influence policy and to counter criticism of their views and activities." Furthermore, "our citizenry has a legitimate and substantial interest in their conduct." What Warren did not note was that they could not initiate criminal prosecutions for libel; only the government could do that.

Warren's disposition was for Butts and against Walker. He concluded that the trial judge's instructions in *Butts* had been close enough to *Sullivan* so that Butts's verdict could stand. Brennan and White largely agreed with Warren but would have sent *Butts* back for a new trial. What seems to have split the three is Warren's conclusion that Butts had suffered enough and deserved to win outright, given the preposterous story about him.

Time, Inc. v. Hill was a privacy case where, because of the ridiculous nature of New York law, the plaintiff could only prevail on his invasion of privacy claim if the statements about him were false. If the invasion of privacy had been true, he would have had no remedy under New York law. The Court responded as if the situation were a libel case and again required the false statements to have been made with actual malice before a plaintiff could recover. The case is best known to Court buffs for the fact that Richard Nixon argued his only Supreme Court case on behalf of Hill and lost 6–3, although in what would turn out to be an irony, both Warren and Fortas, along with Clark, voted for him.

The Hill family had once been taken hostage by an escaped convict and thus had been involuntarily thrust into the media spotlight. Their captivity, combined with a fictionalized version of the event that played on Broadway (*The Desperate Hours*, based on the similarly named novel by Joseph Hayes), was, even years later, "news," in the "public domain," therefore a "matter of public interest." That James Hill would have liked to slide back into obscurity was irrelevant, Brennan explained, because "exposure of the self to others in varying degrees is a concomitant of life in a civilized society." To be sure, a hostage situation and then a Broadway play are not national politics, but "the line between the informing and the entertaining is too elusive for the protection" of freedom of the press.

Sullivan's doctrine may have emphasized the citizen-critic, but subsequent cases, especially *Hill*, moved freeing the press from the risks of damages to the forefront. These were press cases pure and simple, protecting an institution that was vital to the concept of democracy even when it was not discussing government affairs. "We create a grave risk of serious impairment of the indispensable service of a free press if we saddle the press with the impossible burden of verifying to a certainty the facts associated in news articles with a person's name, picture or portrait, particularly as related to non-defamatory matter." That statement suggested a negligence standard might be appropriate, but Brennan immediately rejected that conclusion as placing on the press "the intolerable burden of guessing how a jury might assess the reasonableness of the steps taken to verify the accuracy of every reference to a name, picture or portrait." *Hill* was quite an opinion; furthermore, it pointed to protecting the press in a true privacy case as well, given the newsworthy nature of any information.

Black and Douglas joined Brennan's opinion while separately noting that they adhered to their absolutism. The First Amendment guaranteed that the press was immune from legal scrutiny. The next year the hatchet job on Butts indicated that total immunity for the press would achieve what total power also achieves—absolute corruption. Black and Douglas were undeterred, but beyond self-interested, unthinking members of the press, they never gained any converts. Harlan concurred but would have adopted the negligence standard that Brennan rejected. Harlan believed that there was an important difference between a person involuntarily thrust into the media spotlight and public officials, who necessarily exposed themselves to scrutiny—as factually there is.

Fortas wrote the dissent, which, while stating the importance of a free press, also concluded that privacy was a basic right. That meant some form of accommodation between the two was appropriate and that courts have a "responsibility to preserve values and procedures which assure the ordinary citizen that the press is not above the reach of the law." The Court, the dissenters believed, had simply gone too far, and they would have allowed New York to protect its citizens from the "type of assault" inflicted by the press.

The dissenters were correct in their accusation that the majority was not seeking an accommodation of values. The majority, with its increased certainty about the important role of the press, was applying the "chilling effect" doctrine to give the press ample room to fulfill its role.

In his seminal article on *Sullivan,* Harry Kalven wrote that "the invitation to follow a dialectic progression from public official to government policy to public policy to matters in the public domain, like art, seems to me to be overwhelming."[13] That proved an excellent prediction as the cases subsequent to *Sullivan,* especially *Walker* and *Hill,* demonstrated. What is surprising is that Kalven did not see that the dialectic undermined what he thought was so important about *Sullivan,* its supposed adoption of a seditious libel paradigm. Seditious libel was a dead end, and its use in *Sullivan* allowed the Court to ignore what was new and serious about that case—the phenomenal jump in damages. The Court turned out to be unwilling to police damages, so it policed liability rules instead. These allowed the Court to zero out damages but to do so at the expense of legitimate interests in truth and reputation.

The press was the huge winner in this process, and it is no wonder that the press, on reading the opinions, was generally impressed with the Court's sensitivity. Because the press's professional and economic interests were involved, the public debate on libel was narrow indeed. Brennan's position was taken as the minimum acceptable protection for a sacred institution, the only one with its own constitutional amendment. Then that position was contrasted with what the press deemed the true meaning of the First Amendment, the absolutism long advocated by Black and Douglas. From the press's perspective, once the Court understood the underlying merits of absolutism, a far better world would emerge wherein no one could sue the press or legally question its actions.

Vietnam

Because of the time lag of litigation, the Warren Court saw few cases directly implicating the Vietnam War. The dominant feature of those— the working of the Selective Service System—will be omitted here except as it allowed draftees to challenge their induction by claiming the war was unconstitutional. Antiwar protests produced the major constitutional issue. *Bond v. Floyd* was a revisiting of the World War I issue of speaking strongly against the war effort while *United States v. O'Brien* and *Tinker v. Des Moines School District* raised the newer issue of symbolic speech and demonstrated the limits of judicial tolerance.

Wars are always popular at the beginning. Yet on the Court both Black and Douglas opposed the Vietnam War from its outset. Moreover, unlike Black, Douglas became increasingly vocal. On the other side, Fortas throughout remained a major adviser to Johnson as well as a die-hard supporter of his policies. Thus, Fortas joined with the conservatives, Harlan, Stewart, and White, in dissenting from the 1969 summary reversal of a conviction for threatening the life of the president. At a rally at the Washington Monument, Robert Watts proclaimed that he had been ordered to report for a physical and that he would refuse induction into the armed forces, but if he got a gun "the first person I would want in my sights is LBJ" because shooting the president would be better than shooting his "black brothers" in Vietnam. The majority found that while the statute itself was constitutional, Watts's ramblings were crude hyperbole, not a real threat. (The court of appeals opinion affirming the conviction was written by Warren Burger.)

The Court refused to consider any case that questioned the legality of the war. Douglas, who with increasing adamancy believed the war was illegal because the Tonkin Gulf Resolution was not a true declaration of war and that hostilities of the nature of Vietnam required a congressional declaration, consistently demanded that the Court hear such a case. Presumably, if there ever was a situation where the "political questions" doctrine might apply, determining whether a war was unconstitutional would be a prime case. Could the Court actually declare the war unconstitutional? Could it enjoin the secretary of defense from sending additional troops? Could it require him to bring the troops home? Or at least order them not to fight? Except in self-defense? Would anyone obey such an order? Should anyone? These were real questions. Douglas never answered any of them although it was apparent that he wanted the Court to hold the war unconstitutional and was willing to take his chances on the next step. Only Stewart was willing to vote with him even to hear one of the cases, and there is no reason to believe Stewart would have joined Douglas on the merits. The others simply voted to deny review—as always, without comment.

Like *Sullivan*, the first antiwar speech case—*Bond v. Floyd*—is partially a race case, partially a speech case. Julian Bond was one of the first six African-Americans elected to the Georgia legislature since Reconstruction. Between his election and the legislative session, the Student Non-Violent Coordinating Committee, for whom Bond was the communications director, issued a statement opposing the war and supporting draft resisters. When the legislature met, Bond was refused his seat on the grounds that he could not in good faith take the mandatory legislative oath to support the federal and state constitutions. The other five African-Americans were seated without objection, showing that what triggered the legislative reaction was the antiwar context, perhaps heightened by Bond's race.

Bond had stated that he "endorsed" the SNCC statement because he was against "the" war, against "all" war. He was also against the draft. At the hearing before the legislative committee, he again supported the SNCC statement "without reservation" but went on to note that he had never counseled burning a draft card or breaking any law. Warren's unanimous opinion first stated that "[n]o useful purpose would be served by discussing the many decisions of this Court which establish that Bond could not have been convicted for these statements consistently with the First Amendment." Warren next turned to Georgia's argument that Bond should be held to a higher standard than a mere citizen because he was a legislator. This was rejected with a reminder that "[t]he manifest function of the First Amendment in a representative democracy requires that legislators be given the widest latitude to express their views on issues of policy." Warren followed with *Sullivan*'s already famous line that "debate on public issues should be uninhibited, robust, and wide-open."

Bond was an easy case. What Warren's opinion did not note was that, when statements similar to SNCC's and Bond's had been successfully punished during World War I, the Court had affirmed the convictions. *Bond* was a useful datum on how much First Amendment law had changed in a half century, maybe even a decade, for by the decision the

Court was not only recognizing the necessary sweep of its recent decisions, but also interring the repressive sweep of its World War I decisions.

When the Court next heard a war-protest case, the Tet Offensive was about to begin but, more important, the nonviolent protests of the civil rights movement had receded into a pristine past. The change was most apparent at SNCC, which had gone from leaders like Bob Moses, John Lewis, and Bond to first Stokely Carmichael and then to H. Rap Brown. The organization functionally had become the Non-Student Violent Non-Coordinating Committee. Both civil rights and antiwar demonstrations had too often turned violent, and demonstrators, especially those against the war, appeared to be looking either for television time or new ways to outrage the generation directing the war. David O'Brien, who burned his draft card in the new inflammatory protest, paid the price as Warren wrote an opinion for everyone except Douglas to reject his First Amendment claim. Just as the sit-ins had pushed Black past his limits, the novel and lawbreaking methods of the antiwar protesters pushed everyone but Douglas past his limits. *O'Brien* signaled that the time for tolerance of youth had passed. *Adderley v. Florida* and *Walker v. Birmingham* had been 5–4 cases; *O'Brien* was 7–1.

When O'Brien burned his draft card on the steps of a Boston courthouse to the whirl of CBS cameras, he violated a 1965 amendment to the Selective Service Act that had tightened the existing nonpossession provision to specifically forbid draft-card burning. O'Brien claimed that he was engaged in symbolic speech, and burning his draft card was therefore protected by the First Amendment. Warren first stated that "we cannot accept the view that an apparently limitless variety of conduct can be labeled 'speech' whenever the person engaging in the conduct intends thereby to express an idea." There were limits, and undoubtedly urban rioting passed those limits; so, too, did draft-card burning.

Warren then gave a grudging acknowledgment that O'Brien's action might be deemed an exercise of First Amendment rights and offered a four-part test on the constitutionality of symbolic speech. It could lawfully be prohibited (1) if the regulation was within the government's power; (2) if the regulation furthered an important or substantial government interest; (3) if that interest was unrelated to freedom of speech; and (4) if the restriction on First Amendment rights was no greater than necessary. Having offered the test, Warren did not take it seriously. The government interest in the smooth functioning of the Selective Service System was substantial. Obviously, *that* interest was unrelated to speech. And the restriction was no greater than necessary to facilitate the smooth functioning of the system.

O'Brien also argued that Congress adopted the antiburning provision for the express purpose of suppressing freedom of speech since draft-card burning had become a recognized and highly controversial form of antiwar protest. Warren tersely rejected the argument on the ground that the Court never inquires into motivation and therefore an otherwise constitutional statute does not become unconstitutional on the basis of an illicit legislative purpose. The statement that the Court never looked at motivation was flatly wrong. In the Sunday closing case, *McGowan v. Maryland,* Warren himself had written that if the purpose of the otherwise valid law was to promote religion, then the law was unconstitutional. The Tuskegee gerrymander case, *Gomillion v. Lightfoot,* is also inexplicable without looking at motivation. Thus, Warren's third point about "unrelated to freedom of speech" was not about the law; it was about the government interest supposedly protected by the law. Essentially the third criterion only reached gratuitous restrictions on speech.

Harlan wrote a one-paragraph concurring opinion to note that the majority's analysis should not "foreclose consideration of First Amendment claims in those rare instances when an 'incidental' restriction upon expression . . . has the effect of entirely preventing a 'speaker' from reaching a significant audience with whom he could not otherwise communicate." The words were nice, but their meaning was unclear in application. Only by burning his draft card could O'Brien have communicated with the millions of Americans who watched the *CBS Evening News.*

Douglas dissented but avoided the underlying issue of symbolic speech. Instead, he argued, as he had in his dissents from the denial of certiorari in *Mitchell v. United States* and *Mora v. McNamara,* that the underlying problem was "whether conscription was permissible in the absence of a declaration of war." Because of his fixation on hammering an issue that the others wished to duck, Douglas wasted a chance to show that what occurred to O'Brien was serious and did affect freedom of expression.

Warren asserted that burning a draft card interfered with the smooth functioning of the system, a conclusion undermined by the fact that General Lewis Hershey, the head of the Selective Service, did not believe that the 1965 amendments were necessary. Essentially Warren's four-part test had stated that the Government could prevail on the showing of an important or substantial interest, but he never required the Government to show that it had such an interest. Still, that may have been the least of *O'Brien*'s problems.

The refusal to inquire into legislative motivation saved the Court from the embarrassing facts behind the 1965 amendment. Draft-card burning had become the form of protest du jour in the summer of 1965, and in the heat of a still-popular war, many individuals believed that such conduct was giving aid and comfort to the enemy—that it was treasonous. In reality, it was a modest nuisance for the Selective Service System, which rather efficiently supplied a duplicate card on the request that typically followed a burning.

On August 5, 1965, one day before the Voting Rights Act passed, Mendel Rivers, chairman of the House Armed Services Committee, introduced the amendment to outlaw draft-card burning by declaring it was a "straightforward clear answer to those who would make a mockery of our efforts in South Vietnam by engaging in mass destruction of draft cards."[14] Only one other representative spoke about the measure, William Bray of Indiana, who, in a much longer speech, stated that the "need for this legislation is clear. Beatniks and so-called 'campus cults' have been publicly burning their draft cards to demonstrate their contempt for the United States and our resistance to Communist takeovers." He believed that those burning their cards were out to "destroy American freedom."[15] In the Senate only Strom Thurmond spoke. He viewed draft-card burning as open defiance of "the warmaking powers of the Government" and stated it "must not be tolerated by a society whose sons, brothers, and husbands are giving their lives in defense of freedom and countrymen against Communist aggression."[16] Before August was over, the House passed the prohibition 393–1; the Senate passed it by voice vote without a record of opposition; and then Johnson signed it into law. The law must have been important because rarely is the legislative process so efficient.

Anyone burning the two-inch by three-inch piece of paper was subject to punishment that would last longer than a voluntary enlistment in the armed forces. This produced the single nay in the House as Henry P. Smith of New York, who had been a member of a local draft board, stated that the punishment was "far too excessive for this type of misdemeanor."[17] Indeed. The punishment suggested that burning the draft card was something quite serious because no other federal statute penalized burning a piece of paper so severely, and Smith's statement underscored the obvious; the punishment was keyed not to the conduct of burning a small piece of paper but to the hated message the burning conveyed.

After his conviction, the trial judge offered O'Brien a deal. If O'Brien would ask for and carry a draft card, any sentence would be suspended. O'Brien refused, and the judge sentenced him to six years under the Youth Offenders Act, which meant that he might serve four years at the

Federal Youth Correctional Center in Chillicothe, Ohio. Even those who refused to report for induction in the armed forces received lighter sentences, typically between one and three years. One of O'Brien's stronger arguments was that the Government argued that the statute had nothing to do with protesting the war and then turned around and punished the conduct as if it had everything to do with protesting the war. The court of appeals found O'Brien's First Amendment arguments persuasive, and concluded that he could be validly punished only for failure to possess a draft card and for that offense the sentence imposed was far too excessive. Indeed, O'Brien had argued that the sentence was so disproportionate to the conduct that it constituted cruel and unusual punishment prohibited by the Eighth Amendment. The disposition by the court of appeals in sending the case back for resentencing obviated any need to address the Eighth Amendment claim.

In a virtually unknown facet of Warren's opinion, the Court stripped O'Brien of his Eighth Amendment claim without giving it a minute of appellate review. After Warren had rejected O'Brien's symbolic-speech claim, the appropriate disposition of the case was to vacate the court of appeals order and remand the case to the court of appeals for further action consistent with the Court's opinion. Instead, the Court vacated the judgment of the court of appeals and "reinstate[d] the judgment and sentence of the District Court. This disposition makes unnecessary consideration of O'Brien's claim that the Court of Appeals erred in affirming his conviction on the basis of the nonpossession regulation." The Court was aware of what it was doing because it dropped a footnote stating that other issues in O'Brien's brief—a direct reference to the Eighth Amendment claim at the back of O'Brien's brief—were not properly before the Court, and so the Court did not have to reach them. The Court was quite correct that it had no need to reach those issues. They should first be considered by the court of appeals. But the Court's mandate to skip the court of appeals and reinstate the sentence of the district court deprived O'Brien and the court of appeals of any chance of consideration. Thus, it made any further action in the case not just "unnecessary" but rather impossible. The Court cut out the court of appeals and ordered O'Brien to jail.

Warren engaged in a type of individualized decisionmaking, applicable to one person alone, that has no place in a judicial system that professes any desire for justice and consistency in decisionmaking. Warren took out his anger about the changed nature of dissent on the dissenter who had the misfortune to be present before him. O'Brien brought this to the

Court's attention in a petition for rehearing, but the Court's disposition was not an accident, and therefore the petition was denied without opinion. It was one of the most shameful moments of the Warren Court, ranking with *Naim v. Naim, Ginzburg v. United States,* and *Johnson v. New Jersey.* Douglas, so bored with the Court that he no longer took his job seriously, did not comment. Maybe he did not even notice.

O'Brien came down less than two months after the riots following the assassination of Martin Luther King, Jr., and while students at Columbia University were "liberating" the president's office—by occupying and trashing it—and closing down the university. Fortas had already determined to enter the national debate via a "broadside," *Concerning Dissent and Civil Disobedience,* on the topic of the appropriate limits of dissent. The paperback cover noted that the *New York Times* stated it was "one of the most valuable books of the year" and that 750,000 copies were in print.

Fortas necessarily distinguished between legitimate and illegitimate dissent and drew an extraordinarily bright line. Civil disobedience was legitimate when the law broken was itself unconstitutional. But it was never legitimate when the law broken was itself valid. King, except when ignoring an injunction, had been safe, unlike David O'Brien and the campus radicals and antiwar activists who were engaging in illegitimate dissent that was both "morally as well as politically unacceptable."[18] Fortas's broadside appeared as a pamphlet with a bright red cover— hence his "Little Red Book"—and informed students who were hoping for eventual vindication at the liberal Supreme Court that they were out of luck.

To some extent the liberals' view of antiwar dissent had been presaged two years earlier. For one of his clerkships during the 1966 Term, Brennan had selected Michael Tigar of the University of California's Boalt Hall Law School. Tigar had been a once-in-a-generation student, the runaway number one in his class as well as the editor-in-chief of the prestigious *California Law Review.* He also found time to be a well-known activist on a campus of well-known activists. Unlike his better-known compatriots, however, Tigar understood the boundaries of law. Tigar's clerkship was scheduled to commence in the summer of 1966, but before he started, a right-wing publicity campaign under the slogan "Brown, Berkeley, Brennan"[19] tied Tigar and the Court into the upcoming gubernatorial race in California. By summer, Brennan developed second thoughts. Clyde Tolson, J. Edgar Hoover's right-hand man, began funneling to Fortas for Brennan derogatory information about Tigar and supposed communist links. At their first meeting Brennan asked Tigar if he had attended a Communist Party camp in Paterson, New Jersey. An astonished Tigar responded, "Sir, I have never been to Paterson, New Jersey."[20] Tigar would eventually become one of the nation's leading advocates, but in this, his first important case, he could not save the job nor obtain an explanation from Brennan.

The only conceivable reason for firing Tigar—which Douglas thought was "scandalous" and a "shocking cave-in"[21]—was politics. Tigar was a well-known campus radical, as Brennan had been informed by Boalt Hall faculty members before hiring him, and the Court might come under attack for employing a radical in a sensitive position. Fortas was in Brennan's chambers constantly, lobbying him to fire Tigar. Furthermore, 1966 was a gubernatorial election year in California, and Warren cared deeply about defeating Ronald Reagan, and he did not want Reagan dragging the Court into his standard anti-Berkeley diatribes. But Warren was the chief justice of the United States, not the guardian of liberal California politics, and this episode does not reflect well on either him or Fortas or, especially, Brennan. Tigar, however, like the professional lawyer he was, kept his mouth shut.

After Richard Nixon's election, the Court, in a slightly less hostile mood toward protesters generally, returned to symbolic speech in *Tinker*. Some Des Moines children had worn black armbands to school to protest the war. When the Tinkers refused a request to remove the armbands, they were suspended in accordance with a school policy adopted two days earlier in anticipation of the protest. Fortas first concluded that children had constitutional rights in school, a point consistent with his *In re Gault* opinion two years earlier on the requirements of juvenile justice. Fortas's opinion then stated that the Tinkers' behavior was "closely akin to 'pure speech,'" something he most emphatically had not said about campus demonstrations. Yet this helped explain his "broadside," his vote in *O'Brien*, his opinion in a library sit-in, *Brown v. Louisiana*, and his soon-to-be recounted position on flag burning. What mattered was disruption or serious offense.

Fortas remained enough of a liberal to know that speech could cause some problems and still be protected. Lyndon Johnson might prefer not to hear that chant "Hey, hey LBJ, how many kids did you kill today?" but that was protected anyway. The key was disruption by conduct, not speech. Some discomfort for those who supported the war was to be expected, and even in a school situation authorities had to tolerate speech unless it created a material and substantial disruption of the enter-

prise. "[I]n our system, undifferentiated fear or apprehension of distur-
bance is not enough to overcome the right of freedom of expression."
The only problem, as the flag burning case would show, was that Fortas
could not explain what measure of disruption was too much.

Black, whose speech-conduct distinction necessarily rejected symbolic
speech, wrote an emotional dissent that reflected the problems his family
was having with his teenage grandson (as well as his total estrangement
from Fortas). Black charged the majority with taking over from school
officials "the power to control pupils," and letting students or teachers
"use schools at their whim as a platform" for speech. Geometry class is
about mathematics, and Black believed there was no right whatsoever to
divert other students "to thoughts about the highly emotional subject of
Vietnam." Black concluded with what was truly on his mind—protest
run riot. "[G]roups of students all over the land are already running
loose, conducting break-ins, sit-ins, and smash-ins." It was time for a
halt. Fortas, of course, agreed with the general critique. He and the
majority simply did not think an armband was the equivalent of a smash-
in. Harlan wrote a temperate dissent, recognizing the First Amendment
rights at stake but being willing to override them so long as the school
authorities were motivated by legitimate school concerns.

Two months later, in *Street v. New York,* the Court decided another
symbolic-speech case involving a form of antiwar protest, flag burning,
transported into the civil rights context—a protest over the 1966 shooting of James Meredith by a sniper. Harlan found a way to reverse the
conviction on the possibility that it was based on Street's words, not on
his burning of the flag; the majority could therefore duck the contentious
First Amendment issue. In a highly interesting combination there were
separate dissents each holding that flag burning, whether symbolic
speech or not, enjoyed no constitutional protection. The dissents were
written by Warren, Black, Fortas, and White. Warren referred to Street's
act as "desecration and disgrace." Black's speech-conduct distinction
readily split speech from fire. Fortas, returning to his "broadside," stated
that the flag is "special" and Street's conduct was not protected "merely
because it is an act of flamboyant protest." As with *O'Brien* and Tigar,
Street showed there were limits to the liberalism of some of the liberals.

The Past and the Future

On June 9, 1969, the Court decided two cases that in combination offered an interesting perspective on the Court's First Amendment juris-

prudence. One, *Brandenburg v. Ohio,* returned to the post–World War I statutes prohibiting advocacy of illegal action and resulted in the Warren Court summarizing its free speech jurisprudence. The other, *Red Lion Broadcasting v. Federal Communications Commission,* concerned a radio broadcast, surprisingly an issue the Court had never seen before, and therefore gave the Court the opportunity to apply that free speech jurisprudence to what was clearly the future.

Brandenburg was a local leader of the Ku Klux Klan who, at a Klan rally, attended also by the media, made the typical derogatory remarks about African-Americans and Jews that one expects from the Klan. The rally occurred in the rural part of Hamilton County, Ohio, and tape showed twelve hooded figures, some with firearms, and a large burning cross as a background for Brandenburg's ranting. Brandenburg was convicted of "criminal syndicalism," an early twentieth-century crime consisting of advocating the duty of unlawful action as a means of accomplishing industrial or political reform. He was sentenced to one to ten years, and the Ohio appellate court cavalierly affirmed the conviction as if the First Amendment had been stuck at 1927, or perhaps 1951.

Brandenburg was a short per curiam opinion announcing a new test for the problem of illegal advocacy, the Smith Act crime for which communists from *Dennis* to *Scales* had been tried. Under the new test, a person could not be convicted for advocacy of unlawful action unless the advocacy of lawbreaking was directed toward inciting imminent lawless action and was likely to produce such action. *Brandenburg* thus accepted *Yates*'s conclusion that advocacy was not enough, the words had to constitute incitement, while simultaneously rejecting *Dennis*'s conclusion that it was sufficient that the harm flow from the speech "as speedily as circumstances would permit." Further, the lawlessness had to be likely, not speculative. Not a single communist, from Dennis in 1951 to Scales in 1961, could have been jailed under the *Brandenburg* test.

Black and Douglas would not accept their belated victory. Each concurred to remind the Court of its checkered past and to eschew any part of what they saw as a newly formulated "clear and present danger" test, no matter how speech-protective it might appear.

Brandenburg was an obvious highpoint of the Warren Court's embrace of the First Amendment although it is an insufficiently reasoned per curiam, highly unusual for a case that was ridding the law of a landmark case like *Dennis*. The reason was that Fortas was its author, and he had been forced to resign under pressure and so was no longer on the Court when his opinion came down.

While offering little analysis, *Brandenburg* nevertheless appears to rest on the standard Warren Court conclusion that speech is so important, so vital to a representative democracy, that only the most minimal intrusions, if any, can be tolerated. Government always asserts there are risks to speech, that important social interests are jeopardized by speech. The lessons of *Sullivan-Brandenburg,* not to mention the post-1962 domestic-security cases, were that the government always overstated the risks and interests and always underestimated the value of speech. The Court did not.

Or at least the Court did not when speech came directly out of a mouth or was printed on paper. But when speech was transmitted through the electromagnetic spectrum, the Court joined government generally in underestimating the value of speech and overestimating its potential dangers. Thus, Red Lion Broadcasting could be penalized for criticizing a man who himself recognized no bounds in his criticism of Republican presidential candidate Barry Goldwater.

Red Lion was a tiny AM station located in a Pennsylvania hamlet about sixty miles from York. It had broadcast a "Christian Crusade" tape by the Reverend Billy James Hargis that attacked liberal writer Fred Cook. Cook had previously attacked Hargis and others in the magazine *The Nation* and had been commissioned by the Democratic National Committee to write the hatchet job, *Goldwater—Extremist on the Right,* for the 1964 campaign. And, in fact, the DNC was monitoring Red Lion's broadcasts and advised Cook on requesting reply time on the station and on petitioning the FCC.

The FCC ruled that the Hargis broadcast violated the commission's personal attack rules, which were an offshoot of the better-known Fairness Doctrine. The latter required that if a broadcaster aired one side of a controversial issue, then the broadcaster must air the other side as well. *Red Lion* was a constitutional challenge to the Fairness Doctrine, and the radio station advanced a simple, perfectly framed First Amendment position: The government cannot demand that a speaker who says X about a matter of public interest and concern must then also say non-X. This position seemed more than amply supported by *Sullivan* and especially *Brandenburg,* which had a necessary implication that Brandenburg could not have been punished for failing to afford opportunities for Jews or African-Americans to respond to his diatribe. Why, then, should his rights to speak out depend on whether he spoke in a park or an AM radio station?

The six justices joining White's unanimous opinion rejecting Red Lion's First Amendment claim did so immediately after White's initial circulation and in their remarks to him were inordinately ebullient. Instead of the usual "I agree" or "Join me"—which Warren and Marshall sent—the other justices sent gushing notes. Black wrote that "I am happy to agree to your comprehensive discussion of the vital and important issues involved in this case."[22] Harlan thought White's opinion displayed "great wisdom and skill, and I am glad to join."[23] Brennan stated, "this is a truly superb opinion and I am delighted to join."[24] Stewart stated *Red Lion* was "a very thorough and thoughtful job, and I am glad to join."[25] (Fortas, of course, was gone, and Douglas did not participate in the case.)

For the Court, *Red Lion* turned initially on two issues. Was broadcasting different from publishing or speaking, and, if so, did that matter? The answers were yes. Use of the electronic spectrum placed inherent limits on speech not present in the print medium. Unlike print, the electronic media were limited by scarcity. An implicit premise was that if a medium of communication was scarce, then the government must dictate the content of at least a portion of the speech within the medium. This necessitated a different free speech jurisprudence than anything the Court had created before. The Court, as in so many areas, was up to the task of creation.

White used scarcity to elaborate on a First Amendment fundamentally different from the one the Court had synthesized in *Brandenburg*. Instead of a First Amendment about speakers—like the *New York Times* and Julian Bond—it was one about listeners. The Court made explicit its newer inverted hierarchy: "It is the right of the viewers and listeners, not the right of the broadcasters, which is paramount." What was that right? "To receive suitable access to social, political, aesthetic, moral and other ideas and experiences." How would the right be effectuated? A broadcaster was a "proxy or a fiduciary with obligations" to its audience. The government through the FCC was there, ready and willing, to intervene, to see to it that the broadcaster said what ought to be said. Government assistance in the scope of debate was essential lest the important rights be lost.

The radical nature of *Red Lion* is instantly obvious once its concept is moved elsewhere. Would the rights of readers of a book be paramount to those of its author? Do readers of books have a legal, perhaps constitutional, right to receive suitable ideas? Did Jimmy Carter, in his memoirs, have to treat Ronald Reagan fairly? Should the government create an agency—say a Federal Book Commission—to effectuate these rights?

Red Lion's conclusion that scarcity demanded the creation of an entirely new free speech jurisprudence could be explained in one of three ways. First, broadcasting is so different and so special that a watered-down First Amendment is necessary lest the power of that medium of the press result in a distortion of democracy. To be consistent with *Sullivan,* this rationale assumes that free newspapers are essential to democracy, but free broadcasting poses a threat to it. Second, speech and property are fundamentally distinct, and a claim to speak need not be respected unless its adjoining claim to property ownership is complete. That is, the *New York Times* owns its newsprint, presses, and land, but broadcasters do not own the electromagnetic spectrum; hence, regulating them is like regulating any other economic enterprise, virtually free from constitutional constraints. This rationale assumes that the government has a perfect entitlement to run the airwaves just as it had a perfect entitlement to run the jailhouse grounds in *Adderley v. Florida.* Third, *Red Lion* could be deemed a vote of no confidence in *Sullivan* and the ability of a free press to provide the needed information. As such, it was a vote of confidence in the government to see that the needed information came forth as well as a vote of no confidence in broadcast news at a time it was at a never-to-be-surpassed best.

Red Lion stood First Amendment jurisprudence on its head, denying the past would have relevance to the future, and why it did so demands an answer. One answer is technology. Each justice had been raised in the days of the crystal set, and even the youngest had reached maturity in the age before television. They were sure it was creating an entirely different world.

A second answer is that the justices were less committed to what they had been saying than the opinions had suggested. To be sure, *Brandenburg*'s summary of the meaning of *Yates, Sullivan, Bond v. Floyd,* and others cannot be discarded. But individual justices thought they could create neat and limited exceptions to their general handiwork. Thus, Warren, Black, and Fortas thought they could create a "flag" exception to the First Amendment. Warren, Brennan, and Fortas thought they could create some form of an "obscenity" exception. All but Douglas found a "draft card" exception, and *Red Lion* reflected a similar vote for a "broadcast" exception. Free speech is a powerful force; government was too prone to undervalue it and overstate the risks of its unfettered use—"except" in certain areas. And who could know what other new areas would also be excluded from the Court's supposed standard free speech jurisprudence?

A week after *Red Lion* and *Brandenburg* the Court provided an answer. In *National Labor Relations Board v. Gissel Packing,* the Court unanimously upheld restrictions on employer speech during a union organizing campaign because of statements that lacked "careful phrasing on the basis of objective fact." What had the employer done? It had reminded its employees that once, years before, it had been in a bargaining relationship with a union and that there had been an economically costly strike that had nearly put the company out of business. When the business resumed after the strike ended, the company began nonunion operations.

Gissel involved a Teamsters effort to reunionize the company. In countering the Teamsters, Gissel's president "emphasized the results of the earlier strike which he claimed had 'almost put the company out of business.'" He stated that the company remained on "'thin ice' financially and that a union's only weapon was to strike," and that a strike could lead to the closing of the plant. He claimed the Teamsters were a "strike happy outfit" and always stressed the danger to the company from strikes.

In upholding an unfair labor practice charge against Gissel for threatening the employees on the basis of the above, Warren's opinion explained that the National Labor Relations Act "implements the First Amendment," but that an employer's rights of free speech "cannot outweigh the equal rights of the employees" under the act. There is none of *Sullivan*'s "uninhibited, robust, and wide-open" in this First Amendment; instead, the speaker must be "careful" and "objective." Nor is there need to worry about a chilling effect, nor for that matter a discussion of what, if anything, had been inaccurate in the employer's statements. The employer-speaker can "simply avoid conscious overstatements he has reason to believe will mislead his employees."

While the Court wanted to pretend this was the same First Amendment, *Gissel Packing* simply carved out another exception without acknowledging it. As labor expert Julius Getman notes, "the Court's switch from the marketplace to the laboratory constitutes more than a casual change in metaphor. The laboratory conditions doctrine rests ultimately upon the assumption that free choice is fragile—that it will be undermined by the type of robust debate encouraged by the First Amendment in other areas."[26]

Chapter 13

The End of Obscenity?

A two-inch story on page 78 of the May 10, 1960 *New York Times* reported that the Food and Drug Administration had approved the prescription sale of Enovid, the first oral contraceptive. The pill promised to eliminate the fear of pregnancy from sexual behavior, and newspapers and magazines enthusiastically supported it. Millions of women, especially those in their twenties, began using the pill. Ambassador Clare Booth Luce, otherwise a conservative Republican, expressed a common view: "Modern woman is at last free as a man is free, to dispose of her own body."[1] Helen Gurley Brown more explicitly celebrated female sexual liberation with her 1962 best-seller *Sex and the Single Girl,* whose approach to life paralleled that of the hedonistic and much-envied bachelor, Hugh Hefner, the editor-publisher of *Playboy.* That magazine, with its ingenious linking of sex and upward mobility, passed the million-sales-per-issue mark in circulation at the beginning of the decade. In 1963 Bob Dylan wrote "The Times They Are A-Changing," and nowhere was the title more applicable than to attitudes about and depictions of sex.

At the beginning of the decade an adult could legally purchase for the first time *Lady Chatterley's Lover,* which the Postmaster General had ruled was nonmailable, but the federal court of appeals in New York unanimously held was not obscene. By the decade's end full nudity (at least of women) had become available even on a movie screen (but still not in *Playboy*).

By Warren's retirement, obscenity law seemed to be sufficiently liberalized so that everything then on the open market was protected as long as children and nonconsenting adults were not involved. After protecting those who wished or needed protection for themselves, the law seemed to be "anything goes." The reason for the caveat is simple; until hard-core materials entered the market, which occurred after Warren retired, the solution to the obscenity problem remained in doubt. Yet even a "consenting adults" outcome was far from clear in the mid-1960s when the Court's dominant efforts were, first, to continue *Roth*'s effort to protect serious art and literature and, second, to routinize the bureaucracy of censorship by bringing it out of the dark and under legal control. Because both efforts were successful, the obscenity wars turned to much more explicit material.

Obscenity Procedures

In the mid-1950s New York psychiatrist Frederic Wertham commenced a crusade against violent comic books. Wertham, a would-be twentieth century Comstock, had come to the conclusion that the increase in juvenile crime the nation was experiencing was caused by the influx of horror comics. In 1956 Rhode Island joined his crusade by establishing a Commission to Encourage Morality in Youth. The commission's function was "to educate the public" concerning books unsuitable for children and to recommend prosecution of offending booksellers. Essentially, the state had established a blacklisting operation aimed mostly at comic books, but also at some books that were deemed obscene by a majority of the nine commission members. Thus, when Grove Press shipped 3,380 copies of Henry Miller's *Tropic of Cancer* to three Rhode Island wholesalers, three phone calls from the state's attorney general resulted in 3,380 copies of *Tropic* being returned to Grove Press. When the commission turned on Grace Metalious's *Peyton Place,* which New England censors by providing huge free publicity had catapulted into the century's best-selling novel, and Charles Mergendahl's *The Bramble Bush,* which, if no *Peyton Place,* was nevertheless making good money, Bantam Books, which published the latter, and Dell Publishing, which published the former, sued.

In *Bantam Books v. Sullivan,* Rhode Island argued that the commission was simply an advisory body with no real powers. Brennan didn't believe it because it wasn't true. The commission had been successful in its notices with their implied threats that someone selling a listed book would be targeted for prosecution. Brennan ordered the state to develop procedural safeguards before it listed any book as violating the state's laws. There were two short concurring opinions; Harlan alone dissented.

Bantam Books was in fact of relatively little importance, since by 1960 the systematic efforts to blacklist books had virtually ended. Movies were something else, and *Freedman v. Maryland*, decided two years later in 1965, was therefore far more significant.

Like *Bantam Books*, *Freedman* was a Brennan opinion using his standard technique of conceding to the state the power to accomplish its goals but finding that the way the state exercised its power was inappropriate and unconstitutional. In the case of *Freedman*, Brennan's procedural demands provided the coup de grace to censorship boards throughout the country.

The Maryland film-censorship statute, in common with most in existence, which were held constitutional in 1961 in *Times Film v. Chicago*, required the submission of all movies, even the tamest ones, for prior viewing by the state's board of censors in order to receive the necessary license to exhibit them. Ronald Freedman, with five years in the business managing the Rex Theater in Baltimore, had battled the board over the Louis Malle film *Les Amants (The Lovers)*, and he ultimately prevailed in state court. But the battle was time-consuming, and the board would not always recognize judicial decisions as binding on itself, so Freedman decided to challenge it head on. On November 2, 1962, he phoned the board to inform it that he was about to show a film (*Revenge at Daybreak*, about the Easter 1916 Irish rebellion) that day and that he was not submitting it to the board first. The board conceded that had he submitted the film, it would have been granted a license, but, as expected, Freedman was convicted of exhibiting the film without a license.

Brennan's opinion, while never challenging *Times Film* directly, focuses on the delays inherent in obtaining a license and the procedures needed to minimize, if not eliminate, them. "The administration of a censorship system for motion pictures presents peculiar dangers to constitutionally protected speech. . . . Because the censor's business is to censor, there inheres the danger that he may well be less responsive than a court . . . to the constitutionally protected interests in free expression. And if it is made unduly onerous, by reason of delay or otherwise, to seek judicial review, the censor's determination may in practice be final."

Brennan then spelled out the procedural requirements necessary for any constitutional system of censorship. First, the burden of proof was on the censor. Second, there must be judicial review and the responsibility for initiating it must be on the censors. Third, it must all be done quickly. The censor must act within a specified short time, and so must the reviewing court. Since the Maryland statute did not satisfy these procedures because, surprise, no statute in existence did, it was unconstitutional. Every other justice joined the opinion except Black and

Douglas, who held to their views that obscenity, like other speech, was entitled to full constitutional protection. They noted that they did "not believe any form of censorship no matter how speedy or prolonged it may be is permissible." The other seven, though rejecting such a categorical position, nonetheless interred, as a practical matter, the licensing system by which censorship operated.

Censorship boards, heretofore a staple of twentieth-century urban life, were caught in a vise. On one side, the Court's tightening of the substantive obscenity standard drastically reduced the suppressible materials. On the other side, the procedural requirements of *Bantam Books* and *Freedman* meant that suppression had to be aboveboard, with reasons, and that the censors had to have a budget (provided by the taxpayers) to then seek judicial review of their own actions. It was just too much. Censorship boards vanished overnight without even the benefit of a tepid eulogy. By the end of the decade, in their place the Motion Picture Association of America had adopted its own ratings system to offer some guidance to the public about the sexual content of movies.

Substantive Obscenity

In the decade after *Roth,* while *Peyton Place* was resting at the top of the best-seller lists, the three most famous books involved in obscenity litigation were, first, *Lady Chatterley's Lover,* second, *Tropic of Cancer,* and, finally, *Fanny Hill.* The former two illustrate that at least for most of the Court's first decade of obscenity litigation, the Court's efforts focused on protecting what, by later standards, were defended by mainstream critics as serious attempts at literature and art.

The initial substantive case after *Bantam Books* was *Jacobellis v. Ohio,* which also concerned the Louis Malle film *Les Amants* starring Jeanne Moreau. As the Maryland courts had recognized, and the Ohio courts did not—they still thought of sex and obscenity as synonymous—*Les Amants* was an art film, not a porno film, and it was showing nationwide without incident. *Les Amants,* noted Brennan, had already been "favorably reviewed in a number of national publications, although disparaged in others, and was rated by at least two critics of national stature among the best films of the year." A single love scene in the last reel of the film was "almost entirely" Ohio's reason for finding the film obscene. In a concurring opinion, Arthur Goldberg described the scene as "so fragmentary and fleeting that only a censor's alert would make an audience conscious that something 'questionable' is being portrayed." He then placed it in the context of the movie. "Except for this rapid sequence, the film concerns itself with the history of an ill-matched and unhappy marriage—a familiar subject in old and new novels and in current television soap operas." If Goldberg had only lived long enough, he would have seen more daring, if not anywhere near as well acted, love scenes on prime-time network television. A badly fractured Court, with Warren, Clark, and Harlan dissenting, found the film protected.

Brennan, with only Goldberg joining, tried to decide the case within *Roth*. In doing so he made four points. First, portrayal of sex "is not itself sufficient reason to deny materials protection," and the social importance of a work may not be weighed against its prurient appeal. If it has social importance, it is not obscene. Second, to be obscene, materials must go "substantially beyond customary limits of candor." Third, the community by which those limits are tested is a national, not a local community, since the First Amendment does not "vary with state lines." Fourth and finally, the justices must review an obscenity case de novo and decide for themselves whether the materials are in fact obscene. It might be burdensome and distasteful, but the Court must make its own judgment.

As a result of de novo review, the justices, as Douglas acidly noted, became a full-fledged board of censors for the nation. They perused the materials to determine how explicit and how "serious" everything was. This also inaugurated the tradition of the justices gathering in the Court's basement to view the terrible movies—for *Les Amants* was the last "art" film shown—trapped in obscenity prosecutions (which at least had its humorous side-effects, such as Thurgood Marshall's wisecracks or Harlan's clerks explaining to the near-blind justice what was on the screen).

Black and Douglas stuck to their absolutist position that everything was protected; therefore, they saw no need to join their Brethren in the basement to view any of the materials. Potter Stewart came surprisingly close to their position by indicating that very little, if anything, was obscene. He saw the Court's enterprise as trying to "define what may be indefinable." He would limit obscenity prosecutions to "hard-core pornography." In what became by far his most famous contribution to the genre of legal soundbites, he then wrote: "I shall not today attempt further to define the kinds of material I understand to be embraced within that shorthand description; and perhaps I could never succeed in intelligibly doing so. But I know it when I see it, and the motion picture involved in this case is not that." Unlike domestic communism and mass demonstrations, which posed the risks of violence and disorder, Stewart perceived sexual materials as harmless.

Harlan's dissent reiterated his *Roth* conclusion that a state had great latitude to censor and that this was a sensible accommodation. "I would not prohibit [states] from banning any material which, taken as a whole, has been reasonably found in state judicial proceedings to treat with sex in a fundamentally offensive matter." Ohio operated within these permissible limits, and he would affirm its finding of obscenity. Thus, his position, as he had indicated in *Roth,* was that states were basically free of constitutional restraints when they chose to regulate materials with even minimal amounts of sexual content.

Warren, joined by Clark, also dissented. While adhering to *Roth* as good enough "until a more satisfactory definition" comes about, he took issue both with Brennan's demand that juries apply national rather than local standards and with the requirement of de novo review. States had a right "to maintain a decent society" and in a nation as diverse as the United States, their good-faith application of the *Roth* standard to their local conditions, as he believed occurred in *Jacobellis,* should be respected.

Warren continued to see obscenity as a moral crime. While he was very sympathetic to criminals who he assumed were poor and therefore forced into crime by desperation, he had zero tolerance for sex and gambling. Those were vices, and people engaged in these corrupt practices because they were greedy and degenerate. Once he told a clerk that if someone showed a sexually graphic book to one of his daughters, "I'd have strangled him with my own hands."[2]

That same day the Court held *Tropic of Cancer* not obscene. The publisher, Grove Press, had brought out its edition a year after the favorable decision on its edition of *Lady Chatterley's Lover.* The Justice Department and the Post Office did nothing, but in the states some sixty cases, mostly criminal, were commenced against the book. State supreme courts split on *Tropic*'s obscenity, and Grove Press filed for a writ of certiorari after its defeat in the Florida Supreme Court. Surprisingly, in *Grove Press v. Gerstein,* the Court granted certiorari and reversed immediately without asking for briefs or argument and without explanation except to the citation of the relevant opinions in *Jacobellis.* Warren, Clark, Harlan, and White stated that instead the Court should have denied certiorari, which would have left standing the Florida judgment that *Tropic* was obscene.

The Voting Array

The best interpretation of *Jacobellis* and *Grove Press* was that they established that art and literature were protected under the Constitution even if the material was offensive or sexually arousing. Thus, "a lawyer prominent in the field was quoted by *Time* magazine as saying that it was now 'impossible' for a wholly textual book to be declared obscene."[3]

White was the most inscrutable justice. He concurred in the result in *Jacobellis* without joining any opinion or writing his own, and he voted to deny certiorari in the Florida *Tropic* case. Thus, with no public reasoning whatsoever, he apparently saw a constitutional difference between *Les Amants* and *Tropic of Cancer.*

White's vote, however, was irrelevant because the voting patterns of the justices, especially Stewart's adoption of a hard-core pornography standard, had made Brennan's *the* law of obscenity. In the context of the times, Stewart's position was for all practical purposes a vote with Black and Douglas. Thus, Brennan and Goldberg (and then Fortas) were the deciding votes in all obscenity cases.

Two features of Brennan's *Jacobellis* opinion reinforced his position as the key justice. First, de novo review meant that Brennan and Goldberg, not a jury, would have the final say on the application of *Roth* to the materials. Second, and relatedly, Brennan's conclusion that the relevant community was national meant that areas where materials touching sex received their least welcome reception—the Bible Belt South and localities with high concentrations of Catholics in the North—were to be subjected to the more liberal standards prevailing elsewhere in the nation. National standards, in operation, meant Brennan's standards, for, given the doctrine and the voting patterns, nothing could be obscene unless Brennan said it was obscene.

For six of the justices, the effort to define obscenity was over. They knew what obscenity was or at least what to do about it. Thus, Black and Douglas didn't look to see what it was and didn't care; the First Amendment protected books, magazines, and films completely. Stewart had to check just in case something was "hard-core," but until 1969 nothing involved in obscenity litigation was. (As one of his clerks once quipped to the author, "he said he saw it once as a naval officer in the Mediterranean but has never seen it since.") Harlan, Clark, and White also had reached their stopping points, which were, for the former two, their beginning point in their positions in *Roth*. As it so happened, when White finally explained what he was doing, it too was *Roth*.

This left Brennan, Fortas, and, surprisingly, Warren, each of whom was still not content with the doctrine and intended to fine-tune it to protect everything that deserved protection while allowing the states to suppress the suppressible. This effort required Brennan to abandon his standard technique. Thus, there was no articulating of state interests, no demanding of the least restrictive alternative, no worry, after *Bantam Books* and *Freedman,* about any chilling effect. Indeed, when the Court actually discussed state interests in the 1969 case of *Stanley v. Georgia,* Brennan would not join the opinion. He intended to cut a near-perfect line, protecting serious works of art and literature and creating a buffer zone to minimize misclassification, but he would do so without discussing what the governments thought they were doing.

The 1966 Trilogy

Brennan, Fortas, and Warren worked their positions out in a trilogy of cases in 1966 that offered a variety of materials. *Memoirs v. Massachusetts* brought *Fanny Hill,* that lustful mid-eighteenth-century work to the Court, under its original name, *Memoirs of a Woman of Pleasure.* John Cleland, an otherwise mediocre writer, got lucky with *Fanny Hill* and produced an eloquent, witty, and highly titillating book. It had enjoyed two centuries of clandestine existence because it was so well written, without the vulgarities associated with mid-twentieth-century sexual works. Hence, the frequent characterization, "well-written obscenity."[4] This was Massachusetts's second go at *Fanny Hill;* in 1821 in what is generally regarded as the first suppression of a literary work as obscene in the United States, an illustrated version of the book was banned.

Ginzburg v. United States involved three items, a book, *The Housewife's Handbook of Selective Promiscuity,* a glossy hardcover magazine, *Eros,* and a newsletter, "Liaison." *Handbook,* wrote Brennan, was a short book "purporting to be a sexual autobiography detailing with complete candor the author's sexual experiences from age 3 to age 36." There was ample evidence that doctors and psychiatrists found the book useful in their practices, and the Government did "not seriously contest the claim that the book has worth in such a controlled, or even neutral environment." *Eros* was a coffee-table magazine that cost $10 an issue, a huge amount for a magazine (approximately $50 in current dollars). The copy before the Court had virtually nothing visually sexual except a picture of an African-American man and a white woman, naked at least from the waist up, in an embrace. Obscene in Birmingham perhaps, although not for legitimate reasons, but not outside the South. "Liaison," the biweekly newsletter dedicated to "keeping sex an art and preventing it from becoming a science," was basically a collection of off-color jokes and poems coupled with a synopsis of a professional article on sexual relationships.

Mishkin v. New York was about fetishism, sadomasochism, and homosexuality. There were dozens of cheap "pulp" paperbacks without pictures in the record that Mishkin had commissioned, such as *Cult of the Spankers, The Whipping Chorus Girls, I'll Try Anything Twice,* and *Stud Broad.*

In terms of prurient appeal, *Fanny Hill* was a laydown winner. The commonwealth attorney hit the rationale for obscenity regulation perfectly in his closing argument at trial. He had read the book carefully, and "it did arouse prurient interest and impure thoughts in me. Fortunately I am well adjusted enough so it did not effect my daily life, but I wonder" about others in the commonwealth.[5] *Handbook* was a mediocre second, and *Eros* a distant third; "Liaison" was "a rather silly affair whose ration of prurience was not much larger than its ration of wit."[6] The *Mishkin* materials might arouse their target audience, but they were repulsive rather than prurient to the remainder of the community.

In a stunning outcome, the Court protected only *Fanny Hill,* while consigning Ginzburg and Mishkin to jail. The outcome was the result of Brennan's having reached his limits. At first, he voted that everything in the three cases, *Fanny Hill* included, was obscene. Fortas, while believing obscenity was a "cess-pool problem," nevertheless thought that the "nation was about to turn to another wave of 'book burning,'" and he successfully got Brennan to switch in *Memoirs.*[7] As a result of his flip, Brennan protected the most sexually arousing book, and in the process, just as he had done in *Roth,* he reconceptualized obscenity again and moved the Court closer to Warren's *Roth* view that obscenity was about evil people, like Ginzburg and Mishkin, not evil books.

Mishkin had detailed instructions for those preparing his books. They should be full of sex and lesbian scenes. "The sex had to be very strong, it had to be rough, it had to be clearly spelled out." His contention was that he couldn't be convicted because the average person would be repelled by his pulps. Brennan simply noted that since Mishkin marketed the books to deviants, prurience would be tested by the tastes of his own target audience. It was not the Court's fault that Mishkin's clientele found the books prurient. Black, Douglas, and Stewart dissented.

Ginzburg, who had been convicted of mailing obscene materials and mailing advertisements telling how and where obscene materials might be obtained, had the tougher conviction to leave standing for a very simple reason: None of his three items was even close to obscene under *Roth*. Attorneys following the field assumed that the Court had granted review, not because the case presented any novel points, but rather because the five-year sentence and $28,000 fine imposed on Ginzburg were an obvious injustice. The Government brief offered an open invitation to throw out the convictions by stating that the only way to decide the case was by reading the materials.

Brennan, perhaps serving as Warren's mouthpiece, refused to right the injustice and instead perpetrated it further. First, he lied, implying that *Handbook, Eros,* and "Liaison" might be obscene. Second, while pretending to interpret the federal statute, he "interpreted" it in such a fashion that he created a brand new crime, which Brennan then convicted Ginzburg of committing without the necessity of a trial. Statutes are occasionally rewritten under the guise of interpretation, but there is nothing comparable to what occurred in *Ginzburg*. Warren, Clark, White, and Fortas went along with this shameful travesty of constitutional analysis.

That Ginzburg's materials were not obscene—and therefore the Government was trying to lose—would be clear to anyone who looked at them in the context of the Court's decisions, whether *Roth* or *Jacobellis*. But just as Warren had been offended by the way Stanley Roth conducted his business, the *Ginzburg* opinion is replete with condemnation of how Ralph Ginzburg did his. Where did he seek second-class mailing privileges? Intercourse and Blue Ball, Pennsylvania, but the respective post offices were too small so he settled on Middlesex, New Jersey. This clearly identified him as uncouth. What did he tell prospective customers? That he was taking "full advantage of an unrestricted license allowed by law in the expression of sex and sexual matters." This clearly identified him as a classic American salesman puffing his wares. Furthermore, Ginzburg offered a guarantee of a full refund of any money "if the book fails to reach you because of U.S. Post Office censorship." This added to his unscrupulousness, ironically, because he could not have reasonably believed that there was a real threat of such censorship for such relatively tame materials.

The Court believed that the "leer of the sensualist" (rather than simply the art of the salesman) permeated the advertising and that it was appropriate to "view the publications against a background of commercial exploitation of erotica solely for the sake of their prurient appeal." In a "close" case, the determination of obscenity could be influenced by the circumstances surrounding its distribution, that is, if it were part of "the sordid business of pandering: 'the business of purveying textual or graphic matter openly advertised to appeal to the erotic interest of their customers.'" The latter quote was from Warren's concurring opinion in *Roth* and it explained *Ginzburg*. Ralph Ginzburg was a panderer; pandering should be prohibited; therefore, he was going to jail for pandering, convicted under a statute that did not mention pandering in its text.

Harlan dissented. Since it was a federal case, he offered Ginzburg real First Amendment protection. Here was one time, moreover, when Harlan's devotion to traditional judicial craft served the country well. He noted the "curious result" whereby the statute was ignored and the new offense was "a mere euphemism for allowing punishment of a person who mails otherwise constitutionally protected material just because a jury or a judge may not find him or his business agreeable." Black found that the convictions violated both due process and the First Amendment. Douglas took on the idea of pandering by stating he could not "imagine any promotional effort that would make chapters 7 and 8 of the Song of Solomon any the less or any more worthy of First Amendment protection than does their unostentatious inclusion in the average edition of the Bible" (even if the Court seemingly could imagine such a thing).

Stewart unsuccessfully reminded the majority that censorship is "a hallmark of an authoritarian regime" and "reflects a society's lack of confidence in itself." Like Harlan, Stewart attacked Brennan's redrafting of the federal obscenity statute to include pandering. "The First Amendment applies to Ralph Ginzburg with no less completeness and force than to G. P. Putnam's Sons, the publishers of *Fanny Hill*. In upholding and enforcing the Bill of Rights, this Court has no power to pick or to choose. When we lose sight of that fixed star of constitutional adjudication, we lose our way. For then we forsake a government of law and are left with a government by Big Brother." Stewart was exactly right, and as Brennan announced the result and rationale, Paul Bender, who had argued the case for the Solicitor General's Office, sat with his head buried in his hands, stunned and dismayed by his victory. Later, Thurgood Marshall, in an exchange with some law clerks, playfully stated that he had found the sure way to win at the Court. Obligingly a clerk asked "how?" "Just send Bender up," Marshall quipped, "with instructions to lose." *Ginz-*

burg's only positive point was that it would relieve the Court from the necessity of perusing the materials by focusing on the defendant instead.

Brennan's opinion in *Memoirs* was remarkably short. The Massachusetts courts, in finding *Fanny Hill* obscene, had acknowledged, as considerable expert testimony had claimed, that the book had value. But because its dominant theme was to appeal to prurient interest and because the book was patently offensive because it affronted contemporary community standards relating to the description or representation of sexual materials, it was obscene. That was all *Roth* required; once those two conditions were met, the book was obscene. And because it was obscene, it was deemed utterly without redeeming social value.

In *Memoirs,* Brennan pulled the plug on the "deemed," and instead of assuming the material was worthless, he required the state to prove that the material was utterly without redeeming social value as well as to prove prurience and patent offensiveness. Because a finding of utter lack of value was an independent test, a state could not weigh the prurience and the patent offensiveness of the work against its value in a balancing test. Experts had testified that *Fanny Hill* did have value, and Massachusetts had found that testimony credible; therefore, the book was constitutionally protected.

In addition to standard opinions by Black, Stewart, and Harlan, the more interesting of the separate opinions were those of Clark and White, with Douglas answering the former. White did not believe that just by surviving for a couple of centuries an obscene work became protected by its age (under the theory that its continuous existence demonstrated its value). He did not view social importance as independent of the other two tests and would have stuck with *Roth* as written.

Clark cut loose at obscenity generally. "I have 'stomached' past cases for almost 10 years without much outcry. Though I am not known to be a purist—or a shrinking violet—this book is too much even for me." Clark then turned on Douglas, who had turned on Clark. Douglas claimed there was no proof that obscenity produces any antisocial conduct. In what marked the first effort of a supporter of obscenity regulation to explain why a state should be allowed to restrict the materials, Clark noted that a number of social scientists, police officials, and clergymen linked obscenity to antisocial conduct and believed it had an adverse effect on mental health. Whether or not Clark's noting that some members of these professions believed that obscenity was harmful would constitute the proof Douglas claimed did not exist, Clark made no serious effort to document his assertion, and he made no effort to tie his conclusion into First Amendment doctrine generally. Advocating communism also might cause significant harms (such as extermination of the property-holding classes) and yet it had been constitutionally protected, at least since *Yates*.

Douglas responded to Clark. "We are judges, not literary experts or historians or philosophers. We are not competent to render an independent judgment as to the worth of this or any other book, except in our capacity as private citizens. I would pair my Brother Clark on *Fanny Hill* with the Universalist minister I quote in the Appendix." The appendix contained a sermon condemning the popular Dr. Norman Vincent Peale for narrow-mindedness and supporting the long-dead Cleland. "There is real irony in the fact that Fanny Hill, a rather naive young girl who becomes a prostitute, finds warmth, understanding and the meaning of love and faithfulness amid surroundings and situations which the society, as a whole, condemns as debased and depraved. The issue which a Dr. Peale will never understand, because he is a victim of it himself and which John Cleland describes with brilliant clarity and sensitive persuasion, is that until we learn to respect ourselves enough that we leave each other alone, we cannot discover the meaning of morality." Douglas thereby reinforced his belief that those supporting censorship were narrow-minded Comstockians, accidental relics of the Victorian era and out of step with the necessary conditions of a free modern society.

There was considerable debate about the meaning of the 1966 trilogy, and because they believed that the censors had prevailed, many "legal experts thought another wave of censorship was now in the offing."[8] But *Memoirs* meant another transformation of obscenity law because thereafter the state would have to prove material was "utterly without redeeming social value." The *Memoirs* requirement was a harder task than the route laid out in *Ginzburg* of showing that the defendant was a bad guy who was engaged in the "crass commercial exploitation of sex," as all the pornographers were. Yet because existing statutes were not written in such a way to allow prosecutors to exploit *Ginzburg,* for the time being at least *Memoirs* was the only route available to the states. However unjust, Ralph Ginzburg was sacrificed to save the cause he promoted.

It would be a mistake to see the law as driving the market. Before the 1966 trilogy was handed down, the *New York Times* reviewed the pornographic *Story of O*. The "free publication of 'Story of O' in this country is an event of considerable importance not because the book has more than limited artistic merit (it probably doesn't) or because it is in some way attractive (it isn't) but because it marks the end of any coherent restrictive application of the concept of pornography to books."[9]

To *Redrup*

With obscenity law transformed again, the Court granted review in cases from Arkansas, Kentucky, and New York to focus on a different variant of the *Ginzburg* problem: What level of "scienter," that is, culpable knowledge, should the retailer of sexual materials be required to possess? Must he know the materials are legally obscene or should it be sufficient that he know the materials are intended to arouse a prurient response? Or is scienter simply irrelevant when the materials are obscene? The importance of scienter was highlighted by the conviction of Robert Redrup for selling an undercover agent two paperbacks, *Shame Agent* and *Lust Pool*. Redrup had never heard of them because he just happened to be filling in at work that day for an acquaintance who was ill. The other two cases involved a number of second-string girlie magazines, each searching for the market niche below *Playboy*, of which they were cheap imitations. The pictorial materials in front of the justices, from *Sir* and *Gent* and *Swank* and others, all continued, like *Playboy*, to show breasts and buttocks but to avoid showing pubic hair (which was shown only in nudist magazines, which had been held protected in the immediate aftermath of *Roth*). Kurt Vonnegut had explained the underlying rationale. "Obscenity is any picture or phonograph record or any written matter calling attention to reproductive organs, bodily discharge, or bodily hair. The difference between pornography and art is bodily hair."[10]

Redrup v. New York, the named opinion, and its companions represented the full array of sexually oriented printed matter that was commercially available in most, if not all, of the urban United States in 1967. Hence, a decision about selling these materials would just about cover the field as it was then known, movies excepted inasmuch as they were lagging behind *Playboy* and its cheaper imitators in the explicit picturing of unclothed bodies.

Nothing relating to the abilities of the justices to explain what was obscene had changed in the year since *Memoirs*. Nor were they able to explain what a convenience-store clerk should know about *Swank*. The justices simply threw in the towel. They reversed the obscenity convictions in each of the cases in what is one of the stranger opinions of the Warren era. *Redrup* is a per curiam of four pages that first stated the basic facts of conviction in each case but offered nothing but the name of the materials found obscene. Second, and more important, in a single paragraph the Court stated what was not involved: no kids, no nonconsenting adults, no pandering. Then the opinion offered a one-sentence listing of each of the obscenity positions of every justice save Clark and Harlan, the two dissenters. The final paragraph read in full: "Whichever of these constitutional views is brought to bear upon the cases before us, it is clear that the judgments cannot stand. Accordingly, the judgment in each case is reversed."

The Court could not define obscenity and therefore the necessary scienter, and it gave up trying. For years everyone had known that censors could not distinguish between obscenity and literature. It now turned out that the Court couldn't either. Because it could not define obscenity, for the most part it would treat the issue as if it did not exist so long as the three conditions—no kids, no unconsenting adults, no pandering—were met. In practice, this was a transformation of obscenity law as great as the year before. *Memoirs* protected lustful materials with real value; *Redrup* protected the then-available lustful materials with precious little, if any, value beyond their ability to cause an erection. *Roth*'s work of protecting serious literature was completed with *Jacobellis; Memoirs'* work of protecting sexually arousing materials was cemented by *Redrup*. The surprise vote was Warren's. He had given up. Prosecutors were not interested in his call to create a decent society, so he cast an institutional vote to free the Court from its unhappy role. Fred Graham in the *New York Times* wrote that the Court was "deliberately moving the conflict over 'where to draw the line' on obscenity well back from the conventional fare found on many newsstands."[11] In fact, the Court was going considerably farther.

In the two remaining years of the Warren Court, the majority summarily disposed of three-quarters of all obscenity cases simply by announcing their reversal and citing *Redrup v. New York*. By this process a new verb—"to *Redrup*"—was born. Its definition, to the delight of the constitutional law professors who had created it, was "to summarily reverse an obscenity conviction, without stating any reasons, by citing *Redrup v. New York*" (which itself offered no reasons).

What the Court was doing was obvious, ending the then-existing obscenity prosecutions for adults without taxing itself over the materials. Nonetheless, the justices continued to look at the materials to determine whether their nature was substantially different in a particular case. Between *Redrup* and *Stanley v. Georgia* in 1969, the Court *Redrupped* nineteen cases, denied certiorari in a bare handful, and summarily affirmed one obscenity conviction by a 5–4 vote. The latter involved a film version of Jean Genet's play *Un Chant d'Amour,* where the exhibitors of the film virtually conceded it was obscene but argued that it was being viewed by Berkeley inhabitants who, like the commonwealth attorney reading *Fanny Hill,* could take it.

Because *Redrup* had covered the existing market, everything in existence, save where it was conceded that the materials were obscene, seemed to be okay. The one *Redrupped* movie was *Mondo Freudo,* an ultra-brutal film advertising decadent exhibitions of degradation with scenes "too real for the immature" and including nudity, by which it meant female breasts as depicted in *National Geographic* articles. Yet even the newest market entries, frontal nudity from Denmark, where supposedly the film cameras lingered on the genitals, and the successors to the nudity magazines of the 1950s, which now too focused on the female genitals, also received *Redrup* protection as Vonnegut's observation became obsolete.

The Court thus made a virtue out of its incapacity to make distinctions by ridding itself of the problem. In 1968 and 1969 it wrote only three opinions on obscenity, two of which, *Ginsberg v. New York* on children and *Stanley v. Georgia* on consenting adults, flowed from *Redrup*. The third, *Interstate Circuit v. Dallas,* struck down Dallas's movie-censorship statute as applied to *Viva Maria* as too vague, especially when the censorship board gave no reasons why the movie was not suitable for children. This marked Jeanne Moreau's second successful trip to the Court during the decade, and *Viva Maria,* too risqué for Dallas youth of the 1960s, became a prime-time network movie in the early 1970s.

Children and Adults

Sam Ginsberg, who operated a luncheonette on Long Island that also sold magazines, learned that in obscenity litigation he had an unlucky last name (no matter how it was spelled). He sold a copy of *Sir,* one of the magazines involved in an Arkansas companion case to *Redrup,* to a mature-looking sixteen-year-old who had been sent into the luncheonette by his mother for the purpose of buying the magazine so she could report the sale to the police. Ginsberg's crime was to "sell to minors under seventeen years of age materials defined to be obscene on the basis of its appeal to them, whether or not it would be obscene to adults." In operation, the state deemed girlie magazines as obscene and harmful to sixteen-year-olds without proof of anything more.

Like *Mishkin,* Brennan held that the obscenity standard could vary based on the targeted audience, in this case minors. *Redrup* had indicated such laws would be sustained, and Brennan offered ample reasons to do so. The state has a power to control the behavior of children that exceeds its power over adults. Parents need help parenting and may properly call upon the state to aid them in discharging their responsibilities. Finally, there may exist irresponsible parents, so the state "has an independent interest in the well-being of its youth" and in seeing to it that "they are 'safeguarded from abuses' which might prevent their 'growth into free and independent well-developed men and citizens.'"

Black and Douglas, of course, dissented, with Douglas offering his standard blast at Anthony Comstock. Interestingly, Fortas, but not Stewart, also dissented based on the facts. "The State's police power may, within very broad limits, protect the parents and their children from public aggression of panderers and pushers. This is defensible on the theory that they cannot protect themselves from such assaults. But it does not follow that the State may convict a passive luncheonette operator of a crime because a 16-year-old boy maliciously and designedly picks up and pays for two girlie magazines which are presumably *not* obscene."

While *Ginsberg* supposedly protected children from their own temptations, *Stanley* held that adults weren't children and needed no protection from the state against their own temptations, at least so long as they stayed in their homes. *Stanley* was the mirror of *Mapp v. Ohio.* The principal issue in *Mapp* in the Ohio courts was the right of private possession of obscene materials, but the Court decided the case instead on the Fourth Amendment ground of applying the exclusionary rule to the states. The principal issue in *Stanley* in the Georgia courts was whether a search warrant of a premise for one type of contraband authorized seizure of a different type, but the Court decided it instead on the First Amendment ground of the right to possess obscenity.

Both the Internal Revenue Service and state law enforcement agents thought Robert Stanley was engaged in bookmaking and got a search warrant for his residence authorizing the seizure of all records. They found very little gambling equipment, but in a desk drawer in his bedroom they found three reels of eight-millimeter film. Using a projector and screen found in the living room, they viewed the film, which consisted of "nothing but successive orgies by nude men and women engaging in repeated acts of seduction, sodomy and sexual intercourse."[12] The police were quite correct in concluding that it was obscene under the standards of the day. So, after the viewing, they seized the film and arrested Stanley for possession of obscenity. Stanley unsuccessfully argued that the film should have been suppressed at trial because the search warrant did not authorize its seizure. His weaker argument was that he had the right to possess obscenity for his own use in his home. The reason this argument appeared weaker is that the images on the film went light-years beyond anything that the justices had ever seen at the Court in the prior cases. *Stanley* was the Court's first encounter with stag films, a genre enjoying an under-the-counter existence largely (if not totally) immune from prosecution. The Court granted certiorari to decide the Fourth Amendment question and ruled instead on the First.

Stanley was one of the two important Warren-era opinions of the most junior justice, Thurgood Marshall. His opinion left in shambles the intellectual underpinnings of *Roth* and obscenity regulation in general because he treated the case as if it were a normal First Amendment case where the state would have to explain what it was doing. "If the First Amendment means anything, it means that a State has no business telling a man, sitting alone in his own home, what books he may read or what films he may watch."

Georgia offered the twin interests of obscenity regulation: protection against impure thoughts and minimizing the risks of antisocial behavior because of the effects of voluntary exposure to obscenity by willing adults. For the first time, an opinion of the Court mentioned and dealt with the rationales. "While it may be a noble purpose" to protect someone from bad thoughts, "it is wholly inconsistent with the philosophy of the First Amendment." Whatever the power of the state to protect "public morality," the state cannot premise legislation on the "desirability of controlling a person's private thoughts."

With Georgia's main argument out of the way, Marshall turned to the backup, expressed by Clark in his *Memoirs* dissenting opinion, that exposure to obscenity leads "to deviant sexual behavior or crimes of sexual violence." First, Marshall, like Douglas, was skeptical that there was any real evidence for that proposition; but, second, it did not matter because standard First Amendment doctrine already provided the correct answer. Georgia's argument would authorize a state to prohibit "chemistry books on the ground that they may lead to the manufacture of homemade spirits." Marshall quoted from Louis Brandeis's famous 1927 concurring opinion in *Whitney v. California*: "[A]mong free men, the deterrents ordinarily to be applied to prevent crime are education and punishment for violation of the law."

Although Marshall carefully avoided a frontal rejection of *Roth*, *Stanley* again reinforced the *Redrup* option of limiting regulation to children and unwilling adults. Thus, he distinguished *Roth* because it dealt with public dissemination of materials with the attendant dangers that obscenity might "fall into the hands of children" or that "it might intrude upon the sensibilities or privacy of the general public." In so doing, he recharacterized *Roth* to bring it in line with the *Redrup* caveats.

Roth's two biggest supporters, Brennan and White, could not go along. They joined Stewart in concurring on the Fourth Amendment ground that the films should have been excluded from trial because the seizure was illegal.

There were two ways to read *Stanley*. At its broadest, there was a right to possess obscenity and that right could not be exercised without a right to acquire it. Therefore, a logical extension of *Stanley* would be to hold that adults had the right to acquire, through purchase or importation, the materials they needed for their reading and entertainment in their homes. Combined with *Redrup,* this would create a consenting-adult rule with protection going only to children and nonconsenting adults, combined with limits on pandering. At the narrowest, *Stanley* might just as well have been convicted for taking home movies of himself and a woman engaging in similar practices or for drawing similar pictures. Therefore, the case meant only that if someone managed to get obscenity into his home, he could not be convicted merely for possessing it.

Under the broader reading, *Stanley* would solve the obscenity problem. Under the narrower reading, it was a passing moment. In Marshall's initial draft, he had written of a First Amendment "right to receive, as well as distribute, information and ideas." Harlan wrote him a letter asking him to delete "as well as distribute." Harlan wished to avoid "implications of dilution with respect to our other obscenity cases (which are concerned solely with the right to sell)."[13] There is every reason to believe Brennan and White felt as Harlan did. They were likely to be joined by Richard Nixon's new chief justice, who also might treat *Stanley* as an aberration. If so, then Brennan could place himself again where he was most comfortable as *the* law of obscenity. But if *Stanley* was a serious case, as it seemed to be with its willingness to actually discuss state interests and their relation to individual rights, then Brennan's reign was over, as was the formerly intractable problem of obscenity.

Once the pill became available, the sexual revolution proceeded apace. By the decade's end, Victorianism had been stood on its head with "the

p. 342 Jacobellio + Burver Press established that art + lit.
protected even if obscenity + sexually arousing

p. 340 de novo review Marshall's wisecracks about clerks

p. 340 Black + Douglas absolutist position

p. 340 Douglas acidly noted board of censors formation harmless

p. 340 Potter Stewart define indefinable + "I know when I see it"

p. 341 Harlan's dissent states can censor

p. 341 Warren moral crime daughter quote

p. 355 Roth protected serious lit.
   no kids, nonconsenting adults, no pandering
   Red vop protected no value beyond erection
   + Redvop washorn
   Court ending prosecutions w/o looking at material

belief in sex as the source of personal meaning permeating American society."[14] In late 1967 *Newsweek* ran a signpost story entitled "Anything Goes: Taboos in the Twilight," noting the lost consensus over sexual issues.[15] That summer "thousands of teenagers took literally Scott McKenzie's musical invitation, with its implicit promise of Dionysian revels, to come to 'San Francisco (Be Sure to Wear Flowers in Your Hair).'"[16] *Playboy*'s booming circulation passed the four-million mark (one quarter of whom were college men), second only to *Reader's Digest*, and Hefner made the cover of *Time* magazine in March 1967. A year earlier, William O. Douglas took his fourth wife, twenty-two-year-old Cathleen Heffernan, four years younger than wife number three. In 1966 as well, a book by sex researchers William Masters and Virginia Johnson, *Human Sexual Response*, hardly the easy read of *Fanny Hill*, sold out its first edition in only a week on its way to an unbelievable 300,000 sales and a half-year on the best-seller charts. "After an *AMA Journal* editorial pronounced the work worthy, requests for interviews flooded in. Overnight the pair went from being covert sex researchers to international celebrities."[17] Sex had come out of the closet and into theaters, bookstores, and living rooms. Even Black's wife read *Fanny Hill*, giving it two diary entries. The first was *"Some book!"* Two months later, noting the vote in *Memoirs*, she wrote that it was "terribly obscene."[18]

While low-budget "nudie-cutie" films such as Russ Meyer's *The Immoral Mr. Teas* had been showing in selected urban areas since the beginning of the decade, *The Pawnbroker* in 1965 was the first Hollywood film to show the bare breast of an American. A year later the British import *Blow-Up* offered for the first time in a mainstream film the briefest glimpse of full nudity for those with even better sight and visual reflexes than the excellent vision necessary to have spotted Moreau's exposed nipple in *Les Amants*. As the decade neared its end, however, Meyer shifted from "nudie cuties" to perfect the exploitation film, like *Vixen*, with its big hair, big breasts, and emphasis on implied sex. Russ Meyer films could be explained only as exposure for exposure's sake. These upscale low-budget films (*Vixen* was produced for $72,000), which were not prosecuted, played to increasingly appreciative audiences in urban areas; according to the 1970 President's Commission on Obscenity, *Vixen* grossed just a million dollars less than the contemporaneous James Bond film, *On Her Majesty's Secret Service*.[19]

While Vatican II was updating Catholicism, the American Catholic hierarchy finally acknowledged, as had that of the non-Latin Catholic hierarchies in Europe, that sex in marriage could be for pleasure without regard to procreation. Just as the Catholic Church recognized sex in marriage could be fun, many Americans, married and single, simply dropped the marriage out of that equation. Mainstream Protestantism was well ahead of Catholicism on this, and situational ethics, with its emphasis on free individual choice, was pushing the rigidity of older rules about sex outside of marriage aside. Douglas's quotation of the Universalist minister in the *Memoirs* dissent was illustrative of a split within the religious community on sex and morality. Religious liberals were taking the path of social liberals, just as the latter postulated the former should.

The influx of more sexually explicit materials on the urban markets was not caused by the Supreme Court, but the Court did nothing to attempt to stop it or even to slow it down. It is doubtful it could have, even if it had wished to do so. With the Victorian hegemony on sexual attitudes collapsing, it should hardly be surprising that the cosmopolitan men making up the Court at the end of the second third of the century were not working overtime to prop it up. Some previous Courts might have engaged in a rearguard action to hold to as much of the older order as possible, but that was not this Court's chosen role in any area. The justices may have been troubled, and several were, but the liberals' allies were all on one side of the question of whether to hold to the 1950s standards or to modernize. It is absolutely inconceivable that the justices could have deserted their longtime friends to embrace the mores of their longtime foes.

One contemporary writer with considerable sympathy for the old order nevertheless described many who agreed with him as "Alarmed Citizens (bolstered by most police, almost all prosecutors, and vast numbers of church-goers) who see in today's flood of seeming-pornography the fall of our western civilization; these are the lineal descendants of those who figleaved the Vatican statuary and who bowdlerized Shakespeare."[20] They were Douglas's philistines, who he claimed always held an upper hand in the censorship battle. One was Cincinnati's Charles H. Keating, Jr., who filed seven amicus briefs for Citizens for Decent Literature in the major Warren Court obscenity cases in the antismut phase of his public career. (This also brought him to Washington as a member of both the President's Commission on Obscenity in 1970 and the Meese Commission fifteen years later. With his national contacts in hand, he shifted careers and was a major benefactor of five United States senators, known as the "Keating Five," while, as CEO of Lincoln Savings and Loan, he guided that giant into a spectacular failure during the S&L crisis of the late 1980s.)

American elites were moving, if at a different pace, in the same direction of liberalization. Therefore, as the 1960s progressed, Douglas's philistines (whatever their numbers) were losing, as they typically do, to the elites' changing values. Education was a factor, and with a huge age-cohort moving through college (and purchasing *Playboy*), the demographics all favored change.

Those in the arts and letters viewed Black and Douglas as representing the only sensible view of the First Amendment. It took no courage to be against censorship, and everyone had a favorite story about the idiocy of censors to demonstrate that freedom was the superior choice; thus, even Warren noted that the Chicago censors had banned Walt Disney's *The Vanishing Prairie* because it showed the birth of a buffalo (thereby implying that the beast had engaged in an immoral and forbidden act). Politicians, nevertheless, were not about to stand up and be counted with the Court and obscenity. In the 1968 election year, they fled from Fortas's nomination to be chief justice, but they weren't going to do anything about obscenity, assuming, again, that they could have. (In the early autumn of 1970, the press reported the conclusion of the President's Commission on Obscenity that the laws should reflect a consenting-adults position, and the Senate immediately voted 60–5, with the normal liberals nowhere to be found, to reject the Report before even receiving it.) While attitudes were in motion, the Court allowed them to seek their newer repose without hindrance, without assistance, and, Douglas and Marshall excepted, without enthusiasm.

"With considerable glee," Douglas told his friend Harry Ashmore that "the legal test is whether the material arouses a prurient response in the beholder. The older we get, the freer the speech."[21] But how free? In early 1969 it was still virtually impossible to find hard-core materials on the open market. By the end of the year, the Swedish import *I Am Curious (Yellow)* became the first mass-marketed X-rated film, and this heralded a major market change in which, seemingly almost overnight, hard-core materials became available. But the Court changed too. When Nixon replaced Warren, Black, and Harlan (but not Fortas) with significantly younger jurists for his four appointees, he lowered the cumulative age on the Court by sixty years. Therefore, as Douglas's analysis predicted (although not necessarily because it was correct), the speech became less free, and the combination of *Redrup* and *Stanley* was not the end of obscenity.

Chapter 14

Church and State in a Pluralist Society

University of Chicago law professor Philip Kurland, a former Frank-furter clerk, delivered a screed at the Court in the 1964 "Foreword" to the *Harvard Law Review*. Yet at the end he noted that "[t]he Court has been most fortunate in the enemies that it has made, for it is difficult not to help resist attacks from racists, from the John Birch Society and its ilk, and from religious zealots who insist that the Court adhere to the truth as they know it."[1] Counting the Sunday closing cases as one, the Warren Court had decided only four religion cases when Kurland linked people who supported religious exercises in the schools with racists and Birch-ers. The "zealots," as he so accurately characterized them, cared only about two. The first was *Engle v. Vitale*, prohibiting use in the schools of the New York Regents Prayer. The other, *Abingdon School District v. Schempp*, was decided a year later in June 1963, and it completed *Engle's* work by banning the more overtly denominational religious exercises of reciting the Lord's Prayer and reading verses from the Bible.

After *Schempp*, the *Washington Evening Star* editorialized that the "Court's rulings in the area of religion, although certainly not so in-tended, have already led to a climate of passive and perhaps even active hostility to the religious."[2] Kurland's statement eighteen months later is useful supporting evidence because the fact that he placed "zealots" with racists and Birchers says far more about how mainstream thought, even by secular conservatives, then viewed the publicly religious than it does about the publicly religious themselves. There was a dominant view shared by the well-educated—and therefore the justices of the Court—that religion was a private matter, best left to the homes and the churches. If religion had a public function it was to promote social pro-gress, such as supporting civil rights. Otherwise it should know its place.

358

Bible Reading and the Lord's Prayer

Pennsylvania required the school day to begin with reading, without comment, ten verses from the Bible, with the students allowed to choose among various versions. Baltimore began its school day with readings from the King James version of the Bible, sometimes in conjunction with a recitation of the Lord's Prayer. In both cases, students could be excused at the request of their parents. Instead of asking for an excuse, the Schempps and the Murrays asked that the exercises be ended. The Schempps were Unitarians and claimed that some doctrines purveyed by a literal reading of the Bible were contrary to their religious beliefs. The Murrays were professed atheists who claimed that all the religious doctrines were contrary to their beliefs. While neither argued that they were coerced into participation, their legal claim implied that there were costs to not being in the classroom during the exercises.

Counsel for the Abingdon School District told the Court the Pennsylvania approach was nondenominational, although he quickly admitted under questioning that by nondenominational he meant Protestant. Whatever minimal chance he had evaporated in that answer, for just as government has no business writing prayers, it had no business mandating Protestant devotions in public schools, even though many governments had historically done just that (to an earlier Catholic outcry). The Protestant nature of the exercise made *Schempp* an even easier case than *Engle,* although the Court determined to overlook the easy route in favor of a broader, but less rhetorically inflammatory, decision.

Warren assigned the opinion to Clark for two reasons. First, the Texan was publicly identified as a conservative, not a crazy, on the Court. Second, Clark had gone public the previous summer in defending *Engle* from the firestorm of criticism it engendered.

Although *Schempp,* in invalidating the Bible reading and prayer requirements, completed *Engle*'s work, it could not use *Engle*'s rationale. It is one thing to determine that writing even vacuous prayers is no part of a government's function; it is quite another to suggest that it was not part of Jesus Christ's function.

Clark used *Schempp* to both summarize and create. He avoided the charged language of Jefferson's wall of separation and the rigidity of *Engle* for the more soothing language of neutrality. But it was not the neutrality between religions that would have focused on the Protestant nature of the exercises; instead, it was a neutrality that prohibited government from supporting "the tenets of one or of all religions." To enforce the required neutrality, the Court must inquire whether the law has "a secular legislative purpose and a primary effect that neither advances nor inhibits religion." Applying these principles, it was easy to find that any religious devotions violated neutrality, although Clark sprinkled the opinion with a hint that the exercises weren't as voluntary as the schools were arguing. Clark also dismissed the contention that any constitutional violation was harmless. "The breach of neutrality that is today a trickly stream may all too soon become a raging torrent."

Everyone but Stewart joined Clark's opinion although Douglas, Brennan, and Goldberg, joined by Harlan, concurred as well. There was nice symmetry, and it did not go unnoticed. The *New York Times* reported that "it was particularly noted by courtroom observers that the voice of a Protestant, a Catholic, and a Jew on the Court spoke up for the principle of church-state separation."[3] The Court was implying that whatever one's belief, the Constitution necessarily meant no religious exercises in public schools. The opinion would have been more effective if it were unanimous. (It would also have been more interesting if an evangelical or a charismatic had been on the Court.)

Stewart's dissent was a replay of his *Engle* dissent. He believed the majority was offering a "doctrinaire reading of the Establishment Clause," one that would create "irreconcilable conflict with the Free Exercise Clause." For him, the individual liberty interest in free exercise was paramount, and therefore his concern was whether students were coerced into participation. If they were, then their free exercise rights were violated. But if no one was coerced, then the devotions facilitated free exercise. Possibly because neither the Schempps nor the Murrays challenged them as such, Stewart ignored the fact that the exercises were Protestant; nor did he discuss the abilities of students to engage in private devotions without the aid of teachers.

Of the concurring opinions, only Brennan's merits notice because it implicitly assumed that the Court would be attacked again, as it had been in *Engle,* and Brennan was attempting a preemptive strike. He wrote a seventy-page treatise on what was permissible and what wasn't. He wished to show the critics, both Catholic and evangelical, that "[t]he principles which we reaffirm and apply today can hardly be thought novel or radical. They are, in truth, as old as the Republic itself, and have always been an integral part of the First Amendment as the very words of that charter of religious liberty."

Brennan's opinion was a major effort, and it is persuasive. But it did not persuade the Court's critics. Two months later, speaking to the Aspen Institute, Brennan worried about the Court's opposition—whom he saw as reflexively rejecting the Court without even reading the opinions it declared to be wrong. Brennan could not know whether those opposing *Engle* and *Schempp* had read the opinions, although he probably was on firm ground in assuming they had not. There is no doubt that he believed if they would read him, they would be convinced. But this was naive—note that Stewart was unconvinced—because it assumes, at a minimum, reasoning from shared premises, and those rejecting the Court's conclusions were also rejecting its premises. Moderates might be convinced, but vocal critics were beyond reach, a point the justices would internalize.

Reaction to *Schempp*

The reaction to *Schempp* was nowhere near as intense as that to *Engle*. *Engle* had been a shock out of the blue; *Schempp* was not, having been widely predicted in hearings James Eastland held during the summer of 1962. *Engle* was treated as outrageous by the Catholic hierarchy, while *Schempp* invalidated a Protestant exercise, one that was a major grievance of the Catholic Church during the nineteenth century, indeed the very exercise that helped create an impetus for the establishment of parochial schools. Furthermore, in 1963 Catholic leaders had their sights on far bigger game—federal dollars for parochial schools—and were thus less inclined to worry about prayer in public schools. Some Catholic officials moaned about *Schempp,* but their complaint was very dull compared to *Engle*. The constituency adversely affected was smaller, largely evangelicals and charismatics in the South. The Reverend Billy Graham reflexively reported he was "shocked" and claimed that "prayers and Bible reading have been a part of American public school life since the Pilgrims landed at Plymouth Rock."[4]

Mainstream Protestants rushed to the Court's defense. The chief executive officer of the United Presbyterians, the Reverend Dr. Eugene Carson Blake, was emphatic in his support. "Prayer is cheapened when it is used as a device to quiet unruly children and the Bible loses its moral authority when it is looked upon as a moral handbook for minors."[5] The liberal *Christian Century* took an almost identical stance, referring to the required Bible readings as turning the homeroom exercise "into a talisman which encourages superstition or to make its recitation a meaningless rote. The decision delivers public school children from such ritualistic, potentially harmful exposure to an abuse of Holy Scripture."[6]

As a result, the backlash to *Schempp* was muted and consisted largely of over a hundred pro forma legislative proposals to undo the prayer decisions, not a one of which had a prayer of seeing the light of congressional day on the House floor so long as Emanuel Celler chaired the Judiciary Committee. Frank Becker introduced a newer version of the Becker Amendment the day *Schempp* came down, and by 1964 he successfully pressured Celler into holding hearings. But instead of showing opposition to the Court, the hearings demonstrated that the Court could muster influential religious and academic support against a constitutional amendment. The National Council of Churches, the Baptists, Lutherans, Presbyterians, Seventh-Day Adventists, Unitarians, and the United Church of Christ all opposed an amendment, and the legal department of the National Catholic Welfare Conference advised Catholics to be "very cautious" about supporting any constitutional amendment.[7]

With that kind of religious opposition to overturning *Engle* and *Schempp*, the proposals would have had no chance even if the committee chair were someone other than Celler. At the hearings' end, the *Wall Street Journal*, which opposed the Court, noted there were probably not more than eight members of the Judiciary Committee who still supported the Becker Amendment.[8] The legislative proposals had been free shots where a congressman did not have to worry about consequences. As Robert McCloskey noted, "Congressmen feel that defending prayer is like defending motherhood: it wins them some votes and costs them almost none."[9]

School religious exercises had been largely an eastern and southern phenomenon. In the Midwest only about a third of the schools engaged in the practice; in the West it was less than half that. After *Engle* and *Schempp*, classroom devotions virtually vanished in the East and the West, the former having a 90-percent voluntary compliance rate with the decisions. Elsewhere, the fact that school prayer was unconstitutional did not make it vanish. Like school desegregation suits before the Civil Rights Act of 1964, suits to prevent religious exercises took a plaintiff, and while the consequences were nowhere near those of being an NAACP plaintiff, neither were they nonexistent. A comment in the *Indianapolis Star* helps explain why: "No Supreme Court decision handed down to us because of a disgruntled atheist mother who doesn't want her child to know there is a God should influence our School Board."[10]

In the South, two-thirds of the schools continued as they had before, with decided encouragement from political leaders. The state superintendent of education in South Carolina, for instance, stated *Schempp* would be "ignored."[11] The most vocal politician was George Wallace. He suggested that, if necessary, he would stage a "pray-in" at schools.[12] *Schempp* gave him "a new arrow in his rhetorical quiver: 'Now we find the Court ruling against God.'"[13]

In the Midwest, half the schools continued as before. A study of five noncomplying midwestern communities noted their "homogenous populations" where men of power "are likely to be imbued with a Christian ethic which sees Protestant religious exercises in the public schools as a neutral posture toward religion, because it offends no one of consequence."[14] Those observations apply to the South as well.

This reaction to *Engle* and *Schempp* yields two insights about compliance with the Court. First, opposition to the point of simply ignoring the Court was not limited to issues of race. Second, and perhaps more surprisingly, opposition was not limited to the South even though it was centered there.

Monkey Laws

The only part of the country still seriously fighting Darwin was the South. After World War I, eight southern states had passed "Monkey Laws" prohibiting the teaching of evolution. The Arkansas legislature had refused to adopt an antievolution statute in 1927, the year John Scopes's conviction in his famous "Monkey Trial" in Dayton was affirmed by the Tennessee Supreme Court. So the next year religious fundamentalists went the way of referendum, and the Arkansas voters approved by a 63-percent margin a law prohibiting "teaching the theory or doctrine that mankind ascended or descended from a lower order of animals" or "adopting or using a textbook that teaches" this theory.

By the mid-1960s, with no record of enforcement of the law, administrators in Little Rock, acting on the recommendations of the biology teachers, prescribed a new text that had a chapter setting forth Darwinian theory. One of those teachers from Central High School then sued, claiming she faced a dilemma as to whether to disregard the chapter or instead teach it and face a criminal penalty.

Despite Stanley Kramer's popular 1960 movie *Inherit the Wind*, the Arkansas Supreme Court sustained the antievolution law. Spencer Tracy as the legendary Clarence Darrow was clearly the movie's hero (seconded by Gene Kelly as the caustic H. L. Mencken in his denigration of southern Bible-thumpers). *Inherit the Wind* fully reflected the elite sensibility of the late 1950s, including a belief in the underlying majesty of the idea of law. The Supreme Court unanimously agreed, and in *Epperson v. Arkansas* it gladly followed an updated script by siding with Darrow and Susan Epperson against William Jennings Bryan and the fundamentalists to right the four-decades-old wrong.

Fortas had been a teenager in Memphis during the Scopes trial, and as a Jew from the South he knew what fundamentalism was. Fresh off his battering from the southern senators over his failed nomination to replace Warren, he returned the favor in *Epperson* where the state, understanding the obvious, put up a laconic defense of the statute, causing a couple of the justices to wonder if there really was a controversy at all. While the opinion hinted at an academic-freedom issue, it went off on the seemingly easier grounds that Arkansas had violated the Establishment Clause requirement of neutrality. "The overriding fact is that Arkansas' law selects from the body of knowledge a particular segment which it proscribes for the sole reason that it is deemed to conflict with a particular religious doctrine; that is, with a particular interpretation of the Book of Genesis by a particular religious group." The history of the adoption of the statute demonstrates that "fundamentalist sectarian conviction was and is the law's reason for existence."

In an open-ended reading of history that was not found in the record, Fortas stated that this was not a case where Arkansas had tried to "excise from the curricula of its schools and universities all the discussion of the origin of man. The law's effort was confined to an attempt to blot out a particular theory because of its supposed conflict with the Biblical account literally read." There was, in fact, no showing that Arkansas taught creation from Genesis.

Black and Stewart each concurred on the grounds that the antievolution statute was too vague to enforce. Black's opinion then turned to the majority and found it overbroad and "troublesome." On the one hand, he was not sure that a state hireling could go off and teach whatsoever she pleased to her classes. But more important, he was concerned because of the lack of evidence that Genesis was taught at all. Black thought Fortas had stood neutrality on its head. Since there was no indication that schools taught creation from a literal reading of Genesis, banning Darwin was the actual achievement of neutrality. Neither theory was available to Arkansas high schoolers (in school as opposed to church).

Black was on to something. Darwin could not be banned, but apparently Genesis could. From the perspective of those who believe Genesis, that is anything but neutral. Indeed, it seems that the secular and profane are given a preference over the religious—exactly the underlying argument of those who opposed *Engle* and *Schempp*. If religion was chased from the schools, what would replace it? The answer had to be secularism. California's Episcopal Bishop James Pike, testifying before Eastland's committee, spoke for many when he claimed that *Engle* resulted in the "cutting off the whole spiritual dimension of life, and without even a reference to it. What we have left is a secularist view of life."[15] If that seems overdrawn, one might recall that in *Torcaso v. Watkins* Black had equated theism with nontheism and specifically stated secular humanism was a part of the latter. Quite obviously, those opposing *Engle* and *Schempp* rejected any idea that religion and secular humanism were equals. But worse from their perspective was that *Engle* and *Schempp* were banning religion but not secular humanism from the schools. *Epperson* continued that trend.

Defending Monkey Laws had gone out of fashion with William Jennings Bryan, who concluded that "all the ills from which America suffers can be traced back to the teaching of evolution."[16] The contest of science and modernism versus fundamentalism was nonexistent outside the South, and the national press was uniform in its praise of *Epperson*.

That press, as well as Kurland, would have enjoyed a story Fortas told about the writing of *Epperson*, which, contrary to his usual practice, he did entirely by himself. His former law partners had commissioned a portrait of him for the Yale Law School. The artist had done an impressionistic work, and Fortas was none too pleased. At the time the portrait was sitting in a corner of his office. He told the dean of Yale Law School that while writing *Epperson* he would look at the painting trying to decide whether it indicated mankind "ascended from or descended from apes."[17] One suspects the losers in *Epperson* would understand. Fortas not only rejected their views; as one of the educated elite, he had contempt for them.

Dollars for Catholics

By 1960, Catholic leaders had concluded that the church's parochial schools were "an insupportable burden" on the church and that the necessary remedy was a government subsidy.[18] But, prior to the Civil Rights Act of 1964, substantial federal aid to education, whether to public schools or private schools, had no more of a prayer than the Becker Amendment. Northerners weren't going to fund segregated schools in the South. Southerners didn't trust the federal government and didn't care for Catholics, who wanted their cut of any federal money. The National Education Association (NEA) wanted it all for public schools. And John Kennedy was sensitive to the fact that Protestants thought that he wanted federal aid to education to promote parochial schools.

With the Civil Rights Act on the books and Lyndon Johnson in the White House, the North-South issue dropped out of the equation. Johnson refused to go forward until the NEA and the Catholics settled their dispute, telling Wilbur Cohen, the assistant secretary of Health, Education, and Welfare: "By the way, be sure you don't come out with something that's going to get me right in the middle of the religious controversy."[19] When the teachers and Catholics settled with a compromise whereby aid went to schools with low-income children, both public and private, the Elementary and Secondary Education Act of 1965 went sailing through Congress. By 1968, over four billion dollars of federal money, twelve times the amount of a decade earlier, began to flow through the spigot to the states and their schools.

That a compromise had been reached to begin the flow of dollars did not mean that the public-parochial school interests necessarily agreed on the distribution of the money. Protestants and Jews for the most part (Orthodox Jews being a notable exception) did not believe that taxpayers should be funding parochial education at all. If the Court agreed, then all the money would go to public schools. Catholics believed that parochial schools were serving the nation by educating children and were therefore just as entitled to federal money as their public counterparts. If the Court agreed, then the argument about potential unconstitutionality could no longer be used to limit the amount of money flowing to them.

One problem for both proponents and opponents of aid to Catholic schools was a doctrine called standing, a part of the "case or controversy" requirement of Article III, that relates to who can sue. A plaintiff must have a sufficient personal legal interest in the lawsuit to justify bringing the case. *Frothingham v. Mellon,* a well-established 1923 decision, held that federal taxpayers, suing as taxpayers and citizens, lacked a sufficient personal stake to challenge a federal spending program designed to reduce maternal and infant mortality. Hence, the Maternity Act of 1921, which during that era was of questionable constitutionality, could not be challenged judicially, and, more generally, spending programs could not be challenged by taxpayers even though their taxes were paying for them.

Beginning in 1961, there had been legislative efforts to overturn *Frothingham* for Establishment Clause cases. The Senate version of the Higher

Education Act of 1963 contained a provision authorizing taxpayer suits over aid to education, but it was deleted in the conference committee. There was a Senate bill with similar effect pending in the 90th Congress because *Frothingham* had to be discarded before the religious sides could have their legal war over aid to parochial schools settled in the federal courthouse.

Flast v. Cohen showed that all but Harlan were willing to discard *Frothingham* at least for cases involving aid to religious schools. In *Flast* Warren created an exception to *Frothingham* for situations where there was "a nexus between taxpayer status and the precise nature of the constitutional infringement." The Establishment Clause fit this perfectly since it "operates as a specific limitation upon the exercise by Congress of the taxing and spending power." Congress could not, after all, go around the country funding church construction. As to aiding low-income children in Catholic schools, that would wait for a later day—although another case, *Board of Education v. Allen,* decided that very day, offered considerable guidance.

Douglas, a dissenter in *Allen,* concurred in *Flast* and was chafing at the bit to hold that even a penny of aid for Catholic children was unconstitutional. Seemingly comparing the aid to parochial schools with the problems of race in the South, he first noted "the host of devices used by States to avoid the opening to Negroes public facilities enjoyed by whites." Then he stated: "There is a like process at work at the federal level in respect to aid to religion. . . . The mounting federal aid to sectarian schools is notorious and the subterfuges numerous."

Allen involved a New York law providing textbooks to all children in grades seven through twelve regardless of what school they attended. The state had to approve the texts, but the parochial schools were not limited to those in use in the public schools. White drew on the latitudinarian holding rather than the restrictive language of Black's 1947 opinion in *Everson v. Board of Education,* where the provision of free bus transportation had been sustained as consistent with Jefferson's wall of separation metaphor. White, in keeping with *Schempp,* did not mention the metaphor and instead stated the problem of separation was "one of degree." Applying the *Schempp* test about the purpose and effect of the legislation, White concluded the law was secular because its aim was to benefit children. "The law merely makes available to all children the benefits of a general program to lend school books free of charge." No money and no books were given to the schools, so the "financial benefit is to parents and children." Analogizing to *Everson,* White noted that "perhaps free books make it more likely that some children choose to attend a sectarian school, but that was true of the state-paid bus fares" as well.

The Court's New Dealers Black, Douglas, and Fortas each dissented, stating that they could distinguish books, which were the heart of what school is about, from a bus ride, even if the majority couldn't. But they dissented for different reasons, Fortas because the books the Catholics selected were not the ones used in public schools; Black because the Catholics got books; and Douglas because any religion got something.

Black and Douglas, with their long-standing, thorough-going anti-Catholicism, each responded with his favorite Virginia Framer. Black, as always, embraced Jefferson's metaphor. He ended by asserting the Establishment Clause "was written on the assumption that state aid to religion and religious schools generates discord, disharmony, hatred, and strife among our people, and that any government that supplies such aid is to that extent a tyranny." Douglas, embracing Madison, envisioned priests and nuns craftily selecting texts for the public to buy that would best inculcate the necessary religious positions into the students, though his objection here went beyond his disdain for Catholicism. "It must be remembered that the very existence of the religious school—whether Catholic or Mormon, Presbyterian or Episcopalian—is to provide an education oriented to the dogma of the particular religious faith." Douglas saw the stakes as high—involving attempts to get the "proper" books radiating the "correct" religious views "not only into the parochial school but in the public school as well." He ended with his favorite quote from Madison's *Memorial and Remonstrance* in which Madison states that a government that can coerce three pence for religion is capable of coercing a lot more.

Black and Douglas had reason for their rhetoric. Unlike so many other stands they had taken over the decades, on dollars for religion they had been defeated. As the Catholic journal *America* exulted, "the 'No Aid, Nohow, No Matter What' dogma of certain liberals and fundamentalists is constitutionally dead. . . . It would be fatuous for anyone to fail to recognize what the court has given: a generous definitive endorsement of the place of Catholic and other Church-related schools in American education."[20]

White's child-benefit theory was the theory of the Elementary and Secondary Education Act of 1965, and it was a theory that would sustain a fair amount of aid. Black and Douglas's old-fashioned anti-Catholicism went out of date even before Vatican II, and there was no prospect that on this issue they could succeed in turning the Court around during their lifetimes. Their views on prayer and Bible reading in the schools had prevailed with the support of everyone but Stewart. But here, where a Great Society program was at issue, their normal allies, Warren, Brennan, and Marshall, were with the children and not with their dogmatic reading of the Establishment Clause.

Yet even though Black and Douglas had grounded their views on a combination of Virginia Framers and anti-Catholicism, they had a point. The majority was committed by *Allen* to allowing some types of aid to religious schools and by *Flast* to policing the line of permissible and impermissible aid. Black and Douglas alone spoke of how intense the religious competition for state aid would be, and they alone understood the pressures the Court would feel from the warring religions that wanted to get theirs while hoping the others would not. Dogmatism, as Warren had shown in *Reynolds v. Sims,* can lead to very clear-cut lines, and that is what Black and Douglas had unsuccessfully offered.

Free Exercise

The Court decided only two free exercise cases during the period, and one, *United States v. Seeger,* was on statutory rather than constitutional grounds. The other, *Sherbert v. Verner,* allowed Brennan to turn his *Braunfeld v. Brown* dissent on the free exercise claim against the blue laws into a majority opinion. As in so many other areas, Brennan was able to write an opinion holding that any burden on the exercise of a constitutional right could be sustained only by the showing of a compelling government interest.

Sherbert, a Seventh-Day Adventist, had worked for two years at a textile mill in Spartanburg, South Carolina, when the mill moved to a six-day week for all three shifts. When she refused to work on her Sabbath, she was fired, and she was unable to obtain another job because she continued to refuse to work on Saturdays. South Carolina then rejected her claim for unemployment compensation because state law barred benefits to workers who failed without good cause to accept suitable work when offered, and a refusal to work on Saturday—though not a refusal to work on Sunday—was not good cause.

In holding for Sherbert, Brennan concluded that the state "forces her to choose between following the precepts of her religion and forfeiting benefits, on the one hand, and abandoning one of the precepts of her religion in order to accept work, on the other hand. Governmental imposition of such a choice puts the same kind of burden upon the free exercise of religion as would a fine imposed against her for Saturday worship." Requiring the state to have a compelling interest doomed South Carolina. The best it could offer was a fear of fraudulent claims, something for which it had no evidence. South Carolina's "fear" was just a claim of administrative convenience in different words, and administrative convenience was no longer sufficient—even though an identical claim had provided the rationale for rejecting the free exercise claim in *Braunfeld.*

Besides its complete failure to mention *Braunfeld,* the most interesting facet of the opinion was the argument that, by mandating a religious exemption, the Court was requiring the state to favor religion in violation of the Establishment Clause. Brennan rejected this objection, asserting to the contrary that he was requiring no more than neutrality between religions since South Carolina did exempt those whose Sabbath was on Sunday. His stated rationale, though, went far beyond a simple equality argument that non-Christians should get what Christians have, the ability to have a single day of rest. Brennan's broad language asserted, for example, that someone with a religion requiring, say, two days of rest, or, more realistically, an Orthodox Jew compelled not to work on a variety of holy days throughout the year in addition to Sunday, would be entitled to accommodation.

As Stewart's concurring opinion and Harlan's dissent (with White) showed, they were unpersuaded. Since Stewart had been asserting a primacy of free exercise in *Engle* and *Schempp,* he had no trouble finding that the Free Exercise Clause trumped the Establishment Clause. He suggested the Court had a "duty to face up to the dilemma caused by the religion clauses."

Harlan's dissent rejected the majority's conclusion that what the state had done was the equivalent of a fine on Sherbert's religion. Harlan did not believe Sherbert was denied benefits because she was a Seventh-Day Adventist; he found that in fact she was denied benefits because she refused to work on Saturday. Harlan agreed with Stewart that the majority was forcing South Carolina to incur costs to support a nonmajority religion, but he rejected the view that this was a constitutional command. The state was not constitutionally compelled to carve out an exception for the religious although it could do so if it chose.

Sherbert v. Verner was a major victory for Brennan and his approach. He needed to pick up two more votes than he got in *Braunfeld,* and he got four. Although *Braunfeld* was only two years old, its conception of individual rights already seemed outdated. At one level, the facts were sufficiently different from *Braunfeld* to account for the difference. Requiring someone to take an unwanted day off is not the same as requiring someone to work on her Sabbath. But the approach of Brennan, to shift the burden of proof to the state and then to make it high as well, was an approach that applied to both situations. For the first time in American history, the Court had given the Free Exercise Clause enough substance to invalidate many uncaring burdens placed on non-Christian religions by the state.

Seeger consisted of three conscientious-objector cases where draft boards had denied conscientious-objector status to men who asserted that they were opposed to all war but did not do so in the context of an organized religion. The Court unanimously upheld their claims, not on free exercise grounds, but instead because the Court construed the relevant statute to protect nonreligious beliefs. The Military Training and Selective Service Act of 1948 in §6(j) exempted from military service those who were conscientiously opposed to participation in war in any form because of their "religious training and belief." The statute defined this as a "belief in a relation to a Supreme Being involving duties superior to those arising from any human relation." The statute also stated that this did not include "essentially political, sociological, or philosophical views or merely a personal moral code," language that explained the draft boards' decisions not to grant conscientious-objector status to the three.

Clark read §6(j) to cover anyone whose beliefs occupied a place in his life "parallel to that filled by orthodox belief in God." *Seeger* was thus a case of statutory construction where the Court simply ignored the final qualification that conscientious-objector status not be available to those operating under a "personal moral code." The Court would not have tortured the statute without a good reason, and that reason was, as Douglas's concurring opinion stated, that otherwise §6(j) was unconstitutional. As with *Torcaso,* the statute had distinguished theists from nontheists, and as with *Torcaso,* the Court rejected that as inconsistent with the idea of freedom for religion. Theists, nontheists, and atheists could all claim equality under the Religion Clauses.

Although *Seeger* is typically seen as a Vietnam case, it was not. The Court granted certiorari in the cases three months before the Tonkin Gulf Resolution, and heard argument and voted unanimously for Seeger and the others two months before the first air strikes against North Vietnam while it was still possible to believe that Vietnam was an Asian war for Asian boys, as Johnson had promised during his campaign against Goldwater. *Seeger* was in fact a logical extension of the Court's views in *Torcaso,* a view that the government must take individuals as it finds them rather than in some Judeo-Christian package as it traditionally had. When Clark, Harlan, and White went along, it seems that for the mid-1960s, *Seeger,* like *Torcaso,* easily represented the dominant view.

Griswold v. Connecticut

Connecticut's Planned Parenthood reacted to its defeat in *Poe v. Ullman* by opening a birth-control clinic in New Haven. The clinic lasted ten days before the arrests were made. Estelle Griswold, the executive director of Planned Parenthood, testified in her own defense that "if the Supreme Court had declared this law a nullity, a dead word, and a harmless empty shadow, I do not see how I could commit an offense against it."[21] But she and the head of Yale's infertility clinic were found guilty of giving advice to married couples and fined $100 as accessories.

In *Griswold v. Connecticut,* the anticontraceptive law was back at the Court for the second time in four years and the third time in a quarter-century. Since there was no way the Court could duck the issue again and, by the mid-1960s, even Catholic leaders knew the 1879 law had to go, its invalidation by a policy-oriented Court was a foregone conclusion. The South was an outlier on segregation; the Northeast on contraception; and the Court was tolerating no outliers. The third time would be the charm with only the vote and the rationale at issue.

Yale's Thomas Emerson argued for Griswold and predicted his 7–2 victory perfectly. But no one could predict the rationale, for the problem remained the one that had faced the Court in *Poe.* The Constitution says nothing about contraception or anything close thereto. So explaining why this outmoded and silly law was unconstitutional was no easy task. The only way with a pedigree was substantive due process, whereby the Court could invalidate laws it deemed arbitrary and unreasonable. Yet substantive due process had been a prime doctrine that had led the Court into its confrontation with the New Deal, and it had not been used since the revolution in 1937. In the few cases in which a party had tried to assert it to the Court, the opinions, always by either Black or Douglas, had emphatically rejected it. Bluntly, substantive due process had ceased to exist (or so it seemed).

An advocate must go with the tools available, and Emerson's argument sounded like substantive due process and principally relied on a pair of substantive due process cases from the 1920s and an equal protection case from 1942. One of the substantive due process cases, *Meyer v. Nebraska,* had protected the right to teach German to schoolchildren. The other, *Pierce v. Society of Sisters,* protected a right to send children to private schools. *Meyer* and *Pierce* offered the possibility that substantive due process protected certain family child-rearing functions, and Emerson argued that contraception fit within that pattern too, relying on the equal protection case, *Skinner v. Oklahoma,* in which Douglas struck down a statute that ordered the sterilization of three-time losers who committed blue-collar (but not white-collar) crimes. In an opinion that for the first time used the catchphrase "invidious discrimination," Douglas had labeled procreation as "one of the basic civil rights of man." Emerson also asserted that there was a privacy interest involved and cited every amendment that seemed to offer hope.

Douglas, for the Court, was more impressed by the latter than the former. He immediately rejected the substantive due process argument and tersely reconceived *Meyer* and *Pierce* as First Amendment cases involving restrictions on knowledge. He then returned to his *Poe* dissent and attempted to demonstrate, first, that a right to privacy was a textually-based right, and, second, that the decisions about contraception fit within the right.

He began with First Amendment cases like *NAACP v. Alabama,* which had protected the organization's membership lists and concluded that such cases "suggest that specific guarantees in the Bill of Rights have penumbras formed by emanations from those guarantees that help give them life and substance." In a lead to quick citations to the Third, Fourth, Fifth, and Ninth Amendments, he stated "various guarantees create zones of privacy." Then, at the end of the string cite, he listed, and therefore reconceptualized, *Skinner* as a privacy case. He concluded his series of one-sentence tours through the amendments by stating that the facts involve "a relationship lying within the zone of privacy created by several fundamental constitutional guarantees."

Douglas was trying to tease a right of privacy out of the text of the Constitution so that he could avoid the substantive due process route, which history had shown could not be text-based, but the opinion persuaded no one beyond, perhaps, the four others who were willing to sign on.

The best explanation for the result came in the final several sentences on the meaning of marriage from a person who was twelve months from his fourth. "We deal with a right of privacy older than the Bill of Rights. . . . Marriage is a coming together for better or for worse, hopefully enduring, and intimate to the degree of being sacred. It is an association that promotes a way of life, not causes; a harmony in living, not political faiths; a bilateral loyalty, not commercial or social projects. Yet is an association for as noble a purpose as any involved in our prior decisions." Those sentences demonstrate why marital privacy should be protected in a constitution, and foreshadowed the alternate holding in *Loving v. Virginia* two years later. But neither they nor Douglas's other citations explain whether marital privacy is protected in the United States Constitution.

Goldberg's opinion, for Warren and Brennan, both joined Douglas and additionally tried a tack never taken before. He implied that the Ninth Amendment was the operative clause. That obscure, rarely cited, and never relied-upon amendment reads: "The enumeration in the Constitution, of certain rights, shall not be construed to deny or disparage others retained by the people." James Madison put the Ninth in to deal with the serious textual problem that if certain rights are listed, the list is often taken as complete. The Ninth said that was not necessarily so, and Goldberg interpreted Madison to hold not that there might be, but rather that there were additional rights not listed that the people retained. The question, of course, is how to find out what they were.

To answer this question Goldberg turned to traditional substantive due process methodology. Like Harlan, he felt that to ascertain unenumerated rights the Court "must look to the 'traditions and collective conscience of our peoples' to determine whether a principle is 'so rooted there as to be ranked as fundamental.'" Thus, he quoted approvingly from Harlan's *Poe* dissent to acknowledge that a state could lawfully forbid homosexuality or adultery, but the "intimacy of husband and wife is necessarily an essential and accepted feature of the institution of marriage." Goldberg, in a Brennan-like move, demanded that Connecticut demonstrate a compelling state interest—something, as White's concurring opinion showed, the state could not even come close to doing.

Harlan had said what he meant in his *Poe* dissent, and he chose for the most part to rest on that. The Due Process Clause protects "basic values 'implicit in the concept of ordered liberty'" and is therefore "a living thing." Connecticut had a right to be concerned with "the moral soundness of its people," and accordingly could prohibit "adultery, homosexuality, fornication and incest" but not the use of contraceptives by husband and wife.

White eschewed the warm rhetoric of Douglas, Goldberg, and Harlan, and instead focused on the irrationality of Connecticut's argument—that the anti-use law was designed to deter extramarital relationships. Thus, Connecticut assumed that married people "will comply with the ban in regard to their marital relationships, notwithstanding total nonenforcement in this context and apparent nonenforcibility, but will not comply with criminal statutes prohibiting extramarital affairs and the anti-use statute in respect to illicit sexual relationships, a premise whose validity has not been demonstrated and whose intrinsic validity is not very evident."

Black and Stewart dissented, and each directed his fire at a different target. Black took on Goldberg and Harlan; Stewart took on Douglas, beginning wonderfully by acknowledging the anticontraceptive law was "uncommonly silly. But we are not asked in this case to say whether we think this law is unwise, or even asinine." He noted that Douglas's opinion cited "to no less than six Amendments to the Constitution, but does not say which of these Amendments, if any, it thinks is infringed by the Connecticut law." He rejected the argument that somehow the various constitutional guarantees created a right of privacy. "With all deference, I can find no such general right of privacy in the Bill of Rights, in any other part of the Constitution, or in any case ever before decided by this Court." Nothing, nowhere, nada.

Black's opinion took a quick jab at Douglas before aiming at Goldberg and Harlan. "I get nowhere . . . by talk about a constitutional 'right of privacy' [as if it were in the text]. . . . I like my privacy as well as the next one, but I am nevertheless compelled to admit that government has a right to invade it unless prohibited by some specific constitutional provision."

Turning to his real targets, he accurately noted that substantive due process and Ninth Amendment arguments "turn out to be the same thing—merely using different words to claim for this Court and the federal judiciary power to invalidate any legislative act which the judges find irrational, unreasonable, or offensive." Black denied, as he had for over thirty years, that there were any standards available to decide these questions other than the "personal predilections and prejudices of the judges." Thus, he panned, as he always enjoyed doing, Frankfurter's statement from *Rochin v. California* that the measure of unconstitutionality was whether a state action "shocked the conscience."

Black asserted that the "Court certainly has no machinery to conduct a Gallup Poll." That was correct, but all the justices, save those like Black and Harlan with failing eyesight, had the ability to read Gallup Polls in the *Washington Post* and *New York Times* and, indeed, to read newspapers more generally. Black perceived the stakes as judicial lawmaking without standards; the majority saw them as leaving a relic of the prior century on the books to prevent poor people from having the same family choices as their more affluent compatriots. Black's dissent was the last gasp of the argument that only textually-based rights could be judicially enforced. Truly offensive laws were likely to be unconstitutional because they were truly offensive.

Griswold was a free case. No one could defend the existing debris of Comstockery or its backward cousins in Massachusetts, New York, and Rhode Island, and virtually everyone supported its elimination. In 1960, a Gallup Poll showed that 72 percent of respondents believed that advice on contraception should be available to married couples seeking it. Four years later, another poll showed that even three-quarters of the Catholics surveyed agreed that advice on contraceptives should be freely available. Thus, the Catholic editorial reaction to *Griswold* was generally positive. Hartford's Archbishop Henry O'Brien summed up the typical position: "Catholics, in common with our fellow citizens, recognize this decision as a valid interpretation of constitutional law."[22] That would not be the case four years after Warren retired when Harry Blackmun reinterpreted *Griswold* as a substantive due process case and extended its holding in *Roe v. Wade* to encompass a right of abortion. This outcome was not readily inferable from the *Griswold* opinions, as demonstrated by the fact there were no contemporaneous suggestions that abortion even might be constitutionalized because of the case. A year after Warren retired, Yale's Charles Black, perhaps the most perceptive and sympathetic supporter of the Warren Court, delivered three lectures on "The Unfinished Business of the Warren Court."[23] One of them was entirely devoted to *Griswold* and never mentioned abortion. The same is true of the encyclopedic Lawyer's Edition of Emerson's (with co-authors David Haber and Norman Dorsen) *Political and Civil Rights in the United States.*

Even the staid student-note section in the *Harvard Law Review* displayed a rare trace of humor in a casenote on *Griswold* by dropping a gratuitous footnote at the end of its discussion. "Despite the practice of illegal fornication by Americans of all descriptions throughout our history, the United States has never lost a war."[24] At a time when virtually no law review was published on time, Harvard's legendary dean, Erwin Griswold, was best known for demanding that his copy of the *Harvard Law Review* arrive on his desk during the month listed on its cover. He was also known for reading every word in every issue immediately and conveying his opinions to the editors. If the editors were thinking they could sneak this one by him, they were wrong. He was not amused, and he let them know.

In a rare trace of candor, in the interim between *Griswold* and publication of the Harvard casenote, President Johnson announced that American troops were actively fighting a ground war in Vietnam. It is well the Harvard authors wrote when they did because just as *Roe v. Wade* was handed down in the winter of 1973, American troops pulled out of Vietnam in defeat. Apparently chastened, the *Harvard Law Review* has never returned to the relationship between illegal fornication and martial prowess.

Douglas's concluding statements about marriage are so profound and well written that they are occasionally incorporated by the participants in civil marriage ceremonies. For Douglas, "hopefully enduring" was an apt phrase. When he wrote *Griswold,* he had already exceeded the "one justice, one divorce" limit and his marriage to Joan Martin was on the rocks. When that ended in divorce, it marked his third since joining the Court—to the Brethren's vocal dismay. (At the time his represented 100 percent of the divorces of justices but subsequently Douglas's successor John Paul Stevens divorced his wife. Clarence Thomas holds the only other divorce of a justice, but his occurred seven years before taking his seat.)

It is perhaps surprising how few religion cases the Warren Court decided, given the outcry over *Engle* and the willingness to flout both it and *Schempp.* Frequent pronouncements on church-state issues were a result, in part, of aid to parochial schools and therefore an issue coming after Warren's retirement. Not only were there but a few cases during Warren's tenure, they were decided, even as the decade progressed, with a very high level of agreement. Thus, the last religion case decided, *Presbyterian Church v. Mary Elizabeth Blue Hull Presbyterian Church,* was a unanimous ruling that a civil jury could not decide a property dispute by determining whether the mother church had departed from tenets of the faith (especially since the Georgia jury upheld the local contention that the national church had abandoned the faith by becoming too liberal). Beginning with *Engle* and including the standing decision in *Flast,* there were only eight dissenting votes in the religion cases, and three came from the liberals in *Allen.* That left two each by Harlan and Stewart plus White joining Harlan in *Sherbert v. Verner.* Even adding in the *Griswold* dissents, the numbers hardly change. All in all this bespeaks a high level of agreement about the Religion Clauses; of the controversial areas of the

Warren Court only race could match religion for the justices' coherence and, after the Voting Rights Act, the coherence over race was sharply reduced.

Behind the agreement was the shared concern over sectarianism in a pluralistic society where religion no longer had the prominence among elites it once enjoyed. The almost nuclear reaction to *Engle* showed that the devoutly religious were still willing to impose their dogmas on those who disagreed. It offered a rare but powerful reminder that the eighteenth-century concerns over religious warfare were not just a part of a dated past. A Fortas clerk, from a term where there were no religion cases, told the author that when the topic of religion came up at the Court, the universal reaction of the justices was that religions could not be allowed to capture state and local governments for their own ends. *Schempp* had the identical goal as *Engle*—to remove religion as a source of contention in public life. This was an implicit promise of the Kennedy presidency, and it was one that the Court intended that everyone keep. If it seems somewhat surprising that the promise eroded with *Allen,* it is well to remember that even though Warren Court justices were often dogmatic, they knew when a value was reaching the limits of its usefulness. When a little less separation seemed to help children rather than kindle divisiveness or impose values on the unwilling, the problem was nowhere near as serious, even if Black did argue that the result "bodes nothing but evil to religious peace in this country."

The principal losers—Kurland's "zealots"—also agreed on the results. *Engle* and *Schempp* were wrong, fundamentally and terribly wrong. Because this position was based on taking religion far more seriously and expansively than most Americans, the so-called zealots were not amenable to compromise or persuasion. They therefore did not seem like reasonable people, and so, like Kurland, the justices feared them and worried that they could harm American politics. The zealots reciprocated. Their opposition to the Court was total, if ineffective, and because they overlapped significantly with Douglas's philistines, the Court's liberalization of obscenity law simply gave them yet another reason to believe the Court was taking the nation in exactly the wrong direction—toward an irreligious state.

In retrospect, the 1960s, especially after Goldwater's defeat, were a time for initial organizing by the zealots. The effects were not visible nationally until the end of the 1970s. In the religiously pluralistic society of the 1960s, the Court had terrific support: mainstream Protestants, Jews, and Catholics, the latter's concern having turned almost overnight from prayers in public schools to dollars in parochial schools.

Chapter 15

Policing the Police

Gideon v. Wainwright, mandating that an indigent criminal defendant be provided a lawyer, was the Warren Court's only popular criminal procedure decision. *Gideon* rested on the obvious and powerful insight that without a defendant's having a lawyer at trial there can be no justice. Attorney General Robert Kennedy immediately marked the case's significance, setting the story line for Anthony Lewis's *Gideon's Trumpet.* "If an obscure convict named Clarence Earl Gideon had not sat down in his prison cell with a pencil and paper to write a letter to the Supreme Court, the vast machinery of American law would have gone on functioning undisturbed. But Gideon *did* write that letter and the whole course of American legal history has been changed."[1]

Warren's biographer, Ed Cray, tells the story just as Lewis and Kennedy did. "Clarence Gideon's journey to the Supreme Court of the United States was a piece of storybook Americana: the luckless drifter, in and out of prisons since he was fourteen, the least among men, could appeal to the highest, the most august court of the land. And once there, not only would he be heard, but he would triumph."[2] That summary, wonderfully capturing *Gideon*'s charm, would have been perfect it if added that Abe Fortas became his lawyer at the Court. "No tale so affirmed the American democracy. No story broadcast around the world so clearly proclaimed that not just the rich received justice in American courts."[3]

Gideon's Trumpet

Lewis quickly immortalized *Gideon* with *Gideon's Trumpet,* and eventually Henry Fonda starred as Gideon in a television movie; as a result, the facts are well known. Somewhat less well-known are the facts that twenty-two states filed amicus briefs on Gideon's side and that Florida could gain the amicus support of only Alabama and North Carolina for its claim that an accused could be validly convicted without the aid of counsel; Mississippi and South Carolina were the only other states not offering counsel—hardly, especially in 1963, a stellar lineup. Moreover, hitherto unmined files in the Clark and Douglas Papers reveal that five of the eight justices had already joined an opinion in another case holding that a defendant was entitled to counsel on appeal even if he could not afford a lawyer. If there is a right to counsel after trial, then there surely is a right to counsel at trial. That opinion, however, was not published at the time because the case was put over to the next term so that Fortas could win *Gideon*.

Gideon incorporated the Sixth Amendment right to counsel into the Fourteenth Amendment's prohibitions against state abridgments. The Sixth Amendment guarantee had initially meant that government could not preclude a defendant from retaining a lawyer. Then in 1938 the Court in *Johnson v. Zerbst* construed it to require that indigents be afforded counsel as a necessary ingredient of a fair trial. *Zerbst* was a federal case; four years later, in *Betts v. Brady,* the Court reached the opposite result in a state case.

Gideon's overruling of *Betts* is both interesting and terse, for Black's approach is to show that *Betts* was wrong the very day it was handed down (just as he had claimed in his dissent that day). Thus, *Gideon* agreed with *Betts*'s "assumption, based as it was on our prior cases, that a provision of the Bill of Rights which is 'fundamental and essential to a fair trial' is made obligatory on the States." Then Black used such pre-*Betts* decisions as the Scottsboro case, *Powell v. Alabama*, and *Zerbst* to demonstrate that the right to counsel was known prior to 1942 to be essential to a fair trial. He did not bother to state that in 1963 everyone, save a few southern attorneys general, knew it too.

Harlan concurred to offer *Betts* "a more respectful burial than it has been accorded." He assumed *Betts* had been correctly decided but then had eroded away. The actual legal rule of *Betts* was that counsel was not necessary unless there were "special circumstances" wherein a lawyer's aid was essential. At first all capital cases were found, via a case-by-case analysis, to have the necessary "special circumstances." Then in its 1961 decision in *Hamilton v. Alabama,* the Court issued a blanket decision requiring counsel in all capital cases regardless of circumstances. Furthermore, even in noncapital cases, the last time that the Court had failed to find "special circumstances" was in 1950. Maybe states like Florida had been confused into actually thinking that the law did allow them to refuse an indigent a lawyer, but "to continue a rule which is honored by this Court only with lip service is not a healthy thing and in the long run will do disservice to the federal system." States were entitled to know what the law was, and *Gideon* rightly brought the formal rule into line with the Court's practice. There cannot be a fair trial without the accused having a right to a lawyer.

After the Court reversed Gideon's conviction and ordered a new trial with a lawyer, he was acquitted following a sixty-five-minute jury deliberation of breaking and entering the Panama City poolhall. Fonda's Gideon was the classic innocent man wrongly found guilty. (Or, less charitably, the outcome illustrates why delay in trial is an advantage to the guilty defendant.)

It is easy to understand why *Gideon* was popular. "An untrained, unrepresented, and often uneducated person trying to defend himself as best he can in a public courtroom makes a highly visible and most disconcerting spectacle."[4] Anyone can understand that in a courtroom if one side has a lawyer and the resources of the government and the other side has no money, it is not a fair fight—and not a fair trial. Gideon was in a situation most individuals can identify with, the innocent man in the wrong place at the wrong time. He lost his first trial not because he was guilty, but because he did not have a chance. He won his second trial because he was innocent, and with a level playing field, he had a chance. Justice prevailed. That is the American way. Thus, the *Washington Post* editorialized, "Like the Gideon of old who was summoned by an angel of the Lord to lead Israel and overcome the Midianites, Clarence Earl Gideon championed the cause of justice for all indigent defendants. It is intolerable in a nation which proclaims equal justice under law as one of its ideals that anyone should be handicapped in defending himself simply because he happens to be poor."[5]

Gideon, so wonderfully immortalized in *Gideon's Trumpet*, was lucky. He twice came within a breath of winning without as much as leaving a name, much less his innocence, to history. Even as Warren's clerks followed his directive to search for a good case to overrule *Betts*, Gideon might have found his conviction reversed by a terse per curiam citation either to *Carnley v. Cochran* or to *Douglas v. California*.

A year before Gideon's petition arrived, two other in forma pauperis petitions reached the Court raising indigents' right to counsel issues. Willard Carnley had been convicted of incest and indecent assault upon a minor in Florida without being provided counsel. Although an illiterate as well as an indigent, Carnley, unlike Gideon, may not have initially claimed that he should have been provided counsel. Bennie Will Meyes and William Douglas were convicted in California for robbery and assault with intent to commit murder. They complained that the public defender who had represented them at their trial had been too rushed and had done an inadequate job of defense, and that the two defendants had a conflict of interest, which should have resulted in providing them separate counsel. Then when it came time for appeal, the state did not provide them even one lawyer, and their convictions were affirmed. To their old claims that they needed two lawyers and the one they got wasn't that competent, they added the new claim that on appeal they didn't get a lawyer at all.

The Court granted certiorari in *Carnley* in June 1961 and in *Douglas* the following October. *Gideon* did not arrive at the Court until January 1962, and Florida's response did not come until April 9. *Carnley* was argued in February 1962; *Douglas* on April 17. Certiorari was not granted in *Gideon* until June 4.

At trial the three witnesses against Carnley were his thirteen-year-old daughter, his fifteen-year-old son, and the victim. Carnley's cross-examination was feeble, and he never interposed an objection to anything. Furthermore, the substantive law involved provided several legal options for the defense, which Carnley, not surprisingly, did not pursue. But since Carnley had not requested counsel at trial, the Florida Supreme Court deemed he had waived any right to counsel he might otherwise have had. Carnley could prevail either by overruling *Betts* or within the *Betts* "special circumstances" rule, as his performance could easily be explained by his illiteracy and lack of knowledge of courtroom procedure. If Carnley did have a constitutional right to counsel, then Florida's waiver conclusion was untenable under *Zerbst*.

The justices were ready, but unwilling, to overrule *Betts*. The reason was simple; it was Carnley himself. As Frankfurter explained, it was impossible to "imagine a worse case, a more unsavory case to overrule a long standing decision."[6] Then Whittaker retired and Frankfurter had his strokes, leaving the Court at seven members. Warren was anxious to overrule *Betts*, but he too was reluctant to use *Carnley* as the vehicle if the result was a 4–3 vote. Brennan wrote a special circumstances opinion for a unanimous Court and then held that the record did not support a knowing waiver of the right to counsel. Black and Douglas as well as Warren indicated separately their disdain for *Betts*, with Douglas's opinion rather pointedly reminding everyone that Brennan was previously on record as favoring the overruling of *Betts*. At least four of the remaining seven could thus be counted as ready to overrule *Betts* over a month before certiorari was granted in *Gideon.*

Then, in *Douglas,* with White replacing Whittaker, the four became five. While a 4–3 overruling may be unseemly—because it could be reversed by the addition of the two new justices—an overruling with five votes, by being unassailable, is not.

Douglas also implicated *Betts* in at least two ways. The strongest argument appeared to be that there was a conflict of interest between Meyes and Douglas such that a second public defender should have been appointed for Douglas at trial. This opened two possibilities. First, overruling *Betts* and granting indigents a right to counsel. Second, it could be accomplished, like *Carnley,* within the "special circumstances" exception to *Betts;* a conflict of interest surely is a special circumstance. A second argument, also allowing an overruling of *Betts,* was the right to counsel on appeal.

At Conference, the Court voted 6–2 for Meyes and Douglas, but the justices were unsettled on the rationale. According to Justice Douglas's notes, Warren stated that "we can't say he must have a lawyer on appeal and be denied one at trial."[7] Stewart too claimed that to sustain the defendants' claim meant overruling *Betts,* and he, along with Harlan, indicated a desire to affirm the convictions. Five days later, at a second Conference, White switched his vote. Upon searching the record, he concluded that only Meyes had appealed the conviction and that since the conflict of interest issue applied only to the codefendant, it was not properly before the Court. The justices then voted 6–2, with Douglas and Brennan dissenting, to dismiss certiorari as improvidently granted.

That should have been it, for dismissing a case as improvidently granted rarely produces a public dissent even though not all justices may be happy with the result. Justice Douglas, however, along with Black, had pioneered the public dissent from denial of certiorari, and he also was willing to dissent from a dismissal of certiorari as improvidently granted. At the April 25 Conference, he indicated he would write a dissent, but he was uncharacteristically slow in producing it, perhaps because his second marriage was collapsing, and he was beginning the pursuit of his future wife, Joanie, then twenty-one years old. Thus, the dissent did not circulate until June 18, and it was initially limited to Meyes and the right to counsel on appeal. Black and Brennan immediately joined. Then a quick recirculation added a footnote stating that the record showed that a petition for review in the California Supreme Court had, in fact, been filed on codefendant Douglas's behalf so that, contrary to White's view, his case was properly before the Court. White now agreed with Justice Douglas and sent a letter stating that it was his "view at the outset that both Douglas and Meyes were entitled to relief under *Griffin v. Illinois,* but I was under the impression, apparently wrong, that you and certain other Brethren preferred to face up to the issue of counsel at trial in state cases before deciding the question on appeal via the equal protection route."[8] Warren had also joined, and that meant five votes were on the same opinion and therefore it became, as a Warren memo to the Conference noted, the opinion of the Court.

Douglas held that the Equal Protection Clause required a state to provide counsel for indigents on their first appeal as of right. In so doing, *Douglas* necessarily decided *Gideon* because if defendants have a right to counsel on appeal, it follows a fortiori that they have a right to counsel at trial just as Warren and Stewart had stated at the original Conference. Gideon, whose cert petition had been granted two weeks earlier and who had yet to be assigned counsel, had therefore already won—a result that Harlan's quickly written *Douglas* dissent labeled, in measured under-statement, "incongruous."[9]

The Court met in Conference one last time on June 22, and White switched his vote yet another time. Because Fortas had just agreed to represent Gideon, White concluded that Fortas should have the privilege of arguing the case that interred *Betts* rather than arguing a pro forma case after *Douglas.* The others agreed, and with the 1961 Term having but three days remaining, the Court set *Douglas* for reargument during the next term. It was argued the day after and came down the same day, with the same result, as *Gideon.*

Douglas was essentially the same opinion that Justice Douglas had written the previous term with a couple of fresh sentences added. Instead of finding a Sixth Amendment right to counsel like *Gideon, Douglas* relied on the 1956 decision *Griffin v. Illinois* and its equal protection basis. Just as *Griffin* had required Illinois to provide a transcript to make an indigent's appeal meaningful, so must California provide a lawyer to make the appeal meaningful. "In either case the evil is the same: discrimi-nation against the indigent. For there can be no equal justice where the kind of appeal a man enjoys 'depends on the amount of money he has.'" *Griffin*'s hot rhetoric about equalizing the quality of justice between rich and poor fit like a charm, as it always would in such situations. White stuck with the opinion this time.

Harlan, with Stewart, dissented, finding that the state, with limited resources, could take "reasonable steps to guard against needless expenses" (like providing a lawyer). Once the test was reasonableness, the state necessarily prevailed. Clark also dissented. He noted that 96 percent of the criminal law petitions filed at the Court were filed by a defendant who also lacked a lawyer and therefore reminded the majority of "an old adage which my good Mother used to quote to me, i.e., 'People who live in glass houses had best not throw stones.'" He was unpersuaded by the distinction between first appeal as of right and further discretionary review—the latter being the position that the Court was always in.

Gideon's Trumpet created a canonical history of *Gideon*—from the handwritten petition, to Warren's desire to find such a case, to Fortas's superb advocacy—so much so that when Fortas died, Linda Greenhouse's obituary in the *New York Times* described *Gideon* and Fortas's role more prominently than any of Fortas's own opinions for the Court.[10] The canonical history, while accurate, looks a lot different once the always-neglected *Douglas v. California* is placed in the picture. Certiorari had been granted in *Douglas* three months before Warren's watchful clerks found *Gideon*, and *Douglas* offered the opportunity to overrule *Betts*—although, while better than *Carnley*'s, the record was not the "clean" one the Court was looking for. Five votes for the right to counsel on appeal had already been cast before Fortas was selected as Gideon's appellate lawyer. Gideon, a winner without *Douglas*, was, with *Douglas*, a victor before his case started.

Although neither Lewis, writing in *Gideon*'s wake, nor Cray, three decades later, could have known it, *Gideon* was not an example of a humble, solitary man who, by his faith and dogged determination, was initiating a great change in the criminal justice system—although it may be nice to believe this is true. To be sure, Fortas, with the assistance of a young Yale student (and future Warren clerk), John Hart Ely, produced a masterful brief and did a brilliant job at oral argument, but his efforts were window dressing, following the forms of justice at the Supreme Court just as they had not been followed at trial in Panama City. Even if *Douglas* had not existed, *Betts* was so out of step that had Fortas lost, then a retirement with his beloved violin would have been fitting; with *Douglas* in existence (although not publicly), Gideon could have argued *Gideon* and won 9–0. In retrospect, Harlan's reference to giving *Betts* a "respectful burial" may be more a post hoc explanation for rearguing (and therefore delaying) *Douglas* than for a separate opinion in *Gideon*.

Maybe we celebrate Gideon because he was innocent (that time), while Douglas and Meyes (and probably Carnley) were not. *Gideon* was popular because everyone can picture Fonda's innocent man wrongly in jail;

Jack Palance playing Willard Carnley or Bennie Meyes or William Douglas might be something else. But it should not be so. The principle of equal justice, where both the government and the defendant are represented by counsel, applies not only to the rich and the poor; it applies to the guilty as well as the innocent. However well that sits in the abstract, it is often jarring in reality. When counsel seems to be preventing the police from convicting a criminal, the public reaction is intense and adverse.

Police Interrogation

Gideon closed two eras. It ended the possibility that an indigent could be tried without counsel (unless he so wished). More significantly, *Gideon* was the last important purely southern criminal procedure case. For the rest of the decade the Court decided cases that applied equally to existing northern practices as they did to southern practices. And cases that did not implicitly single out the South were always far more controversial than cases attacking southern backwardness. Furthermore, while criminal procedure cases prior to *Mapp* had typically been disguised race cases, the cases after *Gideon* were often perceived by the public as overtly race cases because urban rioting, crime, and the FBI crime statistics came to merge crime and race in many a white consciousness.

In 1967, according to FBI statistics, in urban areas African-Americans were seventeen times more likely than whites to be arrested for robbery; among those ages ten to seventeen, the relevant arrest rates for whites were 27 per 100,000, while for African-Americans they were an astounding 550 per 100,000. "The FBI's study was only slightly less bleak for violent crimes other than robbery."[11] The other side of the statistics, however, was that African-Americans were disproportionately affected by whatever abuses or inequities there were in the criminal justice system. The Court was already espousing equality of opportunity for African-Americans in every area that came before it. "To be credible equality required not only that the poor Negro be permitted to vote and to attend a school with whites, but also that he and other disadvantaged individuals be able to exercise, as well as possess, the same rights as the affluent white when suspected of crime."[12] As the cases would show, the Court intended to be very credible.

Within a year the justices came to understand there was another powerful insight underlying *Gideon*. By mandating that the state provide lawyers, the Court could create a frontline agency for supervising police practices and this would be more effective than the exclusionary rule in achieving the Court's objectives. Because a lawyer has an obligation of undivided loyalty to the client, the Court could guarantee a vigorous effort to implement its decrees (under the assumption that the attorneys would be neither incompetent nor lax). Had the public understood this was where *Gideon* was leading, it would have looked more like *Mallory v. United States* where the confessed rapist went free because he was not arraigned quickly enough—and therefore been a far less popular decision.

Gideon established the right to counsel, but the justices had long known, as *Mallory* explicitly recognized, that if a defendant confessed before he had counsel, then the trial is reduced to an appeal from interrogation, functionally the formality prior to sentencing. All justices had agreed that a confession was admissible at trial only if it was voluntary. Initially voluntariness meant the absence of physical coercion, but then in the 1940s the Court had expanded voluntariness to preclude mental coercion as well. The Court would look at the totality of the circumstances surrounding the confession to determine if the defendant's will had been overborne. But who knew what the circumstances were since they were, for all practical purposes, invisible? Police interrogations were never taped. Therefore, the witnesses were solely the police officers and the defendant, and they tended to have decidedly different conceptions of what happened behind the closed doors of the interrogation room. When that conflicting evidence is presented, whom does one believe? The officers sworn to uphold the law or the confessed criminal? All too often both sides were shading the truth, but, not surprisingly, the only cases the Court ever saw were those where the police version of events had been credited, what Michigan's Yale Kamisar, one of the most astute critics of the process, aptly labeled a "sanitized" version of what had occurred.[13]

President Herbert Hoover's Wickersham Commission had detailed questionable police practices during interrogation, but legislatures had seen no reason to act. There was no well-organized criminal lobby. Most experts believed that during the three subsequent decades the only important change was minimizing the use of the third degree in obtaining confessions.

With the federal government, the Court dealt with the problem of incommunicado interrogation by its prompt-arraignment rule as exemplified by *Mallory.* Prompt arraignment meant prompt appointment of a lawyer. When a lawyer is involved, there can be a witness in the interrogation room—although a more likely result is that there would be no interrogation at all. Once *Gideon* held that the Sixth Amendment applied to the states, the possibility of also applying *Mallory* became real. In legal terms the question the Court would decide was when did the right to counsel attach: at trial? at arraignment? at custody?

Escobedo v. Illinois

The year after *Gideon*, the Court decided two cases that offered opportunities to explicate the meaning of the right to counsel. One was an obscure federal case, *Massiah v. United States;* the other was the explosive *Escobedo v. Illinois*.

Massiah and a codefendant were indicted for smuggling drugs from South America and were freed on bail. Unbeknownst to Massiah, the codefendant decided to cooperate with the government and agreed to have his car wired. A government agent parked nearby was able to overhear the conversation between the two in which Massiah admitted his guilt. There was no doubt that the confession was voluntary, yet the Court held it inadmissible.

Stewart joined the five liberals to find admission of Massiah's confession violated the Sixth Amendment right to counsel. The result seems explicable only on the ground that if Massiah's lawyer had been present he would have told Massiah not to talk to his codefendant (or presumably anyone else) about the crime. Since Massiah's lawyer was not there, implicitly the Court was holding he should have been. But why? Presumably lawyers have more than one client and cannot be everywhere at once, so why should the lawyer have been in the car? Stewart's answer was that Massiah "was denied the basic protection of counsel when there was used against him at his trial evidence of his own incriminating words, which federal agents had deliberately elicited from him after he had been indicted and in the absence of his counsel."

White, with Clark and Harlan, had an easy time in dissent for it was agreed that the confession had been uttered in an atmosphere wholly without coercion. "Massiah was not prevented from consulting with counsel as often as he wished. No meetings with counsel were disturbed or spied upon. Preparation for trial was in no way obstructed. It is only a sterile syllogism—an unsound one besides—to say that because Massiah had a right to counsel's aid before and during the trial, his out-of-court conversations and admissions must be excluded if obtained without counsel's consent or presence."

The dissent was correct. Yet it was only a dissent. Why did the majority so cavalierly ignore it? One possibility might be that *Massiah* was a disguised electronic surveillance case, but Black (who did not believe the Constitution reached electronics) and maybe another were unwilling to go along. Another was that *Massiah* was serious about no confessions without counsel. As *Escobedo* would show, *Massiah* meant the latter. What was at issue was whether the government should be relying on confessions to prove its cases. The five liberals had concluded it should not. And by interposing lawyers between the defendant and the police, it would not. *Gideon* was being operationalized to deal with confessions first, trial later.

What made *Escobedo* explosive and *Massiah* obscure was that *Escobedo* involved murder, not smuggling—more significantly, Goldberg's opinion for the liberals made explicit their total disdain for confessions and perhaps for modern law enforcement as well. *Escobedo* was a slap in the face of American police by a sharply divided 5–4 Court.

Goldberg began with a sympathetic treatment of the facts from Danny Escobedo's viewpoint. Escobedo was asking for his lawyer. The lawyer, at the police station, was demanding to see his client. There was no doubt that Escobedo had not been coerced into confessing; nevertheless, without one police lie and one significant piece of silence, Escobedo might not have confessed. During his interrogation, the police falsely told Escobedo that he could go home if he implicated another man. The police did not tell him that if he implicated the other, he was implicating himself and that under Illinois law the "admission of 'mere' complicity in the murder plot was legally as damaging as an admission of firing the fatal shots."

Illinois argued, as any state would have, that voluntary confessions are a necessary police tool, and placing a lawyer in the process would "diminish significantly" the number of criminals who confess. The Court agreed that this would happen, but noted that the argument "cuts two ways" because it underscored how critical this stage is to the criminal justice system. Under the Court's doctrine the right to counsel attached at a "critical" stage. If interrogation was a critical stage, then the right to counsel attached, and once counsel is present, confessions are absent.

Next Goldberg claimed that history demonstrated the wisdom of the American system, which he had just described as striking the balance in favor of the right of the accused to be advised by his lawyer of the privilege against self-incrimination. "We have learned the lesson of history, ancient and modern, that a system of criminal law enforcement which comes to depend on the 'confession' will, in the long run, be less reliable and more subject to abuses than a system which depends on extrinsic evidence independently secured through skillful investigation."

After quoting an evidence expert, the Court quoted *Haynes v. Washington,* decided the prior term, for the recognition that "history amply shows that confessions have often been extorted to save law enforcement officials the trouble and effort of obtaining valid and independent evidence." But, of course, that was the reason behind the Court's longstanding rule that a confession was admissible only if it was voluntary.

What followed was a striking paragraph where Goldberg attacked confessions and law enforcement generally, right to the point that the current system was not worth preserving and did not deserve to survive. The paragraph merits quotation in full: "We have also learned the companion lesson of history that no system of criminal justice can, or should, survive if it comes to depend for its continued effectiveness on the citizens' abdication through unawareness of their constitutional rights. No system worth preserving should have to *fear* that if an accused is permitted to consult with a lawyer, he will become aware of, and exercise, these rights. If the exercise of constitutional rights will thwart the effectiveness of a system of law enforcement, then there is something very wrong with that system." It is worth noting what Goldberg did not say—he never suggested there was anything even slightly wrong with that Constitution.

Having condemned the system used across all fifty states, Goldberg retreated to *Escobedo*'s holding. "We hold only that when the process shifts from investigatory to accusatory—when its focus is on the accused and its purpose is to elicit a confession—our adversary system begins to operate, and, under the circumstances here, the accused must be permitted to consult with his lawyer." The sentence has the general and the particular. The general is the shift from the investigatory to the accusatory stage with its acknowledgment that the adversary system then attaches. To a lawyer, this means lawyers. The particular is the specific reference to "circumstances here," which included the fact that, Escobedo, unlike most defendants, already had a lawyer, who was present at the station house and demanding to see his client. The facts of *Escobedo* were wholly atypical; the rhetoric and the rationale were sweeping, and the dissents picked up on the underlying rationale immediately.

White's dissent, like Goldberg's opinion, found nothing wrong with the Constitution. "The Court . . . rel[ies] on the virtues and morality of a system of criminal law enforcement which does not depend on the 'confession.' No such judgment is to be found in the Constitution." White saw the decision as "another major step in the direction of the goal the Court seemingly has in mind—to bar from evidence all admissions obtained from an individual suspected of crime, whether involuntarily made or not." Stewart agreed. He too denied the result flowed from the Constitution and characterized the majority as "perverting the Constitution" by resting on "no stronger authority than its own rhetoric."

White assumed that the majority reached its conclusion as "a necessary safeguard against the possibility of extorted confessions." Law enforcement officers can make mistakes and exceed their authority, but that is unlikely in every case. To the extent the Court relies on a "deep-seated distrust of law enforcement officers everywhere, it is unsupported by relevant data or current material based upon our own experience." Stewart then went a step further and stated the majority opinion "frustrates the vital interests of society in preserving the legitimate and proper function of honest and purposeful police investigations."

The Reaction to *Escobedo*

Both dissents read the majority as going to the heart of law enforcement procedures, and both assumed that confessions would issue only after the state had already sewed up its case against the accused. Therefore, it is hardly surprising that police and prosecutors interpreted the decision, in the words of the Los Angeles Chief of Police William Parker, as "handcuffing the police." Parker, who had previously taken the police lead in criticizing *Mapp,* also, quite accurately if irrelevantly, noted that *Escobedo* "will do nothing to enhance the security of America against crime."[14] The New York City Police Chief Michael J. Murphy agreed, claiming that what the Court was doing "is akin to requiring one boxer to fight by the Marquis of Queensbury rules while permitting the other to butt, gouge and bite."[15]

Historian John Blum states that "*Escobedo* raised the storm against the Court to gale force."[16] Republican presidential candidate Barry Goldwater exclaimed that "no wonder our law enforcement officers have been demoralized and rendered ineffective in their jobs."[17] Cars sporting "Impeach Earl Warren" bumper stickers gained a new companion that proclaimed "Support Your Local Police." At the Republican Convention former President Eisenhower urged delegates "not to be guilty of maudlin sympathy for the criminal who, roaming the street with switchblade knife and illegal firearms seeking a prey, suddenly becomes upon apprehension a poor, underprivileged person who counts upon the compassion of our society and the weakness of many courts to forgive his offense."[18] Goldwater, who found numerous reasons to attack the Court during the campaign, charged the justices "with contributing to the breakdown of law and order in the cities, alleging that the Court's rulings inferred 'that a criminal defendant must be given a sporting chance to go free, even though nobody doubts in the slightest he is guilty.'"[19] No wonder Goldwater claimed that the Court was the most dangerous branch of a very dangerous federal government. Nevertheless, Americans unhappy with the Court were far more upset over school prayer or race.[20]

Escobedo offered every criminal lawyer with a client who had confessed a possible out, and soon the appellate courts were flooded with "*Escobedo*" cases, as confession cases became known for a brief two-year period. With the notable exception of the California Supreme Court, state courts read *Escobedo* narrowly as dealing with the situation of a defendant who, like Escobedo, already had retained counsel. The flood in the state courts soon inundated the Court's docket, but the Court simply held the confession cases, neither granting nor denying certiorari. Meanwhile, Harlem had burned, Watts had burned, and student activists had defeated the university administration at Berkeley; like Eisenhower, Goldwater, Parker, and Murphy, more Americans wondered if there was a correlation between escalating crime and permissive Court decisions. The remains of the Republican Party wasted little time assuring them there was.

The American Law Institute Alternative

In July 1965 *Time* magazine asserted that "the burden is now on Congress and state legislatures which are ideally equipped for the fact finding required to deal with police interrogations in so vast and varied a country as the United States."[21] Whatever *Time* thought, however, Congress's plate was overflowing with Johnson's initiatives, although the Law Enforcement and Assistance Act of 1965 authorized grant money to study police procedures (albeit with a goal of crime prevention, not procedural improvement). State legislatures, with less to do than Congress, had thus far shown little interest in studying how best to deal with the issue of confessions. From appearances, legislatures and their constituents seemed quite satisfied with what the police were already doing.

While state legislatures did nothing, the prestigious American Law Institute decided to investigate the problem of pretrial criminal justice and offer the nation's legislatures its wisdom. Harvard professors James Vorenberg and Paul Bator were in charge of drafting the ALI's Model Code of Pre-Arraignment Procedures, which took the position that the police should be given four hours to question a suspect without his lawyer (although the session would have to be taped). The ALI, whose model statutes were often adopted, was moving into the void that civil liberties supporters of the Court had used to justify the Court's criminal procedure decisions—since no responsible body would deal with the rights of suspects, only the Court was capable of reforming antiquated procedures. With the ALI entering the field and the American Bar Association making it clear that it would adopt the ALI position as well, that justification lost some credibility. Presumably the ALI proposal would receive generous consideration by a number of state legislatures as soon as it was finalized.

Intentionally or not, the proposal looked like an ALI challenge to the Court. Vorenberg was an ex-Frankfurter clerk and Bator was an ex-Harlan clerk. The ALI's establishment membership had a decided Harvard tilt—which to Court supporters meant Frankfurterphiles. The ALI's director, Herbert Wechsler, had authored the era's most influential law review article, "Toward Neutral Principles of Constitutional Law," which, when placed in the context of a number of other articles of a similar genre in the *Harvard Law Review,* offered a formidable challenge to what the Warren majority was doing, whether seen as making the Constitution's promises real or as creating rights where they had not existed before. Liberals, on and off the Court, could perceive the ALI action as an implicit attack on the Court. Judge Henry Friendly of the federal court of appeals in New York, who perfectly fit the Harvard-establishment opposition to the Court, seemed to make the connection clear when he stated during an ALI debate that conditioning police interrogation on the presence of counsel "is not a rule that society will long endure."[22] For civil libertarians the fact that he was accurate was an ignored irrelevancy.

From the fall of 1965 through the following June, the ALI and the Court appeared to be in a race to deal with prearraignment procedure. Vorenberg and Bator, with assistance, produced almost a hundred pages of detailed statutory language and explanatory text. Like *Time,* they justified proceeding by statute rather than adjudication on the express grounds that "a legislature enacting a comprehensive code can evaluate and adjust the various interrelated portions of an interrelated process" better than a court (by which they meant the Court).[23]

In the summer of 1965 Warren had told his incoming clerks that, after a year of not deciding any confession cases, "I think we are going to end up taking an *Escobedo* case this year."[24] In fact it took four in November, one of which was *Miranda v. Arizona,* and two weeks later added a fifth, *California v. Stewart,* where the state supreme court had read *Escobedo* generously. The cases were argued on February 28, March 1, and March 2, and Warren assigned himself the majority opinion for the Court, which after the trade of Goldberg for Fortas was still split 5–4.

The ALI held its annual meeting the third week in May, and *Miranda* did not come down until June 13. The May ALI meeting considered the Model Pre-Arraignment Code. Warren normally addressed the ALI at its first session, but this time he had to postpone his speech until the second session when, it turned out, the ALI was to discuss and vote on Vorenberg's and Bator's work. After his speech, Warren remained on the dais to listen to and perhaps participate in the prearraignment debate (although he did not in fact speak). Fred Graham, the Supreme Court reporter for the *New York Times,* wrote that Warren's presence unsettled the Code's supporters (and Court's critics), and "discussion degenerated into a series of impassioned speeches that produced little more than a consensus not to vote on the proposed interrogation code."[25] The code would be revised in accordance with the ALI discussions and necessarily in accordance with whatever the Court did in *Miranda.* (The code was not adopted until 1975.)

Warren and his liberal allies thus swept the field; neither the ALI nor state legislatures were going to create alternative rules governing interrogation. The criminal procedure revolution was the one area where the Court knew there was no public support for its actions. But it also knew it was right, and it is likely it assumed that the liberals in Congress, like liberals in the academy, knew it too.

Miranda v. Arizona

If *Miranda* is not the most controversial decision by the Warren Court, it is close enough, and it is the most controversial criminal procedure decision hands down (which is where its critics thought the Court had placed the hands of the police just before it put the handcuffs on). *Gideon* required five backward states to change their laws and behavior. *Mapp* required half the states to change theirs. *Miranda* required *all* the states to change theirs. While twenty-two states filed an amicus in *Gideon* asking the Court to require counsel, twenty-seven states filed an amicus in *Miranda* asking the Court to slow down. Only professional civil libertarians thought that the rules were unfairly balanced against the suspected criminal; in 1965 a Gallup Poll already showed 48 percent of Americans registering the view that the Court was too lenient on criminals.

Everyone who reads Warren's lengthy opinion in *Miranda* is struck by its legislative quality. As G. Edward White aptly notes, a "striking feature of the opinion was its disproportionate attention" to the parts of the opinion that have nothing to do with constitutional interpretation.[26] *Miranda* begins with a statement of the new rule—that police must give a person in custody certain warnings about rights. The warnings are so specific that there could be no claim that they flowed directly from the text of the Constitution; furthermore, the decision was abandoning the totality of the circumstances test that had been in use for decades. Next the opinion engages in a lengthy discussion explaining the need for the rule. This is followed by a cursory attempt to ground the decision in prior cases, followed once again by a lengthy discussion of the rule. Then at the end, almost as an afterthought, the opinion turns to the defendants, obviously finds they were not given the warnings the Court had created at the beginning of the opinion, and applying its rule to the facts, comes to the preordained conclusion that the convictions cannot stand.

"Prior to any questioning" the accused must be informed of his rights. First, he "must be warned that he has the right to remain silent." Second, that "any statement he does make may be used as evidence against him." Third, that he has "the right to the presence of an attorney." Fourth, if the suspect cannot afford one, an attorney will be appointed. The accused can waive these rights, but it must be a knowing waiver. Furthermore, if the accused "indicates in any manner and at any stage" he wishes to consult with an attorney, "there can be no questioning." These would shortly and permanently be known as the "Miranda warnings," and police would carry a card on their person listing them.

Having stated its conclusion, the Court turned to the reasons, an extended discussion of "incommunicado interrogation in a police dominated atmosphere." Warren noted that the privacy of the interrogation room "results in secrecy and this in turn results in a gap in our knowledge as to what in fact goes on in the interrogation-room." To fill the gap, he turned to "a valuable source of information," police manuals and their recommended interrogation tactics. There was no showing that any of the police departments in the cases had read, much less used, the manuals the Court was relying upon, but that was irrelevant. The existence of the manuals proved the existence of the methods, and *Miranda* was to govern the methods.

The manuals told a story of police dominance. "When normal procedures fail to produce the needed result, the police may resort to deceptive stratagems such as giving false legal advice." The whole purpose is to "persuade, trick or cajole [the individual] out of exercising his constitutional rights." The environment of the interrogation "is created for no purpose other than to subjugate the individual to the will of the examiner." To be sure, the days of the third degree are past, but the setting "is equally destructive of human dignity. The current practice of incommunicado interrogation is at odds with one of our Nation's most cherished principles—that the individual may not be compelled to incriminate himself."

Thus far everything the Court had said about the police practices aimed directly at requiring counsel at interrogation, and this was consistent with Warren's statement at oral argument that "this is not much different from *Gideon*."[27] But it was different, and the Court stopped short, instead requiring that the police make certain the accused knew what his rights were.

To the obvious argument that the Court was preventing legislatures from acting, Warren responded that it was not. "Our decision in no way creates a constitutional straitjacket which will handicap sound efforts at reform." If there were other methods "which are at least as effective in appraising accused persons of their right of silence," then they may be adopted. Sound efforts at reform, therefore, would take *Miranda* as a floor, not a ceiling.

Warren also denied that the police were being handicapped. "Our decision is not intended to hamper the traditional function of police officers in investigating crime." Police were perfectly free to obtain evidence via lawful searches and seizures and questioning those who were not suspects. They simply had to tell suspects their rights and then respect the suspect's choice to exercise them. From the Court's perspective it was essential to understand that the Court was requiring the states to do only what the FBI already did. Since everyone agreed that the FBI was a superb crime-fighting and crime-solving organization, it followed that state and local police could be too if they followed the example of the Bureau.

There were sharp dissents by Harlan and White. Both saw *Miranda* as having the same purpose as *Escobedo*—to end confessions except after the police had wrapped up their case. Harlan, his face flushed and his voice occasionally faltering with emotion, denounced the decision from the bench as "'dangerous experimentation' at a time of a 'high crime rate that is a matter of growing concern.'"[28] He pounded the bench for emphasis when he stated: "This doctrine has no sanction, no sanction."

White's opinion took the Court head on. The Court's warnings reflected "a deep-seated distrust of confessions." White reminded the Court that the "human dignity" of the defendant was only part of the story; other individuals—victims—were involved. Thus, the Fifth Amendment was "not the sole desideratum" because society has an "interest in the general security," which was of equal weight. Indeed, White saw nothing immoral about asking a suspect whether or not he committed the crime. "The most basic function of any government is to provide for the security of the individual and his property."

By making it harder to obtain a confession, the Court was necessarily having an impact on the system. "In some unknown number of cases the Court's rule will return a killer, a rapist or other criminal to the streets and to the environment which produced him, to repeat his crime whenever it pleases him. As a consequence, there will not be a gain, but a loss, in human dignity." And one of the immediate consequences of *Miranda* was the highly publicized releases of a handful of admitted killers, fully reinforcing White's claim in the public mind.

Fortas accurately acknowledged that *Miranda* was "entirely" Warren's,[29] and when Warren announced the opinion, he also spent a full hour reading it in the Courtroom. While Warren's pressuring Brennan to rid himself of Michael Tigar as a law clerk for the next term looked toward politics and the California election, nothing about *Miranda* related to how it played out politically. It was animated by two strong views tied together by Warren's "sense of the injustice of coercive police practices and his conviction that an omnipresent government could rob its citizens of their dignity and humanity."[30] First, there was a demand for equality. Rich men don't confess right away; the poor shouldn't either. Second, there was the disdain for confessions, which in context merged powerfully with a demand for and belief in professionalism.

Not since *Gideon* and *Douglas* had a decision been so focused on differences between the affluent and the poor. If the police stopped a man of means and wished to interrogate him as a suspect, the first thing he would do was demand to speak to his lawyer. By that very demand he would be spared, first, the indignities of the interrogation room and, second, being convicted for having confessed (since his lawyer would ensure that he would not incriminate himself if the police did not have their case). But the poor, equally obviously, did not have their own law-yers and did not know that they had the right to refuse to speak to the police. It just wasn't fair.

The rich got one kind of justice from the combination of money and knowledge. The poor, lacking both, got a different kind. There was no way the Court could make the poor rich or vice versa, but there was a way the Court could equalize knowledge. Thus, the *Miranda* warnings. Both the majority and the dissents assumed that by equalizing knowledge the decision would equalize behavior. What moved the dissenters was doubt whether it was such a good idea to decrease the number of confessions. The majority, because of its views about professionalism, did not see this as a serious problem.

There was, of course, an anticonfession cast to *Miranda,* but the language was well muted from Goldberg's *Escobedo*. Warren was not so much anticonfession as he was pro-professionalism. He had concluded that the police were using confessions as a shortcut to cover for their own laziness. "I think they are a bunch of lazy people who aren't getting their work done because they are too lazy to get it right."[31] In this respect Warren was comparing police and prosecutors to the way he remembered his own actions as district attorney, and the older he got, the more professional and civil liberties-conscious his old office got. Furthermore, there was the example of the FBI; they warned suspects and they got convictions. Like *Mapp*, *Miranda* was designed to upgrade the police and their practices to the standards of real pros, the FBI. The national government knew how to do things right, and by forcing its example on the states, the Court could force the states to do things right as well. "The Court was not hampering law enforcement, it was ennobling it."[32] Furthermore, like *Mapp*, Warren perceived the move as virtually cost-free. Lazy cops got their man via a confession; a pro got his through serious work. Both got their man, but the professionals always got the right one.

It is hard to believe, but *Miranda* was a compromise. The Court had alternatives and could have gone farther, although the dissenters never gave it credit for not doing so. *Miranda* was a compromise between the old "totality of the circumstances" rule and *Escobedo*'s implication that there could be no interrogation unless counsel was present, a point whose absence in the opinion an otherwise pleased American Civil Liberties Union stated it viewed with "regret."[33] The compromise was to back away from *Escobedo*'s demand of a lawyer (which would have rendered confessions extinct except as part of the plea bargain) and to shift instead to the defendant's waivable right to remain silent. Police, in fact, could rather easily live within the *Miranda* compromise once they understood it, and by the mid-1970s they knew this. In the interim, however, thoughtful observers like Kamisar, who suggested that *Miranda* could have gone further, were not taken seriously in the public debate. The police and politicians reacted to *Miranda* as if the Court had given the criminal the trump card.

The Reaction to *Miranda*

The police, still angry with *Escobedo,* were aghast at *Miranda.* To borrow Blum's imagery, *Miranda* transformed *Escobedo*'s gale into a Force-5 hurricane. There simply were not enough bad things that could be said about the decision and the Court that made it. The executive director of the International Association of Chiefs of Police acidly remarked that "I guess now we'll have to supply all squad cars with lawyers."[34] More typical were the comments by the mayor of Los Angeles, Sam Yorty, and the police commissioner of Boston, Edmund McNamara. Yorty found *Miranda* was "another set of handcuffs on the police department."[35] McNamara complained that "criminal trials no longer will be about a search for truth, but search for technical error."[36]

Across the street from the Court, North Carolina Senator Sam Ervin, a former state-court judge, proclaimed that "enough has been done for those who murder and rape and rob! It is time to do something for those who do not wish to be murdered or raped or robbed."[37] He proposed to enshrine the pre-*Miranda* voluntariness standard into a new constitutional amendment. At hearings that summer, Truman Capote, author of the year-old best-selling *In Cold Blood,* "testified that had the *Miranda* ruling been in effect when the murderers of the Clutter family were captured, the two killers, who were later hanged, would have gone 'scot free.'"[38]

By 1966 crime had emerged "as a major domestic issue" and even Johnson "felt compelled to send Congress a special message" on crime along with legislative proposals and requests for money.[39] But Johnson's efforts toward dealing with crime did not defuse partisanship about "crime in the streets" because that term was "a frequent euphemism for black riots"[40] and crime was a Republican issue. Nixon, actively campaigning for Republican congressional candidates, had "crime in the streets" and riots (along with inflation and high interest rates) as the domestic side of his standard stump speech.

Miranda "galvanized opposition to the Warren Court into a potent political force."[41] Handcuffing the police, coddling criminals; it was easy to disparage the Court. Not surprisingly, *Miranda* offered no help to the

Democrats who, for a number of reasons—the 1964 landslide, off-year elections, LBJ's waning credibility, the failure of guns and butter, as well as crime—suffered major defeats in the 1966 elections. One saw a strong foreshadow of 1968, where Republicans would run on the shorthand "law and order."

No Court decision so quickly moved into popular consciousness. Police shows, long absent from prime-time television, were enjoying a comeback. One of the most popular shows of the 1950s, *Dragnet* starring Jack Webb as Sergeant Joe Friday, had run from 1952 through the 1958 season. Friday's clipped jargon—"Just the facts, ma'am"—showed the police in their best investigative light where they got their man fairly and only changed the names "to protect the innocent." In 1967 *Dragnet* was revived with an older Jack Webb reprising his role. In this post-*Miranda* world, Friday and his partner would give the appropriate *Miranda* warnings prior to interrogation, but they made it clear that this was a hindrance to serious police work. (By contrast in the 1970s, *Hawaii Five-O*'s Steve McGarrett saw *Miranda* exactly as Warren wished, as doing the police a service by making them more professional; the distinction between McGarrett and Clint Eastwood's "Dirty Harry" of the same period could not be more extreme.) In context, it took almost no time for everyone, right down to preteens, to be aware of, and often memorize, *Miranda* warnings. Warren's goal of equalizing knowledge was more successful than he could have dreamed, although hardly for the reasons he assumed. The knowledge equalized, moreover, was of rights, not of any responsibilities to society or other individuals.

Self-Incrimination after *Miranda*

Schmerber v. California, decided a week after *Miranda*, reaffirmed the Court's 1957 decision in *Breithaupt v. Abram* that a blood sample could be unwillingly taken from a person without violating his privilege against self-incrimination. Warren, Black, and Douglas had dissented in *Breithaupt*; Fortas joined them in *Schmerber* where Clark, as the senior justice in the majority, had been more than happy to seal Brennan's vote by assigning him the opinion. (It is ironic that Brennan split with the liberals to create the majority in *Schmerber*, for he explained the increasing post-*Miranda* reluctance to create new liberal rules as resulting from Black's switch where "we lost our fifth vote.")[42]

Brennan's opinion acknowledged the tension between the rhetoric about the purposes of the Self-Incrimination Clause and allowing blood to be taken against the will (albeit by a doctor in a hospital) of a potential drunk driver to prove the case against him. But he also recognized that "the privilege has never been given the full scope which the values it helps to protect suggest." While Schmerber's blood was "an incriminating product of compulsion," it was not testimonial. Hence, it was outside the privilege and could be used to convict him. Brennan did hold the Fourth Amendment might require a search warrant, although not on these facts because the police had ample reason to believe Schmerber had been drunk and if they went to a magistrate for a warrant that evidence might vanish. By determining that blood samples were not governed by the Fifth Amendment, the Court prevented the accused from blocking the police decision. But by holding that the practice was governed by the Fourth Amendment, the Court required the practice to be reasonable and often to be presented first to a magistrate. The Court was thus channeling the law into a regulatory rather than a prohibitory mold.

As a result of *Schmerber,* a defendant may be required to provide, in addition to blood samples, hair samples and handwriting exemplars, be told to stand in a lineup, try on certain clothes, and speak words used by the criminal. But the core of the privilege against self-incrimination—no forced disclosure of testimonial evidence—remained secure. Thus, "Totto" Marchetti and Tony Grosso were convicted for not paying their federal wagering taxes. They defended on the ground that to have paid the taxes would have violated their privilege against self-incrimination by exposing them to prosecution for gambling. The Court, through Harlan, reversed their convictions on the basis of the unanimous decision in *Albertson v. Subversive Activities Control Board* that the SACB's registration order to communists violated their privilege against self-incrimination because it so easily opened them to prosecution under the myriad of laws dealing with communists and subversion. Warren wrote a solo dissent, demonstrating once again his blind spot toward those who offended him by being involved in commercial vice. These were gamblers who thereby had forfeited all their rights. It was one thing for a communist or a murderer to claim the Fifth Amendment; it was quite another for a gambler to do so.

Informants and Undercover Agents

In the 1966 Term, the Court decided a series of cases dealing with informants and undercover agents, and the decisions had an overtly conservative cast. The latent skepticism about informants in the communist cases was nowhere present.

Robert Kennedy set up a special "Get Hoffa Squad"[43] in his Justice Department. Having tangled with Teamsters President James R. Hoffa during his time as counsel to the Senate Permanent Subcommittee on Investigations and then with the Rackets Committee, Kennedy was determined to remove Hoffa from his union position and put him in the federal penitentiary. The squad had thirteen grand juries, sixteen lawyers, and thirty FBI agents going full-time to get it done. Kennedy didn't much care how it was done so long as it was done.

Eventually, while Hoffa was on trial for racketeering, a local Teamsters official, E. G. Partin, approached the government with a proposal to become an informer. The government released Partin from jail, compensated him for services rendered, and enjoyed the fruits of his being privy to all Hoffa's conversations, including those about bribing a juror. In the meanwhile, a jury consultant for Hoffa's lawyer, Z. T. Osborn, Jr., came to the government about the bribery. Two federal judges authorized wiring him, and he taped a meeting with Osborn where they talked about bribing the juror in order to create a hung jury. Both Hoffa and Osborn were convicted of jury tampering, and the Court affirmed both convictions.

Relying on a three-year-old Brennan dissent, Stewart explained in *Hoffa v. United States* that Partin was in Hoffa's entourage by invitation, and Hoffa was just relying on "misplaced confidence" that Partin would not reveal what he learned. The risk of a supposed friend's actually being a government informant "is probably inherent in the conditions of human society. It is the kind of risk we necessarily assume whenever we speak." But, of course, that is not necessarily true. If the Court had upheld Hoffa's or Osborn's claim (in *Osborn v. United States*), it would not be a risk we assume. (*Massiah* was distinguishable because Partin was just a listener while Massiah's codefendant had elicited the incriminating statements.)

A government that can "get" Jimmy Hoffa can get anyone, and in a companion case the Court demonstrated that the defendant personally knowing the informant was not essential. Over a solo dissent by Douglas, *Lewis v. United States* upheld a drug conviction based on the use of an undercover agent. Warren's opinion noted that to solve many types of crime it is necessary to conceal an agent's true identity and that the Constitution does not forbid this essential police tactic nor does it mandate its supervision (unless that informant was wired). *Hoffa, Osborn,* and *Lewis* came down just six months after *Miranda*.

Under some circumstances maybe even police knowledge of the informant was unnecessary. Search warrants are based on probable cause, which often is informant testimony given to police. In *McCray v. Illinois,* a 5–4 Court, through Stewart, held that the defendant could not force the disclosure of the identity of an informant who provided the probable cause for a search warrant. This not only protected informants, it also offered any police who were willing to ignore the law an opportunity to create a fictitious informant in order to obtain a search warrant. Warren, Douglas, Brennan, and Fortas dissented.

Lineups

The prime reason *Miranda* and *Escobedo* rankled so much was that they let the guilty go free. That is a fact about the criminal justice system. Most people caught up in it are not innocent. *Gideon* had offered the rare opportunity to protect the innocent. There was only one further area where that could be done—lineups. Eyewitness identification is notoriously untrustworthy, and "mistaken identification has probably been the single greatest cause of wrongful conviction."[44]

After granting certiorari in the fall of 1966, the Court held in *United States v. Wade* and *Gilbert v. California* that government could not order a lineup for a suspect without his counsel being present. Although these were the Court's first lineup cases, Brennan moved without hesitation to a blanket rule because lineups are "peculiarly riddled with innumerable dangers." One is the "vagaries of eyewitness identification." A second is "the degree of suggestion inherent in the manner in which the prosecution presents the suspect to witnesses" for identification. Once a person has identified the accused in a lineup, the witness is unlikely to recant the identification at trial. Thus, the "first line of defense" is to lessen the hazards by having a lawyer present.

White, joined by Stewart and Harlan, dissented, charging the majority with assuming there was "no adequate source" from which defense counsel could learn about the circumstances of the identification. This was a "treacherous and unsupported assumption" that rested on the conclusion that the defendant will have no idea what is happening. The dissent argued for a "totality of the circumstances" rule, claiming that the tragic mistakes that occur because of eyewitness identification are "as much the product of improper police conduct as they are the consequences of difficulties inherent in eyewitness testimony." On that the Court agreed. A companion case, *Stovall v. Denno,* acknowledged that a "recognized ground of attack" on eyewitness identification was that the lineup was too suggestive.

It took little time for the dissent to prevail fully. In the early 1970s, *Wade* and *Gilbert* were gutted by a pair of decisions holding that the right did not attach prior to indictment and was inapplicable to a photographic identification. A saying about American justice holds that it is better for a hundred guilty men to go free than one innocent man be convicted. The law of eyewitness identification suggests the statement is a bit rhetorical.

The Scope of the Fourth Amendment

Despite *McCray,* in two sets of cases during the 1966 and 1967 Terms the Court extended the scope of the requirement to obtain a search warrant (which then tied in to the so-called *Aguilar-Spinelli* doctrine the Court was simultaneously creating, taking an overly technical view of what information magistrates must have before they can issue warrants). The first set, and by far the less important, *Camara v. Municipal Court* and *See v. Seattle,* overruled the holding of *Frank v. Maryland* that administrative searches needed no warrant. Yet in holding that nonemergency inspections by fire and health officials did require a warrant, the Court watered down probable cause to find that it applied to a geographical area rather than any specific building. Still, Clark, Harlan, and Stewart dissented.

Berger v. New York and *Katz v. United States* were by far the more important for they brought electronic surveillance under the Fourth Amendment and functionally overruled the 1928 case of *Olmstead v. United States* that had produced a classic dissent by Louis Brandeis. In overthrowing *Olmstead*'s trespass rule, Stewart wrote that the amendment protected people, not places, and an individual's reasonable expectation of privacy was what mattered.

Black, whose populist lens had led him to perceive the Fourth as Wall Street's amendment when he served in the Senate, never changed his mind. Thus, he dissented as he normally did from Fourth Amendment expansions for which he could not imagine a Fifth Amendment rationale. He always eschewed the Fourth's rich history, owned no books discussing it, and focused instead on its use of that detested word "reasonable" in its text. As his sympathetic biographer, Roger Newman, notes: "He became fixated with its wording, not its significance."[45] Furthermore, with the Fifth Amendment's having run its course, crime statistics began to impress Black as they already had the four *Miranda* dissenters. "More crime, more crime. Won't it ever stop? We should let the police do their job."[46] With those views, he condemned the majority for construing the amendment so as to keep the Constitution "up to date" or "to bring it in harmony with the times."

Despite overruling *Olmstead, Berger* and *Katz* were not necessarily all that liberal. They looked to supervision, not elimination, of electronic surveillance. If done professionally, there was nothing wrong with the tactic.

Berger and *Katz* thus strongly implied that judicially approved surveillance was valid, and the meaning of that had been explicated in the holding of *Warden v. Hayden,* which came down shortly before they did. Hayden was convicted of armed robbery after a legal search where the police seized items of clothing. The federal court of appeals threw out the conviction on the ground that the clothing was "mere evidence." A 1921 decision, *Gouled v. United States,* had forbidden the seizure of evidence other than that which was the instrumentality or fruit of the crime. Over Douglas's sole dissent concluding that there were zones of privacy that even a legal search could not invade, the Court overruled *Gouled.* The impact of *Hayden* was to guarantee that judicially approved electronic surveillance created admissible evidence.

Hayden marked the thirty-second time the Warren Court had overruled a precedent. There were thirteen more coming in the remaining twenty-five months of Warren's tenure, but *Hayden* was the sole time in the full sixteen years that the new result was more conservative than the prior law.

Stop and Frisk

There was one additional conservative Fourth Amendment case, *Terry v. Ohio,* involving the standard police practice of stopping and frisking individuals who looked suspicious to the police. A Cleveland detective observed three men casing a store for what he assumed was a probable robbery. He approached to question them but frisked them first for possible concealed weapons, which he found on two of them. The two were convicted on weapons charges and claimed the search was unlawful because it was not based on probable cause.

The Court unanimously voted at first to affirm, but, as a Warren clerk noted thirty years later, unanimity "masked an almost complete lack of consensus about just *how* simultaneously to recognize and to cabin this new police authority."[47] Thus, Warren's desire to write a *Miranda*-like opinion was thwarted, and his initial circulation fractured his Court. Then, with Brennan's assistance, he shifted rationales away from probable cause and produced an opinion of the Court for seven justices (with Harlan concurring and Douglas dissenting). Like his initial draft, this final opinion never acknowledged that the detective was white and that the defendants were African-Americans (although it acknowledged that the stops just approved might "exacerbate police-community tensions in the crowded centers of our Nation's cities").

Warren stated that the situation "thrusts to the fore difficult and troublesome issues" involving the security of the officers and the need to circumscribe police authority, and opined: "The exclusionary rule has its limitations as a tool of judicial control." He attempted to avoid the problems by limiting the opinion to the "narrow question posed by the facts before us: whether it is always unreasonable for a policeman to seize a person and subject him to a limited search for weapons unless there is probable cause for an arrest." Answering in the negative, that it is not "always unreasonable," he balanced the magnitude of the intrusion on the individual against the "governmental interest in investigating crime" and concluded that "stop and frisk" was lawful. "[T]here must be a narrowly drawn authority to permit a reasonable search for weapons for the protection of the police officer, where he has reason to believe that he is dealing with an armed and dangerous individual." Then, in the opinion's key words, that sentence continued, "regardless of whether he has probable cause to arrest that individual for crime." With this sentence, the Court for the first time split the Fourth Amendment's search and seizure provisions from its probable cause provisions.

However limited Warren thought his opinion was, *Terry* quickly came to stand for the proposition that a citizen on the street could be legally stopped and frisked because the police had a "reasonable suspicion"— words nowhere joined in Warren's opinion. Any contraband found during the frisk would be admissible even though probable cause was lacking. It is ironic that Warren's desire to write an "annotated stop and frisk statute, *a la Miranda*"[48] was fulfilled, but hardly in the way he wished. A 1972 decision by William H. Rehnquist simply assumed that key unanswered questions in *Terry* had, in fact, been resolved in favor of the police.

Warren's two able biographers classify *Terry* as "practical"[49] and "a considerable bow in the direction of law enforcement."[50] Their restrained comments reflect the fact that *Terry* was at least as significant a victory for the police as *Miranda* had been for the accused and seems a decision out of character for Warren and out of place at the supposed height of the Warren Court, when there apparently were at least five sure votes for liberal results. Warren's former clerk offers an apt observation: "Individually the Justices . . . may have felt differing degrees of sympathy with the arguments of the police, but collectively they were unwilling to be—or to be perceived as—the agents who tied the hands of the police in dealing with intensely dangerous and recurring situations on city streets."[51]

"Collectively," however, had increasingly been inapplicable to Douglas. As he grew older he liked to say that he had only one soul to save and that was his own. He enjoyed a solo dissent as a mark of his individualism, and Warren's move caused Douglas to write. Writing, in turn, both crystallized his views and demonstrated the fundamental split between him and his liberal brethren. He could remember riding boxcars with hobos and Wobblies—the exact types of individuals (along with African-Americans) who were likely to be suspected by police to be up to no good and therefore overly subject to what all too quickly became known as "*Terry* stops."

The dissent was biting, reminiscent of an earlier era. "There have been powerful hydraulic pressures throughout our history that bear heavily on the Court to water down constitutional guarantees and give the police the upper hand. That hydraulic pressure has probably never been greater than it is today. Yet if the individual is no longer to be sovereign, if the police can pick him up whenever they do not like the cut of his jib, if they can 'seize' and 'search' him in their discretion we enter a new regime." The country had; one cannot help but wonder if *Terry* would have been similarly decided two years earlier, but the situation in June 1968 when *Terry* was decided can best be seen through the description of Theodore H. White. "The murder of Robert F. Kennedy, following only eight and a half weeks after the murder of Martin Luther King, had come midway through a year pocked with bombings, arson, demonstrations and random shootings—and had been preceded by three years of riot, crime and summer terror, in a climate of ever-rising hate and fear, to prepare the way for the great concern that now dominated the second half of the campaign of 1968."[52] That great concern was "law and order."

The Politics of "Law and Order"

Miranda was the highpoint of the Warren Court's criminal procedure revolution and set the Court on a collision course with the 1968 presidential election. Furthermore, with criminal cases coming to make up over a fifth of the Court's work product, it did not matter that the Court was decidedly more conservative with decisions like *Schmerber, Lewis, Hoffa,* and *McCray. Miranda,* with its accompanying headlines about confessed killers and rapists going free, towered over everything, and therefore the more conservative decisions did not matter.

Once crime became a major political issue, it was inevitable that something would be done. Liberals neither wanted to discuss the issue nor do anything about it, but when forced to they spoke in terms of the root causes of crime, by which they meant—in Warren's own words—"the degradation of slum life in the ghettos, ignorance, poverty, the drug traffic, unemployment, and organized crime."[53] Conservatives were for law and order, and that translated immediately into getting tough on crime, criminals, and courts.

No one discussed demographics. At least in the second half of the twentieth century, the prime age for criminals has been seventeen to twenty-four, in the late 1960s an age encompassing the baby boomers. With an age cohort like that, it didn't matter where one turned for statistics; they were going to show a huge jump in crime. Thus, the murder rate in the country had more than doubled from 4.6 per 100,000 to 9.2 per 100,000 just between 1963 and 1970. Crime itself was up 139 percent from 1961 levels, the number of police per 1,000 people was up twice the rate of the population growth, and yet clearance rates for crime dropped 31 percent and conviction rates were down 6 percent. During the last weeks of his presidential campaign, Nixon had a favorite line in his standard speech. "In the past forty-five minutes this is what happened in America. There has been one murder, two rapes, forty-five major crimes of violence, countless robberies and auto thefts."[54]

In the spring of 1968, the Omnibus Crime Control and Safe Streets Act, which was a funding bill that had passed the House overwhelmingly the previous session, came before the Senate with proposals in Title II to legislatively repeal both *Miranda* and *Wade,* to deny the Court jurisdiction to hear confession cases where the state supreme court had ruled the confessions voluntary, and to strip the federal courts of their ability to review state convictions through habeas corpus. In a repeat of the outcome a decade earlier, the jurisdiction-stripping proposals were defeated, 52–32 and 54–27. Efforts to delete the *Miranda* and *Wade* repealers failed, however, by votes of 55–29 and 63–21. The bill passed the Senate 72–4 and was accepted by the House 369–17.

As enacted by Title II, confessions, if voluntarily made, were admissible into evidence, and voluntariness was to be tested by the totality of the circumstances. Whether or not a suspect knew of his rights was just one circumstance that "need not be conclusive." *Wade* was directly repealed by the blunt statement that eyewitness testimony was admissible in federal courts. "When Title II burst from the relative obscurity of the Senate Judiciary Committee onto the Senate floor in April of 1968, it was immediately seen as a bald Congressional attempt to rap the Supreme Court's knuckles over crime."[55] Nixon, in denouncing *Miranda* and *Escobedo,* called for the act, Title III of which was a wiretap authorization bill, to pass.

During the debate on Title II, John McClellan placed in the rear of the Senate chamber a large graph of the FBI crime statistics on which he had also placed the names of Court decisions at the date that they had been handed down. "The Supreme Court has set a low tone in law enforcement and we are reaping the whirlwind today! Look at that chart! Look at it and weep for your country—crime spiraling upward and upward and upward. Apparently nobody is willing to put on the brakes."[56] McClellan was correct; it was unmistakable that the crime rate was shooting up at the exact same time that the Court was expanding the rights of criminals. It was also coincidental because of the baby boomers, although no one noticed. Despite urgings by the defeated liberals to veto the act, Johnson signed it a week after Warren announced his intended retirement.

There were obvious arguments that Title II was flatly unconstitutional inasmuch as Congress cannot overrule the Court on a constitutional issue (save for the relatively obscure "dormant commerce clause" decisions involving state regulation of interstate commerce). The arguments were met in two ways. First, there was the counterargument from *Katzenbach v. Morgan,* which had sustained the portion of the Voting Rights Act of 1965 that had enfranchised non-English-speaking Puerto Ricans in New York. One rationale of *Morgan* was that Congress had an independent right to interpret the Constitution. Another was that Congress had superior fact-finding capacity, and it might exercise that ability to show that the Court's prior conclusion was erroneous. Under the first rationale, Congress was simply interpreting the Fifth and Sixth Amendments differently from the Court. Under the second, it was telling the Court that police interrogation was not inherently coercive and therefore the warnings were not necessary. Whichever rationale was adopted, it ran up against Footnote Ten of *Morgan* where Brennan had told Congress that *Morgan* granted a one-way ratchet. Congress could expand rights, but it could not contract them.

It is doubtful if any members of Congress expected the *Morgan* rationale to work. Privately, McClellan told an aide that Title II was "my petition for a rehearing" on *Miranda*.[57] The Senate Committee report took a similar tack in deflecting the claim that the bill was unconstitutional and therefore futile. "After all, the *Miranda* decision itself was by a bare majority of one, and with increasing frequency the Supreme Court has reversed itself. The Committee feels that by the time the issue of constitutionality would reach the Supreme Court, the probability rather is that this legislation would be upheld."[58] After passage the attorney general ordered United States attorneys to follow *Miranda* and *Wade* and not to invoke Title II.

A popular campaign promise of Nixon was that he would replace Ramsey Clark as attorney general. No one bothered much with the obvious, that when a president of a different party is elected, he replaces the entire Cabinet, including the attorney general—for the line about Clark was an applause line. Replacing Ramsey Clark was about getting tough on crime and supporting the peace forces (by which Nixon did not mean those trying to get the United States out of Vietnam quickly).

Nixon echoed the theme of the *Miranda* dissenters and claimed the effect of *Miranda* "has been to very nearly rule out the 'confession' as an effective major tool in prosecution and law enforcement."[59] His punchline during the campaign was that "some of the courts have gone too far in weakening the peace forces against the criminal forces."[60] Everyone knew that "some of the courts" meant the Court.

George Wallace, of course, went further than Nixon. His standard stump speech in 1968 contained a withering attack on the Court. "If you walk out of this hotel tonight and someone knocks you on the head, he'll be out of jail before you're out of the hospital, and on Monday morning they'll try the policeman instead of the criminal."[61] An overwhelming 63 percent of the respondents in 1968 told the Gallup Poll that the Court was too lenient on crime. Between them, Nixon and Wallace overwhelmed Humphrey in the 1968 election by a 57–43 margin.

Jimmy Hoffa was given consecutive four-year sentences for his jury tampering. Just into the second of the two sentences, Nixon commuted his sentence. Four years later Hoffa disappeared, presumably a victim of a mob hit.

Danny Escobedo was freed after his victory despite having arranged for the killing of his brother-in-law. In 1967 he was arrested and subsequently convicted for drug dealing. Thereafter, he was convicted of taking indecent liberties with a child and attempted murder, and as this book comes off the press, he is in prison on federal weapons charges where the judge gave him the maximum, accurately noting "you are a career criminal."[62]

Ernesto Miranda was reconvicted of the kidnapping and rape charges for which he had confessed. At a lineup of suspects for the rape victim, he did a role reversal, and on recognizing the victim said, "That's the girl."[63] (Which was just as well, for she was unsure about the perpetrator.) That evidence was admitted, to his considerable detriment. He was released in 1972 but went back to prison a couple more times over the next few years. When on the outside, he carried police cards with their *Miranda* warnings and autographed them for $1 or $2. Free in 1976, he was stabbed to death over a $3 bet in a poker game. The suspect was arrested, given his *Miranda* warnings, chose to remain silent, and was released pending further investigation. He disappeared and has never been found.

Clarence Gideon, who had come to symbolize the best of the criminal justice system, simply disappeared from view. He reappeared in the news again only in conjunction with Lewis's book, Fonda's film, and Fortas's death. By the time of the latter two occurrences, he was already dead, the innocent man saved by the system who died in such obscurity that he was initially buried in an unmarked grave.

Chapter 16

Policing the Criminal Justice System

Black's opinion in *Gideon* incorporated the Sixth Amendment guarantee of counsel into the Fourteenth Amendment by arguing that *Betts v. Brady* had been wrong for its twenty-one-year existence. Black specifically eschewed any argument that subsequent events mattered, and he uttered not a word about his own theory that the Fourteenth Amendment incorporated the entire Bill of Rights. Thus, neither *Gideon* nor the two-year-old *Mapp v. Ohio* offered much help on why provisions of the Bill of Rights applied against the states, but between them they seemed to offer a solution to the problem of how the Court could guarantee that each criminal trial was fair. In an era when those working in Washington, D.C., believed wisdom rested exclusively within its city limits, the Court recognized that the Bill of Rights offered national standards for criminal procedure regardless of how the states wished to conduct trials, and it quickly applied all the relevant provisions of the Bill of Rights to the states to create minimum national guarantees of fairness in criminal trials. This was but one of a series of steps the Court took that remade the entire American system of criminal justice, from the way juveniles, on the one hand, and capital defendants, on the other, were tried, to the provision of postconviction relief that allowed for a trial of the trial. In the process, the Court's desire to make good policy resulted in an unsettling new definition of constitutional rights.

Incorporating the Bill of Rights

When Warren came to the Court, the only parts of the Bill of Rights that applied to the states were the substantive provisions of the First Amendment's guarantees of freedom of expression and religion and the Fifth Amendment's Just Compensation Clause. *Gideon,* coming down less than two calendar years after *Mapp,* marked the second time the Warren Court had incorporated a Bill of Rights provision. Implicitly the cases had reopened the Black-Frankfurter debates on incorporation and necessarily rejected Frankfurter's position that the Fourteenth Amendment did not incorporate provisions of the Bill of Rights. But neither *Mapp* nor *Gideon* adopted Black's position that the Fourteenth Amendment incorporated all of the Bill of Rights. Both Black and Frankfurter had created intellectually coherent positions. The Court, however, was embracing neither, and it would soon become clear that it was incorporating some, but not all, of the Bill of Rights. The ones deemed good were in; the bad ones were left out. But how could the Court tell which provisions of the Bill of Rights were good and useful and which were bad and outmoded? The answer, of course, was a Brennan opinion, for he did not need an intellectually coherent theory; he wanted realistically coherent results.

Gideon on counsel and *Mapp* on search and seizure had incorporated the two most important criminal procedure aspects of the Bill of Rights. The third potentially important one was the Fifth Amendment's guarantee against self-incrimination, because it dealt generally with the law of confessions as well as the way prosecutors could conduct trials. In fact, though, whether or not the Fifth Amendment's Self-Incrimination Clause applied to the states was just not that important compared to the possibilities available in applying a federal rule on arraignment like *Mallory* to deal with confessions.

Two months after *Gideon,* the Court granted certiorari in a Fifth Amendment case, *Malloy v. Hogan,* and then in the fall of 1963 it granted cert in a second Fifth Amendment case, *Murphy v. Waterfront Commission,* which tested the relationship between state and federal law. The two cases came down the same day, with Brennan writing *Malloy* and Goldberg writing *Murphy,* the latter explaining the meaning of *Malloy*'s having incorporated the Self-Incrimination Clause.

Malloy is a result looking for a reason. On the one hand, Brennan concluded that developments in the areas of coerced confessions and searches and seizures necessitated a reconsideration of the prior conclusion that the Self-Incrimination Clause was not incorporated. Then, on the other hand, Brennan concluded that there was a close connection between the law of searches and seizures and the law of coerced confessions. Hence, the former's incorporation implied that the latter should be incorporated too. If that wasn't much reasoning, it was enough to hold five votes when more reasoning promised to cost votes, since further explanation might show that Brennan's opinion was inconsistent with the total incorporation position of Black and Douglas.

Harlan, with Clark, dissented, seeing Brennan's lack of reasoning as the de facto adoption of the Black position, but the passion that often accompanied one of his federalism dissents was missing. White and Stewart dissented on technical grounds.

Murphy was an investigation by a joint New York-New Jersey commission into work stoppages in New York harbor. The two states granted the witnesses immunity, but the witnesses refused to testify because their testimony might incriminate them under federal law, and states lacked the power to affect federal prosecutions. *Murphy* was in one sense the opposite side of *Escobedo* where Goldberg had questioned police practices that yielded confessions; here he extolled silence. Writing eloquently about the "fundamental values and most noble aspirations" behind the privilege against self-incrimination, Goldberg concluded that whipsawing witnesses between federal and state laws, where one jurisdiction produced evidence under a grant of immunity that then could be used by another, was prohibited. This overruled a pair of decisions from the late 1950s. The Court also held that once a provision of the Bill of Rights was incorporated against the states, then all its auxiliary federal rules came with it. Federalism, as Black and Douglas had long argued, was irrelevant; a constitutional provision applies to the states precisely as it applies to the federal government. Harlan, Clark, and White concurred.

Mapp had opened the incorporation floodgates. Thereafter, any case raising an incorporation issue succeeded. In 1965 the Sixth Amendment provision requiring confrontation of witnesses was incorporated; in 1967 two more Sixth Amendment provisions came in, the right to a speedy trial and the right to compulsory process for obtaining witnesses; in 1968 the final missing Sixth Amendment right—to a jury—was incorporated in *Duncan v. Louisiana*. Finally, on the last day of the Warren Court, the granddaddy of all refusals to incorporate, Cardozo's 1937 opinion in *Palko v. Connecticut*, was overruled as the Fifth Amendment prohibition against double jeopardy was made applicable against the states.

Only *Duncan* attempted an explanation, accurate if also lame, for what the Court was doing. Essentially, the Court looked to two places to determine whether a Bill of Rights provision was incorporated. First, it made a self-referential look to the Bill of Rights itself. Then it looked to state practices, whether by the common law, statute, or state constitution, to see if the right in question was commonly accepted. Since all of the Bill of Rights provisions are matched in the laws of virtually all the states, this reference as well always yields the answer that the right is important. But is it, as *Palko* asked, so important that one could not imagine a civilized system without it? This, White acknowledged, was no longer a relevant question. All the Court wished to know was whether the right was "necessary to an Anglo-American regime of ordered liberty," not whether it was necessary to a perfect regime. Since the Bill of Rights named the right and most states duplicated it, seemingly all the criminal procedure aspects of the Bill of Rights were incorporated.

Given that the Court's approach yielded Black's results, why did the justices not adopt his more coherent approach? The answer, although the Court never gave it, is that there are three guarantees in the Bill of Rights that the justices probably did not like: the right to bear arms, grand jury indictments, and civil jury trials. Black's approach meant those were in. The Court's doctrine of "selective incorporation" meant they could be left out even though they are part of the Bill of Rights and equally as well protected by state law as criminal juries or double jeopardy. Furthermore, given the Court's ability to control the cases it hears, those provisions could be left out without the Court's ever having to justify their exclusion. (And three decades later they are still out, as the Court has never granted certiorari in a case raising their incorporation even though it has had the opportunity.)

The legal changes brought by incorporation after *Gideon* were more dramatic on paper than in practice. The vast majority of states already accorded the accused the rights at issue; like *Gideon*, only a handful of states were affected by each case. In fact, after *Mapp* and *Gideon*, incorporation was easy because the cases did not deal with a controversial issue—such as regulating police practices—but rather with trial procedures that took little to accommodate. *Mapp* was thus the only controversial incorporation case and the subsequent ones, *Gideon* excepted, passed with little notice. Furthermore, as the search and seizure cases from the 1967 and 1968 Terms would illustrate, applying an amendment against the states did not mean that all the implications inherent in the right would turn out to be there. In fact, it might mean that the amendment in operation offered less protection than anyone had previously assumed.

Fair Trial-Free Press

Even as the Due Process Clause was being read to incorporate all the good parts of the Bill of Rights, the Court reversed three convictions on generalized due process grounds holding that either pretrial publicity or the excesses of the press during a trial prejudiced the defendant. The first of the cases, *Rideau v. Louisiana,* involved a defendant whose taped admissions to the sheriff were then aired on a Lake Charles television station on three consecutive days to estimated audiences of 24,000, 53,000, and 29,000 in a parish of 150,000. Rideau's lawyers asked for a change of venue, which the trial judge denied. Three members of the jury had seen the confession on television and two other members were deputy sheriffs (whom the trial judge would not remove for cause). Rideau was convicted of murder, kidnapping, and bank robbery and sentenced to death.

Stewart wrote a terse opinion that concluded that the television program had been Rideau's real trial and everything that followed was reduced to a "kangaroo court." *Rideau* was a year before *Escobedo,* and, interestingly, Stewart noted that "there was no lawyer in the jail to advise Rideau of his right to stand mute." Clark and Harlan dissented, believing that it was sufficient that the jurors had affirmed they could lay aside what they knew and give the defendant a presumption of innocence.

Later that year everyone had to face the issue of the presumption of innocence as Lee Harvey Oswald was pronounced the assassin of President Kennedy first by the Dallas police and then by the entire press. If everyone knew Oswald was the murderer, how could an impartial jury be impaneled? Of course, there was no trial, as the nation then watched Oswald killed by Jack Ruby. Seven "teachers of the administration of criminal justice at the Harvard Law School" wrote the *New York Times* noting the "irony that the very publicity which had already made it virtually impossible for Oswald to be tried and convicted by a jury meeting constitutional standards of impartiality should, in the end, have made such a trial unnecessary."[1] A few days later the American Civil Liberties Union issued a statement concluding that had Oswald lived, he would have been denied all opportunity for a fair trial. The Warren Commission Report, issued ten months after the assassination, had a lengthy section condemning both the police and the press and questioning whether Oswald could have been accorded a fair trial.[2]

Just as his Nuremberg experience as chief prosecutor had seared Robert Jackson's views on totalitarianism, the Warren Commission experience created an indelible mark on Warren's views of the duties of judges and prosecutors to avoid convicting the defendant first in the media and then gaining a second conviction before a jury. Warren, in fact, went further. He did not believe that television and justice were compatible. Fred Friendly, the president of CBS News, on meeting Warren expressed the hope that he would hold the job when television cameras were both on the moon and in the Supreme Court. Smiling, Warren responded that Friendly would have "more luck with the former than the latter."[3]

In 1965 and 1966 the Court, through Clark, reversed two sensational convictions, the first of Texas wheeler-dealer Billie Sol Estes, the second of Cleveland neurosurgeon Sam Sheppard. In 1954 Sheppard, then age thirty, was convicted of bludgeoning to death his attractive, pregnant wife in their bedroom. Sheppard claimed that he had been asleep on a downstairs couch, was awakened by his wife's cry, and had rushed upstairs where he struggled with a "form" who knocked him out. (While in prison, he was immortalized in a popular ABC series that ran from 1963 until 1967 as *The Fugitive*. A 1993 movie with the same name was based on the television series.) Estes, from a West Texas town, was a millionaire by thirty and, more important, a sometime business partner of Lyndon Johnson. The investigation of his case created a sensation when an investigator from the Department of Agriculture was found with five bullet holes from a bolt-action rifle that had to be pumped each time to eject a shell, and the death was pronounced a suicide. According to the *Dallas Morning News*, President Kennedy took "a personal interest in the mysterious death."[4] (Two decades later Estes claimed that Johnson had been in on the decision to kill the investigator. Although a grand jury then determined that the death had not been a suicide, the prosecutor found no corroborating evidence of Estes's charge.)

Estes was ultimately tried and convicted of swindling charges in state court and mail fraud in federal court. Over his objections, photographers were allowed in the courtroom, and the pretrial hearing and parts of the state trial were televised. He claimed that, as such, the proceedings inherently denied him the right to a fair trial. In *Estes v. Texas,* the justices, still unused to the new medium, were badly split—but along no recognizable divide. Black, Clark, Brennan, Stewart, and White voted to affirm the conviction on the ground that cameras per se could not create an unfair trial. Warren, for Douglas, wrote an impassioned dissent calling the trial "a public spectacle and source of entertainment."[5] Using fashionable statements about the power of television—such as "[i]t is common knowledge that 'television . . . can . . . work profound changes in the behavior of the people it focuses on'"—he concluded that television in the courtroom was inherently antithetical to due process of law. Harlan and Goldberg, like the majority, thought Warren's position too extreme but nevertheless believed that on the facts Estes had not been accorded a fair trial.

Warren convinced Clark to switch and thus created a majority to reverse Estes's conviction. Clark's opinion for the Court can easily be read to hold that a televised trial is an unconstitutional trial; indeed, the dissenters thought so. Warren's now-concurring opinion, which Goldberg as well as Douglas joined, explicitly took that position. But Harlan, in addition to joining Clark, wrote separately and stated that he did not believe in a per se rule, and a plausible reading of Clark's opinion is that televising the pretrial hearing live brought the case within *Rideau*. Stewart's dissent for Black, Brennan, and White agreed that cameras in the courtroom were "an extremely unwise policy," but refused "to escalate this personal view" into a constitutional rule and, obviously, also concluded that Estes had not been denied a fair trial. (Because of the parallel federal conviction, Estes was not freed.)

A year later the Court ruled Sheppard was entitled to a new trial because of the carnival atmosphere surrounding his conviction twelve years earlier in one of the many "crime of the century" cases. The trial judge, who was standing for reelection the next month, had denied a motion for change of venue and then essentially turned the case over to the media (apparently with the justification that to do otherwise would violate the First Amendment).

All three Cleveland papers published the names and addresses of all seventy-five people on the jury venire, and during the trial pictures of the twelve jurors appeared over forty times in the Cleveland papers. Inside the bar of the courtroom the judge had erected a long table, one end of which was less than three feet from the jury box, for approximately twenty reporters. Behind the bar the courtroom held four rows of seats, and the judge assigned these for the entire trial. The first was occupied by radio and television, the next two by the print media, and the last was split between Sheppard's family and that of his dead wife. The judge also assigned all available rooms on the courtroom floor to the press, and, on another floor, the room next to the jury deliberation room was occupied by a radio station that continued to broadcast about the case during recesses and while the jury deliberated.

The corridors of the courthouse were filled with reporters, photographers, and press equipment. Private conversations between counsel and the defendant were all but impossible, and reporters "vied with each other to find out what counsel and the judge had discussed, and often these matters later appeared in newspapers accessible to the jury." There were so many errors by the judge that they were not worth counting although Clark listed them numerically. Once—this was number 5—a police officer gave testimony that contradicted parts of Sheppard's written statement. Two days later a radio broadcast labeled Sheppard a perjuror and likened the episode to the Alger Hiss-Whittaker Chambers confrontation. The judge refused to ask the jurors if they had heard the broadcast. The day before the verdict was rendered—"while the jurors were at lunch and sequestered by two bailiffs—the jury was separated into two groups to pose for photographs which appeared in the newspapers." Some sequestration.

Clark quoted a judge below: "In this atmosphere of a 'Roman holiday' for the news media, Sam Sheppard stood trial for his life." Instead of ceding his functions to the press, the trial judge should have "fulfill[ed] his duty to protect Sheppard from the inherently prejudicial publicity which saturated the community and to control disruptive influences in the courtroom." After ten years in prison, Sheppard was entitled to either his freedom or a new trial at the state's choice.

Amazingly there was a dissent—albeit without opinion. The dissenter was Black. Although none of his biographers discuss *Sheppard v. Maxwell,* Douglas did. Black "felt that Sheppard was guilty."[6] Douglas thought so too. (Their intuition was wrong. A jury acquitted Sheppard; more persuasively, DNA evidence recently showed he was not the murderer. The DNA matched that of the Sheppards' handyman, currently serving a life sentence for murdering a woman. Sheppard, who had turned to professional wrestling and the bottle, died just four years after being freed.)

Estes, Sheppard, and the Warren Commission Report spawned a vigorous debate on how to guarantee a fair trial in a notorious case. Some read *Sheppard* and the *Estes* concurring opinion as invitations to gag the press and therefore raised the concern of a conflict between different constitutional amendments. The *Times* had captioned the letter from the Harvard Law professors "Obsession with Public's 'Right to Be Informed' Condemned,"[7] and that caption clearly suggested what was deemed the appropriate balance between the defendant's and the public's rights. Although the debate was not solved during Warren's era, the answers were simpler than the participants thought. Prosecutors and defense counsel, but not the press, could be gagged; jurors could be sequestered; changes of venue could be granted; challenges for cause could be granted. As a result, defendants can get fair trials before impartial juries, the press can report on the cases, and the supposed constitutional conflict vanishes.

Friendly was fired before CBS showed television pictures from the moon. There has even been television from Mars. But no one has ever seen television from the Court.

Habeas Corpus

The most basic legal relationship is between rights and remedies. Yet an often unnoticed aspect of the legal order is that, when constitutional rights start changing, whether by expansion or contraction, it is a safe bet that remedies are changing too. The relationship between rights and remedies is well illustrated by the dramatic changes in habeas corpus wrought by the Warren Court as the means of implementing its sweeping overhaul of police practices and criminal procedure. By the time the Court was done, the substantive reach of the "Great Writ" on this side of the Atlantic bore no relationship to its origins across the ocean. The reason was simple. The Court can review but a handful of the criminal cases claiming constitutional error. But by authorizing federal district courts to hear constitutional claims, the Court could give every convicted defendant an opportunity to present his constitutional claims to a federal court.

Sheppard v. Maxwell is an example. In 1956 the Court denied certiorari. Subsequently Sheppard unsuccessfully sought a writ of habeas corpus in the Ohio courts, and when that was denied, he had the great good fortune to meet F. Lee Bailey, who was just two days past his first anniversary of admission to the bar. Although Sheppard had already spent five years in jail, the timing was propitious. By the time Bailey filed for federal habeas, the Court had expanded the scope of the writ. Instead of "dismissing the writ without reading it," as the district judge suggested,[8] the judge instead agreed with Sheppard that he had been denied a fair trial. The court of appeals reversed; hence, Clark's opinion in *Sheppard v. Maxwell*.

In England, and originally in America, habeas was limited to challenging the legality of pretrial detention. The applicable federal statute, dating from 1867, refers to detention "in violation of the Constitution." Because habeas is about unlawful custody, once the individual had been convicted of a crime, the detention becomes lawful by definition. Nineteenth-century law offered few decisions on the status of American ha-beas. It is clear that it was available to contest whether the convicting court had jurisdiction over the case, since a jurisdictional defect rendered a conviction void and therefore the prisoner was held without constitu-tional authority. By the same token, an unconstitutional law is void and therefore is no law so that a conviction resting on it is also void.

During the first half of the twentieth century, the idea of jurisdictional defect underwent a slow but nevertheless steady accretion so that by the time Warren took his seat it included whether there had been a disregard of the constitutional rights of the accused at the trial. Thus, in *Johnson v. Zerbst* in 1938 habeas was held available to a federal prisoner who challenged his criminal trial at which he had not been provided counsel as he successfully claimed the Sixth Amendment required. For state pris-oners, however, only a denial of due process could be raised on habeas, and under pre-Warren constitutional law, for all practical purposes the only denials of due process were likely to be coerced confessions.

A major doctrinal change in habeas occurred just before Warren took his seat. In *Brown v. Allen,* the Court, through Frankfurter, concluded that a federal district court could hear a due process claim even though the Supreme Court itself was barred from hearing that claim on direct review. Despite the holding, Jackson, in a concurring opinion, described the problem as one of searching for a needle in a haystack where those doing the searching "end up with the attitude that the needle is not worth the search." Jackson's point, that resort to habeas was futile, was prov-able by statistics. In the decade after World War II, there were over 5,000 habeas petitions filed but a mere 82 granted. Of the "lucky" 82, "only a small number were actually released."[9] It is no wonder Jackson thought in terms of needles and haystacks.

Brown v. Allen, equating a constitutional violation with a lack of juris-diction, was a lurking time bomb, although Jackson's opinion shows why few saw it. If there was a sudden expansion of constitutional rights—such as occurred between *Mapp* and *Wade-Gilbert*—then there would be an equal expansion of issues that could be raised on habeas. And, quite obviously, this happened. But before this happened there was one further expansion of habeas, both in actuality and rhetorically.

A pair of 1963 decisions involving confessions and murder convic-tions, *Fay v. Noia* and *Townsend v. Sain,* invigorated federal habeas and offered criminals long in jail the opportunity for freedom. The result of the two cases when combined with *Brown v. Allen* was the creation of the right to try the trial and to do so before a federal fact-finder. The liberal bloc of the Warren Court did not think, like Jackson, in terms of needles and haystacks but rather perceived habeas as the way to police both state judges, who were often hostile to the new approaches in criminal procedure, and the police themselves. Expanding habeas was part and parcel of the expansion of constitutional rights.

Noia was one of three defendants convicted of murder. The sole evidence against them was a signed confession by each. Noia's two codefendants appealed and lost. Noia did not appeal, probably fearing that a new trial might bring the death penalty. When Noia turned to federal habeas, the state made the same argument and one that the Court itself had accepted in 1950: The federal courts had no power to release the defendant because his custody did not violate any federal right since it was pursuant to a conviction that was not appealed. Brennan's 5–4 opinion, resting on a full-fledged, but mythical, history of the "Great Writ," rejected the state's argument. *Noia* held that any state prisoner claiming his constitutional rights had been violated could go to federal court to challenge his conviction once state remedies were first exhausted; if there were no state remedies available (because he had forgone his right to appeal), then the prisoner could go immediately to federal court.

Brennan's rhetorical strategy was talk of the "Great Writ," followed by a lengthy history of British and American practice that offered this breathtaking conclusion about the function of habeas: "Vindication of due process is precisely its historic office." Thus, it was not habeas that was changing so much as the nature of a fair trial as represented by due process of law.

The power of the federal courts "stems from the very nature of the writ." Thus, the fact that neither a state court—nor the Supreme Court itself—could touch a case was not relevant. "[C]onventional notions of finality in criminal litigation cannot be permitted to defeat the manifest federal policy that federal constitutional rights of personal liberty shall not be denied without the fullest opportunity for plenary federal review." Furthermore, the opinion strongly hinted that its conclusions rested not on the federal statute but rather were constitutionally compelled.

The four dissenters were outraged, although Clark's dissent may have been tempered somewhat because he agreed with Jackson's characterization and thus knew that not many prisoners were going to win. Harlan, for Stewart and White, did not care about that. He rightly declared Brennan's opinion had "turned its back on history." Worse, by allowing a single federal judge to overturn a state conviction that state judges could not touch, the majority "struck a heavy blow at the foundations of our federal system."

Operationally, Brennan's "fullest opportunity" permitted a federal trial of the state trial and the police behavior preceding that trial insofar as it was relevant to the underlying claim of a constitutional violation. This received a fuller elaboration in Warren's companion opinion in *Townsend*, which required a hearing when the facts alleged were in dispute. The federal judge had to ascertain historical facts and could not defer to the fact-finding of the state judges unless the state courts had "after a full hearing reliably found the relevant facts." All the justices agreed with the standard, but the four more conservative justices dissented on the application of that standard to the facts of *Townsend*, where the majority reversed the federal courts below and ordered a hearing on the prisoner's allegation that his confession was the result of being given "truth serum" by a police doctor as a supposed aid to the prisoner when he was suffering from drug withdrawal. *Townsend* was the key opinion in getting Sheppard his federal hearing.

Whatever the promise of *Noia* and *Townsend*, the petition for habeas must articulate facts that demonstrate a constitutional violation, and despite Gideon's luck with his handwritten petition, the odds of someone sitting in jail presenting a plausible brief to a court without assistance are slim. No one understood this better than federal judges, and in 1969 in *Johnson v. Avery* the Court held that a prison could not prevent prisoners from helping other prisoners prepare their habeas petitions. Fortas, for all but Black and White, concluded that any other holding would leave illiterate and indigent prisoners without remedies (since the states had no interest in offering legal aid). If they had a meritorious claim, the Court wanted to facilitate its presentation.

Noia offered a huge boon for one special group of inmates. Capital defendants might not win, but they could use habeas to stave off their execution dates in the hopes that future legal developments would offer a chance of success. In the year in which *Noia* was decided, there were twenty-one executions in the country. In 1964, there were fifteen; in 1965, seven; in 1966, only one; in 1967, two; and then they stopped. To be sure, there were other more important factors, but habeas and its promise of delay mattered. Robert Swain, the nineteen-year-old African-American whose death penalty following his rape conviction was affirmed by the Court in 1965 when it rejected his claim that the prosecution had used its peremptory challenges in a racially discriminatory manner, avoided execution thanks to the delays of habeas.

In 1969 alone, there were about 9,000 habeas petitions filed by state prisoners, part of "a writ-writing binge that is unique in the history of penology."[10] Yet despite the rhetorical flourishes and the freeing of Sam

Sheppard, the "Great Writ" remained an illusory hope in the 1960s, very much like winning the lottery, because it was rare indeed for a prisoner to gain ultimate success—in no small part because of the way the Court chose to redefine constitutional rights. When the Court was done, it made clear to everyone that a constitutional right comes into existence on the day the Court announces it. These cases showed that the function of *Noia* was not to retry old cases (and therefore in 1970 the Court ruled that a guilty plea waived the right to seek habeas); it was to retry new cases applying the newly created rules from *Mapp* to *Miranda* to *Wade-Gilbert*. As a civil rights lawyer observed shortly after Warren retired, "federal habeas corpus jurisdiction as it exists at present is proof of a profound skepticism toward criminal adjudication."[11]

State judges understood and resented that skepticism, even though *Noia*, because it seemed like a technical issue of federal jurisdiction, initially passed unnoticed by the press. Strangely, state judges, who had been complaining about federal habeas for over a decade, did not escalate their rhetoric even though the Court had ratcheted up their underlying complaint. One reason may have been that *Brown v. Allen* had already caused the damage; another was that their chosen vehicle for correcting the problem was already in place. Almost unnoticed, state legislatures were proposing a constitutional convention to consider one or more states-rights amendments.

With the Council on State Governments, state chief justices were pushing one of the amendments, the creation of a Court of the Union, composed of themselves, to review Supreme Court decisions affecting federal-state relations. If adopted, it would be a supreme court above the Supreme Court, and not surprisingly it had no fans at the Court.

Using the annual meeting of the prestigious American Law Institute in May 1963 as his forum, Warren attacked the amendments as "radically changing the character of our institutions."[12] Thereafter, heavy hitters from Charles Black to Henry Steele Commager to the AFL-CIO to the Board of Governors of the American Bar Association and the U.S. Conference of Mayors attacked the proposals in every forum available. The strongest language came in an article in the *New York State Bar Association Journal*, which contended that "the threat to our institutions posed by this is as real and as dangerous as the threat of communism."[13] During the summer, the push for amendments just ran out of steam. "Even the council's National Legislative Conference backed away from the amendments at its August 1963 meeting."[14] Thereafter, the proposed amendments themselves began to focus exclusively on preserving legislative jobs by undoing *Reynolds v. Sims,* and this too just petered out between 1965 and 1967. To add insult to injury, while the amendments were dying, the second session of Lyndon Johnson's 89th Congress even codified *Townsend.*

Are New Rights Applicable Retroactively?

In *Gideon*'s wake, Florida opened its prison doors and released almost a thousand convicts who, like Gideon, had been convicted without the benefit of counsel. Florida's action, although drastic, reflected the meaning of constitutional rights. If the accused had a right to counsel at trial, then everyone convicted without counsel had been denied their constitutional rights. While this has a soothing sound, imagine if *Mapp v. Ohio* or *Miranda v. Arizona* were substituted for *Gideon v. Wainwright.* Instead of a thousand Florida prisoners, there would have been thousands upon thousands of prisoners freed from the half of the states that had, prior to 1961, rejected the exclusionary rule or, worse, a total emptying of the nation's jails of everyone whose confession had been introduced into evidence, a group that would include an astonishing number of admitted murderers. The Court understood that such results would not be tolerated, and thus it enthusiastically changed the prevailing constitutional rule that criminal procedure decisions were retroactive. This explains why habeas success rates remained miniscule until the 1970s.

Mapp was initially, and reflexively, applied to all cases on direct review. But that was the next to the last time a major new criminal procedure rule aimed at police or prosecutorial behavior was so applied. A series of cases, from *Linkletter v. Walker* in 1965 to *Desist v. United States* in 1969, tightened and then eliminated retroactive application of the Court's criminal procedure rules unless the purpose of a rule was to protect the innocent. As a result of the Court's decisions, *Gideon* applied to everyone; *Mapp* and *Griffin v. California* (holding that the state cannot comment to the jury on the defendant's choice not to testify) applied to all nonfinal cases; *Miranda* applied to trials beginning after its rule was announced; *Wade-Gilbert* and *Katz* applied only to police conduct occurring after their rules were announced. In each case, the Court became more restrictive.

Brennan, as usual, was given the task of attempting to make sense of what the Court was doing. In *Stovall v. Denno,* a case selected to announce whether a rule—counsel at lineups—created the same day should be applied retroactively, Brennan found three factors dominated the decision: (1) the purpose to be served by the new rule; (2) the extent of reliance by law enforcement on the old rule; and (3) the effect on the administration of justice by the retroactive application of the new rule. Obviously, the third factor was the opening of the prisons, something that would always be an important aspect of retroactivity. It explained fully why *Mapp, Griffin,* and *Miranda* were not retroactive. The second factor seldom seemed to matter; it asked whether police should have anticipated the new decision and that answer was invariably no, so much so that in *Desist* the Court pretended that police should have been surprised to learn that electronic surveillance without a warrant was a Fourth Amendment violation. The first factor asked, in effect, whether the new rules were designed to protect the determination of innocence or to deter police and prosecutors from behavior the Court concluded was violative of the Constitution. If it was the former, like *Gideon,* then the rule was wholly retroactive. But if it was to control police or prosecutors, like the subsequent cases, then retroactivity was out, and the Court could, as it increasingly did, make the rule prospective only.

A year before *Stovall, Johnson v. New Jersey* had held that *Miranda* applied only to trials commenced after it was announced. While this must have seemed innocuous to the Court, the holding immediately caused unanticipated grief. A handful of murderers who had confessed, but whose cases had yet to come to trial, got the benefit of *Miranda* and walked free to an avalanche of adverse publicity for both the Court and *Miranda. Stovall*'s rule precluded any such accidents and therefore any such publicity.

The nonretroactivity cases rested on the conclusion that the Court was free to create whatever rules it wished because "the Constitution neither prohibits nor requires retroactive effect." The justices thus took their cue from a Cardozo quote—"We think the federal Constitution has no voice on the subject"—and used their own voice to create what they assumed was the best possible rule. In so doing, the nonretroactivity cases produced the first two-person split in the liberal bloc as Black and Douglas dissented, while Warren, Brennan, and Goldberg (and then Fortas) joined with Clark, Harlan, Stewart, and White to create the law.

If the nonretroactivity majority appears somewhat of an unusual alliance, it was—the two blocs had joined together for entirely different reasons. Warren, Brennan, and Fortas voted for nonretroactivity because it freed them to do good. They understood that if the criminal procedure rules were retroactive, then there would be a huge backlash against the changes and the Court. Making the decisions nonretroactive muted that backlash. Clark, Harlan, Stewart, and White also wished to minimize the effects of the criminal procedure decisions, not to free them to do more but because they believed the decisions were wrong. They voted nonretroactivity to minimize the damage, not the backlash, the decisions would cause. What these four did not perceive was that the best way to minimize damage was to make the rules retroactive. If a constitutional rule was retroactive, then those creating the rule might be more cautious in doing so. If we perceive the five liberals as addicted to new criminal procedure rules, the other four were unwitting facilitators through their nonretroactivity votes.

Black and Douglas believed not only that the Court was undermining *Noia* but, more important, that it was behaving lawlessly. When *Linkletter* denied the defendant the benefit of *Mapp*, Black called it "a grossly invidious and unfair discrimination against Linkletter simply because he happened to be prosecuted in a State that was evidently well up with its criminal court docket." It was even worse with *Miranda* where, out of scores of confession cases, many involving the death penalty, the Court initially granted certiorari in only four. *Miranda* was the lead case because the justices knew Ernesto Miranda was represented by John P. Frank, a former Black clerk, author of four books on the Court, on friendly terms with all the justices and especially friendly with Black, Warren, and Clark, a frequent advocate before the Court, and a member of both the Advisory Committee on Civil Rules and the American Law Institute; in a word, Frank was connected. The Court could be confident that counsel would do a good job briefing and arguing.

Johnson, involving two capital defendants, Sylvester Johnson and Stanley Cassidy, was selected to announce the nonretroactivity rule. Although *Johnson* was on collateral review, the nonretroactivity rule would have nothing to do with collateral review. Subsequently a fifth case, *California v. Stewart,* was added to the mix because the California Supreme Court had held for Stewart and yet the nonretroactivity rule the Court would announce in *Johnson* would have stripped Stewart of his win. That would have been too unjust. Nevertheless, Stewart and Miranda (and the two others) who got the benefit of *Miranda* were indistinguishable from the scores already on the Court's docket who did not (not to mention the unknown numbers whose convictions were not yet final but who had yet to come to the stage to petition the Court). In the case of Johnson and Cassidy, they were distinguishable on the basis of final-nonfinal judgments, but that was a point the Court found irrelevant. The whole process made a mockery out of the words chiseled on the Court's Marble Palace: "Equal Justice Under Law."

In *Linkletter,* Black had a final observation, one that resonated over the entire area. "The inference I gather . . . is that the rule is not a right or privilege accorded to defendants charged with crime but is a sort of punishment against officers in order to keep them from depriving people of their constitutional rights. In passing I would say that if that is the sole purpose, reason, object and effect of the rule, the Court's action in adopting it sounds more like law-making than construing the Constitution." Whatever the rhetorical power of Black and Douglas, the reality was that they would have emptied America's jails of everyone whose confession had been admitted at trial or who had been convicted with illegally seized evidence—no matter when the police action occurred. The country, by then racked with riots, would not have stood for it. If that was what *Miranda* meant, then *Miranda,* not the prisoners, would have had to go.

In *Desist,* which dealt with the retroactivity of the requirement of *Katz v. United States* that electronic surveillance be pursuant to a court order, Harlan suddenly shifted and adopted at least part of Black and Douglas's conclusion that the Court had been behaving less as a Court and more as a legislature. Harlan reverted to the rule originally announced in *Linkletter;* a new constitutional standard should apply to all cases where there was not yet a final judgment. Harlan acknowledged that he had joined contrary holdings in *Johnson* and *Stovall* but stated that he had done so because he believed that the constitutional holdings of *Escobedo-Miranda* and *Wade-Gilbert* were so wrong that they should be limited at all costs. Now he concluded that the costs had been too high because the costs had turned out to be the Court's ceasing to behave like a judicial body. Harlan believed that the idea of a rule of law had to trump the expediency of prospective holdings. If a rule was a legal rule, then it had to be applied to all nonfinal cases as had been traditional until *Johnson.*

Harlan's opinion showed there was a principled response to Black and Douglas, one that not only conformed to law but made sense as well. Still one cannot help but wonder whether Harlan's new insight stemmed from the fact that every prior retroactivity case involved a constitutional rule that Harlan believed was wrong, while *Katz* had been a decision that Harlan supported. Nevertheless, Harlan's *Desist* dissent was one of his finest contributions.

The majority—always including Warren, Brennan, Stewart, and White—was, however, unwilling to pay Harlan's price. From Warren's and Brennan's perspective, if too many convicted defendants were freed, then the Court might be unable to continue its important and good work in improving police and prosecutorial behavior. If some injustices to individuals occurred, that was an acceptable price to pay for the overall gains to the system. After all, the Court had made a similar judgment in *Brown II* when it held that the rights protected in *Brown* need not be accorded the prevailing parties in the case.

Habeas and nonretroactivity were being molded to achieve a complementary goal. As a result of the nonretroactivity cases, the function of *Noia* and *Townsend* was not to apply constitutional rules to those who found themselves in jail that day. Thus, Warren always bristled when anyone suggested "the impact of the Warren Court innovations in criminal procedure was to turn criminals out of jails to threaten the public."[15] Because of nonretroactivity of the criminal procedure rules, even *Noia* and *Townsend* turned out to be prospective (except for death-row inmates). *Noia* and *Townsend* were to enlist the federal judiciary to police the state courts and the latter's application of the new standards the Court was creating. When the Court announced a new rule, the justices wanted to make sure it was faithfully applied to new cases. Federal judges operating under *Noia* could ensure that reluctant state judges were brought into line.

Can a Constitutional Violation Be Harmless?

Like retroactivity, the Court had yet another significant constitutional change that would operate to keep criminals in jail. Up until the mid-1960s, a constitutional error automatically resulted in reversal of a conviction. After all, constitutional rules were not mere technicalities. But the Court created so many new rules that it was no longer certain that every constitutional violation necessitated a new trial. Adopting the judicial version of the way National Basketball Association referees operate on a "no harm, no foul" basis, the Court authorized state judges to find that constitutional violations did not affect the determination of guilt. Thus, even if some evidence at trial was improperly admitted, a conviction would not be overturned if the defendant was otherwise plenty guilty—because under these circumstances the improper admission of the evidence, while error, was harmless.

The catalyst was the Court's 1965 rule in *Griffin v. California* that prosecutors no longer were free to comment adversely on the defendant's failure to take the stand. The Court concluded that allowing prosecutors to do so placed a burden on the defendant's exercise of his privilege not to testify. Two years later in *Chapman v. California,* the state supreme court had ruled that despite the prosecutor's adverse comment on Chapman's failure to testify, Chapman's conviction was amply supported by the evidence and should be affirmed. While the Court agreed with the California court that some constitutional violations could safely be deemed harmless, it ruled that harmless error had to be tested by a federal standard. The federal standard, which Black then created, was that the state must prove beyond a reasonable doubt that the error was harmless. Stewart concurred, suggesting that the automatic reversal for violations of *Griffin* "seemed best calculated" to deter prosecutors—possibly Stewart was twitting the Court since he had dissented in *Griffin.* Harlan dissented, stating that a state should be allowed to apply its own harmless-error rule.

A further two years later in *Harrington v. California,* the Court concluded that the introduction of a nontestifying codefendant's confession at a joint trial—a violation of the Sixth Amendment's Confrontation Clause—was harmless error under *Chapman.* Douglas's opinion seemed to water *Chapman* down—indeed, Warren, Brennan, and Marshall in dissent claimed it overruled it. Douglas noted that the confession was "cumulative" and the evidence of guilt was "overwhelming." The dissenters noted that the majority opinion had shifted the focus from whether the constitutional error contributed to the conviction to whether the untainted evidence overwhelmingly supported conviction. The dissenters were correct, but Harrington was plenty guilty.

Capital Punishment

From the modern vantage point, it is difficult to realize that as late as 1965 the official policy statement of the American Civil Liberties Union was that capital punishment did not present a civil liberties issue. Nor had the Court spoken a word to the issue—possibly because the Constitution did so explicitly. Stripping out the double negatives, both the Fifth and Fourteenth Amendments textually authorize the taking of a life so long as due process of law is accorded the defendant. For Black, but Black alone, that settled the matter. But Black's defection from his liberal allies was neutralized by the fact that the capital punishment cases began in the 1967 Term and by then the Court was ready to speak. Clark had been replaced by Marshall, and while Marshall was a pragmatic and not an ideological liberal, the mutual reinforcement of race and death created an exception. Marshall, during his twenty-four-year career, never once voted to sustain a capital sentence.

Alexander Bickel wrote of the Court and capital punishment in 1962 that "barring spectacular extraneous events, the moment of judgment on it is therefore a generation or more away."[16] While the Court was silent, capital punishment had been on the wane for some time: in the 1940s, there was an average of 128 executions per year; in the 1950s, 72; between 1960–1962, 48 per year; then but 21 in 1963. Thus, those executed seemed even more randomly selected than those who were released on habeas. "The few men who were selected to die had impressed many a warden, prison chaplain, and penologist as poor, uneducated, friendless, and disproportionately black. Former San Quentin warden Clinton T. Duffy stated flatly that he had never known a person of means to be executed."[17] Although a jury found Sheppard had hit his pregnant wife's head with a blunt object thirty-five times to kill her, he received a life sentence.

At the time Bickel wrote, Warren, Black, Douglas, and Brennan saw capital punishment the same as Frankfurter or Clark or Harlan or Stewart did—as purely an issue of state law. When Warren concluded in *Trop v. Dulles* that expatriation for desertion from the military was cruel and unusual punishment but executing the deserter would not be, he was, on the latter point at least, speaking for everyone. Indeed, as late as 1965 in *Swain v. Alabama,* no justice in either the majority or the dissent even hinted that the issue of death might make the case special. Yet just four years later the Court was taking major strides toward making the death penalty impossible to implement and, therefore, maybe unconstitutional as well.

Bickel's triggering "spectacular extraneous events" were hardly spectacular. One was a Goldberg dissent from denial of certiorari just a year later; the other was the Legal Defense Fund lawyers needing something important to do as "the long golden days of the civil rights movement had begun to wane."[18]

At the beginning of the 1963 Term, Goldberg tried to convince the Court to take two rape cases, *Rudolph v. Alabama* and *Snider v. Cunningham,* where the defendants were sentenced to death. He wrote a short, heavily footnoted dissent to the denial of certiorari that highlighted potential legal issues. Douglas and Brennan joined him, but neither Warren nor Black would provide the necessary fourth vote to grant certiorari and hear the case.

Goldberg's dissent received an interested read by the LDF lawyers, who, like the ACLU, had not thought of the issue as one of civil liberties or civil rights. Marshall's successor, Jack Greenberg, authorized funds to study the issue, and in 1965 the LDF decided to make capital punishment its prime litigation issue. For the LDF, the timing was propitious. First, the "golden days" were in the past, and with the Civil Rights Act of 1964, the Justice Department became the moving force in school desegregation litigation. Second, the NAACP was a civil rights organization and the death penalty disproportionally affected African-Americans. The LDF lawyers, like most who thought they understood capital punishment during this era, mistakenly believed that a defendant convicted of murder was more likely to be sentenced to death if he was an African-American. (It turned out that the race of the victim, not that of the defendant, was the significant factor.) The LDF lawyers correctly understood, moreover, that 90 percent of all rapists sentenced to death were African-American. Finally, the death penalty was mostly a southern problem. Since 1930, 2,306 of the 3,859 executions in the United States occurred in the District of Columbia, the border states, and the states of the Old Confederacy. If lynchings were added in (since many a victim would have been legally executed later), the South's ratio would have been higher. While publicized executions, like those of Ethel and Julius Rosenberg and Caryl Chessman, had ignited debates in the North, like so many other national trends this one had stopped at the Ohio River.

The LDF determined it would represent any capital defendant, whether African-American or white, whether in the North or the South, who requested assistance because everyone on death row had a similar stake in the abolition of the death penalty. The effort would require time and attorneys, and inevitably that meant money. The enormous undertaking might have proven impossible had it not been for a million-dollar grant from the Ford Foundation in 1967.

Once the LDF got involved, death litigation changed in at least three ways. First, for either their appeals or habeas, the poorest and most despised of defendants got superb lawyers, especially former Frankfurter clerk and youthful University of Pennsylvania professor, Anthony Amsterdam, the acknowledged leading advocate of his generation. Second, the LDF had decades of credibility with the Court that it could draw upon. Third, after two executions in 1967, stays of execution, whether individually or statewide, became the order of the day. No person was thereafter executed during Warren's tenure—indeed, until 1977.

During each of the last two terms of the Warren Court, two death penalty cases were argued. In the 1967 Term, *United States v. Jackson* and *Witherspoon v. Illinois* produced results that led many to believe the death penalty was on its last legs. The two from the 1968 Term, *Boykin v. Alabama* and *Maxwell v. Bishop,* had the potential to both substantively and procedurally transform the death penalty, but both were inconclusive.

Jackson involved an appeal from a decision of a district court judge to invalidate the Federal Kidnapping Act, adopted in the wake of the Lindbergh kidnapping and then amended two years later to make kidnapping a potential capital crime when the victim is injured. As the law was written, only a jury could sentence a defendant to death. Therefore, a defendant could avoid any chance of the death penalty either by pleading guilty or requesting a trial by the judge alone. In the case of the former, the defendant waived all his rights; in the case of the latter, he waived his Sixth Amendment right to a jury trial.

Stewart agreed with the judge below that the Federal Kidnapping Act unconstitutionally put the defendant to a choice between avoiding any chance of death or his constitutional right to a jury trial. "[T]he evil in the federal statute is not that it necessarily *coerces* guilty pleas and jury waivers but simply that it needlessly *encourages* them." The Government also argued that the procedure was ameliorative because it permitted defendants to completely avoid the risk of death. Stewart replied that of course Congress could mitigate the severity of a potential sentence, but it could not do so by penalizing those who wished to exercise their constitutional rights.

Stewart then rejected the trial judge's conclusion that the Federal Kidnapping Act was void. A kidnapper could be constitutionally convicted, just not executed. It was a perfect compromise. The death penalty in the Federal Kidnapping Act and seven other federal statutes was void, but no one walked free. Life in prison was a valid substitute for death.

White and Black dissented without passion. The passion came two months later when, joined by Harlan, they dissented in *Witherspoon* when Stewart's majority held that Illinois's so-called "death qualified" jury was unconstitutional because it excluded those opposed, but not necessarily completely so, to capital punishment. Stewart claimed the state had "stacked the deck" to bring about a death sentence. The dissenters responded that "one might much more appropriately charge that this Court has today written the law in such a way that the States are being forced to try their murder cases with biased juries. If this Court is to hold capital punishment unconstitutional, it should do so forthrightly, not by making it impossible for the States to get juries that will enforce the death penalty." The latter, however, was perceived to be *Witherspoon*'s charm.

Witherspoon was an attack on the capital-jury system in Illinois and, by implication, elsewhere. The state allowed the prosecution to remove for cause any potential juror who has "conscientious scruples against capital punishment or is opposed to the same." Forty-seven prospective jurors, half the panel, for Witherspoon's murder trial were removed on this basis even though only five stated that they could not impose the death sentence under any circumstances. One juror was dismissed for cause because she said that she disliked "to be responsible for deciding someone should be put to death."

Witherspoon was convicted and sentenced to death. He argued that the Illinois procedure denied him a jury representing a cross-section of the community, and, in fact, by giving him a death-qualified jury, the state made it more likely that the jury would convict in the first place. Amsterdam wrote a lengthy amicus brief for the LDF that outraged Witherspoon's counsel, for it argued that the constitutional infirmity was not that the jury was more likely to convict but rather that it was more likely to choose death. Witherspoon's argument, if accepted, would have reversed his conviction and set lots of others free as well (including, if logic was a guide, anyone convicted by a death-qualified jury regardless of the sentence imposed); the LDF's argument, if accepted, would have vacated his death sentence and left him and others similarly situated in prison for life.

Stewart's opinion tracked the LDF position. The jury was more prone to vote for death than one drawn from a cross-section of the community. While a state could exclude those who would never, under any circumstances, vote for the death penalty, it must accept others who have lesser opposition. Douglas concurred, but he adopted Witherspoon's position to demand that a jury be taken from the whole community, not just those who might administer death.

Witherspoon was a bombshell because everyone assumed that without a death-qualified jury the death penalty was an impossibility. Somewhere between half and two-thirds of American adults professed opposition to the death penalty. If they could not be completely excluded, it would be a freak jury indeed that would be willing to vote for death. Thus, the Texas attorney general stated that "[i]t would be a very, very remote case where anyone would get the death penalty."[19] The Mississippi attorney general went further, stating "[i]t looks like the Supreme Court has set about to repeal the various death penalty statutes in the States."[20] The Georgia attorney general went all the way; *Witherspoon* would "definitely end capital punishment in Georgia."[21] While there is always the risk of hyperbole, *Witherspoon* did, indeed, look like the end of the death penalty. If only the rarest of juries could be found to impose a capital sentence, then executions, rare already, would look truly "unusual" and be headed for judicial extinction.

At the beginning of the next term, the Court granted certiorari in *Boykin* and *Maxwell*. In context, they looked in part like a mop-up action in *Witherspoon*'s wake and in part like the beginning of the main event, the end of capital punishment.

Edward Boykin, Jr., an African-American, was indicted for committing five armed robberies in Mobile during a two-week period, with takes ranging from $150 to $373. During one of the robberies, he fired a shot that ricocheted into a woman's leg. A witness said she thought Boykin had not intended to hit anyone. Boykin was guilty, and he so pleaded.

Under a unique Alabama procedure, the judge then convened a sentencing jury, held a quick trial on the facts, and informed the jury they could give Boykin anywhere from ten years in the penitentiary to death. After less than an hour of deliberation, the jury returned five death sentences!

On appeal, Boykin argued that death for armed robbery was cruel and unusual punishment prohibited by the Eighth Amendment and further that his court-appointed attorney had not made him aware that a guilty plea could leave him at the risk of electrocution. Like the two denials of cert that produced the Goldberg dissent, *Boykin* could have been a vehicle for ruling that death is cruel and unusual—especially the latter—for a crime that does not involve the death of another. Only nine states authorized death for armed robbery, and while more did so for rape, they still were confined to the South.

The Court, through Douglas, went off instead on the guilty plea. A guilty plea waives all constitutional rights, and waivers of rights must be knowingly made. Douglas ruled that, before accepting the guilty plea, the trial judge was under a constitutional duty to inquire whether the defendant understood the nature and consequences of his plea. Harlan, with Black, dissented, claiming that Boykin had never raised any questions about his plea during the trial proceedings. (Why a legally untrained defendant should be expected to know such questions was left unexplained. But, of course, "Boykin" actually meant Boykin's lawyer, who might have been expected to inform his client. This opens the problems about the actual zeal or competence of lawyers, a subject that the Warren Court, like its successors, studiously avoided.)

Maxwell v. Bishop was the first case to reach the Court that the LDF had developed from scratch for habeas. Maxwell was an African-American sentenced to death for raping a white woman. The LDF put together a statistical study to demonstrate racial discrimination in rape sentencing generally, but the Eighth Circuit, in an opinion by Harry Blackmun, rejected the argument on the ground that the statistics, even if accurate, did not show discrimination against Maxwell individually.

The Court's grant of certiorari specifically limited the LDF to its other two arguments, also rejected by Blackmun, that, first, capital sentencing requires a bifurcated trial and, second, capital sentencing is only constitutional if the legislature sets standards for the jury to follow. The former claim would require that juries in death cases make a determination of guilt in one phase of the trial, which then would be followed by a second phase to determine punishment. The theory behind bifurcation was simple. Many defendants exercise their Fifth Amendment rights not to testify. There are numerous reasons, one of which is that many states authorize the prosecution to question a defendant about prior convictions, and defense attorneys fear that the defendant may be convicted because the prosecution will show he is a bad person deserving jail (or death), whether or not he committed the crime charged. Bifurcation would allow the defendant to exercise his Fifth Amendment right and still, at the second phase, speak to the jury about clemency.

Standardless sentencing was an attack on capital punishment nationwide. The claim was that the state, by not offering the jury guidelines for choosing between life and death, left the jury free to act for any reason or for no reason whatsoever. A death penalty under such circumstances is arbitrary and capricious and therefore violates due process of law. Arkansas responded that the drawing of standards for such an awesome decision was impossible; therefore, if the Court required them, it would necessarily be ending capital punishment in the United States (albeit by indirection). In rebuttal, Amsterdam showed that the state's argument was identical to those of supporters of the English Bloody Code of the eighteenth century, under which there had been 250 capital offenses, and it was claimed that this was a "wise policy of keeping in the net every crime which under any possible circumstances may merit the punishment of death and then letting individual circumstances ferret it out."[22]

Warren, Douglas, Brennan, Fortas, and Marshall agreed with the LDF position on bifurcation. Harlan initially did but then retreated to uncertainty. Stewart and White wanted to reverse Maxwell's sentence on *Witherspoon* grounds (even though the issue had not been raised). Black, alone, would have affirmed. Fortas's resignation intervened, and there was no majority for any position. As a result, *Maxwell* was set for reargument the following term (when the sentence was vacated on *Witherspoon*).

Juvenile Justice

A week after *Miranda,* the Court agreed to hear *In re Gault,* a case challenging all the essential features of the juvenile-justice system, which had developed at the end of the nineteenth century as a humane alternative to treating juvenile offenders (past the age of seven) just like adult criminals. Fortas, who as counsel had helped transform both criminal insanity and counsel for indigents, wanted *Gault* for himself to reform yet another area, and Warren gave the opinion to him. Fortas had written *Kent v. United States,* a federal juvenile case, the year before and had developed decided views on the juvenile-justice system, to wit, that it offered the child the worst of both worlds—neither procedural protections at trial nor solicitous care afterwards. *Gault* is Fortas's major opinion, and, in accordance with Fortas's views that the system needed a total overhaul, it pretty much held the whole juvenile-justice system to be a violation of due process of law.

Gault begins with a sympathetic and not entirely accurate statement of the facts that emphasized the injustice to Gerald Gault—which was real. For making a lewd phone call to a neighbor, he was sentenced to six years, until the age of twenty-one, in a juvenile-detention center. Had Gault been eighteen instead of fifteen, the most he could have received for the offense was two months in jail.

Thereafter, Fortas discussed the origins of the juvenile-justice system, including the theory that the state was operating as *parens patriae* to aid the child. "The constitutional and theoretical basis for this peculiar system is—to say the least—debatable." Thereafter, Fortas catalogs the procedural high-handedness that often attended juvenile proceedings. "Under our Constitution, the condition of being a boy does not justify a kangaroo court."

Any defects in procedure were supposedly outweighed by attendant benefits. "But it is important, we think, that the claimed benefits of the juvenile process should be candidly appraised. Neither sentiment nor folklore should cause us to shut our eyes" to startling data on high rates of recidivism. Relying on a single Russell Sage Foundation study, Fortas stated that "when the procedural laxness of the *'parens patriae'* attitude is followed by stern disciplining, the contrast may have an adverse effect upon the child who feels he has been deceived or enticed." The system simply failed to work as promised decades earlier. "The fact of the matter is that however euphemistic the title, a 'receiving home' or an 'industrial school' for juveniles is an institution of confinement in which the child is incarcerated for a greater or lesser time" and too often not to his benefit.

Having detailed the reasons for the needed changes, Fortas then moved through the Bill of Rights to pick out the provisions that due process would require for juvenile proceedings. Fortas required notice of the charges and hearing, right to counsel, right to cross-examine and confront witnesses, and the privilege against self-incrimination. Fortas did not decide whether there had to be a transcript of the proceedings to facilitate appellate or habeas review, but when he noted that otherwise the juvenile judge could be called as a witness and cross-examined in habeas, he was clearly signaling to the state supreme court what it should order on remand.

The due process decisions with adults had been incremental though rapid. None did so much as *Gault* in one fell swoop; nor did any rely on such thin social science evidence for their conclusions either.

Black, White, Harlan, and Stewart each wrote separately. Black was uninterested in what was fair; he believed that juveniles, like adults, should "be tried in accordance with all the guarantees of the Bill of Rights." White agreed with Fortas's opinion—except for its treatment of self-incrimination, confrontation, and cross-examination, all of which he thought it unnecessary to decide. Harlan believed that no more constitutional restrictions than necessary should be imposed and that any restrictions "should be those which preserve, so far as possible, the essential elements of the State's purpose." He thought those were notice, counsel, and a written record that allowed for judicial review.

Stewart completely opposed constitutionalizing the juvenile-justice system. His dissent looked to the past to offer an unsettling prediction of the future. "The inflexible restrictions that the Constitution so wisely made applicable to adversary criminal trials have no inevitable place in the proceedings of those public social agencies known as juvenile or family courts. And to impose the Court's long catalog of requirements upon juvenile proceedings in every area of the country is to invite a long step backwards into the Nineteenth Century. In that era there were no juvenile proceedings, and a child was tried in a conventional criminal court with all the trappings of a conventional criminal trial. So it was that a 12-year-old boy named James Guild was tried in New Jersey for killing Catharine Beakes. A jury found him guilty of murder, and he was sentenced to death by hanging. The sentence was executed. It was all very constitutional."

Fortas believed changes were necessary to treat juveniles not as adults as they had been in the nineteenth century, and not as outsiders, as they were, but rather as American citizens, deserving procedural protections on the one hand and subsequent help on the other. If legislatures or state judiciaries could not implement the needed correctives, the Court could, and *Gault,* coupled with other factors, led to a wave of legislative revisions of the juvenile-justice system, designed to rid it of its worst defects. Thus, Fortas and his majority and concerned participants would have found Stewart's hyperbolic prediction unbelievable. Was it really thinkable that a nation that seemed to be on the way to abolishing the death penalty would choose to kill, rather than rehabilitate, misbehaving children?

Mentally Impaired Criminal Defendants

Leroy Powell was an alcoholic who, according to his own testimony, lived in Austin, Texas, made $12 a week shining shoes in a tavern, drank wine every day, got drunk at least once a week, and had a hundred convictions of public intoxication since when drunk he typically would eventually lie down in a public place and go to sleep. Powell was cooperative and never a danger to anyone except himself. Despite his numerous convictions, he had never been referred to Alcoholics Anonymous or sent to the state hospital.

When arrested the week before Christmas in 1966, he was convicted and fined $20. He then received a trial de novo in another court of very limited criminal jurisdiction, and his lawyer introduced medical evidence, via a single doctor, that he was a chronic alcoholic and that as an alcoholic had no choice but to drink; therefore, to punish him, a human being who was not morally culpable, was cruel and unusual in violation of the Eighth Amendment. That argument was rejected, and Powell was now fined $50. There was no higher court in Texas to which he could appeal from such a lowly court, so he appealed instead to the Supreme Court, relying on its 1962 decision in *Robinson v. California* that held a statute making it a crime to "be addicted to the use of narcotics" violated the Eighth Amendment.

The underlying debate among the justices was whether *Robinson* and the Eighth Amendment would be read to create a federal constitutional immunity from criminal punishment based on mental impairment. The justices worried about the thinness of both the record and the available knowledge about alcoholism. Should the Court plunge ahead with a rule that would bind the whole nation when it really could not be certain of the underlying problems? Fortas had an answer. "We are similarly woefully deficient in our medical, diagnostic, and therapeutic knowledge of mental disease and the problem of insanity; but few would urge that, because of this, we should totally reject that legal significance of what we do know about these phenomena." Fortas was making an express analogy to an area he believed he knew well. As an advocate fifteen years earlier, in *Durham v. United States* he had helped change the law of insanity by turning it over to trained professionals. Fortas saw *Powell v. Texas* as offering a similar opportunity with alcoholism by requiring the states to decriminalize it and either ignore the alcoholics or turn the problem over to experts. "The alcoholic offender is caught in a 'revolving door'—leading from arrest on the street through a brief, unprofitable sojourn in jail, back to the street and, eventually, another arrest. The jails, overcrowded and put to a use for which they are not suitable, have a destructive effect upon alcoholic inmates."

Durham had begun in 1951 when Monte Durham was arrested for housebreaking. He had been in and out of jail and mental hospitals since the end of the war and was diagnosed by psychiatrists as suffering from "psychosis with psychopathic personality." His insanity defense was rejected at trial, and he was convicted. After his case had been argued on appeal, the federal court of appeals in the District of Columbia appointed Fortas as his counsel and ordered a new round of briefing and reargument. Like *Gideon,* the case was a setup where the court was going to change the law and wanted able help in doing it.

At the time, virtually all courts used the century-old British *M'Naghten* rule for insanity. *M'Naghten* concluded that if, at the time of the crime, the defendant could distinguish right from wrong, then he was not excused by reason of insanity. Fortas, in a brief filled with psychiatric data, labeled *M'Naghten* obsolete and unresponsive to "psychiatric realities and scientific knowledge."[23] In the opinion ruling for Durham, Judge David Bazelon praised Fortas and created a new rule that asked instead whether the act was the product of a mental illness. The reason for the change was that Bazelon, other judges, and most in the mental health profession had concluded that *M'Naghten* kept from the jury relevant mental health evidence. *Durham* would allow juries to know what the professionals already knew.

Durham was nothing short of a judicial vote of confidence in the sophistication of psychiatry. The criminal justice system could be improved by bringing the insights of modern psychology to bear on the issues of causation. Fortas's biographer, Laura Kalman, noted that "a leading psychiatrist expressed his profession's satisfaction when he wrote to Fortas, 'You were largely responsible for the court's decision. . . . We can say, to paraphrase Galileo, "The law *do* move!"'"[24]

With *Robinson* as the fulcrum and *Durham* as the underlying theory, Fortas was ready to reform the law of alcoholism, and Douglas, Brennan, Stewart, and White were ready to join, with the former immediately assigning the opinion to Fortas. Harlan, not surprisingly, was on the other side, but he must have been stunned to be joined by Warren and Marshall as well as Black.

Fortas began by attempting to make the medical case as strong as it could be that alcoholics needed help, not jail. The medical evidence about what to do was hardly overwhelming, but that was of little concern. Fortas could select the best and, as a man of action, was hardly willing to let conflicting or insufficient data paralyze him.

Using *Durham* as an uncited analogy, Fortas employed the medical evidence to show that alcohol shattered Powell's will and, that like those of the insane, his acts were not voluntary. Following *Robinson* and *Durham*, therefore, when an individual does acts over which he has no control, he may not be constitutionally convicted.

Having made his best case about the involuntariness of alcoholism, Fortas disingenuously stated that "the questions for this Court are not settled by reference to medicine or penology" but rather by the principles of the Constitution—by which he meant the six-year-old *Robinson*. The syllogism was ready and, as syllogisms are wont, was easy. *Robinson* holds that "[c]riminal penalties may not be inflicted upon a person for being in a condition he is powerless to change." Chronic alcoholism is a condition that a person is powerless to change. Powell is a chronic alcoholic. Ergo, *Robinson* precludes punishing Powell; any such punishment would be cruel and unusual.

It does not take a long time to discover the hole in Fortas's reasoning as well as the sweep of its logic. Combine *Robinson*, Fortas's *Powell* opinion, and *Durham* and there would be a need "to rework the country's system of criminal law."[25] The hole was obvious; Powell was not punished because he was a chronic alcoholic. He was punished because he was drunk in public. If he stayed in his room and drank himself into a stupor, he would commit no crime. It is when he leaves his premises and ventures into public that Texas became interested in his conduct.

White saw the point and switched his vote to affirm the conviction. He agreed in general with Fortas's Eighth Amendment view but concluded that Powell had produced insufficient evidence to come within it. An "alcoholic is like a person with smallpox, who could be convicted for being on the street but not for being ill, or, like the epileptic, punishable for driving a car but not for his disease."

Marshall, for Warren, Black, and Harlan, also quite sensibly refused to accept the medical conclusions of a judge of a court of limited jurisdiction as true findings of fact. "It goes too far on the basis of too little knowledge." Nor was he as sure of the medical literature as Fortas, Marshall seeing it as less than unitary. But more important, he did not believe that *Robinson* was controlling. Texas "has imposed upon Powell a criminal sanction for public behavior which may create substantial health and safety hazards, and which offends the moral and esthetic sensibilities of a large segment of the community. This seems a far cry from convicting one for being an addict, being a chronic alcoholic, being 'mentally ill or a leper.'" Marshall's plurality thus limited *Robinson* to prohibit statutes creating crimes in terms of "status."

Fortas's law clerk reported that the loss of his *Powell* majority was "a big disappointment," and both the clerk and Kalman see Fortas's effort in *Powell* as "suggesting the depth of Fortas's commitment to the disenfranchised."[26] Perhaps, but this necessarily assumes that either doing nothing or turning the alcoholics over to the treatment of experts—in order, of course, to improve the alcoholics—is a demonstration of commitment to the disenfranchised. Marshall, hardly less committed to the disenfranchised, saw the problem differently. "It would be tragic to return large numbers of helpless, sometimes dangerous and frequently unsanitary inebriates to the streets of our cities without even the opportunity to sober up adequately which a brief jail term provides." Fortas is better characterized not by sympathy to the outsider, but by hubris and faith. He believed in modern science and social science. Tutored by legal realism, he demanded that the best evidence be brought to bear on a problem. Furthermore, he was supremely confident that he knew how to ascertain what the best evidence was. When he finished studying medical, or psychiatric, or social science literature, he knew how to tackle the relevant problem. Once he knew that, he also knew what the Constitution mandated. (Black hated this jurisprudence and had a strong personal antipathy toward Fortas, and just months later he would urge Alabama Senator Lister Hill, who had once been a close friend, to oppose Fortas's nomination as chief justice.)

It is no wonder Fortas is not the patron saint of Mothers Against Drunk Drivers. The same "irresistible impulse" that put Powell on Austin streets places other alcoholics behind the wheel of their cars. They certainly do not want to kill anyone while driving. It is, they claim, their condition, not their actions. To be sure, Fortas could state that being drunk on a sidewalk was a condition, while being drunk behind the wheel of a car was conduct that may be prohibited. Arbitrary lines are a fact of life in the law. But why draw it when a more sound line is already available? Being a chronic alcoholic is a condition; being drunk in public is conduct that may be prohibited.

Powell produced an extraordinary split among the liberals—the first time there were three on each side of a case. Warren, Black (to the limited extent he still was a liberal), and Marshall on the one side; Douglas, Brennan, and Fortas on the other. All were politically well attuned, but votes in *Powell* seem best understood in terms of how ideologically liberal they were and how willing they were to believe their own judgment was infallible. Fortas led the pack with Douglas and Brennan not far behind. Warren and Marshall were also secure in their own judgments but not so sure that when they knew what was in a body of literature they knew everything. Furthermore, while Fortas seemed sure that experts could solve the problems, Warren and Marshall "saw public drunkenness as a practical problem of government."[27] Had Fortas prevailed, some version of *Durham* would have been a federal constitutional mandate; yet *Durham* itself was discarded as unworkable by the D.C. Circuit in 1972.

The cases discussed in this chapter represent a reformist agenda writ large. Little of the criminal justice system escaped the Court's scrutiny and only drunkenness escaped an attempt at reform. A careful reading of White's opinion in *Powell v. Texas* indicates that he agreed with Fortas's reading of the Eighth Amendment to prohibit criminal conviction for some forms of provably involuntary conduct resulting from mental impairment. White just thought the evidence proffered was insufficient. That meant that there were five votes for the Fortas theory but events rendered that vote count moot, and Marshall's plurality opinion to the contrary has subsequently been seen as the authoritative one.

The changes in the criminal justice system were no accidents. Just as the Court was self-consciously changing the rules for police to force expertise and professionalism on their performance, it was changing the rules for prosecutors and judges and trying to ensure that the new rules were followed.

And why not? Congress, especially after the 1964 elections, was taking on poverty. But Congress was not dealing, indeed no one else was, with the aspects of poverty involving criminal justice. Like *Brown* before, the Court acted because no one else would. Furthermore, unlike *Brown,* the

Court also now believed no one else could do it better. Hence, the Court had no interest in alternative solutions. In the mid-1960s the American Law Institute was engaged in studies of criminal justice, but the Court, fully aware of this, could not wait. A majority of the justices were men of action, confident in their own judgment. If wide-scale social engineering of the criminal justice system was necessary—and they certainly believed it was—then who better to do it?

Despite the ambitiousness of the Court's agenda, the cases in this chapter, including *Witherspoon,* were nowhere near so charged as *Mapp* or *Miranda.* They were less visible, with results directed toward the future rather than the present, and left governments with options and criminals in jails. In terms of creating a move to check the Court, these cases are more comparable to the religion and obscenity cases than those regulating the police directly. The latter seemed to affect everyone and were played out against a rising tide of crime that offered headlines to reinforce what seemed to many to be the misguided tack taken by the Court. By contrast, the religion cases were affecting mostly rural Protestants and had the support of liberal Protestants and Jews plus a Catholic hierarchy focused elsewhere. The obscenity cases reflected the temper of the times and because of their interrelation with a profit motive had little impact in communities where the mores denied a market. The criminal-justice-reform cases in this chapter, while mixed, were similar. No one who was positive or neutral about the Court (or liberalism generally) was likely to be shifted negatively by the Court's actions.

Chapter 17

Wealth and Poverty

Judicial review of claims of wealth and poverty were identical at the beginning of the New Frontier. As *Fleming v. Nestor* showed, protection of economic claims was nonexistent. For the wealthy and business, defeats continued to mount up. For the poor, however, the Court created new rights but, unlike the other revolutionary changes beginning with the 1962 Term, the new results came later. Only after Congress committed itself to LBJ's Great Society programs did the Court even consider using the Constitution to aid the noncriminal poor. Then, as Johnson and Congress struggled unsuccessfully to provide both guns and butter, the Court began to see the plight of the poor as having a constitutional dimension.

The Criminal Law Wedge

The Warren Court's most systematic view of poverty came from the steady—and then in its last few terms vastly increased—flow of criminal cases because, as everyone realized, the criminal justice system always sees vastly more individuals near poverty than it does those of means, and this is especially true with crimes of violence. Ernesto Miranda, Danny Escobedo, Bennie Will Meyes, William Douglas, and, of course, Clarence Gideon were quite typical. They were poor and they won. (*Hoffa v. United States* was thus a totally atypical case. Not only did the defendant lose; he was one of three affluent criminal defendants at the Court along with Billie Sol Estes and Sam Sheppard.)

When *Gideon v. Wainwright* and *Douglas v. California* mandated that the states provide indigents with lawyers, the Court did more than order the outward trappings of a fair procedure. *Gideon* and *Douglas* mandated an in-kind wealth transfer to indigent defendants. No matter what it cost or where the money came from, lawyers had to be made available

445

at trial and on appeal. Either the state had to create a legal aid office and employ lawyers itself, or find a way of paying private practitioners to defend the poor, or simply order private practitioners to defend the poor as a price of being a member of the bar. Whichever way it was done, resources were moving from those who had some to those who had much less. Furthermore, this wealth transfer was done in the name of equality complete with the rhetoric from *Griffin v. Illinois.*

Griffin and *Gideon* were first steps of what proved to be an unmistakable, albeit ultimately limited, effort to constitutionalize the welfare state, using coerced wealth transfers to make the lives of the least fortunate better. *Griffin*'s statement that "there can be no equal justice where the kind of trial a man gets depends on the amount of money he has" is at once clearly correct and incapable of being taken literally as a constitutional command. But *Griffin*'s statement could be interpreted as a constitutional aspiration. Before government brought its resources to bear on an individual, it had to provide him with at least some measure of resources to fight back.

Astute commentators during the 1960s readily drew the connection between the Court's criminal procedure revolution and the Johnson administration's "War on Poverty"—parallel efforts at dealing with the same problem. Brennan sent Warren a memorandum during the drafting of *Miranda* urging a downplaying of race because "[i]f anything characterizes the group this opinion concerns it is poverty."[1] Despite *Miranda*'s shift from counsel to warnings, Warren's strongest animating concern was to place the impoverished defendant more closely in the shoes of the wealthier defendant. The Court could not offer cash, but it could and did provide knowledge about rights.

Like Great Society liberals, the justices knew their criminal procedure decisions neither caused nor encouraged criminal activity. Like Great Society liberals, the liberal justices believed that until the root causes of crime were seriously attacked, some Americans necessarily would be forced into criminal activity. The judiciary, of course, lacked the resources and the mandate to alleviate the root causes of crime. But the way those who were brought into the criminal justice system were treated was within the justices' mandate, and the liberal majority refused to add constitutional insult to economic and psychological injury.

Barely Disguised Poverty Cases

Criminal law was not the only area where outcomes had a more significant impact on the poor than the more affluent. *Griswold v. Con-*

necticut on contraceptives, *Board of Education v. Allen* on free textbooks, and *Levy v. Louisiana* on the consequences of illegitimacy can all be understood as poverty cases even though the words poverty and poor never appear in the opinions. The cases were part of a larger movement that was taking definite, but doctrinally uncertain, steps to create a constitutional shield for the poor from "the most elemental consequences of poverty: lack of funds to exchange for needed goods, services, or privileges of access" that the more affluent could purchase with their money.[2]

Before *Griswold*'s precursor, *Poe v. Ullman,* was argued, "a major medical journal, in a story picked up by national newspapers, quoted Connecticut doctors as explaining how the state law affected only those citizens too poor to pay private physicians for diaphragm fittings."[3] Private physicians could—and did—ignore the anticontraceptive law with impunity inasmuch as it allowed contraceptives to be prescribed ostensibly to prevent disease. When the Court refused to rule on the merits in *Poe,* the head of Yale's ob/gyn clinic told a reporter that the result "adds up to the rich getting contraceptives and the poor getting children."[4] *Griswold* remedied this intolerable violation of equal treatment— although not explicitly on equality grounds. With both equality and liberty interests pointing so strongly in the same direction, Connecticut's outdated law had no chance at the Court. The only issue was to be the rationale for explaining its invalidation, and that turned out to be a more difficult proposition than the justices might have expected. (Only *Red Lion Broadcasting v. Federal Communications Commission,* decided at the exact end of the era, offered a situation where liberty and equality interests might be perceived as in conflict, and the result sided with equality.)

Placing the New York textbook case, *Board of Education v. Allen,* on a poverty basis may seem odd, but it is best understood as an adjunct to the compromise between Catholics and public school teachers that allowed federal aid to flow more generously to education. The compromise was that aid would be targeted at disadvantaged students no matter where they attended school. To be sure, New York's textbook law aided all students regardless of circumstances, but for the less affluent, every penny counts and being given free books may be the tipping factor that allows some of the less affluent to leave public schools. This ought to have been true in the era where the Catholic Church was searching for outside funding to keep its schools flourishing.

Although no one said so, *Allen* was the opening shot in the ongoing battle over whether assistance to private schools (or their students) attracts just more students from families with some means or reaches down to the poor as well. The assistance in *Allen* was sufficiently minimal, as well as targeted, that it could have attracted only the less affluent. Was this significant to the Court? It is impossible to know, but *Allen* is a turnaround in Establishment Clause jurisprudence, and, again, liberty and equality interests pointed to the same result.

Levy v. Louisiana and its companion case, *Glona v. American Guarantee and Liability Insurance Co.,* were twin attacks on Louisiana's laws dealing with the consequences of illegitimacy, a status imposed by the state on children born out of wedlock unless the parents subsequently married or the child was "formally" acknowledged by the parent. Everyone knew, without saying, that illegitimacy was overwhelmingly a problem for the poor because the more affluent would demand a marriage (or perhaps secure an abortion) and thereby avoid the stigma that illegitimacy carried for both mother and child.

Levy involved a suit by nonmarital children for the wrongful death of their mother. *Glona* involved a suit by a mother for the wrongful death of her nonmarital child. Had the children been legitimate, both suits could have gone forward, but because the children were not, both were dismissed as not coming within the statutory causes of action for wrongful death. The state supreme court explained that the purpose behind the distinctions between illegitimacy and legitimacy was to deter nonmarital births. In a pair of terse opinions, citing the bastard Edmund's speech in Shakespeare's *King Lear* but little relevant law, Douglas held the distinctions violated the Equal Protection Clause. Illegitimate persons were "humans." The rights in the cases "involve the intimate familial relationship between a child and his mother," and the Court has "been extremely sensitive when it comes to basic civil rights." Douglas bluntly stated that "legitimacy or illegitimacy of birth has no relationship" to the nature of wrongful death, and the idea that these statutes might deter nonmarital childbirth was "farfetched" since it "assumes that women have illegitimate children so that they can be compensated in damages for their wrongful deaths."

Harlan, joined by Black and Stewart, dissented, and like Douglas wrote an opinion short on legal reasoning. Essentially, he concluded that while love knows no bounds, the law does. A state has the right to recognize family relationships, and it is the state's prerogative not to grant children certain rights unless the appropriate legal "formalities" first occur.

Levy and *Glona,* coming down in 1968, were more closely allied with true poverty cases—those where the claim was apparent on the face of the case—because of Douglas's use of equal protection. New doctrine, mostly pushed by Douglas, resting expressly on the premise of equality was being created for the new problems based on lack of resources. The contrast with the beginning of the decade, where Holmes's statement in *Buck v. Bell* (1927) that equal protection was "the usual last resort of constitutional arguments" still was apt, was almost complete. The only poverty case not involving the criminal law was the sad plight of the deported Bulgarian ex-communist, Ephram Nestor, stripped of his social security. Equal protection doctrine, despite Brennan's contrary statement in *Baker v. Carr*, was largely undeveloped outside the area of race except to say in effect that the state could classify however it wished short of manifest irrationality. But beginning in 1966 both of these circumstances began to change.

True Poverty Cases

The transitional case was *Harper v. Virginia Board of Elections* and the $1.50 poll tax to vote in state elections. Douglas reached to *Griffin* and *Douglas* to assert "[l]ines drawn on the basis of wealth or property, like those of race . . . are traditionally disfavored." The statement, if taken seriously, is far more stunning even than *Griffin*'s. The Court's doctrine at the time held that a racial classification, if not per se unconstitutional, was pretty close thereto and could only be justified by extremely important state interests. Was Douglas really equating wealth with race? If so, how? The three Civil War Amendments were certainly about race, but the same cannot be said for wealth. If history alone does not explain why race is legally special, then the facts that it is very visible and immutable could also be called upon. Poverty may or may not be visible. Yet poverty had proven anything but immutable over the course of American history. Douglas had only to look in the mirror for proof.

If the comparison with race was not faulty enough, Douglas also misstated what Virginia had done, for the state had charged an access fee, not drawn a line based on wealth. Virginia demanded $1.50 a year for voting, just as it might demand $2 a year for entry into its state parks. It did not, as *Harper*, taken literally, suggested, ban the poor from voting. Everyone can come up with $1.50 during the course of a year (even if there are more compelling necessities to spend it on).

Unlike Black's statement in *Griffin*, Douglas's opinion in *Harper* could express a constitutional rule as opposed to a mere aspiration. Nevertheless, for the reasons just expressed, it was unlikely to be such a rule; if "poverty" became a "suspect classification" like race, and access fees were equated with discrimination, then a remarkable number of laws were unconstitutional and a true social revolution was underway. But *Harper* did portend something; at a minimum it recognized that constitutional rights might be calibrated to the needs of the poor.

During the 1950s and the early 1960s every southern state plus Arizona, Indiana, Kentucky, Michigan, Missouri, New Hampshire, Oklahoma, and the District of Columbia (the latter under the control of a congressional committee dominated by southerners) adopted policies to deny welfare assistance to children if there was a man in the house who was not their father or stepfather. State welfare policies had to be approved by what was then called the Department of Health, Education, and Welfare, and the "man-in-the-house" regulations were routinely approved because of the prevailing assumption that if a man was capable of living with a woman, he was also capable of supporting her and her family. The only state's man-in-the-house policy that ran afoul of HEW was an Alabama attempt to deny children assistance if the mother had sex with a man in anyone's abode.

During the early 1960s there were occasional newspaper stories about warrantless midnight raids by welfare workers designed solely to ascertain if an unmarried welfare mother was sleeping with a man, the consequence being loss of aid to her children. The result was certainly harsh, but numerous cases, including *Fleming v. Nestor,* stood for the proposition that government payments were not rights but, rather, privileges to be granted or withheld on practically any conditions set by the government.

King v. Smith in 1968 offered the Court its first look at these regulations. Douglas, relying on his recently authored opinions in *Levy* and *Glona,* accurately characterized man-in-the-house regulations as punishing the children for the sins of their mother. An aid-to-children program should focus upon "the economic need of the children, their age, and their other means of support." To rely instead on their mother's cohabitation was "irrational" and "invidious" and therefore a violation of equal protection.

Although the right-privilege distinction was rapidly eroding and perhaps vanishing at the Court in the late 1960s, the other eight justices were unwilling to go as far as Douglas. Warren instead wrote an opinion that concluded that HEW had consistently misconstrued the applicable federal statute and that instead of authorizing man-in-the-house rules, the statute prohibited them. Everyone but Douglas joined Warren's opinion, which ducked the constitutional claim.

If the goal was to duck the hard constitutional questions relating to poverty, it was not achievable, as three cases decided in 1969 showed. Two, *Sniadach v. Family Finance Corp.* and *Shapiro v. Thompson,* supported constitutional claims of the poor, while the third, *McInnis v. Ogilvie,* summarily rejected a challenge to the use of the property tax as a means of funding local education. *Shapiro,* both in result and by Brennan's opinion, was by far the most important and properly overshadowed *Sniadach* and *McInnis.*

McInnis involved the wealth disparities between affluent and poorer school districts and the consequences of states' reliance on local property tax revenues as the principal source of funding for public education. Per-pupil expenditures in Illinois varied between $480 and $1,000. The plaintiffs claimed that students living in poorer districts had less money spent on their education than students in wealthier districts and that property values have no proper relationship to educational spending. Accordingly, use of the local property tax as a funding mechanism denied those students in poorer districts the equal protection of laws. The three-judge federal district court below had dismissed the claim in "a thoroughly unsatisfying opinion,"[5] and so there was neither a trial, nor a record, nor any help figuring out what the case was truly about. Because of a then-existing rule authorizing direct appeal from three-judge district courts to the Supreme Court, there was no intermediate judicial decision to help sort out what was, in fact, a mess, and the Court was forced to deal with the issue. It could affirm or else it could send the case back for a trial; there were no other options. It chose the former but offered no reasons.

The Court's affirmance meant that Illinois's system, as challenged, did not violate the Equal Protection Clause. The affirmance naturally offered support for the proposition that wealth disparities in property tax revenues did not violate equal protection anywhere else either. And a reversal for a trial would have necessarily meant that wealth disparities could violate equal protection. By passing, even by summary affirmance, the Court left the issue for another day and a better conceived case, although it offered no encouragement for such suits. (The other day came four years later when in *San Antonio Independent School District v. Rodriguez,* the Court by a 5–4 vote—Douglas, Brennan, White, and Marshall dissenting—reached the same result as *McInnis,* but with full opinions.)

Sniadach involved Wisconsin's wage garnishment procedure whereby an employer, after being served notice through a simple filing with a clerk of a court by an employee's creditor, was required by state law to withhold a portion of the employee's wages and turn them over to the creditor. Family Finance claimed Sniadach owed it $420 on a promissory note and filed the necessary papers with the clerk of the court to begin garnishment of Sniadach's wages. Sniadach's employer responded that Sniadach made $63.18 a week (roughly $200 in current dollars) after taxes, and it would pay one-half to Sniadach as a statutory subsistence allowance, with the other half to Family Finance. Garnishment would continue until the debt was paid off or until Sniadach prevailed at a trial on the issue of the validity of the $420 debt.

If the debtor-employee challenges the prejudgment garnishment (and therefore the underlying debt) and prevails at trial, then the garnished wages plus statutory interest are refunded. Because it is a prejudgment procedure, there was no state remedy available short of a trial on the underlying debt. Given the realities of litigation, Family Finance's asserted claim would be paid off via the garnishment well before Sniadach would have a day in court to challenge the note.

With only Black dissenting, Douglas made short work of the prejudgment garnishment procedure. Although stating that the question was not whether the Wisconsin law was wise, he also declared that "a prejudgment garnishment of the Wisconsin type may as a practical matter drive a wage-earning family to the wall," which seems an indication that it was in fact not wise. At the time of the case, congressional hearings had focused on garnishment and its ability to give the creditor tremendous leverage over the debtor, and Douglas quoted from them. Indeed, his opinion found that the Constitution already solved the problem without legislation, concluding that "[w]here the taking of one's property is so obvious, it needs no extended argument to conclude that absent notice and a prior hearing," Wisconsin's prejudgment garnishment procedure violated due process. Postjudgment garnishment might be valid, but prejudgment was not.

Black's dissent charged the Court with reviving the "natural law" due process approach and striking the procedure because it "shocks the conscience." He was certainly right on the latter, but unlike the "natural law" due process that Black so enjoyed railing against, Douglas had applied the basic meaning of the textual command of due process: notice and hearing before one is deprived of property.

One additional reason that *McInnis* caused little notice was Brennan's stunning transformation of the law of the poor in *Shapiro*, coming down only a month later. *Shapiro* involved a challenge to Connecticut, Pennsylvania, and District of Columbia welfare regulations that denied aid to the needy until they had lived in the state or DC for one year. The durational residence requirement was justified first as a means of giving aid to those who were truly residents and secondly as a means of forestalling becoming "welfare magnets," that is, attracting in-migration by those seeking simply to gain higher benefits. Unlike *King v. Smith,* there was no doubt that the durational residency requirements conformed to federal law because the relevant statute prohibited durational requirements that were longer than one year. When *Shapiro* was first argued during the 1967 Term, the Court voted 6–3, with Douglas, Fortas, and Marshall in dissent, to uphold the residency requirements precisely because Congress had authorized them.

Warren, the former governor of a high welfare benefits state, took the majority for himself and sustained the congressional authorization and therefore the state statutes, holding that at most they imposed an uncertain, but constitutional, burden on welfare recipients who wish to move to a different state. Warren's opinion reflected the standard post-1937 view that if Congress did anything that related to money, its word was final and its action was constitutional.

Douglas, always happy to find a new provision of the Constitution to rely on, used the Fourteenth Amendment's Privileges and Immunities Clause for his protection of the right to travel, which he found unconstitutionally burdened by the residency requirements. That is, people would be discouraged from exercising their right to travel because of the burden of losing all welfare benefits for a year. Then Fortas circulated a dissent with a direct attack on Warren's analysis as "a total rejection of reality and a resort to debating devices to obscure the palpable and obvious truths," to wit, that the statutes had no other substantial "purpose except to keep needy people out."[6] Fortas's opinion moved Brennan to dissent and caused Stewart, a devotee of a constitutional right to travel, sufficient pause that he was unwilling to cast the deciding vote. So with the term ending, *Shapiro* was set for reargument.

After reargument the Court voted to strike the durational residency requirement, and as the senior justice in the new majority, Douglas chose Brennan rather than Fortas to write the Court's opinion. In doing so, Douglas, who had heretofore been the justice far and away most responsible for undoing Holmes's *Buck v. Bell* statement, gave Brennan the opportunity to synthesize all the equal protection cases of the decade. The key to *Shapiro* is that Brennan explicitly imported his "compelling state interest" test into equal protection analysis, and as Brennan had demonstrated in speech and free exercise cases, no state could ever meet the burden he imposed on it. Brennan was rejecting the post-1937 nationalism that deferred to Congress and instead offering a far different version that assumed that the Court should arbitrate "between government, in its capacity as a large and unfeeling bureaucracy, and destitute welfare recipients, whose very necessities of life were being manipulated."[7] Brennan wrote that deterring travel was an illegitimate state interest and that preserving the state fisc was just not very important. There was always more money available to the state.

Brennan's opinion offered two different theories for demanding that the state justify its law with a compelling interest. One was that the laws burdened the fundamental right to travel. Such an explanation readily placed the voting rights cases from *Reynolds v. Sims* to *Harper* in perspective, for voting too should be deemed fundamental. The other theory focused on poverty. Welfare assistance affects "the ability of families to obtain the very means to subsist—food, shelter, and the other necessities of life." Staying alive surely was as important as casting a ballot or traveling to a new state, and the bare necessities were also fundamental. Or maybe, as *Harper* suggested, poverty cases were being treated like race cases. Whichever, the poor seemed about to fare a lot better than they had prior to 1966.

Harlan's dissent hit on something basic. Just as the pre-1937 Court had used due process to incorporate its policy preferences, so the Warren Court was using equal protection to incorporate its. He closed by noting the decision "reflects to an unusual degree the current notion that this Court possesses a peculiar wisdom all its own whose capacity to lead this Nation out of its present troubles is contained only by the limits of judicial ingenuity in contriving new constitutional principles to meet each new problem as it arises."

Ironically, as the Court made its new move in equal protection, Warren became a dissenter, joined by Black who had opposed much of the equal protection jurisprudence from *Harper* onward. One cannot help but see the former governor remembering 10,000 new Californians entering the state every week and wondering how his government could have met its burdens if Brennan's *Shapiro* had been the law in 1945. It had been a long time since Warren had empathized with government, but here was an area where government had to distribute limited resources and Warren would have protected present residents (and voters), not potential ones.

In a contemporaneous summing up of the Warren Court, Archibald Cox offered a blazing insight—"Once loosed, the idea of Equality is not easily cabined"[8]—which certainly captured the mood generated by

Shapiro. Yet could *Griffin*'s or *Harper*'s rhetoric be the law? A demand of the poor for equal treatment when combined with *Shapiro*'s requirement that the state have compelling interests would mean toppling hundreds, perhaps thousands, of laws that impacted more harshly on the poor. Brennan seemed to be aiming for a truly revolutionary transformation of law, perhaps more so than in the criminal procedure area, for no state had ever prevailed when the Court demanded a compelling state interest. But fate—riots, assassinations, Fortas's resignation, and the ever-mounting costs of the Vietnam War, both psychologically and economically—soon pointed the Court toward a different direction.

Constitutional Claims of Business

The three principal protections of property rights in the Constitution historically have been the Takings Clause, the Due Process Clause, and the Contracts Clause. *Ferguson v. Skrupa* and *El Paso v. Simmons* with but a single dissent rejected constitutional claims under the latter two clauses that matched the unanimous 1962 vote in *Goldblatt v. Hempstead* construing the Takings Clause. These results were consistent with the way the Court was treating the states as well. Thus, when Congress in 1966 extended minimum wage law to cover state-run enterprises, such as hospitals, Harlan's opinion in *Maryland v. Wirtz* (1968) fully sustained the act, brushing aside the state's claim that its sovereignty protected it from congressional incursion. Surprisingly, Douglas (joined by Stewart) dissented.

Goldblatt owned a sand and gravel pit on Long Island where the Township of Hempstead grew rapidly around him. After a state court refused to let Hempstead zone Goldblatt out of business, the town resorted to a "safety regulation" to accomplish the same goal. Clark noted that while the regulations "completely prohibited a beneficial use to which the property has previously been devoted," the regulations were "reasonable" and therefore did not constitute a "taking" that would have entitled Goldblatt to compensation for his loss.

Kansas put Frank Skrupa out of the business of debt adjustment when it barred anyone from consolidating debt unless it was an incident to the practice of law. Black ignored the blatant self-dealing of the legislator-lawyers and instead stated that Kansas "was free to decide for itself that the legislation was needed" without any second-guessing from the judiciary. He reiterated the post-1937 refrain that the Court would not use the "vague contours" of the Due Process Clause "to nullify laws which a majority of the Court believes to be economically unwise." Skrupa should take his claimed injury to the people of Kansas or the state legislature, not the justices of the federal bench.

The Contracts Clause has language much like the First Amendment. It seemingly prohibits *any* state law impairing the obligation of contract. The prohibition had, by 1819, been construed by John Marshall to cover both debtor relief and states unilaterally revising their own contracts (to favor themselves). During the New Deal, the Court virtually gutted the prohibition against debtor-relief laws. In 1965 in *Simmons,* the Court authorized the states to rewrite their own contracts.

As a matter of state policy, Texas sold its extensive public lands as rapidly as possible at the end of the nineteenth century. Given the barrenness of much of the lands and the swings of an agrarian economy, many purchasers were subsequently unable to make the payments. As an inducement to purchase, Texas law had provided that so long as no third-party interests intervened, a defaulting purchaser could reclaim good title by tendering the back interest due. Then in 1941, probably because some of that barren land was atop oil and gas, Texas repealed the reinstatement law and replaced it with a five-year limitation. In *Simmons,* White acknowledged that Texas had modified its own contractual obligations but held it was reasonable to do so because Texas asserted an interest in stabilizing land titles.

(*Simmons* was not an oil and gas case. Simmons's 620 acres of land northwest of El Paso was the projected site encompassing two overpasses on Interstate 10. To the extent Simmons thought that the property's value would jump, he was overly optimistic. It remains very rural.)

Black dissented with a short opinion recognizing that the majority had balanced the Contracts Clause out of the Constitution. He did not explain why the Contracts Clause in *Simmons* was different from the Takings Clause in *Goldblatt,* for neither was subject to his "vague contours" complaint about due process, and the Court had "balanced"—in the sense of requiring the state to have a reason to override the Constitution—in both. Black's was the sole negative vote in these cases. For the other justices the clauses were effectively similar; economic rights of the nonpoor simply did not receive constitutional protection.

The lack of protection of property rights as well as the Court's traditional favoring of labor over business was perfectly clear in the holding of *Amalgamated Food Employees Union v. Logan Valley Plaza* in 1968. Weis Market and Sears, Roebuck and Company were the two original tenants of Logan Valley Plaza, a shopping mall near Altoona, Pennsylvania. Less than two weeks after Weis opened its supermarket at the mall with nonunion employees, Local 590, using employees of other Altoona supermarkets, began picketing in the nearby parcel pickup area, an unleased area controlled by the mall. Ten days later Logan Valley Plaza filed suit against Local 590 to enjoin what it deemed a continuing trespass on its property. The trial court granted the injunction and the state supreme court affirmed, rejecting the union's claim that the First Amendment gave it the right to be there regardless of the landlord's objections.

Under precedents dating back to well before the Warren era, the Court had held that the public streets and sidewalks were appropriate places for picketing and leafleting. Thus, to affirm the injunction would authorize a regime in the suburbs that would be different from that existing down town. "Business enterprises located in downtown areas would be subject to on-the-spot public criticism of their practices, but businesses situated in the suburbs could largely immunize themselves from similar criticism by creating a *cordon sanitaire* of parking lots around their stores." Such a dichotomy, Thurgood Marshall stated, was compelled neither by precedent nor policy.

Like *Adderley v. Florida* before it, the Court did not find the issue of public versus private ownership of the land important, much less dispositive. If people were otherwise invited to be in an area, then they could come with their First Amendment rights; if they were not allowed in the area, then trespass laws could be applied. The Tallahassee sheriff allowed no one in the area; Logan Valley Plaza encouraged people to come. The latter having done so, it could not "substantially hinder" the right to express views on the property.

Marshall noted, as every first-year law student learns, that ownership did not mean "absolute dominion." In a concurring opinion Douglas elaborated that otherwise it would "make 'private property' a sanctuary from which some members of the public may be excluded merely because of the ideas they espouse." As he had in the sit-in cases, Douglas was distinguishing between a business and a home. Black and White disagreed. Each believed that the private ownership of the mall was dispositive against the First Amendment claim because an owner can withdraw his implicit invitation to be there for any reasons the owner chooses.

Thus, by the end of the decade, in a conflict between the First Amendment and property rights, the former was the more important. Although *Logan Valley* can be reconciled with *Adderley* on the basis of the invitation to be on the property, *Logan Valley*'s thrust is more consistent with the *Adderley* dissents, and *Logan Valley* signaled a major First Amendment shift away from *Adderley,* one that is best explained by Marshall having replaced Clark. (The shift was brief; with changed composition *Logan Valley* itself was implicitly overruled in 1972 and explicitly so in 1976.)

Labor and Antitrust Law

If *Logan Valley* is seen not as a First Amendment case but instead as a labor case, its result was perfectly explicable, needing no fancy distinctions. The Warren Court, fully consistent with post-1937 jurisprudence, always favored labor over management. At the era's close it was doing so aggressively.

When at least 30 percent of employees sign cards indicating they wish to have a union represent them for collective bargaining, the National Labor Relations Board will hold a representation election. *NLRB v. Gissel Packing Co.* consisted of three cases raising the similar issue of a union organizing campaign obtaining the signatures from a majority of employees on union authorization cards but not prevailing in a subsequent election.

Because the unions in *Gissel* had a majority of employee authorizations, they demanded that the employers recognize them and bargain without the necessity of an election. Employers rarely, if ever, accede to such a demand because they would rather not have a union. They attempt to justify the refusal, and thus their demand for an election, on the ground that authorization cards are often misleading—a signature may really mean that the employee wishes there to be an opportunity to vote by secret ballot. Thus, cards may be obtained by misrepresentation or some form of coercion could be involved. And the employer may never have had an opportunity to explain why unionization will be a bad idea. Accordingly, employers often deem the cards inherently untrustworthy, and by rejecting the union demand for recognition, an employer can both test the sincerity of the signatures as well as present its side on the issue of unionization. In *Gissel* all three employers took this tack.

The employers also engaged in activities that the NLRB found to threaten retaliation against the employees and thus constitute forbidden unfair labor practices. As a result of the unfair labor practices, one union lost its election, a second gave up on the election campaign after concluding it could not win, and the third blocked the election by filing an unfair labor practice charge and requesting that the NLRB process the complaint before holding the election. In all three cases the NLRB took the unusual step of ignoring the elections and instead concluding that the union was the appropriate bargaining agent; therefore, the employer had a duty to bargain in good faith with the union.

The Court affirmed the NLRB bargaining orders. Although *Gissel* has a number of pro-union holdings (including the one on controlling employer speech discussed at the end of Chapter 12), its most novel holding was that when a union obtains a majority of signatures on authorization cards and the employer engages in unfair labor practices, the NLRB may order collective bargaining—as opposed to a new election—when it finds that, on balance, "the possibility of erasing the effects of past practices and of insuring a fair election (or a fair rerun) by the use of traditional remedies, is slight and that employee sentiment once expressed through cards would, on balance, be better protected through a bargaining order." On its face, if the NLRB so chose, *Gissel* made it considerably easier for a union to organize an employer (although for a variety of reasons, none of which the Warren Court could control, it did not work out this way).

The union victories could be explained, like *Logan Valley,* by a preference for unions over employers. They could equally well, perhaps even better, be explained by the Court's disdain for bigness and its belief that unions were always smaller than employers. In the antitrust area—especially with mergers—the Court's open hostility to bigness was more apparent than in any other area.

In *United States v. Philadelphia National Bank,* the Court construed the Clayton Act's antimerger provision to block Philadelphia's second-largest bank from acquiring its third-largest bank and thus becoming the largest bank in the four-county Philadelphia area (the only area within the state where the banks could do business). Brennan characterized the merger "plainly not a case where two small firms in a market propose to merge in order to be able to compete more successfully with the leading firms in the market." The resulting bank would have held a bit over one-third of the area's bank assets, deposits, and loans. It and the previously largest bank would between them control just under 60 percent of the area's assets, deposits, and loans. Brennan had little trouble concluding that the movement toward oligopoly would lessen competition within the four-county area. Whatever the level of concentration deemed objectionable, this combination had it.

Philadelphia National Bank had argued that it needed to become bigger so that it could better compete with the large New York City banks. Brennan offered several responses, all going to the point that the bank was already big enough for Philadelphia. First, if every bank in the four-county area were rolled into a single bank, that new bank would still not be as large as New York City's largest, and there would be no competition left in Philadelphia. Second, the existing lending limits of the pre-merger banks were adequate for Philadelphia's businesses. "The only businesses in the area which find such limits inadequate are large enough readily to obtain bank credit in other cities."

Brennan's only fancy footwork was to find that the Clayton Act applied to asset acquisitions in addition to stock swaps. The statute was designed, the Court held, to cover "the entire range of corporate amalgamations." Harlan, Stewart, and, interestingly, Goldberg dissented on this point.

In context, *Philadelphia National Bank* seemed to stand for the proposition that a business should not use merger as a means of gaining over a 20-percent market share. Three years later, however, in *United States v. Von's Grocery,* that view came crashing down when a newly merged entity would become a city's second-largest grocery chain but control only 7.5 percent of the grocery business in that city, less than a quarter of the market share of merged banks in Philadelphia.

Von's Grocery involved the merger of Von's, Los Angeles's third-largest supermarket chain, with Shopping Bag, the city's sixth-largest chain. The Court believed that the facts of the postwar Los Angeles market literally spoke for themselves. Von's had grown from fourteen to twenty-seven supermarkets; Shopping Bag from fifteen to thirty-four. Chains with two or more stores increased from 96 to 150. Nine of the top twenty chains acquired stores from smaller rivals. Meanwhile, singly-owned grocery stores decreased from 5,365 in 1950 to 3,818 in 1960 and 3,590 in 1963. Although there was no proof that the Von's-Shopping Bag merger would lessen competition, Black stated the facts just recited "are enough" to demonstrate that the merger should be blocked. As he explained, "where concentration is gaining momentum in a market, we must be alert to carry out Congress's intent to protect competition against ever-increasing concentration through mergers." In a terse final paragraph, the Court ordered the district judge to force Von's to divest itself of Shopping Bag.

Stewart, with Harlan, dissented and aptly charged the majority with writing a legal ode to nostalgia. "No action by this Court can resurrect the old single-line Los Angeles food stores that have been run-over by the automobile or obliterated by the freeway." While stopping the trend toward consolidation in the grocery business was the Court's goal, "the Court's opinion is hardly more than a requiem for the so-called 'mom and pop' grocery stores that are now economically and technologically obsolete in many parts of this country."

Von's Grocery was a return to *Brown Shoe* with a vengeance. Black's opinion explicitly rested on protecting competitors, not consumers. The result of the Von's-Shopping Bag merger might have been to lower prices to consumers, and that is why the Court blocked it—smaller stores might not be able to compete at lower prices. *Von's Grocery* was thus the reverse of *Philadelphia National Bank* where the Court worried about higher prices to the consumer. As the two cases showed, the Court wasn't worried about the consumer at all. The justices wanted to preserve small business as it had been in the disappearing past.

Near the end of his *Von's Grocery* dissent, Stewart stated the principle that he found at work in the merger cases: "[T]he government always wins." No other rational principle could explain *Philadelphia National Bank* and *Von's Grocery* coming down within a three-year period. Stewart's quip was not only 100 percent true, it was barely less accurate when extended to antitrust cases generally. During Warren's tenure, the Court wrote full opinions in forty-eight antitrust cases in which the Antitrust Division was plaintiff, and the government prevailed in forty-five. The Federal Trade Commission did almost as well, winning twenty-four of twenty-six cases decided by opinion. These are astronomical winning percentages—ones that exceed Thurgood Marshall's twenty-seven of thirty-two arguing for the NAACP Legal Defense Fund. (Private plaintiffs in treble-damage antitrust suits did not fare quite as well, winning but twenty of thirty-one cases. Not bad, but not great.)

As G. Edward White notes, antitrust and labor were the two areas where twentieth-century progressives were most successful in translating their economic beliefs into legislation.[9] Their beliefs—principally a fear of the economic power of business—mapped precisely those of the Court's liberal bloc. Warren, Black, Douglas, and Brennan could always find a fifth vote because only Harlan and Stewart, sometimes joined by Fortas, were in disagreement over implementing what the liberals deemed to be congressional goals. As a result of the antitrust and labor cases, when combined with ones involving the Internal Revenue Service—where the government won 77 percent during the entire Warren era—the government maintained a safe harbor where it could regularly prevail.

While the Court was flirting with its new ways to bring constitutional protections to the less affluent, it was simultaneously demonstrating that it had perfected denying protections to business. In figure-skating terms, helping the poor was the free-style program, a work in progress with stunning moves and an occasional spill. Dealing business its defeats was the compulsories, and the Court was good at all the routine moves that the performance required.

IV

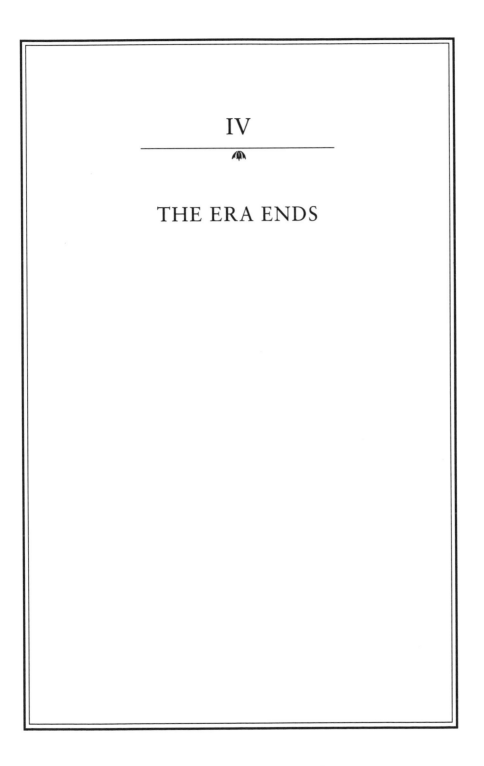

THE ERA ENDS

Retirement

The Saturday before the California presidential primary in June 1968, Warren had been talking politics with his law clerks. He thought Robert Kennedy would win in California and that would catapult him to the presidency. "I read the reports in the papers this morning of the crowds that lined Kennedy's route from the airport to downtown Los Angeles. It persuades me that this man has something that's going to get him elected. I can remember when I was at the peak of popularity running for Governor following the same route from the airport and seeing no one on the streets."[1] Three days later, Kennedy was assassinated, the Democratic Party was in further shambles, and Richard Nixon had a seeming lock on the presidency.

Just a month earlier Nixon had issued a paper, "Toward Freedom from Fear," that was a running attack on the Court's criminal procedure decisions. "From the point of view of the criminal forces, the cumulative impact of these decisions has been to set free patently guilty individuals on the basis of legal technicalities. The tragic lesson of guilty men walking free from hundreds of courtrooms across the country has not been lost on the criminal community."[2] Warren had detested Nixon from their California days; the Republican campaign on "law and order" simply reinforced the decades-old feeling.

It took less than a week for Warren to decide that, at age 77, he could neither outlive a Nixon presidency nor allow him to appoint his successor. Warren would retire immediately and give the appointment to a president he both liked and respected.

Chapter 18

The Last Year

The final year of Earl Warren's tenure as chief justice began unexpectedly on June 5, 1968, when Robert Kennedy was assassinated. It ended on June 23, 1969, with the swearing in of Warren Burger as the fifteenth chief justice of the United States. From beginning to end, the year did not go the way Warren scripted it.

The Fortas Nomination

Once Warren made his decision to deny Nixon the opportunity to appoint his successor, he had Abe Fortas call the president. At the quickly arranged meeting, Warren told Lyndon Johnson that because of his age he felt he should retire and that he wanted Johnson to appoint as his successor a man who felt about the issues as he did. Johnson asked about Fortas as that successor, and Warren gave the expected affirmative response.

Although Warren's formal announcement would be delayed for two weeks, Johnson immediately began lining up support in the Senate, working on Richard Russell for the southerners and Everett Dirksen for the Republicans. Northern Democrats would need no prodding to realize they must either embrace Johnson's choice or else be faced with Nixon's, and both Russell and Dirksen said they would support Fortas. Johnson's initial vote count of the senators was well over seventy.

Warren wrote two retirement letters, one explaining age as the reason for retirement, the other advising the president of his "intention to retire as Chief Justice of the United States effective at your pleasure."[1] When his letters were released two weeks later, they were accompanied by Johnson's official reply that made it all too clear that these two superb politicians were stretching to prevent Nixon from getting an early appointment: "I will accept your decision to retire effective at such time as a successor is qualified."[2] Warren "did not expect others to see his motives so clearly."[3] Yet even the *New York Times* and *Washington Post* thought Warren's pair of letters was fishy; if he meant to resign, he should simply do so.

With the release of the letters came the expected nomination of Fortas. To replace Fortas, Johnson named Homer Thornberry, one of the many Texans who had wisely hitched themselves to Johnson's star and thereby enjoyed the fruits of his success. Thornberry had filled Johnson's seat in Congress and then been put on the federal district court by President Kennedy and elevated to the court of appeals by Johnson. While Johnson was happy to bestow further preferment on Thornberry, the choice was designed to appease Russell and the southern Democrats.

Secretary of Defense Clark Clifford had advised against Thornberry. Clifford thought Fortas an outstanding choice but felt Thornberry would be perceived as a crony and that, combined with Johnson's waning powers, might detract from the Fortas nomination. Clifford begged Johnson to couple Fortas with a nonpolitical Republican. Johnson, supported by Fortas, rejected the advice that might have made Fortas chief justice.

There was no groundswell of support. Only Albert Gore and Wayne Morse, plus Florida's George Smathers, expressed enthusiasm. Northern Democrats were too dispirited watching the Democratic Party slowly but inevitably commit suicide. Death makes the issues of the living seem insignificant; therefore, the northern Democrats did not comprehend that since they liked what the Court had been doing, they should be supporting the president rather than cede the playing field, as well as the election, to the Republicans.

Southern Democrats didn't like the Warren Court and didn't like Fortas either. James Eastland reported that he "had never seen so much feeling against a man as against Fortas."[4] Republicans wanted delay until after Nixon's victory. Robert Griffin of Michigan and John Tower of Texas immediately announced that they opposed a "lame duck" president appointing the new chief justice. Griffin, happy to cheapen a distinguished public career, but unknowingly echoing Clifford's concerns over coupling Thornberry with Fortas, claimed the nomination was cronyism. California Governor Ronald Reagan complained that Warren had no "right to choose which president he thinks should dominate for the next twenty years at the Supreme Court."[5] Reacting on the evening news to the nominations of Fortas and Thornberry, Nixon stated: "It would have been wise for the President to ask Chief Justice Warren to serve in the fall term, thereby leaving selection of the new justices to the next President."[6]

Maybe Johnson's vote count was high; still, the operative assumption was that the votes for cloture on the likely filibuster were there when needed. What the president did not know was that Russell, angered by delays in getting a segregationist friend appointed to the federal bench as promised, had decided against Fortas and cut a secret deal with Griffin to support the Republicans when the time came. In the interim, it was time to bash Fortas and the Court on which he served.

The Senate Judiciary Committee Hearings

The Senate Judiciary Committee called quick hearings and invited Fortas to appear. Only one sitting justice, Brennan, having sat for but four months as a recess appointee, had ever testified at his own confirmation proceedings, and Brennan did so only briefly. Hence, Fortas's appearance was unprecedented, and he would have been well within his rights to claim that the separation of powers precluded his answering questions about the Court. But Fortas was so intelligent, so able, and so arrogant about his intellectual ability that he could not resist the fray, especially since his likely dazzling performance would broaden his support. In his opening statement, he stated he would discuss the work of the Court but in the context of "the constitutional limitations upon me."[7]

When Eastland opened the questioning, his target was separation of powers but not those Fortas had been thinking about. Eastland and others wanted to know about his relationship with the president, for it was long rumored that even after taking his seat in 1965 Fortas had remained Johnson's most trusted adviser. Eastland intended to use separation of powers to attach cronyism to something of substance, but it was a pure fishing expedition. Rumors were one thing, facts another, and Eastland had no facts. Fortas developed a strategy from the very beginning. Since there was no way the senators were going to be able to get at the facts of his relationship with Johnson—the White House would be the source of that—Fortas had an open field and he went anywhere he pleased. Dirksen said Fortas was "awfully good."[8] Philip Hart of Michigan, warming to the nomination, found the performance "superb."[9] Privately in the White House, Johnson aide Joseph Califano found Fortas's testimony so "misleading and deceptive that those of us who were aware of his relationship with Johnson winced with each news report of his appearance before the Senate committee."[10]

In fact, Fortas lied through his teeth. Had he been a prominent adviser on the war, attending numerous key meetings? No, just a few where he restated the arguments of others. A lie. Had he drafted the president's message on sending federal troops to Detroit? No; he had merely been at a meeting. Another lie. Then, to the question whether there were other areas besides Vietnam and the Detroit riots where he had consulted with the president, he not only responded with his usual untruthful "no," he added a gratuitous whopper: "I guess I have made a full disclosure now, because so far as I can recall those are the two things."[11]

Supreme Court justices have advised presidents before—Frankfurter and Douglas with Roosevelt jump to mind, as would Vinson's telling Truman to seize the steel mills because the Court would back him up—but no justice ever went as far as Fortas. According to White House logs, between November 23, 1963, and July 2, 1968, there were 145 face-to-face meetings between Johnson and Fortas. Then there was the red telephone. No justice prior to Fortas had a telephone on his desk with its direct line to the White House. When Fortas was on the phone to Johnson, a light went on in his clerks' office alerting them not to enter his. His relationship with Johnson was enough to easily justify a vote not to confirm; given the ambiguities of past practice, it probably was not an impeachable offense. But his lying to the committee was different. That would have justified his impeachment. Yet behind his last lie—nothing else—was still another impeachable offense.

In the spring of 1966, Fortas met with an assistant director of the FBI and talked of disclosing Robert Kennedy's involvement in an illegal wiretap in a case, *Black v. United States,* dealing with a federal conviction where the Court had denied certiorari and then turned around and asked the Justice Department for further information about underlying authorization for the wiretap. While Hoover wished to finger Kennedy, Kennedy loyalists still in the Justice Department wished the blame to fall on the FBI and specifically its director, J. Edgar Hoover. Attorney General Katzenbach ultimately ordered a compromise explanation, one that referred to prior attorneys general but did not name Kennedy specifically and thus did not provide the White House a desired outcome. Fortas nevertheless concluded that "the entire matter boiled down to a continuing fight for the Presidency" and that "if the facts were made known to the general public it would serve to completely destroy Kennedy."[12]

Talking to a participant (as the FBI was) in a pending case about both that case and presidential politics with an eye to leaking information to "destroy" a political opponent of the president crosses every line of propriety. Had Fortas's conduct been made public, there is no doubt he would have been forced off the Court or impeached. But again, no one who knew the facts was talking. (The following term, Black's conviction was vacated based on the illegal wiretap.)

Back at the hearings, the questioning turned to the Court itself, and here Fortas tried to walk a careful line because he wanted to defend the Court and yet a sitting justice ought not be called on to explain votes or opinions. That, of course, is why he shouldn't have been there in the first place. Sam Ervin, who as a former state-court judge passed as an expert on constitutional law in the Senate, continually condemned the Warren Court for judicial legislation, but Fortas, when he chose to cross the line, could easily best the North Carolina senator. Fortas had taken enough from Eastland, John McClellan, and Ervin, so when Strom Thurmond began his similar tack, Fortas retreated into his above-the-fray pose. As a result, over a period of two hours, Fortas took his version of the judicial Fifth Amendment—"I must ask you to understand and to excuse me from addressing myself to that question. I am under the constitutional limitation that has been referred to during the past two days"[13]—some fifty-nine times. Thurmond grew more hostile, and Fortas began to answer some of the questions, while retreating to his constitutional safe harbor on others. Eventually, in response to an accusation that the Warren Court was responsible for the increase of crime in America, Fortas delivered a lecture on academic studies and crime rates and concluded that "we can do nothing but decide cases, and to the extent that God gives us guidance, decide them on the basis of the Constitution. And that is what I try to do, Senator."[14]

Fourteen years and a couple of hours of not-so-well-pent-up anger came gushing out as Thurmond turned to the 1957 pre-Fortas decision in *Mallory v. United States:* "There was no question Mallory was guilty, yet he went free." In a thunderous tone, Thurmond demanded: "Why did he go free? A criminal, a convict, a guilty man, who committed a serious rape on a lady in this city. Simply because the Court said they held him a little too long before arraignment. Do you believe in that kind of justice?" Fortas sat silent and after a long period took his judicial Fifth again. Thurmond exploded: "Mallory, Mallory, Mallory, I want that word to ring in your ears—Mallory. A man who raped a woman, admitted his guilt, and the Supreme Court turned him loose on a technicality. And who I was told later went to Philadelphia and committed another crime, and somewhere else another crime, because the court turned him loose on technicalities. Is not that type of decision calculated to bring the courts and the law and the administration of justice in disrepute? Is not that type of decision calculated to encourage more people to commit rapes and serious crimes? Can you as a Justice of the Supreme Court condone such a decision as that? I ask you to answer that question."[15]

Never had such hostility to the Warren Court been expressed by senators face to face with a member of the Court. The *Salt Lake Tribune* thought that this "was not the sort of price anyone nominated for high office should have to pay."[16] The *New York Times* concluded that "nothing has emerged that tarnishes his reputation as a vigorous attorney, a highly qualified judge, and a dedicated American."[17]

When the committee finished with Fortas a day later, it was Thornberry's turn. Only four committee members showed up, and they were completely indifferent in their questioning. Thornberry understood and told the president that he did not expect to be returning to Washington on a permanent basis. The senators had made up their mind on Fortas, and that ended Thornberry's chance as well.

Next and last on the list was James Clancy, Charles Keating's partner with Citizens for Decent Literature. What he had to say was that everyone should see the smut that Fortas thought the Constitution protected. Clancy had produced the "Abe Fortas Film Festival," thirty minutes of stills from movies Fortas had held protected by the First Amendment, and he claimed that Fortas had provided the key vote on pornography in forty-nine of fifty-two cases. The claim wasn't wholly accurate, since Fortas's vote had been virtually indistinguishable from Brennan's or Warren's, but it wasn't challenged either (and Warren and Brennan weren't before the committee).

McClellan wanted everyone to have time to study Clancy's pictures, and the result was that the committee delayed its vote until after the August recess and the two parties' conventions. Fortas was dying a slow, public death, and alongside him the Court was being hammered. Clancy helped cement the image that Fortas stood for obscenity and immorality, and that played into Thurmond's basic theme that the Warren Court was responsible for whatever was wrong with America. This was not the summer of '64.

After the hearings, Fortas wrote letters to his two closest friends on the Court, Warren and Douglas. The letters were similar and discouraging. He saw Ervin and Thurmond as "merely reflecting in an articulate way the feelings of others" against the Court. "Every decent constitutional decision in the last three years and for some years prior thereto, has been denounced."[18] "The common element is bitter, corrosive opposition to all that has been happening in the court and the country: the racial progress, and the insistence upon increased regard for human rights and dignity in the field of criminal law."[19] A Gallup Poll showed that Fortas's analysis was apt. To the rare question about the Court, "What type of rating would you give the Supreme Court?," only 8 percent responded excellent and 28 percent good; 32 percent said fair; 21 percent, poor.[20] To provide some comparison, according to the Gallup Poll, Johnson's approval ratings in November 1967 (when Eugene McCarthy decided to challenge him) were 41 percent favorable and 49 percent unfavorable and his handling of the war was at 35–52 percent, surprisingly close to the Court's numbers. Even though "one should treat with considerable distrust surveys that show the Justices losing their prestige,"[21] no one could be happy with such low approvals, especially in an election year.

Fortas, like Thornberry, understood he was in trouble. But unlike Thornberry, Fortas would be on the Court following his defeat, and the Court too was in trouble. New Hampshire's Republican Norris Cotton, whom the administration had counted as a yes, came out no—not because of the specific objections to Fortas but rather "on the broad grounds of principle" against the entire Warren Court.[22]

Defeat

Maintaining the Republican theme from 1966, House Republican Leader Gerald Ford had stated: "I refuse to concede that the elected representatives of the American people cannot be the winner in a confrontation with the Supreme Court."[23] In the ongoing campaign for the presidency, Nixon was blasting the Court to the enthusiastic applause of his audiences, and now the Judiciary Committee was doing the same thing. Fortas was tied to the Warren Court and his hearings were proving Ford a prophet, as those who opposed the Court successfully turned the nomination into a referendum on the Warren Court.

Ironically, Fortas and his supporters hoped Nixon would bail the nomination out. Nixon's only Supreme Court appearance had been in *Time, Inc. v. Hill,* and Fortas's dissent had supported him. Nixon respected Fortas and said so publicly. But Nixon's principal campaign issue was "law and order" and that was tied to both race and attacks on Court decisions, especially *Escobedo* and *Miranda*. Supporting Fortas would undermine the issues, and Nixon had no intention of doing so. He may have respected Fortas, but he was working behind the scenes to block the confirmation.

August and September brought more bad news for Fortas. The Democratic Convention made Chicago look like Prague just the week before. It
was the final act of the party's ongoing suicide. A couple more instances
of Fortas's speechwriting for the president leaked out, thereby undermining his false claim of "full disclosure." But utterly devastating was the
news that Fortas had been paid $15,000 to teach a nine-week seminar
that summer at American University. Compared to his judicial salary of
$39,000, that was a lot of money, and, to make matters worse, it had
been raised by his former law partner Paul Porter from former clients.
This was the coup de grace. It transformed cronyism into conflict of
interest and tied everything—Warren's sudden retirement, the president's lame-duck nomination of a close adviser, and Thornberry—into
an unattractive portrait of insider dealing.

The effort to break the Republican filibuster was pro forma. Fortas
needed 67 votes, and the cloture motion failed 45–43 with an inordinate
number of absences. Fortas immediately asked the president to withdraw
the nomination and called for a halt to the "destructive and extreme
assaults on the Court."[24] Strom Thurmond responded that "this is the
wisest decision Justice Fortas had made since he became a member of the
Supreme Court. I suggest Mr. Fortas now go a step further and resign
from the Court for the sake of good government."[25] In his memoirs,
Johnson wrote that the Fortas loss was "the final blow to an unhappy,
frustrating year."[26]

Nixon had no intention of ceasing his attacks on the Court because he
was running "against Warren and his Court as much as he was running
against his Democratic rival, Senator Hubert Humphrey."[27] The punchline to Nixon's set speech was "some of the courts have gone too far in
weakening the peace forces against the criminal forces."[28] It always
worked. He stepped up his attacks on the Court and promised if he were
elected he would appoint "strict constructionists," judges who would
interpret the law rather than make the law. The slap at the Warren Court
was unstated and unmistakable. Nixon also contrasted his position on
the Court with that of his opponent as if he were debating Humphrey
(which, being so far ahead and having lost the last debates to Kennedy, he
would not). "Whenever I begin to discuss the Supreme Court, Mr. Humphrey acts like we're in church. Mr. Humphrey's respectful silence [on
the controversial criminal procedure decisions] may stem from the fact
that he has spent four years in [Lyndon Johnson's] Obedience School."[29]
Many of the Court's decisions "break down 5–4, and I think that often in

recent years, the five man majority has been wrong, and the four man minority has been right."[30] George Wallace, as usual, was more blunt, accusing the Court of "destroying constitutional government in the country."[31]

The repudiation of the Great Society was almost total. To be sure, Nixon barely bested Humphrey, but when the voters who supported Wallace—who ran on a more atavistic version of Nixon's themes—are added to Nixon's total, 56.9 percent of the voters did not support the Democrats. Historian Alan Brinkley saw it as an emphatic statement "against the antiwar movement, against the counterculture, against violence and for law and order."[32]

After his election, Nixon thought Vietnam was his stronger issue, but given the way Humphrey closed at the end, Nixon's aides, who emphasized domestic issues, seem to have had the better of the debate. Law and order was his key to victory, and while liberals saw it as a code for racism—as with both Nixon and Wallace it was—it was more. Theodore H. White wrote that liberals saw law and order as "the justifying slogan of repression, a repression they felt immediately about to close on the ever expanding freedoms sanctioned by" the Supreme Court.[33] By contrast, many Americans believed that the Supreme Court had been grievously wrong. As the Court's arch-foe Senator Harry F. Byrd understated it during the debate, "[t]oday's Court badly needs to be brought into balance."[34] This was not the fall of '64.

The 1968 Term

Just as the 1968 Term was bracketed by the failure of the Fortas nomination and the swearing in of Warren Burger, so did major cases emphasize the two events. The term's first big case was *Epperson v. Arkansas* and the invalidation of the state's "Monkey Law." This allowed Fortas to gain some revenge on those southern Democrats who had so enthusiastically joined the Republicans in scuttling his nomination. It was also a parting shot at the South by the Court as *Epperson* offered a useful reminder why the South still seemed so backward. Maybe, if fundamentalism could be forced back into the churches and the schools integrated, the South could become more like the Midwest.

A week before the end of the term came the other major case, *Powell v. McCormack*, where the Court claimed for the first time the power to intercede in the internal affairs of Congress, in order, or so it appeared, to protect a corrupt African-American congressman. Furthermore, the fact that Warren's opinion reversed one by his successor made irresistible press and seemingly underscored that an era was over.

In between, however, the occasional splintering of the liberal bloc, heretofore apparent only in the retroactivity cases and the previous term's *Powell v. Texas,* offered the most intriguing development. In *Powell v. Texas,* Warren, Black, and Marshall, joined in the vote by Harlan and White, had defeated Douglas, Brennan, and Fortas (joined by Stewart). *Powell v. Texas* was a victory for the more politically attuned pragmatic liberals and a defeat for their more doctrinaire brothers. The case showed, should anyone have doubted it, that even the most cohesive bloc cannot completely maintain itself over time. Eventually, new applications of old issues or, more likely, new issues will splinter it.

Desist v. United States was yet another retroactivity case. Warren and Brennan remained true to their views that making criminal cases retroactive would hamstring the Court. Douglas continued to believe the Constitution mandated total retroactivity. Black, Harlan, and Fortas all voted the opposite way from their norms although for differing reasons. Black adhered to his *Linkletter v. Walker* dissent, but since his eighteenth-century Constitution could not encompass electronic surveillance, he voted that *Katz v. United States* should not be retroactive. Harlan, as we saw earlier, found his support for *Katz* a reason to rethink his retroactivity votes. Fortas in the meanwhile joined the dissenters because he believed the majority went too far in pretending that *Katz* was a surprise to all.

In June, *Brandenburg v. Ohio* saw Black and Douglas concurring, refusing to accept their belated First Amendment victory where the majority finally agreed with their votes in the communist cases. Then in *Harrington v. California,* they extended harmless constitutional error over the dissents of Warren, Brennan, and Marshall.

Two other cases, *Street v. New York* and *Shapiro v. Thompson,* decided the same day, also created surprising splits in the normal voting blocs. *Street,* the flag burning case, found Douglas, Brennan, and Marshall joining Harlan's opinion avoiding the merits, with Warren, Black, and Fortas dissenting on the merits. For Black, symbolic-speech cases were easy since they were not about speech. For Warren, it was about patriotism; for Fortas, his support of the war and his growing concerns over inflammatory means of protest. *Shapiro* saw both Warren and Black desert their brothers. Warren identified with the plight of the states faced with immigration. *Shapiro*'s rule would have created hardship when placed on the other state programs accommodating the explosive growth. Unlike Douglas, Brennan, Fortas, and Marshall, Warren saw the constitutionalization of added welfare payments from the perspective of a former chief executive who would have to find the money. The other four, however, saw the immense resources of the United States and the crying needs of the poor and assumed the money would be found.

In Black's case, there are many explanations, the best of which is that, with the exception of criminal procedure cases, he was no longer a member of the liberal bloc. Thus, he dissented in *Epperson* on the ability of schools to control teachers, in *Tinker* on the ability of schools to control students, in *Sniadach* on garnishment procedures, and *Daniel v. Paul* on the extension of the public-accommodations provisions of the Civil Rights Act of 1964 to the Lake Nixon Club. He even dissented with Harlan in a criminal procedure case when the Court ducked the death-penalty issue in *Boykin v. Alabama* but nevertheless ruled that Boykin's guilty plea had not been voluntary. During Warren's final year, Black was the least likely of the justices to agree with the Court's results. He did so only 70 percent of the time, a full percentage below Harlan and his lowest number since Warren's first year as chief justice when Black and Douglas constituted the two-man liberal bloc. By contrast, Brennan did so over 98 percent of the time, Marshall 95 percent, and Warren 93 percent. Fortas at 87 percent would have been up with Warren if his votes in the cases handed down after his resignation were counted.

The Fortas Resignation

In true Nixonian form, the new president moved immediately to create a vacancy on the Court in addition to Warren's. Douglas, the Court's most liberal member, seemed the most promising target. He had raised Republican ire for his consistently liberal votes, and when he took twenty-two-year-old Cathleen Heffernan as his fourth wife, there was some grousing that he should be impeached because he was deemed an embarrassment to conventional morality. But maybe there were real reasons too. In October 1966, the *Los Angeles Times* ran a lengthy article by the respected Robert Ostrow on Douglas's relationship with Albert Parvin, a Los Angeles businessman with ties to the Las Vegas gambling industry.[35] Douglas was a very active president of the Albert Parvin Foundation. For this he was paid a yearly salary of $12,000, which was 30 percent of his judicial salary of $39,000. He stated that the money was to cover his expenses traveling for the foundation in its work on international relations, and the explanation appears to have been true. The story raised eyebrows, but they dropped to normal shortly thereafter.

Five days after Nixon's inaugural, the Internal Revenue Service began auditing Douglas's tax returns. Simultaneously, the FBI began gathering data on Douglas's relationship with Parvin. Yet it was Fortas's connections with financier Louis Wolfson and the Wolfson Family Foundation that yielded the vacancy that Nixon wanted to create.

Like so many others, Wolfson had become a client of Fortas's law firm only after Johnson became president. He approached Arnold, Fortas and Porter in 1965 when he was under investigation for securities violations, and he hoped the best-connected firm in the nation could make things well.

Wolfson and Fortas had talked about Fortas's consulting for Wolfson's foundation, but nothing had come of it. Three weeks after Fortas took his seat, he invited Wolfson to Washington where Fortas broached the subject of the consulting agreement. As drafted by Fortas, he would do some unspecified consulting for the foundation in exchange for $20,000 a year for his life and for the life of his wife, Carol Agger, should she survive him. The first year's check arrived in January 1966.

The agreement was a salary supplement pure and simple. Agger and Fortas had made it clear that the pay cut to become a justice was intolerable, and Fortas's friends were arranging to funnel money to him after they received their §501(c) tax deduction on the same money. The American University seminar that derailed his nomination was for the same purpose. But there were differences, important differences. One was that the American University seminar was a one-time shot, and the Wolfson Foundation was for the lives of two people in their fifties. A second was that Louis Wolfson was in deep legal trouble when the arrangement was made and would be heading to jail in the spring of 1969 unless he was pardoned. Whatever Fortas thought about the consulting agreement, Wolfson was cementing a friendship with a person in the highest places of American government who might be able to help him in his time of need.

When one of Fortas's clerks heard through a secretary that the justice had taken money from Wolfson, he warned Fortas that this could mean trouble. Fortas initially responded by telling the clerk to "mind your own business"[36] but he then heeded the good advice and returned the money—eleven months after having received the $20,000 check. Fortas had been stupid, extraordinarily stupid for such an eminent lawyer-adviser, but he had done nothing illegal and by returning the money in the same year it had been received, he did not have to report it as income on his tax return.

In the aftermath of Fortas's failed nomination for chief justice, *Life* reporter William Lambert had come across the barest facts of the story, believing it to be about Fortas's receiving money from the Wolfson Foundation but not paying taxes on it, and therefore tax evasion. (The same information was available to the Republicans during the confirmation battle, but they didn't pursue it because they didn't believe it could possibly be true.) Fortas arranged a meeting between his former partner Paul Porter and Lambert, wherein Porter tried to convince Lambert there was really no story, that Wolfson had given Fortas a check for $20,000 for consulting for the foundation but when it turned out Fortas was too busy, he returned the money. The meeting "only whetted Lambert's interest."[37]

Lambert kept digging, and after January he received help from Nixon's Justice Department. He uncovered some of the relationship between Fortas and Wolfson, with emphasis on the fact that Wolfson was a shady dealer, was in trouble with the Securities and Exchange Commission, was criminally convicted for stock manipulation, and was throwing Fortas's name around liberally, hoping against hope for a presidential pardon. Nixon understood this might force Fortas off the Court, and the Justice Department and FBI gathered what information they could while also encouraging Lambert.

On May 2, Attorney General Mitchell received an advance copy of Lambert's *Life* article entitled "Fortas of the Supreme Court: A Question of Ethics." Mitchell had an aide call every major news organization in town to alert them that *Life* had a big story coming up in its next issue. Indeed, it was. With large pictures of the two principals, *Life*'s caption asked: "Why would a man of his legal brilliance and high position do business with a well-known corporate stock manipulator known to be under federal investigation?"[38] But this was all Lambert had: an association between Fortas and Wolfson with its implication of quid pro quo. Lambert did not know about the dual-lifetime arrangement.

Lambert's story started things churning, and Fortas had no choice but to respond. Making the cardinal mistake of acting as his own lawyer, he issued an unsatisfying, incomplete, but lawyerlike, statement, which caused the *Washington Post* to editorialize that if he could not offer a better explanation, Fortas "can best serve himself, the Court on which he serves, and the country by stepping down."[39] The *Times* editorialized the same day that the "dignity of the Supreme Court requires the most exhaustive disclosure of every aspect of the Wolfson affair."[40] Liberals deserted him immediately, and a "poll by the *New York Times* could find *no* Democrats in Congress now supporting Fortas."[41]

The key moment occurred two days after the *Life* story when an IRS subpoena to the Wolfson Foundation produced the 1966 letter of agreement between Fortas and Wolfson. The letter quickly moved from IRS to the Justice Department, and aides met Mitchell at 1 A.M. when he landed at National Airport. After they showed it to him, Mitchell could not stop repeating, "It can't be real."[42] But it was, and once it became public, Fortas's time remaining on the Court would be measured in days—seven to be exact. Mitchell briefed Nixon in the morning and then arranged a meeting with Warren to show him the newly acquired documents. Mitchell intended to rely on Warren's well-known moral probity to complete the administration's goal of removing Fortas.

Warren immediately recognized the implications of a justice with a lifetime contract for both himself and his wife with a criminal; he copied the documents, and from that moment he worked to force the resignation. Monday-morning quarterbacks have suggested that he should have told Mitchell that this was a matter for the Justice Department, not for the Court. But the Court always protects itself under attack, and this was just such a time. Fortas's nomination as chief justice had been turned into a referendum on the Warren Court, and now his scandal might be turned into a rerun with implications for the legacy of the Court. Warren did not know, as the FBI would soon learn, that Fortas had never lifted a finger to help Wolfson, and probably Warren would not have cared either.

News of the meeting was quickly leaked by the administration, and *Newsweek* reported on the attorney general's "backstairs call on Chief Justice Warren. The message: there was still more damaging material in the Fortas file—and it was sure to surface unless Fortas withdrew."[43] The *Newsweek* piece was perfect for Nixon because its innuendo asked readers to think the worst, even though by then the FBI knew that the worst did not exist because Fortas, in fact, wisely refrained from doing anything to help Wolfson. With its goal in sight, however, the Nixon administration kept this exonerating information under wraps and also kept enthusiastic Republicans from filing impeachment resolutions. The administration instead intended to reinforce Warren's pressure, with the press administering the coup de grace so the resignation would not appear to have anything to do with partisanship. Thus, while "doing its best to appear circumspect," the administration urged reporters to keep digging.[44] John Ehrlichman stated, "I never discourage you guys from trying to do better."[45] Reporters set up a command post in front of the Fortas townhouse in Georgetown and commenced what would soon become the obligatory death vigil.

Fortas meanwhile received conflicting counsel and lacked firm support from the iron-willed Douglas, who was in South America. Black, who had secretly urged Alabama Senator Lister Hill to vote against Fortas the previous year, now urged Fortas to resign. Douglas arrived back in Washington too late; he urged Fortas not to yield, but Fortas was already there. Agger had told him to give up. "The hell with it. It's not worth it to live this way."[46] On May 13, Fortas met with the Brethren to tell them what he was going to do, and he gave Warren a two-sentence letter of resignation the next day. His judicial career had been even shorter than Johnson's presidential career, but unlike Johnson, who could return to Texas, Fortas was left in the capitol. But even his old law firm, now Arnold and Porter, where he had been managing partner and Agger remained a senior partner, would not take him back.

A week later, in recognition of the changed ethical climate, Douglas resigned from the Parvin Foundation. Two years later, *Life* published a survey of constitutional law scholars rating all the Supreme Court justices prior to Nixon's appointees. In anticipation of the ethical blindness that would descend upon the profession generally, Fortas was rated—along with Brennan, Douglas, and Harlan—as near great.[47]

The End of the 1968 Term

After Fortas's resignation, the 1968 Term, with but five weeks to go and all but one of the major cases handed down, was essentially over. The First Amendment pair of *Brandenburg v. Ohio* and *Red Lion Broadcasting v. FCC* came down together on June 9. A week later, *Powell v. McCormack* told Congress and the nation that the Court could and would supervise Congress's decisions to exclude duly-elected members. Beyond *Powell v. McCormack*'s result, the press was able to note that the Warren opinion reversed the holding below by Warren Burger, his now-confirmed successor.

June 23 was the last day of the Warren Court. Two criminal procedure decisions, *Chimel v. California* on the search of homes incident to a valid arrest and *Benton v. Maryland* on the incorporation of the Double Jeopardy Clause into the Fourteenth Amendment, overruled three prior cases. Indeed, *Benton* signed the death certificate to Benjamin Cardozo's famous *Palko v. Connecticut*. Unlike that Court thirty-two years earlier (also including Hugo Black), this Court had come to the conclusion that the guarantee against double jeopardy in criminal cases was indeed fundamental to a system of justice. Warren must have enjoyed overruling Frankfurter's beloved *Palko* as well as the knowledge that the votes in these cases were so solid that they could not be overruled by the addition of the two new justices.

Chimel was the 132nd time the Supreme Court had overruled one of its own precedents. *Benton* was number 133. Sixteen years earlier, when Warren took his seat, only 88 cases had overturned earlier ones. Thus, in a period less than one-tenth the existence of the Court, the Warren Court had overturned 50 percent as many decisions as had their predecessors. Still, the Court seemed to be slowing down just a bit. *Chimel* and *Benton* brought the 1968 Term overrulings to four. The prior term had seen six cases overrule existing cases, but that was one down from the Court's all-time record of seven during the 1966 Term. For a Court that in *Cooper v. Aaron* said that the Constitution meant exactly what the Court said it meant, it was a fitting end, underscoring how much that Constitution had changed in sixteen years.

June 23, 1969

The spectators on the 1968 Term's last day included the secretary of state, the attorney general, the senior Justice Department officials, J. Edgar Hoover, the president of the American Bar Association, several past presidents of the ABA, and, of course, Nixon. It was no wonder they were present, for the old order was vanishing right before them. Fortas, the unexpected casualty, was barely gone. Warren was literally at his last hour as chief justice. The feeble Black, still burning at Warren for making age (six years under Black's) a reason for retirement, but hanging on in hopes of gaining the longevity record, was a certain future vacancy. The ever more antiestablishment Douglas was the next target of the administration. This was neither the retirement Warren wanted nor the one he expected a year earlier.

Nixon was there to acknowledge Warren's retirement and then watch the swearing-in of the man his 1968 campaign had described as the anti-Warren. Warren had seen the choice coming. Months before Nixon made his selection, Warren had correctly guessed it would be Burger. The reasoning was basic; Burger was as prominent a critic of the Warren Court as existed in the judiciary, and his reputation as such was enhanced with a 1967 attack on the Court in Nixon's favorite weekly, *U.S.*

News & World Report. Burger saw to it that Nixon received a copy of
the article "What to Do about Crime in the U.S."—but in fact Nixon was
already familiar with it.[48] As a judge of the federal Court of Appeals for
the District of Columbia, Burger had attacked as excessive the new procedural protections and habeas-caused delays that favored the criminal
defendant. Like Warren, he was a large, handsome man who avoided
legal theory like the plague. Unlike Warren, he was a pure law-and-order
judge who thought that the criminal justice system had been tilted unfairly, unwisely, and unconstitutionally toward the criminal and away
from justice.

Burger had engaged in a very successful campaign for preferment, and
his nomination had been signaled in late April when Nixon made him the
only lower court judge at a White House dinner honoring Warren's
retirement. Six days after Fortas's resignation, Nixon informed Burger he
was the choice and then went on national television to announce it.
Eighteen days later, the Senate confirmed the nomination by a 74–3 vote.

After *Chimel, Benton,* and a third criminal procedure victory for the
defendant were announced, Warren recognized his old California adversary who was wearing the cutaway coat and striped trousers that by
tradition the advocate for the United States always wore. Nixon became
the first president ever to speak at the Court and gave a gracious farewell
to Warren, wherein he complimented Warren's dignity, integrity, and
fairness. Nixon then tied these traits to the symbol of the Court in America. The only possible criticism, if criticism it was, came in four sentences:
"These 16 years without doubt, will be described by historians as years
of greater change than any other in our history. And that brings us to
think of the mystery of Government in this country, and for that matter
the world, the secret of how Government can survive for free men.
Change without continuity can be anarchy. Change with continuity can
mean progress."

Apparently Warren took the words as a slap at him and the Court
because in response he spoke of continuity. "I might point out to you,
because you might not have looked into the matter, that [this Court] is a
continuing body as evidenced by the fact that if any American at any time
in the history of this Court—180 years—had come to this Court he
would have found one of seven men on the Court, the last of whom, of
course, is our senior Justice, Mr. Justice Black. Because at any time an
American might come here he would find one of seven men on the bench
itself shows how continuing this body is and how it is that the Court
develops consistently the eternal principles of our Constitution in solving

the problems of the day. We, of course, venerate the past, but our focus is on the problems of the day and the future as far as we can foresee it."

A minute later, he finished his reply and turned to the business of the Court, announcing that all submitted cases had been disposed of and that the term had ended. He then called on the Clerk of the Court to read the Commission of the Chief Justice-designate. The clerk did; Warren administered the oath of office to Burger and ended the Warren Court with the words, "I present the new Chief Justice of the United States."

That summer, on a major street running over Red Mountain in Birmingham, the billboard proclaiming IMPEACH EARL WARREN came down. That summer Neil Armstrong and Buzz Aldrin walked on the moon and returned safely to earth.

Chapter 19

What Was the Warren Court?

Almost eight decades ago Benjamin Cardozo observed that "the great tides and currents which engulf the rest of men do not turn aside in their course and pass judges by."[1] So, too, with the Warren Court, a historically unique Court operating during a historically unique era. When Anthony Lewis asked Archibald Cox how it felt "to be present at the second American Constitutional Convention,"[2] he had captured the logical congruence of a Court filled with accomplished, confident, powerful men and *Cooper v. Aaron*'s immodest conclusion that the Court's pronouncements were synonymous with the Constitution. Then and now when supporters and critics alike are asked for a neutral adjective to describe the Warren Court's work, revolutionary is the overwhelming choice.

Even if one assumes—contrary to the sharply divided vote in *Brown v. Board of Education* when Fred Vinson was chief justice—that segregation was an unconstitutional result waiting to be announced, there was nothing pointing toward the judicial reapportionment of legislative bodies, the federalization of criminal procedure, the protection of sexually arousing depictions, or the safeguarding of the economic rights of the poor in mid-century constitutional doctrine. A revolutionary body is necessarily one that is engaged in making a sharp break from the past, and constitutional doctrine in 1953 (or even 1962) bore few relationships to constitutional doctrine in 1969.

The only comparable judicial period in American history was that initiated by Owen Roberts's "switch in time that saves nine." Yet even more than the New Deal Court, the Warren Court was engaged in a fundamental discarding of older law. In the eight years encompassing 1937–1944, the New Deal Court created a new constitutional order, as it overruled thirty cases (two-thirds as many as had been overruled in the

Court's previous history). The New Deal transformation, however, was largely limited to three areas: the expansion of national power, the withdrawal of constitutional protection for economic claims, and an incipient civil liberties jurisprudence. In the seven years encompassing 1963–1969, the Warren Court overruled thirty-three prior decisions. When Warren replaced Vinson, the Court had overruled eighty-eight cases in its history. When Warren introduced Burger as the new chief justice, forty-five more precedents had been confined to the scrap heap of history—with a record seven in a single term—and the changes were in virtually all constitutional areas save those settled by the New Deal. As *Brown v. Board of Education*, *Baker v. Carr*, *Miranda v. Arizona* roll off the tongue, the appellation is, indeed, revolutionary.

Over the past generation no one has more warmly, consistently, and ably defended the Warren Court than Yale's Owen Fiss. In his tribute to his former employer, William J. Brennan, on the latter's retirement, Fiss listed the accomplishments of the Court he reveres so much. Because his statements so accurately capture the dominant view of the Warren Court, they merit quoting at some length.

> In the 1950s, America was not a pretty sight. Jim Crow reigned supreme. Blacks were systematically disenfranchised and excluded from juries. State-fostered religious practices, like school prayers, were pervasive. Legislatures were grossly gerrymandered and malapportioned. McCarthyism stifled radical dissent, and the jurisdiction of the censor over matters considered obscene or libelous had no constitutional limits. The heavy hand of the law threatened those who publicly provided information and advice concerning contraceptives, thereby imperiling those most intimate of human relationships. The states virtually had a free hand in the administration of justice. Trials often proceeded without counsel or jury. Convictions were allowed to stand even though they turned on illegally seized evidence or on statements extracted from the accused under coercive circumstances. There were no rules limiting the imposition of the death penalty. These practices victimized the poor and the disadvantaged, as did the welfare system, which was administered in an arbitrary and oppressive manner. The capacity of the poor to participate in civic activities was also limited by the imposition of poll taxes, court filing fees, and the like.
>
> These were the challenges that the Warren Court took up and spoke to in a forceful manner. The result was a program of constitutional reform

almost revolutionary in its aspiration and, now and then, in its achievements. Of course the Court did not act in a political or social vacuum. It drew on broad-based social formations like the civil rights and welfare rights movements. At critical junctures, the Court looked to the executive and legislative branches for support. . . . Yet the truth of the matter is that it was the Warren Court that spurred the great changes to follow, and inspired and protected those who sought to implement them.[3]

Fiss's description and prescription illustrate that there were very serious problems in the United States, but thanks to the courageous action of the members of the Court, all the problems were alleviated and some were solved completely—except gender equality before the law, which Fiss didn't mention because the Court did nothing about it during Warren's tenure (although Congress importantly addressed it in the Equal Pay Act of 1963 and the Civil Rights Act of 1964). To elaborate on Fiss and the standard history of the Warren Court, we need to look at the problems that Court tackled, how the outcomes may be explained, and where the cases came from.

Footnote Four

Fiss offers a useful starting point to consider the conventional view, well expressed in John Morton Blum's *Years of Discord,* that the Court was "really" operating as Footnote Four of *United States v. Carolene Products* (1938) dictated.[4] Footnote Four was Harlan Fiske Stone's proclamation that the Court should and would protect the basic rights of the individual while simultaneously withdrawing constitutional protection from economic behavior. Specifically, Footnote Four directs the Court, first, to police the electoral process, that is, carefully scrutinize laws regulating voting and political expression. Second, Footnote Four demands special protection for discrete and insular minorities, that is, those who even in a well-functioning political process may not be able to form coalitions and thus may be subject to discriminatory legislation. African-Americans are, because of the Fourteenth Amendment and American history, the quintessential discrete and insular minority. A more economical way of expressing the second point is that the Court should protect those who need protection. Third (albeit in its first paragraph), Footnote Four suggests that the Court ought to enforce specific commands of the Bill of Rights. This paragraph, added to Harlan Fiske Stone's footnote by Chief Justice Charles Evans Hughes, had a decided overlap with the other two paragraphs because it was intended to guarantee protection for speech and religion claims.

All the cases involving African-Americans, criminal defendants, and the poor generally fit within Footnote Four with no difficulty. Since these encompass a huge amount of the Court's constitutional work, it is no wonder that the conventional wisdom so well captured by Blum, following the path initially articulated by Alpheus Thomas Mason and then indelibly crafted by John Hart Ely, has associated the Warren Court with Footnote Four. These areas give Footnote Four a large and immediate leg up.

Footnote Four seems to fit two other major areas, reapportionment and free speech, well indeed (once the pre-1963 communist cases are doubly excluded because not only do they involve speech, the communists were, as well, an extraordinarily discrete and insular minority despised by all). The reapportionment cases, like those involving African-Americans as discrete and insular minorities, are a quintessential fit, albeit under the first heading of policing the electoral system (although one must assume that rural voters are not discrete and insular minorities). Virtually all the First Amendment cases similarly fit. The exceptions are extending *New York Times v. Sullivan* to private figures like Wally Butts and to privacy concerns like those of James Hill. Nevertheless, these can be picked up by the final catchall of enforcing the specific provisions of the Bill of Rights.

With a single exception, a similar explanation of reliance on the First Amendment handles cases involving religion and morality: prayer, Bible reading, monkey laws, and sexual materials. That exception, however, is *Griswold v. Connecticut* and the right to use contraceptives. Quite obviously there is no constitutional text on contraception, nor can the right to contraception be related to access to the political process. That leaves only discrete and insular minorities. Unless *Griswold* is reconceived as a poverty case, finding the relevant discrete and insular minority is impossible. Could it be people who wish to prevent ill-timed children? They could easily be a majority. Protestants, perhaps? At 40 percent of the state's population such a conclusion would result in Catholics being a discrete and insular minority in all other states except Massachusetts and Rhode Island. Footnote Four was designed in part to protect religious dissenters, not mainstream religions. *Griswold* is correctly decided not because it fits within Footnote Four, but because the law affected the most intimate part of the marital relationship and was wholly out of place in mid-century America and everyone—the Connecticut Catholic hierarchy included—knew it.

Footnote Four offered a judicial ideology that paralleled Kennedy-Johnson liberalism. First, it expanded rights under the Mae West assumption that one can never have too much of a good thing. Second, and fundamentally, like the Great Society, it focused on those most in need of help.

Neither expanding rights nor helping those whom the political processes excluded were unproblematic. Despite Brennan's assumptions in *Katzenbach v. Morgan,* it is hardly clear that rights are a one-way street. Vigorous rights of speech, however vital, necessarily detract from rights of reputation and privacy, to name but two. Nor can the analysis be ended by noting rights of speech have a constitutional dimension while the others do not—because what is at issue is the scope of the constitutional dimension. When we move from liberty to the equality dimension of Footnote Four, the operative premise is that the Court is helping those who cannot secure help through the political process. Yet the Great Society was aimed precisely at benefiting society's least fortunate. For a brief period, at least, those the Court was ready to help were those the national (but not state) legislature was enthusiastically helping. That is not going against the grain; that's redundancy.

The case for Footnote Four is virtually perfect once *Griswold* and the pre-1963 communist cases are excluded. Yet it is interesting that only once in Warren's sixteen years did an opinion of the Court cite Footnote Four—and that too was a footnote in *Katzenbach v. Morgan* for the proposition that "states can be required to tailor carefully the means of satisfying a legitimate state interest when fundamental liberties and rights are threatened." Brennan's separate opinion in *Braunfeld v. Brown* offered the era's only other citation to Footnote Four, and that was for the unexceptional proposition that religion was special. (The *Carolene Products* holding—that it sure didn't take much to sustain economic regulation—was itself cited three times during the era.) If Footnote Four was the Court's Rosetta Stone, it was seldom on public display.

The Geography of Constitutional Violations

Fiss's bill of particulars levels twelve charges at America. Only three apply to the national government (excluding, as Fiss implicitly did, the horribly malapportioned Senate, which because of the text of the Constitution the Court could not fix). First was McCarthyism with its background of national security concerns. The federal government was far and away the major exposer and prosecutor of domestic communists—although California, New York, and New Hampshire were also active in exposing former communists and attempting to deny them current public employment. Second was obscenity. Customs and Post Office agents as well as United States attorneys fought the evils that depictions of sex supposedly created, but not any more vigorously than states with large concentrations of Catholics. Finally, federal capital punishment for murder and kidnapping was, by later times, standardless, but it was also in complete remission. Capital punishment for murder, rape, or robbery in the states was also standardless and active. This is especially true of the southern states, which used crimes not involving death as a means to sentence to death African-American defendants who violated the norms of white supremacy—thereby offering another issue on which the South had separated itself from the nation.

Fiss's "America" is on to something—although not necessarily what Fiss had in mind. In large part Fiss is accurately describing the South, especially the Deep South. To be sure, he has added in some Catholic flavor, but once the two are combined, they largely explain why his America was not a pretty sight. Local elites were imposing outmoded values, and the national government was not doing anything about it. In fact, the dominant motif of the Warren Court is an assault on the South as a unique legal and cultural region.

By 1953 the South had created, by law and custom (backed by whatever force necessary), a caste system based on white supremacy. From laws against miscegenation, to laws mandating segregation, to subterfuges maintaining a basically all-white electorate, to the use of peremptory challenges to ban African-Americans from juries, to the enforced customs of better jobs for whites, to mandating social deference—every white was called Mr., Mrs., or Miss while all African-Americans were called by their first names—the southerners lived in a society that told all whites, no matter how poor, ignorant, or illiterate, that they were better than any African-American.

This was the society that the Court set about dismantling in *Brown*. With the huge and essential reinforcements provided by the Civil Rights Act of 1964 and the Voting Rights Act of 1965, the effort to transform the "southern way of life" was successful as a legal matter—only racially based peremptory challenges survived. As a result, the legal regime of race was nationalized with a single operative standard for the entire country. But the effort was not a national one. It was directed exclusively at the South and was designed to force the South to conform to northern—that is, national—norms. Recall that, with the exception of the two referenda cases, *Reitman v. Mulkey* and *Hunter v. Erickson*, all the Court's civil rights cases were from and directed at the South.

The Court's civil rights jurisprudence intertwines with its free speech jurisprudence, and after 1962 the former leads to the methodology that invalidates the dated but remaining aspects of McCarthyism. *Gibson v. Florida Legislative Investigating Committee* was the key battleground because either the domestic-security jurisprudence or the civil rights jurisprudence would prevail. When it was the latter and when it was combined with the contemporaneous *NAACP v. Button,* the Court had developed the tools that it would turn on the remnants of McCarthyism. Vagueness, overbreadth, and chilling effect washed away the former balancing that found the need for self-preservation always paramount. Nevertheless, it is essential to realize that the Court did not find the domestic-security program unconstitutional until long after any actual or political need for the program had passed. As late as the Kennedy administration, the Court was sustaining everything the federal government wished to do and, of course, was initially willing to apply the domestic-security jurisprudence to Florida's attack on the NAACP.

Even the most celebrated First Amendment transformation, the constitutionalization of libel in *Sullivan,* was part of the civil rights struggle. There had been no prior hints that the justices thought libelous statements were constitutionally protected. To the contrary, very solid dicta indicated that they weren't. But *Sullivan's* civil rights context made all the earlier statements untenable. Similarly, the quick extension of *Sullivan's* "actual malice" standard from public officials to public figures in *Associated Press v. Walker* occurs in the civil rights context of the riot at Ole Miss. If the *Saturday Evening Post's* hatchet job on Wally Butts had come to the Court alone, the easy extension of *Sullivan* in *Walker* might not have occurred. And again, although the World War I relic that overly sharp criticism of a war effort could justify jail time was eradicated, that decision was made in the context of the Georgia legislature's refusal to seat Julian Bond, the former communications director of the Student Non-Violent Coordinating Committee.

Virtually the entire law of mass demonstrations came from civil rights, with *Edwards v. South Carolina* implicitly rejecting the idea of a heckler's veto. Even as the progression stopped at *Adderley v. Florida,* it was sufficient to protect most of the later nonviolent antiwar protests over Vietnam. When Warren left the Court, the First Amendment was far more protective than it had ever been, and without the South it is unlikely that it could have had either such breadth or such depth, for the only area where the South did not offer important insights of the intertwining of free speech and civil rights was obscenity.

As noted, obscenity law flowed from localities with a high concentration of Catholics (and also from the South as more titillating materials entered the mainstream). When the Court began its efforts, its goal was to protect serious art and literature from the censor's hand. To accomplish this, some breathing space was necessarily created involving less than serious art and literature—*Fanny Hill,* for instance—and it turned out that, given *Memoirs v. Massachusetts,* the Court could find no acceptable stopping place. In George Wallace's words, the Court could not distinguish constitutionally between "smut and great literature."[5] But its important cases came from New York, Rhode Island, Massachusetts, and Ohio and bear the heavy overtones of the pre–Vatican II Catholic Church, as did Connecticut's enforcement of its Comstock-era anticontraceptive statute. In these decisions, the Court was bringing urban Catholic communities into the American mainstream. These remaining little pockets of censorship were out of place in an America where *Playboy* was gaining a circulation that rivaled *Reader's Digest* and Masters and Johnson's *Human Sexual Response* could become a runaway bestseller.

The Court's handful of religion cases paralleled the geography of the obscenity cases. They were either from the South or from the arc running from New England through the Middle Atlantic states where laws already on the books acquired the backing of the local Catholic hierarchies.

For the quarter-century prior to *Mapp v. Ohio,* the Court's criminal procedure cases were thinly disguised race cases (although the cases discussed in text, with the exception of *Mallory v. United States,* would not lead a reader to this conclusion). As such, they were disproportionately southern. Beginning with *Mapp v. Ohio,* the criminal procedure decisions become national, one legal rule always implicating the South but also affecting large parts of the remainder of the country. The national impact of criminal procedure decisions is what made *Mapp, Escobedo v. Illinois,* and *Miranda* so unpopular. The purely southern cases—like *Gideon* and the incorporation of the other "fair trial" procedures of the Sixth Amendment—were either popular or unnoticed, except in the handful of affected jurisdictions. Nevertheless, with these southern exceptions, the criminal procedure decisions were not about bringing backwaters into the mainstream. They were about improving the performance of police, prosecutors, and judges. Thus, their goal was to force state systems to behave like they assumed the FBI, United States attorneys, and the federal courts behaved.

The two remaining items in Fiss's list of twelve evils were confined neither to the South nor to religiously dominated backwaters. Malapportioned legislatures were everywhere, and the arbitrariness of the welfare system was virtually universal. But, of all the areas of Fiss's critique, the Court did less with welfare than with anything else. It struck down man-in-the-house rules and durational residency requirements and, after Congress passed and the states ratified the Twenty-Fourth Amendment, it also struck down the poll tax in the remaining five southern states that had it. The man-in-the-house regulations were not exclusively southern, but well over half the states that had them were. Deterring in-migration was never a southern problem in the first seven decades of the century, and durational residency requirements were a protection of the northern and western states from influxes of the (often southern) poor. *Shapiro v. Thompson* is an excellent example of the Court's acting not to strike at the South or some other backwater, but to impose enlightened views of welfare policy upon reluctant bureaucracies and legislatures.

While the South had some of the most starkly malapportioned legislatures, Illinois, Vermont, Connecticut, and California could compete with anyone. Malapportionment was not a regional problem; rather, it was a problem for the ever-increasing urbanization of post–World War II America. The days when farmers could properly dominate American politics had long since passed by the 1960s. The reapportionment decisions, especially *Reynolds v. Sims,* were explicitly designed to transfer political power from rural America to urban America with its new suburbs. Farmers may have been popular in the Senate, but they had no friends at the Court. *Reynolds* moved power from a backwards rural elite to, the Court could well believe, the more educated urbanites who better understood that the prime problem of American life was no longer World War I price parity for crops.

The geography of constitutional violations downsizes Fiss's America considerably. It is the South by an overwhelming margin. Then it picks up urban areas of Catholic dominance. When dealing with the federal government, the Court nibbled at McCarthyism in 1956 and 1957, then retreated to its 1951 stance, and then, commencing in 1963, ended the domestic-security program. The attack on the welfare system began only in 1968 and consisted of, at most, three decisions. Prior to 1968 the law of welfare was *Fleming v. Nestor,* that is, government may do as it pleases. The two truly national areas were reapportionment with its assault on rural political dominance and the criminal justice revolution with its twin demands of professionalism and a fair trial for the defendant. If discrete and insular minorities are the key, then possibly the Court could be better seen as attacking (rather than protecting) them on a national (rather than a local) scale: the white South, the pre–Vatican II

Catholic hierarchy, rural legislators, the local criminal justice system, and those remaining few who believed domestic communists were a threat to the nation.

As the previous ten chapters have demonstrated, the Court was a functioning part of the Kennedy-Johnson liberalism of the mid and late 1960s. Indeed, a prime reason that liberals were and remain captivated by the Warren Court is that it represents the purest strain of Kennedy-Johnson liberalism. The Warren Court seemed to combine Kennedy's rhetoric with Johnson's ability to do the deal. Unlike congressional politics, there was never a need to compromise over money (and therefore the value placed on a right), and the Court could never be tainted with Vietnam. No wonder liberals and law professors believe the "Warren Court got the Constitution right once and for all."[6] The Warren Court demanded national liberal values be adopted in outlying areas of the United States and that the rural dominance of state legislatures, which it believed were precluding necessary solutions to urban problems, be broken. In the criminal procedure area, it took the lead as the branch of government most familiar with the problems and most capable of supervising the solutions. The Court's belated welfare decisions were an assault on both national and local bureaucracies, but in moving toward constitutionalization, the Court was several years behind the Great Society in creating new rights.

Public Values

The Warren Court completed the eradication of federalism, once a cherished and innovative part of the American constitutional order. The New Deal revolution had rejected the Framers' belief that limiting the scope of the national government protected the individual. What remained of federalism thereafter celebrated difference and experimentation, and this was the Warren Court's target. Because there were better solutions and those were known in Washington, D.C., it made no sense to authorize weaker solutions—especially when they came at the expense of rights all Americans were deemed to hold. Federalism served no ascertainable purpose except to authorize local—and typically southern—oligarchies to impose their backwards and often arbitrary views on those unfortunate enough to live within their jurisdictions. By nationalizing rights and reducing federalism to an empty concept—a "watered-down Bill of Rights" was the acerbic characterization of Black and Douglas—the Warren Court reflected the view that states were impediments to the achievement of a better, fairer America. With Congress and the president as working partners, the Court hoped to achieve this vision of America because that was what the nation deserved and therefore what the Constitution mandated.

While there had been persistent attacks on the Court during Warren's first decade, once the 85th Congress adjourned in August 1958, they came largely from the South and the fringes. Then Barry Goldwater made the Court a prime campaign issue in 1964, attacking the school prayer, reapportionment, and criminal procedure decisions as exercises of "raw and naked power."[7] These attacks moved the Court's results into two-party American politics, albeit through a candidate widely perceived as a right-wing extremist. Goldwater's other radical ideas, such as ending social security, selling the TVA, or having a real war, maybe with nukes, in southeast Asia, never again surfaced in a presidential campaign. But his perhaps premature attack on the Court for its "obsessive concern for the rights of the criminal defendant"[8] had staying power and became a staple of American politics as the Republicans institutionalized it. Race and crime metastasized into the politics of "law and order," and being tough on crime was deemed to necessitate an attack on liberal judges.

Mapp had initiated the shift in criminal cases from the South to the nation generally. *Escobedo* accelerated the shift, and *Miranda* cemented the Court and the release of violent criminals in the public mind. As this was occurring, crime statistics took their huge jump, and many politicians, led by Richard Nixon, played the demagogue and argued that liberal Supreme Court decisions were causing the increase in crime. Even if that claim was discounted totally, the public wanted criminals in jail, and to the extent that *Mapp* and *Miranda* appeared to make that task more difficult, they were resented. Furthermore, even if members of the public could not repeat either what the Court said or did, they knew a criminal procedure revolution was proceeding apace, and they didn't like it.

Beyond the crime statistics were the annual summer riots, commencing in 1964 and peaking in the "Long Hot Summer" of 1967. Television brought into every home the senseless violence, the wanton looting, the buildings burning. Liberal Democrats held with the Kerner Commission that the riots were symptomatic of America's developing into two societies, one white and one black, separate and unequal. Republicans, joined by southern Democrats, blamed the riots on the rioters and liberals, especially judges, who excused the criminal behavior.

For southern Democrats, "law and order" was a second godsend.

Attacking the Court for being soft on communism had lost its salience, so still hating the Court because of *Brown,* now they could publicly hate it because of coddling criminals. The hearings on the Fortas nomination for chief justice were dominated by the former segregationists blasting Fortas and the Court for the criminal procedure decisions. The obscenity and prayer cases were the added glue: efficient causes capable of fully explaining moral depravity and a society going to hell.

To some extent, of course, the Court was being dragged down with other liberals by the unpopularity of Johnson's Vietnam War and the unrealistic promises of the Great Society. But other, deeper factors were at work. For its first decade, the Warren Court was able to decide cases on the basis of "an idealized set of public values" that it could presume that all Americans (with the exception of ignorant outliers) shared:[9] ending segregation, moving past Victorianism, leaving religion as a personal decision in the home or church, "one person, one vote," and precluding police from using the third degree.

Idealized values, however, began to look different in practice than in the abstract when the criminal procedure decisions brought home a new meaning. Warren had argued in his *Jacobellis v. Ohio* dissent that the states had the right to maintain a decent society. While he was talking of a smut-free world, far more basic were the citizens' expectations that criminals would be apprehended, convicted, and incarcerated. John McClellan, who graphed the rising crime rate along with liberal criminal procedure decisions, was not alone in believing the latter caused the former. Sam Ervin's charge that "enough has been done for those who murder and rape and rob! It is time to do something for those who do not wish to be murdered or raped or robbed"[10] rang true. Many Americans, no matter how they voted, believed with the Republicans that the police "should not be unnecessarily handicapped in their efforts to prevent crime and apprehend criminals."[11] Similarly, with Vietnam and the beginnings of inflation squeezing both national and personal resources, not all Americans shared the Court's belief that welfare recipients were a class peculiarly in need of special constitutional protections against government.

As James Patterson's magisterial *Grand Expectations* demonstrates, the 1960s generally were a time when a consensus over public values was disintegrating. The Court was part and parcel of this phenomenon, and as an outgrowth the Court became a political issue because its values were deemed political and wrongheaded by a significant sector of the politicians and electorate. In his important blueprint for the future, the youthful Kevin Phillips wrote that Republicans could "hardly ask for a better target than a national Democratic Party aligned with Harvard, Boston, Manhattan's East Side, Harlem, the *New York Times* and the liberal Supreme Court."[12] The fact that the Republicans could perceive the Court as too much like liberal Democrats foreshadowed the conclusion that discrete and insular minorities were synonymous for liberal special interest groups. The initial Democratic response, to lecture Americans about constitutional guarantees, was as unsatisfying as it was unsuccessful. The response of law professors, that the Court was simply enforcing the Constitution, was no more successful with conservatives. Dissents, and there were always dissents after the 1963 Term, demonstrated the availability of alternative readings of the Constitution.

Some, but hardly all, of the Warren Court's advances stuck. The antidiscrimination principle of *Brown* is sacrosanct as is one person, one vote. (It is affirmative action and racial redistricting where the modern controversies lie.) The Warren Court's free speech jurisprudence has lasted as well, aided by a quarter-century of domestic quiescence following Vietnam and Watergate. By contrast the liberal criminal procedure decisions, while never overruled, have largely been gutted and there is precious little clamor to resurrect them. In between, the height of the Wall of Separation between church and state never was firmly established and remains hotly contested. More recently, even federalism is enjoying a comeback. Set in its era, the Warren Court does look revolutionary. Decades later the results that have lasted have a decided majoritarian cast.

Three Warren Courts

The Warren Court burst onto the national scene with *Brown*. Then after *Brown II,* it began the process of dismantling the domestic-security program that had grown up during the McCarthy era. This phase of the Warren Court came to a halt with the 1957 decisions, and the next phase varies between stalemate and retreat for a period of almost five years. Without any means to decide the domestic-security cases on technicalities, the Court once again, as it had in 1951, sustained the program as consistent with the First Amendment. With race, the Court shifted from school desegregation to simply trying to keep the NAACP in business in the face of a southern attack where states often adopted methods perfected in the domestic-security area. Most constitutional law scholars have not appreciated this initial break—probably because the domestic-security retreat does not fit well with a story about unfolding progress after the ill-starred *Dennis v. United States* decision. And in protecting the NAACP, the Court adopted methods that would shortly thereafter dismantle the outdated domestic-security programs.

Like most constitutional law scholars, I agree that following Frankfurter's retirement the Court dramatically changed, and almost three-quarters of the overrulings occurred thereafter. Part III of the book details the changes and the Court's aggressive willingness to implement liberal values, like those being articulated across the street in Congress and at the end of Pennsylvania Avenue at the White House, once the fifth vote was secured.

Using quantitative rather than qualitative measures, political scientists Jeffrey Segal and Harold Spaeth have placed the transformation one year earlier. They accurately note that the jump in civil liberties victories at the Court between the 1960 and 1961 Terms is genuinely significant—from 54.3 percent to 79.6 percent[13]—and that the latter percentage is far more consistent with the later terms than with the terms in the 1950s. Yet using the 1960 Term as the break would leave the NAACP losing both *Gibson* and *Button* in the Court's most robust era. Such a conclusion seems inherently wrong. Segal and Spaeth's data do not pick up the votes in *Gibson* and *Button* because they were set over to the next term following Whittaker's retirement, and in the 1962 Term they come down as civil liberties victories. The outcomes and events illustrate why quantitative data can offer insights but must be supplemented by qualitative information to avoid questionable conclusions.

Like everyone else, I view the 1962–1968 Terms as largely harmonious. Yet it would be a mistake not to note that, after *Miranda* and another summer of rioting, the civil liberties results are less exuberant after the 1965 Term, even after Thurgood Marshall replaces Tom Clark. The most noticeable term, however, is the 1966 Term, immediately following *Miranda,* where the percentage of civil liberties victories is much lower than any term of the 1960s (while being much higher than all but one term of the 1950s). Yet that very term saw a then-record-tying six overrulings.

With these splits over time it is difficult to describe a single Warren Court. The Court that (temporarily) ceased its efforts to order school desegregation in 1958 adamantly ordered "results now" in 1968. The Court that found George Anastaplo unfit for the Illinois bar in 1961 concluded that the federal government could not bar admitted communists from working in defense facilities in 1967. The membership of the

Court had changed, and the political climate in which the Court operated also changed.

The Warren Court?

It is perhaps appropriate to end with a return to the book's title and a frequently used pair of words—the Warren Court. Was it truly the Warren Court? That question is designed to provoke the response, "Wasn't it really the Brennan Court?" which three very able scholars, Dennis Hutchinson,[14] Sanford Levinson,[15] and Robert Post,[16] have answered in the affirmative. No one agreed with the results of the Court more than Brennan as he led the pack all through the 1960s, voting with the majority an astronomical 96–98 percent of the time. Furthermore, Brennan was the Court's designated doctrinalist, the person to whom Warren turned when he needed a difficult majority result translated into an opinion that could hold the voters together. The clearest example was *Baker v. Carr*, where Brennan was selected to write the historic opinion because he was more likely than anyone else to bring Potter Stewart's fifth vote along. Brennan's claim thus flows from his being the man who both created the Court's doctrine and then most agreed with its results.

Brennan's major problem is *Brown*. He joined the Court two years later, and it is impossible to think of the era without *Brown* as its beginning. To be sure Brennan would have joined *Brown*, and he did draft *Cooper v. Aaron*, but he was on the New Jersey Supreme Court when the century's greatest case came down.

Brennan is the author of major opinions in *Baker, Sullivan,* and *Green v. New Kent County*. In retrospect, these may well be more important than Warren's *Brown, Reynolds,* and *Miranda,* but they were not more important or more controversial during the era covered. Additionally, Brennan was the Court's "law" of obscenity and he created the doctrinal techniques that slew the domestic-security program—even as he avoided Warren's use of them in delivering the coup de grace in *United States v. Robel*. But Warren too authored other important decisions from *Flast v. Cohen* to *Robel* to *Powell v. McCormack*. When all is said and done, however, basing a decision about whose Court it was on secondary opinions seems to miss the point.

Concluding that the Warren Court should be principally associated with Warren does not denigrate Brennan's influence. Stonewall Jackson's importance is not reduced by the fact that the Army of Northern Virginia is known as "Lee's Army." An enormously able lieutenant—Brennan, as well as the far less dependable Hugo Black and William O. Douglas—can make an outstanding general look even better. (A great general also needs worthy opposing generals, and Felix Frankfurter and John Marshall Harlan offered the necessary foils.)

Over time, Brennan became the most important justice of the second half of the twentieth century, but that achievement is based on his full thirty-four-year career. Had it been but a thirteen-year career no one would make the assertion in the prior sentence. The claim that the Warren Court was really "the Brennan Court" seems largely based on reading Brennan's subsequent career backward or defining a different era (well past Warren's retirement). Even Frank Michelman's new tribute to Brennan basically ignores his contributions during Warren's era to focus on his post-1970 jurisprudence.[17] It is also well worth remembering that in the mid-1960s some commentators were suggesting it was really "the Black Court"—a claim that no one would take seriously today.

No one claimed that it was the Brennan Court while Warren sat. Not only had Brennan's illustrious career just begun, but he was largely unknown. No billboards proclaimed "Impeach Bill Brennan." No body investigating political assassinations was called the "Brennan Commission."

Warren was more important in the first of the three periods of the Court during his tenure (because of *Brown*), least important during the second (because of Frankfurter's switch in the domestic-security area). But during the entire era, the public face of the revolutionary Court was its dignified, genial chief justice, who even Nixon stated exemplified "dignity, integrity, and fairness."[18] When all the discussions are over, CBS commentator Eric Sevareid needed but a single word to explain why the Court was identified with Warren rather than anyone else. Warren possessed that rarest of traits—"gravitas."[19]

The legendary lawyer-political scientist Thomas Reed Powell, who taught Douglas Constitutional Law at Columbia and gave him a C, but was best known for a quarter-century at the Harvard Law School, offered a definition of the legal mind that was perfect and therefore has never been bettered: A legal mind is a mind that can think of one of two inseparably connected things without thinking of the other. Law professors have first-rate legal minds. When they think of the Warren Court, they see what Part III calls "history's Warren Court" without seeing history. They see the Court ordering an end to racial discrimination, creating political equality as well as an end to McCarthyism, requiring religion to quit the public schools and appear in public only to march for justice, moving the death penalty toward its deserved grave, demanding an administration of criminal justice that conforms to the strictures of *Griffin-Gideon-Douglas*, providing the most needy among us with treatment characterized by equal concern and respect. They see a Court that was better than any Court had ever been. To paraphrase Robert Kennedy, "some ask 'why?'; they ask 'why not?'"—meaning why not again, right now?

One message of this book echoes what political scientists have been preaching for decades on end: The Court does not operate in a vacuum. Therefore, all the good things bestowed on American society in the 1960s did not come from judicial decisions alone. Fiss may believe that "the truth of the matter is that it was the Court that spurred the great changes to follow, and inspired and protected those who sought to implement them."[20] But, in fact, that belief is only partially true. The Warren Court definitely did inspire a generation of lawyers, Fiss and myself included, who worshiped it. Liberal law professors came to have what Fiss displays and what Laura Kalman calls a "religious and mystical" view of the Warren Court.[21] Like many a devout communicant, Fiss believes that the Court spurred the great and positive changes of the 1960s and 1970s. But that does not make it so.

Another message of this book is that a nostalgia for the Warren Court is necessarily a nostalgia for the 1960s. The same impulses that produced the "I Have a Dream" speech and the sanitation strike in Memphis five years later, that sent Neil Armstrong and Buzz Aldrin to the moon and John and Robert Kennedy to Arlington Cemetery, that caused four African-American students to sit in at Woolworth's in Greensboro and hundreds of demonstrators to gather in Chicago for the Democratic National Convention, that sang "Blowing in the Wind" and "White Rabbit," that authored *Catch 22* and *The Housewife's Handbook of Selective Promiscuity*, that filmed *Dr. Strangelove* and *The Green Berets*, that placed Viola Liuzzo in Alabama and George Wallace in Michigan, that witnessed the New Frontier and the New Nixon, that celebrated the withdrawal of Soviet missiles from Cuba and the introduction of American combat units in Vietnam, that sent youths to Mississippi for "Freedom Summer" and to San Francisco for the "Summer of Love," that offered a Great Society for America and a TVA for the Mekong River, that unleashed idealism and produced hubris, that witnessed old virtues and verities that Earl Warren represented, like integrity, patriotism, and family, begin their slide out of style—well, those impulses created history's Warren Court, too. Only a legal mind could separate them.

Chronology

November 1952   Dwight Eisenhower elected president
June 1953   School segregation cases set for reargument
July 1953   Korean War cease-fire
September 1953   Chief Justice Fred Vinson dies of heart attack

October Term 1953
October 1953   Earl Warren replaces Vinson
December 1953   *Playboy* commences publication
February 1954   *Irvine v. California*
March 1954   U.S. hydrogen bomb at Bikini Atoll
April 1954   Army-McCarthy Hearings
  Barsky v. Board of Regents
May 1954   *Brown v. Board of Education*
  Bolling v. Sharpe
  Galven v. Press

October Term 1954
December 1954   Senate condemns Joseph McCarthy
March 1955   John Marshall Harlan replaces Robert Jackson
  Williamson v. Lee Optical
May 1955   *Brown v. Board of Education*
June 1955   *Peters v. Hobby*

October Term 1955
October 1955   *Lucy v. Adams*
November 1955   *Toth v. Quarles*
  Mayor of Baltimore v. Dawson
  Holmes v. Atlanta
December 1955   Montgomery bus boycott
  American Federation of Labor and Congress of
    Industrial Organizations merge
February 1956   Nikita Khrushchev's "Secret Speech" denouncing Stalin
March 1956   "Southern Manifesto"
  Naim v. Naim

	Ullmann v. U.S.
	Florida ex rel. Hawkins v. Board of Control
April 1956	*Pennsylvania v. Nelson*
	Slochower v. Board of Education
	Griffin v. Illinois
	Communist Party v. Subversive Activities Control Board
June 1956	*Black v. Cutter Laboratories*
	Kinsella v. Krueger
	Reid v. Covert
	Cole v. Young
	Interstate Highway Act

October Term 1956
October 1956	William J. Brennan replaces Sherman Minton
	Suez Crisis
November 1956	Hungarian Rebellion crushed
	Mesarosh v. U.S.
	Eisenhower reelected
	Gayle v. Browder
February 1957	*Butler v. Michigan*
	Ferguson v. Moore-McCormack Lines
March 1957	Charles Whittaker replaces Stanley Reed
May 1957	*Schware v. State Bar*
	Konigsberg v. State Bar
June 1957	*Textile Workers Union v. Lincoln Mills*
	U.S. v. duPont
	Jencks v. U.S.
	Reid v. Covert
	Watkins v. U.S.
	Sweezy v. New Hampshire
	Yates v. U.S.
	Service v. Dulles
	Mallory v. U.S.
	Roth v. U.S.
September 1957	Arkansas National Guard blocks Little Rock desegregation
	Eisenhower sends federal troops to Little Rock

October Term 1957
October 1957	Soviet Union launches Sputnik
	Florida ex rel. Hawkins v. Board of Control
March 1958	*Perez v. Brownell*
	Trop v. Dulles

May 1958 *International Association of Machinists v. Gonzales*
June 1958 *Kent v. Dulles*
           Beilan v. Board of Education
           Lerner v. Casey
           NAACP v. Alabama
           Speiser v. Randall

Special August Term 1958
September 1958 *Cooper v. Aaron*

October Term 1958
October 1958 Potter Stewart replaces Harold Burton
November 1958 *Shuttlesworth v. Birmingham*
March 1959 *Bartkus v. Illinois*
May 1959 *Frank v. Maryland*
June 1959 *Vitarelli v. Seaton*
           Lassiter v. Northampton Board of Elections
           Uphaus v. Wyman
           Barenblatt v. U.S.
           Harrison v. NAACP
           Kingsley Pictures v. Board of Regents

October Term 1959
January 1960 *Kinsella v. Singleton*
February 1960 First "sit-in": Greensboro, North Carolina
               Bates v. Little Rock
June 1960 *Hannah v. Larche*
           Fleming v. Nestor
           Eaton v. Price

October Term 1960
November 1960 John F. Kennedy elected president
               Gomillion v. Lightfoot
December 1960 *Boynton v. Virginia*
               Shelton v. Tucker
February 1961 *Wilkinson v. U.S.*
               Braden v. U.S.
April 1961 Yuri Gagarin orbits the earth
            Bay of Pigs invasion
            Burton v. Wilmington Parking Authority
            Konigsberg v. State Bar
            In re Anastaplo
May 1961 Freedom Rides
          McGowan v. Maryland
          Braunfeld v. Brown

June 1961	*Communist Party v. Subversive Activities Control Board*
	Scales v. U.S.
	Noto v. U.S.
	Torcaso v. Watkins
	Poe v. Ullman
	Mapp v. Ohio
	Cafeteria Workers v. McElroy
August 1961	Berlin Wall

October Term 1961

November 1961	*Hoyt v. Florida*
December 1961	*Garner v. Louisiana*
March 1962	*Baker v. Carr*
April 1962	Felix Frankfurter suffers strokes
	Byron White replaces Charles Whittaker
	Carnley v. Cochran
June 1962	*Brown Shoe v. United States*
	Engle v. Vitale
September 1962	Riot at Ole Miss

October Term 1962

October 1962	Arthur J. Goldberg replaces Frankfurter
	Vatican II commences
	Cuban Missile Crisis
January 1963	*NAACP v. Button*
February 1963	*Bantam Books v. Sullivan*
	Edwards v. South Carolina
March 1963	*Townsend v. Sain*
	Gideon v. Wainwright
	Douglas v. California
	Gray v. Sanders
	Fay v. Noia
	Gibson v. Florida Legislative Investigating Committee
April 1963	Good Friday March in Birmingham
	Ferguson v. Skrupa
May 1963	*Peterson v. City of Greenville*
	Lombard v. Louisiana
	Watson v. Memphis
June 1963	*Goss v. Board of Education*
	Medgar Evers assassinated in Mississippi
	Abingdon School District v. Schempp
	Sherbert v. Verner
	U.S. v. Philadelphia National Bank

August 1963	March on Washington
September 1963	Church bombing in Birmingham kills four children
	Senate ratifies atmospheric nuclear test ban treaty
October Term 1963	
November 1963	Ngo Dinh Diem killed in South Vietnamese coup
	President Kennedy assassinated
February 1964	*Wesberry v. Sanders*
March 1964	*New York Times v. Sullivan*
May 1964	*Massiah v. U.S.*
	Griffin v. Prince Edward County
June 1964	Freedom Summer
	Reynolds v. Sims ⁻
	Lucas v. Colorado 44th General Assembly
	Malloy v. Hogan
	Senate passes Civil Rights Act
	Andrew Goodman, James Chaney, and Michael Schwerner killed in Mississippi
	Barr v. City of Columbia
	Robinson v. Florida
	Jacobellis v. Ohio
	Bell v. Maryland
	Bouie v. City of Columbia
	Escobedo v. Illinois
	Aptheker v. Secretary of State
July 1964	Civil Rights Act
	Four days of rioting in Harlem
August 1964	Gulf of Tonkin Resolution
	Democratic Convention "compromise" of two seats rejected by Mississippi Freedom Democratic Party
September 1964	Warren Commission releases report
October Term 1964	
October 1964	Free Speech Movement, Berkeley
	Khrushchev deposed
November 1964	Lyndon Johnson elected president
December 1964	Occupation of Berkeley Administration Building
	McLaughlin v. Florida
	Heart of Atlanta Motel v. U.S.
	Katzenbach v. McClung
	Hamm v. Rock Hill
January 1965	*El Paso v. Simmons*
	Cox v. Louisiana
February 1965	Operation Rolling Thunder

                          Malcolm X assassinated
        March 1965   *Freedman v. Maryland*
                          "Bloody Sunday" in Selma
                          U.S. v. Seeger
                          Swain v. Alabama
                          First official combat troops land in South Vietnam
        April 1965   *Dombrowski v. Pfister*
                          First non-Monday opinion: *Harman v. Forssenius*
        May 1965   *Lamont v. Postmaster General*
        June 1965   *U.S. v. Brown*
                          Griswold v. Connecticut
                          Linkletter v. Walker
        July 1965   Formal acknowledgment of ground war in Vietnam
        August 1965   Voting Rights Act
                          Six days of rioting in Watts

    October Term 1965
        October 1965   Abe Fortas replaces Arthur Goldberg
        November 1965   *Albertson v. Subversive Activities Control Board*
        December 1965   Vatican II ends
        January 1966   *Evans v. Newton*
        February 1966   *Brown v. Louisiana*
        March 1966   *South Carolina v. Katzenbach*
                          Memoirs v. Massachusetts
                          Ginzburg v. U.S.
                          Mishkin v. New York
                          Harper v. Virginia Board of Elections
        April 1966   *Elfbrandt v. Russell*
                          Publication of *Human Sexual Response*
        May 1966   *U.S. v. Von's Grocery*
        June 1966   *Miranda v. Arizona*
                          Katzenbach v. Morgan
                          Stokely Carmichael of SNCC calls for "Black Power"
                          Johnson v. New Jersey
                          Schmerber v. California

    October Term 1966
        November 1966   Ronald Reagan elected California governor
                          Adderley v. Florida
        December 1966   *Bond v. Floyd*
                          Hoffa v. U.S.
        January 1967   *Time, Inc. v. Hill*
                          Keyishian v. Board of Regents
        February 1967   *Chapman v. California*

March 1967	Martin Luther King leads his first antiwar March
May 1967	*Redrup v. New York*
	In re Gault
	Reitman v. Mulkey
	H. "Rap" Brown replaces Stokely Carmichael as head of SNCC
June 1967	"Long Hot Summer" of northern rioting begins
	Six Days War
	Loving v. Virginia
	Berger v. New York
	Curtis Publishing v. Butts
	U.S. v. Wade
	Gilbert v. California
	Walker v. Birmingham
July 1967	Five days of rioting in Newark
	Four days of rioting in Detroit
	Federal troops sent to Detroit
October Term 1967	
October 1967	Thurgood Marshall replaces Tom Clark
December 1967	*U.S. v. Robel*
	Katz v. U.S.
January 1968	*Marchetti v. U.S.*
	Grosso v. U.S.
	Tet Offensive
March 1968	Johnson announces he will not run for reelection
April 1968	Martin Luther King assassinated
	U.S. v. Jackson
	Ginsberg v. New York
	Student takeover at Columbia University
May 1968	*Levy v. Louisiana*
	Glona v. American Guarantee & Liability Insurance Co.
	Duncan v. Louisiana
	Amalgamated Food Employees Union v. Logan Valley Plaza
	U.S. v. O'Brien
	Green v. New Kent County
June 1968	*Witherspoon v. Illinois*
	Robert Kennedy assassinated
	Terry v. Ohio
	Flast v. Cohen
—	*Board of Education v. Allen*

Earl Warren announces retirement
King v. Smith
Jones v. Alfred H. Mayer
Powell v. Texas
Johnson nominates Abe Fortas as Chief Justice and
    Homer Thornberry as Associate Justice

July 1968   Senate hearings on Fortas-Thornberry
August 1968   Warsaw Pact troops invade Czechoslovakia
Democratic National Convention in Chicago

October Term 1968
October 1968   Fortas withdraws as nominee for Chief Justice
November 1968   Richard Nixon elected president
Epperson v. Arkansas
December 1968   Apollo 8 circles the moon
January 1969   *Hunter v. Erickson*
February 1969   *Johnson v. Avery*
Tinker v. Des Moines School District
March 1969   *Shuttlesworth v. Birmingham*
McInnis v. Ogilvie
April 1969   *Stanley v. Georgia*
Street v. New York
Shapiro v. Thompson
May 1969   Fortas resigns
June 1969   *U.S. v. Montgomery County Board of Education*
Boykin v. Alabama
Harrington v. California
Daniel v. Paul
Sniadach v. Family Finance Corp.
Red Lion Broadcasting v. FCC
Brandenburg v. Ohio
Powell v. McCormack
NLRB v. Gissel Packing Co.
Kramer v. Union Free School District
Chimel v. California
Benton v. Maryland
Warren Burger replaces Earl Warren
July 1969   Neil Armstrong and Buzz Aldrin land on the moon

$\mathscr{N}otes$

1. The Supreme Court, 1935–1953

1. Arthur M. Schlesinger, Jr., *The Politics of Upheaval*, 488 (1960).
2. *6 Public Papers and Addresses of Franklin D. Roosevelt*, 122, 130, 126 (1937).
3. *Time*, April 5, 1937, at 13.
4. Frank Freidel, *Franklin D. Roosevelt*, 229 (1990).
5. Bruce Ackerman, *We the People: Transformations*, 334 (1998).
6. William E. Leuchtenburg, *The Supreme Court Reborn*, 142 (1995); for a revisionist position, see Barry Cashman, *Rethinking the New Deal Court* (1998).
7. The text of Footnote Four reads as follows:

   There may be narrower scope for operation of the presumption of constitutionality when legislation appears on its face to be within a specific prohibition of the Constitution, such as those of the first ten amendments, which are deemed equally specific when held to be embraced within the Fourteenth. See *Stromberg* v. *California*, 283 U.S. 359, 369–370; *Lovell* v. *Griffin*, 303 U.S. 444, 452.

   It is unnecessary to consider now whether legislation which restricts those political processes which can ordinarily be expected to bring about repeal of undesirable legislation, is to be subjected to more exacting judicial scrutiny under the general prohibitions of the Fourteenth Amendment than are most other types of legislation. On restrictions upon the right to vote, see *Nixon* v. *Herndon*, 273 U.S. 536; *Nixon* v. *Condon*, 286 U.S. 73; on restraints upon the dissemination of information, see *Near* v. *Minnesota ex rel. Olson*, 283 U.S. 697, 713–714, 718–720, 722; *Grosjean* v. *American Press Co.*, 297 U.S. 233; *Lovell* v. *Griffin, supra*; on interferences with political organizations, see *Stromberg* v. *California, supra*, 369; *Fiske* v. *Kansas*, 274 U.S. 380; *Whitney* v. *California*, 274 U.S. 357, 373–378; *Herndon* v. *Lowry*, 301 U.S. 242; and see Holmes, J., in *Gitlow* v. *New York*, 268 U.S. 652, 673; as to prohibition of peaceable assembly, see *De Jonge* v. *Oregon*, 299 U.S. 353, 365.

   Nor need we enquire whether similar considerations enter into the review of statutes directed at particular religions, *Pierce* v. *Society of Sisters*, 268 U.S. 510, or national, *Meyer* v. *Nebraska*, 262 U.S. 390; *Bartels* v. *Iowa*, 262 U.S. 404; *Farrington* v. *Tokushige*, 273 U.S. 484, or racial minorities, *Nixon* v.

Herndon, supra; Nixon v. *Condon, supra:* whether prejudice against discrete and insular minorities may be a special condition, which tends seriously to curtail the operation of those political processes ordinarily to be relied upon to protect minorities, and which may call for a correspondingly more searching judicial inquiry. Compare *McCulloch* v. *Maryland,* 4 Wheat. 316, 428; *South Carolina* v. *Barnwell Bros.,* 303 U.S. 177, 184, n. 2, and cases cited.

8. Samuel Walker, *In Defense of American Liberties,* 109 (1990).
9. The *Japanese Relocation Cases* are *Korematsu* v. *United States,* 323 U.S. 214 (1944), and *Ex parte Endo,* 323 U.S. 283 (1944). They were preceded by *Hirabayashi* v. *United States,* 320 U.S. 81 (1943), sustaining the West Coast curfew that applied only to those of Japanese ancestry. Despite *Endo's* holding that Japanese-Americans who could prove their loyalty must be released on habeas and the Roosevelt administration's knowledge that by the summer of 1944 there was no threat whatsoever, there were no releases prior to the 1944 presidential election.
10. William H. Rehnquist, *The Supreme Court Then and Now,* 97 (1987).

I. Beginnings: Prologue

1. Thomas Dixon, *The Leopard's Spots: A Romance of the White Man's Burden,* 244 (1902).
2. Charles A. Lofgren, *The Plessy Case,* 197 (1987).
3. 49 *Landmark Briefs and Arguments of the Supreme Court of the United States,* 389 (Philip B. Kurland and Gerhard Casper, eds., 1975).
4. Bernard Schwartz, *Super Chief,* 72 (1983).

2. *Brown*

1. J. Harvie Wilkinson, *From Brown to Baake,* 6 (1979).
2. Douglas Conference notes, quoted in Michael J. Klarman, "Civil Rights Law: Who Made It and How Much Does It Matter?," 83 *Georgetown Law Journal* 433, 444 (1994).
3. Richard Kluger, *Simple Justice,* 698 (1976).
4. *The Memoirs of Earl Warren,* 3 (1977).
5. 49 *Landmark Briefs and Arguments of the Supreme Court of the United States,* 32–33 (Philip B. Kurland and Gerhard Casper, eds., 1975).
6. Warren to Conference, May 7, 1954, Tom Clark Papers, Box 27A.
7. Alpheus Thomas Mason, *The Supreme Court from Taft to Warren,* 207–208 (1968).
8. C. Vann Woodward, *The Strange Career of Jim Crow,* 131 (2d rev. ed. 1966).
9. Mark V. Tushnet, *Making Civil Rights Law,* 142 (1994).
10. William Faulkner, "A Letter to the North," *Life,* March 5, 1956, at 51–52.
11. U.S. Brief at 6; reprinted in 49 *Landmark Briefs* at 121.

12. U.S. Brief at 7; id. at 122.

13. U.S. Brief at 4; id. at 119.

14. U.S. Brief at 7; id. at 122.

15. Philip Elman, "The Solicitor General's Office, Justice Frankfurter, and Civil Rights Litigation," 100 *Harvard Law Review* 817 (1987).

16. *New York Times,* May 18, 1954, at 1.

17. Mary Dudziak, "Desegregation as a Cold War Imperative," 40 *Stanford Law Review* 61, 113 (1988).

18. *New York Times,* May 18, 1954, at 19.

19. *New York Times,* May 19, 1954, at 1.

20. *Memoirs of Earl Warren,* at 6–7.

21. Herbert Brownell (with John Burke), *Advising Ike,* 193–194 (1993).

22. Tushnet, *Making Civil Rights Law,* at 216.

23. *New York Times,* May 18, 1954, at 18.

24. Kluger, *Simple Justice,* at 710.

25. *Time,* May 24, 1954, at 21.

26. Kluger, *Simple Justice,* at 710; Benjamin Muse, *Ten Years of Prelude,* 18 (1964).

27. Woodward, *Strange Career,* at 149.

28. Dewey Grantham, *The South in Modern America,* 212 (1994).

29. Id. at 206.

30. Muse, *Ten Years,* at 17.

31. Quoted in Kluger, *Simple Justice,* at 711.

32. Id. at 710.

33. Id.

34. Id.

35. 100 *Congressional Record* 7254 (1954).

36. Numan Bartley, *The Rise of Massive Resistance,* 68 (1969).

37. *New York Times,* May 24, 1954, at 19.

38. Juan Williams, *Thurgood Marshall,* 230 (1998).

39. *New York Times,* May 19, 1954, at 18.

40. Kluger, *Simple Justice,* at 710.

41. Doris Kearns Goodwin, *Lyndon Johnson and the American Dream,* 252 (rev. ed. 1991).

42. 100 *Congressional Record* 6748 (1954).

43. Wilkinson, *From Brown,* at 29.

44. 100 *Congressional Record* 6748 (1954).

45. Quoted in Muse, *Ten Years,* at 19.

46. *New York Times,* May 18, 1954, at 14.

47. David W. Southern, *Gunnar Myrdal and Black-White Relations,* 71–99 (1987).

48. Idus A. Newby, *Challenge to the Court: Social Scientists and the Defense of Segregation 1954–66* (1969).

49. Alexander Bickel, "The Original Understanding and the Segregation Decisions," 69 *Harvard Law Review* 1, 2 (1955).

50. Quoted in Michael J. Klarman, "*Brown,* Originalism, and Constitutional Theory," 81 *Virginia Law Review* 1881, 1930 (1995).
51. 100 *Congressional Record* 6749 (1956).
52. June 1, 1955 (responding to *Brown II*).
53. 49A *Landmark Briefs,* at 527–528.
54. Brownell, *Advising Ike,* at 179.
55. Roy E. Carter, Jr., "Segregation and the News: A Regional Content Study," 34 *Journalism Quarterly* 3, 10 (1957).

3. Implementation

1. 49A *Landmark Briefs and Arguments of the Supreme Court of the United States,* 1308 (Philip Kurland and Gerhard Casper, eds., 1975).
2. 49 *Landmark Briefs,* at 321.
3. Mark V. Tushnet, *Making Civil Rights Law,* 212 (1994).
4. Richard Kluger, *Simple Justice,* 594 (1976).
5. 49A *Landmark Briefs,* at 1167–68.
6. Id. at 1154.
7. 49 *Landmark Briefs,* at 322.
8. 49A *Landmark Briefs,* at 1154.
9. Tushnet, *Making Civil Rights Law,* at 225.
10. 49A *Landmark Briefs,* at 522.
11. Id. at 1150.
12. Tushnet, *Making Civil Rights Law,* at 219.
13. Philip Elman, "The Solicitor General's Office, Justice Frankfurter, and Civil Rights Litigation," 100 *Harvard Law Review* 817, 827 (1987).
14. *New York Times,* June 1, 1955, at 1.
15. Id. at 26; *New York Times,* June 2, 1955, at 15.
16. *New York Times,* June 1, 1955, at 27.
17. Id. at 1.
18. Id. at 26 (quoting *Los Angeles Times* editorial, "The Reasonable Will Agree").
19. *New York Times,* June 3, 1955, at 1.
20. Benjamin Muse, *Ten Years of Prelude,* 29 (1964).
21. The *Richmond News Leader* was so proud of the editorials that it put them in booklet form under the title "Interposition" and made them available to anyone; bulk orders went for 25 cents a booklet. All subsequent citations to the editorials are from the booklet.
22. December 30, 1955, at 35.
23. November 23, 1955, at 11.
24. December 30, 1955, at 35 (emphasis in original).
25. November 22, 1955, at 6.
26. January 23, 1956, at 42.
27. The resolution was also printed in the booklet at 51–54.

28. Walter F. Murphy, "Book Review," 67 *Yale Law Journal* 1505 (1958).

29. C. Vann Woodward, *The Strange Career of Jim Crow,* 154 (2d rev. ed. 1966).

30. Quoted in J. Harvie Wilkinson, *From Brown to Baake,* 74 (1979).

31. 102 *Congressional Record* 4515–16 (1956).

32. Dewey W. Grantham, *The South in Modern America,* 210 (1994).

33. Anthony Lewis, *Portrait of a Decade,* 39 (1964).

34. Tushnet, *Making Civil Rights Law,* at 237.

35. Id. at 268.

36. Tom P. Brady, *Black Monday,* 45 (1955).

37. Neil McMillen, *The Citizen's Councils,* 237 (1971).

38. Dan T. Carter, *The Politics of Rage,* 84 (1995).

39. Id. at 233–234.

40. Elizabeth Jacoway, "The Southern Palladium," in *W. J. Cash and the Minds of the South,* 112, 124 (Paul D. Escott, ed., 1992).

41. Brady, *Black Monday,* at 45.

42. William Attwood, "Fear Underlies the Conflict," *Look,* April 3, 1956, at 26.

43. Id.

44. Paul Brest and Sanford Levinson, *The Processes of Constitutional Decision-Making,* 583 (3d ed. 1992).

45. Joel Williamson, "Wounds Not Scars," 83 *Journal of American History* 1221, 1228 (1997).

46. *Voices of Freedom,* 3 (Henry Hampton and Steve Fayer, eds., 1990).

47. Walter F. Murphy, *The Elements of Judicial Strategy,* 193 (1964).

48. Elman, "The Solicitor General's Office," at 847.

49. Dennis Hutchinson, "Unanimity and Desegregation," 68 *Georgetown Law Journal* 1, 63–64 (1979).

50. Tushnet, *Making Civil Rights Law,* at 304.

51. Juan Williams, *Thurgood Marshall,* 247 (1998).

52. Nicholas Lemann, "The Lawyer as Hero," *New Republic,* March 13, 1993.

53. Press Conference of March 24, 1956, quoted in James C. Duran, *A Moderate among Extremists,* vi (1981).

54. Charles J. Pach, Jr., and Elmo Richardson, *The Presidency of Dwight Eisenhower,* 141 (1991).

4. Domestic Security

1. Harvey Klehr, John Earl Haynes, and Kyrill M. Anderson, *The Soviet World of American Communism,* 6 (1998).

2. James T. Patterson, *Grand Expectations,* 188–189 (1996).

3. *Time,* March 6, 1950, at 17.

4. Quoted in Bernard Schwartz, *Super Chief,* 155 (1983).

5. David Caute, *The Great Fear,* 57–59 (1978).

6. 102 *Congressional Record* 7341 (1956).

7. Walter F. Murphy, *Congress and the Court,* 88–89 (1962).

8. 102 *Congressional Record* 6383 (1956).

9. Id. at 6384.

10. *U.S. News & World Report,* May 18, 1956 at 50.

11. Murphy, *Congress and the Court,* at 89.

12. 102 *Congressional Record* 6386 (1956).

13. Id.

14. Id. at 6385.

15. *Time,* June 25, 1956, at 16.

16. Ed Cray, *Chief Justice,* 322 (1997).

17. 102 *Congressional Record* 10,174 (1956).

18. Murphy, *Congress and the Court,* at 91–95.

19. Stephen J. Wermiel, "The Nomination of Justice Brennan," 11 *Constitutional Commentary* 515 (1995).

20. Patterson, *Grand Expectations,* at 53.

21. 103 *Congressional Record* 10,624 (1957).

22. Quoted in Schwartz, *Super Chief,* at 230.

23. Tinsley Yarbrough, *John Marshall Harlan,* 190 (1992).

24. *New York Times,* June 18, 1957, at 32.

25. I. F. Stone, *The Haunted Fifties,* 203 (1963) (from June 24, 1957).

26. *New York Times,* June 27, 1957, at 1.

27. Murphy, *Congress and the Court,* at 118.

28. Quoted in Schwartz, *Super Chief,* at 284.

29. *The Memoirs of Earl Warren,* 322 (1977).

30. Id. at 323.

31. Id.

32. *Washington Post and Times-Herald,* quoted in Murphy, *Congress and the Court,* at 114.

33. *New York Post,* quoted in id. at 114.

34. 103 *Congressional Record* 10,296 (1957).

35. *New York Times,* July 8, 1957, at 15.

36. Murphy, *Congress and the Court,* at 116.

37. 103 *Congressional Record* 15,972 (1957).

38. Id. at 12,806.

39. Id. at 12,807.

5. Glimpses of the Future

1. *New York Times,* February 9, 1954, at 20.

2. 103 *Congressional Record* 12,810 (1957).

3. Id. at 11,645.

4. *Hearings before the Special Subcommittee to Study Decisions of the Supreme*

Court of the United States of the Committee on the Judiciary, 85th Cong., 2d Sess., Part I, at 42 (1957).

5. Quoted in Bernard Schwartz, *Super Chief,* 226 (1983).
6. *New York Times,* November 8, 1955, at 21.
7. 98 *Congressional Record* 912 (1952).
8. *Senate Committee on the Judiciary, Treaties and Executive Agreements: Hearings,* 83rd Cong., 1st Sess., 136–137 (1953).
9. *United States v. Kennerley,* 209 Fed. 119, 120 (S.D.N.Y. 1913).
10. *United States v. One Book Called "Ulysses,"* 5 F. Supp. 182, 184 (S.D.N.Y. 1933).
11. Schwartz, *Super Chief,* at 224.
12. *Wall Street Journal,* June 5, 1957, at 12.
13. *New York Times,* June 9, 1957, §IV, at 7.

II. Stalemate: Prologue

1. *Public Papers of the Presidents, 1958,* at 337.
2. James T. Patterson, *Grand Expectations,* 301 (1996).
3. Quoted in Walter F. Murphy, *Congress and the Court,* 173 (1962).
4. Id.
5. Id. at 174.
6. 104 *Congressional Record* 2011 (1958).
7. Gerald Gunther, *Learned Hand,* 648 (1994).
8. Learned Hand, *Bill of Rights,* 42 (1958).
9. Id. at 54.
10. Id. at 73–74.
11. Gunther, *Learned Hand,* at 654–655.
12. William F. Buckley, Jr., and L. Brent Bozell, *McCarthy and His Enemies* (1954).
13. *New York Times,* March 16, 1958, at E10.
14. Rogers to James Eastland, March 4, 1958, *Hearings on S. 2646, before the Subcommittee to Investigate the Administration of the Internal Security Act,* Senate Committee of the Judiciary, 85th Cong., 2d Sess., Part 2, at 573–574 (1958).
15. Murphy, *Congress and the Court,* at 164.
16. Id. at 163.
17. S. Rep. No. 1586, at 49; Gunther, *Learned Hand,* at 656.
18. Murphy, *Congress and the Court,* at 211.
19. 104 *Congressional Record* at 18,750 (1958).
20. John Morton Blum, *Years of Discord,* 137–38 (1991).
21. Joseph Rauh, "The Truth about Congress and the Court," 22 *The Progressive* 30 (November 1958).
22. *The Memoirs of Earl Warren,* 313 (1977).

23. Robert G. McCloskey, "Reflections on the Warren Court," 51 *Virginia Law Review* 1229, 1258 (1965).

6. Domestic Security after Red Monday

1. Ellen Schrecker, *No Ivory Tower,* 171 (1986) (Slochower resigned rather than go through the next hearing).
2. *Report of the Committee on Federal-State Relationships as Affected by Judicial Decisions,* 27–29 (1958). The *Report* is more accessible in C. Herman Pritchett, *Congress versus the Supreme Court 1957–60,* 141–159 (1961).
3. *Time,* Sept. 1, 1958, at 15.
4. "Who Writes Decisions of the Supreme Court?" *U.S. News & World Report,* December 13, 1957, at 74 (when asked about the article after he joined the Court, Rehnquist told a college class that "it was written by a young man who was full of himself").
5. *New York Times,* May 1, 1958, at 27.
6. Walter F. Murphy, *Congress and the Court,* 226 (1962).
7. Id.
8. Michael Barone, *Our Country,* 303–305 (1990).
9. 105 *Congressional Record* 3379 (1959).
10. Ed Cray, *Chief Justice,* 389–390 (1997).
11. Bernard Schwartz, *Super Chief,* 281 (1983).
12. *New York Times,* March 2, 1960, at 36.
13. Schwartz, *Super Chief,* at 320.
14. Erwin Griswold, "Absolutes in the Dark," 8 *Utah Law Review* 167, 172 (1963).
15. Charles Black, "Mr. Justice Black, the Supreme Court and the Bill of Rights," *Harper's,* February 1961, at 63.
16. Harry Kalven, *A Worthy Tradition,* 269 (1988).
17. *New York Times,* June 7, 1961, at 40.
18. Doris Kearns Goodwin, *Lyndon Johnson and the American Dream* (rev. ed. 1991).
19. James T. Patterson, *Grand Expectations,* 157 (1996).

7. Little Rock and Civil Rights

1. *Public Papers of the Presidents of the United States: Dwight D. Eisenhower, 1957,* at 546.
2. Sherman Adams, *First-Hand Report: The Story of the Eisenhower Administration,* 355 (1961).
3. Anthony Lewis, *Portrait of a Decade,* 43 (1964).
4. Id. at 45.
5. Id. at 44.
6. James T. Patterson, *Grand Expectations,* 415 (1996).

7. Quoted in Mary L. Dudziak, "The Little Rock Crisis and Foreign Affairs," 70 *Southern California Law Review* 1641, 1685 (1997).

8. Mark V. Tushnet, *Making Civil Rights Law,* 259 (1994).

9. Melba Pattillo Beals, *Warriors Don't Cry: A Searing Memoir of the Battle to Integrate Little Rock's Central High,* 241 (1994).

10. 54 *Landmark Briefs and Arguments of the United States Supreme Court,* 714 (Philip Kurland and Gerhard Casper, eds., 1975).

11. *New York Times,* September 30, 1958, at 30.

12. *Voices of Freedom,* 52 (Henry Hampton and Steve Fayer, eds., 1990).

13. Bernard Schwartz, *Super Chief,* 303 (1983).

14. Monroe Billington, "George Wallace," in *Encyclopedia of Southern Culture,* 1200 (1989); Dan T. Carter, *The Politics of Rage,* 96 (1995).

15. Tushnet, *Making Civil Rights Law,* at 283.

16. Id. at 277.

17. William Chafe, *Civilities and Civil Rights,* 99 (1980).

18. John Morton Blum, *Years of Discord,* 69 (1991).

19. Mark Stern, *Calculating Visions,* 61 (1992).

20. Id.

21. Robert Weisbrot, *Freedom Bound,* 25 (1990).

22. Michael Barone, *Our Country,* 354 (1990).

23. Lewis, *Portrait of a Decade,* at 113.

24. Blum, *Years of Discord,* at 72.

8. The Transition

1. Alan Westin, "Also on the Bench: 'Dominant Opinion,'" *New York Times Magazine,* October 21, 1962, reprinted in *The Supreme Court under Earl Warren,* 63 (Leonard Levy, ed., 1972).

2. *New York Times,* June 29, 1962, at 11.

3. *The Memoirs of Earl Warren,* 316 (1977).

4. *New York Herald Tribune,* July 5, 1962, at 18, quoted in Philip Kurland, "The Regent's Prayer Case," 1962 *Supreme Court Review* 1, 2 n.4.

5. *New York Times,* June 27, 1962, at 34.

6. *Wall Street Journal,* June 27, 1962, at 14.

7. Kurland, "The Regent's Prayer Case," at n.5.

8. Id.

9. Id.

10. *New York Times,* June 27, 1962, at 20.

11. *New York Times,* June 26, 1962, at 17.

12. Id.

13. Kurland, "The Regent's Prayer Case," at n.7.

14. John D. Weaver, *Warren: the Man, the Court, the Era,* 260 (1967).

15. Kurland, "The Regent's Prayer Case," at n.7.

16. *New York Times,* June 27, 1962, at 20.

17. Leo Katcher, *Warren: A Political Biography,* 463 (1967).

18. Weaver, *Warren,* at 258.

19. William Beaney and Edward Beiser, "Prayer and Politics," 13 *Journal of Public Law* 475, 482 (1964).

20. *New York Times,* June 27, 1962, at 20.

21. Kurland, "The Regent's Prayer Case," at 3.

22. Francis J. Lally, "Points of Abrasion," 210 *Atlantic* 78 (August 1962).

23. *New York Times,* June 28, 1962, at 12.

24. Douglas Laycock, "The Underlying Unity of Separation and Neutrality," 46 *Emory Law Journal* 43, 57 (1997), summarizing John T. McGreevy, "Thinking on One's Own: Catholicism in the American Intellectual Imagination, 1928–60," 84 *Journal of American History* 97 (1997).

25. Bernard Schwartz, *Super Chief,* 391 (1983).

26. *New York Times,* April 28, 1965, at 50.

27. Roger Traynor, "*Mapp v. Ohio* at Large in the Fifty States," 1962 *Duke Law Journal* 319, 335; *People v. Cahan,* 44 Cal. 2d 434, 282 P.2d 905 (1955).

28. Id. at 342.

29. Quoted in Yale Kamisar, "On the Tactics of Police-Prosecution Oriented Critics of the Courts," 49 *Cornell Law Quarterly* 436, 437 (1964).

30. Id. at 439.

31. *Memoirs of Earl Warren,* at 306.

32. Ed Cray, *Chief Justice,* 379 (1997).

33. Schwartz, *Super Chief,* at 412.

34. Cray, *Chief Justice,* at 380.

35. Brief of the United States Amicus Curiae in *Baker v. Carr* at 17.

36. Id. at 55.

37. Robert McCloskey, "Foreword: The Reapportionment Case," 76 *Harvard Law Review* 54, 58–59 (1962).

38. Chester Newland, "Press Coverage of the United States Supreme Court," 17 *Western Political Quarterly* 15, 29 (1964).

39. *New York Times,* March 28, 1962, at 1.

40. *New York Times,* March 29, 1962, at 17.

41. McCloskey, "Foreword," at 57.

42. "The Shame of the States," *New York Times Magazine,* May 18, 1958, at 12.

43. Schwartz, *Super Chief,* at 425.

44. Id.

45. Nicholas Katzenbach, "Some Reflections on *Baker v. Carr,*" 15 *Vanderbilt Law Review* 829, 836 (1962).

46. Westin, "Also on the Bench: 'Dominant Opinion.'"

47. Cray, *Chief Justice,* at 368.

48. Id.

49. Schwartz, *Super Chief,* at 391.

50. Ken Gormley, *Archibald Cox,* 170 (1997).

III. History's Warren Court: Prologue

1. Arthur M. Schlesinger, Jr., *Robert Kennedy and His Times,* 392 (1969).
2. Id. at 393.
3. Dennis Hutchinson, "'The Ideal New Frontier Judge,'" 1997 *Supreme Court Review* 373, quoting from Benjamin C. Bradlee, *Conversations with Kennedy,* 69 (1975).
4. Id. at 394.
5. David L. Stebenne, *Arthur J. Goldberg,* 317 (1996).
6. Bruce Allen Murphy, *Fortas,* 180 (1990).
7. See Chapter 1, note 7.

9. To the Civil Rights Act

1. Mark Stern, *Calculating Visions,* 72 (1992).
2. James T. Patterson, *Grand Expectations,* 477 (1996).
3. Taylor Branch, *Parting the Waters,* 656 (1988).
4. Arthur M. Schlesinger, Jr., *Robert Kennedy and His Times,* 334 (1978).
5. John Morton Blum, *Years of Discord,* 75 (1991).
6. Patterson, *Grand Expectations,* at 475.
7. Dan T. Carter, *The Politics of Rage,* 11 (1995).
8. Tony Freyer, "Hugo Black and the Warren Court in Retrospect," in *The Warren Court in Historical and Political Perspective,* 94 (Mark V. Tushnet, ed., 1993).
9. Robert Weisbrot, *Freedom Bound,* 58 (1990).
10. Branch, *Parting the Waters,* at 753.
11. Blum, *Years of Discord,* at 106.
12. Id.
13. Id. at 759.
14. Id. at 760.
15. Michael Barone, *Our Country,* 354 (1990).
16. Arthur M. Schlesinger, Jr., *A Thousand Days,* 964–965 (1965).
17. C. Vann Woodward, *The Strange Career of Jim Crow,* 181 (2d rev. ed. 1966).
18. Gerald Rosenberg, *The Hollow Hope,* 131 (1991).
19. Weisbrot, *Freedom Bound,* at 82.
20. Taylor Branch, *Pillar of Fire,* 132 (1998).
21. Roger Newman, *Hugo Black,* 545 (1994).
22. Hugo L. Black and Elizabeth Black, *Mr. Justice and Mrs. Black,* 96 (1986).
23. Patterson, *Grand Expectations,* at 484.
24. Theodore H. White, *The Making of the President 1964,* 304 (1965).
25. Branch, *Pillar of Fire,* at 232.
26. Blum, *Years of Discord,* at 145.
27. Stern, *Calculating Visions,* at 161.
28. Doris Kearns Goodwin, *Lyndon Johnson and the American Dream,* 191 (rev. ed. 1991).

29. Id. at 192.
30. Patterson, *Grand Expectations,* at 544.
31. Eric Goldman, *The Tragedy of Lyndon Johnson,* 69 (1969).
32. *New York Times,* June 20, 1964, at 11.
33. *New York Times,* July 16, 1964, at 13.
34. *New York Times,* August 20, 1963, at 11.
35. 22 *Congressional Quarterly* 2534 (1964).
36. *New York Times,* September 4, 1964, at 12.
37. *New York Times,* September 17, 1964, at 28.

10. Revamping the Democratic Process

1. *New York Times,* March 30, 1962, at 1, 12.
2. David E. Kyvig, *Explicit and Authentic Acts,* 354 (1996).
3. Theodore H. Sorenson, *Kennedy,* 535 (1965).
4. Kyvig, *Explicit Acts,* at 356.
5. Alfred Kelly, "Clio and the Court: An Illicit Love Affair," 1965 *Supreme Court Review* 119, 136.
6. Note, "Partisan Gerrymandering," 42 *Stanford Law Review* 1549, 1555 (1990).
7. 110 *Congressional Record* at 16,061 (1964) (statement of October 29, 1948, read into the *Congressional Record,* July 8, 1964).
8. Robert Dixon, Jr., *Democratic Representation,* 199 (1968).
9. Id. at 214.
10. *Washington Post,* June 12, 1966, at E4.
11. Anthony Lewis, "A Talk with Warren on Crime, the Court, the Country," *New York Times Magazine,* October 19, 1969, reprinted in *The Supreme Court under Earl Warren,* 164 (Leonard Levy, ed., 1972).
12. Dixon, *Democratic Representation,* at 462.
13. Jack H. Pollock, *Earl Warren,* 209 (1979).
14. *New York Times,* June 21, 1964, §IV at 3.
15. Anthony Lewis, "The Legacy of the Warren Court," in *The Warren Court: A Retrospective,* 398 (Bernard Schwartz, ed., 1996).
16. Ken Gormley, *Archibald Cox,* 176 (1997).
17. Jerold Israel, "On Charting a Course through the Mathematical Quagmire," 61 *Michigan Law Review* 107, 122 (1963).
18. 110 *Congressional Record* at 20,236–37 (1964).
19. Id. at 20,223–25.
20. Id. at 20,220.
21. *New York Times,* August 9, 1964, §IV at 8.
22. Kyvig, *Explicit Acts,* at 375.
23. Walter F. Murphy and Joseph Tanenhaus, "Publicity, Public Opinion, and the Court," 84 *Northwestern Law Review* 985, 996 (1990).
24. Kyvig, *Explicit Acts,* at 379.

25. *New York Times,* June 23, 1969, at 24.
26. Doug McAdam, *Freedom Summer,* 24 (1988).
27. Anthony Lewis, *Portrait of a Decade,* 177 (1964).
28. Neil McMillen, "Black Enfranchisement in Mississippi," 43 *Journal of Southern History* 364 (1977).
29. Dan T. Carter, *The Politics of Rage,* 223 (1995).
30. Taylor Branch, *Pillar of Fire,* 437 (1998).
31. James T. Patterson, *Grand Expectations,* 556 (1996).
32. Id. at 557.
33. Doris Kearns Goodwin, *Lyndon Johnson and the American Dream,* 228 (rev. ed. 1991).
34. Patterson, *Grand Expectations,* at 579.
35. Allen J. Matusow, *The Unraveling of America,* 182 (1984).
36. Dewey Grantham, *The South in Modern America,* 240 (1994).
37. Robert Weisbrot, *Freedom Bound,* 134 (1990).
38. Mark Stern, *Calculating Visions,* 223 (1992).
39. Patterson, *Grand Expectations,* at 581.
40. Robert Dallek, *Flawed Giant,* 198–199 (1998).
41. *New York Times,* March 8, 1965, at 1.
42. Grantham, *The South,* at 228 (emphasis in original).
43. Patterson, *Grand Expectations,* at 583.
44. Goodwin, *Lyndon Johnson,* at 229.
45. Id.
46. Grantham, *The South,* at 240.
47. Stern, *Calculating Visions,* at 227.
48. Weisbrot, *Freedom Bound,* at 152–153.
49. Archibald Cox, "Constitutional Adjudication and the Promotion of Human Rights," 80 *Harvard Law Review* 91, 107 (1966).
50. *New York Times,* March 25, 1966, at 40.
51. The Court was quoting from volume 11 of Lawrence H. Gipson, *The British Empire before the American Revolution,* 222 (1965).
52. *New York Times,* June 17, 1969, at 36.

11. After the Civil Rights Act

1. James L. Sundquist, *Politics and Policy,* 281 (1968).
2. Thomas B. Edsall and Mary D. Edsall, *Chain Reaction,* 49–50 (1991).
3. Robert Weisbrot, *Freedom Bound,* 160 (1990).
4. David J. Garrow, *Bearing the Cross,* 360–361 (1986).
5. Doris Kearns Goodwin, *Lyndon Johnson and the American Dream,* 305 (rev. ed. 1991).
6. Michael Barone, *Our Country,* 418 (1990).
7. Allen J. Matusow, *The Unraveling of America,* 363 (1984).

8. *Ramparts,* June 15, 1968, at 40.

9. Clark Kerr, "The Multiversity," *Harper's,* November 1963; Clark Kerr, *The Uses of the University* (1963).

10. Matusow, *Unraveling,* at 317–318.

11. Id. at 318.

12. David Lance Goines, *The Free Speech Movement,* 489 (1993).

13. Weisbrot, *Freedom Bound,* at 186.

14. Id.

15. Id. at 196.

16. Matusow, *Unraveling,* at 365.

17. *New York Times,* July 19, 1967, at 42.

18. Matusow, *Unraveling,* at 366.

19. Weisbrot, *Freedom Bound,* at 264.

20. Jules Whitcover, *The Year the Dream Died,* 124 (1997).

21. Weisbrot, *Freedom Bound,* at 220.

22. John Morton Blum, *Years of Discord,* 270 (1991).

23. *New York Times,* June 13, 1967, at 26.

24. Whitcover, *The Year the Dream Died,* at 7.

25. Id.

26. Hugo L. Black and Elizabeth Black, *Mr. Justice and Mrs. Black,* 122 (1986).

27. *New York Times,* June 13, 1967, at 26.

28. Charles Alan Wright, *The Law of the Federal Courts,* 231 (3d ed. 1976).

29. Id.

30. Quoted in Dan T. Carter, *The Politics of Rage,* 306 (1995).

31. Ed Cray, *Chief Justice,* 451 (1997).

32. Brief for Appellants, *McLaughlin v. Florida,* 1963 Term, No. 11 at 13.

33. Andrew Kull, *The Color-Blind Constitution,* 170 (1992).

34. Charles Black, "Foreword: State Action," 81 *Harvard Law Review* 69 (1967).

35. Roger Newman, *Hugo Black,* 568 (1994).

36. Mark V. Tushnet, *Making Constitutional Law,* 12 (1997).

37. Id. at 19.

38. Id.

39. Id. at 25.

40. Robert Dallek, *Flawed Giant,* 406 (1998).

41. Goodwin, *Lyndon Johnson,* at 307.

42. Tushnet, *Making Constitutional Law,* at 25.

43. *Washington Post,* September 1, 1967, at A20.

44. Tushnet, *Making Constitutional Law,* at 26.

45. J. Harvie Wilkinson, *From Brown to Bakke,* 108 (1979).

46. Id. at 109.

47. Id. at 110.

48. *New York Times,* April 10, 1966, at 38.

49. Wilkinson, *From Brown,* at 104.

50. Id. at 101–102.

51. *Briggs v. Elliot,* 132 F. Supp. 776, 777 (E.D.S.C. 1955).
52. *Singleton v. Jackson Municipal School District,* 355 F.2d 865, 869 (5th Cir. 1965).
53. *United States v. Jefferson County School Board of Education,* 372 F.2d 836, 866 (5th Cir. 1966).
54. Id.
55. Id. at 869.
56. Brennan to Clark, May 23, 1963, in Tom Clark Papers, Box A145 and William J. Brennan Papers, Box 177.
57. Harlan to Goldberg, May 20, 1963, quoted in David O'Brien, *Storm Center,* 254 (1986).
58. Bernard Schwartz, *Super Chief,* 706 (1983).
59. Blacks, *Mrs. Black,* at 193.
60. Wilkinson, *From Brown,* at 118.
61. Tushnet, *Making Constitutional Law,* at 70.
62. Blacks, *Mrs. Black,* at 222.
63. Lewis Steel, "Nine Men in Black Who Think White," *New York Times Magazine,* October 13, 1968, reprinted in *The Supreme Court under Earl Warren,* 82 (Leonard Levy, ed., 1972).

12. Freedom of Expression

1. Laura Kalman, *Abe Fortas,* 271 (1990).
2. Benjamin C. Bradlee, *Conversations with Kennedy,* 69 (1975).
3. Harry Kalven, "The New York Times Case: A Note on the 'Central Meaning of the First Amendment,'" 1964 *Supreme Court Review* 191.
4. *New York Times,* March 29, 1960. A huge blowup of the ad is an appendix to the Court's opinion in *Sullivan.*
5. Anthony Lewis, *Make No Law,* 11 (1991).
6. Quoted in Lucas A. Powe, Jr., *The Fourth Estate and the Constitution,* 83 (1991).
7. Ronald Rotunda, "The Warren Court and Freedom of the Press," in *The Warren Court: A Retrospective,* 89 (Bernard Schwartz, ed., 1996).
8. Powe, *Fourth Estate,* at 86.
9. Id. at 87.
10. Brief of Abernathy, *Abernathy v. Sullivan,* a companion case to *New York Times v. Sullivan,* at 29.
11. *New York Times,* November 16, 1965, at 34.
12. *New York Times,* May 25, 1965, at 1.
13. Kalven, "Central Meaning," at 221.
14. 111 *Congressional Record* 19,871 (1965).
15. Id. at 19,871–72.
16. Id. at 20,433.
17. *New York Times,* August 11, 1965, at 14.

18. Abe Fortas, *Concerning Dissent and Civil Disobedience,* 124 (1968).
19. Andrew Kopkind, "Brennan v. Tigar," *New Republic,* August 27, 1966, at 21.
20. *Washington Post,* September 29, 1997, at D1.
21. Robert Woodward and Scott Armstrong, *The Brethren,* 77 (1979).
22. Black to White, May 27, 1969, in William J. Brennan Papers, Box 183.
23. Harlan to White, May 28, 1969, in William J. Brennan Papers, Box 183.
24. Brennan to White, May 28, 1969, in William J. Brennan Papers, Box 183.
25. Stewart to White, May 27, 1969, in William J. Brennan Papers, Box 183.
26. Julius Getman, "Labor Law and Free Speech," 43 *Maryland Law Review* 4, 12 (1984).

13. The End of Obscenity?

1. James T. Patterson, *Grand Expectations,* 360 (1996).
2. Ed Cray, *Chief Justice,* 327 (1997).
3. Charles Rembar, *The End of Obscenity,* 416 (1968).
4. Id. at 435.
5. Id. at 335.
6. Id. at 424.
7. Bruce Allen Murphy, *Fortas,* 458 (1988).
8. John Heidenry, *What Wild Ecstasy,* 83 (1997).
9. *New York Times,* March 2, 1966, at 39.
10. Kurt Vonnegut, *God Bless You, Mr. Rosewater,* 71, 72 (1965).
11. *New York Times,* May 9, 1967, at 20.
12. *New York Times,* April 8, 1969, at 1.
13. Harlan to Marshall, March 13, 1969, in Thurgood Marshall Papers, Box 53.
14. John D'Emilio and Estelle Freedman, *Intimate Matters,* 327 (1988).
15. *Newsweek,* November 3, 1967.
16. Allen J. Matusow, *The Unraveling of America,* 297 (1984).
17. Heidenry, *What Wild Ecstasy,* at 33.
18. Hugo L. Black and Elizabeth Black, *Mr. Justice and Mrs. Black,* 127, 134 (1986).
19. 3 *Technical Report of the Commission on Obscenity and Pornography: The Marketplace,* 65–66 (1970).
20. Richard Kuh, "Censorship with Freedom of Expression," in *Censorship and Freedom of Expression,* 131 (Harry Clor, ed., 1970).
21. Harry Ashmore, "Doubling the Standard," 62 *Virginia Quarterly Review* 70, 71 (Winter 1986).

14. Church and State in a Pluralist Society

1. Philip Kurland, "Foreword: 'Equal in Origin and Equal in Title to the Legislative and Executive Branches of the United States Government,'" 78 *Harvard Law Review* 143, 176 (1964).

2. *Washington Evening Star,* June 18, 1963, quoted in *Religious Liberty in the Supreme Court,* at 166 (Terry Eastland, ed., 1993).

3. *New York Times,* June 18, 1963, at 1.

4. *New York Times,* June 18, 1963, at 27.

5. *New York Times,* June 18, 1963, at 29.

6. *The Christian Century,* July 3, 1963, reprinted in *Religious Liberty in the Supreme Court,* at 168.

7. *New York Times,* June 23, 1964, at 2.

8. *Wall Street Journal,* June 16, 1964, at 3.

9. Robert McCloskey, "Principles, Powers, and Values," 1964 *Religion and Public Order* 3, 28 (Donald A. Gianella, ed.).

10. William Beaney and Edward Beiser, "Prayer and Politics," 13 *Journal of Public Law* 475, 486 (1964).

11. *New York Times,* June 18, 1963, at 27.

12. Beaney and Beiser, "Prayer and Politics," at 486.

13. Dan T. Carter, *The Politics of Rage,* 162 (1995).

14. Kenneth Dolbeare and Phillip Hammond, *The School Prayer Decisions,* 11 (1971).

15. Beaney and Beiser, "Prayer and Politics," at 480.

16. Peter Irons, *The Courage of Their Convictions,* 210 (1992).

17. Laura Kalmen, *Abe Fortas,* 275 (1990).

18. 12 *Church and State,* No. 11 at 3 (1960) (quoting Father Robert Drinan, dean of Boston College Law School).

19. Robert Dallek, *Flawed Giant,* 182 (1998).

20. *America,* June 22, 1968, at 786.

21. David Garrow, *Liberty and Sexuality,* 212 (1994).

22. Id. at 256.

23. Charles Black, "The Unfinished Business of the Warren Court," 46 *Washington Law Review* 3 (1970).

24. "*Griswold v. Connecticut:* The Supreme Court, 1964 Term," 79 *Harvard Law Review* 56, 165 n.22 (1965).

15. Policing the Police

1. From a speech quoted on the dust jacket of Anthony Lewis, *Gideon's Trumpet* (1964).

2. Ed Cray, *Chief Justice,* 405 (1997).

3. Id. at 405–406.

4. Yale Kamisar, "The Warren Court and Criminal Justice," in *The Warren Court,* 139 (Bernard Schwartz, ed., 1996).

5. *Washington Post,* August 11, 1963, at E4.

6. Quoted in Bernard Schwartz, *Super Chief,* 408 (1983).

7. Conference Notes, April 20, 1962, in William O. Douglas Papers, Box 1290.

8. White to Douglas, June 20, 1962, in William O. Douglas Papers, Box 1290.

9. Tom Clark Papers, Box A137.

10. *New York Times,* April 7, 1982, at 1, 15.

11. Fred P. Graham, *The Self-Inflicted Wound,* 91 (1970).

12. A. Kenneth Pye, "The Warren Court and Criminal Procedure," 67 *Michigan Law Review* 249, 256 (1968).

13. Yale Kamisar, "A Dissent from the *Miranda* Dissents," 65 *Michigan Law Review* 59, 86 (1966).

14. Cray, *Chief Justice,* at 457.

15. *New York Times,* May 14, 1965, at 39.

16. John Morton Blum, *Years of Discord,* 210 (1991).

17. Paul L. Murphy, *The Constitution in Crisis Times,* 381 (1972).

18. Theodore H. White, *The Making of the President 1964,* 241–242 (1965).

19. Murphy, *Crisis Times,* at 381.

20. Walter F. Murphy and Joseph Tanenhaus, "Public Opinion and the Supreme Court," 32 *Public Opinion Quarterly* 31, 36 (1968).

21. *Time,* July 16, 1965, at 23.

22. *Proceedings of the 43rd Annual Meeting of the American Law Institute,* 250 (1966).

23. Graham, *The Self-Inflicted Wound,* at 169.

24. Cray, *Chief Justice,* at 455.

25. Graham, *The Self-Inflicted Wound,* at 175.

26. G. Edward White, *Earl Warren,* 269 (1982).

27. Schwartz, *Super Chief,* at 588.

28. *New York Times,* June 14, 1966, at 1.

29. Schwartz, *Super Chief,* at 589.

30. White, *Earl Warren,* at 270.

31. Cray, *Chief Justice,* at 328.

32. White, *Earl Warren,* at 275.

33. *New York Times,* June 14, 1966, at 25.

34. *Newsweek,* June 27, 1966, at 21–22.

35. Schwartz, *Super Chief,* at 593.

36. Liva Baker, *Miranda, Crime, Law and Order,* 176 (1983).

37. *New York Times,* July 23, 1966, at 54.

38. Baker, *Miranda,* at 201.

39. Robert Dallek, *Flawed Giant,* 373 (1998).

40. Allen J. Matusow, *The Unraveling of America,* 214 (1984).

41. Kamisar, "The Warren Court and Criminal Justice," at 119.

42. Roger Newman, *Hugo Black,* 570 (1994).

43. Arthur M. Schlesinger, Jr., *Robert Kennedy and His Times,* 291 (1978).

44. Kamisar, "The Warren Court and Criminal Justice," at 130.

45. Newman, *Hugo Black,* at 554.

46. Id. at 559.

47. Eric C. Dudley, Jr., "*Terry v. Ohio,* the Warren Court and the Fourth Amendment: A Law Clerk's View," 72 *St. John's Law Review* 891, 893 (1998).

48. Dudley to Earl Warren, February 29, 1968, quoted in John Q. Barrett, "Deciding the Stop and Frisk Cases: A Look inside the Supreme Court's Conference," 72 *St. John's Law Review* 749, 816 (1998).

49. Cray, *Chief Justice,* at 468.

50. White, *Earl Warren,* at 277.

51. Dudley, *"Terry v. Ohio,"* at 893.

52. Theodore H. White, *The Making of the President 1968,* 188 (1969).

53. *The Memoirs of Earl Warren,* 317 (1977).

54. Stephen E. Ambrose, *Nixon,* vol. 2 at 201 (1989).

55. Graham, *The Self-Inflicted Wound,* at 319.

56. 114 *Congressional Record* 14,146 (1968).

57. Graham, *The Self-Inflicted Wound,* at 320.

58. S. Rep. No. 1097 at 51 (90th Cong., 2d Sess. 1968).

59. Graham, *The Self-Inflicted Wound,* at 284.

60. Ambrose, *Nixon,* at 154.

61. Graham, *The Self-Inflicted Wound,* at 10.

62. *Chicago Daily Law Bulletin,* November 2, 1995, at 1.

63. Baker, *Miranda,* at 13.

16. Policing the Criminal Justice System

1. *New York Times,* December 1, 1963, at 10E.

2. *Report of the President's Commission on the Assassination of President John F. Kennedy,* 201–242 (1964).

3. Bernard Schwartz, *Super Chief,* 543 (1983).

4. Robert Dallek, *Flawed Giant,* 39 (1998).

5. Schwartz, *Super Chief,* at 543.

6. William O. Douglas, *The Court Years,* 142 (1980).

7. *New York Times,* December 1, 1963, at 10E.

8. F. Lee Bailey, *The Defense Never Rests,* 66 (1971).

9. Charles Alan Wright, *Law of the Federal Courts,* 246 (3rd ed. 1976).

10. Fred P. Graham, *The Self-Inflicted Wound,* 109 (1970).

11. Michael Meltsner, *Cruel and Unusual,* 94 (1973).

12. David E. Kyvig, *Explicit and Authentic Acts,* 372–373 (1996).

13. William Fennell, "The States' Rights Amendments," 35 *New York State Bar Association Journal* 466–467 (1963).

14. Kyvig, *Explict Acts,* at 374.

15. G. Edward White, *Earl Warren,* 272 (1982).

16. Alexander Bickel, *The Least Dangerous Branch,* 242 (1962).

17. Meltsner, *Cruel and Unusual,* at 70.

18. Id. at 36.

19. Id. at 124.
20. Id.
21. Id.
22. Id. at 165.
23. Laura Kalman, *Abe Fortas,* 180 (1990).
24. Id.
25. Mark V. Tushnet, *Making Constitutional Law,* 181 (1997).
26. Kalman, *Fortas,* at 259, 260.
27. Tushnet, *Making Constitutional Law,* at 183.

17. Wealth and Poverty

1. Brennan to Warren, May 11, 1966, in Bernard Schwartz, *Super Chief,* 591 (1983).
2. Frank I. Michelman, "Foreword: On Protecting the Poor through the Fourteenth Amendment," 83 *Harvard Law Review* 1, 9 (1969).
3. David J. Garrow, *Liberty and Sexuality,* 171 (1994).
4. Id. at 197.
5. Michelman, "Foreword," at 48.
6. Bernard Schwartz, *The Unpublished Opinions of the Warren Court,* 306–307 (1985).
7. Robert Post, "William J. Brennan and the Warren Court," in *The Warren Court in Historical and Political Perspective,* 123, 128 (Mark V. Tushnet, ed., 1993).
8. Archibald Cox, *The Warren Court,* 6 (1968).
9. G. Edward White, *Earl Warren,* 301 (1982).

IV. The Era Ends: Prologue

1. Bernard Schwartz, *Super Chief,* 680 (1983).
2. Quoted in Liva Baker, *Miranda, Crime, Law and Order,* 211 (1983).

18. The Last Year

1. Bernard Schwartz, *Super Chief,* 682 (1983).
2. Bruce Allen Murphy, *Fortas,* 270 (1988).
3. G. Edward White, *Earl Warren,* 312–313 (1982).
4. Laura Kalman, *Abe Fortas,* 329 (1990).
5. Ed Cray, *Chief Justice,* 498 (1997).
6. Murphy, *Fortas,* at 302.
7. Kalman, *Fortas,* at 336.
8. Murphy, *Fortas,* at 406.
9. Kalman, *Fortas,* at 339.

10. Robert Dallek, *Flawed Giant,* 518 (1998).
11. Kalman, *Fortas,* at 338.
12. Id. at 314.
13. Murphy, *Fortas,* at 423.
14. Id. at 426.
15. Id. at 426–427.
16. Id. at 438.
17. *New York Times,* July 20, 1968, at 26.
18. To William O. Douglas, quoted in Kalman, *Fortas,* at 348.
19. To Earl Warren, quoted in Murphy, *Fortas,* at 450.
20. *New York Times,* July 10, 1968, at 10.
21. Walter F. Murphy and Joseph Tanenhaus, "Publicity, Public Opinion, and the Court," 84 *Northwestern Law Review* 985, 994 n.35 (1990).
22. Murphy, *Fortas,* at 449.
23. Paul Murphy, *The Constitution in Crisis Times,* 440 (1972).
24. Stephen E. Ambrose, *Nixon,* vol. 2 at 199 (1989).
25. Murphy, *Fortas,* at 525.
26. Lyndon B. Johnson, *The Vantage Point,* 547 (1971).
27. Robert Woodward and Scott Armstrong, *The Brethren,* 10 (1979).
28. Ambrose, *Nixon,* at 154.
29. Id. at 201.
30. Quoted in Liva Baker, *Miranda, Crime, Law and Order,* 245–246 (1983).
31. Dan T. Carter, *The Politics of Rage,* 339 (1995).
32. Jules Whitcover, *The Year the Dream Died,* 474 (1997).
33. Theodore H. White, *Making of the President 1968,* 188 (1969).
34. 114 *Congressional Record* 26,144 (1968).
35. *Los Angeles Times,* October 16, 1966, summarized in James Simon, *Independent Journey,* 392–393 (1980).
36. Murphy, *Fortas,* at 209.
37. Kalman, *Fortas,* at 361.
38. *Life,* May 9, 1969, at 32–33 (originally available May 4).
39. *Washington Post,* May 6, 1969, at A18.
40. *New York Times,* May 6, 1969, at 46.
41. Murphy, *Fortas,* at 560 (emphasis in the original).
42. Kalman, *Fortas,* at 367.
43. *Newsweek,* May 19, 1969, at 29 (originally available May 10).
44. Kalman, *Fortas,* at 370.
45. Id.
46. Id. at 372.
47. *Life,* October 15, 1971, at 59.
48. Warren E. Burger, "What to Do about Crime in U.S.," *U.S. News & World Report,* August 7, 1967, at 70.

19. What Was the Warren Court?

1. Benjamin N. Cardozo, *The Nature of the Judicial Process,* 168 (1921).
2. Anthony Lewis, "The Legacy of the Warren Court," in *The Warren Court: A Retrospective,* 398 (Bernard Schwartz, ed., 1996).
3. Owen Fiss, "A Life Twice Lived," 100 *Yale Law Journal* 1117, 1118 (1991).
4. See Chapter 1, note 7.
5. Dan T. Carter, *The Politics of Rage,* 425 (1995).
6. Bruce Ackerman, *We the People: Transformations,* 419 (1998).
7. *New York Times,* September 12, 1964, at 1.
8. Quoted in Liva Baker, *Miranda, Crime, Law and Order,* 41 (1983).
9. Stephen M. Griffin, "Legal Liberalism at Yale," 14 *Constitutional Commentary* 535, 551 (1997).
10. *New York Times,* July 23, 1966, at 54.
11. *New York Times,* December 20, 1965, at 23.
12. Kevin Phillips, *The Emerging Republican Majority,* 287 (1969).
13. Jeffrey A. Segal and Harold J. Spaeth, "Decisional Trends on the Warren and Burger Courts," 73 *Judicature* 104 (1989).
14. Dennis Hutchinson, "Hail to the Chief," 81 *Michigan Law Review* 922 (1983).
15. Robert G. McCloskey, *The American Supreme Court,* 150 (revised by Sanford Levinson, 1994).
16. Robert Post, "William J. Brennan and the Warren Court," in *The Warren Court in Historical and Political Perspective,* 123 (Mark V. Tushnet, ed., 1993).
17. Frank I. Michelman, *Brennan and Democracy* (1999).
18. *New York Times,* June 24, 1969, at 24.
19. Ed Cray, *Chief Justice,* 515 (1997).
20. Fiss, "A Life Twice Lived," at 1118.
21. Laura Kalman, *The Strange Career of Legal Liberalism,* 4 (1996).

Bibliography

A Note on Primary Sources

The primary source for any discussion of the Supreme Court is the opinions of the Court found in the volumes of the *United States Reports*. The Warren Court handed down approximately 1,750 opinions during its sixteen years, and they provide the data for understanding the Warren Court. These are found in fifty volumes of the *United States Reports* running from 346 U.S. to 395 U.S. The text of this book discusses about 15 percent of these cases. Several major areas—from tax to administrative law generally—constituting at least as large a percentage of the Court's work as discussed in the text are omitted entirely even though these areas would also illustrate what highly successful litigants the various departments of the federal government were.

Statistics about voting behavior were taken from the United States Supreme Court Judicial Database, 1953–1992 (ICPSR study number 9422, Fifth ISCSR release, March 1994) for which Harold J. Spaeth was the principal investigator. These data can be obtained from the Inter-university Consortium for Political and Social Research, P.O. Box 1248, Ann Arbor, Michigan, 48106. Initial results were published by Jeffrey A. Segal and Harold J. Spaeth, "Decisional Trends of the Warren and Burger Courts," 73 *Judicature* 103 (1989). Joseph L. Smith, then a Ph.D. candidate in the Department of Government at The University of Texas and now an assistant professor at Grand Valley State University, did the statistical work for me. Observant readers may notice that the rates of interagreement among pairs of justices are uniformly higher than those reported annually in the *Harvard Law Review*. The *Review* records two justices as having voted together only if they sign the same opinion. The analyses presented here count two justices as voting together if they agree on which party should prevail even if they do not sign the same opinion.

Briefs in the cases are available in depository libraries, like Tarlton Law Library at the University of Texas, or on microfiche, or, in some cases, in volumes 49–68 of *Landmark Briefs and Arguments of the Supreme Court of the United States: Constitutional Law* (Philip Kurland and Gerhard Casper, eds., 1975). Sometimes the briefs will show legal arguments avoided by the Court or facts that do not appear in the opinions. In the case of *Brown v. Board of Education*, for instance, they make quite clear that the NAACP was arguing for a race-neutral standard and in *Loving v.*

Virginia that the NAACP for the first time abandoned its prior claim that racial classifications were always arbitrary.

Because this is an external rather than an internal history of the Court, I placed little interest or reliance on the papers of the individual justices. I systematically worked through only one set of papers, those of Tom Clark, housed in the Tarlton Law Library. I took a highly selective look at the papers of Hugo L. Black, William J. Brennan, William O. Douglas, and Thurgood Marshall at the Library of Congress. I did not have access to Brennan's end-of-term memoranda, which are likely to be the most informative part of his papers.

Both Warren and Douglas published memoirs, *The Memoirs of Earl Warren* (1977) and *The Court Years* (1980), respectively. Warren's has some useful information although it has been mined so well by his able biographers that there is little if any reason to consult it. Douglas's is simply unreliable. Better than either is the diary of Black's second wife, published as the second half of Hugo L. Black and Elizabeth Black, *Mr. Justice and Mrs. Black* (1986). Mrs. Black was in love and in awe, and at times she successfully recorded Black's every thought.

During virtually all of the Warren Court, the *New York Times* had either Anthony Lewis or Fred Graham as its Supreme Court correspondent, a position Lewis virtually created during his tenure. Thus, the *Times* was not only the newspaper of record; it was blessed with as able Court reporters as any newspaper has had. I gave considerable credit to their analysis of the implications of cases because whether or not the analysis was correct, it did reflect what the best people thought contemporaneously with an opinion.

The notes cite far more law review articles from the Warren era than from the later period. This again reflects my decision to understand a case as it was understood when it came down, not as it has come to be understood subsequently. I have profited immeasurably from law review commentary over the past thirty years and it has informed my thinking, but I did not turn to post-Warren literature to comprehend what a Warren Court case meant.

I have sprinkled some polling results, typically Gallup, into the text. Maybe more so than other polling data they should be taken with a grain of salt. Polls rarely questioned people about their feelings on the Court and constitutional issues. Hence, any given snapshot could be off, although the fact that I cited the data means that it seems "more or less" correct to me. The only systematic polling on the Court was done by Walter F. Murphy and Joseph Tanenhaus in 1964, 1966, and 1975. Their data, which are more sophisticated than anything Gallup or others created, are consistent with my results (although more favorable to the Court). The articles are cited in Walter F. Murphy and Joseph Tanenhuas, "Publicity, Public Opinion, and the Court," 84 *Northwestern Law Review* 985, 989 n.17 (1990).

Finally, I should note, as the text sporadically indicates, that I did contact a small number of ex-law clerks to ask them specific questions about a case or an issue. There was nothing systematic about how I did this. If I had a question and thought an ex-clerk I knew might be able to help, I then tried to get in contact with that person. If I had omitted all this limited information, it would make no dent in the text.

Selective Bibliography of Secondary Sources

The Supreme Court Generally

Cornell W. Clayton and Howard Gillman, eds., *Supreme Court Decision-Making* (1999)

Clare Cushman, ed., *The Supreme Court Justices* (1993)

Robert Dahl, "Decision Making in a Democracy: The Supreme Court as National Policy-Maker," 6 *Journal of Public Law* 279 (1957)

John Hart Ely, *Democracy and Distrust* (1980)

Leon Friedman and Fred Israel, eds., *The Justices of the United States Supreme Court* (5 volumes, 1980)

Mark A. Graber, "The Non-Majoritarian Difficulty," 7 *Studies in American Political Development* 35 (1993)

Kermit L. Hall, *A Comprehensive Bibliography of American Constitutional Law and Legal History* (5 volumes, 1984)

Kermit L. Hall, ed., *The Oxford Companion to the Supreme Court* (1992)

Donald L. Horwitz, *The Courts and Social Policy* (1977)

William Lasser, *The Limits of Judicial Power* (1988)

Leonard Levy, ed., *Encyclopedia of the American Constitution* (4 volumes, 1986)

Alpheus Thomas Mason, *The Supreme Court from Taft to Burger* (1979)

Robert G. McCloskey, *The American Supreme Court* (revised by Sanford Levinson, 1994)

Walter F. Murphy, *The Elements of Judicial Strategy* (1964)

David O'Brien, *Storm Center* (4th ed. 1996)

H. W. Perry, *Deciding to Decide* (1991)

Gerald Rosenberg, *The Hollow Hope* (1991)

Stuart A. Scheingold, *The Politics of Rights* (1974)

Martin Shapiro, *Law and Politics in the Supreme Court* (1964)

G. Edward White, *The American Judicial Tradition* (rev. ed. 1988)

The Warren Court

Alexander Bickel, *Politics and the Warren Court* (1965)

Alexander Bickel, *The Supreme Court and the Idea of Progress* (1970)

Archibald Cox, *The Warren Court* (1968)

Owen Fiss, "A Life Lived Twice," 100 *Yale Law Journal* 1117 (1991)

Kermit L. Hall, "The Warren Court: Yesterday, Today, Tomorrow," 28 *Indiana Law Review* 319 (1995)

Morton J. Horwitz, *The Warren Court and the Pursuit of Justice* (1998)

Michael J. Klarman, "Rethinking the Civil Rights and Civil Liberties Revolutions," 82 *Virginia Law Review* 1 (1996)

Leonard Levy, ed., *The Supreme Court under Earl Warren* (1972)
Robert G. McCloskey, *The Modern Supreme Court* (1972)
Bernard Schwartz, *Super Chief* (1983)
Bernard Schwartz, ed., *The Warren Court: A Retrospective* (1996)
"Symposium," 67 *Michigan Law Review,* No. 2 (1968)
Mark V. Tushnet, ed., *The Warren Court in Historical and Political Perspective* (1993)

The Justices

Leonard Baker, *Brandeis and Frankfurter* (1984)
Liva Baker, *Felix Frankfurter* (1969)
Howard Ball, *A Defiant Life* (1999)
Howard Ball, *Hugo L. Black* (1996)
Howard Ball and Philip J. Cooper, *Of Power and Right* (1992)
Robert Burt, *Two Jewish Justices* (1988)
Ed Cray, *Chief Justice* (1997)
Harry N. Hirsh, *The Enigma of Felix Frankfurter* (1981)
Dennis Hutchinson, *The Man Who Once Was Whizzer White* (1998)
Laura Kalman, *Abe Fortas* (1990)
Philip B. Kurland, *Mr. Justice Frankfurter and the Constitution* (1971)
Bruce Allen Murphy, *Fortas* (1988)
Roger Newman, *Hugo Black* (1994)
James Simon, *Independent Journey* (1980)
David L. Stebenne, *Arthur J. Goldberg* (1996)
Mark V. Tushnet, *Making Civil Rights Law* (1994)
Mark V. Tushnet, *Making Constitutional Law* (1997)
Melvin Urofsky, *Felix Frankfurter* (1991)
Steven Wasby, ed., *"He Shall Not Pass This Way Again"* (1990)
G. Edward White, *Earl Warren* (1982)
Tinsley Yarbrough, *John Marshall Harlan* (1992)

Great Cases

Liva Baker, *Miranda, Crime, Law and Order* (1983)
David J. Garrow, *Liberty and Sexuality* (1994)
Richard Kluger, *Simple Justice* (1976)
Anthony Lewis, *Gideon's Trumpet* (1964)
Anthony Lewis, *Make No Law* (1991)

Doctrinal Areas

Robert G. Dixon, Jr., *Democratic Representation* (1968)
Fred P. Graham, *The Self-Inflicted Wound* (1970)

Harry Kalven, *A Worthy Tradition* (1988)
Yale Kamisar, "The Warren Court and Criminal Justice," *The Warren Court* (Bernard Schwartz, ed., 1996)
Philip Kurland, ed., *Church and State* (1975)
Douglas Laycock, "The Underlying Unity of Separation and Neutrality," 46 *Emory Law Journal* 43 (1997)
Robert B. McKay, *Reapportionment* (1965)
Michael Meltsner, *Cruel and Unusual* (1973)
John T. Noonan, Jr., *The Lustre of Our Country* (1998)
Lucas A. Powe, Jr., *The Fourth Estate and the Constitution* (1991)

American Politics

Henry J. Abraham, *Justices and Presidents* (3d ed. 1993)
Stephen E. Ambrose, *Nixon* (Volume 2, 1989)
Michael Barone, *Our Country* (1990)
John Morton Blum, *Years of Discord* (1991)
Herbert Brownell, *Advising Ike* (1993)
Robert Dallek, *Flawed Giant* (1998)
Doris Kearns Goodwin, *Lyndon Johnson and the American Dream* (rev. ed. 1991)
David E. Kyvig, *Explicit and Authentic Acts* (1996)
Allen J. Matusow, *The Unraveling of America* (1984)
Paul J. Murphy, *The Constitution in Crisis Times 1919–69* (1972)
Walter F. Murphy, *Congress and the Court* (1962)
James T. Patterson, *Grand Expectations* (1996)
C. Herman Pritchett, *Congress versus the Supreme Court* (1961)
Arthur M. Schlesinger, Jr., *A Thousand Days* (1965)
Mark Stern, *Calculating Visions* (1992)
Theodore H. White, *The Making of the President 1964* (1965)
Theodore H. White, *The Making of the President 1968* (1969)

The South and Civil Rights

Taylor Branch, *Parting the Waters* (1988)
Taylor Branch, *Pillar of Fire* (1998)
Dan T. Carter, *The Politics of Rage* (1995)
David J. Garrow, *Bearing the Cross* (1986)
Dewey W. Grantham, *The South in Modern America* (1994)
Henry Hampton and Steve Fayer, eds., *Voices of Freedom* (1990)
Michael J. Klarman, "*Brown,* Racial Change, and the Civil Rights Movement," 80 *Virginia Law Review* 7 (1994)
Anthony Lewis, *Portrait of a Decade* (1964)

Neil McMillen, *The Citizen's Councils* (1971)
Benjamin Muse, *Ten Years of Prelude* (1964)
Robert Weisbrot, *Freedom Bound* (1991)
J. Harvie Wilkinson, *From Brown to Bakke* (1979)
C. Vann Woodward, *The Strange Career of Jim Crow* (2d rev. ed. 1966)

Index of Cases

General Index